October 4–7, 2016
Biopolis, Singapore

I0036243

Association for Computing Machinery

Advancing Computing as a Science & Profession

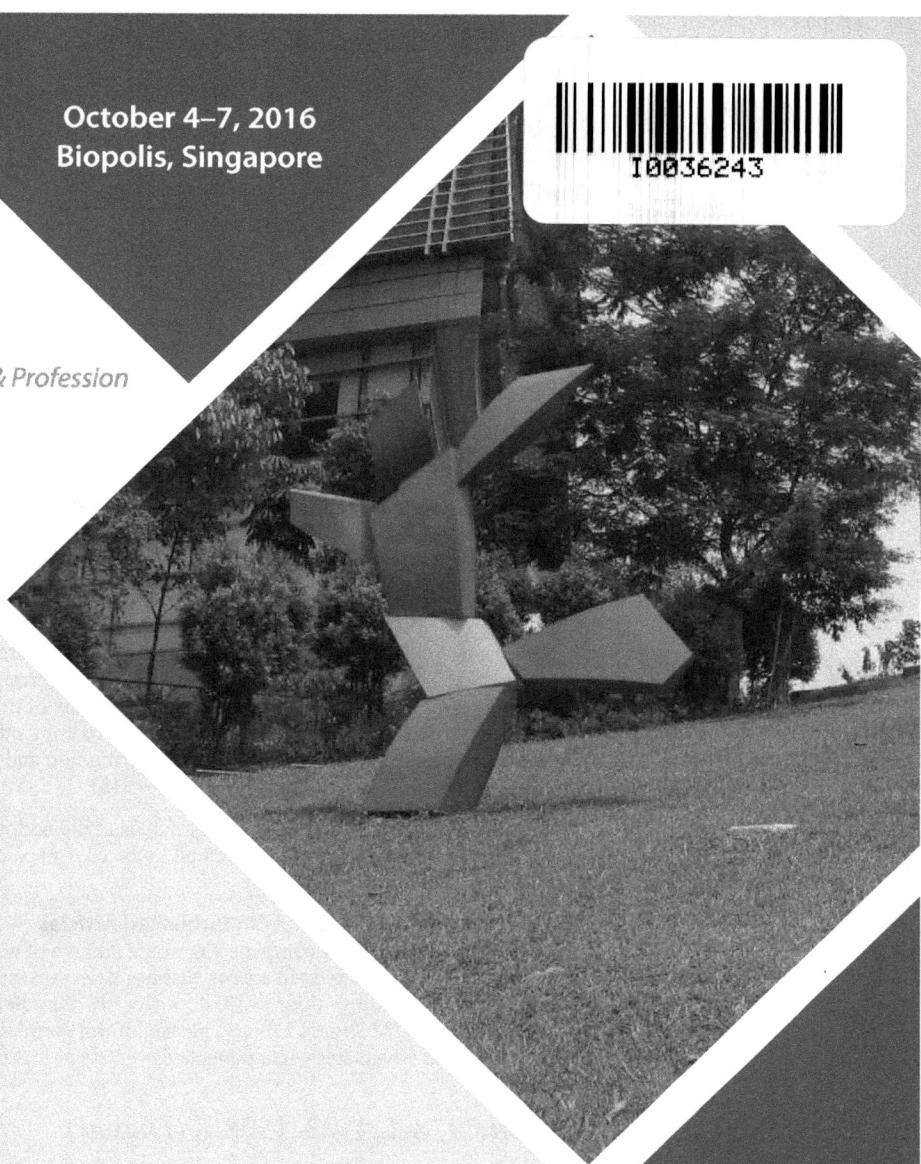

HAI'16

Proceedings of the Fourth International Conference on
Human Agent Interaction

Sponsored by:
ACM SIGCHI

In cooperation with:
Chinese and Oriental Languages Information Processing Society

Technical Sponsors:
IEEE Computer Society and IEEE SMC

Association for Computing Machinery

Advancing Computing as a Science & Profession

The Association for Computing Machinery
2 Penn Plaza, Suite 701
New York, New York 10121-0701

Notice to Past Authors of ACM-Published Articles

ISBN: 978-1-4503-4508-8 (Digital)

ISBN: 978-1-4503-4683-2 (Print)

Additional copies may be ordered prepaid from:

ACM Order Department
PO Box 30777
New York, NY 10087-0777, USA

Phone: 1-800-342-6626 (USA and Canada)
+1-212-626-0500 (Global)
Fax: +1-212-944-1318
E-mail: acmhelp@acm.org
Hours of Operation: 8:30 am – 4:30 pm ET

Printed in the USA

HAI 2016 Chairs' Welcome

It is our great pleasure to welcome you to *The Fourth International Conference on Human-Agent Interaction* (HAI 2016) and the vibrant city of Singapore. HAI has grown beyond our expectations in last three years and this year's HAI continues its tradition of being the relevant forum for presentation of research results and experience reports on leading edge issues of Human-Agent Interaction. HAI gathers researchers from fields spanning engineering, computer science, psychology, sociology and cognitive science while covering diverse topics including Human-Virtual/Physical agent interaction, communication and interaction with smart home/smart cars, and modeling of those interactions.

The mission of the conference is to share novel quantitative and qualitative research on human and artificial agent interaction and identify new directions for future research and development. HAI gives researchers and practitioners a unique opportunity to share their perspectives with others interested in the various aspects of human-agent interaction.

The theme for HAI 2016 is "Machine learning methods and multimodal interfaces to achieve social intelligence in robots, avatars, and virtual characters". The programme for HAI 2016 includes two exciting keynote talks by the world leaders in areas related to human-agent interaction: Prof. David Hsu of the National University of Singapore and Prof. Leila Takayama of University of California, Santa Cruz and Researcher, Hoku Labs. We encourage participants to attend them.

This year, we saw a record number of submissions in full paper, late-breaking poster as well as workshop proposal categories. The programme committee has unanimously remarked on the exceptional quality of this year's submissions and had a tough time playing the role of the gatekeeper with the acceptance rate of 43.9%. Our final programme features 29 oral presentations, 46 poster presentations, 2 tutorials and 3 workshops. All of them present latest research results and ideas of interest to HAI researchers. It will also be a good avenue for researchers from all over the world to discuss and network, hopefully generating new ideas and seeding new collaborations.

In addition to the stimulating conference programme, Singapore, with its tourist attractions, cultural diversity and top-notch quality cuisine, is one of the all-time favourite place to visit. With a recent conferment of 29 Michelin Star restaurants which include affordable hawker stalls, we hope that you will get a chance to explore Singapore and enjoy the sumptuous culinary experience in the vibrant city state.

HAI 2016 @ one-north would not be a great success without the dedicated team behind the scene. On behalf of the Organising Committee, we would like to thank the Advisory Board for their advice, the Technical Programme Committee and hundreds of reviewers led by the Programme Chairs for their contributions to a wonderful technical programme. We would like to express our gratitude to the keynote speakers, tutorial speakers and workshop organisers for augmenting the programme of this edition of the HAI conference series. In addition, the Organising Committee works tirelessly to ensure the quality of the conference and the best experience for the delegation. We would also like to thank our corporate sponsors, Hokuyo and Orcadesign. They enabled us to provide a better experience while keeping the registration fee affordable. Finally, we would also like to thank ACM SIGCHI, our in-cooperation partner; as well as the IEEE System, Man and Cybernetics Society, Singapore Chapter and IEEE Computer Society, Singapore Chapter, our technical co-sponsors.

We hope that you will find this program interesting as well as thought provoking and that the symposium will provide you with a valuable opportunity to share ideas with other researchers and practitioners from institutions around the world.

Wei-Yun Yau
HAI 2016 General Co-Chair
A*STAR Institute for Infocomm Research,
Singapore

Takashi Omori
HAI 2016 General Co-Chair
Tamagawa University,
Tokyo, Japan

Shengdong Zhao
HAI 2016 Program Co-Chair
National University of
Singapore, Singapore

Hirotaka Osawa
HAI 2016 Program Co-Chair
University of Tsukuba, Japan

Giorgio Metta
HAI 2016 Program Co-Chair
Italian Institute of Technology,
Italy

Table of Contents

Main Track Session III: Modelling Interactions

Session Co-Chairs: Sho Sakurai *(University of Electro-Communications)* and Yugo Takeuchi *(Shizuoka University)*

Main Track Session IV: Emotions and Inner States

Session Co-Chairs: Tomoko Koda *(Osaka Institute of Technology)* and Adam Miner *(Stanford University)*

Main Track Session V: Extending Body Image
Session Co-Chairs: Hirotaka Osawa *(University of Tsukuba)* and Tetsushi Oka *(Nihon University)*

Main Track Session VI: Human Characteristics
Session Co-Chairs: Hideyuki Nakanishi *(Osaka University)*
and Andreea Ioana Niculescu *(A*STAR Instittue for Infocomm Research)*

Main Track Session VII: Communication Cues
Session Co-Chairs: Kazunori Terada *(Gifu University)* and Tomo Wantanabe *(Okayama Prefectural University)*

Keynote Lecture II

Poster Session II

Main Track Session VIII: Interaction Tactics
Session Co-Chairs: Michita Imai *(Keio University)* and Yusuhike Kitamura *(Kwansei Gakuin University)*

Main Track Session IX: Supporting Work
Session Co-Chairs: Andreas Kipp *(Bielefeld Universtiy)* and Yoshimasa Ohmoto *(Kyoto University)*

Poster Session III

Main Track Session X: Agents for Real-world
Session Co-Chairs: Tomoko Yonezawa *(Kansai University)*
and Luis Fernando D'Haro *(A*STAR Institute for Infocomm Research)*

HAI 2016 Organizing Committee

Honorary Chair: Haizhou Li, National University of Singapore, Singapore

General Chairs: Wei Yun Yau, A*STAR Institute for Infocomm Research, Singapore
Takashi Omori, Tamagawa University, Japan

Advisory Board: Sonia Chernova, Georgia Institute of Technology, USA
Yiannis Demiris, Imperial College London, UK
Michita Imai, Keio University, Japan
Hideaki Kuzuoka, University of Tsukuba, Japan
Minho Lee, Kyungpook National University, Korea
Yukie Nagai, University of Osaka, Japan
Tetsuo Ono, Hokkaido University, Japan
Hyeyoung Park, Kyungpook National University, Korea
Yugo Takeuchi, Shizuoka University, Japan
Britta Wrede, University of Bielefeld, Germany
Seiji Yamada, National Institute of Informatics, Japan
James Young, University of Manitoba, Canada

Program Chairs: Giorgio Metta, Italian Institute of Technology, Italy
Hirotaka Osawa, University of Tsukuba, Japan
Shengdong Zhao, National University of Singapore, Singapore

Finance Chairs: Rafael Banchs, A*STAR Institute for Infocomm Research, Singapore
Lei Wang, A*STAR Institute for Infocomm Research, Singapore

Local Organization Chairs: Minghui Dong, A*STAR Institute for Infocomm Research, Singapore
Zhiyong Huang, A*STAR Institute for Infocomm Research, Singapore
Swee Lan See, A*STAR Institute for Infocomm Research, Singapore

Publicity Chairs: Yan Wu, A*STAR Institute for Infocomm Research, Singapore
Yanyu Su, Suzhou BoZhon Robot Co., Ltd, China

Publication Chairs: Eng Siong Chng, Nanyang Technological University, Singapore
Yugo Hayashi, Ritsumeikan University, Japan

Awards Chairs: Martin Dunn, Singapore University of Technology and Design, Singapore
Ellen Yi-Luen Do, National University of Singapore, Singapore
Ayse Kucukyilmaz, University of Yeditepe, Turkey

Poster & Tutorial Chairs: Dimitri Ognibene, Universitat Pompeu Fabra, Spain
Keng Peng Tee, A*STAR Institute for Infocomm Research, Singapore

Workshop Chairs: Marcelo Ang Jr., National University of Singapore, Singapore
Ai Ti Aw, A*STAR Institute for Infocomm Research, Singapore

HAI 2016 Sponsors & Supporters

Organisers:

COLiPS

Institute for Infocomm Research
A*STAR

In-Cooperation with:

acm In-Cooperation

SIGCHI

Technical Sponsors:

IEEE COMPUTER SOCIETY
SINGAPORE CHAPTER

IEEE SMC
Systems, Man, & Cybernetics Society
SINGAPORE CHAPTER

Silver Supporters:

HOKUYO

orcadesign

Official Travel Partner:

来这里 ComeLah

Robots in Harmony with Humans

David Hsu

National University of Singapore

Abstract

In early days, robots often occupied tightly controlled environments, for example, factory floors, designed to segregate robots and humans for safety. Today robots "live" with humans, providing a variety of services at homes, in workplaces, or on the road. To become effective and trustworthy collaborators, robots must understand human intentions and act accordingly in response. One core challenge here is the inherent uncertainty in understanding intentions, as a result of the complexity and diversity of human behaviours. Robots must hedge against such uncertainties to achieve robust performance and sometimes actively elicit information in order to reduce uncertainty and ascertain human intentions. Our recent work explores planning and learning under uncertainty for human-robot interactive or collaborative tasks. It covers mathematical models for human intentions, planning algorithms that connect robot perception with decision making, and learning algorithms that enable robots to adapt to human preferences. The work, I hope, will spur greater interest towards principled approaches that integrate perception, planning, and learning for fluid human-robot collaboration.

Short Bio

David Hsu is a professor of computer science at the National University of Singapore, a member of NUS Graduate School for Integrative Sciences & Engineering (NGS), and deputy director of the Advanced Robotics Center. His current research focuses on robotics and AI.

He received B.Sc. in computer science & mathematics from the University of British Columbia, Canada and Ph.D. in computer science from Stanford University, USA. After leaving Stanford, he worked at Compaq Computer Corp.'s Cambridge Research Laboratory and the University of North Carolina at Chapel Hill. At the National University of Singapore, he held the Sung Kah Kay Assistant Professorship and was a Fellow of the Singapore-MIT Alliance. He is currently serving as the general co-chair of IEEE International Conference on Robotics & Automation 2016, the general chair of Robotics: Science & Systems 2016, a steering committee member of International Workshop on the Algorithmic Foundation of Robotics, and an editorial board member of Journal of Artificial Intelligence Research. He and his team of colleagues and students won the Humanitarian Robotics and Automation Technology Challenge Award at the International Conference on Robotics & Automation (ICRA) 2015 and the RoboCup Best Paper Award at IEEE/RSJ International Conference on Intelligent Robots & Systems (IROS) 2015.

HAI'16, October 4–7, 2016, Biopolis, Singapore.
ACM ISBN 978-1-4503-4508-8/16/10.
DOI: http://dx.doi.org/10.1145/2974804.2993927

Perception of Animacy
by the Linear Motion of a Group of Robots

Momoka Nakayama
The University of Tokyo
nkym@iis.u-tokyo.ac.jp

Shunji Yamanaka
The University of Tokyo
design-lab@iis.u-tokyo.ac.jp

ABSTRACT

With the advancement of technology, the number of domestic robots used in day-to-day life is expected to increase. We think that it is important for people to perceive animacy in robots in order to develop relationships with them. In this study, we report the proposal and development by our research of a group of five robots shaped like cubes, and equipped with a simple mechanism that allowed them to move in a straight line in order to test certain hypotheses. We showed our group of robots at several exhibitions, where visitors interacted with them. We analyzed how participants' impressions of the robots changed as they began to move. To this end, we used the semantic differential (SD) method in questionnaires. The results revealed that our robot system could convey the impression of being animate to users because of its movement, in spite of its abstract shape and simple mechanism. We also determined that such movement can help improve the relationship between a human user and a robot.

Author Keywords

Interactive; group robots; perception; animacy; likeability; linear motion

ACM Classification Keywords

H.5.m. Information Interfaces and Presentation (e.g. HCI): Miscellaneous

INTRODUCTION

With the startling advancement in technology in the last few decades, the use of robots has been introduced to a variety of fields. In recent years, robots have been developed not only for such traditional uses as factory floors and nursing care, but also for employment in daily domestic life, as exemplified by robots such as 'Pepper'[3] and 'OHaNAS'[4]. Robots for domestic use in particular need to be able to easily communicate with a human. For this purpose, it is necessary for the human to feel familiar and comfortable with the robot. One of the ways of bringing this about is through the imitation by the robot of the actions of another human or a pet animal.

HAI'16, October 04-07, 2016, Biopolis, Singapore.
Copyright © 2016 ACM ISBN 978-1-4503-4508-8/16/10 ...$15.00.
http://dx.doi.org/10.1145/2974804.2974806

The purpose of a related study (Yamaoka et al. [10]) was to develop animate or 'lifelike' behaviors for robotic communication based on developmental psychological categorization. This development is expected to make human–robot interaction more natural. Based on their findings, the authors of the study proposed a design guide for developing lifelike robots. These suggestions were implemented to create lifelike behavior in a humanoid robot, the results of which are shown below. A motion capturing system was used to implement the guide. This system has allowed us to leapfrog technological developments in terms of the sensing abilities of robots:

1. Robots can move depending on the movement of a partner without direct contact with it.

2. A partner can become both a host and a guest in an interaction with robots.

3. Robots move as if they have their own will or purpose.

The purpose of these guides was to create interactions that encouraged people to consider the robot as a living creature. In other words, a person could develop some kind of intimacy with the robot. To achieve this, robots were provided with a complicated mechanical structure to function, appear, and behave like a human. However, according to related studies on factors effecting human perception of animacy, Heider et al. [6] showed that people perceived a connection with geometrical figures that moved similarly to humans. In a subsequent study (Tremoulet et al. [9]), it was proposed that the perception of animacy arises naturally when an object's motion evinces intent or purpose. Arita et al. [1] investigated whether 10-month-old infants expected others to talk to a humanoid robot. Their results suggested that infants interpreted an interactive robot as a communicative agent and a non-interactive robot as an object. Their findings implied that infants categorized interactive humanoid robots as some type of human beings. Therefore, interactions clearly have an impact on our perception of affinity with others, including robots. These findings show that specific instances have a greater influence on one's perception of an object than its shape, which tends to imitate humans or pets. For example, Itou et al. [8]) developed a pendulum-type robot with unstable behavior, like an infant, that explored unconscious behaviors and interactive spaces of the caregiver. Fukuda et al. [5] carried out an investigation using the educational robot 'e-puck', which features a simple appearance. They found that the movements with 1/f randomness made observers perceive animacy stronger than those that had no randomness when observers interacted with the robot. This suggests that interaction can have an effect on the human perception of animacy in robots. These studies yielded a number of key observations. The movement of an object is one of the most important factors in a person's perception of it. Its actions create an interaction with the human observer. Interactive movements, which contain irregular elements such as unconscious behaviors or 1/f random movements, have a greater influence on perception than movements that are regular. Conventional robots can move with the help of an extensive network of actuators, sensors, and mechanisms. These robots imitate humans or pets in order to appear more likeable to a human user. However, we think that even if a robot's shape is abstract, it can effectively communicate with people and create the perception of animacy in users through simple movements. In this way, inexpensive domestic robots can be designed that can communicate effectively with their human users, thus allowing more people to use and own robots. Our research group developed a group of five robots that were shaped like cubes, and featured a simple mechanism that allowed them to move in a straight line. Figure 1 shows an image of these robots. They could interact with users and move irregularly, which made it easier for users to connect with them. Each

Figure 1. The appearance of the robots used in our study

of the five robots was equipped with a simple sensor, in addition to simple movements and control structures. However, they were designed to share their interactions with one another and move autonomously. In designing this movement, we considered the movement of animals in the initial stages of their evolution before the brain develops, with responses only stemming from nerves corresponding to that input. By contrast, simpler, more conventional robots are developed to interact with users using many sensors and complicated movements, mechanisms, and control algorithms. These mechanisms were designed in a manner similar to those of an animal that controls its body by using its brain. However, we expect that our simple robotic system can develop biological behavior more easily than conventional systems. Moreover, we displayed this robot system at the iii Exhibition 17 at the University of Tokyo for five days (2015/11/12 - 2015/11/16), where people interacted with our robots. During the exhibition, we analyzed people's remarks and interactions with the robots. Using this data, we gathered the users' impressions of the robotic system. We also documented the adjectives

that people used to describe their perceptions of animacy in these robots. We used these results to create a questionnaire using the SD method during an art exhibition in Shinjuku-Isetan (2016/2/17 - 2016/2/22) for six days, where our robotic system was exhibited as well. In order to verify the effect the amount of robot gives to animacy perception, we carried out interviews in MAKING MAKE exhibition that took place at the University of Tokyo Institute of Industrial Science, University of Tokyo (2016/7/13 - 7/16).We concluded that our system helped build affinity with human users due to its movement, in spite of its abstract shape. This movement improved the relationship between human users and our robots. We plan to apply our design to various robots in future work.

ROBOT SYSTEM CONFIGURATION

Design Policy

We designed the robot in the shape of a geometrical cube in order to discourage the impression of the robot as a creature. We made this decision because our purpose was to investigate how movement creates the perception among humans of animacy in robots without relying on their appearance. Moreover, we limited the movement of the robots to linear reciprocal movement in order to eliminate movement arising out of the human–robot perception relationship. The robots' appearance is shown in Figure 1. We refer to the design policy proposed by Yamaoka et al. [10]. The robotic system was equipped with the following functions.

1. To join an interaction without contact, we installed infrared distance measuring sensors at the front and rear of each robot.

2. In order to facilitate interactions, each robot could change its speed and direction depending on how far it was from other robots.

3. Each sensor could measure the distance between a robot and an obstacle in any direction. Using this distance information, the robots could use a simple control program that caused a chain reaction and coupled oscillation.

Hardware

The internal constitution of the robot is shown in Figure 2. We used infrared distance measuring sensors (PSD sensors), module GP2Y0A21, made by Sharp Corporation. We attached a polypropylene cube to a Tamiya Mini 4WD model. The robots were equipped with a microcomputer-compatible Arduino UNO to control the motor. We controlled the forward and reverse rotations of the IC motor driver, manufactured by Toshiba Corporation, and the semiconductor TA7291P. A summary of the specifications of the robots is provided Table 1.

Length Width Height	15cm 15cm 15cm
Weight	564g
Maximum velocity	0.15m/s
Maximum acceleration	0.016m/s^2

Table 1. The specifications of the robots

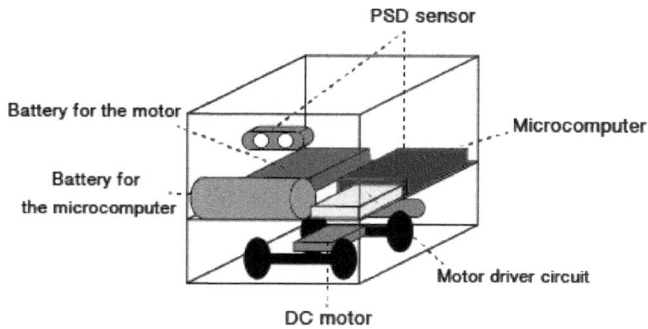
Figure 2. Internal constitution of the robots

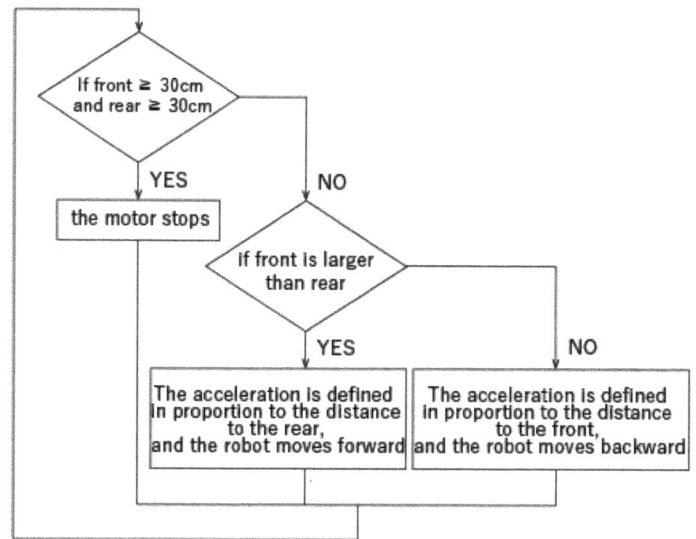
Figure 3. The control flow of the robots

Control Configuration

The control flow of the robots is shown in Figure 3. Each of the five robots was controlled independently by a micro-computer installed in it. Figure 1 and Figure 4 show how the robots were arranged in a line along their direction of motion. The infrared distance measuring sensors were located at the front and rear of each robot. Each sensor could measure the distance between a robot and an obstacle in each direction. If this distance was greater than 30 cm, and if the distances were equal, the robot stopped moving. If there was a difference, the robot moved in the direction of the larger distance. Accelera-tion was defined in proportion to the distance between a robot and an obstacle. We set a time constant formed by the mass and the torque of the driving motor of the robot to about 1 second, because 1 second is close to the period of breathing and heart beat of human. Further more we set the gain of the control loop to high level. The vibration was deliberately caused by this gain to create a movement that feels natural to human. Using this control rule and data from the PSD sensor, the robot reacted not only to the distance an anteroposterior robot, but also to an approach from a person interacting with it. We called such a person 'a user.' The robots advanced in the direction that reduced the distance between an object and the user when the user approached the robot. This one-dimensional movement satisfied the first and second design policies. Furthermore, because the robots were controlled proportionally to the distance between an obstacle and the speed of the robot, the coupled oscillation in the anteropos-terior direction defined the movement of the robots. We cre-ated random behavior using a simple mechanism and control program. The linear motion of the group of robots is shown in Figure 4. Further, when a user stopped approaching, the robots' coupled oscillation converged, and they finally stabi-lized and halted at an equal distance from all obstacles. While users observed this stabilization of movement, they were re-garded as 'guests of the interaction.' However, by allowing the user to approach a robot that was vibrating, we permitted the movement of the robots to either become complicated or converge. As a result, they could become the 'hosts of the interaction.'

EVALUATION CONFIGURATION

For the group of robots, we tested whether users perceived them as lifelike creatures or an, and whether the relationship

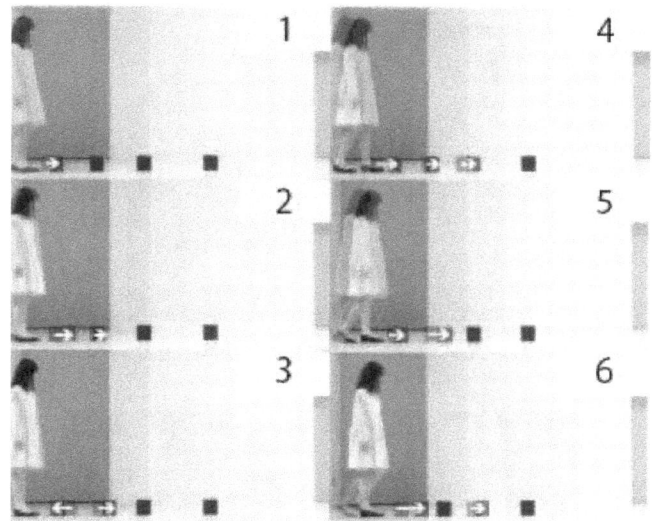
Figure 4. The linear motion of the group of robots

between the human and the robot improved due to their move-ment. We displayed the robots in two exhibitions and used the SD method for evaluation. We recorded users, with permis-sion secured beforehand, as they associated with the robots in the first exhibition. Once we had analyzed the record-ings, we extracted the remarks made by each user express-ing impressions of the robots. We picked out the adjectives that described their perceptions of animacy in these robots in the remarks. In the second exhibition, we designed the ques-tionnaire based on the SD method using the adjectives that had been derived from the impressions of these robots in the previous exhibition. We distributed the questionnaire to vis-itors to the exhibition, and analyzed the results using the SD method. We then investigated changes in users' impressions of the moving robots.In the third exhibition, in order to verify the effect the amount of robot gives to animacy perception, we carried out two types of interviews in MAKING MAKE exhibition that took place at the University of Tokyo Institute of Industrial Science, University of Tokyo (2016/7/13 - 7/16).

EVALUATION OBSERVATION

Evaluation Observation Purpose and Observation Method

The purpose of these observations was to discover how users reacted to the robots according to the adjectives they chose to describe their impressions. Furthermore, we attempted to determine whether the adjectives that they had used revealed a perception of animacy of the robots. The robots were displayed in the iii Exhibition 17 at the University of Tokyo for five days (2015/11/12 - 2015/11/16). Figure 5 shows the display of the robots and Figure 6 shows an image taken during the exhibition.   After explaining to users how to han-

Figure 5. Display of robots

Figure 6. The iii exhibition

dle the robots, we conducted an experiment where they were required to move the robots by handling them. This experience was defined as 'the users experiencing the robots.' We recorded users who had authorized us to do so as they interacted with the robots. We carried out the recording experiments for three days (November 12, 14, and 15). During this, we recorded 153 men and 87 women interacting with the robots.

The Results of Observations, and Discussion

We analyzed the videos, and considered the actions and remarks of the users. Furthermore, we recorded the number of

Remark contents	Men	Women	Total
Cute	14	27	41
Moving unsteadily	1	1	2
Like a creature	1	1	2
Attachment to the movement	1	0	1
Like a dove running away	1	0	1
call out to the robots, go for it	0	1	1
apologize for the robots	0	1	1
seems to be trouble	0	1	1

Table 2. The result of evaluative observations

people who made remarks that evinced affinity towards the robots, such as 'cute' or 'looks like a creature,' as they experimented with the robots, even though nothing in the design encouraged the idea of animacy. We show the statistics concerning the number of people who interacted with the robots in Table 2. We explain below why we think the users considered the robots 'cute.'

- All five robots vibrated and recoiled.

- The users felt that the robots seemed to be troubled due to their vibrations.

- Slow speed.

- Vibrating in a group.

- When vibrating, the robots' motors made a 'tictac' sound.

- When the robots move vibrate, they sounded like babies.

We grouped adjectives from people's reports that had been derived from their impressions of the robots, and mapped these impressions. The map is shown in Figure 7. Furthermore, the adjective pairs are given in Table 3 .

In the exhibition,we recorded the comments given to this robot. After extracting the comments, we classified them, corresponding to the four shown in the following.

1. Figurative languages that specifically shows an example of living creatures

2. Adjectives that indicates the characteristics of the movement

3. Adjectives normally used for living creatures

4. Adjectives that indicates cuteness

This classification figure shown in Figure 7. In addition, we extracted an adjective derived from the above-mentioned four kinds of grouping, adjective pair, figurative languages. Although it is subjective, we referenced the adjective pair groups which are used in the SD method by Inoue et al.[7] and Bartneck et al.[2], and the dictionary. Also as we translate, we referenced to the Bartneck et al's.

EVALUATION EXPERIMENT

Our research group designed the questionnaire used during the exhibition. It used adjectives from users' stated impressions of the robots during the evaluative observation. During the art exhibition in Shinjuku-Isetan (2016/2/17 - 2016/2/22)

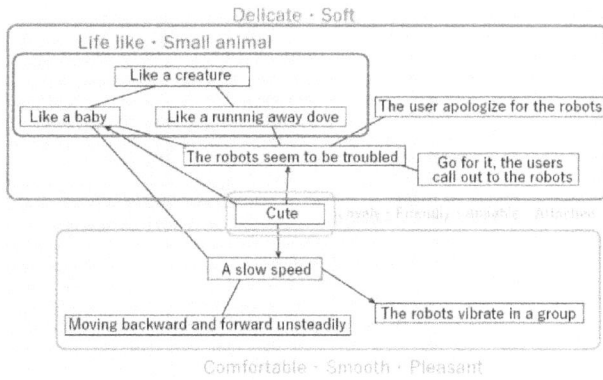

Figure 7. Map of users' impressions

Pair of adjectives
Strong-Weak
Stiff-Soft
Artificial-Lifelike
Unconcern-Lovely
Unfriendly-Friendly
Dislike-Like
Monotonous-Pleasant
Rough-Smooth
Gloomy-Cheerful

Table 3. Pair of adjectives from the analysis

for six days, we distributed questionnaires among 29 men and 28 women.

Questionnaire Design

We designed the questionnaire using the SD method. Since we were distributing the questionnaire during the exhibition, we reduced the number of questions to six items in order to not tire users. These items were extracted from the grouping experiment. Table 4 shows the pairs of adjectives used in the questionnaire. Because the questionnaire was written in Japanese, we used Bartneck [2] as a reference to aid with translation.

No.	Pair of adjectives
1	Monotonous-Pleasant
2	Unfriendly-Friendly
3	Gloomy-Cheerful
4	Stiff-Soft
5	Strong-Weak
6	Artificial-Lifelike

Table 4. Pairs of adjectives used in the questionnaire

Experimental Method

We separately performed each experiment, and had an experimenter answer the questionnaire on openFrameworks using a PC mouse. We prepared the questionnaire by digitizing seven phases with different adjective pairs and allowing the experimenter to choose the best match according to the impression of the robots. Below, we detail the experimental procedure:

1. The experimenter explained the experiment to a participant.

2. The experimenter did not tell the participant that the robots could move and were interactive. The experimenter distributed the questionnaire, recording the user's impressions of the robots standing in a line.

3. The participant recorded his/her age and sex.

4. The participant chose the best impression for the static robots.

5. The experimenter explained to the participant the mechanism of the robot, and how to operate it.

6. The participant operated the robot.

7. The participant chose the best impression.

After letting the participants evaluate their impressions of the robots before they knew that they could move, we performed impression evaluation using the same questionnaire. It was easy to compare how the users' impression of the robots changed during the course of the experiment.

Experimental Results and Remarks

Figure 8 shows the results of the experiment. From the movement of the robots, the impressions were positive (affirmative) and the level of significance was less than 2 percent for all items. Furthermore, the impressions were affirmative and the level of significance was less than one percent, except for item No. 5. This result showed that users' impressions of the robots changed due to their movement. Moreover, item No. 6 indicated the change in users' perceptions of animacy in the robots, as it depended on the perception that they were 'lifelike.' The level of significance of this observation was less than one percent in the movements of the robots. The results strongly indicated that the movement of the robots induced in the users the perception of animacy.

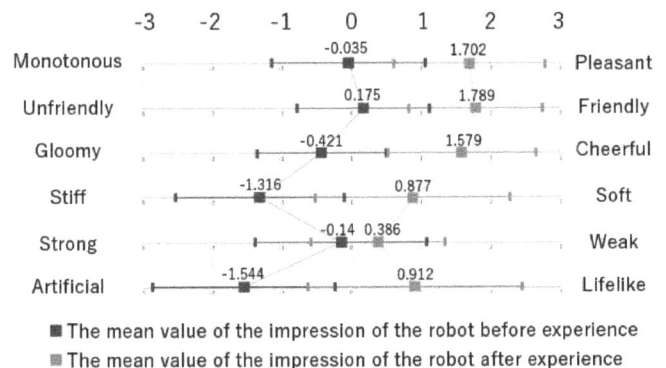

■ The mean value of the impression of the robot before experience
■ The mean value of the impression of the robot after experience

Figure 8. The appearance of the robots

Hearing questionnaire

In order to verify the effect the amount of robot gives to animacy perception,we carried out the following two types of interviews at the University of Tokyo MAKING MAKE Exhibition (2016/7/13 - 7/16).

Interview 1: The users contacted first with one robot, second with three robots, and finally with five robots. After the users contacted with three types, they selected subjectively which type felt most like living creatures.

Interview 2: Referencing Takahashi et al.,we created five choices below. After the users contacted with five robots, we let users select multiple choices which seemingly represent the way robots move.

- move synchronously
- move taking cooperation
- move interacting other robots
- move independently
- move random

Interview 1 was carried out with 37 people. The results are shown in Figure 9. While 7 people answered they percepted animacy in one robot, 14 people in three robot, and 16 people in five robot. Interview 2 was carried out with 33 people, which we obtained 54 votes in total. This is shown in Figure 10. "Move interacting other robots" gathered 31 votes, followed by "move independently" with 9 votes, "move taking cooperation" with 6 votes, "move random" with 5 votes, "move synchronously" with 3 votes.

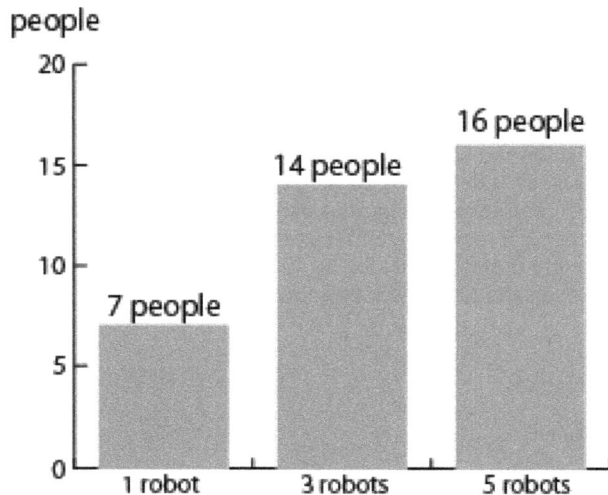

Figure 9. the graph of users' impressions about number of robots

From Hearing 1, It is suggested that users percept animacy to plural number of robots stronger than one robot. However, significant difference between three and five was difficult to admit. From hearing 2, animacy perception of this robot is recalled not from coordinated movement of several robots, but from the interaction of individual independent robots.

CONCLUSION

The five robots used in these experiments were shaped like cubes. This shape was chosen because it eliminated any emotional connection in the users to the idea of the robots being live creatures. Therefore, we conclude that we, as humans, assume that inanimate objects are not lifelike. This

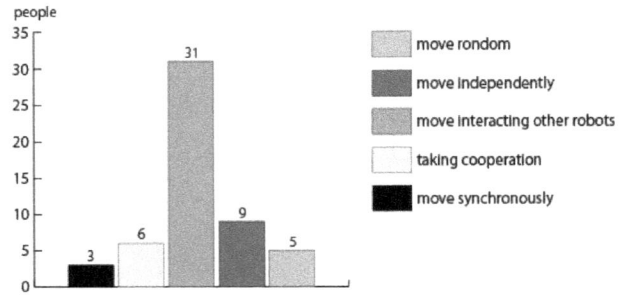

Figure 10. the graph of users' impressions about robots

was evident from the results of the questionnaire, when the robots had been stationary. Then, as the robots moved, the participants' impressions significantly changed. Through the robots' movements, we found that the affinity between the users and the robots improved. This perception was generated by the movement of the robots. We estimated that there was an equilateral correlation in the perception of the robot and animacy between users and the robots. In future research, we intend to show by collecting more data that the perception of animacy can improve the relationship between a person and the robot. The robots and their movements were implemented using simple mechanisms, which were nonetheless effective in improve the affinity between users and the robots. We intend to apply this mechanism to a situation where this kind of affinity is needed. This kind of mechanism should be considered in future use because of its practical nature.

REFERENCES

1. Arita, A. Can we talk to robots? ten-month-old infants expected interactive humanoid robots to be talked to by persons. *Cognition*, B49-B57 (2005).

2. Bartneck, C. Measurement instruments for the anthropomorphism, animacy, likeability, perceived intelligence, and perceived safety of robots. *International Journal of Social Robotics*, 1(1) (2009), 71–81.

3. FUKUDA, H., and UEDA, K. Interaction with movements of robot influences animacy perception. *Human-Agent Interaction Symposium*, 1F-2 (2007).

4. Heider, F., and Simmel, M. An experimental study of apparent behavior. *The American Journal of Psychology Vol. 57*, No. 2 (Apr., 1944), 243–259.

5. Inoue, M., and Kobayashi, T. The research domain and scale construction of adjective pairs in a semantic differential method in japan. *Jap.J.of Educ.Psychol. Vol.33*, No.3 (1985), 253–260.

6. Ito, N. Pelat : Exploring a 'field' emerged from the human-unstable robot interactionpelat. *Human-Agent Interaction Symposium*, P-1 (2014).

7. P.D.Tremoulet, and J.Feldman. The influence of spatial context and the role of intentionality in the interpretation of animacy from motion. *Perception and Psychophysics vol.68*, no.6 (2006), 1047–1058.

8. SoftBank. Softbank mobile and aldebaran unveil 'pepper' - the world's first personal robot that reads emotions. `http://www.softbank.jp/en/corp/group/sbm/news/press/2014/20140605_01/`, 2014. (accessed 2016-4-18).

9. TAKARATOMY. Product information omnibot series. `http://www.takaratomy.co.jp/products/omnibot/`. (accessed 2016-4-18).

10. Yamaoka, F. The design guide for 'lifelike' communication robots based on developmental psychology findings. *Journal of the Robotics Society of Japan Vol.25*, No.7 (2007), 1134–1144.

Exploring Social Interaction with Everyday Object based on Perceptual Crossing

Siti Aisyah binti Anas, Shi Qiu, Matthias Rauterberg, Jun Hu
Eindhoven University of Technology,
Department of Industrial Design,
5600 MB, Eindhoven, The Netherlands
{s.a.b.anas, sqiu, g.w.m.rauterberg, j.hu}@tue.nl

ABSTRACT
Eye gaze plays an essential role in social interaction which influences our perception of others. It is most likely that we can perceive the existence of another intentional subject through the act of cathing one another's eyes. Based on the notion of perceptual crossing, we aim to establish a meaningful social interaction that emerges out of the perceptual crossing between a person and an everyday object by exploiting the gazing behavior of the person as the input modality for the system. We investigated in literature the experiments that adopt the perceptual crossing as their foundation, lessons learned from literature were used as input for a concept to create meaningful social interaction. We used an eye-tracker to measure gaze behavior that allows the participant to interact with the object by using their eyes through active exploration. It creates a situation where both of them mutually becoming aware of each other's existence. Further, we discuss the motivation for this research, present a preliminary experiment that influences our decision and our directions for future work.

Author Keywords
Perceptual crossing; eye tracking; gaze sensitive object; human-object interaction; social interaction.

ACM Classification Keywords
H.5.m. Information Interfaces and Presentation (e.g. HCI): Miscellaneous.

INTRODUCTION
The growing maturity of sensor technology allows engineers to transform everyday object and make it smart enough for effortless interaction with users. Human perceptual sensing capabilities seem becoming limited and in many cases underappreciated as the technology grows. It seems that people are looking for perfection without even realizing that they are missing something that they normally use to experience the world - their capabilities to interact in this world. Taking coffee machine as an example, we simply push a button, and its all done for us. Of course, technology helps us in so many ways, but through this technology, we experience our everyday object without meaningful, and expressive interaction.

We are capable of experiencing and interacting with the world in very different ways because of our built-in multitude of senses - sight, hearing, taste, smell and touch. We have these abilities that seem to fade away as the technology evolves through the years. This world is full of things that are right in front of us, but we did not realize their existence unless we expect to see them. We interact and experience things around us effortlessly without being aware of it. Taking the experience of looking into the mirror and seeing the image reflected back. We perceive ourselves as the image starts to mimic our behavior. The image looks back, and our gaze crosses each other. However, most of us do not realize the existence of the mirror, the object which helps us to make sure that we are still the same person we were yesterday. What if the mirror was *aware* that we are looking at it and we get the feeling that the mirror *looks back* at us? How could the mirror respond and what could it do to *look back* at us? The psychoanalyst, Jacques Lacan believe that the act of seeing is a reciprocal process [5]. According to him, each object has a certain presence that makes him feel of being looks back. "*I see and I can see that I am seen, so each time I see, I also see myself being seen.*" However, not everyone can feel the same as Lacan sees things. Indeed, we tend to less appreciate the act of seeing things in front of us. The presence of objects that make our live complete is nothing more than just an object. The question remains, though, on how can we make the object and the person aware of each other's existence. Under what situation can we experience meaningful social interaction with everyday object? What if we change the way we look at things and the things we look at change in the sense that it reacts to our gaze? Can we create situations when we look at something and it "looks" back at us?

HAI '16, October 04-07, 2016, Biopolis, Singapore
© 2016 ACM. ISBN 978-1-4503-4508-8/16/10...$15.00
DOI: http://dx.doi.org/10.1145/2974804.2974810

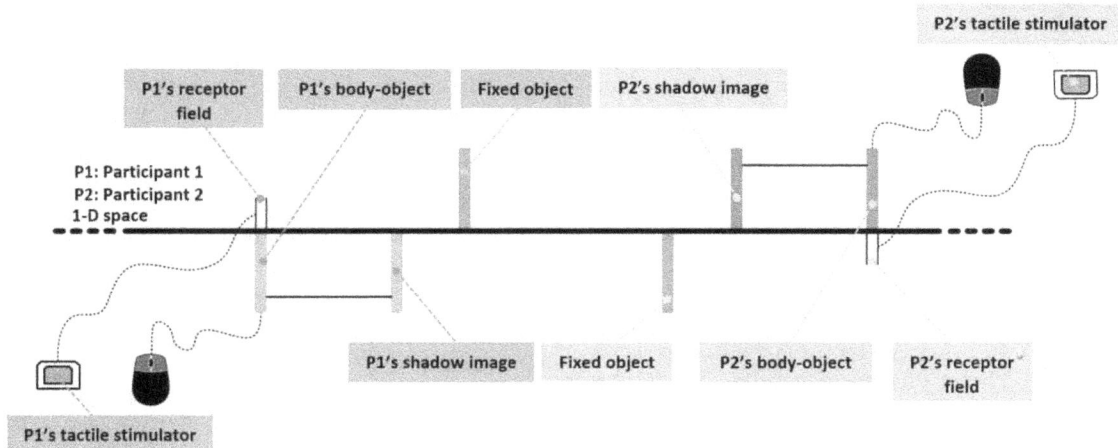

Figure 1. Virtual environment of Auvrey et. al's perceptual crossing paradigm [1].

RELATED WORK

Perceptual Crossing Paradigm

Auvrey et al.'s [1] perceptual crossing paradigm (PCP) is a well-known paradigm for studying real-time interaction and has been used by many researchers in different areas to investigate factors involved in perceiving each other's existence. In their experiment [1], pairs of participants in separate rooms explored a one-dimensional virtual space using a computer mouse and received tactile stimuli on the index finger of the other hand if they encountered something in space. There were three objects that participants could encounter: the partner's body-object, a fixed object and the shadow image which movement was identical to their partner's body-object. The only difference between the body-object and the shadow image was that the former was responsive to the perceptual crossing (both participants would receive tactile stimuli when they encountered each other). The task was to click the mouse button when the participants believed that they perceived the presence of their partner (see Figure 1). The results indicated that participants clicked more often when they encountered the partner's body-object. The participants' ability to distinguish all three objects resulted from active exploration and shared perceptual activity that influenced their behavior during real-time interaction and not because they consciously recognized the differences between three of the objects. When they encountered each other, both of them received tactile stimulation. They would reverse the direction of their body-object that caused them to performed the same oscillatory behavior. The co-dependence of the two participants to coordinate their behavior influenced them to create a stable interaction.

Froese et al. [6] later continued to investigate the dynamics of interaction process based on PCP by using Evolutionary Robotics simulation modeling. There were two agents in the simulation, and they needed to locate each other's presence. Once both agents successfully established perceptual crossing, they needed to maintain the interaction until the end

of the trial. For this task, both agents seemed to depend on the duration of the stimulation to differentiate whether they encountered their partner, the static object or their partner's shadow image. That has led to a conclusion that the agents might use individual strategy to carry out the task and not because they mutually perceived each other. Based on this result, the team created another task where they switched the receptor field of both agents. The agents should be able to complete the task if they mutually depended on each other during interaction process even though they could not rely on their receptor field at the individual level. As predicted, the agents successfully established perceptual crossing that self-organizes out of the interaction process. It is arguable that both agents perceived one another because they were actively forming the interaction based on their individual efforts to stay in contact rather than relying on each other during interaction process. The creation of the last task was to prove the validity of this argument. Instead of mutually responding toward each other, agents were required to remained in contact with their partner's shadow image. If both agents depend on their individual strategy to complete this task, stayed in contact with the shadow image would be easy. It turned out that both agents could not meet the task requirement successfully. Unstable interaction occurred when they were trying to interact with the shadow image, hence prevented the establishment of perceptual crossing from occurring out of the interaction process. However, during exploration, when both agents found each other, they somehow sustained the interaction even though the task required them to stay in contact with their partner's shadow image. It showed that the interaction process itself shaped the behavior of the agents rather than depending on the individual strategy to complete the task.

Lenay et al. [12] studied the emergence patterns produced by the participants during the interaction process in a two-dimensional virtual space. The task of this experiment was still the same as Auvrey's PCP where participants needed to clicked when they encountered their partner's body-object.

Through active exploration, participants employed several criteria based on their trajectory in space and time. The act of anticipation formed when sufficient regularity occurred during interaction with a fixed object. Participants expected the stimulation to be consistent when they perceived a fixed object. The act of surprised to differentiate between a fixed object with their partner's body-object and the shadow image (the other). When participants encountered a fixed object, the stimulation should be regular (the act of anticipation) as the object did not move in space. However, when they failed to establish these regularities (the act of surprised), it can be concluded that they were in contact with the other. The other's existence were unpredictable but could also retain its presence if the other was their partner's body-object. Logically, these criteria employed by the participants were based on the encountered of two intentionalities during the perceptual crossing. The participants did not need to recognize each other before they established perceptual crossing. It is because they mutually responded during perceptual crossing that led them to recognize each other.

Lizuka et al. [13] investigated whether participants could differentiate the interaction to be live or recorded. Based on Auvrey et al.'s PCP but without the static object and the shadow image in the virtual space, participants would encounter two kinds of body-objects. One was the body-object controlled by their partner. The other was the recorded body-object from the previous trial. The participants faced difficulties at the beginning but after several trials, they developed a turn-taking behavior. During the live interaction, Participant 1 (P1) oscillated at the body-object of Participant 2 (P2) while P2 stayed at one place and identified P1's oscillatory behavior. When P1 stopped moving and oscillating, P2 would repeat the same behavior as he/she recalled from P1. The establishment of turn-taking behavior by P1 and P2 made this strategy useful in determining whether the interaction was live or not. Lizuka et al. also extended this experiment by investigating whether non-communicative behavior could become communicative when both participants encountered each other. In this experiment, pairs of participants needed to decide whether they confronted with an identical or different shape (sharp,# or square,□) displayed on the monitor. After several trials, both participants learned to take turns and communicated by exchanging oscillation patterned to represent each shape that they confronted during the trial. If they saw a sharp, the oscillation patterned become more frequent and fast. If they saw a square, the movement of the oscillation become slower. Lizuka et al.'s experiment showed that during the interaction process, participants were capable of developing turn-taking behavior to communicate with each other through non-verbal interaction.

Deckers et al. [4] proposed six design notions to establish perceptual crossing between a person and an artefact. *Focus the Senses*, *Active Behavior Object*, *Subtleness*, *Reaction to External Event*, *Detecting Active Behavior Subject*, *Reflecting Contextual Noise*, and *Course of Perception in*

Time were implemented by them in designing an artefact which they addressed as the *perception pillar plus* (*PEP+*). *PEP+* was a square pillar embedded with eight ultrasonic sensors, and 17 static matrices of LEDs mounted on top surface of the pillar. An experiment conducted between *PEP+* and the participant concluded that most of the participants managed to achieve shared perception with the artefact that was one of the vital element during perceptual crossing. The possibility of experiencing reciprocal perception improved the participant's feeling of beeing involved during interaction with the artefact within the environment.

Lesson Learned from Perceptual Crossing
Social interaction can emerge out of the perceptual crossing. Even though participants do not have any conscious recognition to interact with each other, but through active exploration in real-time, they can perceive one another and mutually become aware of their partner's existence. This process is crucial for them to understand the social interaction [2]. Social interaction often lead to a social understanding based on the collective properties gain during the interaction process. Traditionally, social understanding is built upon how we predict and interpret other people's behavior or action. However, the concept of PCP is to concentrate on the interaction process rather than focusing on how individual figures out the others, but taking interaction as a medium to recognize and to engage with one another [9]. An example was during the encounter with the body-object and the shadow image in the aforementioned experiments. The experimenter's intuition was the difficulties that participants might face differentiating the body-object with the shadow image as both of the object move in the same manner. However, during the interaction process, when participants encounter the shadow image, they established unstable interaction which leads them to avoid the shadow image and proceed to explore the space until they perceive a stable interaction [1].

One can also observe in the aforementioned experiments several patterns adopted by participants during the interaction process. The act of surprise and anticipation when they encountered the body-object, fixed object and the shadow image that helped them to recognize which is which [12]. They learned the turn-taking behavior to distinguish whether the interaction was live or not [13]. They managed to use this turn-taking behavior as a strategy to communicate with each other by controlling their oscillation patterned [13].

During the simulation, it seemed that both agents might come out with an individual strategy to differentiate the objects they encountered [6]. However, when the experimenter switched the receptor field of both agents and changed the task to which they needed to stay in contact with the shadow image of the other agent, both agents somehow managed to establish perceptual crossing but failed to interact with the shadow image. Both agents preferred to stay in contact with each other even though the task told them no to do so. The interaction process influenced both agent's behavior to establish perceptual crossing.

All of these behaviors, patterns and criteria were established during active exploration that self-organized out of the interaction process without any explicit interpretation of the other interactor. It did not concern on the individual's ability to act in order to complete the task, but the shared perceptual activity was the most important part that influences their behavior to act during the interaction. They learned to appreciate each other existence in the very limited resources. Even though it required some time, eventually they managed to perceive each other's presence. Variations of results gained from the aforementioned experiments provoke inspiration to design interactive devices that can establish meaningful social interaction with a person during the interaction process itself.

MOTIVATION

This research is motivated to appreciate human capabilities and to create opportunities to experience social interaction that emerges out of the perceptual crossing with an everyday object. We aim to design an interactive everyday object that is sensitive to the perceptual crossing by depending on the user's gaze behavior as the input modality for the system. Giddens et al. [7] addresses that social interactions is a process of acting and reacting toward people around us, and it can be in any forms of verbal and nonverbal communication. Since visual modality is dominant for most individuals and as the matter of fact, our eyes serve as the focal points of our body, our gaze behavior is an essential type of nonverbal communication. We use our eyes to perceive others and to signal our intentions [8]. Hence, we decided to make use the role of gaze in developing social interaction with an object. Through active exploration, we wanted to establish a situation where the person and the object could coordinate their behavior so that both of them would mutually become aware of each other existence.

PROTOTYPE

Mechanical Actuating

To design an object that can perceive while being perceived, it needs to possess distinctive characteristics that allow it to be engaged in live dyadic interactions. We decided to use a coffee cup as our first everyday object that we commonly use in our daily lives. Figure 2 shows the exploded view drawing of the coffee cup. Table 1 outlines the explanation for each part.

The purpose of this design is to allow the cup the ability to react during interaction with the user. We believe that by adding the coffee cup with elements of dynamic behavior, the user can experience social interaction with it, and the cup's movement is triggered only when they look at it. To control the movement of the cup, we used gears as part of the working mechanism.

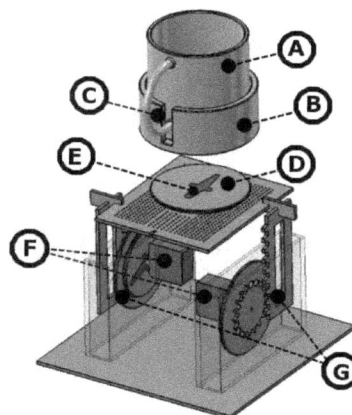

Figure 2. Exploded view drawing of the coffee cup.

Part	Explanation
A	The coffee cup
B	The cup's holder to hold the cup securely on top of the base Below
C	The slot to grip the cup's handle
D	The base to control the cup's rotation (rotate left or right)
E	Servo horn
F	Combination of rack and pinion to allow the cup to move vertically (up or down)
G	Servo motors to control the movement of the cup

Table 1. The explanation for each part of the design.

A pinion is a typical round gear, and a rack is a straight bar with teeth that allow it to engage with the pinion's gear teeth. When the pinion rotates, it causes the rack to move corresponding to the pinion, thereby enable the cup to move up if the pinion rotates clockwise, or move down if the pinion rotates counterclockwise (see Figure 3).

Figure 3. The coffee cup moves up when the pinion rotates clockwise.

The cup's holder (B) and the base (D) are securely fixed together with plastic screws. This base is attached to a servo horn where one servo motor control the rotation of the coffee cup to a specified position (see Figure 4). We used acrylic plastic as the material for the mechanical parts and Adobe

Illustrator to generate the design for laser cutting. The coffee cup (A) and the cup's holder (B) were modeled using Rhino3D and fabricated using Ultimaker's 3D printer.

Figure 4. The coffee cup rotates to a specified position (from left to right).

Sensing: Eye Tracking

To track the gaze behavior in real-time, we need a device that can measure the participant's eye positions and movements. The Eye Tribe Tracker is an affordable eye tracker that can detect and determine the point of gaze defined by a pair of (x,y) coordinates with an average efficiency of 0.5° to 1.0° of visual angle and it connects to a USB 3.0 port on a laptop. It comes with software that allows client applications to access the underlying tracker's server to obtain a real-time stream of gaze data in raw and smoothed forms. To create a system that is responsive toward the user's eye gaze, we developed a Java program to calculate and reveal the location of the gaze point on the screen. A graphical user interface (GUI) with 15 targeted area is created to detect the point of interest where the user fixates in real-time. Figure 5 depicts the interface of the program. When the user fixates on one of the targeted areas, the system will activate the correspond circle (large red circle) to indicate that the user is now looking at that point (example: Point 3, Point 7). The small red dot indicates the user's current point of gaze. We assigned each targeted area with a command. Once the targeted area is activated, this command is sent out to an Arduino over a wireless Bluetooth connection.

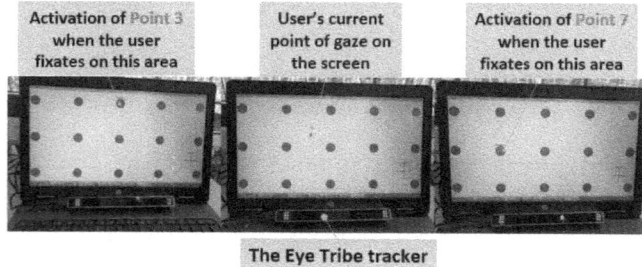

Figure 5. The interface of the system.

Processing and Behavior

To enable the coffee cup to interact and respond towards the user's eye gaze, the position of the cup is carefully pre-determined, and must be within the eye tracker's tracking area. From Figure 6, it can be seen that the position of the coffee cup is equal to Point 7 from the GUI. The eye tracker detects the user's eye gaze, and if the user's gaze point

correspond to the position of the coffee cup, a command is sent out via Bluetooth adapter from the laptop to a Bluetooth module connected to an Arduino.

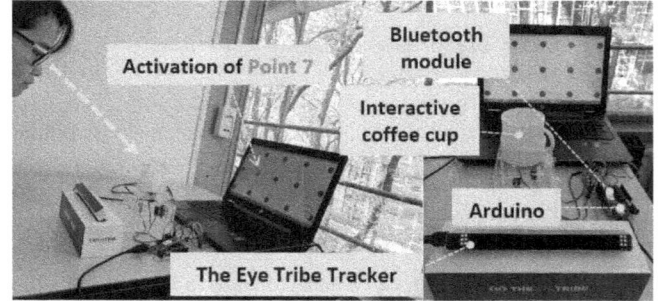

Figure 6. A user is fixating at the interactive coffee cup.

This microcontroller process the signal received from the module, and it generates behavior to the interactive coffee cup. There are four modes of behavior that the interactive coffee cup could display when the user is looking at it. For this experiment, Arduino will decide which mode displayed to the user in a random manner. If the user is not looking at the cup, it will go back to its initial state. Table 2 shown the type of behavioral patterns of the interactive coffee cup. These patterns depend on the degrees of rotation that the servo motors will rotate during interaction with the user. All of these patterns were created to be use in future experiment where the user will engage more with the coffee cup. *Breathing* happen when the coffee is still in the cup and the user ignore the cup (by not looking at it) for a while. *Shivering* occur when the temperature of the coffee in the cup drop to a certain value. *Playing* result when the user fixates at the cup for a certain time but does not pick it up to drink the coffee. *Dancing* happens when the cup is empty, and the user is looking at the cup.

Type	Behavioral patterns	Mode
0		Initial state
1		Breathing
2	This behavior causes the coffee cup to vibrate.	Shivering

Type	Behavioral patterns	Mode
3		Playing
4		Dancing

Table 2. Coffee cup's behavioral patterns.

EXPERIMENT

Participants

15 participants, nine men, and six women, between the ages of 26 to 38 participated in the experiment. Seven of them is a Ph.D. student, five are currently not working, and three of them work as an engineer from various field.

Setup

We want to investigate whether participants can perceive the behavior of the coffee cup that will only react when they look at it. We decided to place a normal coffee cup beside the interactive coffee cup. We expect the participant to compare both cups and explore the environment by shifting their gaze during the experiment. Can the participant and the cup perceive each other behavior during his/her active exploration? Figure 7 illustrate the experimental setup. The placement of the interactive coffee cup was very crucial and must correspond with the system's targeted area. The position of the participant was also important and must be paralleled to the eye tracker's tracking area. It is necessary to center aligned the tracker and adjusted it towards the participant's face for the maximum trackability. When the participant gazes at the setup, the eye tracker extracted the gaze coordination and compared it with the pre-determined position of the interactive coffee cup. If matched, a command is sent via Bluetooth and Arduino will display the behavioral patterns of the interactive coffee cup to the participant in a random manner.

Since eye gaze is not a very typical input modality used for interaction in a real environment and mostly confined to the digital or virtual world, we want to investigate whether participants realize that their eye gaze is being exploited by the system that allows them to interact with the coffee cup. If the participant look away from the interactive coffee cup, it will go back to its initial state (type 0). If the participant fixates at the interactive coffee cup, it will react (random mode) to indicate *"I see you looking at me. Hence, I will respond."*

Normally, we rely heavily on sight to guide our movements that lead to appropriate actions [15]. However, for this experiment, we want the participants to appreciate the joy of experiencing social interaction with an object by simply looking at it and without the needs for them to act during the ongoing experiment.

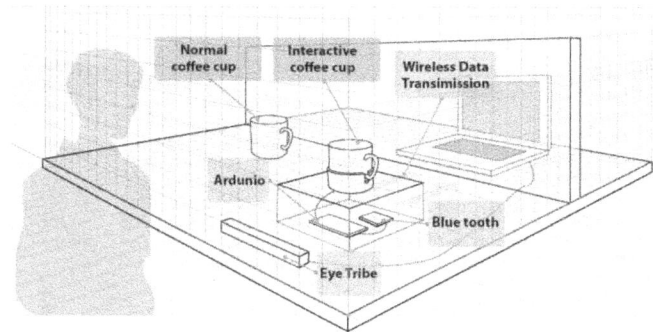

Figure 7. Overview of the setup.

Procedures

The participants were told to sat in front of a desk where the normal and the interactive coffee cup were placed. The instructions were rather simple. We instructed the participants to observe both coffee cup, and at the end of the experiment, they filled out a questionnaire. After that, we asked two open-ended questions related to the participant's perception regarding both cups. If the open-ended question leaves the participants confused, we explained to them the concept and motivation behind this research and asked them to participate in the experiment once again. Participants followed the same instructions and filled out the same questionnaire for the second time.

Questionnaire

We decided to measure the participants experienced with the interactive coffee cup by using the User Experience Questionnaire (UEQ) [10]. The questionnaire consists of 6 scales with 26 items. *Attractiveness* indicates the overall impression of the product. *Perspicuity* illustrates the difficulty of participants to get familiar and learn how to use the product. *Efficiency* is the ability of participants to solve the task without unnecessary effort. *Dependability* indicates if participants feel in control during the interaction process. *Stimulation* shows the excitement and motivation of participants to use the product. *Novelty* indicates whether the product is innovative, creative and able to catch the participant's interest [10]. Two open-ended questions regarding the participant's experienced during observation of both coffee cups were constructed and delivered to them. The questions were; *what is the difference between these two cups* and *did the participant realize that his/her gaze is making the cup react*. Verbal and non-verbal responses gathered from the participants were also recorded for future references and were used to complement the findings from the UEQ.

RESULTS

We categorized the findings from the UEQ into two, the before and the after condition. The first experiment was *the before condition* where the participants were instructed to observed the coffee cups without knowing the motivation behind the experiment. The second experiment was *the after condition* where the participants were asked to participate in the experiment once again after we explained to them the objectives of this research. Figure 6 shows the scores for all scales based on findings from the UEQ.

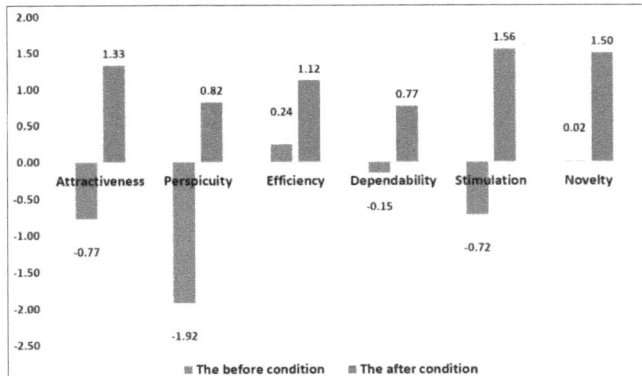

Figure 6. Graph of the six UEQ scales

From the graph, the overall scores indicated clearly the difference for each scales between the before and the after condition. The participant's responses to the open-ended questions may explain these findings. 13 out of 15 participants faced the difficulties to explain the differences between the regular coffee cup with the interactive one other than the former was a static object, and the later was embed with mechanical behaviors that allowed the cup to show random movements. The same participants also did not realize that their gaze influenced the interactive cup to react. The cup perceived participants' gaze, but participants did not perceive the cup's reaction to their gaze at the same time. Since the task was to observe on both objects without any further instructions or explanation, most of the participants seemed to be confused on why the interactive cup was suddenly showing some behaviors and why at some time it stopped interacting. The participant's gaze tended to focus more on the interactive cup rather than to compare and to observe their gaze with the other normal coffee cup. They felt that the cup was interacting on its own that attracted them to fixate on the interactive cup. They were also busy trying to interpret the behavior shown by the coffee cup which was rather new to them and if the cup's behavior was related to their action or influenced by the environment. However, after the second attempt, the graph show major improvements on the scores indicating positive feedback from participants. They started to explore both objects actively and realized that their gaze indeed influenced the cup's behavior. It was after being told the motivation behind this research that they felt the *existence* of the cup rather that just simply an object that could demonstrate random movement. Four of the participants found the interactive cup *playful* and *very responsive*. Six of the participants felt that the cup was trying to communicate with them, but they could not interpret it as the behavior was very random and unrecognizable. Others

thought that the cup was a toy. Participant 3 said: "*I cannot believe that we can interact with the cup just by depending on our eye gaze. It is fascinating and new.*" Participant 5 said: "*It is weird to see the cup with this kind of behavior, but I like the idea behind this research.*" Participant 10 said: "*This research can attract children to observe their surroundings rather than spending more time with the touchscreen. Like my kids!*". Furthermore, all of the participants did not realize the function of the eye tracker in front of them. They thought that it was just part of the interactive design.

DISCUSSION

The observation during experiments, findings from the UEQ and feedback gathered from the participants gave us some hints regarding on why the user did not perceive the behavior of the coffee cup while the coffee cup perceive the user's gaze behavior and the future if this research. These can be summarized as follows:

- Active exploration is crucial in social interaction

The accuracy of the interactive cup that can react once it detects the presence of someone's gaze does not give much impact on the participant's feeling of mutually becoming aware of each other's existence. The interaction process needs to be improved in this context. In PCP, active exploration during the interaction process is crucial to make both subjects feel the presence of each other. We cannot simply depend on the accuracy of the input to produce the output or participants will face difficulties to understand the environment. We need to consider on how to build the relationship through active exploration which can lead to the discovery of each other presence. The establishment of the relationship can be developed when the object and the subject understand and recognize each other's behavior.

- Behavior of the interactive object

It is not necessary to design an interactive object that has unique features to perform perceptual crossing. "Unique" here means that overloading too many new features to an existing everyday object will divert our primary purpose of creating social interaction with the object. Perhaps, the use of properties already built in the object can be modified to create unique characteristics. An analog clock, for example, its mechanical behavior of controlling the moving hands can be altered as part of its unique features that can be used to perform perceptual crossing. Otherwise, participants will be preoccupied constructing internal interpretation of the object's behaviors that is very new to them rather than realizing the interaction process with the object.

- The identity of the system

For the system to have its identity, it needs to consider stages of data processing cycle and not to rely on producing an output whenever the system detect an input. This method is crucial in PCP as the system needs to actively explore and become familiar with the environment first in order to recognize the presence of the others. Possibly, the system should self-organize its behavior during the interaction process rather than depend on a set of predefined rules. The system should consider to analyze the characteristics of the gaze behavior, interpret the necessary gaze information and exploit the gaze behavior to produce relevant output [14]. However, the system must not consume too much time for its behavior to emerge, or participants might lose interest to interact as there is no feedback coming from the system in time.

- The eye tracking metrics

To develop the system's identity during the interaction process, it needs to understand the participant's gaze behavior since it is the only reliable input modality that the system can use. Gaze behaviors can reveal our point of interest. The eye tribe tracker enables us to collect and measure gaze data in real-time. It can detect the points of gaze of the participants. The time spent observing the point and traces of fixation patterns from a specific point to another reflects how participants scan the environment. These eye tracking metrics are useful to draw a better picture in obtaining direct feedback from participants while they interact with the object [3], which can contribute to the development of the system's behavior.

CONCLUSION AND FUTURE WORK

From our preliminary experiment, even though the task was rather simple, we gain insights that can guide us in creating meaningful social interaction between a person and an everyday object. The accuracy of the system to produce the output is important when both the subject and the object perceive each other rather than to depend on the accuracy of the sensor to detect an input and straightaway produce the output without considering the interaction process. The object should identify and adopt the behavioral patterns of the subject through the learning process and coordinate its behavior once it recognizes the subject. Furthermore, to design an interactive everyday object, we need to investigate and fully utilize the characteristic of the existing object. The object's behavior needs to be relevant to the object itself. This way, we can reduce internal representations constructed by the subject and allow the subject to appreciate the social interaction with the object that can emerge out of the perceptual crossing during the interaction process. Unless we want to attract the subject's attention, then a "unique" design should be applicable.

We view the work describe in this paper as a starting point for our research. We intend to create a system that can detect human's gaze behavioral patterns which will influence the system's ability to respond during perceptual crossing. We also intend to develop a complete framework that can enable a person to experience social interaction with everyday objects by depending on his/her gazing behavior.

ACKNOWLEDGMENTS
We thank our colleagues at the Design Intelligence research group who give suggestions and ideas for this project. This research received funding from the Ministry of Higher Education, Malaysia and Universiti Teknikal Malaysia Melaka (UTeM).

REFERENCES
[1] Auvray, M., Lenay, C. and Stewart, J. 2009. Perceptual interactions in minimalist virtual environment. *New Ideas Psychol.* 27, (2009), 79–97.

[2] Auvray, M. and Rohde, M. 2012. Perceptual crossing: the simplest online paradigm. *Frontiers in Human Neuroscience.* 6, (2012), 181–194.

[3] Bergstrom, J.R. and Schall, A. 2014. *Eye Tracking in User Experience Design.* Morgan Kaufmann.

[4] Deckers, E., Lévy, P., Wensveen, S., Ahn, R. and Overbeeke, K. 2013. Designing for perceptual crossing: applying and evaluating design notions. *International Journal of Design.* 6, (2013), 41–55.

[5] Elkins, J. 1997. *The Object Stares Back. On the Nature of Sensing.* Simon and Schuster, Inc.

[6] Froese, T. and Di Paolo, E.A. 2009. Modeling social interactions as perceptual crossing: an investigation into dynamics of the interaction process. *Connection Science.* 22, (2009), 43–68.

[7] Giddens, A., Duneier, M., Appelbaum, R.P. and Carr, D. 2013. *Introduction to Sociology.* W. W. Norton & Company.

[8] Gobel, M.S., Heejung, S.K. and Richardson, D.C. 2015. The dual function of social gaze. *International Journal of Cognitive Science.* 136, (2015), 359–364.

[9] De Jaegher, H. 2009. Social understanding through direct perception? Yes, by interacting. *Consciousness and Cognition.* 18, (2009), 535–542.

[10] Laugwitz, B., Held, T. and Schrepp, M. 2008. Construction and evaluation of a User Experience Questionnaire. *USAB.* 5298, (2008), 63–76.

[11] Lenay, C. and Stewart, J. 2012. Minimalist approach to perceptual interactions. *Frontiers in Human Neuroscience.* 6, (2012), 98–115.

[12] Lenay, C., Stewart, J., Rohde, M. and Ali Amar, A. 2011. You never fail to surprise me: the hallmark of the Other. Experimental study and simulations of perceptual crossing: *Interaction Studies.* 12(3), (2011), 373–396.

[13] Lizuka, H., Marocco, D., Ando, H. and Maeda, T. 2012. Turn-taking supports humanlikeness and communication in perceptual crossing experiments. *Virtual Reality Short Papers and Posters (VRW) IEEE.* (2012), 1–4.

[14] Nakano, Y.I., Conati, C. and Bader, T. 2013. *Eye Gaze in Intelligent User Interfaces. Gaze-based Analyses, Models and Applications.* Springer.

[15] Noe, A. 2006. *Action in Perception (Representation and Mind series).* A Bradford Book.

Pre-scheduled Turn-Taking between Robots to Make Conversation Coherent

Takamasa Iio
Osaka University / JST ERATO
Osaka, Japan
iio@irl.sys.es.osaka-u.ac.jp

Yuichiro Yoshikawa
Osaka University / JST ERATO
Osaka, Japan
yoshikawa@irl.sys.es.osaka-u.ac.jp

Hiroshi Ishiguro
Osaka University / JST ERATO
Osaka, Japan
ishiguro@irl.sys.es.osaka-u.ac.jp

ABSTRACT

Since a talking robot cannot escape from errors in recognizing user's speech in daily environment, its verbal responses are sometimes felt as incoherent with the context of conversation. This paper presents a solution to this problem that generates a social context where a user is guided to find coherency of the robot's utterances, even though its response is produced according to incorrect recognition of user's speech. We designed a novel turn-taking pattern in which two robots behave according to a pre-scheduled scenario to generate such a social context. Two experiments proved that participants who talked to two robots using that turn-taking pattern felt robot's responses to be more coherent than those who talked to one robot not using it; therefore, our proposed turn-taking pattern generated a social context for user's flexible interpretation of robot's responses. This result implies a potential of a multiple robots approach for improving the quality of human-robot conversation.

Author Keywords

Human robot interaction; Multiple robots' conversation;

ACM Classification Keywords

H.5.2. User Interfaces – *Interaction styles*.

INTRODUCTION

Social robots which talks to a user in daily environment have been widely developed, such as museums [1, 2], expositions [3], receptions [4], shops [5], stations [6], shopping malls [7] and elementary schools [11, 12].

Such robots are considered to be adopting a scenario based approach, in which a robot leads a conversation along a scenario pre-designed on the domain of its application. Figure 1 shows two examples of a conversation following such a scenario based approach. In these examples, a robot asks something (Question), a user answers to the question (Answer), the robot gives a back-channel feedback (Back-

channel feedback), and finally the robot responds to user's answer. The robot leads a conversation by choosing a behavior including speeches and gestures along this scenario. This approach has a merit that a conversation continues naturally as long as a user says something expected by scenario designers.

However, such a scenario based approach has a serious problem that when a robot fails to recognize user's answer, its response seems incoherent to the answer; in other words, the robot chooses a behavior incoherent to the answer. See the recognition failure case of Figure 1. It shows that the robot failed to recognize user's answer; the robot caught the

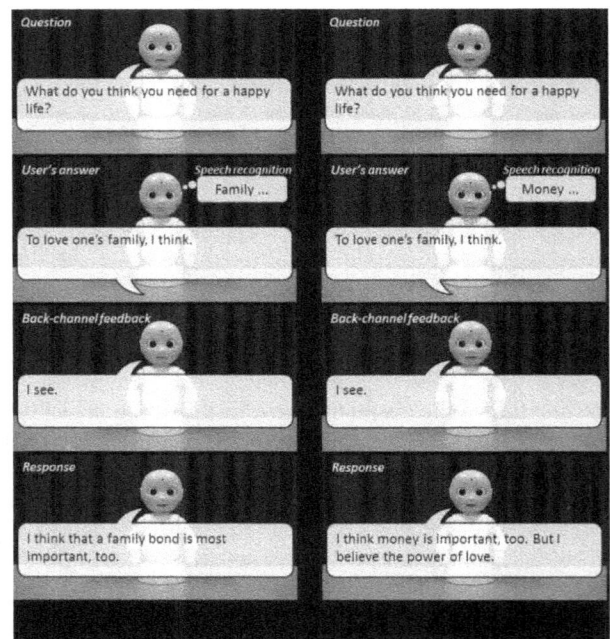

Figure 1. Two examples of a conversation based on a scenario based approach. The left conversation shows a coherent case, and the right conversation shows an incoherent case. The robot first asks a user about what the user need for a happy life (Question). Then, the user answers to the question and the robot tries to recognize user's speech at that time (Answer). After that the robot gives a back-channel feedback (Back-channel feedback). Finally, the robot responds the answer according to the recognition results (Response). In recognition success case the robot caught the correct word 'Family,' but in recognition failure case it caught the incorrect word 'Money' due to misrecognition.

HAI '16, October 04-07, 2016, Biopolis, Singapore
© 2016 ACM. ISBN 978-1-4503-4508-8/16/10..$15.00
DOI: http://dx.doi.org/10.1145/2974804.2974819

incorrect word 'Money', instead of the correct word 'Family.' This misrecognition caused the robot to choose a behavior incoherent to the answer. Therefore, even though the user said she needed to love one's family, the robot responded as if the user said she needed to get money. It will make the user feel robot's response to be incoherent.

We try to solve this problem by generating a social context in which a user feels that robot's responses seem coherent, even though the responses were actually incoherent to user's answer. This paper presents a novel turn-taking pattern for generating such a social context by two robots behaving cooperatively. Furthermore, we explain two experiments to investigate whether our turn-taking pattern generates a social context. Finally, we report and discuss the experimental results.

TURN-TAKING DESIGN FOR SOCIAL CONTEXT
We designed a turn-taking pattern for generating a social context where a user feels robot's response to be coherent. This turn-taking pattern is produced by pre-scheduled behaviors of two robots.

First, we introduce a background to our idea that two robots cooperate to generate a social context. Next we explain how to make a turn-taking pattern from such cooperated behaviors.

Background of cooperating multiple robots
Research in the field of human robot interaction has suggested that cooperating multiple robots have a potential merit for improving user's impression [8-10].

Hayashi et al also developed robots as a passive-social medium, in which multiple robots converse with each other [10]. They conducted a field experiment at a station to investigate the effects of the robots. As a result, they found that people were more likely to stop to listen to a conversation of two robots than one robot. This research suggested that a social context generated by two robots attract user's attention.

Arimoto et al reported that a social context built by a bystander robot have a positive effect on user's impression of a conversation [8]. This research focused on a situation that the user talked to a robot remotely controlled by another person. Arimoto et al found that the users who talked to the robot with a bystander robot felt the remote-controlled robot to be more made eye contact with and to be less ignored than those who talked to it without the bystander robot. According to Arimoto et al, the robot's gaze which is seemingly meaningless in a conversation could get to make sense in a social context that the bystander robot produced.

Those findings suggest that the power of a social context generated by cooperative behaviors of two robots. Based on those suggestions, we designed a turn-taking pattern generated by cooperated behaviors of two robots.

Social Context built by Cooperating Two Robots
As shown in the recognition failure case of Figure 1, when the robot fails to recognize user's answer to robot's question,

robot's response seems incoherent. To build the social context that allows a user to feel the robot to be coherent, we designed the following turn-taking pattern in that situation:

1. A robot asks something to a user. (Question)

2. The user answer to the question. (Answer)

3. The robot gives back-channel feedback; for example, "I see" and "un-huh". (Back-channel feedback)

4. The robot says an interjection to itself; for example, "Um..." and "Hmm..." (Interjection)

5. Another robot responds to user's answer. (Response)

Figure 2 demonstrates this turn-taking pattern. The first, second and third steps in the pattern are almost same as a usual communication pattern shown in Figure 1. The third step is actually optional but back-channel feedbacks could be used to make the conversation sound like natural. They can be also used as a way to buy time for speech recognition.

The fourth and fifth steps are different from the usual communication pattern. The robot says an interjection in the fourth step, and another robot responds to user's speech in the fifth step.

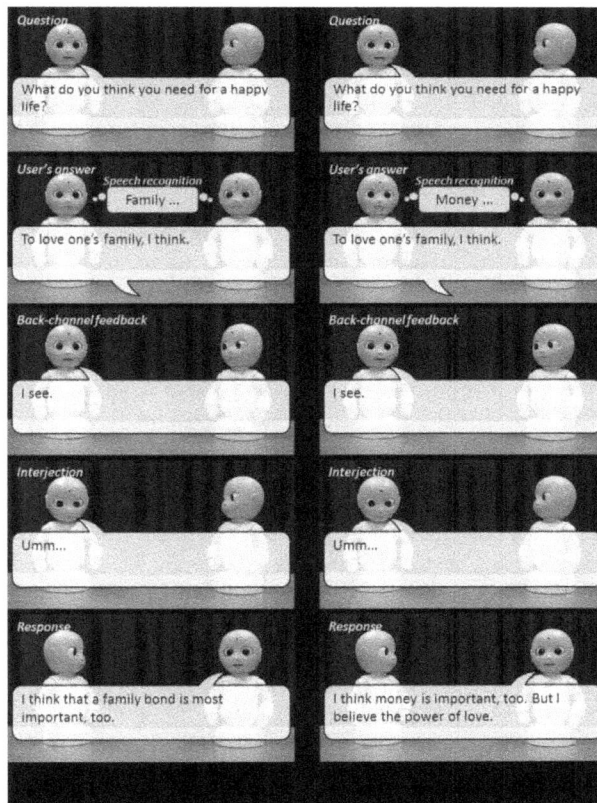

Figure 2. Two examples of a conversation, in which a social context is built by the robots behaving cooperatively. The left conversation shows a recognition success case, and the right conversation shows a recognition failure case. In both cases, robot's response seems to be coherent despite whether the recognition is successful or not.

This turn-taking pattern creates an opportunity for a user to flexibly interpret robot's response. First, see the recognition success case of Figure 2. This is an example of a conversation that the robots successfully recognize user's speech. At the fourth step of the example, the left robot who asked a question to the user seems to be thinking of user's answer because of its interjection, and also the right robot seems to be concerned with the left robot. At the fifth step, the right robot says that a family bond is important. This opinion is same as the user's. Therefore, the user would feel the right robot to approve of the user's opinion. The right robot looks clearly coherent because it gives a response consistent with user's speech as same as the example of the recognition success case of Figure 1.

Next, we consider the example of a conversation shown in the recognition failure of Figure 2, which is a case that the robots fail to recognize user's speech; for instance, the robots did not catch the correct word 'Family' but the incorrect word 'Money.' At the fourth step of the example, as mentioned above, the left robot just pretends to consider about user's answer due to its interjection, and also the right robot seems to be concerned with the right robot. At the fifth step, the right robot says that the power of love is more important that money. This opinion misses the point of user's answer because the user does not say anything about money. However, this conversation relatively looks coherent. This is because it seems that the left robot believes that money is important and the right robot represents its own opinion against that consideration of the left robot. This social context elicits user's imagination to the conversation and enables such a flexible interpretation.

In summary, the turn-taking pattern we proposed builds a social context in which enable a user to interpret robot's response in two ways.

EXPERIMENT 1

We conducted an experiment to explore the efficacy of a turn-taking pattern we designed. In the experiment, we investigate whether the turn-taking pattern enables a user to feel a conversation to be coherent or not. For this investigation, the turn-taking pattern was compared with a usual turn-taking pattern that one robot talks.

Design

Experiment 1 had two conditions. One condition was one-robot condition, in which participants talked to a single robot that behave in a usual turn-taking pattern. The usual turn-taking pattern is almost same as the proposed turn-taking pattern except for being only one robot and not using interjections. The other condition was two-robots condition, in which participants talked to two robots that behave in the proposed turn-taking pattern. The experimental scenes of these conditions are shown in Figure 3.

All participants experienced both conditions; in other words, this experiment was designed as a within-subject experiment.

Environment

We illustrated the environment of the experiment in Figure 4. In one-robot condition, the robot was put on the center of the desk. In two-robots condition, the two robots were symmetrically arranged on the desk. Participants were seated in front of the robot(s). There was an operator for controlling the robot(s) out of sight of the participants.

Robot

We employed CommU, which is a social conversation robot developed by VSTONE, in our system. This robot is a desktop size, which is with a height of 304 mm, a width of 180 mm and a depth of 131 mm. The robot has three DOFs for its west, three DOFs for its neck and two DOFs for each eye so it flexibly controls its gaze as shown Figure 5. This flexible gaze control is important for humanlike social behaviors such as turn-taking in a conversation, establishing engagement via eye contact, expressing its attention.

The robot was operated by the external PC in Figure 4. The PC parsed an action sequence script containing scheduled robot commands, which are Say, Gesture, Look and Wait and sent the commands to the robot(s). The robot played sound file corresponding to say command and moved motors of each axis from gaze or gesture command. Wait command

Figure 3. Experimental scenes. The left picture shows one-robot condition, and the right one shows two-robots condition.

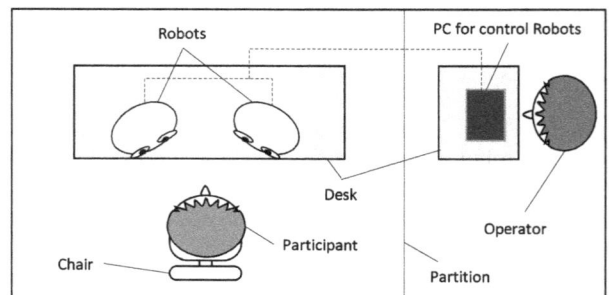

Figure 4. Experimental environment.

Figure 5. CommU

makes the robot(s) pause until an input from an operator (see the next section).

Operator

Since our conversation system pauses a conversation program to wait for participant's response whenever the robot(s) asked something to a participant, the conversation system needed the end of participant's voice activity to resume the conversation program. If failure of voice activity detection happens, the conversation system resumes the program during participant's speech, in other words it interrupts her speech. It will cause the decrease of participant's sense of conversation. Since this side effect makes the analysis of effects of the proposed conversation method complicated, we needed to guarantee the accuracy of voice activity detection. Therefore, we had a human operator detect participant's voice activity instead of using an automatic detection technology (e.g. Wizard of Oz method).

The operator sat out of sight of a participant and listened to her speech shown in Figure 4. The operator pushed the resume button that sends the signal to resume the conversation program when detected the end of participant's voice activity.

Procedure

First, participants read and signed a consent form of this experiment, which was reviewed and approved by a third-party organization review board. We gave the following instruction to the participants: "In this experiment you talk to a robot (robots). Since the robot(s) sometimes ask you something, you should answer the question. Please naturally talk with the robot(s) as you talk with another person."

After this instruction, the participants moved to the experimental space and were seated in front of the robot(s) as shown in Figure 4. After participants sat, the operator started to run a scenario file of either two conditions. The robot(s) proceeded a conversation according to the scenario.

When the conversation finished, we let the participants to move to another space and answer a questionnaire. After that, the participants returned the experimental space, and then they talked again the robot(s) in another condition. The participants answered the same questionnaire again after that second conversation.

Participant

Participants were native speakers of Japanese. In this experiment a total of 16 subjects participated (Female: 8, Male: 8). The average of their age was 21.5 (SD=1.77).

Questionnaire

We asked four questions to evaluate the sense of conversation. We used 7-point Likert scale to score the questions.

Q1. I felt robot's responses to my speeches almost made sense. (Coherence)

Q2. I felt I discussed deeply with the robot. (Discussion)

Q3. I felt the robot was friendly. (Friendliness)

Q4. I felt I wanted to talk to the robot again. (Talking again)

We asked Q1 to investigate whether a proposed turn-taking pattern enabled a user to feel a conversation to be more coherent than a usual turn-taking pattern of one robot. If the proposed turn-taking pattern had an effect on making a conversation coherent, it might have a potential to improve the quality of the conversation; therefore, we asked Q2 for this verification. Q3 and Q4 were asked because they were important elements for sense of conversation, which is for the user to sense that he or she talked to the robot well.

Results

Figure 6 shows the results of questionnaire in each condition. We explain the results each item.

Q1. Coherence.
The means of scores of Q1 were 2.63 (SD=1.73) and 4.13 (SD=2.00) in one-robot condition and two-robots condition, respectively. We analyzed the results by Wilcoxon's sign rank test because the data was not assumed as normal. This result indicated a significant difference between these conditions (T=4.5, n=10 $p<.05$). It suggests that participants of two-robots condition felt the conversation to be more coherent than those of one-robot condition.

Q2. Discussion.
The means of scores of Q2 were 2.56 (SD=1.37) and 4.13 (SD=1.54) in one-robot condition and two-robots condition, respectively. The results of Wilcoxon's sign rank test indicated a significant difference between these conditions (T=3.5, n=13, $p<.01$). It suggests that participants of two-

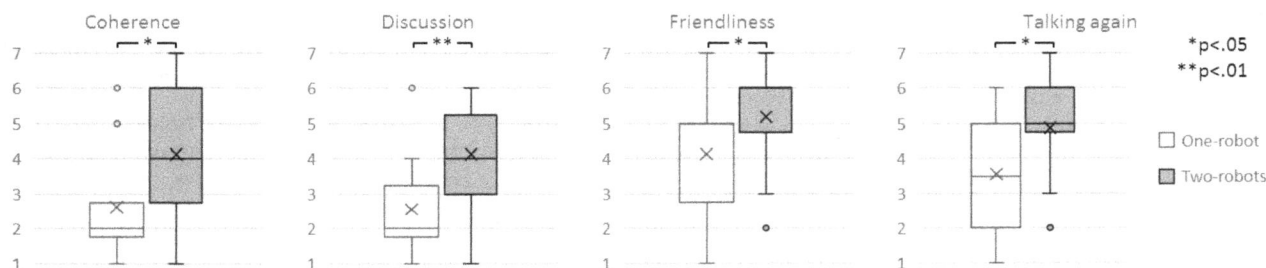

Figure 6. Results of Experiment 1.

22

robots condition felt to be discussed more deeply with robots than those of one-robot condition.

Q3. Friendliness.
The means of scores of Q3 were 4.13 (SD=1.69) and 5.19 (SD=1.29) in one-robot condition and two-robots condition, respectively. Wilcoxon's sign rank test showed a significant difference between these conditions (T=13, n=12, p<.05). It suggests that participants of two-robots condition felt the robots to be more friendly than those of one-robot condition.

Q4. Talking again.
The means of scores of Q4 were 3.56 (SD=1.73) and 4.88 (SD=1.27) in one-robot condition and two-robots condition, respectively. Wilcoxon's sign rank test indicated a significant difference between these conditions (T=3, n=11, p<.01). It suggests that participants of two-robots condition felt to want to talk to the robots again more than those of one-robot condition.

Discussion
These results suggested that the proposed turn-taking pattern of two-robots made a conversation coherent and improved the conversation's quality more than a usual turn-taking pattern of one robot. Furthermore, it could increase user's impression of friendliness and talking again more than the usual turn-taking pattern. We show a part of cases observed in the experiment which seem to keep a conversation coherent (R0, R1 and H mean Robot 0, Robot 1 and Human, respectively).

Case 1

```
R0-> H: Anyway, do you think robots need human-
likeness?
H ->R0: Yeah, I think it's necessary.
R0-> H: I see.
R0-> H: But...
R1-> H: I think it is absolutely necessary for
robots which communicate with humans, too.
```

Case 2

```
R0-> H: Anyway, do you think robots need human-
likeness?
H ->R0: I think case by case.
R0-> H: I see.
R0-> H: But...
R1-> H: I think it is absolutely necessary for
robots which communicate with humans, too.
```

Even though each participant of these cases says different opinion, the conversations looks coherent. Case 1 looks as if R0 have different opinion from the participant and R1 agrees with him/her. In case 2, R0 seems to disagree to the participant as well as case 1, but R1 looks to voice R0's opinion. If there was only one robot in those conversations, the conversation of case 2 would have been incoherent when the robot did not use an interjection (e.g. the word 'But...') and that of case 1 would have been also incoherent when the robot used an interjection.

Case 3

```
R0-> H: Robots cannot eat. How do you think about
this?
H ->R0: Oh, that's too pity.
R0-> H: I see.
R0-> H: Umm...
R1->R0: I think very bad, too. Because electricity
does not tasty.
```

Case 4

```
R0-> H: Robots cannot eat. How do you think about
this?
H ->R0: I think it is good because you do not feel
hungry.
R0-> H: I see.
R0-> H: Umm...
R1->R0: I think very bad, too. Because electricity
does not tasty.
```

These cases also look coherent thanks to communication of two robots. In case 3, a participant can know R0's idea but can understand R1 reacted to his/her pity. Meanwhile, in case 4, a participant can imagine as if R1 reflects understanding of what R0 is feeling. Those conversations would be incoherent in the case of only one robot as well as case 1 and 2.

However, the results might have been just the effect of using two robots; in other words, there is a possibility to get the same results just by using two robots without the proposed turn-taking pattern.

EXPERIMENT 2

Overview
We conducted another experiment to explore whether the proposed turn-taking pattern owes the efficacy suggested in Experiment 1 to using multiple robots or interjections by the robots. For this investigation, in Experiment 2, the turn-taking pattern with interjections was compared with the almost same a turn-taking pattern without interjections.

Design
Experiment 2 also had two conditions. One condition was without-interjection condition, in which participants talked to two robots that behave in the communication pattern without interjections. The other condition was with-interjection condition, in which participants talked to two robots that behave in the communication pattern with interjections; therefore, it is same as two-robots condition of Experiment 1.

All participants experienced both conditions; in other words, this experiment was designed as a within-subject experiment.

Environment, Robot, Operator and Procedure
Experiment 2 employed the same experimental environment, robot and operator role as Experiment 1. The experimental procedure was also same as Experiment 1

Participant

Participants were native speakers of Japanese. In this experiment a total of 15 (Female: 7, Male: 8) subjects participated. The average of their age was 19.8 (SD=1.05).

Questionnaire

We used the same questionnaire as we used in Experiment 1 to compare the results of Experiment 2 with those of Experiment 1.

Results

Figure 7 shows the results of questionnaire in each condition. We explain the results each item.

Q1. Coherence.

The means of scores of Q1 were 3.67 (SD=1.25) and 4.53 (SD=1.2) in without-interjection condition and with-interjection condition, respectively. The results of Wilcoxon's sign rank test indicated a significant difference between these conditions (T=4, n=10, p<.05). It suggests that participants of with-interjection condition felt the conversation to be more consistent than those of without-interjection condition.

Q2. Discussion.

The means of scores of Q2 were 4 (SD=1.32) and 4.47 (SD=1.36) in without-interjection condition and with-interjection condition, respectively. Wilcoxon's sign rank test indicated no significant difference between the conditions but showed significant trend (T=3, n=7 p<.1). The results suggest that participants of with-interjection condition might feel to be discussed more deeply with the two robots than those of without-interjection condition.

Q3. Friendliness.

The means of scores of Q3 were 5.2 (SD=1.28) and 5.47 (SD=1.09) in without-interjection condition and with-interjection condition, respectively. The results of Wilcoxon's sign rank test showed no significant difference between the conditions (T=10.5, n=7, n.s.).

Q4. Talking again.

The means of scores of Q4 were 4.33 (SD=1.74) and 5 (SD=1.55) in single and duo condition, respectively. Wilcoxon's sign rank test did not indicate a significant difference between the conditions (T=8, n=7, n.s.).

Discussion

Comparing Experiment 1 and Experiment 2

The results of Experiment 2 showed that robot's interjection enabled a user to feel a conversation coherent. It suggests that robot's interjection by two robots succeeded in building a social context that enables a user to interpret robot's response coherent. Furthermore, the results suggested that decrease of such incoherence might give participants an impression that they deeply discussed with the robots.

On the other hand, we could not find the efficacy of robot's interjection on the friendliness of the robots and the feeling of wanting to talk again. The results of Experiment 1 showed the significant effects in those items. It indicates that the difference of using a one robot and two robots. Using two robots is considered to improve the friendliness and to feel a user to want to talk again. These results are similar trends as previous works [8, 10]

Limitation and Future works

The analysis of Experiment 1 and Experiment 2 did not consider the rate at which robot's responses was actually corresponding to participant's utterances. If the rate is higher, the scores of each questionnaire item will be higher. To precisely explore the effect of the proposed method, we need to correct the experimental data. This detailed analysis is a future work.

CONCLUSION

This paper presented a pre-scheduled turn-taking pattern in which two robots behave cooperatively to generate a social context where a user to feel robot's responses to be coherent, even though the responses are actually inconsistent with user's answer.

We conducted two experiments to investigate effects of this turn-taking pattern. The results of the experiments suggested that our turn-taking pattern made by cooperated behaviors with interjections of two robots enables a user to feel a conversation to be more coherent and a discussion to be more deep than a usual turn-taking pattern of one-robot and a turn-taking pattern of two robots without interjections. It suggests that a turn-taking pattern with interjections could build a social context where a user interpreted robot's speech.

These results that a social context generated by multiple robots makes conversation coherent are novel in the field of human-robot interaction research. It will contribute the

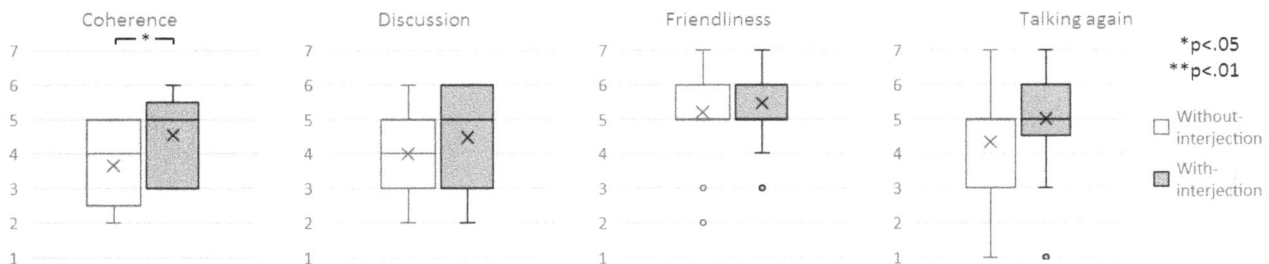

Figure 7. Results of Experiment 2.

development of the research of the design of human robot interaction.

REFERENCES

1. W. Burgard, et al., The Interactive Museum Tour-Guide Robot, National Conf. on Artificial Intelligence (AAAI1998), pp. 11-18, 1998.

2. S. Thrun, et al., Minerva: A Second-Generation Museum Tour-Guide Robot, IEEE Int. Conf. on Robotics and Automation (ICRA1999), pp. 1999-2005, 1999.

3. R. Siegwart, et al., Robox at Expo.02: A Large Scale Installation of Personal Robots, Robotics and Autonomous Systems, vol. 42, pp. 203-222, 2003.

4. R. Gockley, et al., Designing Robots for Long-Term Social Interaction, IEEE/RSJ Int. Conf. on Intelligent Robots and Systems (IROS2005), pp. 1338-1343, 2005.

5. H.-M. Gross, et al., Shopbot: Progress in Developing an Interactive Mobile Shopping Assistant for Everyday Use, IEEE Int. Conf. on Systems, Man, and Cybernetics (SMC2008), pp. 3471-3478, 2008.

6. M. Shiomi, et al., A Semi-Autonomous Communication Robot - a Field Trial at a Train Station -, ACM/IEEE Int. Conf. on Human-Robot Interaction (HRI2008), pp. 303-310, 2008.

7. T. Kanda, M. Shiomi, Z. Miyashita, H. Ishiguro and N. Hagita, A Communication Robot in a Shopping Mall, IEEE Trans. on Robotics, vol. 26, pp. 897-913, 2010.

8. T. Arimoto, Y. Yoshikawa, H. Ishiguro, Cooperative Use of Multiple Robots for Enhancing Sense of Conversation without Voice Recognition, SIG-SLUD, B5(2), 76-77, 2015 (In Japanese)

9. T. Takahashi, M. Kanbara, N. Hagita, A Social Media Mediation Robot to Increase an Opportunity of Conversation for Elderly: Mediation Experiments Using Single or Multiple Robots, Technical Committee on Cloud Network robotics (CNR), 113(84), 31-36, 2013. (In Japanese)

10. K. Hayashi, D. Sakamoto, T. Kanda, M. Shiomi, S. Koizumi H. Ishiguro, T. Ogasawara and N. Hagita, Humanoid robots as a passive-social medium - a field experiment at a train station -, ACM/IEEE 2nd Annual Conference on Human-Robot Interaction, pp. 137-144, 2007

11. M. Shiomi, T. Kanda, I. Howley, K. Hayashi, N. Hagita, Can a Social Robot Stimulate Science Curiosity in Classrooms?. International Journal of Social Robotics, 1-12. 2015.

12. T. Kanda, R. Sato, N. Saiwaki and H. Ishiguro, A two-month Field Trial in an Elementary School for Long-term Human-robot Interaction, IEEE Transactions on Robotics, 23(5), pp. 962-971, 2007.

Do Synchronized Multiple Robots Exert Peer Pressure?

Masahiro Shiomi
ATR-IRC
Kyoto, 619-0288, Japan
m-shiomi@atr.jp

Norihiro Hagita
ATR-IRC
Kyoto, 619-0288, Japan
hagita @atr.jp

ABSTRACT

In human-human interaction, peer pressure is a major social influence on people's thoughts, feelings, and behaviors. The larger the group of people, the more social influence it exerts. In this paper, we investigate whether multiple robots and their synchronized behaviors exert peer pressure on people, as in human groups. We developed a multiple robot controller system that enables robots to perform precise synchronization. In the experiment, we prepared a setting that resembled previous experiments that investigated peer pressure between people and robots. The participants answered questions after hearing the robots' answers, only some of which were incorrect. Our experiment results showed that the influence of the synchronized multiple robots increased the error rates of the participants, but we found no significant effects toward conformity.

Author Keywords

Human-robot interaction; group interaction; peer pressure

ACM Classification Keywords

H.5.2. User Interfaces – *Interaction styles*

INTRODUCTION

Human decision making is strongly influenced by others. In particular, the power of the many is one famous social influence from others. For example, Sherif investigated a conformity effect in an ambiguous situation and showed that participants willingly followed the opinions of others, even though they admitted objections to them [1]. Asch experimentally investigated the impact of the majority's influence and concluded that participants conformed to other people's incorrect choices [2, 3]. Asch also investigated how peer pressure is strengthened by an increase in the number of the sources of such influence. Other literature identified the social influences of relationships among people's thoughts, feelings and behaviors [4, 5]. Midden et al. investigated the persuasive effects of a group of virtual agents with Asch paradigm [6].

HAI '16, October 04-07, 2016, Biopolis, Singapore
© 2016 ACM. ISBN 978-1-4503-4508-8/16/10…$15.00
DOI: http://dx.doi.org/10.1145/2974804.2974808

Can robots exert a social influence, like peer pressure, on people? Even though people regard a robot as a different being from humans, they do view it as a social being [7, 8]. This attitude is helpful for understanding how people are influenced by robots. Several researchers investigated the effects of answering this question in the human-robot interaction research field and showed that robots influence people's decisions [9, 10]. Even though these research works showed that people's decision making is influenced by robots, the power of such influence is relatively weak compared to the effect from humans.

Another question must be confronted. Do multiple robots exert more social influence? Since the practice of installing groups of robots like Pepper in real shops continues to advance worldwide, understanding their social influence is critical. However, the answer to that question remains unknown because how multiple social robots exert social influence hasn't been extensively addressed by the human-robot interaction research field. Do people change their decisions if a number of robots oppose them? Are people more likely to follow the opinions of unanimous robots?

This paper addressed these questions by investigating the effects of peer pressure from multiple robots with a relatively large number of robots (Fig. 1). The power of influence from robots is probably weaker than from humans, and past research reported that the size of the group is important to increase conformity [2]. We also investigated the effects of the synchronized behaviors of multiple robots, which are designed to increase conformity by showing unanimity because past research work reported that it increases the power of social influence [2].

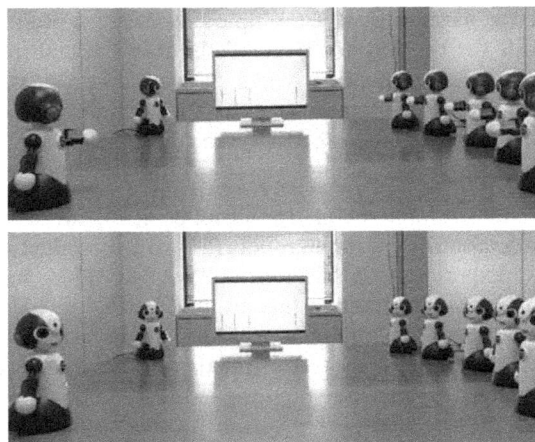

Fig. 1 Synchronized behaviors of multiple robots

RELATED WORKS

Social influence from a single robot

Many robotics researchers have investigated the social influence from a single robot in the human-robot interaction research field with an approach that resembles human-computer interaction research works [11] [12]. For example, researchers unveiled the effects of a robot's social facilitation, which is the tendency for people to perform differently in the presence of others (i.e., a robot) than when they are alone. The existence of physical robots influenced the performances of people in simple tasks, similar to human existence [13] [14].

Nagakawa et al. focused on social influence due to the unique feature of physical robots in the physical interaction between a robot and people and reported that a robot's physical interaction motivates people during simple and monotonous tasks [9, 10]. Shinozawa et al. clarified that physical presence affects human decision making more greatly than a screen-agent in the real world [15]. These social influences of robots can be exploited for commercial purposes, and real robots have already been installed for advertisements in daily environments like shopping malls [16] [17].

Even though these research works provided rich knowledge about the social influences of robots on people, they mainly focused on a single robot effect, not a multiple robot effect. It remains unknown whether using multiple robots increases the social influence from robots to people. In this paper, we unveil the effects of multiple robots under the context of social influence.

Interaction with a group of robots

Some research works focus on using multiple robots in human-robot interaction contexts. Sakamoto et al. developed a passive social medium using two robots and investigated its effectiveness for information-providing services in open public environments [18]. Kory et al. used two robots for a storytelling-task to improve children's language-learning [19]. Leite et al. also focused on storytelling with multiple robots and reported that interactive narratives with multiple robots are a promising approach for the development of children's social-related skills [20]. These research works showed the effectiveness of using multiple robots to transfer information to people. However, since their focuses are different from peer pressure from robots, such research is different from ours.

Similar to our motivation, Brandstetter et al. investigated peer pressure from multiple robots [21] in a reproduction of Asch's experiment with four robots or four human experimenters. They investigated the levels of pressure from the robots in both non/ambiguous situations. As in the original experiment, they confirmed peer pressure effects with human experimenters, but the robots did not show any significant effects of peer pressure. In this research work, we also use multiple robots to investigate peer pressure

from robots. The main differences between our research work and Brandstetter's work is the number of robots and the synchronized behaviors.

DESIGN

Task design

In this study, which resembles Brandstetter's work [21], we prepared visual judgment tasks along the lines of Asch's experiments [2, 3] by considering aspects of the Sherif experiment: ambiguous situations for conformity effects [1]. Fig. 2 shows an example of the line tasks in this study, where the participants have to identify the corresponding lines from candidates A to C.

On the left side are displayed three lines whose lengths differ from the correct line in a range of +/- 1 to 3 mm. One of the three lines corresponds to a line on the right side labeled "?". The right side line has three different lengths: 50, 100, and 150 mm. Since these lines look ambiguous, distinguishing them might be difficult for participants.

System design

We referred to both the Asch and Brandstetter experiments to determine the number of robots for our study. Asch investigated the relationships between conformity and group size [22]. The former increased immediately when a group had three people and did not appreciably increase by adding more people (Fig. 3). On the other hand, Brandstetter's experiment with four robots showed that using more robots over the saturation number in the human case did not exert peer pressure on people, even in ambiguous situations [21]. Therefore, at least four robots were inadequate to create peer pressure from them.

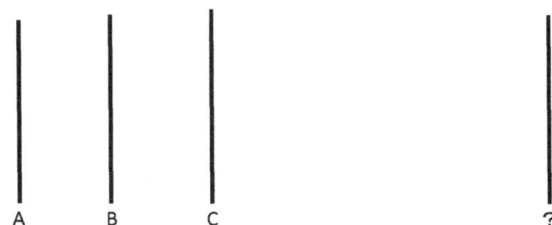

Fig. 2 Example of line task

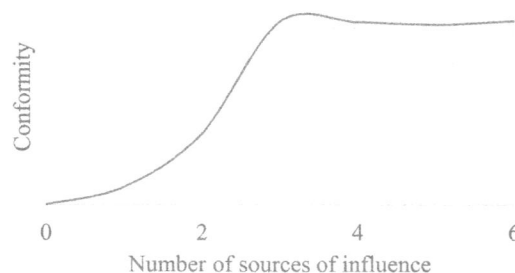

Fig. 3 Relationships between conformity and group size, original graph [22]

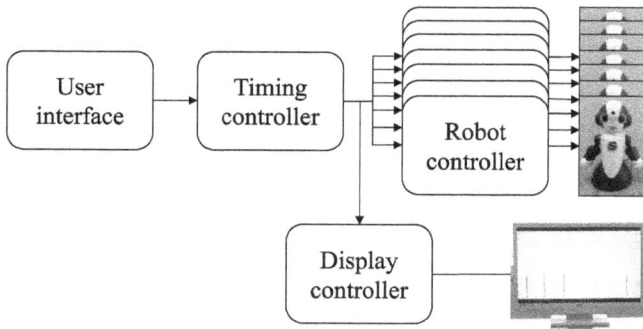

Fig. 4 System overview

After considering these research works, we chose six robots, which is two more than the saturation number in the human case. To increase the power of many, we also investigated the effects of the synchronized behaviors of robots. Since past work reported that unanimity increases the power of social influence [2], we believe that showing unanimity by synchronized behavior will increase the power.

Since the effects of such a large number of robots and their synchronized behaviors remain unknown under the context of peer pressure, our design includes heuristic points. But we believe that investigating these effects will be helpful to understand how people are influenced by interaction with a group of robots. By considering both the task and system design, we developed an experiment system for this study and described its details in the next section.

SYSTEM CONFIGURATION

Figure 4 shows an overview of our multiple robot controller system that consists of the following five components: user interface, timing controller, robot controller, display controller, and a robot. The total number of robots was seven: an MC robot and six answerers. All of the systems are connected through a wired/wireless LAN. The details of each component are described as follows.

User interface

To simultaneously control multiple robots, we developed a simple user interface with several buttons that are used to send a scenario to the timing controller. Each scenario includes information about when and which robot will execute a behavior (motion and speech sets) and shows images on the display. These scenarios are analyzed by the timing controller and sent to both the robot and display controllers. The operator controls the start timing of each scenario by the user interface, but after sending a scenario, each robot automatically behaves as defined by the scenario.

Timing controller

This module synchronizes each robot behavior and precisely shows images on the display. When an operator sends a scenario to the timing controller, it generates command sets for each robot, displays images by analyzing

the scenario, and sends the command set and the start timing to each controller. To avoid influence from the network delay, each controller is connected to the same NTP server to synchronize the clocks between PCs.

Robot controller

The robot controller manages a robot's behavior, which is motion and speech sets. In advance we prepared robot behaviors and registered them to each robot controller, which executes a registered behavior based on the timing information from the timing controller. When a behavior is executed, it controls each motor and starts to play a robot's sound.

Display controller

The display controller manages the displayed images and shows an image based on the timing controller's signal.

Robot

We used "Sota," which is an interactive humanoid robot characterized by its humanlike physical expressions. It has two DOFs in its arms, three in its head, and one in its waist. Its hands are soft material to ensure safety. The robot is 280 mm tall and is equipped with a CCD camera and microphones. Since Sota's CPU is Edison, users can connect and control it by Wi-FI. We used a corpus-based speech synthesis to generate speech [23].

EXPERIMENT

Hypotheses and Prediction

Based on human science literature, the power of math exists in the context of social influence, e.g., peer pressure [2, 24]. These research works also report that the size of the group and unanimity increases such social influences. On the other hand, in human-robot interaction research fields, other kinds of social influences exist, such as social facilitation [9, 10], but no peer pressure effect by multiple robots has been observed yet [21]. To investigate whether multiple robots can exert peer pressure, we employ more robots than past research work [21] and synchronized behaviors to increase unanimity, which is related to the power of peer pressure. If our system effectively produces synchronized behaviors among multiple robots, people will feel more pressure than from just non-synchronized multiple robots. This pressure will probably cause more errors during the experiments and create conformity to the robot answers; peer pressure from robots will be observed. Based on these considerations, we made the following predictions:

Prediction 1: The synchronized behaviors of multiple robots will produce more feelings of pressure during the interactions than the non-synchronized multiple robots.

Prediction 2: People will make more mistakes and act in conformity with the robot answers when they interact with the synchronized multiple robots than those who interact with non-synchronized multiple robots or do not interact with them at all.

Environment

We conducted an experiment in a laboratory room. Fig. 5 shows a map of the environment. Seven robots (one MC and six answerers) and a display were placed on the desk in room A. The MC robot is on the right of the display, and the other six robots are answerers. The operator is placed in room B, sends start signals to the robots, and monitors the entire system. The participants were placed in front of the display, and the distance between them and the display was 180 cm. We recorded all of the experiment's data with two cameras and one microphone.

Participants

Twenty people (10 women and 10 men, who averaged 35.5 years of age, S.D 9.7) participated in the experiment. In the experiment, 18 participants made at least one error in all of the conditions. We targeted these 18 individuals to evaluate how the robot's behaviors influenced their answers.

Conditions

We used a within-participant experiment design to evaluate and compare the effects of multiple robots and their synchronization behaviors. In each condition, the number of trials was 18 and errors on 12, as in Asch's experiment.

Sequence condition

This condition reproduces Asch's experiment with multiple robots. In the beginning, the MC robot requests that a participant answer a question after the robot to the participant's right answered it. Each robot looked at the next answerer after responding to the question (Fig. 6, left; the fifth robot is answering and the fourth robot is looking at the fifth robot). Therefore, the five robots first answered the question in order, then the participant answered it (Fig. 6, right; the participant is answering and the fifth robot is looking at the participant), and finally the sixth robot answered, too. After the sixth robot answered, the MC robot asked the next question. The answers of all the robots were identical, but they made errors on 12 of the 18 trials.

Synchronization condition

This condition investigated the effects of the synchronized behaviors of the robots. Here, the MC robot requested that a participant answer a question after all the robots had already answered. However, unlike the *sequence* condition, all the robots simultaneously answered the question (Fig. 7, left); they looked at the participant after they answered the question in unison. Therefore, first the six robots simultaneously answered the question, and then the participant answered it (Fig. 7, right). The answers of all the robots were the same; they again made errors on 12 of the 18 trials.

Alone condition

This condition investigated the ratio of the correct answers of the participants without the robot's behaviors. In this condition, the MC robot requested that a participant answer a question alone, and then the MC robot immediately asked the next question after the participant answered the robot. During the condition, the other six robots did nothing.

Procedure

Before the first session, the participants were given a brief description of our experiment procedure. Since the experiment had a within-participant design, each participant joined three sessions of different conditions. We counterbalanced the order of the conditions, the answer labels, and the basic lengths of the lines. The participants filled out questionnaires after each session.

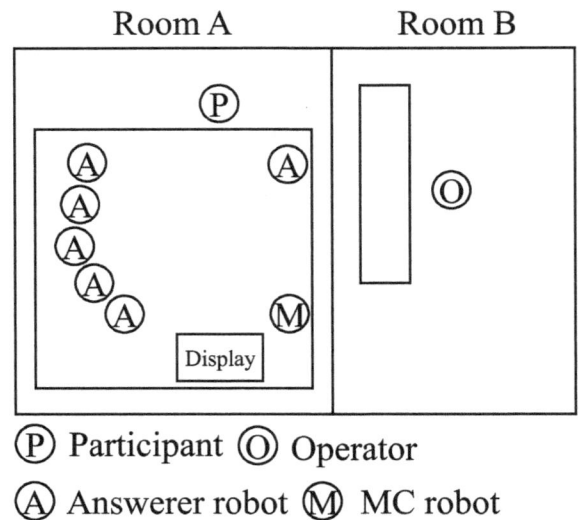

P Participant **O** Operator
A Answerer robot **M** MC robot

Fig. 5 Experiment environment

Fig. 6 Experiment scenes in *sequence* condition

Fig. 7 Experiment scenes in *synchronization* condition

Measurements

In this experiment, we used a questionnaire to measure on a 1-to-7 point scale one subjective item: the feeling of pressure from the robots. We also measured two objective items: the ratio of correct answers when the robots made mistakes and the ratio of conformity to wrong answers.

RESULTS

Verification of Prediction 1

Figure 8 shows the questionnaire results of the degree of pressure. We conducted a paired t-test and found a significant difference among the conditions (t (1, 17) = 3.03, $p<.01$, $r=0.59$. Prediction 1 was supported.

Verification of Prediction 2

Figure 9 shows the ratios of correct answers when the robots made mistakes in both the *sequence* and *synchronization* conditions and the *alone* condition (i.e., without robots). First, we conducted a one-factor within subject ANOVA of the ratios to investigate whether robot pressure caused more errors in the participants. The results showed a significant difference among the conditions (F (2, 34) = 3.26, $p=.05$, partial $\eta^2=.58$). Multiple comparisons with the Bonferroni method revealed a significant trend: *synchronization* > *alone* ($p=.07$), but no significance between *sequence* and *synchronization* (p =.51) and *sequence* and *alone* (p =.74).

We also conducted a paired t-test on the ratio of the participants' conformity to the robots' mistakes to investigate whether the participants conformed with them (Fig. 10). The results did not show a significant difference among the conditions (t (1, 17) = 1.21, $p=.24$). Prediction 2 was partially supported.

DISCUSSION

Relationship between perceived pressure and mistakes

Even though the experimental results did not show conformity by synchronizing multiple robots, it showed interesting phenomenon. Thus, participants make more mistake under *synchronization* condition than *alone* condition, but did not follow robots' answers. These results would suggest that the perceived pressure did not relate to the power of peer pressure, or the total power of perceived pressure is not enough to make peer pressure; because the average of the perceived pressure at the *synchronization* condition is larger than *sequence* condition but it was less than middle (four). If the robots could make more pressures, the latter assumption, i.e., whether the total power of perceived pressure related to conformity, can be unveiled; this is one of interesting future works.

Here another question arises. Do perceived pressures influence mistakes? In fact, the participants reported more feelings of pressure from the robots under the *synchronization* condition than the *sequence* condition. On

the other hand, they probably felt less pressure from the robots under the *alone* condition because only the MC robot was working. Therefore, we analyzed the correlation between the perceived pressure and the ratios of the correct answers to understand the details of their relationship.

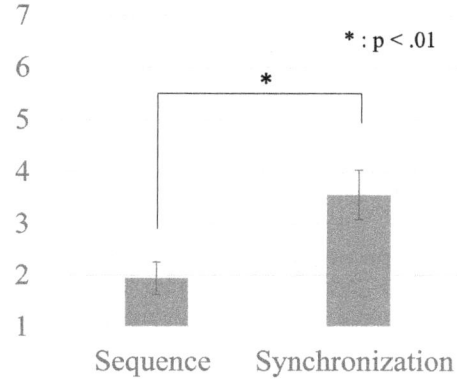

Figure 8. The questionnaire result of the degree of pressure

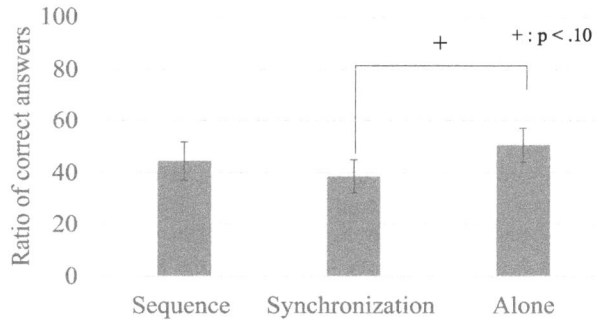

Fig. 9 Ratios of correct answers in all conditions

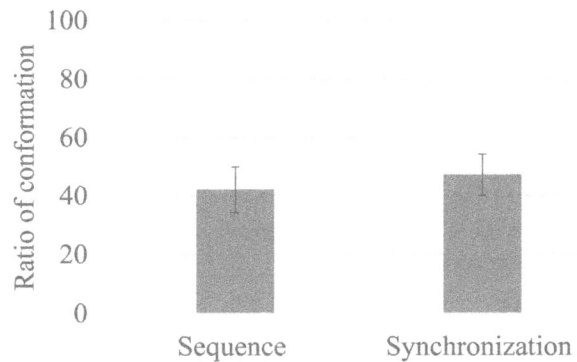

Fig. 10 Ratios of conformity in both *sequence* and *synchronization* conditions

Correlation analysis using the Pearson correlation did not reveal any statistical significance in both the *sequence* condition (Pearson correlation = -.29, p = .24) and the *synchronization* condition (Pearson correlation = -.05, p = .85). This result indicates that the perceived pressure did not have any correlation to the ratio of the correct answers. We must investigate other kinds of variables to explain these phenomena, for example, why the participants made more errors in the *synchronization* condition. Even though our findings did not clearly explain what feelings are related to the ratio of mistakes, this research provides one implication. We need a careful behavior design about using multiple robots because their synchronization behaviors might cause incorrect human judgments, such as deceptive advertising uses.

Why didn't the participants conform to the robots?
More robots and their synchronization behaviors were still insufficient to create conformity among the participants in our current settings. Here we discuss what factors are essential to cause people to conform to robots.

First, people perceive robots as different from humans [7, 8]; they do not treat them as humans. If a robot were to establish a rapport or a social relationship with people, their responses might be different. In this research work we did not include any interaction design or context to create such relationships between the robots and the participants.

Another perspective is the authority of the robots. If people felt great respect for them, their opinions might change. Geiskkovitch et al. reported that a robot's authority influenced people's behavior [25]. They investigated whether participants continued to perform a tedious task under a robot's direction by controlling its authority and concluded that its perceived authority status was more strongly correlated to obedience.

Robot appearance and size are also related to the power of pressure. When people face larger or stronger robots, they might feel physical pressure. In this study, the participants probably did not experience such pressure. After the experiments, several participants described the synchronized robots as cute. We also investigated their feelings of enjoyment about their interaction with the robots, and these results showed significant differences between the *sequence* and *synchronization* conditions by paired t-test ($p<.01$). This results indicated that participants felt more enjoyment under the *synchronization* condition than the *sequence* condition.

Limitations
Since this study investigated the effects of peer pressure from multiple robots, we cannot generalize about our predictions from it. Even though this experiment showed that pressure effects increased the mistakes of people by synchronized multiple robots, it still did not show peer pressure. It was also conducted within the framework of an academic study.

The participants only had limited interaction with desktop-sized robots. Thus, the effect shown in the experiment might be moderated if they interacted with a robot with a different appearance or size. Of course, the number of interacting robots would also influence the experiment results; we only used six robots.

Only adults participated in our experiment. Moreover, the number of participant was 20 and we did not evaluate other factors such as gender, age and cultures. If children or seniors were to interact with our robot, they might perceive a different level of peer pressure from the synchronized multiple robots. Also, the effects of pressure from multiple robots are related to ethical issues. We conducted this experiment under an academic context, but we need to carefully design multiple robot behaviors in real world contexts. These limitations will be tested in the future, perhaps with different kinds of robots or societal contexts.

CONCLUSION
In this research work, we focused on the effects of peer pressure from multiple robots. Even though previous research reported less peer pressure from multiple robots, the effects of synchronized behaviors that increase pressure remain unrevealed. To investigate the effects of peer pressure from synchronized multiple robots, we conducted a within-subjects experiment in which multiple robots provided incorrect answers under an ambiguous situation.

Our experimental results indicated that synchronized multiple robots exerted more pressure on participants, as we assumed, and increased their error rate more than a situation where these robots did not provide incorrect answers. However, the peer pressure effects are not completely clear from the experiment. We believe that our findings will provide several implications to the development of robot applications that simultaneously use multiple robots, especially for commercial or advertising purposes.

ACKNOWLEDGMENTS
This research work was supported by JSPS KAKENHI Grant Number 15H05322, and 16K12505.

REFERENCES
1. M. Sherif, "A study of some social factors in perception," *Archives of Psychology (Columbia University)*, 1935.
2. S. E. Asch, "Opinions and social pressure," *Readings about the social animal,* vol. 193, pp. 17-26, 1955.
3. S. E. Asch, "Effects of group pressure upon the modification and distortion of judgments," *Groups, leadership, and men. S*, pp. 222-236, 1951.
4. R. W. Spencer, and J. H. Huston, "Rational forecasts: On confirming ambiguity as the mother of conformity,"

Journal of Economic Psychology, vol. 14, no. 4, pp. 697-709, 1993.

5. V. Griskevicius, N. J. Goldstein, C. R. Mortensen, R. B. Cialdini, and D. T. Kenrick, "Going along versus going alone: when fundamental motives facilitate strategic (non) conformity," *Journal of personality and social psychology,* vol. 91, no. 2, pp. 281, 2006.

6. C. Midden, J. Ham, and J. Baten, "Conforming to an Artificial Majority: Persuasive Effects of a Group of Artificial Agents," *Persuasive Technology: 10th International Conference, PERSUASIVE 2015, Chicago, IL, USA, June 3-5, 2015, Proceedings*, T. MacTavish and S. Basapur, eds., pp. 229-240, Cham: Springer International Publishing, 2015.

7. P. H. Kahn Jr, T. Kanda, H. Ishiguro, N. G. Freier, R. L. Severson, B. T. Gill, J. H. Ruckert, and S. Shen, ""Robovie, you'll have to go into the closet now": Children's social and moral relationships with a humanoid robot," *Developmental psychology,* vol. 48, no. 2, pp. 303, 2012.

8. K. Hayashi, M. Shiomi, T. Kanda, and N. Hagita, "Are Robots Appropriate for Troublesome and Communicative Tasks in a City Environment?," *IEEE Transactions on Autonomous Mental Development,* vol. 4, no. 2, pp. 150-160, 2012.

9. M. Shiomi, K. Nakagawa, K. Shinozawa, R. Matsumura, H. Ishiguro, and N. Hagita, "Does A Robot's Touch Encourage Human Effort?," *International Journal of Social Robotics,* pp. 1-11, 2016.

10. K. Nakagawa, M. Shiomi, K. Shinozawa, R. Matsumura, H. Ishiguro, and N. Hagita, "Effect of Robot's Whispering Behavior on People's Motivation," *International Journal of Social Robotics,* vol. 5, no. 1, pp. 5-16, 2012.

11. B. Reeves, and C. Nass, *How people treat computers, television, and new media like real people and places*: CSLI Publications and Cambridge university press, 1996.

12. B. J. Fogg, "Persuasive technology: using computers to change what we think and do," *Ubiquity,* vol. 2002, no. December, pp. 5, 2002.

13. S. Woods, K. Dautenhahn, and C. Kaouri, "Is someone watching me?-consideration of social facilitation effects in human-robot interaction experiments," in Computational Intelligence in Robotics and Automation, 2005. CIRA 2005. Proceedings. 2005 IEEE International Symposium on, pp. 53-60, 2005.

14. N. Riether, F. Hegel, B. Wrede, and G. Horstmann, "Social facilitation with social robots?," in Human-Robot Interaction (HRI), 2012 7th ACM/IEEE International Conference on, pp. 41-47, 2012.

15. K. Shinozawa, F. Naya, J. Yamato, and K. Kogure, "Differences in effect of robot and screen agent recommendations on human decision-making," *International Journal of Human-Computer Studies,* vol. 62, no. 2, pp. 267-279, 2005.

16. H.-M. Gross, H.-J. Böhme, C. Schröter, S. Mueller, A. König, C. Martin, M. Merten, and A. Bley, "Shopbot: Progress in developing an interactive mobile shopping assistant for everyday use," in Systems, Man and Cybernetics, 2008. SMC 2008. IEEE International Conference on, pp. 3471-3478, 2008.

17. M. Shiomi, D. Sakamoto, T. Kanda, C. T. Ishi, H. Ishiguro, and N. Hagita, "Field Trial of a Networked Robot at a Train Station," *International Journal of Social Robotics,* vol. 3, no. 1, pp. 27-40, 2010.

18. D. Sakamoto, K. Hayashi, T. Kanda, M. Shiomi, S. Koizumi, H. Ishiguro, T. Ogasawara, and N. Hagita, "Humanoid Robots as a Broadcasting Communication Medium in Open Public Spaces," *International Journal of Social Robotics,* vol. 1, no. 2, pp. 157-169, 2009.

19. J. Kory, and C. Breazeal, "Storytelling with robots: Learning companions for preschool children's language development," in Robot and Human Interactive Communication, 2014 RO-MAN: The 23rd IEEE International Symposium on, pp. 643-648, 2014.

20. I. Leite, M. McCoy, M. Lohani, D. Ullman, N. Salomons, C. K. Stokes, S. Rivers, and B. Scassellati, "Emotional Storytelling in the Classroom: Individual versus Group Interaction between Children and Robots," in HRI, pp. 75-82, 2015.

21. J. Brandstetter, P. Racz, C. Beckner, E. B. Sandoval, J. Hay, and C. Bartneck, "A peer pressure experiment: Recreation of the Asch conformity experiment with robots," in Intelligent Robots and Systems (IROS 2014), 2014 IEEE/RSJ International Conference on, pp. 1335-1340, 2014.

22. D. Forsyth, *Group dynamics*: Cengage Learning, 2009.

23. H. Kawai, T. Toda, J. Ni, M. Tsuzaki, and K. Tokuda, "XIMERA: A new TTS from ATR based on corpus-based technologies," in Fifth ISCA Workshop on Speech Synthesis, pp., 2004.

24. S. E. Asch, "Effects of group pressure upon the modification and distortion of judgments."

25. D. Y. Geiskkovitch, D. Cormier, S. H. Seo, and J. E. Young, "Please Continue, We Need More Data: An Exploration of Obedience to Robots," *Journal of Human-Robot Interaction,* vol. 5, no. 1, pp. 82–99, 2015.

NAMIDA: Sociable Driving Agents with Multiparty Conversation

Nihan Karatas
Toyohashi University of
Technology
Toyohashi, Japan
karatas@icd.cs.tut.ac.jp

Soshi Yoshikawa
Toyohashi University of
Technology
Toyohashi, Japan
yoshikawa@icd.cs.tut.ac.jp

Michio Okada
Toyohashi University of
Technology
Toyohashi, Japan
okada@tut.jp

ABSTRACT

We propose a multi party conversational social interface NAMIDA through a pilot study. The system consists of three robots that can converse with each other about environment throughout the road. Through this model, the directed utterances towards the driver diminishes by utilizing turn-taking process between the agents, and the mental workload of the driver can be reduced compared to the conventional one-to-one communication based approach that directly addresses the driver. We set up an experiment to compare the both approaches to explore their effects on the workload and attention behaviors of drivers. The results indicated that the multi-party conversational approach has a better effect on reducing certain workload factors. Also, the analysis of attention behaviors of drivers revealed that our method can better promote the drivers to focus on the road.

Author Keywords

Multi party conversation, context aware interaction, cognitive workload, NAMIDA

INTRODUCTION

The habits of a significant amount of drivers reveal the need for location-based information during long hours behind the wheels. Many drivers tend to use their mobile devices even though this action can easily divert a driver's attention, increasing the risk of accidents. Although the in-vehicle infotainment (IVI) systems are designed to meet a driver's needs inside a car, these systems also require both attention to initiate and frequent attention to monitor the system. [17] suggests that, the risk of a traffic accident increases exponentially the longer for a driver takes his or her eyes off the road.

Some newer generation IVI systems that facilitate the driver's ability to pay attention to the road by utilizing Bluetooth, windshield projection as well as, gesture and speech recognition technologies [23], [5]. Nevertheless, these systems are still very reactive and distraction is inevitable. So that, human

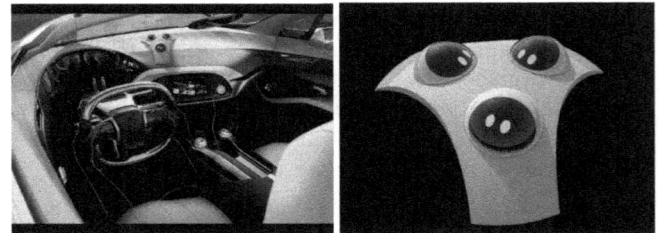

Figure 1. Base unit of NAMIDA, designed to be secured on the dashboard of the car within the peripheral vision of the driver *(left)*. With movable heads and eyes, NAMIDA projects a life-like appearance *(right)*.

factor researchers suggest that these technologies are not any less dangerous than the devices that require a driver's eyes or hands. Therefore, when designing an IVI system, it is crucial to examine the mental workload of drivers.

A driver's mental process plays a very critical role during a driving maneuver. Once the mental workload reaches an unacceptable level, driving safety may suffer [11]. As information receiving technology becomes more intelligent and complex, engineers face the challenge of developing a communication channel between drivers and IVI systems that takes into consideration a design with a method of interaction that is more natural and intuitive. Barton et al. [3] claimed that human brain has evolved to be highly adaptive in social interactions therefore, people tend to anthropomorphize the technology. From the drivers' perspective, we believe that, it is crucial to interact with an IVI system, that is perceivable as an animated entity, in such a social, natural and familiar manner to reduce the mental workload and creating a more sociable environment inside a car.

Recently, some car manufacturers have focused on developing robotic interfaces as in-car companions to deliver the necessary information and monitor the driver's state of alertness while interacting with the driver socially [24], [27], [19]. Further, though the collaborative work of MIT and Audi, AIDA (Affective Intelligent Driving Agent) can leverage a driver's mobile device and deliver personal, vehicle and city information by speech coupled with expressive body movements [30]. In AIDA research, it was determined that AIDA, as an expressive robot and a static-mounted agent, could decrease the mental workload of a driver and prevent distractions as opposed to a mobile phone. Nevertheless, the driver needs to maintain constant interaction with AIDA and takes on burden of managing and sustaining the conversation/interaction (e.g. asking questions of and responding to the system) for the purpose of acquiring the demanded information. We believe that, such kind a one-to-one conversation approach cannot diminish the mental workload of the driver sufficiently because of the above reasons.

The conversational structure of a driving agent system should be very smooth, well designed and aimed at reducing the workload. Bakthin [1] explained a persuasive conversation structure through analyzing the relationship between the hearer and addresser in the state of hearership and addressivity. Under driving conditions, we have to focus more on addressivity. In a one-to-one communication modality, when the system directs individual words towards to driver (addressivity), the driver is compelled to react to the addresser through a verbal or non-verbal channel (hearership), which creates a mental workload. For the purpose of decreasing the workload, what would happen if we could increase the number of robots such that the hearership burden can be taken on by another robot in the system?

Yoshiike et al. [31] have studied a system called MAWARI, which consists of three social robots who can conduct multi-party conversations as an interactive social medium. The results of this study showed that three MAWARI robots could reduce the workload on users through its communication modality. Besides, Suzuki et al. [29] claims that the one-to-one communication method not only requires active involvement of the subject in the conversation, but allows only one-sided individual information, which limits a conversation's range. On the other hand, a multi-party conversation, one that includes different personalities, gives a user the opportunity to obtain information from different aspects.

Ishizaki et al. [14] explained that multi-party conversation not only presents new topics/details, but it also lessens the stress of conversation initiation. In such a multi-party conversation, there are certain roles for the participants and these roles shift according to the verbal or non-verbal behaviors/cues of the participants. Goffman [9] introduced the concept of "footing", which explains the participant roles in a conversation. In a more than two-party conversation (multi-party), we can define the main roles as: speaker, addresser and side-participant. The role of a participant when he/she doesn't contribute to the conversation becomes that of "bystander".

Suzuki et al. [29] claimed that when a subject is in a dyadic interaction with a single entity (one-to-one communication), he/she is heavily forced to interact with it. Existing in the same environment with an agent (or agents) loads the conversational roles to the individual. That is why even when the entity performs a monologue, since the only interlocutor in the environment is one individual, he/she will be under a conversational burden. Likewise, the presence of two entities will still bring the conversational load to the subject at least as a side-participant. However, the presence of three entities and their conversation within each other yields a situation where the subject can escape the conversational burden as a bystander.

In this vein, we propose a NAMIDA configuration that consists of three, sociable, robotic interfaces that can perform a multi-party conversation (Fig. 1). We designed the concept of NAMIDA as friendly companions who can navigate the driver, give information/suggestions about surroundings, monitor the drowsiness and entertain the driver. In this study, we initially developed NAMIDA robots as conversational agents that only give information about the nearby places. We believe that a multi-party conversation approach, unlike a one-to-one conversation, allows for an alleviation of the hearership burden of driver by allocating the work overload among the NAMIDA interfaces. Thence, we can diminish the instances of directed utterances toward the driver, allowing the driver to obtain the necessary information exclusively by listening to the conversation from other participants (robotic interfaces).

In our study, we examined the effects of multi-party conversation on the workload and attentional behaviors of drivers as well as the effects of communication. This study is presented roughly in our previous work [16]. However, in the current paper, we discuss our communication design and utterance generation model in more detail and discuss the objective evaluation of attention behaviors.

DESIGN OF THE SYSTEM
We implemented NAMIDA as virtual, embodied social agents contained in a small display (Fig. 1). NAMIDA consists of one base unit that attaches to the dashboard of a car, containing three movable heads with one degree of freedom each. This is designed to reduce the number of modalities involved in a conversation and thereby reduce the mental workload.

Appearance
Since NAMIDA is conceptualized as fitting onto the dashboard of car, it will be in the driver's peripheral vision. In this manner, we adopted a minimal design policy that attempts to minimize the appearance of an agent's competence being overestimated or underestimated by the human user [20], [2]. The round-shape display of NAMIDA allows for the positioning of their eyes with one degree of freedom. We used three different discernible colors (red, green and blue) for composing the eyes, and varied the voices of the three imply that each NAMIDA character is a different personality. This design approach will minimialize the attention getting from the driver and also allow us to integrate the user's participation in the conversation in the future implementation of this study.

Utterance Generation Mechanism
Recently, research in human-robot interaction (HRI) has tackled not only the conveyance of content to users, but also the style of the transmission of information. Psychological studies suggest that the appearance and behavior of machines has the potential to influence human perceptions of as well as human behaviors toward machines [21], [4], [12]. The behaviors that allow humans to engage in social interactions in a relatively harmonious atmosphere can be defined as politeness [18]. Since driving can be a stressful act that can put people on edge, using a model that minimizes offensive statements and relieves stress by using polite utterances, even though the utterances would not be directed at the driver, has significant

Table 1. NAMIDA utterances coupled with nonverbal behaviors (turn-initial elements, hedges and nonverbal behaviors indicated)

TCU/TRP	Non-verbal behaviours	Turn-initials	Hedges
TCU	Eye gaze towards addresser and side participant	TI1:"a-a", TI2:"ano-", TI3:"anone", TI4:"anosa", TI5:"e-tto", TI6:"e-ttone", TI7:"etto", TI8:"etto-", TI9:"ne-ne", TI10:"ntto", TI11:"nttone"	
TRP	Eye gaze towards addresser		H1:"ne", H2:"kedo", H3:"tte", H4:"ka"

importance. In this regard, the communication design of a driving agent system should be designed around a politeness approach to elicit positive behaviors from the driver. In order to apply a polite-utterance model, we followed the linguistic cues described by Itani [15].

Another important point is to maintain the transitions between the utterances. Ford et al. [7] suggests that humans employ turn-initials for changing direction, error handling and enhancement to maintain the liveliness of a conversation. In this study, the utterances emerged from informal, polite Japanese language, utilizing the turn-initials and hedges shown in Table 1. Within each utterance, the agents use turn-initials or hedges randomly. As a voice synthesis engine, we employed Wizard Voice (ATR-Promotions).

In addition, persuasive behaviors of agents may function as a tool to induce changes in human behavior [10]. Ohshima et al. [25] showed that merging the utterance mechanism with bodily movements (head rotating and eye gazing) leads to a persuasive impression for human. To ensure a persuasive communication design, we have also integrated some non-verbal social cues such as eye gazing and orienting the head towards the speaker or addresser based on the conversation phase.

Conversational Structure
During everyday informal conversations, the role of speaker, addresser and other participants intuitively alternates on turn-taking bases. Sacks et al. [28] introduced the components in a turn-taking system: 1) a Turn Construction Unit (TCU) defines an utterance as a whole turn, 2) a Transition Relevance Place (TRP) corresponds to the end of a TCU where the turn could legitimately pass from one speaker to another, and 3) a Turn Allocation Component (TAC) describes how the next turn is allocated among the participants (by the current speaker's selection or self-selection).

We built a conversational structure based on the above pattern. In order to emphasize the change of direction, dummy error-handling of the conversation and the lessening of face-threatening acts, the speaker conducts turn-initials within the utterances. Also, for the purpose of indicating the TRPs at the end of each TCU and softening the utterance, the speaker chooses a hedge. In this way, it becomes easy for the driver to recognize when the speaker will be able to start or end the turn in each TCU. We followed such a strategy to make the conversation turns perceived as natural, and also to take into consideration the driver joining into the conversation based on the turn-taking system for the future implementations.

EXPERIMENTAL PROTOCOL
We set up an experiment with two conditions, one-to-one communication based NAMIDA (OOCN) and multi party conversation based NAMIDA (MPCN). Each participant performed a mock-driving routines by watching a projected driving simulation on a big wall while communicating with each NAMIDA conditions respectively. In the simulation, the driver was in streets where he/she has been for the first time with high buildings, shopping malls, restaurants and ordinary houses. In each condition, NAMIDA robots introduce the environment to the driver. We employed the same utterance patterns for both NAMIDA conditions. However, the turn-taking is occurred between the three agents only in the MPCN condition by allocating the script among them. With the OOCN condition, the same content was uttered through one agent. The symbol (...) in the extracts below represents a pause of about 1.0-1.5 seconds.

Condition1
The subject is always the addresser and receives the relevant, location-based information from OOCN while the agent is always the speaker. The conversational turn doesn't change in terms of the subject's roles. Below is an extract from a conversation under the OOCN condition:

```
1 Turn 1  N1:  [TCU I think, this is
2    a very nice street.]  [TRP](...)
3 Turn 2  N1:  [TCU There
4    must be
5    an old temple
6    around here.]  [TRP]
7 Turn 3  N1:[TCU This is amazing
8    isn't it?][TRP] (...)
```

Condition2
The participant is always bystander and receives the location-based information from the MPCN. During a turn changes in the conversation, subject's roles are changing as well. Below is an extract from a conversation under the MPCN condition:

```
1 Turn1  N1:  [TCU I think, this is
2    a very nice street.]  [TRP](...)
3 Turn2  N3:  [TCU Oh, really?]  [TRP]
4 Turn3  N2:  [TCU Yes.][TRP]
5    [TCU There,
6    must be
7    an old temple
8    around here.]  [TRP]
```

```
9 Turn4   N3:[TCU This is amazing
10   isn't it?][TRP](...)
```

Experiment Setup

In total, 14 participants of ages varying from 20 to 35 years old (average age of 23.15) took part in the experiment within a counterbalanced measures design. Since the interaction between the participants and the system was limited, we kept each session approximately 5 minutes in length to maintain a high level of concentration of the participants. All participants had a driving license.

Upon arrival, each participant was given an orientation about the experiment and their task. They were informed to memorize the content of the conversation that involves information about nearby places. We gave this task to the participants, because in a real life driving case, drivers would like to remember the new places they have seen where might be interesting to visit afterwards. We expected that in MPCN condition, the participants would recall the information better than the OOCN case. At the end of the each session, participants are given five questions about their recollection of the conversation under both conditions.

We measured the experiment objectively and subjectively. As a subjective approach, we employed a Driving Activity Load Index (DALI) questionnaire in which the participants were required to answer five questions related to the five demands of mental workload. Each question had scale of 1 to 5 to rank participant opinion. As an objective approach, we recorded the driver's eye-gaze behaviors with the Eye Tribe Tracker in order to measure the attention behavior of each participant.

RESULTS

Workload Factors

In order to evaluate the mental workload, after each experimental session, the participants received the DALI questionnaire. Then we applied a paired t-test to determine if there was a statistical difference between the MPCN and OOCN cases.

Driving Activity Load Index (DALI)

DALI (Driving Activity Load Index) is a SWAT technique, which was proposed by [26] as a revised version of the NASA-TLX and adapted to driving tasks. It includes six predefined factors: attention, interference, situation stress, visual, auditory and temporal demands. However, in our study, we used five factors, excluding the interference factor because this factor is most suitable when it is used in a real driving environment. One of the main advantages of DALI is the possibility to identify the origins of the driver's workload and allowing for improvement of the proposed system at this identified level.

Each DALI factor has been calculated based on the subjects' ratings according to the work of [26].

Attention Demand: 88% and 85% of the participants answered the memorization questions correctly for the MPCN and OOCN, respectively. The participants' recall of the information showed no significant difference across the two conditions (p=0.409>0.05). However, the t-test for attention demand of the DALI revealed a significant difference (t(13)=2.10,

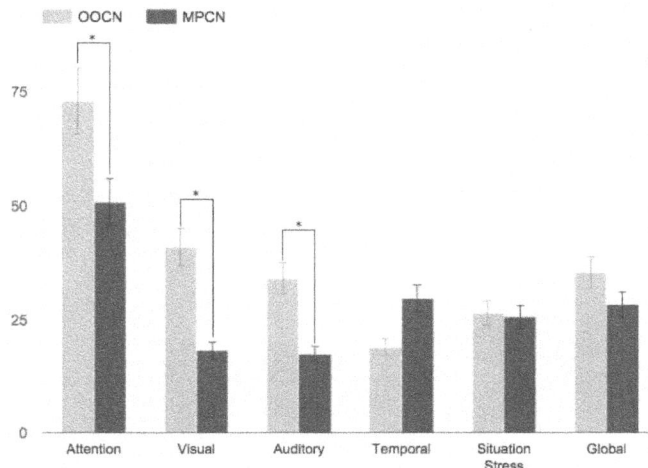

Figure 2. The results of the DALI factors under the OOCN and MPCN cases.

P<0.05, significant) (Table 2 and Fig. 2). According to these results, the OOCN required more attention than the MPCN with regard to remembering the presented information.

Visual Demand: There was a significant difference in visual demand (t(13)=2.86, P=0.009<0.01, highly significant) (Table 2 and Fig. 2). This reveals that the participants had to exert more visual effort for the OOCN as compared with the MPCN because of the directed utterances by the interface.

Auditory Demand: There was also a significant difference in auditory demand (t(13)=1.83, P=0.0449<0.05, significant) (Table 2 and Fig. 2). These results indicate that the participants allocated less auditory effort when listening to the MPCN as compared with the OOCN. This was because the driver was excluded from the conversation, yet could listen and discern the presented information.

Temporal Demand: We found relatively high, yet non-significant difference for this demand (t(13)=-1.10, P=0.145>0.05, non-significant). This may be because of more utterance generated by the MPCN compared with the OOCN during the same period of time (Table. 2 and Fig. 2).

Situation Stress: This factor also does not show a significant difference (t(13), P=0.45992>0.05, non-significant) (Table. 2 and Fig. 2). This may be because the experiments were conducted in a mock driving environment rather than a more realistic driving simulation or in a real-world environment.

Global Value: Overall, the global value didn't show significant difference between the MPCN and the OOCN (t(13) = 0.81, P=0.224>0.05, non-significant) (Table. 2 and Fig. 2). We can claim that this is because of the non-significant results of temporal and situation stress demands, and the relatively higher rate of temporal demand for the MPCN case.

From the Fig. 2, we can infer that the MPCN required significantly less attentional, visual and auditory efforts of participants than with the OOCN. A mock driving environment and higher utterance generation of the MPCN may have had an

Table 2. Dimensions of DALI, based on context and the associated questionnaire with significant and non-significant dimensions of MPCN and OOCN indicated.

Dimention	Mean value (standard error)		Pairwaise t-test t(d.f.) = t-value p <0.05 (significant)	Results
	OOCN	MPCN		
Attention demand	73.14 (8.55)	51.00 (28.34)	t(13) = 2.10 p = 0.033 <0.05	Significant
Visual demand	41.14 (18.72)	18.28 (9.75)	t(13) = 2.86 p = 0.009 <0.05	Significant
Auditory demand	34.28 (17.71)	17.5 (17.62)	t(13) = 1.83 p = 0.0449 <0.05	Significant
Temporal demand	19.00 (23.78)	29.81 (16.43)	t(13) = -1.10 p = 0.144 >0.05	Non-significant
Situation Stress	26.66 (16.32)	(25.71 (16.94)	t(13) = 0.10 p = 0.459 >0.05	Non-significant
Global Value	35.50 (5.50)	28.46 (6.67)	t(13) = p = 0.224 >0.05	Non-significant

effect on the temporal and situation stress demands. This circumstance can be the reason for observing the non-significance found in the global value.

Attention Behavior of Driver

During a driving activity, the eye gaze of a driver should be on the road as much as possible. However, the eye gaze behavior can be easily altered with a one-to-one communication-based driving agent system due to the reasons mentioned before.

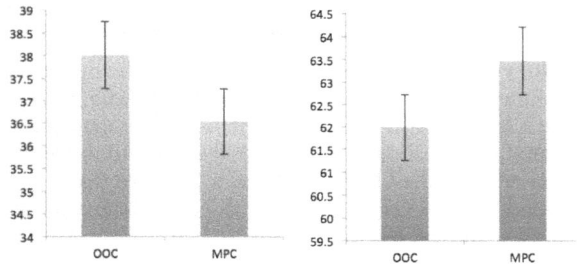

Figure 3. Results showing of the percentage of the eye gazes on the NAMIDA system (*left*) and on the road (*right*) during the simulation.

We hypothesized that a multi-party conversation-based driving agent system required less eye-gaze contact, consequently helping the driver to focus on the road. For this purpose, in our two-session experiment, we tracked the participant's various eye-gaze behaviors during the driving simulation with the NAMIDA system.

Since the eye gaze movements provide significant cues about the attention behaviours of the user ([8], [6], [13]), we utilized an eye gaze tracker to understand the users' visual demand allocation between the NAMIDA system and the simulation.

To track a participant's eye gaze, we divided the attention region into two different areas and then counted the number of the driver's attention frames for the NAMIDA interface and also on the road (driving simulation). The eye gaze tracking system allowed us to capture approximately 30 frames/second.

According to the results, 63.46% frames were detected on the simulation road during the MPCN session while 61.98%

frames were detected for the OOCN session (Fig. 3). The eye gaze data also showed that, the participants exert comparatively more attention to the NAMIDA under the OOCN condition (38.01%) rather than the MPCN condition (36.53%).

Trend line Analysis

Research in HRI suffers from the limited time of interactions during experiments. It may not be possible to predict relatively longer interactions from shorter-timed experiment extrapolation. However, a trend line analysis can help to identify the trends of user behaviors and forecast future interactions. For the purpose of interpreting the attention behaviors of the participants in our study, we applied a trend line analysis and then fit the user data in a mathematical model to estimate the future tendency of behaviors, using a regression model.

Within the trend line analysis, with the OOCN case, we obtained a negative linear regression with a slope of $m=-0.751$ and a coefficient of determination of $R^2=0.424$, on the road, and a positive regression with a slope of $m=0.751$ and a coefficient of determination of $R^2=0.424$, on NAMIDA. The above Fig. 4 shows the decline and incline of eye gaze behavior during five minutes of the OOCN experiment. The coefficient of determination, equal to 0.424, on both the road and NAMIDA, indicates that about 48% of the variation in eye gaze data can be explained by the participants reducing their attention on the road while increasing their attention on NAMIDA, in the OOCN case, over time. This would be considered a good fit to the data in the sense that it would substantially improve the ability to predict the eye gaze behavior of the participants.

On the other hand, with the MPCN case, we obtained a negative linear regression with a slope of $m=-2.238$ and a coefficient of determination of $R^2=0.897$, on NAMIDA, and a positive regression with a slope of $m=2.238$ and a coefficient of determination of $R^2=0.897$, on the road. Again, Fig. 4 shows the decline and incline of eye gaze behavior during five minutes of the MPCN experiment. The coefficient of determination, equal to 0.897, on both the road and NAMIDA, indicates that about 89% of the variation in eye gaze data can be explained by the participants reducing their attention on NAMIDA while increasing their attention on the road, in the

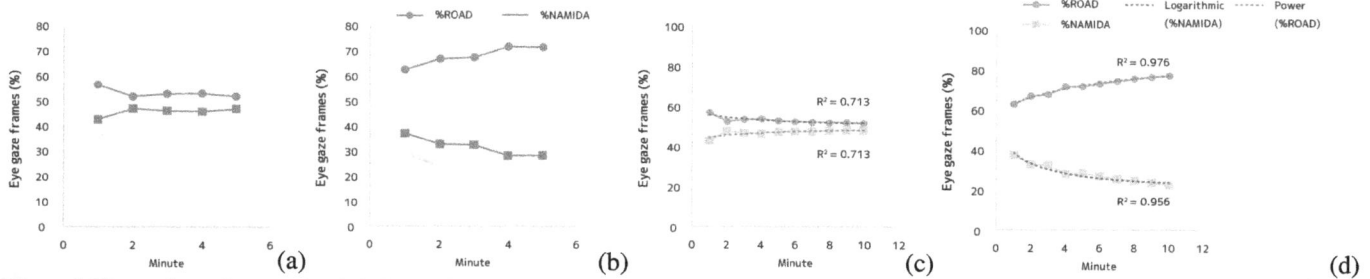

Figure 4. Figure shows the attention behviours of the subjects. The current trend of OOCN *(a)* and MPCN *(a)*, also the regression model of OOCN *(c)* and MPCN *(d)*

MPCN case, over time. This result can be considered a very good fit to our data in the sense that it would substantially improve the ability to predict the eye gaze behavior of the participants.

In order to predict eye gaze behavior, we fit our results into a statistical model. For the OOCN case, we obtained a power regression, for the road, with a coefficient of determination of $R^2=0.713$ and a logarithmic regression, on NAMIDA, with a coefficient of determination of $R^2=0.713$. Fig. 4 shows the declining and inclining attention behavior trend for the road and the NAMIDA system over a five-minute period. Since both the power regression and logarithmic regression models show high correlation coefficients (R^2), these models can be taken as good predictors in explaining the future trend of variation in eye gaze behaviors.

In the MPCN case, we obtained a logarithmic regression with a coefficient of determination of $R^2=0.972$, for the road, and a Power Regression with a coefficient of determination of $R^2=0.956$ for NAMIDA. Fig. 4 shows the inclining and declining attention behavior trend on the road and the NAMIDA system over a five-minute period. Since both the power regression and logarithmic regression models show high correlation coefficients, these models can be taken as good predictors in explaining the future trend of variation in eye gaze behaviors.

DISCUSSION

In the current research, we argued the effects of a multi-party conversation based robotic agent and a one-to-one conversation based robotic agent on drivers' mental workload and attention behavior of the driver. The proposed design of the multi-party conversation system employs well-established turn-taking and role-changing techniques. We hypothesized that coupled with the utterance generation, eye gazing and agent body movements, MPCN will create a more enjoyable, natural and intuitive environment in which easier to follow and overhear the conversation instinctively and, thus, reduce the mental workload demands. Although, we couldn't observe significant difference on the global value of DALI, we can infer that in the OOCN case, the participants felt the responsibility of the conversation by the directed utterances from the system, which requires more mental resources, as can be seen in resulting in more attentional behaviors that indicate distraction (e.g., staring at the NAMIDA longer). Table. 2 and Fig. 2 show the significant and non-significant differences

between the mental workload factors observed in the MPCN and OOCN.

The results showed from the memorization test that recalling the given information during the conversation in both experimental cases had a non-significant effect unlike our expectation. A reason of this may be the ceiling effect that was caused by the relatively short duration of the experiment and the places that have been mentioned in the conversation were remarkable and easy to remember. On the other hand, as in the experiment of [22], the roles of a participant in the conversation didn't affect information recall. That is, may be we can say that the significantly higher rate of the attention demand of DALI in the OOCN implies that the participants (as addressers) exerted more attentional effort when memorizing the information. On the other hand, overhearing the same content via the MPCN, required less attentional demand as a cognitive component of the workload.

We claim that the reason for the high rates of attention demand for the DALI, in both cases, can be found in the fact that the NAMIDA interfaces are in the form of embodied social agents rather than physical robotic agents. Since the research proves that a social robotic agent provides more natural and intuitive interaction with humans over that of an embodied agent ([30]), we were not able to obtain as less attention demand value as we would have using a physically developed social robot. This will be involved in the next challenge for this project.

We also observed significant differences between the perceptive components (visual and auditory factors) of the workload. Considering the visual and auditory factors of each session, we observed very low values of these demands that displayed in the situation where the driver has to memorize the presented information from MPCN. Taking into account the fact that in both situations, the driver relied on the auditory information coming from the system, due to having the conversational burden as an addresser in OOCN, the driver was obligated to be in direct interaction with the system which emerged as the visual and auditory efforts of the driver. Since direct interaction by the one-to-one communication required more workload than overhearing by a multi-party conversation as the nature of the communication model, it was relevant to find the highly significant difference for these workload factors as we expected. At this point a sound-only communicative agent system can be thought to eliminate the visual factor of the workload. However, our aim is to provide a social, natural and familiar communication manner that would be possible by employing animated entities. We believe that this kind of interaction can be more enjoyable and effective in reducing the other factors of the workload (e.g. situational stress).

The non-significant yet higher rate of temporal demand in the MPCN (Table 2 and Fig. 2) can be the reason of more robots (with different voices) generating the utterance occurring in this case than the OOCN in a same period of time. However, we believe that in an unscripted, real-time interaction case, both cases would demonstrate less temporal demand, with MPCN requiring the least. It is because, in a real-time interaction scenario, the participants would take interactive roles: in the MPCN, a participant would take on one of the roles of speaker, addresser, side-participant or by-stander, while in the OOCN case, the role would be only speaker or addresser. Due to the higher conversation responsibility of the OOCN as the research [29] mentioned, participants would feel less temporal demand in the MPCN. We also observed non-significant and relatively low ratings in situational stress demand section (Table 2 and Fig. 2). This might be because the agents provided a natural way of communication that relieved stress. Another reason might be the experiments were performed in a mock driving environment and the participants were relaxed during the experiments. In a realistic driving simulation, the results might change.

The trend-line analysis results supported the subjective findings for visual demand in the DALI by showing decreasing eye-gaze instances on the NAMIDA system during the MPCN case, and incremental eye-gaze behaviors on the road, unlike with the OOCN (Fig. 4). The coefficients of determination for the visual attention on the road and NAMIDA system ($R^2=0.424$, $R^2=0.897$, respectively) revealed a good fit to the eye-gaze data such that we could predict the eye-gaze behaviors for the next five minutes.

Therefore, we fit our results into a statistical model to predict the tendency of the interaction based on the user's attention towards to the NAMIDA system. For the OOCN case, we obtained a power regression for the road with $R^2=0.713$ and a logarithmic regression for NAMIDA with $R^2=0.713$. Also, for the MPCN case, we obtained a logarithmic regression for the road with $R^2=0.972$ and a power regression on NAMIDA with $R^2=0.956$ (Fig. 4). With the high correlation coefficients, these results are reliable data in predicting the next five minutes of conversation/interaction between the users and the NAMIDA system. We can infer that the MPCN exhibits considerable potential in reducing eye gaze behaviors on an in-car agent system, yet it enhances the attentional focus on the road.

The low number of participants and the recruitment of mostly male subjects limited our results and ability to make broader generalizations. Ideally, a study with more participants, across a wider age range with more gender balance, using/not using the conventional in-car navigation system would produce more reliable results in terms of the affects of both systems on the drivers. Because we conducted our experiment with Japanese participants, the cultural context of our study constitutes an-

other limitation: the fact that Japanese participants are more accustomed to robotic interfaces.

CONCLUSION & FUTURE WORK

The proposed multi-party conversation based social interface of NAMIDA presents a unique interaction between a car and driver. As a social interface, it has been designed to assist drivers by conducting a context-aware interaction during a drive. We believe that this conversation approach is enjoyable as it requires less attention in obtaining necessary information. We designed an experiment to verify our hypothesis by comparing two different cases, MPCN and OOCN, in a mock driving environment. In the current research, we examined how it is becomes possible to reduce the certain workload factors of a driver by comparing a multi-party conversation-based, social-embodied system with a one-to-one conversation-based system in terms of mental workload and attention behavior.

We evaluated our proposed system using a DALI questionnaire, a trend analysis of the eye-gaze data gathered during the experiments and a subjective impression questionnaire. The results of DALI revealed that even though the MPCN cannot fulfill all the workload factors, it induced less cognitive and perceptive components of workload. That is, overhearing the location-based information via a conversation between the sociable agents required significantly less attentional, visual and auditory efforts. It has been also shown that, MPCN required less eye gaze behavior during the experimental conditions. Thus, the trend analysis demonstrated that our proposed multi-party conversation-based system is promising in reducing the attention behavior on the system over use. Our future study will involve the driver in the multi-party conversation by considering the instant condition (in behavioural and workload aspect) of the driver. We will also work on to generalize the results and investigate the different aspects of the multi-party conversation on drivers during a real-time interaction with physically developed robotic agents.

ACKNOWLEDGMENTS
This research has been supported by Grant-in-Aid for scientific research of KIBAN-B (26280102) from the Japan Society for the Promotion of Science (JSPS).

REFERENCES
1. Mikhail M Bakhtin. 1986. The Problem of Speech Genres (Vern W McGee, övers.) I Caryl Emerson & Michael Holquist (Red.), Speech Genres & Other Late Essays (ss. 60-102). (1986).

2. Christoph Bartneck, Dana Kulić, Elizabeth Croft, and Susana Zoghbi. 2009. Measurement instruments for the anthropomorphism, animacy, likeability, perceived intelligence, and perceived safety of robots. *International journal of social robotics* 1, 1 (2009), 71–81.

3. Robert A Barton and Robin IM Dunbar. 1997. 9 Evolution of the social brain. *Machiavellian intelligence II: Extensions and evaluations* 2 (1997), 240.

4. Judee K Burgoon, Joseph A Bonito, Artemio Ramirez, Norah E Dunbar, Karadeen Kam, and Jenna Fischer.

2002. Testing the interactivity principle: Effects of mediation, propinquity, and verbal and nonverbal modalities in interpersonal interaction. *Journal of communication* 52, 3 (2002), 657–676.

5. Jerome F DiMarzio. 2008. *Android*. Tata McGraw-Hill Education.

6. Luke Fletcher and Alexander Zelinsky. 2009. Driver inattention detection based on eye gaze - Road event correlation. *The international journal of robotics research* 28, 6 (2009), 774–801.

7. Cecilia E Ford and Sandra A Thompson. 1996. Interactional units in conversation: Syntactic, intonational, and pragmatic resources for the management of turns. *Studies in interactional sociolinguistics* 13 (1996), 134–184.

8. Alexandra Frischen, Andrew P Bayliss, and Steven P Tipper. 2007. Gaze cueing of attention: visual attention, social cognition, and individual differences. *Psychological bulletin* 133, 4 (2007), 694.

9. E. Goffman. 1979. Footing. *Semiotica* 25, 1-2 (1979), 1–30.

10. Jaap Ham and Cees JH Midden. 2014. A persuasive robot to stimulate energy conservation: the influence of positive and negative social feedback and task similarity on energy-consumption behavior. *International Journal of Social Robotics* 6, 2 (2014), 163–171.

11. Sandra G Hart and Lowell E Staveland. 1988. Development of NASA-TLX (Task Load Index): Results of empirical and theoretical research. *Advances in psychology* 52 (1988), 139–183.

12. Pamela J Hinds, Teresa L Roberts, and Hank Jones. 2004. Whose job is it anyway? A study of human-robot interaction in a collaborative task. *Human-Computer Interaction* 19, 1 (2004), 151–181.

13. Takahiro Ishikawa. 2004. Passive driver gaze tracking with active appearance models. (2004).

14. Masato Ishizaki and Tsuneaki Kato. 1998. Exploring the characteristics of multi-party dialogues. In *Proceedings of the 17th international conference on Computational linguistics-Volume 1*. Association for Computational Linguistics, 583–589.

15. Reiko Itani. 1995. *Semantics and pragmatics of hedges in English and Japanese*. Ph.D. Dissertation. University of London.

16. Nihan Karatas, Soshi Yoshikawa, P Ravindra S De Silva, and Michio Okada. 2015. NAMIDA: Multiparty Conversation Based Driving Agents in Futuristic Vehicle. In *Human-Computer Interaction: Users and Contexts*. Springer, 198–207.

17. Sheila G Klauer, Feng Guo, Bruce G Simons-Morton, Marie Claude Ouimet, Suzanne E Lee, and Thomas A Dingus. 2014. Distracted driving and risk of road crashes among novice and experienced drivers. *New England journal of medicine* 370, 1 (2014), 54–59.

18. Geoffrey Leech. 2005. Politeness: is there an East-West divide. *Journal of Foreign Languages* 6, 3 (2005).

19. BYD Company Ltd. 2012. Qin:Asocialrobotforanewplug-inhybrid vehicle. (2012).

20. Nobuyoshi Matsumoto, Hiroyuki Fujii, Miki Goan, and Michio Okada. 2005. Minimal design strategy for embodied communication agents. In *Robot and Human Interactive Communication, 2005. ROMAN 2005. IEEE International Workshop on*. IEEE, 335–340.

21. Youngme Moon and Clifford Nass. 1996. How âĂĲrealâĂİ are computer personalities? Psychological responses to personality types in human-computer interaction. *Communication research* 23, 6 (1996), 651–674.

22. Bilge Mutlu, Toshiyuki Shiwa, Takayuki Kanda, Hiroshi Ishiguro, and Norihiro Hagita. 2009. Footing in human-robot conversations: how robots might shape participant roles using gaze cues. In *Proceedings of the 4th ACM/IEEE international conference on Human robot interaction*. ACM, 61–68.

23. Feels Like Driving in Future Navdy Inc. 2013. https://www.navdy.com/. (2013).

24. In Automotto Nissan Motor Company Ltd., PIVO: An in-car robotic assistant. 2005. (2005).

25. Naoki Ohshima, Yusuke Ohyama, Yuki Odahara, P Ravindra S De Silva, and Michio Okada. 2015. Talking-Ally: The Influence of Robot Utterance Generation Mechanism on Hearer Behaviors. *International Journal of Social Robotics* 7, 1 (2015), 51–62.

26. Annie Pauzié, J Manzan, and Nicolas Dapzol. 2007. Driver's behavior and workload assessment for new in-vehicle technologies design. In *Proceedings of the 4th International Driving Symposium on Human Factors in Driver Assessment, Training, and Vehicle Design. Stevenson, Washington*.

27. Pioneer and iXsResearch Corp. 2010. Carnaby:anin-carrobotic navigation assistant. (2010).

28. Harvey Sacks, Emanuel A Schegloff, and Gail Jefferson. 1974. A simplest systematics for the organization of turn-taking for conversation. *language* (1974), 696–735.

29. Noriko Suzuki, Yugo Takeuchi, Kazuo Ishii, and Michio Okada. 2000. Talking eye: Autonomous creatures for augmented chatting. *Robotics and autonomous systems* 31, 3 (2000), 171–184.

30. Keith J Williams, Joshua C Peters, and Cynthia L Breazeal. 2013. Towards leveraging the driver's mobile device for an intelligent, sociable in-car robotic assistant. In *Intelligent Vehicles Symposium (IV), 2013 IEEE*. IEEE, 369–376.

31. Yuta Yoshiike, P Ravindra S De Silva, and Michio Okada. 2011. MAWARI: a social interface to reduce the workload of the conversation. In *Social Robotics*. Springer, 11–20.

Are You Talking to Me?
Improving the Robustness of Dialogue Systems in a Multi Party HRI Scenario by Incorporating Gaze Direction and Lip Movement of Attendees

Viktor Richter[1] Birte Carlmeyer[1] Florian Lier[1]

Sebastian Meyer zu Borgsen[1] David Schlangen[1] Franz Kummert[1]

Sven Wachsmuth[1] Britta Wrede[1]

ABSTRACT

In this paper, we present our humanoid robot *Meka*, participating in a multi party human robot dialogue scenario. Active arbitration of the robot's attention based on multi-modal stimuli is utilised to observe persons which are outside of the robots field of view. We investigate the impact of this attention management and addressee recognition on the robot's capability to distinguish utterances directed at it from communication between humans. Based on the results of a user study, we show that mutual gaze at the end of an utterance, as a means of yielding a turn, is a substantial cue for addressee recognition. Verification of a speaker through the detection of lip movements can be used to further increase precision. Furthermore, we show that even a rather simplistic fusion of gaze and lip movement cues allows a considerable enhancement in addressee estimation, and can be altered to adapt to the requirements of a particular scenario.

ACM Classification Keywords

I.2.9 Robotics; I.5.5 Implementation: Interactive systems; I.2.11 Distributed Artificial Intelligence: Intelligent agents; I.2.7 Natural Language Processing: Speech recognition and synthesis; I.4.8 Scene Analysis: Motion, Shape, Color; I.5.2 Design Methodology: Feature evaluation and selection; I.2.10 Vision and Scene Understanding: Modeling and recovery of physical attributes

Author Keywords

dialogue systems; multi-party; multi-modal; interaction; autonomous robot; attention management; speaker; addressee

[1]Bielefeld University (CITEC), 33615 Bielefeld, Germany
[vrichter,bcarlmey,flier,semeyerz]@techfak.uni-bielefeld.de
d.schlangen@uni-bielefeld.de
[franz,swachsmu,bwrede]@techfak.uni-bielefeld.de

HAI '16, October 04-07, 2016, Biopolis, Singapore
©2016 ACM. ISBN 978-1-4503-4508-8/16/10. . . $15.00
DOI: http://dx.doi.org/10.1145/2974804.2974823

INTRODUCTION

In the context of Human Robot Interaction (HRI), it has become increasingly apparent that social and interactive skills are indispensable in order to build an intuitive, natural communication via speech, gestures, and facial expressions [4][10]. Moreover, *socially correct* interaction is desired. Therefore, Dautenhahn [8] already proposed a *"robotiquette"*, a set of "social rules for robot behaviour that is comfortable and acceptable to humans" in 2007. In a series of HRI studies [33], it was classified as socially interactive, in contrast to socially ignorant, that the robot took an interest in the humans activity and that it was actively *looking* at the human. Dautenhan further argues, that "a robot that serves as a companion in the home [...] needs to possess a wide range of social skills which will make it acceptable for humans. Without these skills, such robots might not be 'used' and thus fail in their role as an assistant." This finding is also confirmed in [9][12][15] – to only mention a few. To this end, the robotics community puts considerable effort into the development of "attentive systems" capable of interactively directing the robot's attention towards the human and vice versa [22][5][8][13].

While it is already a complex task to correctly direct the robot's attention in a 1:1 interaction between a human and a robot, this complexity significantly increases in a 1:N scenario where a robot needs to participate in a mixed interaction with, and between, multiple persons at the same time. Hence, single user HRI allows for multiple design simplifications for a situated robot. To give an example, it is sufficient to direct the robot's attention, via gaze for instance, towards its *sole* interaction partner or a potential focus of discourse. Moreover, the conversational roles in a single user interaction are limited to *speaker* and *addressee* [32]. Thus, usually all dialogue acts produced by the human interaction partner are targeted at the robot and therefore do not need to be verified or tested.

In contrast, in case of a multi user interaction, these simplifications may become a hindrance to the interaction dynamic. Additional conversational roles, like *ratified* (intended to listen) by the speaker or *side participant* (not part of the present dialogue act) emerge [32]. These additional roles will have a negative impact on the human-robot interaction dynamic if not considered and designed correctly in the robot's behaviour capabilities.

Figure 1. The Meka M1 Mobile Manipulator robotic-platform.
Image ©Johannes Wienke

The assumption that all dialogue acts are directed towards the robot does not hold in a multi user scenario. Users may also direct their gaze and/or speech towards another human instead of the robot. Thus, in the worst case scenario, the robot will react to every speech recognition result – even if it is not addressed. This may lead to refusal or even exclusion of the robot from the interaction. Subsequently, due to the fact that users recognize and negotiate conversational roles among each other, a robot will negatively influence the interaction whether or not this is intended. Moreover, Mutlu et al. [24] already showed that the gaze behaviour of a robot has a significant impact on conversational roles and participation of people in a multi person interaction. This effect was also confirmed in [31]. Therefore, if a robot is not capable of distinguishing multiple conversation partners and also exhibits this distinction, via directed attention for example, the human-robot interaction will become less natural, unintuitive and in the worst case – unacceptable. Finally, in case of a mobile robot, it is not safe to assume that all interaction partners are always located in front of the robot or any other "visible" location. It is also not safe to expect that a human interaction partner is always willing to move to the area where the robot is able to recognize them. Therefore, a robot must possess capabilities that allow for spacial localization and recognition of potential interaction partners in a dynamic environment, not only using vision but also other modalities. Moreover it needs to recognize if this potential partner is expressing an intention to communicate.

In this contribution we present our humanoid *Meka* (Figure 1), participating in a multi party human robot dialogue scenario. We investigate the impact of attention management and addressee recognition on the robot's performance to distinguish utterances directed at it from communication between humans. Taking into consideration the aforementioned issues and requirements, we formulate the following hypotheses:

1. Mutual gaze, as a means of yielding a turn to someone, can be used to facilitate the decision to whom an utterance was directed.

2. Recognition of lip movements can be used to validate an interaction partner as producer of perceived speech, and thus further increases the accuracy of addressee recognition.

3. Mutual gaze and lip movement recognition complement each other, and therefore can be combined in a simple, logical manner to further enhance the addressee recognition performance.

To test our hypotheses we conducted a proof of concept evaluation where the robot participated in a multi party human-robot interaction. During the interaction the robot was occasionally addressed, e.g., to provide information or execute a simple command. In this scenario the robot is required to direct its attention towards spatially distributed interaction partners. At the same time it needs to be able to react to robot-directed speech (addressee recognition) while ignoring interpersonal dialogue. To this end, we evaluate approaches to addressee recognition utilizing different types of visual cues, i.e. mutual gaze at the end of utterances, detection of lip movements, and logical combinations of these.

RELATED WORK

With respect to control of a robot's attention Ruesch [28] et al. presented a bottom up approach using the iCub robot based on audio-visual saliency. However, in their work face recognition as a social cue was not considered. Moreover, the evaluation was not carried out in the context of an human robot interaction (HRI) scenario. Breazeal [5] et al. introduced an attention system using the Kismet robot which implements bottom-up saliency and top-down habituation capabilities only using visual features. By changing weights between features, they generated different behaviours of their robot with respect to gaze preferences in the scene. Lang [21] et al. introduced a person tracking and anchoring system using the mobile robot BIRON. The presented system allowed the robot to identify and follow speakers based on the fusion of face detection results, sound source localization and laser scan data. However, the system is not able to instantly switch its communication partner due to a fixed interaction decay period and was only evaluated for speaker localization but not addressee recognition.

A further important question for our work is the effect of a robot's behaviour on the participants of an ongoing interaction. Bruce [6] et al. showed that actively turning to human interaction partners significantly increases their willingness to interact. Moreover, Mutlu [24] showed that shifting a robot's attention via looking behaviour during an interaction, can impose a conversational role on participants.

With regard to addressee recognition, Li [23] et al. fused features from upper body posture, face, gaze and lip-movement detection and emotion recognitions to calculate which person would most likely want to interact with their system. The calculated results were used to interact with the presumably most attentive person in the systems field of view. However, they do not take into consideration towards which participant an utterance was directed. In [3], Bohus et al. use a virtual avatar on a screen. They evaluate their system's turn taking performance in multi party interaction and observe that errors in addressee recognition have a negative impact on the quality of their turn taking model. [2] further elaborate on this model. They use sound source localization for speaker detection and classify the speaker'e visual focus of attention (vfoa) (based

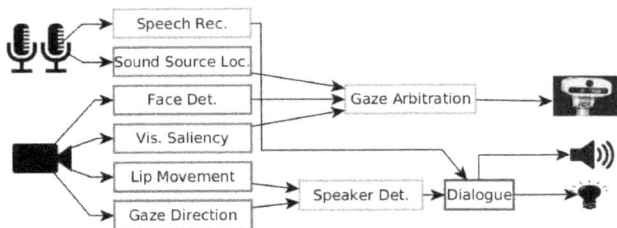

Figure 2. Overview of the robot's components for speaker/addressee recognition, gaze arbitration and dialogue management. ©*Sebastian Meyer zu Borgsen*

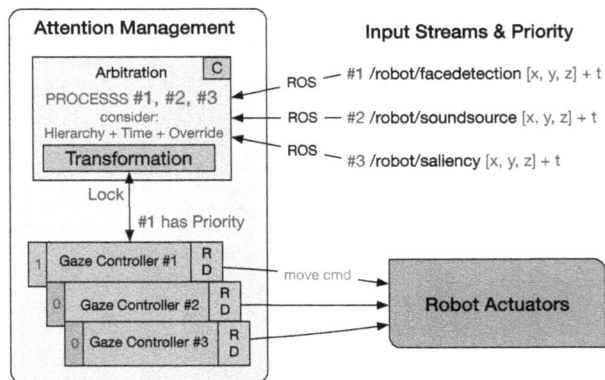

Figure 3. Overview of the attention management system. ©*Florian Lier*

on head poses) as addressee of the speech. The work by [31] eliminates the problem of speaker recognition by utilizing close talking microphones. Their robotic head *Furhat* considers itself addressee, when a speaker looked at it at some time during speech production. They further evaluate different turn taking cues produced by the robot in multi party interaction. Using the resulting data [17] creates a data driven classification after which utterance the robot should take the turn, utilizing voice activity, syntax, prosody, head pose of both persons, movement of cards, and dialogue context. Another data driven approach is realized in [16] where proportions of time a speaker/partner is looking at the robot/partner during utterances and contextual features are used to classify whether a *Nao* was addressed.

The presented work above assumes that all participants are visible throughout the whole interaction. Additionally, [3] and [31] (and therefore [17] too) used an external static camera not affected by the agent's actions. [23] and [16] implicitly require all participants of the interaction to reside within the robots field of view. Thus, while there exists a large body of research on robot attention modelling and addressee recognition, we go beyond these approaches by (1) taking into account more realistic settings (i.e. that it is not always possible to see all present interaction partners at once) and (2) by providing an evaluation of turn taking cues within a multi party setting with respect to correct attention management and addressee recognition.

SYSTEM DESCRIPTION

The humanoid robot platform *Meka* is part of the Cognitive Service Robotics Apartment (CSRA)[1] research project. It is used to explore research questions related to human-robot-interaction in smart-home environments. It's core software system (Figure 2) running on the robot consists of a speaker/addressee recognition, a gaze arbitration component and a dialogue system. These components include further sub-modules to process camera and stereo microphone input streams. The system controls the robot and is capable of producing speech output and triggering external actuators in the apartment, such as switching the light on/off.

Robot Platform

Amongst many other sensors, the M1 Mobile Manipulator robotic-platform *Meka* (Figure 1) features a *PrimeSense* Carmine RGBD camera to receive RGB images. Furthermore, a laser range finder allows to gather spacial information about the environment. Two microphones allow to retrieve audio in stereo. A real-time-enabled computer controls the robot hardware. With the compliant force controlled actuators including four-fingered hands the robot can grasp objects and execute human-interpretable gestures. An omni-directional base and lift-controlled torso enables navigating in complex environments. In total, the robot is equipped with 37 motor-powered joints. It has 7 per arm, 5 per hand, 2 in the head, 2 in the torso and 9 joints actuate the base including the z-lift. The motors in the arms and hands are Series Elastic Actuators (SEAs)[26], which enable fine force sensing.

Attention Management

The robot's attention management system is based on hierarchical prioritization of multi-modal sensor input streams. We realized this subsystem, which is openly available on github[2], as follows (Figure 3).

In general, the attention management system is sensor- and robot-independent. This is achieved by a) abstracting multi-modal sensor input via middleware data streams and b) an easily exchangeable robot control interface. Supported middleware implementations are Robot Operating System (ROS)[27] and Robotics Service Bus (RSB)[34].

Input data streams are a series of typed sensor messages consisting of a global target position [x,y,z] and a time stamp (t). Usually, these streams contain the position of a face detection result, a sound source or an interesting location in the robot's environment. The arbitration component is set up using a global configuration file (C). In this file topic names of N desired input streams, e.g., */robot/facedetection*, their associated data type, priority, timeout, control strategy, control mode, and override values are defined. Based on this configuration, the arbitration component continuously reads sensor messages – starting with the stream that has the highest configured priority. If the time stamp of the current message is *not* older than its

---

[1]https://www.cit-ec.de/de/content/
cognitive-service-robotics-apartment-ambient-host

[2]https://github.com/CentralLabFacilities/simple_robot_gaze

pre-defined maximum timeout value (100 milliseconds for example), the current position is transformed from the global target position into the robot's field of view. If the time stamp is "too old" or if there is no new message at all, the next priority (stream) is evaluated. Besides the arbitration component, the attention management system implements a so-called gaze controller per configured input stream. A gaze controller holds a reference to the robot driver (RD) and an activation flag.

Essentially, the robot driver implements the interface to the robot's hardware, its hardware abstraction layer or control API. The robot driver can be easily exchanged for a desired target platform, e.g., for NAO or iCub. However, after the current input message has been verified and the position has been transformed, the corresponding gaze controller is activated by toggling its activation flag and a movement command is sent to the robot. The control strategy of a gaze controller can be either configured to open- or closed loop. In case of an open control strategy, the command is issued and no further processing is required. In case of a closed-loop strategy, the command is issued and the arbitration component is locked until the desired position is reached. Moreover, the control mode can be set to relative or absolute positioning. These modes are required for sensors that move along with the robot (relative), a camera in the robot's head for instance, or fixed sensor setups (absolute). The attention management component features an override mode. If a preconfigured threshold is exceeded, the default hierarchy is temporarily disabled and the highest priority is instantly shifted to the input stream which triggered the override. In our setup we configured the attention management system as follows.

The highest priority were face detection results, the second highest priority were sound source localization results and the third highest priority were results produced by the visual saliency component. We activated the override feature for all three input streams which enabled the robot to initially look at a person and instantly shift it's attention towards another location where a loud sound or a visually salient spot was detected. This made it possible to dynamically and spontaneously shift the attention of the robot towards potential communication partners, even if they where not in the robot's field of view.

Addressee Recognition

To assess the gaze direction of currently observable persons the gaze detector from Schillingmann et al. [29] is used. The implementation was extended to be able to receive video data via ROS and publish its results, containing relative gaze directions and face landmarks [19] for all observed persons via RSB for further processing.

Based on this data, the addressee recognition component classifies its current speaking state for each person observed and whether the person maintains mutual gaze with the robot or not. Mutual gaze is assumed when a person keeps its gazing direction within a range of α around the robots head. To classify a person's speaking state we inspect its facial landmarks over a predetermined time period. When the variance of the distance between the horizontally centred points of the inner lips exceeds a threshold, the person is classified as currently

Figure 4. The experimental set up as used in a pre-study.

speaking:

$$Speaking(p_n) = \begin{cases} yes & \text{when } \mathrm{Var}(X_n) > d \\ no & \text{else} \end{cases}$$

where p_n is the n-th observed person and X_n is the set of its inner lip distances during the last Δ_t. The constants $\Delta_t = 600ms$, $\alpha = 12°$ and $d = 1.5$ were estimated in advance to produce reasonable results. Finally, the robot is classified as addressee if the person is speaking while maintaining mutual gaze with it.

Dialogue Management

For verbal communication we use a combination of the incremental natural language processing toolkit InproTK[1] and the human-robot dialogue manager Pamini[25] that have been integrated in [7]. MaryTTS[30] is used for speech synthesis and Sphinx[20] for speech recognition. A simple dialogue act generation module produces human dialogue acts based on keyword-spotting on the incremental ASR results, e.g., *action requests* such as "turn on/off the light", *information requests* such as "What time is it?" or *confirmations/negations*. The dialogue manager receives these results and processes them in sequence based on the current state of the interaction and the results of the addressee recognition.

STUDY SETUP & METHOD

In this section, the study setup and applied evaluation methods will be described in detail by elaborating on the experimental setup and the data recording and annotation.

Experimental set up

Figure 4 depicts the experimental set up. Three participants are sitting around the table in the CSRA, one participant is sitting on the sofa and two in the armchairs. On the table are 15 small slips of paper available with the following set of possible tasks or questions for the robot: (i) *turn on/off the light*, (ii) ask for the *current time*, (iii) whether a *call* or (iv) *delivery* has been missed, (v) request about *possible experiments* or (vi) which *data is getting recorded*, and (vii) ask for more *information about the Zen-garden* in the apartment.

The multi party interaction consists of two parts: interpersonal communication and human robot interaction. In the first phase a participant picks one of the tasks from the table, chooses another member of the group and tell him/her to issue the current task/question to the robot. In the second part of the interaction the chosen participant has to gain the attention of the robot and repeat the request addressing the robot. The participants were told to repeat their utterance a maximum of three times if the robot did not react. During the experiment, results of the speech recognition were evaluated and – if possible – executed, only if the robot was recognized as addressee of the utterance. This was only the case if mutual gaze at the end of the utterance and lip movements were detected, and allows us to evaluate other, more permissive, strategies later on (using the recorded interactions). The grammar chosen for speech recognition was relatively small because it was not subject of the evaluation.

Data Recording and Annotation

All interactions were recorded via two network-enabled Basler cameras and one Rode NT55 omni-directional microphone mounted at the ceiling of the apartment to cover the whole interaction area. Additionally, the robot's internal PrimeSense camera video stream has been recorded. Moreover, we collected various system events such as speech recognition results, generated dialogue acts and detailed information of the addressee recognition component. These consist of facial landmarks, gaze recognition results, and classification results for mouth movement, mutual gaze, and addressee.

For annotation purposes, the two top-down videos, the audio track and system events were merged into one ELAN[35] file (for further information about this process cf. [14]).

The study has been carried out with German native speakers. In total, we recorded approximately 53 minutes of interaction in 5 trials with 2 female and 13 male participants in total. A typical trial takes approximately 10 minutes. Altogether the dialogue system detected 874 human dialogue acts, 152 of these would have triggered a verbal response or a corresponding system action (light on/off). In order to evaluate the means of different approaches to addressee recognition, a ground truth annotation was carried out for each dialogue act.

RESULTS

To assess the performance of different approaches to addressee recognition, task specific utterances are extracted and classified into "robot is addressee" (positive condition) and "robot is not addressee" (negative condition). Comparing the classification results of the different approaches yields the corresponding 2x2 confusion matrix, which can be used to calculate accuracy, recall and precision (cf. Figure 5).

As baseline approach we accepted all results from the speech recognition (C_0). This approach does not reject tasks, thus its recall is 100% and the accuracy equals the prevalence of the dataset for the robot being addressed (84%, for an interpretation of this rather high amount of tasks addressed towards the robot see section: DISCUSSION).

We compare the results of the baseline test with the following approaches:

- (C_l) *lip movement* Accept tasks only when movement of the lips was detected.

- (C_g) *mutual gaze* Accept tasks only when mutual gaze with the robot was detected.

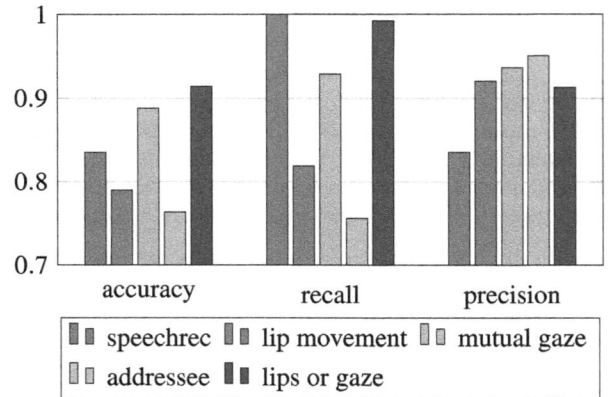

Figure 5. Accuracy, recall and precision of different addressee recognition approaches.

- (C_a) *addressee* Accept tasks only when the robot was recognized as addressee. This requires both mutual gaze and lip movement, and is the condition that was actually used throughout the trials.

- (C_x) *lips or gaze* Accept tasks when either lip movement or mutual gaze (inclusive disjunction) were detected.

As depicted in Figure 5 it is evident that *mutual gaze* can preserve a high recall (93%) compared to the baseline. The detection of lip movements does not perform as well (82%) as the baseline, and the conjunction of lip movement and mutual gaze detection C_a achieves only 76% recall. The accuracy of C_l and C_a is lower than the baseline's accuracy too. In contrast, the accuracy of C_g (89%) and C_x (91%) is higher than the baseline's accuracy. All non-baseline conditions show a precision of $> 90\%$, with a maximum of 95% for C_a in contrast to the baseline precision of 84%.

Many interactions between the participants in our scenario were not recognized as tasks by the robot. The resulting recognitions of short statements were out of context and therefore could be automatically rejected by the dialogue system (see section: Data Recording and Annotation). This results in the relatively unbalanced prevalence of the dataset, with 84% of the tasks actually addressed at the robot. The ratio between statements directed at the robot and statements exchanged between the participants is rather specific to our scenario. We therefore calculated the diagnostic odds ratio (DOR) for all conditions. This measure is an indicator of test quality, like accuracy, but decoupled from the prevalence of the test set. A DOR of x can be interpreted as: *The odds of being correctly classified as addressee are x times higher than the odds of being falsely classified as addressee.* [11].

Considering the DOR, all conditions perform better than the baseline C_0 with C_x indicating the best performance (cf. Figure 6). In contrast to the accuracy results, the conjunction of mutual gaze and lip movement detection has a higher DOR than lip movement detection only. This shows that the addressee recognition is, in general, more reliable than C_l.

We looked into the ten cases in which the robot was addressed but failed to look at the respective speaker. While in 3 of

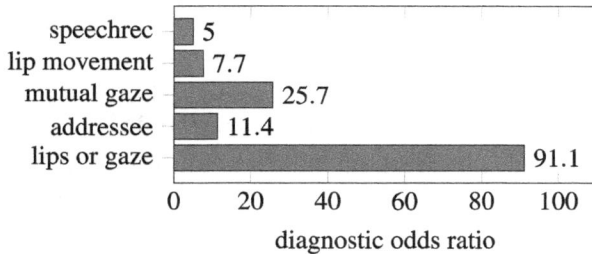

Figure 6. Diagnostic odds ratio of different addressee recognition approaches.

these cases none of the approaches' (C_l, C_g, C_a, C_x) cues were identified, mutual gaze with the chosen attendee was involved in 6 of the other cases. Mouth movements were misclassified twice, once because an attendee had to laugh.

DISCUSSION

There are multiple reasons for the relatively high amount of tasks directed towards the robot (84%) in contrast to tasks recognized from interpersonal speech (16%). First, participants used a much more variable wording and lower voice in interpersonal speech, decreasing the probability of the robot recognising a task. Additionally, in one trial, the participants resorted to showing the task descriptions to each other instead of stating the tasks. Finally, the addressee recognition – needing the highest certainty for acceptance – often rejected tasks, forcing the participants to repeat their assignment.

Nonetheless, the results show that detection of mutual gaze at the end of an utterance improves the accuracy and precision when recognizing whether or not a robot was verbally addressed. This confirms our first hypothesis.

Detection of lip movements does not perform that well in our scenario. When used as a single feature for addressee recognition in our scenario it has a much lower accuracy than the baseline, which means that our second hypothesis could not be confirmed. Additionally, it results in low accuracy and recall in the *addressee* condition where we require both mutual gaze and lip movements.

However, this does not eliminate lip movements as a feature per se. When mutual gaze and lip movement detection is used in conjunction, the system shows a high precision of 95%, which makes it more suitable for scenarios where the robot is rarely addressed. The result produced by *lips or gaze* reach the highest accuracy and DOR of all tested approaches, showing that a simple logical combination of mutual gaze and lip movement information increases the performance of addressee recognition, and thus confirms our third hypothesis.

Furthermore, we observed that in multiple cases the robot was addressed but did not detect mutual gaze or lip movements. One explanation for this is that either of these features could not be recognized at the relevant moment due to movements of the robots head and the resulting motion blur. Another explanation is that the robot sometimes did not look at the speaker when the task was stated and executed. While in such cases the focused person did not speak, there are multiple reasons for

other persons to establish mutual gaze, which allows the robot to recognize itself as addressee although it is not looking at the speaker. For instance: in multi party interaction people do not only look at the speaker but also at the addressee [18]. This is especially valid while a turn is transferred from one agent to another, where the attention is typically directed towards the agent most probable to take the turn [32]. However, the exact reasons for this apparent supplementing of the two features are subject to further investigation.

Considering that it was impossible to see all participants of the interaction at once in our scenario ,it is evident that the generic attention management, combining bottom-up and top-down saliency features, provides a considerably good basis for addressee recognition using only visual features. This results in the observation that already a simple addressee recognition can increase the performance of an agent in a multi party interaction. Nevertheless another consequence is that the attention module has a direct impact on the quality of addressee recognition.

LESSONS LEARNED & FUTURE WORK

The first observation is that the attention module sometimes triggers unintended behaviour of the robot. In only a few cases the participants had difficulties to acquire the robot's attention while it looked at another person. This is based on the fact that face detection results have the highest priority. Although it is possible to override this attention cue, e.g., verbally, this becomes difficult in the case of multiple persons speaking simultaneously (habituation).

A second observation is that people do not always wait until the robot looks at them. Occasionally they are already talking while the robot is still turning around. Often, in this case it is not possible to align visual features, such as gaze, and speech recognition results. In addition, an addressee recognition based solely on visual features is very challenging during head movements due to motion blur. Based on these observations other modalities or arbitration mechanisms should be considered.

We believe that the proportion of recognized dialogue acts may be different in long term multi party interaction. In our scenario most of the recognized dialogue acts were actually addressed towards the robot. We expect that in long term multi party interactions the dialogue acts not addressed to the robot will increase. In such cases addressee recognition becomes even more important. Therefore we additionally should consider scenarios with more interpersonal communication for evaluation.

However, with the recorded dataset we are able to tackle some of these issues. We will now be able to train and test different classifiers for lip movement detection to improve the accuracy of the classification of this visual feature. Furthermore, we will investigate different approaches for data fusion. On the one hand, a more sophisticated model for late feature fusion could be used. On the other hand, it is possible to explore various techniques for early fusion based on the raw data.

In addition, our observations show that the integration of other modalities is required. For instance, information from the attention management could be used in addressee recognition and vice versa. Apart from these low level features, we want to investigate the inclusion of high level features. One example are the speech recognition results. The verbal addressing of the robot by either using its name or the word "robot" should be exploited in order to improve the results of the addressee recognition.

We are also interested in the evaluation of the influence of such an attentive system on the subjective ratings of the robot by the participants. Therefore, we will carry out further experiments to measure different key concepts in HRI such as anthropomorphism and likeability of the robot.

CONCLUSIONS

In this work we investigated the impact of attention management and addressee recognition on a robot's capability to distinguish utterances directed at it from communication between humans. A multi party interaction study was carried out and the recordings annotated with ground truth information. Based on the evaluated results, we can show that attention management facilitates addressee recognition, especially in situations where it is not possible for the robot to see all participants of the interaction at the same time. It can further be verified that mutual gaze at the end of an utterance, is a meaningful signal for turn yielding. Verification of a speaker through the observation of lip movements decreases false positive addressee recognitions. Furthermore, already simple logical combinations of gaze and lip movement classifications yield good performance when it comes to finding out who is being addressed. However, more work is required to create a fusion model that performs well in all situations or can be tuned for a specified precision or accuracy in a continuous way. Extra effort is needed to enhance the interoperation between attention management and addressee recognition in order to be able to cope with some of the observed corner cases.

ACKNOWLEDGMENT

This work was supported by the Cluster of Excellence Cognitive Interaction Technology "CITEC" (EXC 277) at Bielefeld University, which is funded by the German Research Foundation (DFG), and by the German Federal Ministry of Education and Research (BMBF) via the KogniHome project (project number: 16SV7054K).

REFERENCES

1. Timo Baumann and David Schlangen. 2012. The InproTK 2012 Release. In *NAACL-HLT Workshop on Future Directions and Needs in the Spoken Dialog Community: Tools and Data*. 29–32. http://nbn-resolving.de/urn:nbn:de:0070-pub-25145558

2. Dan Bohus and Eric Horvitz. 2010. Facilitating multiparty dialog with gaze, gesture, and speech. In *Ieeernational Conference on Multimodal Interfaces, Workshop on Machine Learning for Multimodal Interaction*. 1. DOI: http://dx.doi.org/10.1145/1891903.1891910

3. Dan Bohus and Eric Horvitz. 2011. Multiparty turn taking in situated dialog: Study, lessons, and directions. In *Special Interest Group on Discourse and Dialogue*. http://dl.acm.org/citation.cfm?id=2132903

4. Cynthia Breazeal. 2003. Toward sociable robots. *Robotics and Autonomous Systems* 42, 3 (2003), 167–175.

5. Cynthia Breazeal and Brian Scassellati. 1999. A Context-dependent Attention System for a Social Robot. In *International Joint Conference on Artificial Intelligence*. 1146–1151. http://dl.acm.org/citation.cfm?id=1624312.1624382

6. Allison Bruce, Illah Nourbakhsh, and Reid Simmons. 2002. The role of expressiveness and attention in human-robot interaction. In *International Conference on Robotics and Automation*, Vol. 4. 4138–4142. DOI: http://dx.doi.org/10.1109/ROBOT.2002.1014396

7. Birte Carlmeyer, David Schlangen, and Britta Wrede. 2014. Towards Closed Feedback Loops in HRI: Integrating InproTK and PaMini. In *Workshop on Multimodal, Multi-Party, Real-World Human-Robot Interaction (MMRWHRI '14)*. 1–6. DOI: http://dx.doi.org/10.1145/2666499.2666500

8. Kerstin Dautenhahn. 2007. Socially intelligent robots: dimensions of human–robot interaction. *Philosophical Transactions of the Royal Society of London B: Biological Sciences* 362, 1480 (2007), 679–704. DOI: http://dx.doi.org/10.1098/rstb.2006.2004

9. Boris De Ruyter, Privender Saini, Panos Markopoulos, and Albert Van Breemen. 2005. Assessing the Effects of Building Social Intelligence in a Robotic Interface for the Home. *Interacting with Computers* 17, 5 (2005), 522–541. DOI:http://dx.doi.org/10.1016/j.intcom.2005.03.003

10. Terrence Fong, Illah Nourbakhsh, and Kerstin Dautenhahn. 2003. A survey of socially interactive robots. *Robotics and Autonomous Systems* 42, 3 (2003), 143–166. DOI:http://dx.doi.org/10.1016/S0921-8890(02)00372-X

11. Afina S. Glas, Jeroen G. Lijmer, Martin H. Prins, Gouke J. Bonsel, and Patrick M.M. Bossuyt. 2003. The diagnostic odds ratio: a single indicator of test performance. *Journal of Clinical Epidemiology* 56, 11 (2003), 1129–1135. DOI: http://dx.doi.org/10.1016/S0895-4356(03)00177-X

12. Marcel Heerink, Ben Kröse, Vanessa Evers, BJ Wielinga, and others. 2008. The influence of social presence on acceptance of a companion robot by older people. *Journal of Physical Agents* 2, 2 (2008), 33–40. DOI: http://dx.doi.org/10.14198/JoPha.2008.2.2.05

13. Patrick Holthaus. 2014. *Approaching Human-Like Spatial Awareness in Social Robotics - An Investigation of Spatial Interaction Strategies with a Receptionist Robot*. Ph.D. Dissertation. Bielefeld University.

14. Patrick Holthaus, Christian Leichsenring, Jasmin Bernotat, Viktor Richter, Marian Pohling, Birte Carlmeyer, Norman Köster, Sebastian Meyer zu Borgsen, René Zorn, Birte Schiffhauer, Kai Frederic Engelmann, Florian Lier, Simon Schulz, Philipp Cimiano, Friederike Eyssel, Thomas Hermann, Franz Kummert, David

Schlangen, Sven Wachsmuth, Petra Wagner, Britta Wrede, and Sebastian Wrede. 2016. How to Address Smart Homes with a Social Robot? A Multi-modal Corpus of User Interactions with an Intelligent Environment. In *International Conference on Language Resources and Evaluation* (23-28).

15. Patrick Holthaus, Karola Pitsch, and Sven Wachsmuth. 2011. How Can I Help? *International Journal of Social Robotics* 3, 4 (11 2011), 383–393. DOI: http://dx.doi.org/10.1007/s12369-011-0108-9

16. Dinesh Babu Jayagopi and Jean-Marc Odobez. 2013. Given that, should i respond? Contextual addressee estimation in multi-party human-robot interactions. In *Human-Robot Interaction*. 147–148. DOI: http://dx.doi.org/10.1109/HRI.2013.6483544

17. Martin Johansson and Gabriel Skantze. 2015. Opportunities and Obligations to Take Turns in Collaborative Multi-Party Human-Robot Interaction. In *Special Interest Group on Discourse and Dialogue*. 305–314.

18. Martin Johansson, Gabriel Skantze, and Joakim Gustafson. 2014. Comparison of Human-Human and Human-Robot Turn-Taking Behaviour in Multiparty Situated Interaction. In *Workshop on Understanding and Modeling Multiparty, Multimodal Interactions*. 21–26. DOI:http://dx.doi.org/10.1145/2666242.2666249

19. Vahid Kazemi and Josephine Sullivan. 2014. One millisecond face alignment with an ensemble of regression trees. In *IEEE Conference on Computer Vision and Pattern Recognition*. 1867–1874. DOI: http://dx.doi.org/10.1109/CVPR.2014.241

20. Paul Lamere, Philip Kwok, Evandro Gouvea, Bhiksha Raj, Rita Singh, William Walker, Manfred Warmuth, and Peter Wolf. 2003. The CMU SPHINX-4 speech recognition system. In *IEEE International Conference on Acoustics, Speech and Signal Processing*, Vol. 1. Citeseer, 2–5.

21. Sebastian Lang, Marcus Kleinehagenbrock, Sascha Hohenner, Jannik Fritsch, Gernot a Fink, and Gerhard Sagerer. 2003a. Providing the basis for human-robot-interaction. In *International Conference on Multimodal Interfaces*. 28. DOI: http://dx.doi.org/10.1145/958432.958441

22. Sebastian Lang, Marcus Kleinehagenbrock, Sascha Hohenner, Jannik Fritsch, Gernot A. Fink, and Gerhard Sagerer. 2003b. Providing the Basis for Human-Robot-Interaction: A Multi-Modal Attention System for a Mobile Robot. In *International Conference on Multimodal Interfaces*. DOI: http://dx.doi.org/10.1145/958432.958441

23. Liyuan Li, Qianli Xu, and Yeow Kee Tan. 2012. Attention-based addressee selection for service and social robots to interact with multiple persons. In *Proceedings of the Workshop at SIGGRAPH WASA*, Vol. 1. 131. DOI: http://dx.doi.org/10.1145/2425296.2425319

24. Bilge Mutlu, Toshiyuki Shiwa, Takayuki Kanda, Hiroshi Ishiguro, and Norihiro Hagita. 2009. Footing in human-robot conversations. In *Human Robot Interaction*, Vol. 2. 61. DOI: http://dx.doi.org/10.1145/1514095.1514109

25. Julia Peltason and Britta Wrede. 2010. Pamini: A Framework for Assembling Mixed-Initiative Human-Robot Interaction from Generic Interaction Patterns. In *Special Interest Group on Discourse and Dialogue (SIGDIAL '10)*. 229–232.

26. Gill A Pratt and Matthew M Williamson. 1995. Series elastic actuators. In *Human Robot Interaction and Cooperative Robots*, Vol. 1. IEEE, 399–406.

27. Morgan Quigley, Ken Conley, Brian Gerkey, Josh Faust, Tully Foote, Jeremy Leibs, Rob Wheeler, and Andrew Y Ng. 2009. ROS: an open-source Robot Operating System. In *International Conference on Robotics and Automation Workshop on Open Source Software*, Vol. 3. 5.

28. Jonas Ruesch, Manuel Lopes, Alexandre Bernardino, Jonas Hornstein, Jose Santos-Victor, and Rolf Pfeifer. 2008. Multimodal saliency-based bottom-up attention a framework for the humanoid robot iCub. In *International Conference on Robotics and Automation*. 962–967. DOI: http://dx.doi.org/10.1109/ROBOT.2008.4543329

29. Lars Schillingmann and Yukie Nagai. 2015. Yet another gaze detector: An embodied calibration free system for the iCub robot. In *International Conference on Humanoid Robots*. 8–13. DOI: http://dx.doi.org/10.1109/HUMANOIDS.2015.7363515

30. Marc Schröder and Jürgen Trouvain. 2003. The German Text-to-Speech Synthesis System MARY: A Tool for Research, Development and Teaching. *International Journal of Speech Technology* 6, 4 (2003), 365–377. DOI: http://dx.doi.org/10.1023/A:1025708916924

31. Gabriel Skantze, Martin Johansson, and Jonas Beskow. 2015. Exploring Turn-taking Cues in Multi-party Human-robot Discussions about Objects. In *International Conference on Multimodal Interaction*. 67–74. DOI: http://dx.doi.org/10.1145/2818346.2820749

32. David Traum. 2004. Issues in Multiparty Dialogues. In *Workshop on Agent Communication Languages*. 201–211. DOI:http://dx.doi.org/10.1007/978-3-540-24608-4_12

33. Michael L Walters, Kerstin Dautenhahn, Sarah N Woods, Kheng Lee Koay, R Te Boekhorst, and David Lee. 2006. Exploratory studies on social spaces between humans and a mechanical-looking robot. *Connection Science* 18, 4 (2006), 429–439. DOI: http://dx.doi.org/10.1080/09540090600879513

34. Johannes Wienke and Sebastian Wrede. 2011. A Middleware for Collaborative Research in Experimental Robotics. In *IEEE/SICE International Symposium on System Integration (SII)*. 1183–1190. DOI: http://dx.doi.org/10.1109/SII.2011.6147617

35. Peter Wittenburg, Hennie Brugman, Albert Russel, Alex Klassmann, and Han Sloetjes. 2006. Elan: a professional framework for multimodality research. In *Language Resources and Evaluation Conference*, Vol. 2006. 5th.

Tracking Human Gestures under Field-of-View Constraints

Keng Peng Tee
A*STAR Institute for
Infocomm Research
Singapore
kptee@i2r.a-star.edu.sg

Yuanwei Chua
A*STAR Institute for
Infocomm Research
Singapore
ychua@i2r.a-star.edu.sg

Zhiyong Huang
A*STAR Institute for
Infocomm Research
Singapore
zyhuang@i2r.a-star.edu.sg

ABSTRACT

This paper presents a control design for a desktop telepresence robot that guarantees satisfaction of field-of-view (FOV) constraints when dynamically tracking multiple points of interest on a person. The multi-point tracking problem is solved by complementing centroid tracking with local constraint satisfaction that is achieved by local integral barrier functions active only in small regions near the FOV limits. Such a control provides an aggregate view of the points of interest on the person and ensures that none of them goes out of view. A simulation study illustrates the performance of the proposed control in comparison with a conventional control.

Author Keywords

Gesture; Tracking; Constrained Control; Field-of-View

INTRODUCTION

An important ingredient for engaging human-robot interaction is the visual understanding of human action in relation to a task or an environment. Before this challenging feat can be accomplished, multiple salient points need to be simultaneously tracked and maintained in the field of view. There are numerous works on vision-based tracking of human action in both the computer vision and robotics literature (see [5] for an overview). A visual tracker for mobile platforms has been proposed for human tracking based on a component-based descriptor that is adaptable and suitable for representing humans [3]. These works tend to focus on visual detection methods rather than tracking control, and they do not address field-of-view constraint satisfaction.

Many of the works that do deal with field-of-view constraints involve the control of nonholonomic mobile robots with vision systems [6, 9, 1], or eye-in-hand robotic manipulators [2, 4]. These robots typically contain more degrees of freedom (DOFs) than a 2-DOF pan-tilt robot, and thus offer more tractable means of solving the FOV problem. For pan-tilt robots, only two inputs are available to control multiple (more than two) output pairs and ensure that all of them satisfy FOV constraints, leading to an underactuated control problem.

Permission to make digital or hard copies of part or all of this work for personal or classroom use is granted without fee provided that copies are not made or distributed for profit or commercial advantage and that copies bear this notice and the full citation on the first page. Copyrights for third-party components of this work must be honored. For all other uses, contact the owner/author(s).

HAI '16 October 04-07, 2016, Biopolis, Singapore

© 2016 Copyright held by the owner/author(s).

ACM ISBN 978-1-4503-4508-8/16/10.

DOI: http://dx.doi.org/10.1145/2974804.2980477

In this paper, we design control for a desktop telepresence robot with pan-tilt actuation [7]. The robot is required to track multiple points of interest on a person (e.g. body gestures) without any of the points escaping from the FOV. This is important for the robot to accurately interpret gesture commands or perceive human intention. We use local integral barrier functions [8] active only in small regions near the FOV limits, and complement this local constraint satisfaction with centroid tracking for an aggregate view of the points of interest. The control ensures that the robot is able to track the multi-point centroid without any point leaving the FOV at any time.

PROBLEM FORMULATION

Consider a pan-tilt robot, with a camera mounted on the tilt link, that tracks m points of interest (e.g. head, hands) on a user who is moving about in front of the robot. Let $X_{c_j} = [x_j, y_j, z_j]^T$, $j = 1, ..., m$, be the camera-centric coordinates of each point of interest, and $q = [\psi, \theta]^T$ the pan and tilt angles of the robot in the *base frame* (see Figure 1). Since the camera is mounted on the tilt link, the camera frame is oriented with respect to the base frame by

$$^bR_c = \begin{bmatrix} \cos\psi\cos\theta & -\sin\psi & \cos\psi\sin\theta \\ \sin\psi\cos\theta & \cos\psi & \sin\psi\sin\theta \\ -\sin\theta & 0 & \cos\theta \end{bmatrix} \quad (1)$$

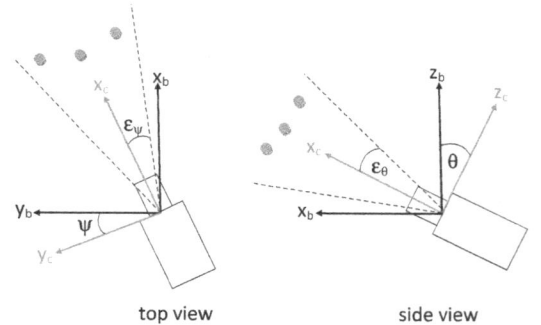

Figure 1. Base frame (x_b, y_b, z_b), camera frame (x_c, y_c, z_c), joint angles (ψ, θ) and FOV limits $(\varepsilon_\psi, \varepsilon_\theta)$ for the pan-tilt robot.

We can compute, via geometrical relationship with the measured positions of the points of interest, the pan and tilt errors in the *camera frame*, denoted by e_{j_ψ} and e_{j_θ} respectively:

$$e_{j_\psi} = \tan^{-1}\left(\frac{y_j}{x_j}\right), \quad e_{j_\theta} = \tan^{-1}\left(\frac{-z_j}{x_{j_r}}\right) \quad (2)$$

for $j = 1,...,m$, where

$$x_{j_r} = x_j \cos e_{j_\psi} + y_j \sin e_{j_\psi} \qquad (3)$$

is the x-coordinate of an intermediate frame after the original camera frame is rotated by e_{j_ψ} about its z-axis.

The equations of motion for the pan-tilt robot are:

$$M(q)\ddot{q} + C(q,\dot{q})\dot{q} + G(q) = \tau \qquad (4)$$

where $M(q) \in \mathbb{R}^{2\times 2}$ is a symmetric positive definite matrix, $C(q,\dot{q})\dot{q} \in \mathbb{R}^2$ the Coriolis and centrifugal forces, $G(q) \in \mathbb{R}^2$ the gravitational forces, $\tau \in \mathbb{R}^2$ the input torque.

Taking into account the change of coordinates between the pan and tilt velocities in the base and camera frames, we can rewrite the dynamics in the form:

$$\dot{e}_j = J\eta + d_j(t), \qquad j = 1,...,m$$
$$\dot{\eta} = M^{-1}(-C\eta - G + \tau) \qquad (5)$$

where $e_j = [e_{j_\psi}, e_{j_\theta}]^T$, $\eta = [\dot{\psi}, \dot{\theta}]^T$, $J = -\text{diag}(\cos\theta, 1)$, and $d_j(t)$ the rate of change of the pan and tilt errors in the camera frame due to human movements.

The control objective is to stabilize the centroid of the pan and tilt errors, $\bar{e} = \frac{1}{m}\sum_{j=1}^{m} e_j$ about the origin. At the same time, all the points of interest must be kept in the field of view (FOV) at all times, i.e.

$$|e_{j_\psi}(t)| < \varepsilon_\psi, \quad |e_{j_\theta}(t)| < \varepsilon_\theta, \quad \forall t \geq 0, j = 1,...,m \qquad (6)$$

where $\varepsilon_\psi, \varepsilon_\theta > 0$ are the FOV limits.

We define a *safety zone* by the set:

$$\Omega_s = \{|e_\psi| \leq \underline{\varepsilon}_\psi, |e_\theta| \leq \underline{\varepsilon}_\theta\} \qquad (7)$$

where $\underline{\varepsilon}_\psi < \varepsilon_\psi$ and $\underline{\varepsilon}_\theta < \varepsilon_\theta$. When any point of interest ventures out of this safety zone, the respective barrier function becomes active in ensuring that it never leaves the FOV.

ASSUMPTION 1. *The differences between the respective error and the centroid components, for $j = 1,...,m$, are bounded as follows:*

$$\max_j |e_{j_\psi} - \bar{e}_\psi| < \underline{\varepsilon}_\psi, \quad \max_j |e_{j_\theta} - \bar{e}_\theta| < \underline{\varepsilon}_\theta \qquad (8)$$

CONTROL SYNTHESIS FOR PAN-TILT ROBOT

The multi-point problem is solved by complementing centroid tracking with local constraint satisfaction that is achieved by local integral barrier functions active only in small regions near the FOV limits. This is an underactuated problem, where only 2 inputs are available to control $2m$ outputs. Fortunately, our application of human tracking allows us to make a reasonable assumption (Assumption 1) about the spread of the m points of interest. As a result, 2 control inputs are sufficient to ensure that all m points of interest remain in view at all times.

Define a positive constant $\Delta\varepsilon_\psi = \varepsilon_\psi - \underline{\varepsilon}_\psi$, and consider the barrier function:

$$V(e_1,...,e_m) = V_a(\bar{e}) + \sum_{j=1}^{m} V_{b_j}(e_j) \qquad (9)$$

where

$$V_a = \frac{1}{2}\bar{e}^T\bar{e}, \quad V_{b_j} = V_{b_{j_\psi}}(e_{j_\psi}) + V_{b_{j_\theta}}(e_{j_\theta})$$

$$V_{b_{j_\psi}} = \begin{cases} \int_{\underline{\varepsilon}_\psi}^{e_{j_\psi}} \frac{\Delta\varepsilon_\psi^2(\sigma - \underline{\varepsilon}_\psi)}{\Delta\varepsilon_\psi^2 - (\sigma - \underline{\varepsilon}_\psi)^2} d\sigma, & \underline{\varepsilon}_\psi < e_{j_\psi} < \varepsilon_\psi \\ 0, & |e_{j_\psi}| \leq \underline{\varepsilon}_\psi \quad (10) \\ \int_{-\underline{\varepsilon}_\psi}^{e_{j_\psi}} \frac{\Delta\varepsilon_\psi^2(\sigma + \underline{\varepsilon}_\psi)}{\Delta\varepsilon_\psi^2 - (\sigma + \underline{\varepsilon}_\psi)^2} d\sigma, & -\underline{\varepsilon}_\psi > e_{j_\psi} > -\varepsilon_\psi \end{cases}$$

$$V_{b_{j_\theta}} = \begin{cases} \int_{\underline{\varepsilon}_\theta}^{e_{j_\theta}} \frac{\Delta\varepsilon_\theta^2(\sigma - \underline{\varepsilon}_\theta)}{\Delta\varepsilon_\theta^2 - (\sigma - \underline{\varepsilon}_\theta)^2} d\sigma, & \underline{\varepsilon}_\theta < e_{j_\theta} < \varepsilon_\theta \\ 0, & |e_{j_\theta}| \leq \underline{\varepsilon}_\theta \quad (11) \\ \int_{-\underline{\varepsilon}_\theta}^{e_{j_\theta}} \frac{\Delta\varepsilon_\theta^2(\sigma + \underline{\varepsilon}_\theta)}{\Delta\varepsilon_\theta^2 - (\sigma + \underline{\varepsilon}_\theta)^2} d\sigma, & -\underline{\varepsilon}_\theta > e_{j_\theta} > -\varepsilon_\theta \end{cases}$$

We denote $\xi = \eta - \alpha$, and design the control as

$$\tau = -K_\xi \xi + M\dot{\alpha} + C\alpha + G - J^T v \qquad (12)$$
$$\alpha = -J^{-1}Kv \qquad (13)$$

where $K_\xi > 0$, $K = \text{diag}(k_\psi, k_\theta) > (1/2)I$, and

$$v = \left(\frac{dV_a}{d\bar{e}} + \sum_{j=1}^{m} \frac{dV_{b_j}}{de_j}\right)^T \qquad (14)$$

It can be shown, using BLF-based Lyapunov control synthesis and stability analysis [8] arguments, that the control (12) ensures that the points of interest always remain in the FOV, i.e.

$$|e_{j_\psi}(t)| < \varepsilon_\psi, \quad |e_{j_\theta}(t)| < \varepsilon_\theta \quad \forall t \geq 0, j = 1,...,m$$

SIMULATION RESULTS

In this simulation study, we choose 3 points of interest, namely the head and both hands. Two trajectories are simulated, one minimum-jerk and the other sinusoidal. The minimum-jerk trajectory describes a rightward (human-centric) reach with the right hand and an upwards reach with the left hand. The sinusoidal trajectory describes a purely up-and-down motion with both hands extending downwards on the down motion and upwards on the up motion.

To illustrate the necessity of the barrier functions in ensuring FOV constraint satisfaction, we simulate the response of an alternative controller that simply stabilizes the error centroid $\bar{e}$ and does not rely on barrier functions V_{b_j} to prevent each e_j from escaping the FOV:

$$\alpha = -J^{-1}K\bar{e}$$
$$\tau = -K_\xi \xi + M\dot{\alpha} + C\alpha + G - J^T\bar{e} \qquad (15)$$

Figures 2-4 show the results of the proposed control (12) corresponding to the minimum-jerk trajectories. In Figure 2, we see the head and hand paths in the yz plane (camera frame). Although the triangle joining the 3 points of interest changes shape and orientation according to the relative motion between the human and camera, the centroid of the triangle converges to the origin as a result of the proposed control, ensuring that the camera captures human action in an aggregate manner.

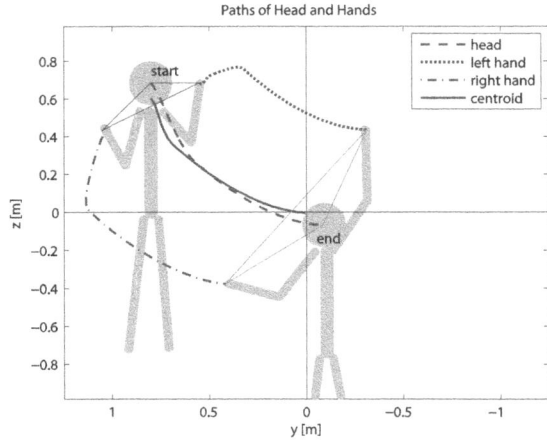

Figure 2. Path of head, hands, and centroid w.r.t. camera frame for the minimum-jerk human trajectory. The centroid converges to the origin. Stick figures depict the start and end human body pose.

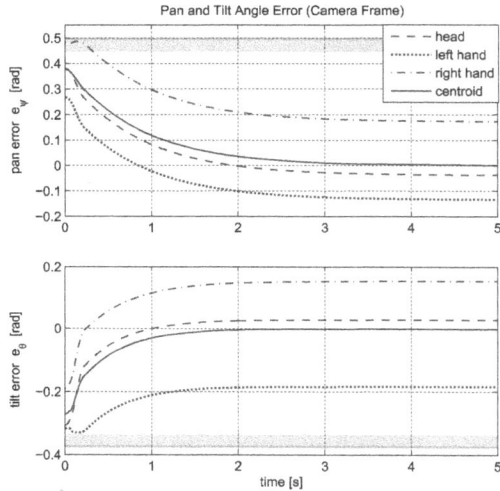

Figure 4. Positions of points of interest in camera frame for the minimum-jerk human trajectory. Gray regions mark unsafe regions where barrier functions are active.

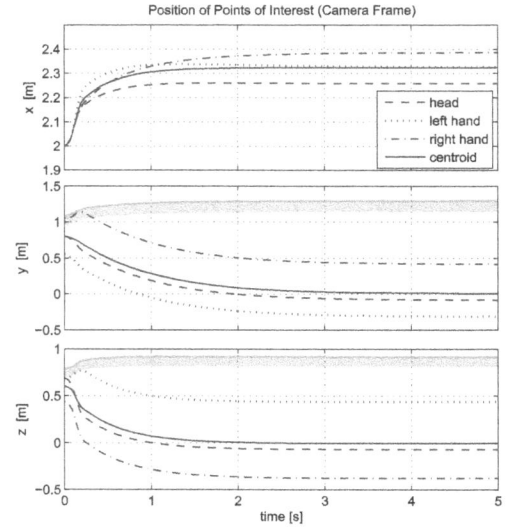

Figure 3. Visual tracking error angles in the camera frame for the minimum-jerk human trajectory. Gray regions mark unsafe regions where barrier functions are active. All error angles remain within FOV limits and the centroid converges to zero.

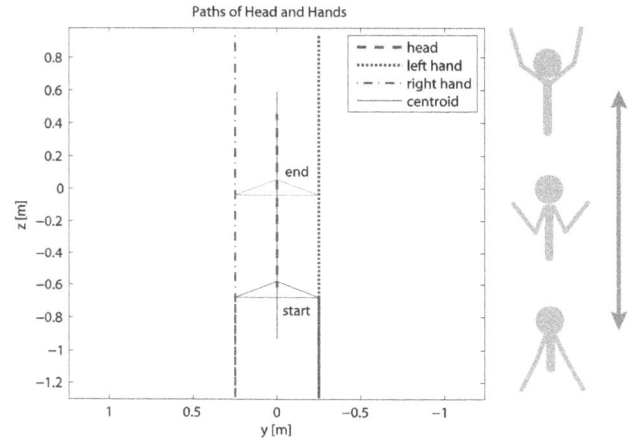

Figure 5. Path of head, hands, and centroid w.r.t. camera frame for the sinusoidal human trajectory. Stick figures on the right illustrate human upper body poses at select points.

Figure 3 shows that the visual tracking error angles in the camera frame for each point of interest are always bounded within the respective FOV limits. Note that the pan error for the right hand approaches the FOV (pan) limit closely due to the fast outward movement. However, once it enters the unsafe region, the barrier functions (10)-(11) become active and effectively prevents it from transgressing the limit, thus keeping the right hand in view. The centroid of these error angles converge to zero. Similarly, the centroid of the positions of the points of interest in the camera frame also converge to zero, as observed in Figure 4.

Figures 5-7 show similar results for the sinusoidal human trajectory. Since the first two thirds of the movement is aggressive, the unsafe regions are triggered 4 times by both hands,

as seen in error and position trajectories in Figures 6 and 7. Despite this challenging condition, the controller is able to prevent the hands from escaping the field of view.

Finally, simulation of controller (15) for the sinusoidal human trajectory shows that it is unable to keep all points of interest in view all of the time. There are a total of 6 instances where one of more points of interest exceeded the FOV limits by a significant amount. Note that this simulation result appears more benign than what an actual scenario would be, because we allow the system states to be simulated even though visual input is lost. In an actual scenario, losing view of one of more points of interest can distort the centroid representation drastically and lead to instability.

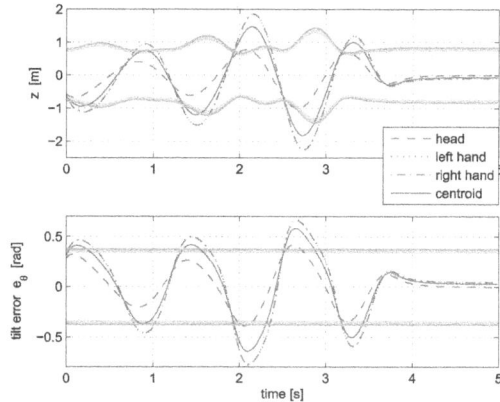

Figure 8. The points of interest escape from the field of view when barrier functions are not used in the control.

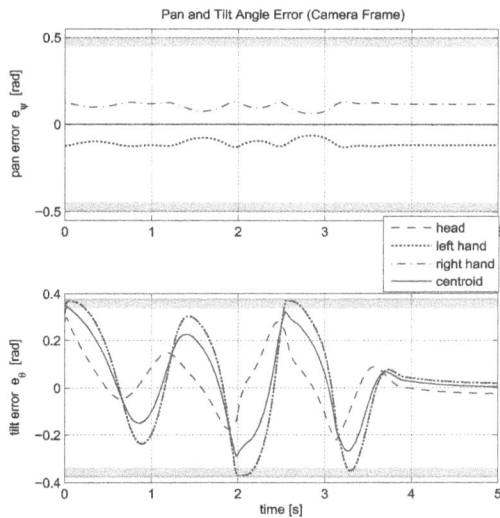

Figure 6. Visual tracking error angles in the camera frame for the sinusoidal human trajectory.

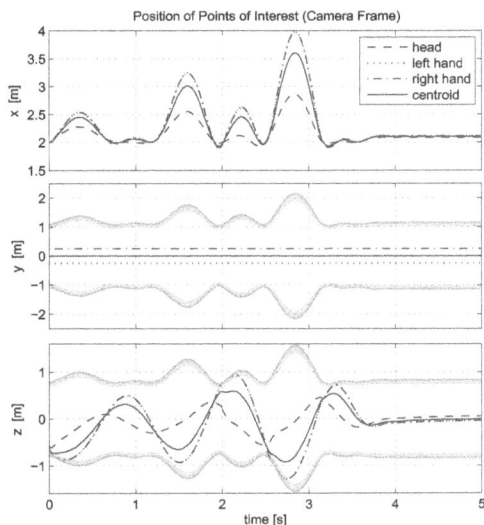

Figure 7. Positions of points of interest in camera frame for the sinusoidal human trajectory.

CONCLUSION

This paper has presented a control that provides an aggregate view of the points of interest on the person and ensures that none of them goes out of view. By exploiting the fact that multiple points on the same person are bounded about the centroid, we are able to circumvent the underactuation problem. Simulation shows that the proposed control with barrier functions is effective for tracking the centroid of multiple points of interest on a person with FOV constraint satisfaction, but a conventional control is unable to ensure that the points of interest remain in view at all times.

REFERENCES

1. S. Bhattacharya, R. Murrieta-Cid, and S. Hutchinson. 2007. Optimal paths for landmark-based navigation by differential-drive vehicles with field-of-view constraints. *IEEE Trans. Robotics* 23, 1 (2007), 47–59.

2. J. Chen, D. M. Dawson, W. E. Dixon, and V. K. Chitrakaran. 2007. Navigation function-based visual servo control. *Automatica* 43, 7 (2007), 1165–1177.

3. S. Frintrop, A. Konigs, F. Hoeller, and D. Schulz. 2010. A component-based approach to visual person tracking from a mobile platform. *International Journal of Social Robotics* 2, 1 (2010), 53–62.

4. O. Kermorgant and F. Chaumette. 2011. Combining IBVS and PBVS to ensure the visibility constraint. In *IEEE/RSJ International Conference on Intelligent Robots and Systems (IROS)*. 2849–2854.

5. T. B. Moeslund, A. Hilton, and V. Kruger. 2006. A survey of advances in vision-based human motion capture and analysis. *Computer Vision and Image Understanding* 104 (2006), 90–126.

6. P. Salaris, D. Fontanelli, and L. Pallatino. 2010. Shortest paths for a robot with nonholonomic and field-of-view constraints. *IEEE Trans. Robotics* 26, 2 (2010), 269–281.

7. K.P. Tee, R. Yan, Y. Chua, Z. Huang, and S. Liemhetcharat. 2014. Gesture-Based Attention Direction for a Telepresence Robot: Design and Experimental Study. In *IEEE/RSJ International Conference on Intelligent Robots and Systems (IROS)*. 4090–95.

8. K. P. Tee and S. S. Ge. 2012. Control of State-Constrained Nonlinear Systems Using Integral Barrier Lyapunov Functionals. In *Proc. 51st IEEE Conference on Decision & Control*. 3239–3244.

9. A. Widyotriatmo, G.Y. Hong, and K.S. Hong. 2010. Configuration control of a wheeled vehicle using vision system with limited field of view. In *International Conference on Control, Automation and Systems*. 76–81.

Whispering Bubbles: Exploring Anthropomorphism through Shape-Changing Interfaces

Shi Qiu, Siti Aisyah binti Anas, Jun Hu
Department of Industrial Design
Eindhoven University of Technology
{SQIU, S.A.B. Anas, J.Hu}@tue.nl

ABSTRACT

In anthropomorphic design, there has been increasing interests in using kinetic motion and shape changing of the physical objects as a medium to communicate with people. In this paper, we introduce an interactive installation named Whispering Bubbles to explore anthropomorphism through shape-changing interfaces embedded in a physical space. It aims to provide a poetic place for people to whisper with the organically shaped objects (bubbles), to help people release mental stress in their modern lives. When a person approaches bubbles within a given distance, slight up-and-down movements of the bubbles will be activated by infrared sensors embedded in the space; when a person stands nearby a bubble and whispers to it, the bubble will "hear" with its sound detector and be triggered to bend towards the person, indicating engagement in listening. A scale model is implemented to explore and demonstrate interactions.

Author Keywords
Anthropomorphism; shape changing; kinetic design

ACM Classification Keywords
H.5.2. Information interfaces and presentation: User Interface.

INTRODUCTION
Anthropomorphism describes the tendency to imbue the real or imagined behavior of nonhuman objects with humanlike characteristics, motivations, intentions, or emotions [1]. "Anthropomorphism" originates from the Greek "*anthropos*" for "human" and "*morphe*" for "shape" or "form" [2]. In the field of Human-Robot Interaction (HRI), one approach to enhance people's acceptance of the robots is the attempt to increase a robot's familiarity by using anthropomorphic (humanlike) design and "human social" characteristics [3]. In the design of socially interactive object, anthropomorphism can be reflected in the object's form, behavior (e.g. motion), and interaction (e.g. modality) [3]. It uses anthropomorphism to increase the

HAI '16, October 04-07, 2016, Biopolis, Singapore
ACM 978-1-4503-4508-8/16/10.
http://dx.doi.org/10.1145/2974804.2980481

acceptance of the socially interactive object and facilitate the interaction. People tend to respond more positively to an object that displayed humanlike behavioral characteristics (emotions, facial expression) in contrast to a purely functional design [4][5][6][7].

The phenomenon of ascribing intentions and animacy to simple shapes based on motion has been intensively studied in (developmental) psychology [8]. In the field of Human-Computer Interaction (HCI), there has been increasing interests in using shape changing of physical objects as a medium to communicate with people. Parkes et al. addressed it is the innate ability for people to be engaged by the lifelike qualities of motion, allowing them to employ the movement of objects as a tool for communication and engagement, and allowing inanimate objects to become partners in people's interactions [9]. The inanimate objects could become "alive" if they have organic and life-like movements. This approach is commonly used for engendering emotion. Togler et al. proposed a novel type of home appliance: a thrifty water faucet. Through a servo motor construction, it was enabled to move and behave in life-like manners by continuous and small movements. These movements enriched the impression of a living object stepping into a dialogue with the user [10]. Seoktae Kim et al. also designed the Inflatable Mouse that was a volume-adjustable user interface. It simulated breathing to "express the motion of taking a nap when it is not in use." [11]. Attributing familiar humanlike qualities to a less familiar non-humanlike object can serve to make the object more familiar, explainable, or predictable[1].

In this paper, we present an interactive installation named Whispering Bubbles to explore anthropomorphism by merging shape-changing technology, which is widely used in HCI field. It aims to provide a poetic place for people to whisper with organically-shaped objects (bubbles), to help people release their mental stress in the modern lives. The kinetic interactions of the bubble (e.g. breathing and bending postures) are designed to be mimetic of a living organism, aiming provoking emotional responses.

PERSONA & SCENARIOS
Persona and scenarios were developed at early stages of the concept design. Instead of considering human behavior and experience through formal analysis and modeling of well-specified tasks, scenario-based design is a relatively lightweight method for envisioning future use possibilities

[12]. Here we identify two typical scenarios of Whispering Bubbles in our design:

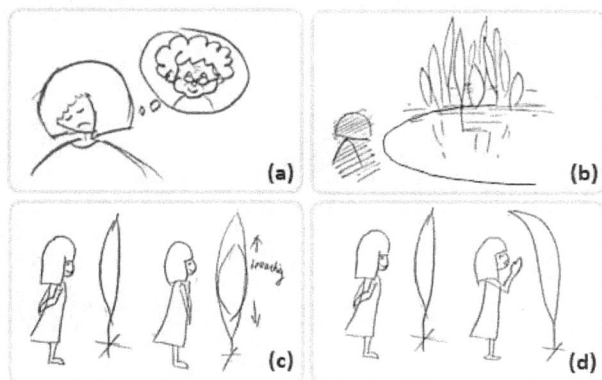

Figure 1.Sketches of the scenarios (sketches provided by Yangzi Li).

Persona

Emily is a student who continues her master study abroad. Being fresh to a new place, she feels lonely and often misses her hometown, especially her grandma who accompanied with her in her childhood. Sometimes, she dreams of talking to her grandma and sharing all her unhappiness. Her grandma is a good listener, who is helpful in releasing her pressure and making her feel better (Figure 1 (a)).

Scenario 1: Up-and-Down Movements

One day, she walks to a repulse bay and many translucent bubbles are located there. She is attracted by their elegant appearances. She walks towards them (Figure 1 (b)). When she is approaching, one cluster of bubbles softly moves up and down. The shape changing of the bubbles looks like "breathing". In her eyes, they are no longer inanimate bubbles and they become "alive" now. When she passes by, the bubbles move up and down one after the other to send "greetings" to her (Figure 1 (c)).

As illustrated in this scenario, when a person approaches bubbles within a given distance, slightly up-and-down movements of bubbles will be activated by infrared sensors embedded in the physical environment.

Scenario 2: the Bending Posture

Emily walks along with the path and after a while she stops walking and stands near a bubble. She cannot help murmuring: "I feel so tired now and I could not handle all the things well …" At that time, the nearby bubble gently bends to her as a posture for offering comfort (Figure 1 (d)). "Thank you, bubble. You seem willing to listen to me, which reminds me of my grandma. She always has patience to listen to me when I feel sad." She says.

In this scenario, when a person stands nearby a bubble and whispers to it, the bubble will "hear" by its sound detector and be triggered to bend to the person, which indicates engagement in listening. The bending posture of the bubble

also creates close and private space for the person to whisper.

WHISPERING BUBBLES SYSTEM

We design our Whispering Bubbles system from two aspects: 1) kinetic and shape-changing design; 2) circuit and system design.

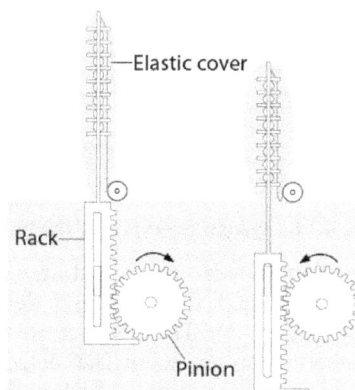

Figure 2.Mechanism of the up-and-down movement.

Kinetic and Shape-Changing Design

In the kinetic design, bubbles have two primary postures as described in the scenarios: up-and-down movements and the bending posture. To enable the bubble to move up and down, a rack-and-pinion system is proposed as the working mechanism. It is made of a pair of gears that can convert rotary motion to linear motion. As shown in Figure 2, the pinion is driven by a servo motor to rotate clockwise or counterclockwise. It drives the nearby rack to move up or down correspondingly. A thin rod follows the rack to go up and down to trigger the shape change of the elastic cover outside.

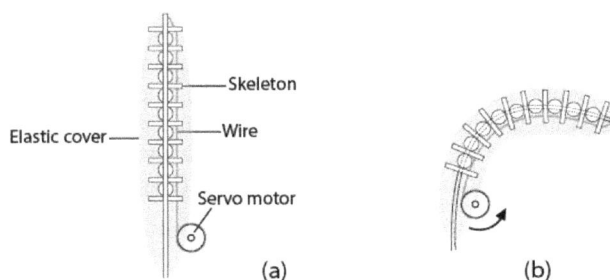

Figure 3.Mechanism of the bending posture.

A bending skeleton consists of plastic rings, plastic beads and a thin elastic rod. The thin elastic rod passes through rings and beads and both of them are arranged at intervals. They are used to guide a wire that, when exerted a force on, bend the skeleton (Figure 3). Allocating the force by many hinges achieves an organic bending movement. When the wire is pulled by the servo motor, it causes the skeleton with the elastic cover to bend towards that direction.

System Design

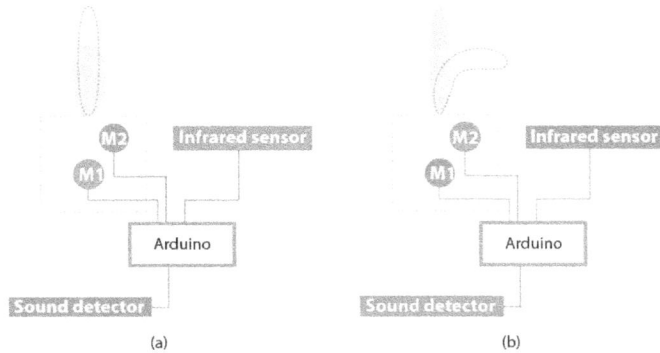

Figure 4.The system overview of the bubble.

Each of the bubbles is controlled by an Arduino microcontroller connected with a sound detector and an infrared sensor (Figure 4). The distance that the infrared sensor can detect is up to 80cm.The detection distance between the human and the bubble is adjustable as long as it is within the range of 10 cm to 80 cm. The sound detector is used to detect presence of voice coming from the human. This sensor will convert sound into analog voltage. It is possible to read the amplitude of sound coming from the human's voice by programming the Arduino to convert the analog voltage into digital representation. Based on this reading, the Arduino will compare and make sure that it is the amplitude of sound coming from the human and not from the surroundings.

As the human passes by one of the bubble, the infrared sensor will detect his/her presence and it will give signal to Arduino. Arduino will send a message to Motor 1 (M1) that triggers the bubble to move up and down as the indication that the bubble acknowledges the human is passing by (Figure 4 (a)). If the human approaches the bubble and starts to communicate verbally to the bubble, the sound detector will detect the voice and transmit the signal to Arduino so that it can process the signal (based on the amplitude of the sound) and control Motor 2 (M2) that drives bubble to bend towards the human (Figure 4 (b)).

SCALE MODEL

An interactive scaled model was exhibited at Hong Kong Polytechnic University with the dimensions of approximately 800 mm x 1000 mm x 500 mm (Figure 5). The mechanic parts were fabricated of acrylic sheets with 2 mm thick (Figure 6). Adobe Illustrator and a laser cutter were used to design and fabricate gears and supporting parts. We used a white net fabric tube with high elasticity to make the physical appearance of the bubble. This particular material could make a big shape change when it was stretched.

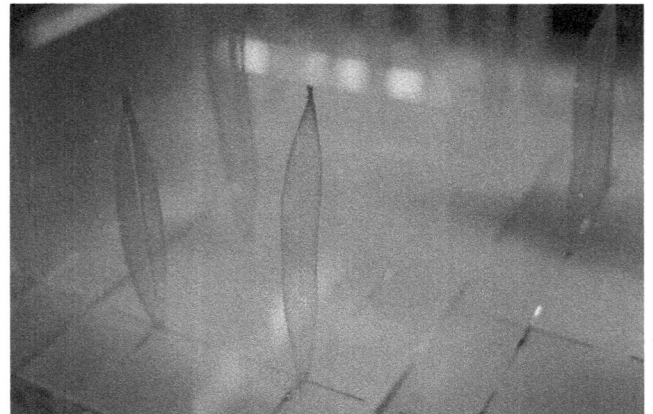

Figure 5.The scale model of Whispering Bubbles.

Figure 6.The mechanic parts of the scale model were fabricated with acrylic sheets.

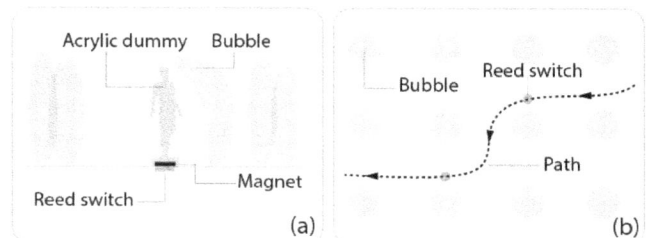

Figure 7.An example of the acrylic dummy interacted with the bubble in the scale model.

The scale model consisted of five servo motors, five reed switches, one Arduino Mega 2560 development board and one LED strip. We used reed switches as a replacement for infrared sensors and sound detectors in the scale model. The reed switch is operated by applying magnetic field. When a magnet is near to the reed switch, it will be actuated. An acrylic dummy with the magnet was used to interact with the bubble in the scale model (Figure 7 (a)). A path was embedded three reed switches (Figure 7(b)). When the dummy was moving along the path approaching one of the reed switches, it was actuated to trigger the nearby servo motor to cause bubble to change its shape. The LED strip was located on the bottom of the scale model to display different colors of light. The LED lights through the transparent acrylic materials created a dreamlike atmosphere of the Whispering Bubbles.

CONCLUSION

A growing number of the research has been carried out to investigate the human-shaped objects and objects using humanlike behavior in the interaction with people. In this paper, we presented the concept of Whispering Bubbles: an interactive installation to explore anthropomorphism through shape-changing interfaces in the environment. It aims to provide a poetic place for people to whisper to the organically shaped objects. We also emphasized the aesthetic feeling of material and lighting in prototyping to provide a better user experience. The scale model was implemented and exhibited at Hong Kong Polytechnic University. In our future work, we will implement the full-size installation of Whispering Bubbles. After that, we will plan a user experiment to measure the user experience when the people interact with Whispering Bubbles.

VIDEO

The link to the Whispering Bubbles video:
https://vimeo.com/142078880

ACKNOWLEDGEMENTS

This research is supported by the China Scholarship Council and facilitated by Eindhoven University of Technology. We also thank the support from Yangzi Li, Xueting Xie, Michael Fox, Tequila Chan and Michael Lai in Hong Kong Polytechnic University.

REFERENCES

1. Nicholas Epley, Adam Waytz and John T. Cacioppo. 2007. On seeing human: a three-factor theory of anthropomorphism. *Psychological review*, 114(4), 864.

2. Brian R. Duffy. 2002. Anthropomorphism and robotics. *The Society for the Study of Artificial Intelligence and the Simulation of Behavior*, 20.

3. Julia Fink. 2012. Anthropomorphism and human likeness in the design of robots and human-robot interaction. In *International Conference on Social Robotics*, 199–208.

4. Friederike Eyssel, Frank Hegel, Gernot Horstmann, and Claudia Wagner. 2010. Anthropomorphic inferences from emotional nonverbal cues: A case study. In *19th International Symposium in Robot and Human Interactive Communication*, 646–651.

5. Laurel D. Riek, Tal-Chen Rabinowitch, and Bhismadev Chakrabarti. 2009. How anthropomorphism affects empathy toward robots. In *Proceedings of the 4th ACM/IEEE international conference on Human robot interaction*, 245–246.

6. Mullen, Carol A. 1999. The media equation: How people treat computers, television, and new media like real people and places. *International Journal of Instructional Media*, 26(1), 117.

7. Sören Krach , Frank Hegel, Britta Wrede, Gerhard Sagerer, Ferdinand Binkofski and Tilo Kircher. 2008. Can machines think? Interaction and perspective taking with robots investigated via fMRI. *PloS one*, 3(7), e2597.

8. Henny Admoniand Brian Scassellati. 2012. A multi-category theory of intention. In *Proceedings of COGSCI*, vol. 577, no. 2012, 1266-1271.

9. Amanda Parkes, Ivan Poupyrev, and Hiroshi Ishii. 2008. Designing kinetic interactions for organic user interfaces. *Communications of the ACM* 51, no. 6, 58-65.

10. Jonas Togler, Fabian Hemmert, and Reto Wettach. 2009. Living interfaces: the thrifty faucet. In *Proceedings of the 3rd International Conference on Tangible and Embedded Interaction*, 43-44. ACM.

11. Seoktae Kim, Hyunjung Kim, Boram Lee, Tek-Jin Nam, and Woohun Lee. 2008. Inflatable mouse: volume-adjustable mouse with air-pressure-sensitive input and haptic feedback. In *Proceedings of the SIGCHI Conference on Human Factors in Computing Systems*, 211-224. ACM.

12. Mary Beth Rosson and John M. Carroll. 2009. Scenario based design. *Human-computer interaction. Boca Raton, FL*, 145-162.

Model-Driven Gaze Simulation for the Blind Person in Face-to-Face Communication

Shi Qiu[1], Siti Aisyah binti Anas[1], Hirotaka Osawa[2], Matthias Rauterberg[1], Jun Hu[1]

[1]Department of Industrial Design
Eindhoven University of Technology
{SQIU, S.A.B. Anas, G.W.M.Rauterberg, J.Hu}@tue.nl

[2]Faculty of Engineering, Information and Systems
University of Tsukuba
osawa@iit.tsukuba.ac.jp

ABSTRACT

In face-to-face communication, eye gaze is integral to a conversation to supplement verbal language. The sighted often uses eye gaze to convey nonverbal information in social interactions, which a blind conversation partner cannot access and react to them. In this paper, we present E-Gaze glasses (E-Gaze), an assistive device based on an eye tracking system. It simulates gaze for the blind person to react and engage the sighted in face-to-face conversations. It is designed based on a model that combines eye-contact mechanism and turn-taking strategy. We further propose an experimental design to test the E-Gaze and hypothesize that the model-driven gaze simulation can enhance the conversation quality between the sighted and the blind person in face-to-face communication.

Author Keywords

Eye contact; eye tracking; conversation quality

ACM Classification Keywords

H.5.2. [Information Interfaces and Presentation]: User Interfaces, K.4.2 [Computers and Security]: Social Issues – Assistive technologies for persons with disabilities.

INTRODUCTION

Gaze and eye contact are of importance in the development of trust and deeper relationships [1]. McNeill emphasizes that nonverbal cues such as mutual gazes are integral to a conversation and that ignoring them means ignoring part of the conversation [2]. Nonverbal cues also play an important role for the blind people in social interactions. Some findings were reported in an investigation of twenty blind people [3]. They were interviewed about the nonverbal signals for face-to-face communication with the sighted people. Some blind people in the investigation tended to wear the black glasses to hide their eyes in face-to-face communication. One possible reason was their eyes were conspicuously unattractive, and/or deformities might be present which made the person less appealing to others [4]. The other reason was some of them were not able to control the appropriate eye gestures. For example, one blind person had an illness of nystagmus and she could not control the movement of the eyeball. It was easier to cause the misleading of the sighted towards her eye gaze gestures. As a blind person, she often feels difficult to meet people, because she cannot see and establish eye contacts with the sighted people. Van Hasselt [4] pointed out, lack of eye contact might cause the sighted to feel that the blind person was not fully in communication. The impatience, discomfort, or intolerance of the sighted is an important factor in determining the possible extent of the involvement for the blind person. In this paper, we present E-Gaze glasses (E-Gaze), a reactive system based on the eye-tracking technology. It simulates gaze for the blind person to react and engage the sighted in face-to-face conversations. It is designed based on a model that combines eye-contact mechanism and turn-taking strategy. We further propose a user experiment to test the sighted person's responses to different gaze patterns of the E-Gaze, worn by the blind person, in a dyadic-conversation scenario.

RELATED WORK

Several previous studies on simulating gaze behaviors concentrated on turn-taking phenomena that linked gaze behaviors with speaking and listening modes in conversations. Cassell et al. proposed a new approach to design conversational agents that exhibit appropriate gaze behavior. The exchange of looks between participants was related to both information threads and the exchange of turns during the flow of conversation[5]. Heylen et al. reported an experiment that investigated the effects of different eye gaze behaviors of a cartoon-like talking face on the quality of human-agent dialogues. The result demonstrated that the gaze strategy using a turn-taking model significantly affects the dialogue quality [6]. Garau et al. described an experiment to investigate the importance of eye gaze between humans in four mediated conditions: video, audio-only, random-gaze avatars and inferred-gaze avatars. In inferred-gaze, gaze was tied to turn taking in the conversation. The result showed that the inferred-gaze avatar significantly outperformed the random-gaze model and also outperformed audio-only model [7].

HAI '16, October 04-07, 2016, Biopolis, Singapore
ACM 978-1-4503-4508-8/16/10.
http://dx.doi.org/10.1145/2974804.2980482

E-GAZE GLASSES

We presented our design concept of E-Gaze in a previous study [8]. It is a wearable device, worn by the blind person as glasses (Figure 1) and displays two basic gaze patterns: "look at" and "look away" from the sighted based on whether the blind person is talking. When the blind person starts talking, E-Gaze will "look away" from the sighted to concentrate on what the blind person is going to say; when she ends talking, E-Gaze will "look at" the sighted to establish the "eye contact" when giving the sighted an opportunity to take the turn. If the sighted stares at E-Gaze, E-Gaze will "look away" to avoid the long gaze.

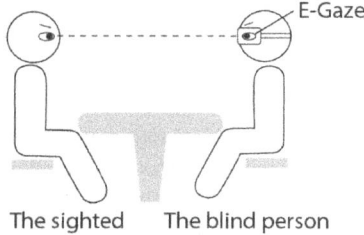

Figure 1.Design concept of the E-Gaze.

Model-Driven Gaze Simulation

A number of studies that investigated the role of gaze in human-avatar communication and provided the evidence that proper eye gaze behavior of the avatar elicited more natural responses in human users[6][7]. Most avatar systems display gaze behaviors based on turn-taking strategies rather than being reactive. In reactive systems, the sighted person's gaze behavior should trigger an instant response from the avatar side which in turn influences the user, resulting in a tightly coupled feedback loop [9]. These reactive responses can be triggered by tracking eye gaze from the sighted.

In our gaze model, E-Gaze is capable of reacting to the sighted person's current gaze using an eye tracker. The gaze model combines eye contact mechanism with turn-taking strategy which can distinguish while listening and while speaking modes in a conversation flow. We basically copy the timing of the eye gaze from research on dyadic conversations between a human and a humanoid avatar [7][10]. In this model, whenever the sighted is looking at E-Gaze, it displays "look at" eye gaze and tries to establish the eye contact with the sighted. The timing of E-Gaze "look at" and "look away" is slightly adapted depending on whether the blind person is talking or listening to account for the fact people look more at the person when listening than when speaking[1].

More specifically, we define four states of the sighted in the dyadic conversation with the blind person: `looking at & speaking (LS)`, `looking at & quiet (LQ)`, `looking away & quiet (AQ)` and `looking away & speaking (AS)`. The blind person also has the same four states since they are peer-to-peer in the conversation. The state machine diagram (Figure 2) describes four states and

their transitions. The corresponding eye gaze animations of each state are presented as follows:

`LS`: when the sighted is speaking and she is looking towards E-Gaze, E-Gaze displays a "look at" eye gaze for 2.5 seconds to establish an eye contact with the sighted and then "look away" for 1.6 seconds. After that, E-Gaze displays an average frequency of 17 "look at" glances per minute if the state continues. For "look at" partner gaze (Figure 3(a)), E-Gaze eyes focus directly ahead. There are two types of the "look away" eye gaze: left look away (Figure 3(b)) and right look away (Figure 3(c)). In order to avoid repeated eye gaze animation, E-Gaze randomly displays one of the "look away" eye gaze animations.

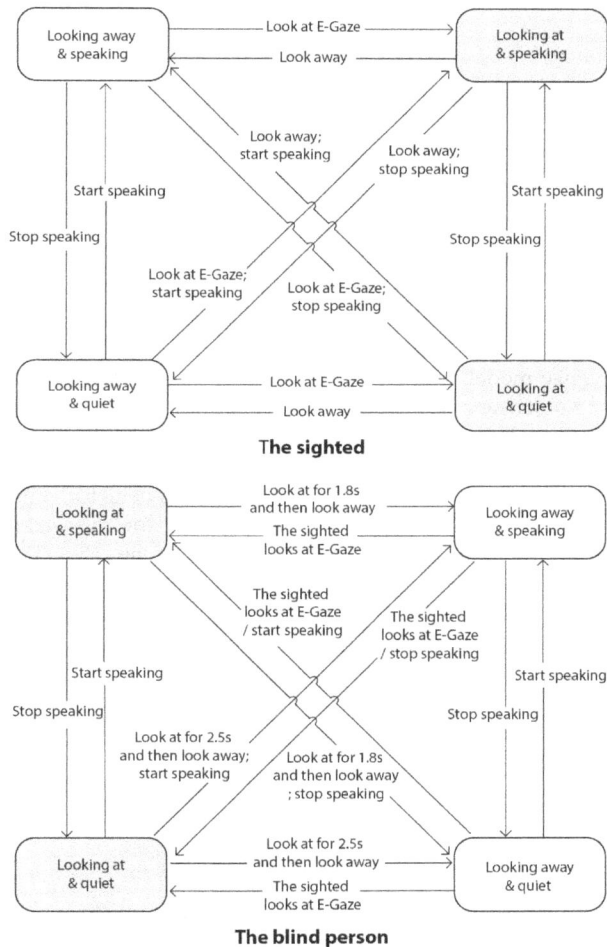

Figure 2.The state machine diagram of the sighted and the blind person with E-Gaze in a dyadic conversation. The sighted and the blind person can establish the eye contact in LS and LQ states.

`LQ`: when the sighted is not speaking and she is looking towards E-Gaze, E-Gaze displays a "look at" eye gaze for 1.8 seconds to establish an eye contact with the sighted then "look away" for 2.1 seconds. After that, E-Gaze displays an average frequency of 14 "look at" glances per minute if the state continues.

AQ: when the sighted is not speaking and she is not looking towards E-Gaze, E-Gaze displays a "look away" gaze for 2.1seconds to concentrate on what the blind person is going to say. After that E-Gaze displays an average frequency of 14 "look at" glances per minute if the state continues.

AS: when the sighted is speaking and she is not looking towards E-Gaze, E-Gaze displays an average frequency of 17 "look at" glances per minute if the state continues.

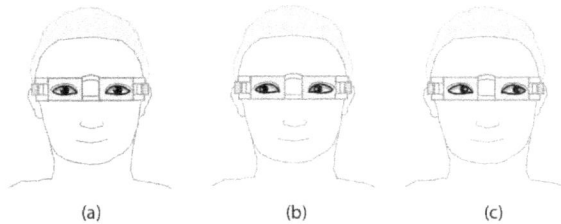

(a)　　　　　(b)　　　　　(c)

Figure 3 Face-on views of E-Gaze looking "at" and "away".

System

In the previous study[11], we used an Eye Tribe Tracker to detect the eye gaze from the sighted. The sighted used her gaze to control five gaze animations of the E-Gaze: look up, look down, look left, look right and look at. The system was programmed in Java. In this work, the system implements the gaze model. The gaze animation of the E-Gaze is driven by two sensors: the gaze signal from the Eye Tribe and the audio signal from the sound detector. The Eye Tribe is used to detect the gaze signal from the sighted to provide input for eye contact mechanism, while the sound detector is used to detect the blind person's speaking for turn-taking strategy. The E-Gaze system consists of an Eye Tribe Tracker, an Arduino microcontroller, a Bluetooth module, two uOLED-160-G2 display modules with an embedded GOLDELOX graphics processor, a sound detection sensor module and a physical glasses-shaped prototype fabricated using a 3D printer (Figure 4). Figure 5 shows the overview of the E-Gaze.

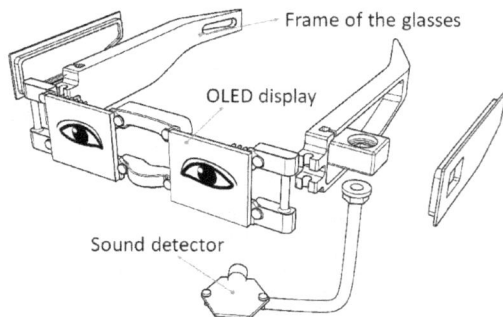

Figure 4.The exploded view of the prototype for the E-Gaze

In a dyadic-conversation setting, in order to detect the blind person's speaking clearly, the sound detector is fixed on a flexible rod that can be adjusted to near her mouth (Figure 4). We lower the sensitivity of the sound detector, to make it only detect the speaking from the blind person rather than

the sighted. We use the real human's eye gaze video to display on OLED display. It needs to be saved onto the SD card in a raw format readable by GOLDELOX graphics processors.

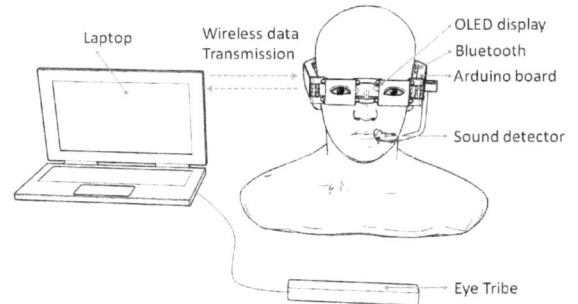

Figure 5.Overview of the E-Gaze system.

For the calibration, a graphical user interface (GUI) with 15 targeted area is created to detect the point of the interest where the sighted fixates in real-time (Figure 6(a)). When the sighted fixates on one of the target areas, the E-Gaze system activates the corresponding area to display the red points. It indicates that the sighted is now looking at the direction of the target area. The target area is parallel with the E-Gaze, so when the laptop is removed after calibration (Figure 6(b)), the sighted is equal to looking at the E-Gaze.

When the sighted looks at the E-Gaze, the system sends the command to the Arduino over a wireless Bluetooth connection. To enable the E-Gaze to interact and respond to the sighted person's eye gaze, the position of the E-Gaze is predetermined, and should be within the Eye Tribe Tracker's tracking area. The Eye Tribe Tracker detects eye gaze from the sighted, and if her gaze point corresponds to the position of the E-Gaze, a command is sent out via Bluetooth adapter from the laptop to a Bluetooth module connected to the Arduino. At the moment, E-Gaze displays a "look at" eye gaze to establish the eye contact with the sighted.

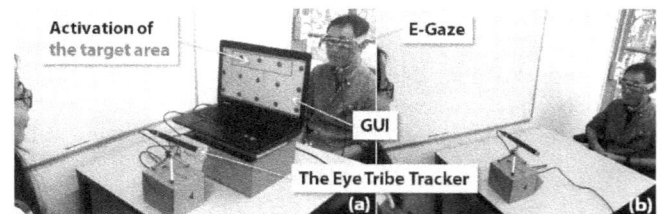

Figure 6.(a)Calibration;(b)E-Gaze.

EXPERIMENTAL DESIGN

We have planned an experiment that uses the E-Gaze system as a test bed to find out how the sighted perceive the blind person with the E-Gaze in face-to-face communication. The purpose of the experiment is two-fold: first to test whether simulating the eye appearance image for the blind person improves the conversation quality with the sighted in face-to-face communication compared to not having the eye gaze image (i.e. E-Gaze without gaze display and it is used only as the black glasses). The second, we are particularly interested in finding out which gaze patterns are appropriate for the blind person in communication. Does the model-driven gaze simulation improve the conversation quality with the sighted compared to constant gaze and random gaze? Based on the literature review, we hypothesize that the model-driven gaze simulation for the blind person can enhance the conversation quality between blind and sighted people in face-to-face communication. A between-subject experiment will be conducted and it includes four conditions (E-Gaze without gaze simulation, E-Gaze with constant gaze, E-Gaze with random gaze and E-Gaze with the model-driven gaze simulation). The level of conversation quality will be measured using questionnaires with four subjective measures: relatedness, partner closeness, engagement and partner evaluation.

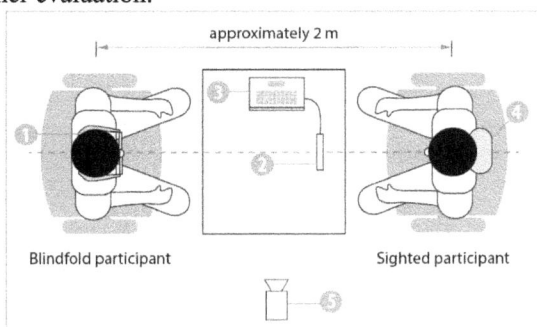

Figure 7.Overhead view of the experiment: (1) E-Gaze; (2) Eye Tribe Tracker; (3) Laptop; (4) the pillow to fix the neck of the sighted participant; (5) observation camera.

In the experiment, a specific goal is to exam the responses of the sighted towards E-Gaze. We will use the blindfolded but sighted participants as an alternative to the blind user. The participants will be 96 student volunteers from the university. They are divided into pairs to have dyadic conversations. One of each pair will wear the blindfold and the E-Gaze. Two participants sit face-to-face to have a conversation. There is a table between two participants on which the Eye Tribe Tracker connected to a laptop is placed. The Eye Tribe Tracker will be installed 40 to 60 cm away from the sighted participant. When the Eye Tribe Tracker is calibrated, the eye tracking software calculates the sighted participant's eye gaze coordinates with an average accuracy of around 0.5 to 1 degree of visual angle. In order to stabilize and track accurate eye gaze, we will place a pillow on the chair to fix the neck of the sighted participant. The observation camera captures the whole dyadic-conversation. Figure 7 shows an overview of the setup. In the next step, we will involve some real blind users to participate in the experiment.

CONCLUSION

We presented a functional prototype of the E-Gaze glasses based on the Eye Tribe tracking system to simulate the model-driven gaze for the blind person, to enhance the engagement between the sighted and the blind person in face-to-face communication. In our future work, we will implement a user experiment that uses the E-Gaze system as a test bed to find out how the sighted perceives the blind person with E-Gaze in face-to-face communication.

REFERENCES

1. Michael Argyle and Mark Cook. 1976. *Gaze and mutual gaze*. Cambridge University Press.

2. David McNeill.1992. *Hand and mind: What gestures reveal about thought*. University of Chicago Press.

3. Shi Qiu, Jun Hu, and Matthias Rauterberg.2015. Nonverbal Signals for Face-to-Face Communication between the Blind and the Sighted. In *Proceedings of International Conference on Enabling Access for Persons with Visual Impairment*, 157–165.

4. Vincent B. Van Hasselt.1983. Social Adaptation in the Blind. *Clinical Psychology Review*, 3(1), 87–102.

5. Justine Cassell, Obed E. Torres, and Scott Prevost.1999. Turn taking versus discourse structure. In *Machine conversations*, 143-153, Springer US.

6. Dirk Heylen, Ivo van Es, Anton Nijholt, and Betsy van Dijk. 2005. Controlling the gaze of conversational agents. In *Advances in Natural Multimodal Dialogue Systems*, 245-262, Springer Netherlands.

7. Maia Garau , Mel Slater, Simon Bee, and Martina Angela Sasse. 2001. The impact of eye gaze on communication using humanoid avatars. In *Proceedings of the SIGCHI conference on Human factors in computing systems*, 309–316.

8. Shi Qiu, Hirotaka Osawa, Jun Hu, and Matthias Rauterberg. 2015. E-Gaze: Create Gaze Communication for People with Visual Disability. In *Proceedings of the 3rd International Conference on Human-Agent Interaction*, 199–202.

9. Michael Kipp and Patrick Gebhard.2008. Igaze: Studying reactive gaze behavior in semi-immersive human-avatar interactions. In *Intelligent Virtual Agents*, 191–199.

10. Nikolaus Bee, Johannes Wagner, Elisabeth André, Thurid Vogt, Fred Charles, David Pizzi, and Marc Cavazza.2010. Discovering eye gaze behavior during human-agent conversation in an interactive storytelling application. In *International Conference on Multimodal Interfaces and the Workshop on Machine Learning for Multimodal Interaction*.

11. Shi Qiu, Siti Aisyah Anas, Hirotaka Osawa, Matthias Rauterberg, and Jun Hu.2016. E-Gaze Glasses: Simulating Natural Gazes for Blind People. In *Proceedings of the TEI'16: Tenth International Conference on Tangible, Embedded, and Embodied Interaction*, 563–569.

Investigation of Practical Use of Humanoid Robots in Elderly Care Centres

Zhuoyu Shen
National Junior College
Singapore
shenzhuoyu3@gmail.com

Yan Wu
A*STAR Institute for
Infocomm Research Singapore
wuy@i2r.a-star.edu.sg

ABSTRACT

The global trend of population ageing has magnified the shortage of qualified staff in the elderly care industry. This study evaluates the feasibility and user experience of introducing robots in elderly care services. A robot instructor was being benchmarked against a human instructor administering two types of activities with 41 elderly participants. The results show that robot was more effective and better preferred by users over human instructor on instructing physical exercise, while reaching similar level of effectiveness and user acceptance on information delivery. Additionally, user perception of robots improved after the robot experiment session. These findings could be useful for future design of robots for elderly users and for social robots in general.

Author Keywords

Human-robot interaction; social robotics; humanoid robots

INTRODUCTION

Singapore has one of the fastest growing ageing population in the world. Residents aged 65 years and above made up 11 per cent of the resident population in 2014 [9]. Meanwhile, the elderly care landscape in Singapore is far from ideal. One major problem is the shortage of qualified elderly care staff to keep up with the burgeoning demand. This problem is shared by many ageing societies across the globe. Recently, using assistive robot technologies has emerged as a solution [2]. In nursing homes, robots cooperate with caregivers to remind elderly to take medicine, assist elderly on daily activities such as eating and walking [14, 3], encourage social interaction [6] and provide psychological support [13, 12].

It is, however, worth-noting that people's attitude towards robot technologies varies with age [7]. Scopelliti et al found that older people were significantly more suspicious of technology, and showed a more negative emotional response towards robots [11]. A closer examination is hence needed on user acceptance when designing robots for the elderly [4, 5]. In other word, how should assistive robots be designed and used so that they are better welcomed by elderly users, and

what are the tasks that robots are most useful for when used in elder care?

Current studies on robotics for the elderly have mostly focused on system functionalities or user perception alone [10, 14, 8]. Little attention is paid on comparing robots with its human counterparts, whom the robots will ultimately be employed to assist and relieve. In this work, we benchmark a robot against a human instructor performing similar tasks with groups of senior citizens. In our approach, a humanoid robot is used to instruct groups of elderly on simple physical exercises and to teach them factual information. The robot's performance is then compared against that of the human instructor under a similar controlled setting, through a series of analyses of the participants' responses.

HYPOTHESES

Six hypotheses were established for this study.

Hypothesis 1: Robot instructor is objectively more effective than human on instructing physical exercise.

Hypothesis 2: Human instructor is objectively more effective than robot when delivering factual information.

Hypothesis 3: Participants evaluate robots more positively after than before the robot-instructed session.

Hypothesis 4: Participants evaluate the robot instructor as more suitable for instructing the physical exercise than delivering factual content.

Hypothesis 5: Participants report a clear preference for the robot instructor over human on instructing physical exercise when asked to directly compare the two instructors.

Hypothesis 6: Participants report a clear preference for the human instructor over robot on delivering factual information when asked to directly compare the two instructors.

METHODOLOGY

We use control experiment to compare the robot instructor with the human instructor on two types of activities. There are two within-subject factors: instructor (robot, human) and instruction content (physical activity, factual information). Participants are instructed on the two types of content by both robot and human, one after the other. The order of the instructors is counterbalanced among the participants. Each instructor engages the participants for 15 min. Mandarin, the participants' mother tongue, is used throughout this experiment.

HAI '16, October 04-07, 2016, Biopolis, Singapore
ACM 978-1-4503-4508-8/16/10.
http://dx.doi.org/10.1145/2974804.2980485

Instructors

Robot instructor

Aldebaran NAO, a 58cm-tall humanoid robot was used. Its movements and speech are preprogrammed on a time-line using Choregraphe SDK. The robot uses audio recording of the human instructor as its "voice". This avoids confusion caused by the robot's accent and eliminates bias due to participants' voice preference. NAO is set on its Autonomous Life mode, by which it identifies and gazes at human faces within its visual range, mimicking the natural eye contact of a human speaker with the audience.

Human instructor

The human instructor is a staff member from Lions Home for the Elders. No participants knows the instructor personally prior to the experiment. During the physical activity coaching, the human instructor follows approximately the same pace as the robot and is instructed not to adjust her pace according to the participants'. The instructor strictly follows the script set for her and the robot. Both instructor remain standing in one place throughout the period of instruction. Apart from natural eye contact and hand waving, she does not make extra movements to attract attention. These restrictions ensures that the differences are only on delivery media and content, but not on delivery style.

Instruction Content

Physical activity

The instructors conduct demonstration on simple joint exercise and ask participants to follow the exercise. The exercise is adapted from a set of exercises provided by Pek Kio Community Centre senior living programme, consisting of 5 movement sets. All movements are easy-to-follow, minimizing the effect of familiarity on execution accuracy. Both instructors count the beats aloud while demonstrating.

Factual information

The instructors deliver facts and healthy living tips related to common health problems such as diabetes, coronary heart disease and dementia to the participants. Each instructor delivers a different set of information so as not to reinforce memory of the same content in the second session. Both sets of information are about 300 words.

EXPERIMENTS

Survey data is collected before, in-between and after the two sessions. Two aspects, effectiveness and participant evaluation of the two instructors, are measured and compared. Additionally, elderly users' evaluation of the robot before and after the experiment is also studied.

Objective evaluation of effectiveness

Physical Exercise

To examine the effectiveness of the physical exercise, we use two criteria set by the elderly care centre to evaluate the performance and compliance in all the exercise sets:

Joint bending (J): Whether the participants reach the desired level of joint bending specified in the exercise description provided by the centre on each beat.

Movement sync (V): Whether the participants are able to sync the exact speed of their movements to the instructor on each count. The maximum beat count difference allowed is two counts, i.e. a participant fails to sync on a particular count, if he or she is in a position two counts ahead or behind.

We analyse the performance of participants in the exercise by observing the video recording of the experiment. Each participant is judged on both criteria over $5 \times 32 = 160$ beat counts, and receives two performance scores: Joint bending (J) and Movement sync (V). The highest score for both criteria is 160. One mark is deducted from the respective highest score for each count the participant fails to meet the aforementioned criteria. Each participant also receives a total score (T) calculated as J+V.

Factual information

To assess the effectiveness of factual information delivery, a set of 8-item choice recognition test is given to participants immediately after the factual content is delivered by each instructor. Each item asks the participant to determine whether a statement has been presented during the session. There are 8 statements for each instructor, 4 that occurs and 4 otherwise. This reflects the attention level paid to the instructor.

Evaluation of the robot

General perception of robot is measured both before and after the two sessions, based on participants' responses to ten five-point semantic differential scales (1 and 5 denote that the robot is best described by the negative and positive adjectives respectively) concerning the following robot descriptions: unfriendly/friendly; dangerous/safe; rigid/natural; vague/distinct; inaccessible/accessible; empty/full; dull/exciting; cold/warm; passive/active; unintelligent/intelligent. Participants are also asked to choose their preferred robot instructed content (physical exercise v.s. factual information delivery).

Direct comparison

Additional questions ask participants to directly compare the two instructors, to understand the participants' preferences. On each type of instructed content, participants are asked to choose the one they like more and feel that is more effective between the robot and human instructor.

RESULTS

A total of 41 elderly from Lions Home for the Elderand Pek Kio Community Centre senior living programme sparticipated had completed the experiment. There were 25 female participants (61%) and 16 male participants (39%). Participants' age ranged from 67 to 86 (M=73, S.D.=4.84). Half of the participants (n=20) were instructed by the human first, the other half (n=21) were instructed by the robot first.

Objective evaluation of effectiveness results

Paired samples t-test was used to compare the data collected from objective evaluation of effectiveness of two instructors. In support of hypothesis 1, the physical exercise instructed by robot was significantly more effective than that of human instructor (Figure 1). The average total score (T)

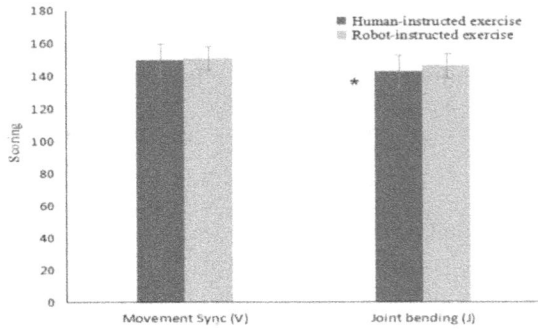

Figure 1. Results of objective effectiveness of physical exercise conducted by human and robot instructors. Significant difference is marked by asterisks (*).

for each participant during robot-instructed physical exercise (M=297, SD=10.9) was significantly higher than during human-instructed physical exercise(M=291, SD=14.4); t(40)=2.52, p <.05. Though J under robot-instructed condition was significantly higher than under human-instructed condition, V under robot-instructed condition was only somewhat significantly higher than under human-instructed condition. The robot's main strength was its ability to motivate participants to reach the desired level of joint bending.

The effectiveness of factual content delivery showed no significant difference between the two instructors. Average number of correct answers under robot instruction (M=6.88, SD=1.14) was similar to that under human instruction (M=6.90, SD=1.02); t(40)=0.0835, p¿.10. Hence, hypothesis 2 was not supported by the result. The robot and human instructor were about equally effective when delivering factual information.

Evaluation of robot results

Table 1. Participants' evaluation of the robot on 5-point semantic differential scales before and after the instruction session with robot

Adjective pair	Before	After
Unfriendly / Friendly	4.17	4.33
Dangerous / Safe	3.34	4.27
Rigid / Natural	3.56	3.83
Vague / Distinct	3.37	3.46
Inaccessible / Accessible	4.07	4.34
Empty / Full	3.88	4.07
Dull / Exciting	4.12	4.27
Cold / Warm	3.34	3.98
Passive / Active	4.00	4.20
Unintelligent / Intelligent	4.63	4.37
Mean	3.85	4.11

Participants' perception of robots enhanced after the robot-instructed session, supporting hypothesis 3. The average score on the five-point semantic differential scales of the ten adjective pairs increased towards the positive end (from M=3.85 before, to M=4.11 after) as shown in Table 1. Scale that demonstrated greatest level of improvements were dangerous/safe (from M=3.34 before to M= 4.27 after).

Participants rated the robot as more suitable for instructing physical activity than delivering factual information, supporting hypothesis 4. More participants reported that the robot-instructed physical activity was more enjoyable (n=35, 85.4%), useful (n=24, 58.5%) and they were more willing to accept a robot instructor for physical exercise in future(n=31, 75.6%) than for factual information delivery.

Direct comparison results

Table 2. Participant responses to items for direct comparison of the robot and human instructors

Description	Human	Robot	Equally
Liked more for physical activity	0(0%)	38(92.7%)	3(7.3%)
More effective for physical activity	7(17.1%)	8(19.5%)	26(63.4%)
Liked more for information delivery	6(14.6%)	17(41.4%)	18(44.0%)
More effective for information delivery	7(17.1%)	4(9.8%)	30(73.2%)

The results of direct comparison of human and robot instructors supported hypothesis 5. Participants demonstrated a strong preference for the robot instructor over the human instructor on instructing physical exercise (Table 2). Specifically, majority (92.7%) of the participants reported they liked the robot instructor when doing physical activity more than the human instructor, while the remaining 7.3% all viewed the two as equally likeable. On subjective effectiveness, the robot instructor received a slightly higher vote (19.5%) than robot instructor (17.1%).

Hypothesis 6 was not well-supported by the direct comparison results. For information delivery, participants also seemed to prefer the robot instructor (Table 2). Only 14.6% participants liked human instructor more, compared to the 41.4% for robot instructor. On subjective effectiveness, majority (73.2%) of the participants felt both were equally effective. 17.1% participants felt the human was more effective, higher than the 9.8% of the robot. Although the human instructor were perceived as more effective, participants still had a strong inclination towards the robot instructor as agent for information delivery.

DISCUSSIONS

The result of the study showed the robot instructor was more suitable for physical activity instruction than information delivery, both in terms of objective effectiveness and subjective evaluation. Countering hypotheses 2 and 6, the robot was not significantly less effective or less preferred than the human instructor for information delivery. In fact, it reached similar level of objective effectiveness as human instructor, and was even liked by more participants for this purpose. Additionally, participants' perception of robots in general improved after the robot-conducted session.

Countering the overall perception improvement, participants seemed to perceive robots as slightly less intelligent after(M=4.36) the session than before (M=4.63). One explanation for the decreased rating of robot intelligent might be that the session content was rather repetitive and predictable, and the robot did not actively interact with the participants during the session. According to [1], predictability and lack of interaction make agents appear less intelligent. However, the same study pointed that predictability also potentially makes agents appear less frightening for inexperienced users. This may also explain why participants generally perceived robots as safer and more friendly after the session.

However, it is worth noting that the human instructor was under various restrictions for variable control purpose. Further studies can use higher level of audience engagement techniques to reassess the effectiveness of a robot speaker with respect to a human speaker. Also, despite the effort of ensuring the robot and human had the same instruction style, humanoid robot was still a novel occurrence for most elderly. Novelty may potentially enhance participants' subjective rating of the robot. To further investigate the novelty factor, future studies should use the robot to facilitate activities over a prolonged period, such as one year. Objective effectiveness test and user perception evaluation are to be conducted consistently throughout the course of the year, to minimize novelty level.

CONCLUSION

Based on the results of the study, we concluded that humanoid robots have great potential as agents for exercise coaching and information delivery for elderly users. It was encouraging to see that the robot could motivate the elderly to do exercises effectively better than the human instructor, while still having the same level of effectiveness on information delivery. Overall, it remains a challenging task to explore the design principles of robots meant for elderly users, to achieve the goal of letting robots share and reduce the workload of humans in elderly care services.

ACKNOWLEDGEMENTS

The authors would like to thank Lions Home for the Elders and Pek Kio Community Centre, the staff members and the participating residents, with special thanks to J. Heng, J. Ang and I. Teo for their help in the preparation and execution of the study.

REFERENCES

1. Kerstin Dautenhahn. 1999. Robots as social actors: Aurora and the case of autism. In *Proc. CT99, The Third International Cognitive Technology Conference, August, San Francisco*, Vol. 359. 374.

2. Steven Dubowsky, Frank Genot, Sara Godding, Hisamitsu Kozono, Adam Skwersky, Haoyong Yu, and Long Shen Yu. 2000. PAMM-a robotic aid to the elderly for mobility assistance and monitoring: a helping-hand for the elderly. In *Robotics and Automation, 2000. Proceedings. ICRA'00. IEEE International Conference on*, Vol. 1. IEEE, 570–576.

3. Juan Fasola and Maja J Matarić. 2012. Using socially assistive human–robot interaction to motivate physical exercise for older adults. *Proc. IEEE* 100, 8 (2012), 2512–2526.

4. Priska Flandorfer. 2012. Population ageing and socially assistive robots for elderly persons: the importance of sociodemographic factors for user acceptance. *International Journal of Population Research* 2012 (2012).

5. Takayuki Kanda, Hiroshi Ishiguro, and Tom Ishida. 2001. Psychological analysis on human-robot interaction. In *Robotics and Automation, 2001. Proceedings 2001 ICRA. IEEE International Conference on*, Vol. 4. IEEE, 4166–4173.

6. Cory D Kidd, Will Taggart, and Sherry Turkle. 2006. A sociable robot to encourage social interaction among the elderly. In *Robotics and Automation, 2006. ICRA 2006. Proceedings 2006 IEEE International Conference on.* IEEE, 3972–3976.

7. Tineke Klamer and Somaya Ben Allouch. 2010. Acceptance and use of a social robot by elderly users in a domestic environment. In *Pervasive Computing Technologies for Healthcare (PervasiveHealth), 2010 4th International Conference on-NO PERMISSIONS.* IEEE, 1–8.

8. Michael Montemerlo, Joelle Pineau, Nicholas Roy, Sebastian Thrun, and Vandi Verma. 2002. Experiences with a mobile robotic guide for the elderly. In *AAAI/IAAI*. 587–592.

9. Department of Statistics Singapore. 2014. Resident Population Profile. (2014). http://www.singstat.gov.sg/statistics/latest-data

10. Miguel Sarabia, Tuan Le Mau, Harold Soh, Shuto Naruse, Crispian Poon, Zhitian Liao, Kuen Cherng Tan, Zi Jian Lai, and Yiannis Demiris. 2013. iCharibot: Design and Field Trials of a Fundraising Robot. In *Social Robotics*. Springer, 412–421.

11. Massimiliano Scopelliti, Maria Vittoria Giuliani, and Ferdinando Fornara. 2005. Robots in a domestic setting: a psychological approach. *Universal Access in the Information Society* 4, 2 (2005), 146–155.

12. Kazuhiko Shinozawa, Byron Reeves, Kevin Wise, Sohye Lim, Heidy Maldonado, and Futoshi Naya. 2003. Robots as new media: A cross-cultural examination of social and cognitive responses to robotic and on-screen agents. In *Proceedings of Annual Conference of Internation Communication Association*. 998–1002.

13. Kazuyoshi Wada, Takanori Shibata, Tomoko Saito, and Kazuo Tanie. 2003. Effects of robot assisted activity to elderly people who stay at a health service facility for the aged. In *Intelligent Robots and Systems, 2003.(IROS 2003). Proceedings. 2003 IEEE/RSJ International Conference on*, Vol. 3. IEEE, 2847–2852.

14. Haoyong Yu, Matthew Spenko, and Steven Dubowsky. 2003. An adaptive shared control system for an intelligent mobility aid for the elderly. *Autonomous Robots* 15, 1 (2003), 53–66.

User Generated Agent: Designable Book Recommendation Robot Programmed by Children

Yusuke Kudo†1
Tsukuba City, Japan
s1520775@u.tsukuba.ac.jp

Wataru Kayano†1
Tsukuba City, Japan
s1520770@u.tsukuba.ac.jp

Takuya Sato†1
Tsukuba City, Japan
s1311125@u.tsukuba.ac.jp

Hirotaka Osawa†1
Tsukuba City, Japan
osawa@iit.tsukuba.ac.jp

ABSTRACT

School libraries are required to promote the habit of reading books in elementary school children. It is necessary to cultivate children's interest in books to achieve this goal. In this paper, we propose a user-generated agent (UGA) that introduces books. Elementary school children can program the behavior of the UGA themselves. The UGA not only cultivates the children's interest in the book introduced by the agent, but also their motivation for the presentation by allowing them to design the contents of the agent. We promote the habit of reading by allowing the children to modify the agent's design and giving them the opportunity to refine their ability to promote books.

Keywords
Agent robot; HAI; Designable; Book introduction

1. INTRODUCTION

The development of numerous multimedia outlets provides children with several information channels. However, these media also keep children away from literature. It is necessary for children to cultivate the habit of reading. The Ministry of Education, Culture, Sports, Science and Technology in Japan is demanding an effective guide to promote the habit of reading as a part of school education. School libraries are required to effectively fulfill their function as a guide to the habit of reading.

Book recommendations by children themselves are proposed as a solution for the above problem. In this method, the children themselves create recommendations for books and introduce them to other children. This result is expected to be more effective than guidance by teachers, because it provides for mutual education in children.

We propose a new method called a user generated agent (UGA) that supports reading in children using an agent (UGA robot) that they can edit themselves. In the UGA, the children themselves can create the motion, appearance, and guiding content for the book agent by organizing its design. The UGA robot behaves as a child avatar when introducing books to other children. Figure 1 shows examples of the UGA robot face.

HAI '16, October 04-07, 2016, Biopolis, Singapore
ACM 978-1-4503-4508-8/16/10.
http://dx.doi.org/10.1145/2974804.2980489

Figure 1: Design examples of UGA robot face.

The UGA was not designed simply to enhance children's interest in the introduced books, but also helps the children promote the books using the agent as a mediator. We expect that the UGA will improve the children's ability to promote books, which will also affect their motivation for reading. Tanaka et al. [1] proposed the learning by teaching method in human-agent interaction (HAI) using a care-receiving robot (CRR). They hypothesized that using the CRR would make it possible to construct a new educational framework with the goal of promoting children's spontaneous learning through their teaching the robot.

If children can design the agent, it creates the CRR relationship between the children and the UGA. We hope that children are interested in books.

This paper is organized as follows. Section 2 describes the requirements for the introduction of books. Section 3 describes the implementation of the agent to achieve the UGA. The plans for the experiment are shown in section 4, and the results and future challenges are shown in section 5.

2. REQUIREMENT FOR UGA

The UGA is a social agent. However, rather than being programmed by professionals, it is designed by the children themselves. There are several specific requirements for achieving the UGA.

When the children come to the library, they can ask the agent about a title or genre, or request recommendations for a book that they might want to read. The agent then introduces the child to a book. Consequently, children can develop an interest in books.

---

†1University of Tsukuba

We also believe that facial expressions and body movements are important to reflect the children's interest.

Non-verbal information is also used by children and plays a critical role [2].

Thus, we believe that allowing the agent to change its facial expression will allow children to be attracted to the agent and content, and generate more interest in reading books. The agent needs to show an interest in the children by displaying the six basic emotions proposed by Ekman [3]. In addition, if children can design the emotions, it will be possible to see their own feelings expressed by the agent.

Ono et al. [4] verified the importance of the information transmitted by the body's synchronous behavior in human-robot interaction.

The agent imitates the synchronous behavior of the children when moving its body. Children then become interested in the things at which the agent is pointing.

The UGA needs to be easily designed by children. If a child can easily design the agent's appearance and speech content, they will have more interest in introducing their favorite books through the agent. Using these methods, the agent introduces books that attract the children's interest.

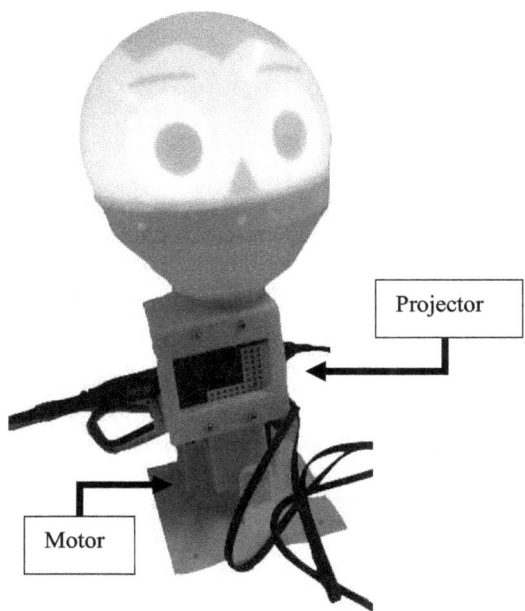

Figure 2: Appearance of UGA

3. USER GENERATED AGENT (UGA)

3.1 UGA robot

3.1.1 Hardware

We created a UGA robot, as shown in Figure 2, in order to introduce books.

(1) Face
A projector is attached to the UGA, and it projects the UGA's face

(2) Actuator

Figure 3 shows an example of the motion of the UGA. Two servo motors are installed in the UGA. These make it possible to move the UGA at any angle in the longitudinal and transverse directions

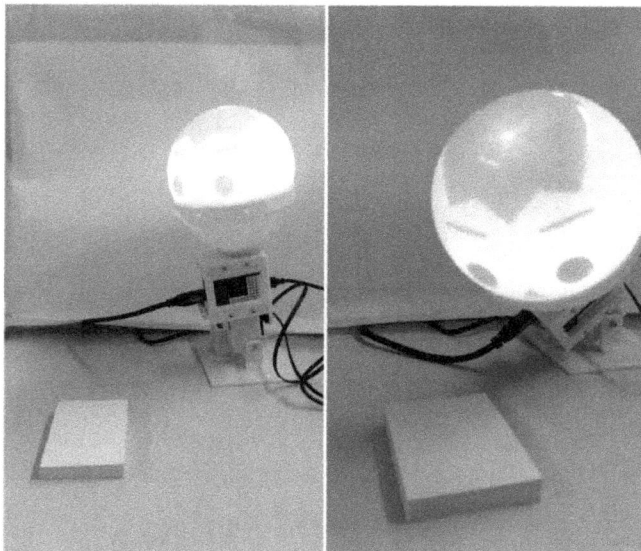

Figure 3: Example of the motion of UGA

(3) Speaker
A speaker is attached to the UGA, and it produces a voice in the direction of the children.

3.1.2 Software

Figure 4 shows a system configuration diagram of the UGA, which has the features shown below.

(1) Voice interaction
The UGA has the functions of voice recognition and voice synthesis, which allow it to perform vocal interaction.

(2) Flexible facial expression
The UGA's face is a projection. This allows it to change faster than a mechanical face, because facial expressions are produced at a rate of 60 frames per second. Figure 5 shows an example of an emotion being expressed by the UGA. It is also possible to create a rich variety of facial expressions by changing the shape, size, color, eyes, nose, and mouth.

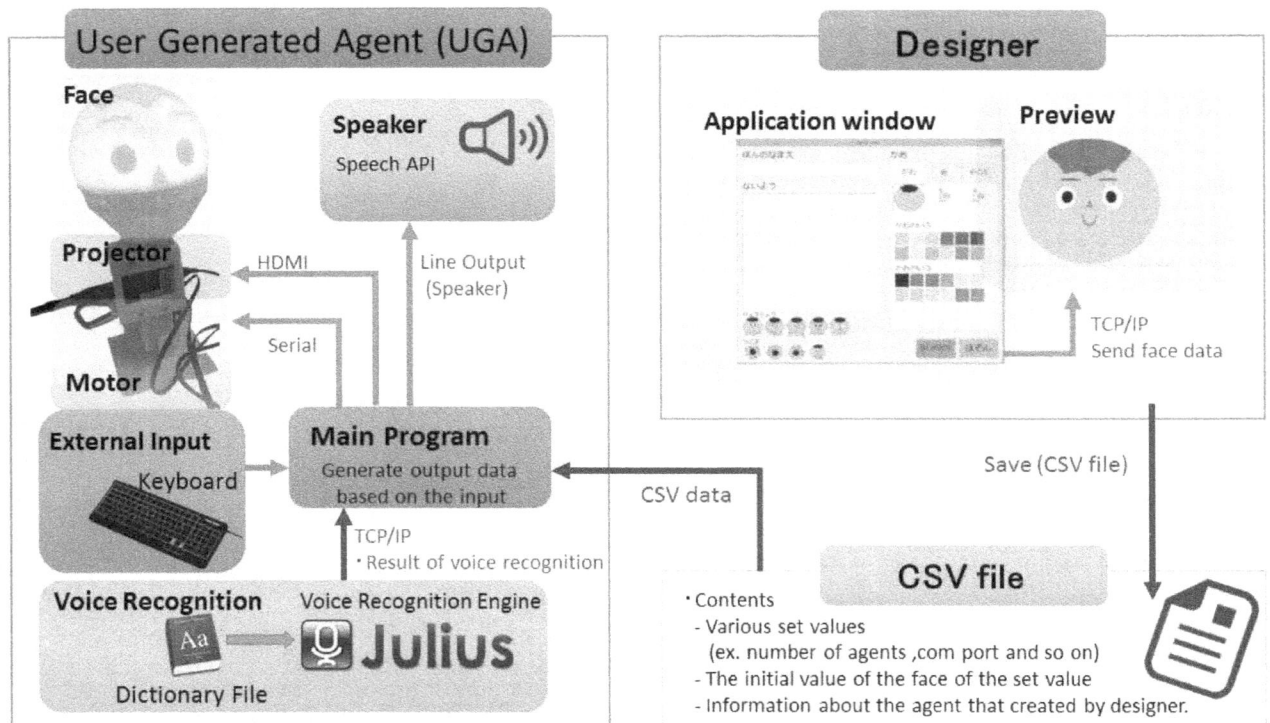

Figure 4: System configuration

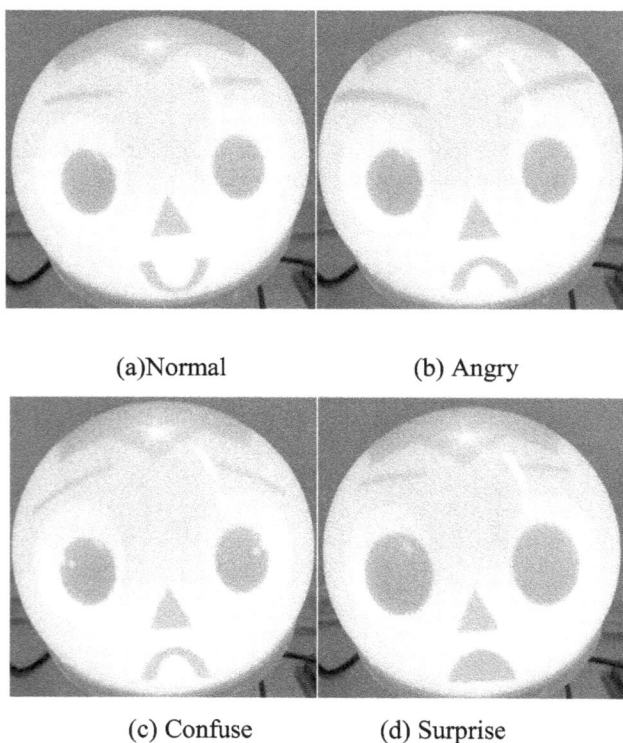

(a)Normal   (b) Angry

(c) Confuse   (d) Surprise

Figure 5: Example of the emotion of UGA

3.2 Designer Application

We show the design software for children in Figure 6. Children can select the robot's facial color, hair, eyes, and each part's size. Children can input talking words of agent, and also can insert several movements and facial actions using the emoticons shown at the bottom left of Figure 6. Children can easily organize the introduction of books.

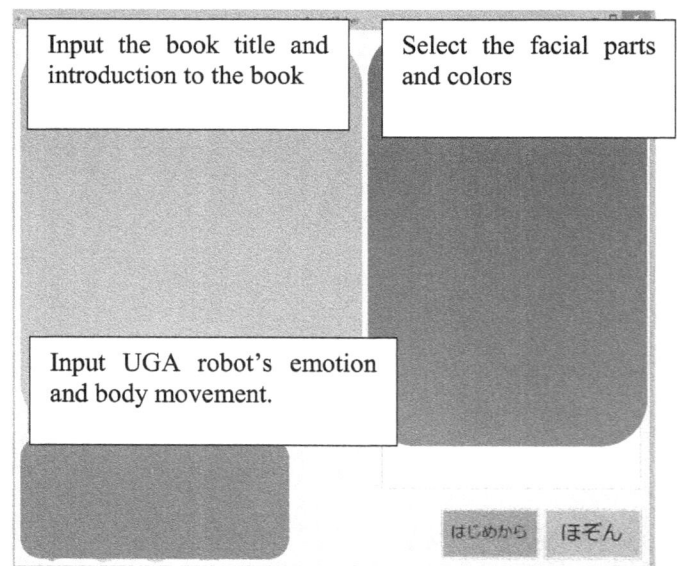

Figure 6: Designer application

4. PLANS FOR EXPERIMENT

The outline of an experiment is shown below.

We took the UGA to an elementary school and allowed the children to create book introductions. After installing the UGA in the library, it introduced books to other children.

Before the experiment, we gave a demonstration in the elementary school (Figure 7). We investigated the children's reactions and improvements.

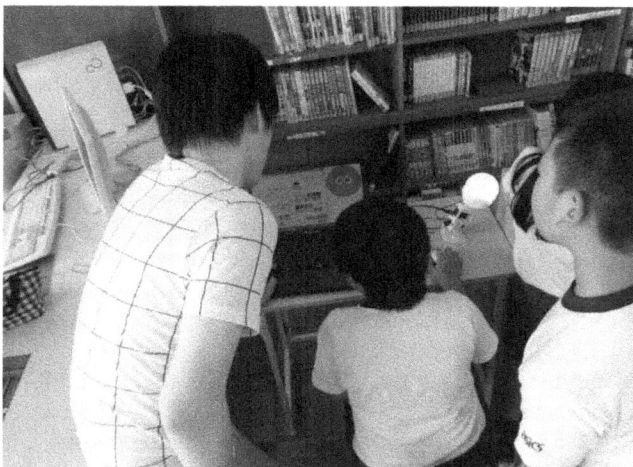

Figure 7: Demonstration in elementary school

In the demonstration, we obtained feedback from the children. Some of this feedback is shown below.

1. The synthesized voice is unnatural.

2. The designer has too little color variation for the facial parts.

We will improve the software based on this feedback.

We also plan to install sensors on bookshelves to acquire information about the books that get picked up or borrowed.

This will allow us to evaluate the changes in the children's motivation for reading.

5. CONCLUSIONS AND FUTURE ISSUES

We proposed the UGA to promote an interest in reading. We then developed the facial expressions, speech, voice recognition, and motions of the UGA.

We will improve the UGA design applications by adding an easy interface to allow children to participate in the design. We are planning to evaluate the UGA in the library of an elementary school.

ACKNOWLEDGEMENTS

This work was partially supported by JSPS KAKENHI 26118006A.

REFERENCES

1. Fumihide Tanaka and Shizuko Matsuzoe. 2012. Care-Receiving Robot to Promote Children's Learning by Teaching : Field Experiments at a Classroom for Vocabulary Learning. *Journal of Human-Robot Interaction* 1, 1: 78–95.

2. Elizabeth Brey and Kristin Shutts. 2015. Children Use Nonverbal Cues to Make Inferences About Social Power. *Child Development* 86, 1: 276–286.

3. Paul Ekman and Maureen O'Sullivan. 1979. The role of context in interpreting facial expression. *Journal of Experimental Psychology: General* 117, 1: 86–88.

4. Tetsuo Ono and Michita Imai. 2001. A model of embodied communications with gestures between humans and robots. *23rd meeting of the Cognitive Science Society*, 760–765. Retrieved May 19, 2014 from http://citeseerx.ist.psu.edu/viewdoc/summary?doi= 10.1.1.394.7902

Cross-cultural Study of Perception and Acceptance of Japanese Self-adaptors

Takuto Ishioh
Graduate School of Information Science and Technology,
Osaka Institute of Technology
Osaka, Japan
m1m16a03@st.oit.ac.jp

Tomoko Koda
Graduate School of Information Science and Technology,
Osaka Institute of Technology
Osaka, Japan
koda@is.oit.ac.jp

ABSTRACT

This paper reports our preliminary results of a cross-cultural study of perception and acceptance of cultural specific self-adaptors performed by a virtual agent. There are culturally-defined preferences in self-adaptors and other bodily expressions, and allowance level of expressing such non-verbal behavior are culture-dependent. We conducted a web experiment to evaluate the impression and acceptance of Japanese culture specific self-adaptors and gathered participants from 8 countries. The results indicated non-Japanese participants' insensitivity to the different types of self-adaptors and over sensitivity to Japanese participants' to stressful self-adaptors.

Author Keywords

HAI; human-agent interaction; intelligent virtual agents; gesture; self-adaptors; non-verbal behavior; evaluation; culture-specific behavior; cross-culture;

ACM Classification Keywords

H.1.2 User/Machine Systems, Software psychology; H.5.2 User Interfaces, Evaluation/methodology;

INTRODUCTION

Intelligent virtual agents (IVAs) that interact face-to-face with humans are beginning to spread to general users, and HAI research is being actively pursued. IVAs require both verbal and nonverbal communication abilities. Among those non-verbal communications, Ekman classifies gestures into five categories: emblems, illustrators, affect displays, adapters, and regulators [1]. Self-adaptors are non-signaling gestures that are not intended to convey a particular meaning [2]. They are exhibited as hand movements where one part of the body is applied to another part of the body, such as picking one's nose, scratching one's head and face, moistening the lips, or tapping the foot. Many self-adaptors are considered taboo in public, and individuals with low emotional stability perform more self-adaptors,

HAI '16, October 04-07, 2016, Biopolis, Singapore
ACM 978-1-4503-4508-8/16/10.
http://dx.doi.org/10.1145/2974804.2980491

and the number of self-adaptors increases with psychological discomfort or anxiety [2, 3, 4].

Because of its non-relevance to conversational content, there has not been much HAI research done on self-adaptors, compared with nonverbal communication with high message content, such as facial expressions and gazes. However, self-adaptors are not always the sign of emotional unstableness or stress. Blacking states self-adaptors also occur in casual conversations, where conversant are very relaxed [5]. We focus on these "relaxed" self-adaptors performed in a casual conversation in this study. If those relaxed self-adaptors occur with a conversant that one feels friendliness, one can be induced to feel friendliness toward a conversant that displays self-adaptors. We apply this to the case of agent conversant, and hypothesize that users can be induced to feel friendliness toward the agent by adding self-adaptors to the body motions of an agent, and conducted two experiments.

The first experiment evaluated continuous interactions between an agent that exhibits self-adaptors and without [6]. The results showed agents that exhibited relaxed self-adaptors were more likely to prevent any deterioration in the perceived friendliness of the agents than agents that have no self-adaptors. In addition, people with higher social skills harbor a higher perceived friendliness with agents that exhibited relaxed self-adaptors than people with lower social skills. Thus, we expect that it would be possible to improve humanness and friendliness of agents by implementing self-adaptors in them. The second experiment evaluated interactions with agents that exhibit either relaxed self-adaptors or stressful self-adaptors in a desert survival task. The result suggests the need to tailor non-verbal behavior of virtual agents according to conversational contents between an agent and a human [7].

This paper reports a preliminary result of our consecutive experiment that deals with cultural issues. Our two previous experiments used only Japanese participants for evaluation and did not consider cultural differences. However, there are culturally defined preferences in types of gestures and expressive methods of gestures [8]. Therefore, we can assume that there are cultural differences of expressing and perceiving self-adaptors as well as gestures.

We focus on cultural differences of perception and evaluate the impression of the agents with Japanese self-adaptors in this experiment. We hypothesize that "when the agent performs Japanese-specific self-adaptors, Japanese participants have better impression than non-Japanese participants".

EXPERIMENTAL METHOD

We used a female 3D model using Poser 7[1] for the agent's appearance and created animations with three sets of conditions: "agents that exhibit relaxed self-adaptors (RA hereafter)", "agents that exhibit stressful self-adaptors (SA hereafter)", and "agents that exhibit beat gestures (BE hereafter)". The self-adaptors implemented for RA are the three types implemented in [6]. These relaxed adaptors were extracted based on the results of video analysis of the conversations between 20 pairs in a Japanese university. We found the following three types of self-adaptors occurred most frequently in most pairs: "touching hair," "touching chin," and "touching nose." Each stroke occurred once as a one-off action with a narrow range of hand movements. The timing was either at the beginning or at the end of an utterance. The self-adaptors implemented for SA are the three types implemented in [7]: "head-scratching", "neck-scratching", and "chin-scratching". A stressful self-adaptor is a scratching action which occurs a number of times over a wider range of hand movements than a relaxed self-adaptor [9]. We implemented beat gestures to the agent as a control condition. A beat gesture is a rhythmic gesture used in conjunction with speech to emphasize certain words or phrases [10]. RA is shown in Fig. 1, SA is shown in Fig. 2 and BE is shown in Fig. 3.

The experiment was conducted on the web to gather participants from all over the world. Participants were given a fake instruction to evaluate reliability of an e-learning agent. They watched three movie clips where the agent talks about three different topics (i.e., origin of pasta, history of ice cream, panda's diet) assigned to them randomly. The agent performs either RA, SA or BE in one movie clip. They answer a questionnaire on the impression of the agent, namely, perceived friendliness, intelligence, emotional stability, naturalness, after they finish watching each movie clip. They repeat the same task three times until they experience all three conditions. A post-experiment questionnaire was conducted to evaluate social and individual acceptance of the self-adaptors used in the experiment.

Fig. 1. Agent Exhibiting Relaxed Self-adaptors

Fig. 2. Agent Exhibiting Stressful Self-adaptors

---

[1] http://poser.smithmicro.com/poser.html

Fig. 3. Agent Exhibiting Beat Gestures

RESULTS & DISCUSSION

We gathered 29 participants from Japan and 15 from 8 countries, (i.e., USA, France, Germany, New Zealand, Korea). We performed two-way ANOVA with repeated measures on the results of the impression evaluation questionnaire with two factors; self-adaptor (RA, SA and BE) and participants' nationality (Japanese (JP hereafter) or non-Japanese (NJ hereafter)). We examined whether there are differences in the impressions of the agents according to the types of self-adaptors and the participant's nationality. Fig. 4, 5, 6 show comparison of perceived friendliness, perceived intelligence, and perceived emotional stability of the agent between the JP and NJ respectively. Each question was rated with a 7 point Likert scale.

Firstly, for the results of the perceived friendliness of the agents, no main effect of self-adaptors was found. There is an interaction between self-adaptors and nationality ($F=5.79$, $p<0.01$). The results of multiple comparison showed significant differences of perceived friendliness rated by JP between SA and BE ($F=7.43$, $p<0.01$) and RA and SA ($F=14.81$, $p<0.01$). (see Fig.4). In both comparisons, SA was rated as significantly less friendly than RA or BE by JP. However such difference was not found in the ratings by NJ, and NJ's ratings were constantly lower than the median score in any self-adaptor condition.

Secondly, the perceived intelligence ratings showed similar results (see Fig.5). There is an interaction between self-adaptors and nationality ($F=8.06$, $p<0.01$). Again, SA was rated as significantly less intelligent than RA or BE by JP. However, such difference in perceived intelligence was not found in any ratings by NJ, and NJ's ratings were stayed flat around the median score in any self-adaptor condition.

Thirdly, in terms of perceived emotional stability (see Fig. 6), there is an interaction between self-adaptors and nationality ($F=17.04$, $p<0.01$). Again, SA was rated as significantly less emotionally stable than RA or BE by JP. However, such difference in emotional stability was not found in the ratings by NJ between RA and SA. However, BE was rated as significantly less emotionally stable by NJ than JP, and than RA and SA. The reason for the low rating of BE by NJ is that the way JP and NJ perform beat gestures are different. Japanese culture-specific beat gesture is performed as palm down movements, which was implemented in BE. However, we were informed by some of the foreign participants that they always perform beat gestures as palm faced up. Japanese beat gesture was interpreted as "Calm down, be quiet." Thus we assume the palm down beat gesture was interpreted as aggressive as an e-learning instructing agent by NJ.

To summarize the impression of the agents, when the agent performed the relaxed-self-adaptors, impression evaluations made by the Japanese participants are higher than the ones made by non-Japanese participants. However, impression evaluations of the Japanese are lower than the one made by non-Japanese when the agent performed the stressful self-adaptors. Evaluations made by non-Japanese were constantly low across all conditions. These results partially support our hypothesis only to the case of relaxed self-adaptors and beat gestures.

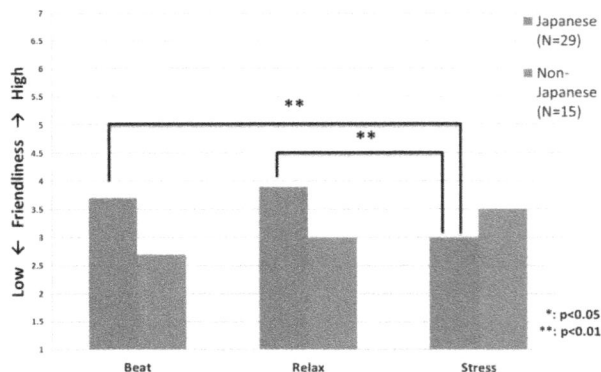

Fig. 4. Comparison of Friendliness Scores between Japanese and Non-Japanese

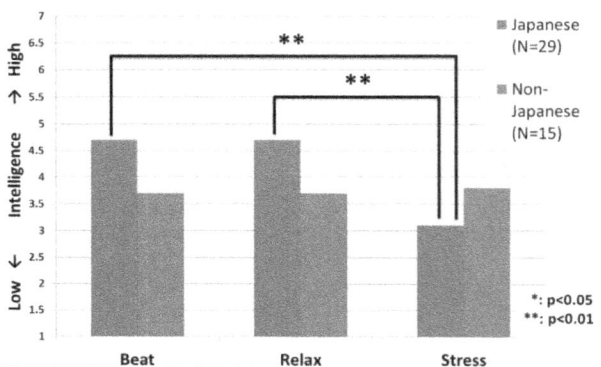

Fig. 5. Comparison of Intelligence Scores between Japanese and Non-Japanese

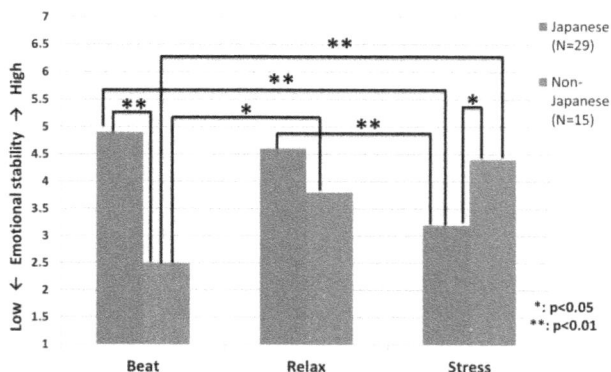

Fig. 6. Comparison of Emotional Stability Scores between Japanese and Non-Japanese

Although the results suggested cultural differences in the impression of stressful self-adaptors, it is important to investigate whether the agent's behaviors and hand movements were perceived as natural. The result of perceived naturalness of agent's behavior is shown in Fig. 7. There is an interaction between self-adaptors and nationality (F=8.43, p<0.01). Cultural differences were seen in RA and BE. JP felt significantly higher naturalness toward RA (F=15.35, p<0.05) and BE (F=25.89, p<0.05) than NJ. Similar to the impression analyses above, JP felt significantly less naturalness toward SA than RA (F=13.11, p<0.01) and BE (F=16.92, p<0.01), while NJ's perception of naturalness stayed low across any self-adaptor conditions. Similar to Fig. 6, BE was perceived as significantly less natural by NJ.

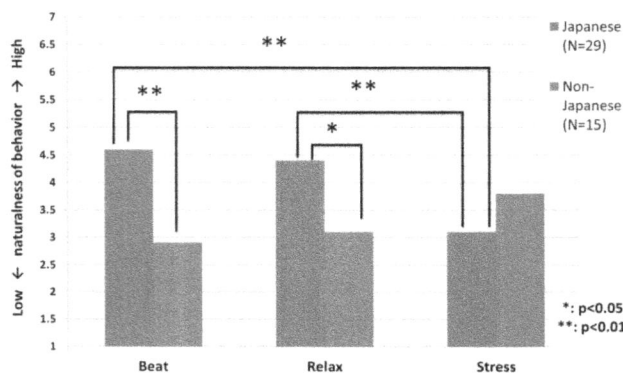

Fig. 7. Comparisons of Naturalness of Behavior Scores by Japanese and Non-Japanese

Finally, we examined whether the self-adaptors used in this experiment were considered taboo or not individually and culturally, since most self-adaptors were considered taboo if shown in public. The results of participants' personal acceptance of agent's behaviors and social acceptance in their home countries are shown in Fig. 8 and 9 respectively. JP evaluated the personal acceptance of SA significantly lower than RA (F=54.04, p<0.01) and BE (F=54.04, p<0.01). JP's personal acceptance of SA is significantly lower than NP (F=8.60, p<0.01). These results indicate Japanese rigorous attitude and little acceptance to stressful self-adaptors. The results of previous research suggested that the participants unconsciously expect agents to behave in a manner that is appropriate to the topic of conversation as we do with humans [7]. Since the participants were instructed to evaluate reliability of an e-learning agent, JP evaluated the appropriateness of the behavior for an e-leaning instructor that led to rigorous evaluations.

However, NJ didn't change their appropriateness evaluation according to the type of self-adaptors. There is a possibility that the reason for constant evaluation ratings across any self-adaptors by NJ is that NJ did not notice the differences of self-adaptors used in the experiment, since we used self-adaptors extracted from dyad conversation video recordings between Japanese university students. Only JP noticed the differences of the self-adaptors and lowered their evaluation on the agent with stressful self-adaptors.

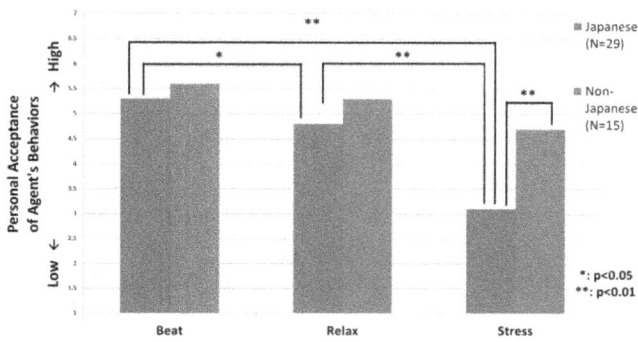

Fig. 8. Participants Personal Acceptance of Agent's Behaviors

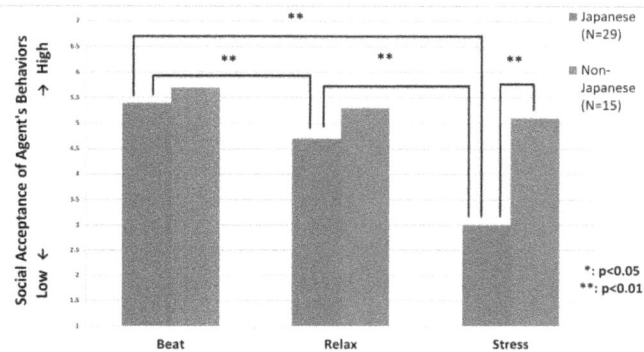

Fig. 9. Social Acceptance of Agent's Behaviors in Participants' Home Country

CONCLUSIONS

This experiment compared impressions of an e-learning instructor agent with Japanese specific self-adaptors rated by Japanese and non-Japanese participants. Our hypothesis "when the agent performs Japanese-specific self-adaptors, Japanese participants have better impression than non-Japanese" was partially supported only to the case of relaxed self-adaptors. The results suggest Japanese' significantly low evaluations and over sensitivity toward stressful self-adaptors compared to the ones by non-Japanese participants. This negative impression can be explained by lower social acceptance toward stressful self-adaptors among the Japanese participants. The Japanese participants evaluated the agent performing stress self-adaptors were not appropriate as an e-learning instructor.

On the contrary, the non-Japanese participants were insensitive to the differences in the types of Japanese culture specific self-adaptors. However, they reacted negatively to the Japanese culture specific beat gestures, which are closely coordinated with speech and add meaning to the content.

In order to investigate different impression and sensitivity to culture specific self-adaptors and their influences to interactions, future study should investigate culture-specific self-adaptors shown in other countries, implement them with agents, and conduct a cross-cultural experiment with larger number of participants and countries.

ACKNOWLEDGEMENT
This research is partially supported by JSPS KAKENHI JP2633023.

REFERENCES

1. Ekman, P., 1980. Three classes of nonverbal behavior, Aspects of Nonverbal Communication, Swets and Zeitlinger.

2. Waxer, P., 1988. Nonverbal cues for anxiety: An examination of emotional leakage. In Journal of Abnormal Psychology, 86, 3: 306-314.

3. Ekman, P., Friesen, W.V., 1972. Hand movements. In Journal of Communication 22, pp. 353-374.

4. Argyle, M., 1988. Bodily communication. Taylor & Francis.

5. Blacking,j.(ed)., 1977. The Anthropology of the Body, Academic Press.

6. Koda, T. and Higashino, H., 2014. Importance of Considering User's Social Skills in Human-agent Interactions. In Proc. of ICAART2014, 115-122.

7. Koda, T., and Mori, Y., 2014. Effects of an agent's displaying self-adaptors during a serious conversation. In: T. Bickmore et al. (Eds.): IVA 2014, LNAI 8637, 240–249, Springer-Verlag.

8. Aylett, R., Vannini, N., Andre, E., Paiva, A., Enz, S., Hall, L., 2009. But that was in another country: agents and intercultural empathy. In Proc. of International Conference on Autonomous Agents and Multi-agent Systems, 1: 329-336.

9. Neff, M., Toothman, N., Bowmani, R., Fox Tree, J. E., Walker, M., 2011. Don't Scratch! Self-adaptors Reflect Emotional Stability. In Vilhjalmsson, H. H. et al. (Eds.): IVA 2011, LNAI 6895, 398-411. Springer-Verlag.

10. D.McNeil., 1992. Hand and Mind: What Gestures Reveal about Thought, The University of Chicago Press.

Modulating Dynamic Models for Lip Motion Generation

Singo Sawa
Graduate School of
Informatics, Kyoto University
Kyoto, Japan
sawa@vision.kuee.kyoto-
u.ac.jp

Hiroaki Kawashima
Graduate School of
Informatics, Kyoto University
Kyoto, Japan
kawashima@i.kyoto-u.ac.jp

Kei Shimonishi
Graduate School of
Informatics, Kyoto University
Kyoto, Japan
simonisi@vision.kuee.kyoto-
u.ac.jp

Takashi Matsuyama
Graduate School of
Informatics, Kyoto University
Kyoto, Japan
tm@i.kyoto-u.ac.jp

ABSTRACT

Generation of natural human motion is one of key techniques for multimodal dialogue systems with a human-like avatar. In particular, natural and expressive lip motion synthesis is necessary to make conversation between a user and an avatar richer. However, such expressive lip motion is often difficult to be generated automatically because it can be changed depending on phonemic context and prosody. To address this difficulty, we introduce a novel motion generation method on the basis of the modulation of a set of dynamic models learned from neutral motion data. As a suitable model for lip motion generation, we adopt a hybrid dynamical system, which consists of linear dynamical systems for each motion unit and a symbolic automaton for switching between these units. We show that, from the viewpoint of control theory, it is possible to modulate linear dynamical systems for various types of motion. Early results demonstrate the applicability of the proposed method using lip motion synthesis for simple phoneme sequences.

ACM Classification Keywords

H.5.1. Information Interfaces and Presentation (e.g. HCI): Multimedia Information Systems

Author Keywords

Lip motion generation; hybrid dynamical system; linear dynamical system; modulation; optimal control.

INTRODUCTION

Automatic generation of natural human motion from data becomes more important than ever before. It is not only important for movie and game productions but is widely required for

HAI '16 October 04-07, 2016, Biopolis, Singapore

© 2016 Copyright held by the owner/author(s).

ACM ISBN 978-1-4503-4508-8/16/10.

DOI: http://dx.doi.org/10.1145/2974804.2980499

human agent interaction. For example, while speech dialogue systems that interact with a user by voice are becoming popular recently, presenting an avatar in such dialogue systems can convey richer information through multimodal interaction with a user.

Above all, lip motion synthesis of an avatar is necessary to make conversation natural and expressive. Here, a lip moves more complicatedly than other parts such as hands and legs, following his/her intention and utterance. It can be changed by prosody like speaking rate or volume of voice, and also by the preceding and succeeding phonemes [9]. To treat this difficulty, the simplest solution is concatenating each motion from data of motions collected in every phonemic context and every prosody; however, it is not realistic because enormous amount of data that cover all variety of motion is needed. To overcome this problem, we introduce a novel motion generation technique on the basis of modulating dynamic model for neutral lip motion depending on phonemic context and prosody, assuming that a generative model can be learned in each phoneme from image sequences of lip motion.

Methods to automatically synthesize motion from data has been studied in many fields such as lip-sync and dance-motion synthesis. Although a hidden Markov model (HMM) is commonly used [1, 4, 9], the dynamic property of a motion trajectory is not represented in this model, and additional morphing techniques are used to generate smooth trajectories. From this viewpoint, HMM is not suitable to modulate motion systems dynamically in each phonemic context and prosody; thus, in this paper we focus on models where each temporal segment can be represented by a dynamical system [8].

Lip movement can be considered as a sequence of motion units switching one to another, roughly corresponding to phoneme series. Therefore, an appropriate generative model for such movement should include a dynamic motion model for every unit and a symbolic event model to represent switching among motion units. As such, we consider that a hybrid dynamical system, which consists of a linear dynamical system for each motion unit and an automaton for switching units, is suitable to model such movements [5, 7].

The contribution of this paper is as follows: given that typical dynamic models for a set of motion units have been learned from measured data, we propose a framework to modulate the model dynamics themselves to generate various natural and expressive human motion. As a particular example, we focus on the application of lip-sync necessary for multimodal dialogue system, and address the problem of generating natural lip motion by modulating the dynamic models depending on phoneme context and prosody.

HYBRID DYNAMICAL SYSTEM
A hybrid dynamical system used in this paper consists of two layers. The upper layer models the switching of motion units by discrete event systems, and here each symbol, which is called a mode, is specified in this layer during motion generation. In the case of lip motion, one mode is roughly corresponding to a single phoneme or a transition between phonemes. The lower layer models the dynamics of each motion unit, and a sequence of lip shapes is generated by a certain dynamical system having one-to-one correspondence to a mode specified in the upper layer.

The lower layer: Linear Dynamical System
Time-invariant linear dynamical system (LDS) is used for the models in the lower layer, where time evolution of the state of the system is represented by a difference equation. The state z_t can be calculated from feature vectors y_t such as coordinates of feature points for lip shape. The relations between a state z_t, a compressed feature x_t and an original feature vector y_t at time t are described by the following three equations:

$$z_t = A^{(m)} z_{t-1}, \tag{1}$$

$$x_t = z_t + \mu^{(m)}, \tag{2}$$

$$y_t = C x_t + c_0. \tag{3}$$

The equation (1) is a state equation where a system matrix $A^{(m)}$ defines the dynamics of lip motion. This matrix is time-invariant since the system is time-invariant in the same mode, switching depending on a mode m specified in the upper layer. The upper suffix (m) of $A^{(m)}$ indicates that a system matrix can be different between each mode; however, we will omit this suffix unless there is a need to clearly indicate the mode m. The equation (2) separates a time-invariant bias from a state of the system. The bias $\mu^{(m)}$ defines a point attractor of the dynamical system when the system is stable, and it switches depending on the modes as well as a system matrix. The equation (3) is an output equation, which represents the dimensionality reduction of a vector from an original feature y_t to a compressed feature x_t. The output matrix C and the output bias c_0 in this equation are calculated by principal component analysis similarly to [6]. In summary, the parameters required for generating lip motion corresponding to mode m are as follows: a system matrix $A^{(m)}$, a state bias $\mu^{(m)}$, an initial compressed feature $x_{ini}^{(m)}$, and a duration length $L^{(m)}$. When a mode switches after $L^{(m)}$ unit times, these parameter set will be switched to the parameter set for the next mode m'.

The upper layer: Probabilistic Finite Automaton
The discrete system in the upper layer defines a timed probabilistic finite automaton. The next mode and its duration length are stochastically determined depending on the current mode.

MODULATION METHODS TO LDS
We consider the modulation to a linear dynamical system for human motion as the operation of properly changing the system matrix of the system, since it determines the time evolution of an autonomous LDS. Here we take two things into consideration: (1) keeping the features of a system matrix already learned from neutral motion data, and (2) modifying the features of the same matrix in order to fit phonemic context and prosody. We suppose that conditions to the system for motion generation can be given by states at segment boundaries such as the initial state and the final state, temporal elements such as speaking rate and duration lengths, or energy function for modulation. Thus, the question is how to design an algorithm that outputs a new system matrix by using existing one together with these newly given conditions during a generation phase. This section explains that a modulation for these given conditions can be achieved by changing the original model using a framework of the state feedback control.

The proposed framework can be seen as the generalization of a batch-based motion generation method, which solves a large linear equation to find a trajectory that satisfies given dynamic constraints and boundary conditions. In what follows, we first introduce a batch-based method, and then explain how the method can be interpreted from the viewpoint of the state feedback control. Finally, we explain our proposed modulation framework, where a variety of given conditions can be incorporated using an optimal control technique.

Motion Generation using a Batch Method
A batch-based method is one of standard motion generation methods in the field of robotics and computer graphics. Given boundary conditions, an initial state $z_{ini} := x_{ini}^{(m)} - \mu^{(m)}$, and a final state $z_{fin} := x_{ini}^{(m')} - \mu^{(m)}$, of a linear dynamical system with system matrix A, its state equations at every time can be integrated into the following equation [8] [1]:

$$\mathbf{Mz} = \mathbf{b}, \tag{4}$$

$$\mathbf{M} = \begin{pmatrix} I & & & 0 \\ -A & I & & \\ & \ddots & \ddots & \\ & & -A & I \\ 0 & & & -A \end{pmatrix}, \mathbf{z} = \begin{pmatrix} z_2 \\ z_3 \\ \vdots \\ z_{L-1} \\ z_L \end{pmatrix}, \mathbf{b} = \begin{pmatrix} A z_{ini} \\ 0 \\ \vdots \\ 0 \\ -z_{fin} \end{pmatrix}.$$

Note that constraints $z_1 = z_{ini}$ and $z_{L+1} = z_{fin}$ are imposed in this equation. Since the equations $A z_{t-1} = z_t$ $(t = 2, ..., L+1)$ are not satisfied at the same time in general, we minimize the

---
[1] The second order dynamics in [8] is not considered here for simplicity.

sum of error ϕ expressed by the following equation:

$$\underset{\{z_t\}}{\text{minimize}} \ \phi = \sum_{t=2}^{L+1} ||z_t - Az_{t-1}||^2, \quad (5)$$

$$\text{subject to } z_1 = z_{\text{ini}}, \ z_{L+1} = z_{\text{fin}}.$$

The solution of this optimization is given by equation (6) using a pseudo-inverse matrix $\mathbf{M}^+$ of $\mathbf{M}$,

$$\mathbf{z} = \mathbf{M}^+\mathbf{b}. \quad (6)$$

Here, $\mathbf{z}$ is the result of a generated state trajectory.

Motion Generation with State Feedback

The above method cannot deal with other conditions except for boundary conditions (i.e., initial and final states), since the states is directly changed without modulation of the dynamics. Here, we consider taking another way to incorporate given conditions: changing the system matrix itself.

As for an example of changing the system matrix, a constraint is imposed on the poles of the system (i.e., eigenvalues of the system matrix) for dynamic texture generation [3, 10]. To generate end-less periodic change of textures, a dynamic model (i.e., LDS) behind the generated signal should be *oscillatory system*, i.e., some poles of the system are on the unit circle in the complex plane (in the pole plot) and the rest are inside the circle. Therefore, generation of desired image sequences can be recast as a pole assignment problem in [10], where closed-loop feedback is introduced for dynamical systems. Following this method, we interpret the batch-based method as a problem of state-feedback controller design.

Figure 1 is the block diagram of the dynamic model for general motion. The next state z_t is generated from a given modulation input u_{t-1} and its output from the neutral dynamic model Az_{t-1}, based on the state equation (7) and the objective function (8):

$$z_t = Az_{t-1} + u_{t-1}, \quad (7)$$

$$\phi = \sum_{t=1}^{L} u_t^\top u_t, \quad (8)$$

where the following equation defines state feedback at a certain time t:

$$u_t = F_t z_t. \quad (9)$$

Using equations (7) and (9), we can eliminate the modulation input u_{t-1} and obtain equations (10) and (11). Note that the system matrix A_t now depends on time t and it is changed by state feedback at every moment. This model can represent keeping features of the existing dynamics and modifying features by given conditions:

$$z_t = A_t z_{t-1}, \quad (10)$$

$$A_t = A + F_t. \quad (11)$$

Modulation Method based on Optimal Control

Since we exploit the switching of LDSs for motion generation, we are interested in generating not periodic motion but transient motion from each of LDSs. While a pole assignment

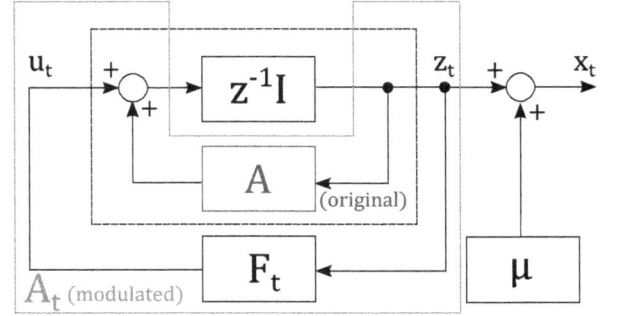

Figure 1. Block diagram of modulation to a linear dynamical system

method can be used for periodic sequence generation [10], other conditions should be considered for transient motion generation. For example, the vicinity of a final state should be considered to synthesize smooth motion in each segment represented by one mode (i.e., one LDS). It can be assumed that $\mu^{(m)} = x_{\text{ini}}^{(m')}$, if the duration length L is long enough for the state sequence to converge. However, this assumption cannot be applied in our case because the length of segments can be short in many situations. Therefore, we can design an objective function that includes weights for the vicinity of the final state. A possible choice for such objective functions is

$$\underset{\{z_t\},\{u_t\}}{\text{minimize}} \ \phi = \sum_{t=1}^{L} \left(z_t^\top Q z_t + u_t^\top R u_t \right) + z_{L+1}^\top P_{L+1} z_{L+1}, \quad (12)$$

$$\text{subject to } z_1 = z_{\text{ini}}, \ z_{L+1} = z_{\text{fin}},$$

where P_{L+1}, $Q \geq 0$, $R > 0$, and all of these matrices are symmetric. The first term determines the velocity of convergence and the second term defines the energy to modulate the system as we mentioned before. The last term imposes a penalty on the deviation from the final state. This is a natural extension of the equation (8) because this objective function is equivalent to that equation when $P_{L+1} = Q = 0$, $R = I$ where I denotes the identity matrix. This minimization is known as a linear quadratic regulator problem in the field of modern control. As the duration length is finite, this problem can be solved using dynamic programming similar to finite-horizon optimal regulator problem. As a result, the following equation (13) can be found as a solution.

$$\begin{cases} P_t &= A^\top P_{t+1} A + Q + (P_{t+1}A)^\top F_t, \\ F_t &= -(R + P_{t+1})^{-1}(P_{t+1}A). \end{cases} \quad (13)$$

Finally, eliminating the modulation input u_t yields the following equation (14):

$$\begin{cases} P_t &= Q + A_t^\top P_{t+1} A, \\ A_t &= (R + P_{t+1})^{-1} RA. \end{cases} \quad (14)$$

EXPERIMENT

We obtained a sequence of 20 feature points for lip shapes on two-dimensional space by using CLM-Framework [2], recording a sequence of lip motion when five vowels /aiueo/ was uttered. Then, after calculating three-point moving average for noise removal, we compressed 40-dimensional feature vectors y_t into three-dimensional vectors x_t using principal component

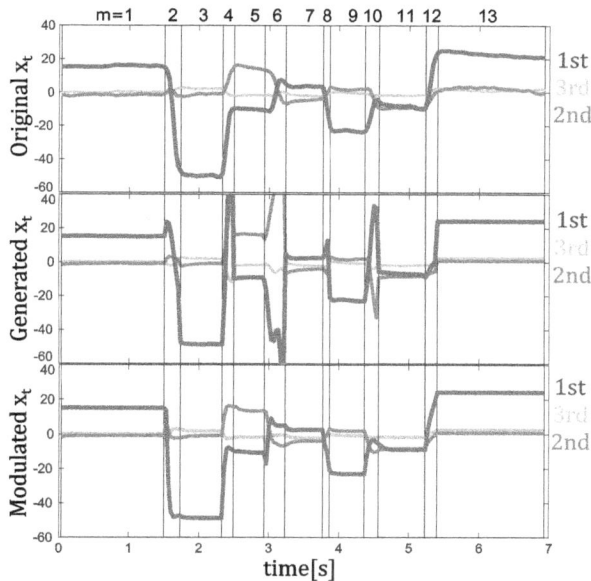

Figure 2. Three-dimensional compressed features and modes of lip motion. The upper is the original sequence, the middle is a generated sequence without modulation, the lower is a generated sequence with modulation.

analysis as shown in equation (3). We segmented the sequence of compressed feature vectors x_t, and calculated the parameters of the linear dynamical system in each mode similarly to [7].

Figure 2 (top) is an original sequence of compressed features x_t and its segmentation. Here we replace the following parameters in equation (12): $P_{L+1} = pI, Q = qI, R = (1-q)I$ ($p \in \mathbb{R}_+, q \in [0,1]$). Figure 2 (middle) shows the result of a generated sequence of compressed features x_t by using a method equivalent to the batch method, namely we substituted $p = 0, q = 0$. Large fluctuation can be seen at the periods when the modes switch. On the other hand, the result of modulating the dynamics shown in Figure 2 (bottom) is very close to the original sequence, where $p = 10, q = 0.1$ were used. It is found that such a sequence can be generated by the modulation using a proper objective function even if the point attractor is not close to the final state, for example, in mode 6.

CONCLUSION

The present paper proposed a method to modulate dynamic models learned from typical motion data. The proposed method can be used to generate a variety of natural motions. While the experimental result only demonstrates that

the method can generate a smooth lip motion, our future work will consider the extension of the objective function and investigate how the method can be applied to generate natural and expressive lip motion depending on phoneme context and speech prosody.

ACKNOWLEDGMENTS

This work was supported by JST, PRESTO.

REFERENCES

1. Robert Anderson, Bjorn Stenger, Vincent Wan, and Roberto Cipolla. 2013. Expressive Visual Text-to-Speech Using Active Appearance Models. In *Proc. of CVPR '13*. 3382–3389.

2. Tadas Baltrusaitis, Peter Robinson, and Louis-Philippe Morency. 2013. Constrained Local Neural Fields for Robust Facial Landmark Detection in the Wild. In *Proc. of ICCVW '13*. 354–361.

3. Byron Boots, Geoffrey J Gordon, and Sajid M. Siddiqi. 2008. A Constraint Generation Approach to Learning Stable Linear Dynamical Systems. In *Proc. of NIPS '07*. 1329–1336.

4. Matthew Brand. 1999. Voice Puppetry. In *Proc. of SIGGRAPH '99*. 21–28.

5. Christoph Bregler. 1997. Learning and Recognizing Human Dynamics in Video Sequences. In *Proc. of CVPR '97*. 568–574.

6. Gianfranco Doretto, Alessandro Chiuso, Ying Nian Wu, and Stefano Soatto. 2003. Dynamic Textures. *IJCV* 51, 2 (2003), 91–109.

7. Hiroaki Kawashima and Takashi Matsuyama. 2005. Multiphase Learning for an Interval-Based Hybrid Dynamical System. *IEICE Trans. Fundamentals* E88-A, 11 (2005), 3022–3035.

8. Yan Li, Tianshu Wang, and Heung-Yeung Shum. 2002. Motion Texture: A Two-level Statistical Model for Character Motion Synthesis. *ACM TOG* 21, 3 (2002), 465–472.

9. Sarah L. Taylor, Moshe Mahler, Barry-John Theobald, and Iain Matthews. 2012. Dynamic Units of Visual Speech. In *Proc. of SCA '12*. 275–284.

10. Lu Yuan, Fang Wen, Ce Liu, and Heung-Yeung Shum. 2004. Synthesizing Dynamic Texture with Closed-Loop Linear Dynamic System. In *Proc. of ECCV '04*. 603–616.

Magnetic Dining Table Interface and Magnetic Foods for new Human Food Interactions

Nur Ellyza Abd Rahman[1], Azhri Azhar[1], Kasun Karunanayaka[1], Adrian David Cheok[1],
Mohammad Abdullah Mohamad Johar[1], Jade Gross[2], Andoni Luis Aduriz[2]
[1]Imagineering Institute Iskandar Puteri, Malaysia and
[2]Mugaritz,Errenteria,Gipuzkoa,Spain
{amira, nurafiqah, kasun, adrian}@imagineeringinstitute.org,
{jade, info}@mugaritz.com

ABSTRACT

This poster paper discuss the concept of magnetic table interface and magnetic foods. This interface introduces new human-food interactions such as modifying weight, levitation, movement, and dynamic textures for our daily used food and utensils using a strong magnetic field formed by an array of Bitter electromagnets. To make foods and cutleries interactive, we add edible magnetic material on the food such as iron and iron oxides, and make cutleries with magnetic materials. We expect that this system will alter our food consumption behaviours and make the whole experience much more interactive and enjoyable.

ACM Classification Keywords

H.5.m. Information Interfaces and Presentation

Author Keywords

Multisensory Experiences; Magnetic User Interfaces; Magnetic Table; Magnetic Foods; Levitation

INTRODUCTION

Food is one of the basic humans need. It can be considered as a media that creates connections and interactions among people. Some recent research in HCI have introduced new food interactions and experiances such as remote co-dining, virtual and augmented foods [10, 9]. By using the recent advancements of the technology, Internet and multi sensory communication, our attempt in this research is to make food and food eating behaviours much more interactive. We try to combine the properties of magnetic fields in to food and cutleries and create new experiences such as modifying weight, attraction, repulsion, levitation, vibration, rotation, and modifying texture dynamically. We expect this kind of system will lead the people enjoying their food better. Our concept is shown in the Figure 1.These new food interactions will be implemented by making the food and utensils magnetic and manipulating them dynamically using a strong magnetic field

HAI '16 October 04-07, 2016, Biopolis, Singapore

© 2016 Copyright held by the owner/author(s).

ACM ISBN 978-1-4503-4508-8/16/10.

DOI: http://dx.doi.org/10.1145/2974804.2980504

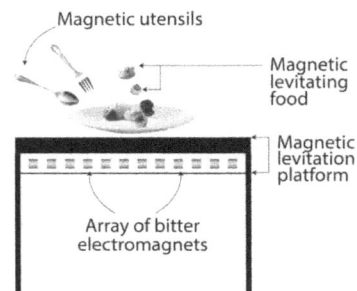

Figure 1. The conceptual image of 'Magnetic Dining Table and Magnetic Food' Interface: This interface will introduce new interactions for food and utensils such as modify weight, levitation, movement, and dynamic textures.

that will be generated from below the surface of the table. An array of Bitter electromagnets [1] will be used for this purpose.

LITERATURE REVIEW

The proposed Magnetic table interface would require about 2T to 3T magnetic field to create these interactions. while considering about a suitable electromagnet technology for our system, we compared conventional electromagnets [1], superconductor electromagnets [3] and bitter electromagnets [1]. However, the suitable one that fits into our requirements was the Bitter plate electromagnets since conventional electromagnets produce less than 2T field and superconductor electromagnets needs more specific needs such as liquid gases [3]. The idea of the Bitter electromagnets was demonstrated by Francis Bitter by producing strong magnetic field up to 45T using his electromagnet design [1]. Then, Berry. et. al. [4] shows that even a living frog can be float on the bore of 20T magnetic field generated by a Bitter magnet.

Some materials that have magnetic properties and can be found in our body are bismuth, silver, copper and gold. However, first three are not suitable to add to the foods in higher quantities and gold is difficult to magnetize. Among the iron enriched foods and vitamins in our meal contain iron or iron oxides are used [7]. Therefore, currently we are concentrating more on adding iron and iron oxide as powder to the food.

METHOD

The proposed system is divided into two parts. They are,

Copper Thickness	Insulation Thickness	Cross-sectional m^2	Area cm^2	No of Turn	Field (T)	Space Factor	Power,P Watt	Resistance,R Ω
1	1	1.73E-5	1.73E-1	50	0.0941	0.999913	38.9061	0.0024
0.9	0.9	1.55E-5	1.55E-1	56	0.1045	0.999893	48.0316	0.00297
0.8	0.8	1.38E-5	1.38E-1	63	0.1176	0.999865	60.0789	0.00375
0.7	0.7	1.21E-5	1.21E-1	72	0.1344	0.999823	79.39608	0.0049
0.6	0.6	1.04E-5	1.04E-1	84	0.1568	0.999759	108.0628	0.00667
0.5	0.5	8.63E-6	8.63E-2	100	0.1882	0.999654	155.6008	0.00961
0.4	0.4	6.91E-6	6.91E-2	125	0.2352	0.999459	243.0987	0.01501
0.3	0.3	5.18E-6	5.18E-2	167	0.3135	0.999038	432.0696	0.02669
0.2	0.2	3.45E-6	3.45E-2	250	0.4699	0.997839	971.4765	0.06005
0.1	0.1	1.73E-6	1.73E-2	500	0.9363	0.991412	3871.3077	0.24021

Table 1. Analytical calculation results for Bitter electromagnet design (100A current supply)

Thickness of copper (mm)	Field (T)
1	0.1002
0.9	0.1112
0.8	0.1250
0.7	0.1427
0.6	0.1661
0.5	0.1986
0.4	0.2467
0.3	0.3246
0.2	0.4699
0.1	0.8086

Table 2. The effect of the thickness of the copper plate vs. the field produced in Bitter electromagnets

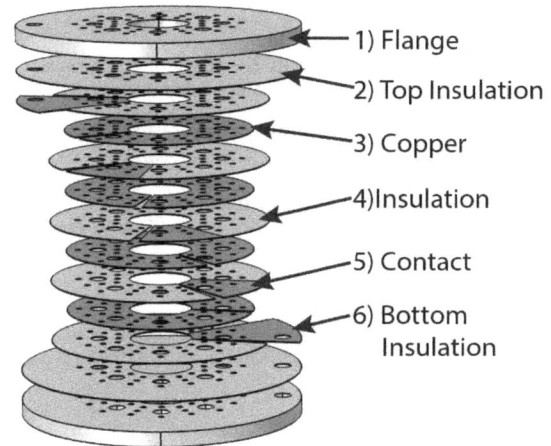

1) Flange
2) Top Insulation
3) Copper
4) Insulation
5) Contact
6) Bottom Insulation

Figure 2. Bitter Electromagnet Design

1. Magnetic Field Control Platform.

2. Magnetic foods and magnetic utensils.

Magnetic Field Control Platform

Magnetic table will be developed by placing an array of electromagnet under the table, and a controller circuit is used to control the magnetic field pattern. Bitter electromagnets (shown in Figure 2) will be designed according to the Francis Bitter's previous paper [5]. Our first Bitter electromagnet prototype will generate a magnetic field close to 0.5T. After we make the first prototype and conduct testing, we are planing to gradually improve our designs until we reach 2T to 3T range. These electromagnets will be developed either by using the multilayer PCB technology or metal stamping technology.

Calculation for a Bitter electromagnet was demonstrated using a spread sheet software, so that we can change parameters whenever we want and see the results instantly. We decided to choose the thickness of the copper plate less than or equal to 1mm [6] because the copper thickness does affect the total magnetic flux produced by the electromagnets as shown in Table 2. Based on the analysis, the electromagnet is set to be 10cm high, the outer radius is 3cm, inner radius of the hollow

section is 1cm, and the supply current to the magnet is 100A. The height of the electromagnet will change the number of turns required for the electromagnet. The coil resistance need to be between 0.02Ω and 0.2Ω and the space factor must be greater than 0.7 [5].

Analysis result shows copper plate with thickness of 0.1mm to 0.4mm (with a difference of 0.1mm) are suitable for making the Bitter electromagnet as in Table 1. Therefore, copper thickness of 0.2mm is chosen for our first bitter design because it is more practical to make and test in laboratory environment (limitations of power requirements and technology). The insulation thickness must be the same as the copper thickness [5]. With the selected parameter, the bitter electromagnet is estimated to produce 0.4699T (4699 Gauss). The 2D simulation result for the Bitter electromagnet is as shown in Figure 3. The copper and insulation thickness is reduced to 0.1mm to consider the hole that present in the actual electromagnet design. It produce 0.4236T (4236 Gauss) when 250 turns of bitter plate is supplied with 100A. Actual electromagnet pro-

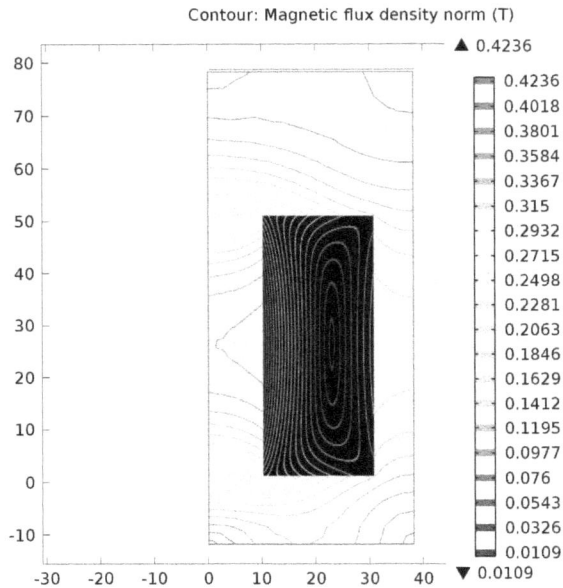

Contour: Magnetic flux density norm (T)

Figure 3. Software simulation in 2D-axisymmetry format. The area filled in black represents the right hand side cross section of the Bitter Electromagnet (note that the left hand side cross section is not shown in the simulation). Y axis represents the height and X axis represent the radius of Bitter Electromagnet. Value X=0 line represents the center of the electromagnet (X=0 to X=10 is right hand side of the center hole) and value Y=0 represents the bottom of the electromagnet. The maximum flux generated by this magnet would be 0.4236 T at the center.

totype may produce approximately the same result since both results from analytical calculation and software simulation show almost the same.

A microcontroller based firmware and a computer program will be used to control the circuit and thus controlling the magnetic objects above the table. A custom made electromagnet controller circuit will be designed to power up Bitter electromagnet. These electromagnet will produce considerable amount of heat during the operation, thus it is important to decide method of cooling. Therefore, we are designing a water based cooling system based on the theories discussed by McAdams [8].

Magnetic Food and Magnetic Utensils

Magnetic foods and Magnetic utensils will be placed on top of the Magnetic table interface.Custom-made foods with permanent magnet(s) replacing the seed(s) inside will also be tested. In addition, we will look in to powder like materials that can be added into the food such as iron since it is a known fact that iron enriched cereals can be movable on a smooth surface by using a weak magnetic field [2] and other suitable ferromagnetic materials.

The magnetic utensils will be magnetized in three different methods. First method is to use ferromagnetic or ferrimagnetic material for utensils and use a magnetizer to magnetize them. Secondly, permanent magnets can be embedded into the utensils. Lastly, small battery powered electromagnets can be embedded into the utensils and control the flux dynamically.

CONCLUSION

This paper discussed about the development of Magnetic Table Interface and Magnetic Foods using magnetic fields and materials. The proposed platform will be a dining table and the weight of cutlery will be manipulated during the dining by using magnetic fields. This interface would be a perfect fit for collaborative dining; serving the floating dishes, changing weight, and change the textures dynamically would add new experiences to the food interactions.One of our future objectives is to study the influence of changing weight of utensils on the consumption of food. This interface would be useful to introduce new food interactions and modify food consumption habits in future applications in the fields of human-computer interaction, new media, mixed reality, medicine and also entertainment computing.

ACKNOWLEDGEMENTS

The authors would like to thank greatly and acknowledge Michael Herrera and the other members in Imagineering Institute, Malaysia for their helpful contributions for this research.

REFERENCES

1. 2016. Bitter electromagnet. (2016). https://en.wikipedia.org/wiki/Bitter_electromagnet.

2. 2016. Magnetic Cereal. (2016). https://www.kjmagnetics.com/blog.asp?p=cereal-contains-iron.

3. SH Autler. 1960. Superconducting electromagnets. *Review of Scientific Instruments* 31, 4 (1960), 369–373.

4. Michael Victor Berry and Andre Konstantin Geim. 1997. Of flying frogs and levitrons. *European Journal of Physics* 18, 4 (1997), 307.

5. F Bitter. 1936. The design of powerful electromagnets Part II. The magnetizing coil. *Review of Scientific Instruments* 7, 12 (1936), 482–488.

6. The National High Magnetic Field Laboratory. 2009. Making resistive magnets. (2009). https://nationalmaglab.org/news-events/feature-stories/making-resistive-magnets.

7. Alexis Little. 2016. Magnetism and Food. (2016). https://prezi.com/paipcqdgxopr/magnetism-and-food/.

8. William H McAdams. 1954, Heat transmission. (????).

9. Kjartan Nordbo, David Milne, Rafael A Calvo, and Margaret Allman-Farinelli. 2015. Virtual Food Court: A VR environment to Assess People's Food Choices. In *Proceedings of the Annual Meeting of the Australian Special Interest Group for Computer Human Interaction.* ACM, 69–72.

10. Jun Wei, Adrian David Cheok, and Ryohei Nakatsu. 2012. Let's have dinner together: evaluate the mediated co-dining experience. In *Proceedings of the 14th ACM international conference on Multimodal interaction.* ACM, 225–228.

A Study on Trust in Pharmacists for Better HAI Design

Jia Qi Lim
Singapore, Singapore
7114140320@nygh.edu.sg

Nicole, Sze Ting Lim
Singapore, Singapore
7114140265@nygh.edu.sg

Maya Zheng
Singapore, Singapore
7114140360@nygh.edu.sg

Swee Lan See
Singapore, Singapore
slsee@i2r.a-star.edu.sg

ABSTRACT

Trust is a fundamental element in human cooperation and a critical factor in determining the success of human-human communications. This paper investigates trust in pharmacists and their customers and provides an insight into how trust is being established to effect human-human and human-agent interactions (HAI), in order to promote better design of robotic agents, such as a robot pharmacy-advisor, in support of the healthcare industry.

Author Keywords

Trust; Human-Agent Interaction; Pharmacy, Pharmacist; Robot design

ACM Classification Keywords

H.1.2: User/Machine Systems; H.3.4: Systems and Software; H.3.5 Online Information Services; H.5.2 User Interfaces; J3 Life and Medical Sciences

INTRODUCTION

There is a growing need for robotics in high-risk industries and situations, such as emergency rooms, evacuation protocols, etc.. However, there remains underlying uncertainties in users due to safety concerns about the use of these intelligent agents. Many people still do not feel fully comfortable placing their lives into the hands of such robots, which are not socially accepted in most high-risk industries. Thus, it is necessary to engender trust for more natural human-agent interactions (HAI) [1].

In the context of this study, we seek to investigate and understand how trust is being established between pharmacists and their customers. This trust is important for a customer to follow the advice and recommendation of drugs and treatment given by the pharmacist, in the hopes of recovering and to facilitate more readily acceptable and pleasant human-agent interactions [2, 3], such as between a robot pharmacy-advisor and its user.

Purpose of Research

To study trust in pharmacist-customer interactions, we would look into the roles of the pharmacist and the client to

HAI '16, October 04-07, 2016, Biopolis, Singapore
ACM 978-1-4503-4508-8/16/10.
http://dx.doi.org/10.1145/2974804.2980507

elicit the factors that contribute to the quality of trust established in their conversational interactions. These observations could be useful when it comes to the designing and programming of suitable features of an intelligent agent (robot) to help pharmacists meet increasing needs for more immediate and comprehensive healthcare, improving pharmaceutical business and the health of individuals at the same time. Then, through analyzing user's reported symptoms, the robot could help assess and provide advice in similar way to that of a human pharmacist as well as establish trust with the user.

METHODOLOGY

Studying Trust in Human-Human Interaction

Factors hypothesised to affect trust positively
In this research, we conduct surveys and interviews with the pharmacists and the customers at various commercial pharmacies. In designing the questionnaire, three factors, namely, perceived ability, perceived congeniality, and perceived emotional sensitivity of the pharmacist, were taken into consideration since these are factors that could affect trust and credibility in human-human interactions [5, 6, 7].

The perceived ability of the pharmacist depends significantly on how s/he displays his or her knowledge and experience. This definitely affects the perceived credibility of the pharmacist, ultimately affecting a customer's decision to trust the pharmacist's judgement and purchase the prescribed medicine or follow his/her advice.

However, while many customers may presume that robots have better memory and more reliable database than human pharmacists, most customers also seek the empathy and understanding of a professional pharmacist and trust that the pharmacist's emotional sensitivity will result in a more suitable prescription.

Due to the brief nature of interactions between pharmacist and customer, the customer will tend to make some assumptions about the general character of the pharmacist based on some social cues. For example, "how friendly, courteous, and positively predisposed" the pharmacist is could be attributed to other positive characteristics, such as sincerity and trustworthiness [4].

Data collection
To gain a deeper understanding of the trust in pharmacist-customer interactions that we plan to simulate in our robot, we are in progress of finalising the data collected from ten human pharmacists and thirty adult customers at major

pharmacies at shopping malls, using a designed questionnaire approved by an appropriate institutional review board.

Data analysis
We will employ a statistical analysis method to analyse the data collected. The participants' responses will be populated into the SPSS software to determine and report the relationship between each of three above-mentioned factors and trust.

Prototype Design
With the research findings from the field study, we could then discuss and further evaluate how trust can be engendered within the user interface for better HAI. On top of that, the suggestions made by customers and pharmacists on the design of the robot will be taken into consideration, so that the robot will be able to meet the needs of real users.

Prototype Testing
To assess the reliability and effectiveness of the final prototype, forty human volunteers would be invited to interact with the robot pharmacy-advisor and evaluate the credibility of this agent. They would also be asked to assess the relevant factors found to affect trust in interactions between human customers and pharmacists. Their feedback will also allow us to ensure that the design of our robot actually appeals to its target users and prompts them to accept and use the robot without fear or uncertainty in the studied context.

CONCLUSION
In the process of this research, we observed the unwillingness of potential users to accept the idea of having a robot that could support a human pharmacist in a pharmacy due to the fear of human pharmacists being replaced by robots, doubts of a robot's qualifications to provide professional services, and uncertainties about safety of using a robot for such purposes (as expected). This is a typical challenge when it comes to HAI and we are positive that this research is meaningful and the findings would be useful to creating more acceptable agents, especially for high-risk industries. If we aim to make progress in the use of robotics in high-risk industries such as healthcare, we need to first seek ways to establish trust between robots and their human users, to allow people to begin accepting robots socially.

Future Direction
This research proposed the design concept of a robot pharmacy-advisor and highlighted the fact that users are still unwilling to accept the use of robots in certain professions or real world scenarios. How to engender trust in HAI stills remains a challenge and this paper seeks to shed some light upon this obstacle. Although this study focused on the perceived ability, perceived congeniality, and perceived emotional sensitivity of the pharmacist, the unavoidable subjectivity in the interpretation of these factors limits the development of the prototype in this research. In future studies, we could investigate other factors affecting trust in human-human interactions, such as body language or the use of specific words in conversation, that perhaps would be able to effect better HAI.

ACKNOWLEDGEMENTS
We would like to thank the Ministry of Education (Singapore) and the Institute for Infocomm Research, A*STAR for the support of this research project under the Science Mentorship Programme.

REFERENCES
1. Cameron, D., Aitken, J., Collins, E., Boorman, L., Fernando, S., MaAree, O., Martinez Hernandez, U., and Law, J. 2015. Framing Factors: The Importance of Context and the Individual in Understanding Trust in Human-Robot Interaction. In *IEEE/RSJ International Conference on Intelligent Robots and Systems* (IROS).

2. Hedges, K. 2012. Trust the ultimate gatekeeper. In *The power of presence*. American Management Association, USA.

3. Lohani, M., Stokes, C., McCoy, M., Bailey, C. A., & Rivers, S. E. 2016. Social Interaction Moderates Human-Robot Trust-Reliance Relationship and Improves Stress Coping. In *The Eleventh ACM/IEEE International Conference on Human Robot Interaction*, pp. 471-472. IEEE Press.

4. McLeod, S. A.. 2010. *Attribution Theory*. [on-line]. Available: www.simplypsychology.org/attribution-theory.html. (Accessed 4 June 2016).

5. Paine Schofield, C. B., and Joinson, A.N. 2008. Privacy, trust, and disclosure online. In *Psychological Aspects in Cyberspace: Theory, research, applications*, Barak, A. (Ed.). Cambridge University Press, USA.

6. Wagner, A. R., and Arkin, R. C.. 2011. *Recognizing situations that demand trust*. Atlanta: IEEE.

7. Zaltman, G., Moorman, C., Deshpande, R.. 1993. Factors Affecting Trust in Market Research Relations. *Journal of Marketing, Vol. 57(1)*, pp. 81-101.

Development of a Simulated Environment for Recruitment Examination and Training of High School Teachers

Masato Fukuda, *Hung-Hsuan Huang, Tetsuya Kanno, Naoki Ohta, Kazuhiro Kuwabara
College of Information Science and Engineering, Ritsumeikan University
Kusatsu, Japan
*hhhuang@acm.org

ABSTRACT

While the environment of schools become more and more complicated, the improvement of teachers' skills in teaching and management is required. In this study, we focus on the development of a Wizard-of-Oz (WOZ) platform of simulated school environment, which can be utilized for teacher training or the examination of teacher recruitment from remote. This system is comprised of two front ends, one is a simulated classroom for the trainee, the other one is the interface for the system operator / investigator. The virtual classroom contains a number of virtual students who are controlled by the operator from the remote. The operator can observe the trainee from a dedicated interface and control the behaviors of any individual student as well as the atmosphere of the whole class. The whole-class atmosphere created by relatively large number of students is modeled as a concentration-arousal two dimensional space. The prototype system is evaluated with subject experiment and the results are reported.

ACM Classification Keywords

H.1.2 User/Machine Systems: Human Factors; H.5.2 User Interfaces: Evaluation/methodology; I.2.1 Applications and Expert Systems: Games, Natural language interfaces

Author Keywords

Virtual Agents; Application for Education; Group Atmosphere; Affective Interface

INTRODUCTION

According to the fundamental policy for development of educational human resources, published by Board of Education of Tokyo in 2007, the environment of school education problems is getting more complex and diverse with the evolvement of the whole society. Along with this situation, it is getting more and more difficult for teachers to adopt themselves to the problems which do not occur dozens of years ago. For example, the complains which go too far from overprotective guardians or the students isolated on social media of the Internet by their classmates, or increasing suicides of the students who met bullying. Since failed treatments may cause permanent stress of the young students, trainees and novice teachers are demanded to accumulate their experience and to improve their knowledge before the actual deployment to schools.

In order to deal with the diversity of problems, teacher trainees need not only knowledge but also repeated practice to learn from experience. In Japan, however, the training of teachers mainly relies on classroom lectures in colleges and is compensated with the practice for a relatively short period, say only two to three weeks in actual schools. Even though there may be some chances for practicing teaching skills in the class of teacher-training course in the colleges, these practices are usually conducted by peer role-playings in small number of participants and are far from real situations where they have to face dozens of teenagers. The teacher-training programs in Japan obviously lacks the practice in teaching skill and the admission of classes. The result is, many young teachers left their jobs in the first year due to frustration and other mental issues.

In this paper, we propose a virtual-reality (VR) platform of simulated school environment with computer graphics (CG) animated virtual students. The trainees can interact with the virtual students in this immersive and realistic virtual classroom and practice their teaching and admission skills. Besides the training purpose, the system is considered to be able to be used in the examination of teacher recruitment as well. The virtual students are operated by an operator the examination investigator from remote with a dedicated interface.

RELATED WORKS

Virtual environments have also been shown to be an effective tool for various training tasks. Jones et al. [2] developed a job interview simulation platform, which supports social training and coaching in the context of job interviews. Williamon et al. [5] designed and tested the efficacy of simulated performance environments as a new training facility for musician trainees. Kenny et al. [3] designed the training systems of mental therapeutic with virtual simulated patients.

On the other hand, few studies have focused on the training system of teachers in virtual environment. TechLive [1] is one of the examples. This application is also a VR simulated classroom with operator(s). In this system, one opera-

HAI '16 October 04-07, 2016, Biopolis, Singapore

© 2016 Copyright held by the owner/author(s).

ACM ISBN 978-1-4503-4508-8/16/10.

http://dx.doi.org/10.1145/2974804.2980508

tor can only control one of the virtual students by selecting pre-defined animation sequences or driving it with a motion capture device in real-time. There are no severe issues in the US where the number of students in a class is small. However, due to more limited resources, the number of students in one class is much larger in Japan. How to efficiently and realistically control dozens of students at the same time is not a trivial problem. Our work addresses this by proposing an atmosphere model that is described in the next section.

PROPOSED VIRTUAL CLASSROOM SYSTEM

In designing the virtual classroom system, there were two fundamental issues have to be considered. The first one is the level of autonomy of the virtual students. The second one is the number of virtual students.

During the planned multimodal interaction between the virtual students and the trainee, in responding the trainee's speech, and sensor like MS Kinect. In order to drive the virtual students, they have to be equipped with an autonomous behavior model, i.e. when should the virtual students do what to whom. Obviously, good literatures for designing such kind of models are not available. Data collection of real students is another candidate but is not practical due to privacy issues. Therefore, we concluded to develop a WOZ (Wizard-of-Oz) platform where knowledgeable operators control virtual students to compose realistic scenarios in the virtual environment. The history of the operator's operations and the responds from the trainees can thus be analyzed and be used in the design process of the autonomous virtual students in the future.

In this study, the simulation system is supposed to be controlled by experts, that means, the number of operators may be limited and is not available when needed. The design of the remote operating interface allows the same expert to engage multiple simulation sessions without physical moving. This can also help to keep the conditions fair, especially when the system is used as an examination of teacher recruitment.

Fig. 1 shows the basic layout of the proposed system. This system is comprised of two front ends, one is a simulated classroom for the trainee, the other one is the interface for the system operator / investigator. Fig. 2 shows the user interface for the trainee and the WOZ operator, respectively. The expected usage of the system is: the front end of Fig. 2(a) is projected on a life-size large screen (say 100 inches or even larger) while one trainee stands in front of the screen and practice his/her teaching skill. The trainee's teaching is captured by a Web cam and is displayed at the operator's interface (Fig.2(b)) in real-time. Operator's interface has two scroll bars so as to control the level of concentration-arousal parameters. In addition, eight buttons express pre-defined representative states so that the operator can control the whole class more easily. The operator can control atmosphere of the virtual classroom using this interface in reacting to the performance of the trainee. In addition, the operator can trigger the animations like sitting, sleeping, raising hand and posing to a specific virtual student. Every virtual student's motion are always synchronized between the trainee interface and operator interface. That virtual classroom was created by Unity

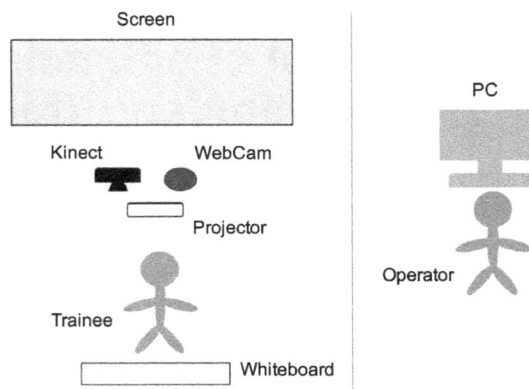

Figure 1. System layout of the proposed simulated environment

3D game engine. For the CG models of students, we adopted Daichi Character Pack freely available at "Game Asset Studio."

Basic Survey on Schools 2015 published by the Ministry of Education, Culture, Sports, Science and Technology, Japan figured out that the average number of students of one class is 28.2 in Japan [1]. With this relatively larger number, it is impractical to operate them one by one in a simultaneous manner. Not only an individual virtual student but also the whole group of virtual students needs a way to be controlled efficiently and to be perceived realistically.

We divided the control of virtual students into two modes, *individual* mode and *whole-class* mode. When the operator choose an arbitrary student, that student will shift to the individual mode and then the operator can fully control that student manually. By default, all virtual students are in the whole-class mode and are controlled by an atmosphere model. The atmosphere model serves as a template and all the virtual students together create the atmosphere of their group. This atmosphere is supposed to be the feedback sent from the operator to the trainee. The trainee can then adopt his/her teaching style in responding to the atmosphere. The class atmosphere is model is defined to be driven by two elements, *concentration* and *arousal*. which are inspired from the two dimensional circumplex model of affected proposed by Russell [4] . The concentration-arousal space is defined as the follows:

Concentration: how much the students are concentrating on the lecture. How well the trainee is explaining important topics of the lecture.

Arousal: the activity level of the students. How well the trainee is keeping the interest of the students.

The idea is: the values of these parameters have the effect in the possibility of the virtual students to express corresponding behaviors. For example, in a low-concentration, low-arousal, many of the virtual students may show sleepy animation, while in a high-concentration, high-arousal situation, the virtual students may concentrate in the lecture, take memos,

---

[1] http://www.mext.go.jp/b_menu/toukei/chousa01/kihon/1267995.htm

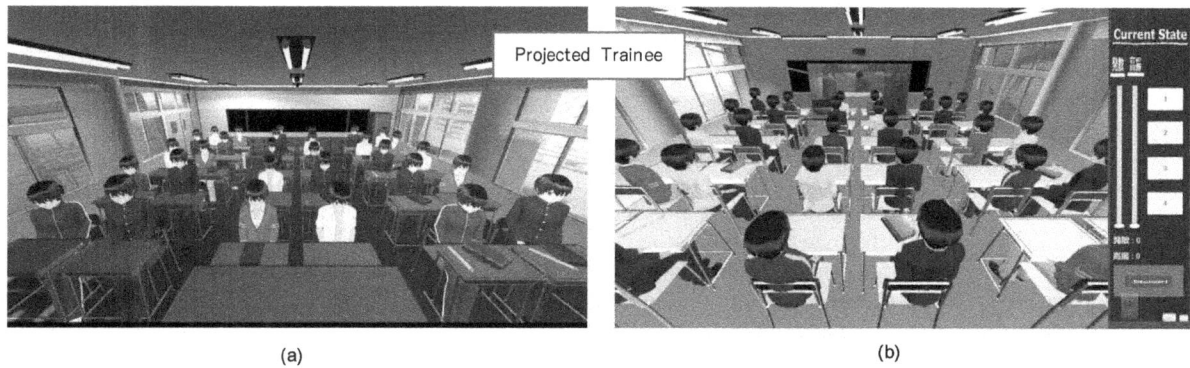

Figure 2. User interface of the proposed system. (a) the interface for trainee (b) the interface for the WOZ operator (wizard)

nodding frequently and so on. The probability for each virtual student to do certain behavior is manually assigned.

EVALUATION EXPERIMENT

In order to evaluate the proposed system, we conducted an evaluation experiment where subjects actually use the system for teaching skill practice sessions. Nine students of our college were recruited as the participants of the evaluation experiment. These participants were divided to three levels regarding to their experience in teaching. Three of them have no educational experience at all (L1), three of them are in the teacher-training course in our university or work as a cram school teacher with teaching experience less than 100 hours (L2), three of them have experience more than 100 hours (L3). The 100-hour criterion was determined from the approximation of a part-time job as two to threes hours per week for one year. We issued the materials for high-school level mathematics to the participants and asked them to prepare a 10-minute lecture prior to the experiment. The subject, mathematics was chosen because all of the subjects major in computer science, and we expect that more whiteboard-writing movements can be observed. During the experiment, the participants were organized to three groups where each group is comprised with one member from each level. For each group, every participant made a lecture while the other two members in that group played the operator role at the same time. Fig. 3 shows one scene of the use of the system in the evaluation experiment.

After each experiment session, every participant filled two questionnaires sheets, one as an operator and the the other one as a trainee. Table1 shows the results of the questionnaire survey. The questions with ID starts with alphabet, "O" are the ones as the operator role while the "T" questions are the ones as the trainee role. All questions are answered in the scale from 5 to 1 in the range of strongly agree to strongly disagree.

Overall, the system was evaluated as quite satisfying since most of the items exceed 4.0, and most of the participants expect that the system could be useful if it is further improved (T14). The system is higher evaluated in the items related to human-agent interaction. The virtual students reflect the

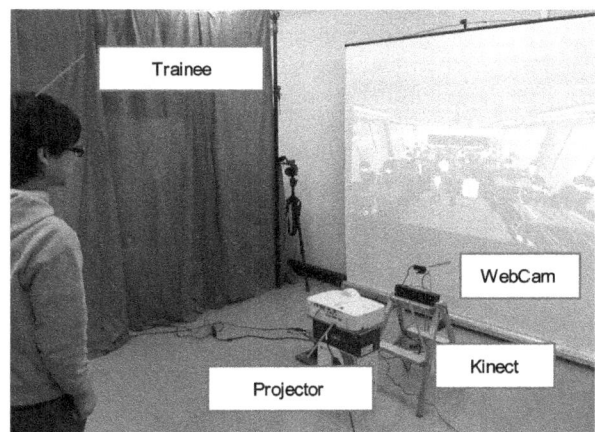

Figure 3. One scene of the use of the system in the evaluation experiment

intention of the operator and the trainee reacted to that. However, it is lower evaluated in the aspects related to the immersive environment. Also, some participants reported the inconvenience that they cannot walk into the class. During the experiment, there were some situations that the trainee could not successfully communicate with the virtual student. This is due to the limited number of pre-recorded voice track. In the actual field of education, students may have numerous number of behavior patterns so that it is impossible to implement all of them.

It is interesting that L1 participants often evaluated the system with relatively low scores (T07, T12: 2.67. Average: 4.00), while L2 participants often evaluated the system with high scores (O02, O10, T02, T14: 5.0. Average: 4.41). With the small number of participants, although it is hasty to draw conclusion at this time point, the results may come from the different level in the concern to education. Also, the L1 participants who has low experience seem to be less attentive to the environment and the virtual students.

CONCLUSIONS AND FUTURE WORKS

This paper presented a Wizard-of-Oz (WOZ) platform of simulated school environment, which can be utilized for teacher

Table 1. Questionnaire results of the evaluation experiment

ID	Question	L3	L2	L1	Avg.
O01	The system is comprehensive to operate.	4.00	4.67	4.67	4.44
O02	The virtual students can be operated in reflecting my intention.	4.00	5.00	4.67	4.67
O03	I can make the virtual students to say what I want them to say.	4.00	4.33	3.67	4.00
O04	The projected trainee looks coherent to the virtual classroom.	3.67	4.67	3.33	3.89
O05	It is easy to observe the projected trainee.	4.33	3.67	4.33	4.11
O06	I can operate the atmosphere in reflecting my intention.	4.33	4.67	4.00	4.33
O07	The behaviors of the virtual students had influence on the trainee.	4.67	4.67	4.33	4.56
O08	The utterances of the virtual students had influence on the trainee.	4.33	4.33	4.33	4.33
O09	The whole 30 virtual students can create some kind of atmosphere.	4.33	4.67	3.33	4.11
O10	The trainee reacted to the change of atmosphere.	4.67	5.00	4.33	4.67
T01	I feel that I was really teaching in a classroom.	4.67	4.00	3.67	4.11
T02	I could teach without being aware of the cameras.	4.00	5.00	4.33	4.44
T03	I felt that I was really standing in a classroom.	3.00	4.00	3.67	3.56
T04	The behaviors of the virtual students looked natural.	4.00	3.33	3.67	3.67
T05	The speech of the virtual students sounded natural.	3.33	4.00	4.00	3.78
T06	The number of virtual students is appropriate.	4.67	4.00	4.67	4.44
T07	The virtual students were listening to my lecture.	3.33	4.00	2.67	3.33
T08	I felt intimidated by the 30 students.	4.00	4.67	4.67	4.44
T09	The virtual students reacted to my instruction.	3.33	4.67	3.33	3.78
T10	I felt the atmosphere of a classroom.	4.00	4.33	3.67	4.00
T11	If there were less students, it could be more difficult to feel the atmosphere.	4.00	4.67	4.33	4.33
T12	I felt the change of the atmosphere.	4.33	4.33	2.67	3.78
T13	By using the system, it is possible to improve my teaching skill.	4.33	4.67	4.67	4.56
T14	By using a further improved version of the system, it is possible to improve my teaching skill.	4.67	5.00	4.67	4.78
T15	It is better to use this system to improve my teaching skill than the rehearsal with two people.	4.00	4.00	4.33	4.11
	Average	4.08	4.41	4.00	4.17

training or the examination of teacher recruitment from remote. This system is comprised of two front ends, one is a simulated classroom for the trainee, the other one is the interface for the system operator / investigator. The operator can control the group of students with an atmosphere model which is defined with concentration and arousal of virtual students. The prototype system is evaluated with subject experiment and the results show that it is generally satisfying with some drawbacks.

We plan to use this system to gather more trainee-operator interaction sessions. By analyzing the relationship with the reactions (both verbal and non-verbal signals) of the trainee toward the virtual students' behaviors and the performance evaluation from expert operators, we hope that we can conduct an automatic evaluation model of the performance of teacher trainees. Based on these results, we plan to develop a fully autonomous virtual classroom and conduct field tests in the future.

REFERENCES

1. Roghayeh Barmaki and Charles E. Hughes. 2015. Providing Real-time Feedback for Student Teachers in a Virtual Rehearsal Environment. In *17th International Conference on Multimodal Interaction (ICMI 2015)*. 531–537.

2. Haza el Jones, Nicolas Sabouret, Ionut Damian, Tobias Baur, Elisabeth Andrre, Kaska Porayska-Pomsta, and Paola Rizzo. 2014. Interpreting social cues to generate credible affective reactions of virtual job interviewers. In *arXiv:1402.5039v2*.

3. Patrick Kenny, Thomas D. Parsons, Jonathan Gratch, Anton Leuski, and Albert A. Rizzo. 2007. Virtual Patients for Clinical Therapist Skills Training. In *Proceedings of the 7th International Conference on Intelligent Virtual Agents (IVA'07)*. Paris, France, 192–210.

4. James A. Russell. 1980. A Circumplex Model of Affect. *Journal of Personality and Social Psychology* 39, 6 (1980), 1161–1178.

5. Aaron Williamon, Lisa Aufegger, and Hubert Eiholzer. 2014. Simulating and stimulating performance: introducing distributed simulation to enhance learning and performance. *Frontiers in Psychology* 5, 25 (February 2014), 1–9.

Ex-Amp Robot: Physical Avatar for Enhancing Human to Human Communication

Ai Kashii
Keio University, Faculty of
Environment and Information Studies
Fujisawa, Japan
tisbee@ht.sfc.keio.ac.jp

Kazunori Takashio
Keio University, Faculty of
Environment and Information Studies
Fujisawa, Japan
kaz@ht..sfc.keio.ac.jp

Hideyuki Tokuda
Keio University, Faculty of
Environment and Information Studies
Fujisawa, Japan
hxt@sfc.keio.ac.jp

ABSTRACT

Our research focuses on creating a robotic system that aids human-to-human communication. The robot acts as a personal companion that understands the user's emotions and helps express them alongside the user. First, the user's facial expression is detected through a connected camera device and relays the retrieved information to a humanoid robot. The humanoid robot then performs physical gestures that match the detected emotion. By using this system, those who are unable to freely move their own bodies can add a physical component to their communication method. In this paper, we have determined the efficacy of translating detected facial expressions into robot movements. Through experiments and surveys, we determined whether our proposed 'Ex-Amp Robot' helped enhance the communication of a hypothetically tetraplegic user.

Author Keywords

Facial expression detection; humanoid robot; gesture; communication; disability; body language; bodily presence.

ACM Classification Keywords

I.2.9. Artificial Intelligence: Robotics: Commercial Robots and Applications.

INTRODUCTION

There are diverse needs in society with which robots could lend a hand, whether it is in children's education, at retirement homes, or with customer service.

'Ex-Amp Robot', short for Expression Amplifying Robot, is a system in which a humanoid robot amplifies a human emotion by offering according robotic gestures and speech.

In this system, the users' facial expressions are continually captured from a video camera source so that the robot can perform gestures best suited to express the detected user's emotions in real-time. By having a robot by their side, users unable to move their own bodies may enjoy physical

HAI '16, October 04-07, 2016, Biopolis, Singapore
ACM 978-1-4503-4508-8/16/10.
http://dx.doi.org/10.1145/2974804.2980509

aspects of communication that would otherwise be absent. The physical expressions help to put an impact on parts of conversations, which would help raise conversation quality of such users.

REAL-LIFE ISSUES: TWO USE CASES

Around the world, there are many people who are unable to physically express their emotions to their peers, whether it is due to lack of physical existence due to remoteness or disabilities preventing the person from creating gestures.

Remoteness

People who are in remote places are unable to communicate physically. Skype, a popular video chat application, is a form of virtual communication. Other communication methods, such as phone calls and instant messeging, also lack physical aspects of communication. If two remote people could use robots as avatars to sense each other's physical existence, it would help them acknowledge each other's real-time emotion and state-of-being without being physically together. Therefore, this new method of communication would allow new aspects of propinquity to be shared by separated people. By sensing physical movement representative of an absent person's emotions, people may be able to better understand each other, which would enhance the current norm of communication. Figure 1 is a hypothetical setup in which a robotic avatar could be used to represent users in remote places.

Physical Disability

In addition to remoteness, people who are physically disabled, such as those who have paralysis, are also unable to create gestures and move their bodies to communicate physically. According to research by Mehrabian (1972), 55% of communication lies within body language [6]. For those who are unable to move their own bodies to communicate their message, using a personal robot as their second body would serve to expand their communication methods. By having the robot create body movements, these users could enhance their communication with their peers. The requirements for this use case are as follows:

- Facial expressions must detect the users' subtle expressions and correctly identify matched emotions

- Robots must preform body movements and gestures that suit the correctly identified emotions

- The timing of robot reactions must not disturb the conversation tempo of the user and conversation partner

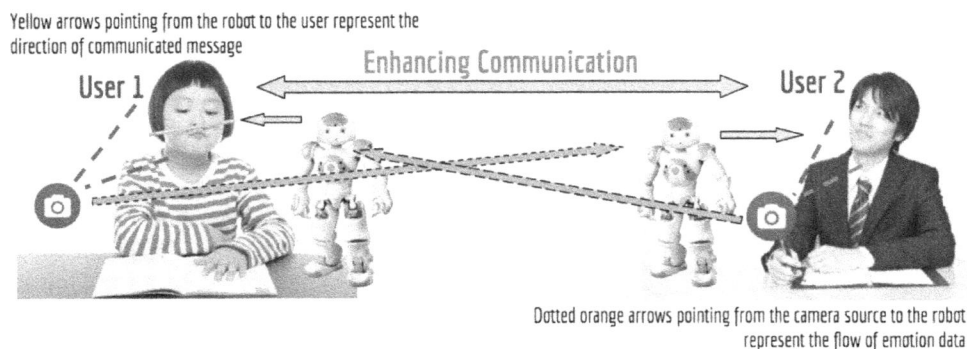

Yellow arrows pointing from the robot to the user represent the direction of communicated message

Enhancing Communication

User 1

User 2

Dotted orange arrows pointing from the camera source to the robot represent the flow of emotion data

Figure 1. Two users in remote places can experience physical communication using robot avatars.

- The conversation partner should be able to naturally understand and accept the robot's actions

In this paper, we will be discussing this use case in further detail.

RELATED RESEARCH

One related research to remote physical communication includes Pillow Talk by Little Riot [5]. This system allows couples to sleep to their partners' heartbeats using a pair of devices and wristbands. When a user wears the wristband, it monitors the user's heart rate and sends the information to their partner's device. The device, which can create thumping movements in sync with the partner's heart rate, allows the partner to sleep feeling their partner's heartbeats through a pillow. This experience offers a romantic and soothing physical connection between remote couples that are unable to share a bed. It helps remote users share their existence and strengthens physical aspects of communication. Similar to the intentions of this product, we would like to create a system that allows remote users to share not only their existence, but also their feelings and emotions in real time.

In Li's study, communication of emotion in social robots was tested through simple head and arm movements. They demonstrated in their research that "ratings of lifelikeness [in robot gestures] were found to be related to the number of arm movements (but not head movements) in a gesture" [4]. Therefore, we have decided that arm movements were key in designing the robot reaction gestures. Bates also states that "appropriately timed and clearly expressed emotion is a central requirement for believable" robotic agents [2]. Without the tuning of specific gestures and verbal cues, a physical avatar is not fully useful. Robots must have believability; in other words, conversation partners must be able to take in and understand the robot's expressions for the robot to be effective in aiding communication.

OriHime is a communication robot that serves as a representation of remote users including disabled and remote people [8]. By using this robot, users can see the robot's surrounding environment and converse with others as though they are in the same room. It creates motions according to the user's choice of preset answers. Some of the action buttons include "Yes", "Hey", and "Hug". 'OriHime eye' targets users with incurable neuromuscular disease and allows them to control their robot through gaze tracking technology. Our research targets a similar disabled audience; however, it differs in two areas:

1. The Ex-Amp Robot uses a fully humanoid robot that has legs and arms that represent the physique of human beings more truly

2. Detected emotion data, a tuple of an emotion label (text) and a level value (1-100%) is published

Our research focuses on creating absent body language; therefore, a humanoid robot helps conversation partners to visualize and better understand the user's body language compared to non-humanoid robots. Also, representing emotion according to detected expressions is a truer representation of the user than manual user response operation. There are various research on emotion detection not only through facial expression analysis, but also speech and other multimodal information [3, 7].

ROBOT SYSTEM

As previously mentioned, the Ex-Amp Robot has two unique use cases. For this research, we focused on creating a system targeted towards users with physical disabilities.

Approach

We first set a camera before the user's face to capture facial expressions. The captured information is relayed to the robot, which moves its body according to the detected emotion. Using the Ex-Amp robot, the user is able to experience an enhanced method of communication, as the conversation partner will be able to receive physical aspects of communication— something that would otherwise be absent from a paralyzed person. This proposed system is specifically targeted towards people who are physically disabled but have full capacity of creating facial expressions.

System Configuration

For facial expression detection, we revised Affectiva's released code of AffdexMe [1]. This iPhone application allows real-time emotion detection (Figure 2). With advanced facial analysis features, it identifies a face and scales emotion values extracted from an iPhone camera.

The system connects this facial expression detection application and a robot with a third party MQTT service. We chose to work with a cloud MQTT service, since it is location independent and allows for continuous subscription and publishing that would integrate well with both the iPhone and robot's application code. Its continuous and instant service allowed for data signals to be transferred quickly enough to suit the speed of a natural human conversation. Figure 3 shows the system configuration diagram of the system, and Figure 4 shows the four main action-reactions of the robot, which include speech and gestures for the emotions joy, anger, sadness, and disgust.

In short, the list below describes the system flow:

1. Camera captures facial expression to identify user's emotion

2. Detected emotion data is published onto a designated MQTT channel

3. The robot, subscribed to the designated MQTT channel, receives the message

4. Robot performs gestures when the expressions joy, sadness, anger, and disgust are detected at a level higher than 80%

EXPERIMENTATION

We conducted experiments by having 7 people experience a conversation with the robot intermediate. All experimentees were asked to take part in two 5-minute conversations to experience being both the user and the conversation partner. 6 out of the 7 experimentees were female, and all experimentees had previous knowledge and/or experience with the NAO robot. At the end of each experimentation session, we conducted a survey to collect feedback of impressions. We asked questions to be answered on a scale of 1 to 10, 10 being strongly agree. Table 1 lists the survey questions and the average rating of responses to each survey question.

Figure 2. Smartphone application. Using the iPhone's inside camera, the application continuously captures and measures facial features to return degrees of emotion values in real time.

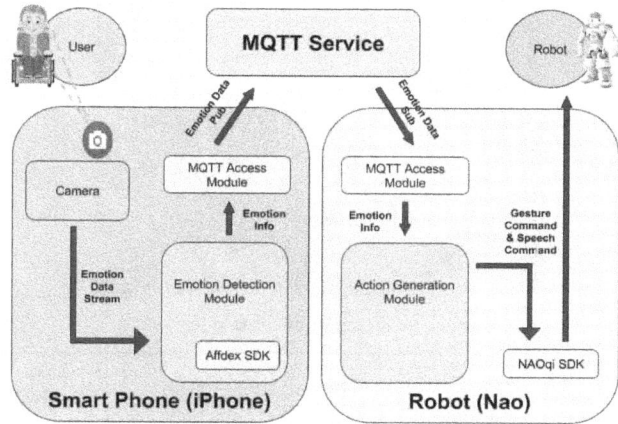

Figure 3. System Configuration Diagram.

Figure 4. Action Reactions (gestures and dialogue) of the robot for each expression.

Experimentation Setup

For the experiment, two experimentees sat facing each other for casual conversation. Figure 5 shows the experiment setup layout. The experimentee on the couch played the role of the paralyzed user, while the conversation partner sat across facing both the user and the Ex-Amp Robot. Through the experiment, we stressed to have the users imagine themselves as paralyzed, with no ability to move their limbs. The iPhone was set in front of the user with a thin clear rod, which avoided the setup from disturbing the conversation. The robot was mounted on a rack to match the eye-level of the conversation partner.

Experimentation Result

Through experimentation, we found that on average, users felt that communication was more enhanced with a Robot intermediate at a 7.5 rating. On the other hand, the conversation partners felt that they were able to better understand the user's emotions at an average rating of 6.0. The higher rating for the user was most likely due to the

Figure 5. Experiment setup layout.

Questions	Ave. Rating
Did this system enhance your communication as a user?	7.5
Did you feel you understood the other person better as a conversation partner?	6.0
Was the robot annoying?	2.8
Was the system fun to use?	8.1
How accurately did the robot actions match the conversation content?	4.0
Did the robot actions derail the conversation?	4.3
Would you want to use the system again?	7.5
What would you rate the timing and speed of the system?	9.3
Did you feel a need to comment on the robot to keep a natural conversation going?	7.5
What do you rate the accuracy of expression recognition?	7.8

Table 1. Average rating responses to each survey question.

sense of purpose, whereas the conversation partners felt uneasy using this new method of physical communication. Some were unsure where to look and who to face, as the iPhone partially blocked their view of the user's face.

Average rating for the accuracy of the robot gestures to the conversation content was 4.0. This will be discussed in further detail in the next section. The level of annoyance of the system was rated at 2.8 and using this Ex-Amp system was deemed 'fun' at an average of 8.1 points; therefore, in general, most people had good impressions of using the intermediary robot for enhancing communication.

DISCUSSION AND FUTURE WORK
The accuracy of the robot gestures to the conversation content was given a poor rating of 4.0 on average. The reason may be due to the predominant Japanese culture that values under-expressiveness and showing respect to others. In a culture where it is natural to hide true feelings with a smile to be polite, many users felt that their smiles were correctly detected but the emotion "joy" was inappropriate for the conversation context.

CONCLUSION
The hypothesis that having an expression amplifying robot system would help enhance the communication between users with physical disabilities and their conversation partners was deemed valid, as results showed that experimentees felt their communication was enhanced and emotions better communicated using this system. The successful points of this experiment were the accuracy of the facial detection and the quick speed of the robotic gesture translations. The existence of the humanoid robot allowed for a conversation-friendly atmosphere, and users were able to enjoy their experience using this robot as an intermediate. However, it can be clearly noted from results that robot gestures did not always match the conversation context. To improve on this aspect, multimodal features, such as context sorting and keyword recognition would be necessary. Moreover, with the recognition of more types of micro expressions, this research could potentially prove how much a robot could aid mutual understanding and enhance human-to-human communication.

We wish to further pursue this research by testing the system on users at elderly care facilities as well as testing for remote use.

REFERENCES
1. Affdex, "White Paper: Exploring the Emotion Classifiers Behind Affdex Facial Coding". 10 Mar. 2016. http://www.affectiva.com/wp-content/uploads/2014/09/Whitepaper___Exploring_Affdex_Classifiers.pdf.

2. J. Bates. The role of emotion in believable agents. Source Communications of the ACM archive, 37(Issue 7):122 – 125, July 1994.

3. Busso, Carlos, "Analysis of Emotion Recognition using Facial Expressions, Speech, and Multimodal Information". ICMI '04. 2004 Oct. 13-15.

4. Li, J. and Chignell, M., 2011. Communication of emotion in social robots through simple head and arm movements. International Journal of Social Robotics, 3(2), pp.125-142.

5. Little Riot, "About Pillow Talk". Web. 1 May 2015. http://www.littleriot.com/pillow-talk/.

6. Mehrabian, A. "Nonverbal Communication," New Brunswick: Aldine Transaction, 82, 1972.

7. M. Suwa, N. Sugie and K. Fujimora, "A preliminary note on pattern recognition of human emotional expression," in International Joint Conference on Pattern Recognition, pp. 408-410, 1978

8. Orylab, "OriHime", 2 Aug. 2016 https://orihime.orylab.com/.

Interaction in a Natural Environment: Estimation of Customer's Preference Based on Nonverbal Behaviors

Hidehito Honda
The University of Tokyo
Tokyo, Japan
hitohonda.02@gmail.com

Ryosuke Hisamatsu
The University of Tokyo
Tokyo, Japan
r-his@fg8.so-net.ne.jp

Yoshimasa Ohmoto
Kyoto University
Kyoto, Japan
ohmoto@i.kyoto-u.ac.jp

Kazuhiro Ueda
The University of Tokyo
Tokyo, Japan
ueda@gregorio.c.u-tokyo.ac.jp

ABSTRACT

We examined the interaction in face-to-face selling situation. In particular, we examined how customer's nonverbal behaviors were related to their preference in a natural environment. We found that customers' body posture could be a good predictor about their preference. We also found that estimation on customer's preference could be achieved from two nonverbal behaviors better than single behavior. We discuss the present contributions toward constructing the efficient agent systems.

Author Keywords

nonverbal behaviors; estimation of preferences; interaction in the natural environment

ACM Classification Keywords

H.5.m. Information interfaces and presentation (e.g., HCI): Miscellaneous; J.4 [Social and behavioral Sciences]

INTRODUCTION

Recent studies on human-computer interaction have shown that people can effectively interact with an agent when the agent behaves like a human, and that nonverbal behaviors (e.g., facial expression, posture, eye contact, gesture) play an important role in such interaction (e.g., [2, 7, 11]). In estimating user's preference and recommend products or services based on the estimated preference, if a computer agent can utilize the information about users' nonverbal behaviors in estimating their preference, the estimation will be more effective.

Previous studies [1, 6, 9, 10, 12] have shown that nonverbal behaviors (e.g., gaze direction, body posture, prosody or head position) are correlated with people's mental states (e.g., interest, persuasiveness, or satisfaction). Thus, nonverbal behaviors will be good predictors for people's mental state.

Toward constructing the agent which can estimate users' preference based on their nonverbal behaviors and propose an appropriate products or services, it is necessary to examine the relationship between nonverbal behaviors and

preference in a natural environment. Although many previous studies have examined the relationship between people's nonverbal behaviors and their mental states in a laboratory experiment to clarify their significant relationships, few studies have been conducted in a natural environment. In a natural environment, human behaviors are highly complicating and it is not sure whether previous findings in laboratory settings are true in a natural environment. Given that people behave with multiple nonverbal behaviors in a natural environment, multiple nonverbal behaviors may be effective predictors. Actually, psychological studies have suggested that people's mental states can be estimated using multiple nonverbal behaviors more effectively (e.g., [2, 3, 5, 8]).

In order to examine the above issue, we conducted an experiment about face-to-face selling situation in a natural environment and examined interaction in such environment. In particular, we examined how nonverbal behaviors were related to people's preference in a natural environment.

EXPERIMENT

Participants

Ten shop clerks (M_{age} = 30.20, SD_{age} = 5.47, they were all women) and fifteen customers (11 women and 4 men, M_{age} = 50.93, SD_{age} = 10.47) participated in this experiment. The shop clerks were actual workers for a travel agency company. For the customers, we recruited people who were interested in travel with families and wanted to consult about their travel plans.

Experimental procedure

We conducted a travel consultation task (see Figure 1). In this task, a customer consulted a shop clerk about travel plan, and the shop clerk proposed some travel plans. Each customer participated in the consultation task for two different shop clerks, and each shop clerk participated for three different customers (in total, we conducted 30 consultation tasks). Consultation time was limited to thirty minutes. During consultation, the shop clerk was required to estimate the customer's preference on travel plan and to propose a plan based on the estimation on customer's preference.

HAI '16, October 04-07, 2016, Biopolis, Singapore
ACM 978-1-4503-4508-8/16/10.
http://dx.doi.org/10.1145/2974804.2980512

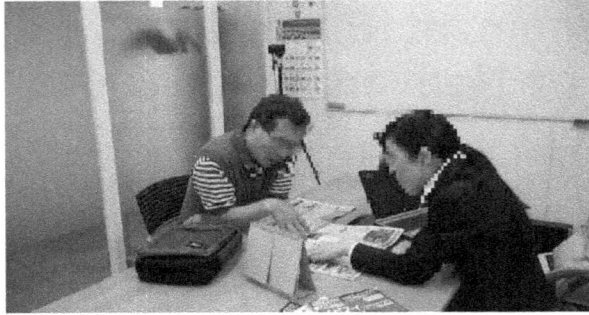

Figure 1. Travel consultation task.

In order to enhance natural interaction during the consultation, we did not have any controls except for the consultation time. After the consultation, customers were asked to answer questionnaire about plans proposed by the shop clerk during consultation (three to six plans were proposed in one consultation). Customers were asked to rate how they felt the proposed plan using 7 point scale (1: not attractive at all, 7: very attractive).

Each consultation was recorded with video.

RESULTS

We focused on the following customer's nonverbal behaviors, which were salient during consultations: Customer gazes at the clerk (hereafter, CG), Customer's body leans forward (hereafter, LF), Customers puts their hand on the cheek (hereafter, HC), and Customer's nodding (hereafter, CN). For each video data, we put annotations on nonverbal behaviors using ELAN (https://tla.mpi.nl/tools/tla-tools/elan/). In particular, we put the information about when each nonverbal behavior started and ended during 30 minutes' consultation.

We analyzed these nonverbal behaviors with the following procedure. First, we calculated the proportion of times each behavior appeared both while the customer was proposing a plan and during 30 seconds after the plan was proposed. For example, when a shop clerk proposed a plan for 20 seconds (e.g., she talked about a specific hotel as a recommendation for 20 seconds), we examined the behaviors for 50 (30 + 20) seconds. Hereafter, we call this period, *proposal period*. Suppose that CG, LF, and HC appeared for (10sec, 10sec, and 5sec) during the proposal period. The calculated proportions were (0.2, 0.2, and 0.1). Thus, these values indicate the proportions of behavioral appearance during the proposal period. As to CN, we counted the number of appearance during the proposal period. We used these values as the measure of appearance of behavior to in the following analyses.

Table 1 shows the distribution of customer's rating (attractiveness for proposed plan) in questionnaire. More than 50% of rating was highly scored (6, 7). Based on this result, we regarded ratings of 6 and 7 as strong preference and those of 1-5 as weak preference. Figure 2 shows distribution of appearance of the four nonverbal behaviors: CG, LF, HC and CN. It was found that nonverbal behaviors generally

appeared with small proportion (or low frequency) during the proposal period. Accordingly, we dichotomized appearance of nonverbal behavior into strong or weak appearance based on median value. That is, when the proportion (or frequency) of appearance was more than or equal to median value, we regarded the appearance as strong appearance. Otherwise, the appearance was regarded as weak appearance. In the following statistical analyses, we used these dichotomized variables.

Table 1. Distribution of customer's rating for proposed plan.

1	2	3	4	5	6	7
0.009	0.073	0.027	0.145	0.164	0.300	0.282

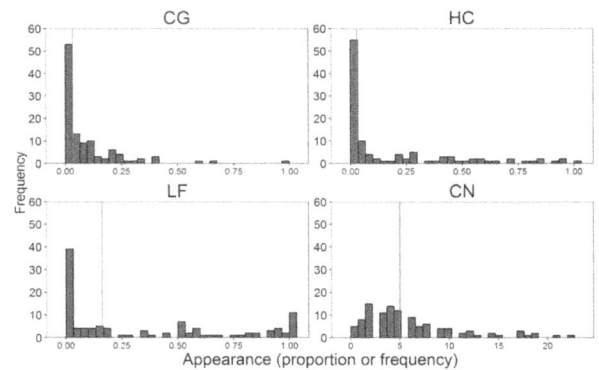

Figure 2. Distribution of appearance of nonverbal behaviors. The solid red line indicates the median value.

Estimation of preference based on nonverbal behaviors

In order to examine whether nonverbal behaviors could estimate customer's preference, we conducted the following logistic regression analyses.

Strength of preference was used as dependent variable (1; strong preference, 0; weak preference), and strengths of appearance in nonverbal behaviors were used as independent variables (1; strong appearance, 0; weak appearance). In this model, we assumed the main effects of the four nonverbal behaviors. In addition, we assumed second-order interaction. In particular, we assumed that interactive effect occurred when two nonverbal behaviors co-appeared strongly. Thus, we defined values of interaction variables in the logistic regression analyses by multiplication. For example, the values of interaction in CG and HC took 1 when they co-appeared strongly. Otherwise, the values took 0.

We first assumed the model including main effects of CG, HC, LF, and CN and second-order interactions of CG/HC, CG/LF, CG/CN, HC/LF, HC/CN, and LF/CN. Based on this model, we examined whether each of the variables (i.e., main effects and interactions) had effective explanation powers on the dependent variable using a stepwise method. Here, each least effective coefficient was deleted until the elimination of a coefficient no longer led to a better model. We used AIC as a criterion in this examination.

We found that the model including interactions of HC/LF and LF/CN was the best model. Table 2 shows estimated coefficients for this model. Although the two interactions, HC/LF and LF/CN, were selected as the independent variables as the best model, only LF/CN was significant.

Note that the two interaction variables in the best model comprised of LF, suggesting that LF would correlate with the mental state indicating preference. Thus, we examined proportions of strong preference as a function of behavioral strength for HC/LF, LF/CN, and LF. Figure 4 shows the results of this examination. It was found for all three behaviors, the proportion of strong preference was significantly higher when behavioral strength was strong than when it was weak ($p < .05$, Fisher's exact test). Although there was not significant differences in proportion of strong preference in strong behavioral appearance between any pair of nonverbal behaviors ($p > .1$, Fisher's exact test), the proportion of strong preference in HC/LF or LF/CN was higher than that in LF. These results suggested that although LF alone might be a good predictor for preference, accuracy of estimation on the preference could be improved by focusing on multiple nonverbal behaviors.

Table 2. Estimated coefficients for the best model in the logistic regression analysis.

Variable	Estimated value	Z-value	
Intercept	-0.23	-0.93	
HC/LF	0.91	1.64	
LF/CN	1.12	2.35	*

*p < .05

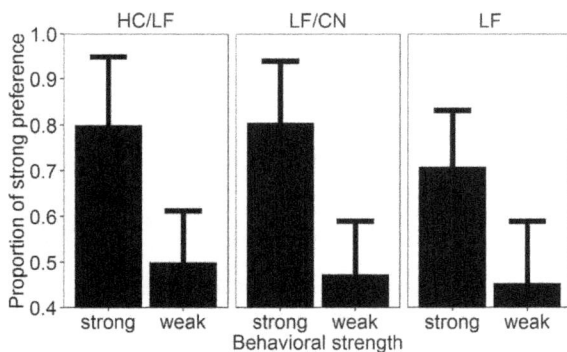

Figure 4. Proportion of strong preference as a function of behavioral strength. Error bar denotes 95% confidence interval.

DISCUSSION

Our findings are summarized with the following two points: First, in estimating customer's preference through face-to-face selling situation, customer's leaning forward behavior can be a good predictor about her/his preference. Second, customer's preference can be more accurately estimated from the predictor comprised of two nonverbal behaviors, i.e. LF/CN.

Our findings showed that body posture (i.e., customer's body leans forward) was a good predictor for customer's preference. Previous study have reported the analogous findings in the experimental setting (e.g., [9]). These findings indicate that body posture is strongly related to people's mental state in many situations.

As we described before, few previous studies have examined how nonverbal behaviors and preference are related in a natural environment wherein human behaviors are complicating. Our findings suggest that nonverbal behaviors can be a good predictor in such environment. In particular, when multiple nonverbal behaviors are used for predictors, the accuracy of prediction on preference will increase.

These findings suggest that in constructing an agent which recommends appropriate products or services on the basis of estimation on customer's preference, the agent can make accurate estimations about customer's preference based on customer's multiple nonverbal behaviors.

ACKNOWLEDGMENTS

This research was a collaborative work between Ueda Laboratory at the University of Tokyo and JTB Tourism Research & Consulting Co. The experiment conducted in this research was supported by JTB Tourism Research & Consulting Co., JTB Tokyo Metropolitan Corp, and JTB Corp. This research was supported in part by Grant-in-Aid on Innovative Areas (NO. 26118002).

REFERENCES

1. Jeremy N. Bailenson and Nick Yee. 2005. Digital Chameleons: Automatic Assimilation of Nonverbal Gestures in Immersive Virtual Environments. Psychol. Sci. 16, 10 (October 2005), 814–819.

2. Tanja Bänziger, Marcello Mortillaro, and Klaus R. Scherer. 2012. Introducing the Geneva Multimodal expression corpus for experimental research on emotion perception. Emotion 12, 5 (October 2012), 1161–1179.

3. Olivier Collignon et al. 2008. Audio-visual integration of emotion expression. Brain Res. 1242 (November 2008), 126–135.

4. Andrew J. Cowell and Kay M. Stanney. 2005. Manipulation of non-verbal interaction style and demographic embodiment to increase anthropomorphic computer character credibility. Int. J. Hum. Comput. Stud. 62, 2 (February 2005), 281–306.

5. Beatrice de Gelder and Jean Vroomen. 2000. The perception of emotions by ear and by eye. Cogn. Emot. 14, 3 (May 2000), 289–311.

6. Shinya Fujie, Yasushi Ejiri, Hideaki Kikuchi, and Tetsunori Kobayashi. 2005. Recognition of

positive/negative attitude and its application to a spoken dialogue system. IEICE Trans. Inf. Syst. (Japanese Ed. J88-D-II, 3 (2005), 489–498.

7. Katherine Isbister and Clifford Nass. 2000. Consistency of personality in interactive characters: verbal cues, non-verbal cues, and user characteristics. Int. J. Hum. Comput. Stud. 53, 2 (August 2000), 251–267.

8. Marc Mehu and Laurens van der Maaten. 2014. Multimodal Integration of Dynamic Audio–Visual Cues in the Communication of Agreement and Disagreement. J. Nonverbal Behav. 38, 4 (2014), 569–597.

9. Selene Mota and Rosalind W. Picard. 2003. Automated Posture Analysis for Detecting Learner's Interest Level. Comput. Vis. Pattern Recognit. Work. 2003. CVPRW '03. Conf. 5 (2003), 49.

10. Yoshimasa Ohmoto, Takashi Miyake, and Toyoaki Nishida. 2012. Dynamic estimation of emphasizing points for user satisfaction evaluations. In Proceedings of the 34th Annual Conference of the Cognitive Science Society. 2115–2120.

11. Lingyun Qiu and Izak Benbasat. 2009. Evaluating Anthropomorphic Product Recommendation Agents: A Social Relationship Perspective to Designing Information Systems. J. Manag. Inf. Syst. 25, 4 (April 2009), 145–182.

12. William T. Stoltzman. 2006. Toward a social signaling framework: Activity and emphasis in speech. (Doctoral dissertation, Massachusetts Institute of Technology).

Ear Ball for Empathy:
To realize the sensory experience of people with Autism spectrum disorder.

Taisuke Murakami
Aichi Shukutoku University
2-9, Katahira, Nagakute-city,
Aichi Prefecture, Japan.
taisum@asu.aasa.ac.jp

ABSTRACT

Autism spectrum disorder (ASD) are characterized by difficulties in sensory integration and a body image which differs from the normal, healthy one. In order to enable healthy people to experience and thus develop a deeper understanding of the different body image that people with developmental disorders possess the author is pursuing research into the simulation of sensory experiences common to ASD. This study focuses on a particular sensory characteristic of ASD where difficulty is experienced in locating the source of sound in an environment and the development of a device for simulating the sense of hearing experienced in such a disorder. Workshops for children were carried out using the developed device, with interviews indicating that the majority of participants experienced feelings of ambiguity in relation to their own senses. Such a feeling in one's sensory boundaries is a phenomenon which is common in ASD research. It was concluded that the device developed in this study allowed people to vicariously experience the senses of people with ASD.

Author Keywords

Autism spectrum disorder, Integration of sense, Workshop of children

ACM Classification Keywords

B.1.1 [Hardware]: *Hardwired control* H.5.5 [Information Systems]: Sound and Music Computing.

INTRODUCTION

Is it possible to share a picture of the world held by another person who has a different sensory experience from your own? The present author has approached this question through studies on ASD. The way people with ASD cognize the world is different from typically developing

HAI '16, October 04-07, 2016, Biopolis, Singapore.
ACM 978-1-4503-4508-8/16/10.
http://dx.doi.org/10.1145/2974804.2980516

(TD) people because of different sensory integration between them. For this reason, people with ASD may have a unique picture of the world. The present author does not look at people with ASD as someone that should be more normal or healthier, but as the one who perceive various things in the world in a different manner from TD people. This world is made up of a diverse spectrum of world images, and the present author is searching for a way of constructing the world based on these pluralistic images of the world.

PROJECT DESCRIPTION

ASD is a disorder where people have problems integrating their senses, and it is believed that they have a different body image from the one TD would have. The present author is working on research to simulate the ASD sensory experience in order for TD people to grasp the ASD body image and deepened the understanding of it. This study focused on the unique sensorial characteristics of people with ASD, and we developed a device that simulates their sense of hearing. [Figure 1]

Figure 1. The Device.

By using that device, we hold a workshop for children and interviewed them. It was made clear that many of them had an experience that their sense of the self and others became blurred. This type of sensory experience that blurs the boundary between the self and others is a phenomenon that has been commonly reported in the studies done by people with ASD. Thus, it is believed that the device developed for this study is able to give TD people the ASD sensory experience. [Figure 2]

Figure 2. A workshop for children.

About the Device that was Created
We developed a device that gives people the ASD sensory experience by simulating the sense of hearing that people with ASD experience. First, we made a binaural microphone in the shape of human ears to capture the sounds within space in the same manner that humans do. [Figure 3]

Figure 3. A binaural microphone.

To spatially separate the voices the subject actually heard by his ears and the voices from the binaural microphone, headphones were prepared to receive the voices that were captured and wirelessly sent by the binaural microphone. Then, the binaural microphone and wireless transmitter were installed into a sphere approximately the size of a child's head, which was made to be portable. [Figure 4]

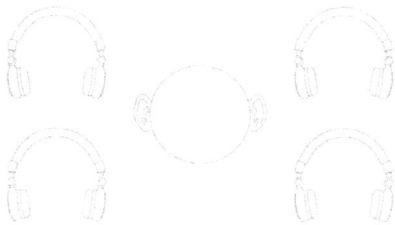
Figure 4. A binaural microphone and wireless headphones.

In this way, the person wearing the headphones was able to hear the voices from the binaural microphone in their ears; however, the direction the binaural microphone was facing to was not the same as the direction that the subject was facing to. This type of device design separates the person wearing the headphone's aural sense of direction (caused by the time difference in sound between both ears) from their bodily sense of direction. This allowed for an experience as if one's own physical body was separate from one's sense of hearing.

The Device Caused Experiences
The device made by the present author has been announced primarily for children's workshops. One of the main announcements was made at the French Art center Le CUBE in 2011, and a children's workshop was held at Acclimatation Park in Bois de Boulogne, France in 2012. This workshop developed a variety of games by using the device. [Figure 5]

Figure 5. Children wearing the headphones sit in a circle.

One such game has four children wearing headphones sit in a circle and have a conversation with one another while passing around the binaural microphone sphere. When they do this, they do not know where other voices come from. In the interview that was conducted after this game, many of the children said that they could not figure out which one was their own voice. Moreover, one child said that his sense of the self and others was confused during the game and he felt like he became a different child. Thus, it is believed that simulating different sensory experiences between ASD and TD and creating a place to realize such people with ASD has demonstrated pluralistic possibilities in the way people perceive the world according to different sensory experiences.

Acknowledgements
I would like to thank Professor Satoru Takahashi who provided carefully considered feedback and valuable comments. I would also like to thank Professor Motomi Toichi who provided technical help and sincere encouragement.

REFERENCES
1. AXEL BRAUNS, Buntschatten und Fledermause, Hamburg: Hoffmann und Campe Verlag, 2002.

2. NAOKI HIGASHIDA, The Reason I Jump, London: SCEPTRE, 2013.

3. TEMPLE GRANDIN, Thinking in Pictures, New York: Doubleday, 1995.

Process of Agency Identification Based on the Desire to Communicate in Embodied Interaction

Takafumi Sakamoto
Graduate School of Science and Technology,
Shizuoka University
3-5-1 Johoku, Naka-ku, Hamamatsu, Shizuoka
4328011, Japan
dgs14010@s.inf.shizuoka.ac.jp

Yugo Takeuchi
Graduate School of Science and Technology,
Shizuoka University
3-5-1 Johoku, Naka-ku, Hamamatsu, Shizuoka
4328011, Japan
takeuchi@inf.shizuoka.ac.jp

ABSTRACT

Humans can communicate because they adapt and adjust their behavior to each other. We hypothesize that developing a relationship with others requires coordinating the desire to communicate and that this coordination is related to agency identification. To model this initial phase of communication, we created an experimental environment to observe the interaction between a human and an abstract-shaped robot whose behavior, moving on the floor and rotating, was mapped by another human. The participants were required to verbalize what they were thinking or feeling while interacting with the robot. At present, we do not have a sufficient number of participants, and experiments and data analysis are ongoing. We must verify the effects of interaction patterns and inspect what type of action and reaction are regarded as signals that enhance interpersonal interaction.

Author Keywords

Interaction; agency; communication relationship;

ACM Classification Keywords

H.1.2. User/Machine Systems: Human information processing

INTRODUCTION

Humans have the social ability, such as theory of mind, to adjust their behavior according to the behavior and mental states of others [9]. In addition, to behave without being affected is an important adjustment in our social life, exemplified through situations such as passing someone in a crowd or sitting next to a stranger in a public space. The behavior of objects, on the other hand, is normally regarded as inanimate or lacking emotion. Despite this, we often treat computers as agents [10]. Whether or not we recognize others or objects as agents, which have a mental state and are able to regulate their own behavior, depends on actual interaction. Some

HAI'16, Oct 04–07, 2016, Biopolis, Singapore
© 2016 Copyright held by the owner/author(s).
ACM ISBN 978-1-4503-4508-8/16/10.
DOI: http://dx.doi.org/10.1145/2974804.2980518

research also indicates that social cognition is embodied interaction [4, 2]. In this study, we hypothesize the process of interaction that develops into interpersonal relationship as the initial phase of communication and try to model it.

Human-human communication, such as language, facial expression, gaze, gesture, posture, and spacing, is carried out intricately and simultaneously. To model the process of establishing a relationship, we need to narrow these elements down to one simple element. Humans manipulate distance between others based on context or relationship [5]. Approaching someone normally indicates a level of interest in that person. Spatial interaction is observed in many animals; therefore it appears to be a primitive and basic interaction. Thus, we focus on spacing coordination as a starting point to simplify modeling. Research on minimum interaction indicates that people recognize other people without cues provided beforehand because of our ability to form extemporaneous joint action or turn-taking with each other [1, 6]. However, little research has been done on interaction when the participants have no prior knowledge of or context for, such as experimental tasks, the interaction partner. These participants attempt to interact with their partner from the beginning because they are motivated to complete tasks. We assume that the initial phase of communication has the aspect of participants coordinating interest in or wanting to communicate with their partners. We need to consider the situation in which participants are able to ignore their partner's behavior or are not interested in the partner. Our experiment is carried out with no instruction about interaction with the partner. In order to clarify how people behave and coordinate relationships in the initial phase of communication, we conducted an experiment in which the participants interact with an ostensibly unknown artifact whose behavior actually mirrors another participant's movement. By modeling this process, artifacts, such as a robot, become able to form relationships adaptively with humans, estimate human desire to communicate, or display a specific pattern of notification of communication.

INITIAL COMMUNICATION PHASE

In this section, we describe our concept of the initial communication phase and our research method. We assume that the initial communication phase has two aspects: mutual behavioral coordination depending on the desire to communicate and the process of agency identification. Interaction between humans and encountering entities that possess physical bodies always is affected, even if the entities do not move at all. Despite this, we are able to ignore entities that are irrelevant to us. We assume that embodied interaction is carried out subconsciously before initiating conscious interaction (Figure 1). In this subconscious interaction, some specific pattern or message causes human cognitive activity to be concerned about the entity's mental state. This interaction then progresses to the next phase in which both actors coordinate their desire to communicate with each other. As an example, when we need directions in an unfamiliar place, we look for someone to ask by gazing at or approaching a person we believe can help. Naturally, we can direct this signal depending on our own desire to communicate.

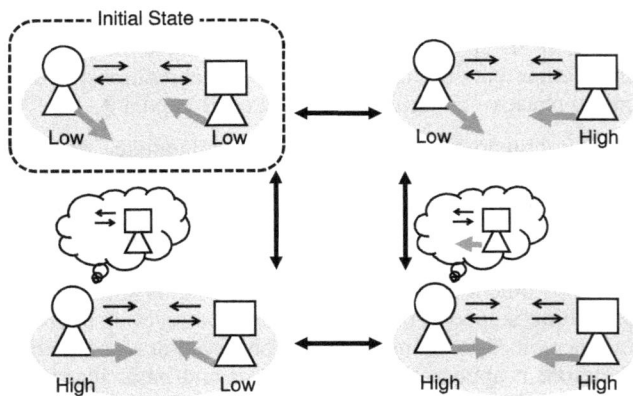

Figure 1. State of desire to communicate

In human communication, we can immediately identify human partners. The human brain possesses an area that is specifically designed to detect the human body [3]. In addition, as the phenomenon of "biological motion" illustrates [7], we have a specific perception for recognizing human body movement. On the basis of these abilities, other people are regarded as agents with which we can communicate. On the other hand, artifacts, especially non-humanoid, non-animal, or abstract-shaped robots, must build a social relationship beyond just being objects (Figure 2). The artifacts' behavior must convey to human abstract thinking that their motions contain some intention or meaning. We hypothesize that some interaction pattern or joint action formed subconsciously on the physical level acts as a signal. Because the interaction partner has been already recognized as an agent, this does not continue. When interaction collapses, the partner seems to be regarded as an object. We assume that a social relationship can repeatedly form and collapse through interaction.

A think-aloud method is useful for investigating changes in mental states regarding an object. Without clues, it is difficult to segment physical interaction. By getting participants to speak about their thinking or feelings during interaction, we can identify the interaction and the development of recognition of the interaction partner can be observed. We also aim to detect any cues that indicate that the object is being perceived as an agent with a mental state.

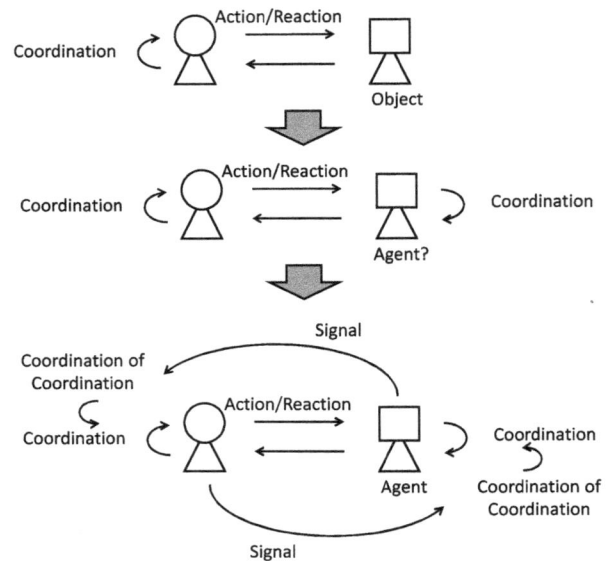

Figure 2. Agency identification

PREVIOUS EXPERIMENT

In our previous study, we conducted an experiment in which the participants interacted with a robot that had only one function: moving on the floor. Synchronizing motion is possibly a cue to start recognizing a robot as an agent (Figure 3). Some research indicates that synchronization of behavior between humans occurs unconsciously and is necessary for joint action with others [8, 11]. Thus, we can conclude that synchronizing motion with objects causes a phase shift from the initial phase in our hypothetical model. However, whether behavior including synchronization is accidental or not is unclear and difficult to determine from our previous experiment. Furthermore, it is too difficult for us to identify the desire to communicate because we confuse the mutual coordination of desire and the process of identification of agency, such as testing the regularity of behavior. To solve this problem, in this study, we use a robot that can perform a rotating motion in addition to moving about the floor. In this way, behaviors can obviously indicate whether the robot can think or not and whether it desires or doesn't desire to form a relationship.

EXPERIMENT

In this section, we describe the details of our experiment for investigating the process of how people realize that an interaction partner has the ability to construct a communication relationship and wants to establish a relationship with them. We observed interaction between humans and robots. It is difficult for participants to recognize that a robot's motion corresponds with another participant's motion without interaction. However, the robot's behavior is certainly capable of building an interpersonal relationship through interaction. Therefore, we observed the interaction between a human and a robot that was not previously perceived as an agency, but behaves as an agent. In addition, we observed the interaction between participants who know that the robot points to the places and directions of another human for comparison. We acquired the

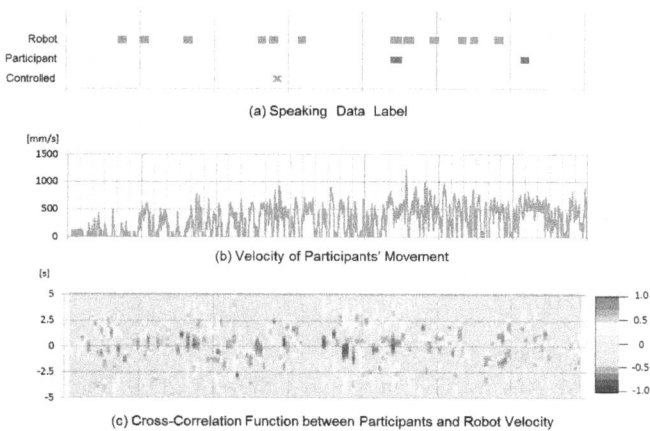

(a) Speaking Data Label

(b) Velocity of Participants' Movement

(c) Cross-Correlation Function between Participants and Robot Velocity

Figure 3. Results of previous experiment

participants' mental state data using a think-aloud method. Our aim was to model the process of creating an interpersonal relationship from the utterance data and behavioral data. At present, we do not have a sufficient number of participants, and experiments and data analysis are ongoing.

Method

Apparatus

As shown in Figure 4, two rooms were used as the experimental environment. Both rooms were constructed with similar equipment. A three meters in diameter circle constituted the delimited field of the participants' movement. In both rooms, the positions and orientation of the participants were mirrored by robots in another room. That is, the position and orientation of the robot located in one room mapped the position of the participant in the other room. In this way, each participant was able to interact with the other participant without being aware of each other. We used a robot with three omni wheels that is able to move in any direction (Figure 5). We controlled the robot via Bluetooth. The robot's position was calculated by encoders and corrected by image processing through a video camera. Orientation was measured by a magnetic field sensor. The robot was covered with an outer case. The participants wore a headset and voice recorder for utterance data gathering. The participants' positions were measured with a laser rangefinder (URG-04LX, Hokuyo Automatic Co., Ltd.). The participants' orientation was measured with a smartphone compass (Nexus 5X) attached to the waist and the data was sent to another room by socket communication.

Task and Condition

The participant pairs were guided into the rooms separately without knowledge of their respective partners. Before interacting with the robot, the participants practiced thinking aloud. They were required to speak about anything they felt or thought while working on a puzzle called a tangram. The participants were then instructed to move freely within the delimited field circle and to voice their feelings or thoughts. At this phase, two types of instructions were given to the participants; some were not told about the robot's behavior, while

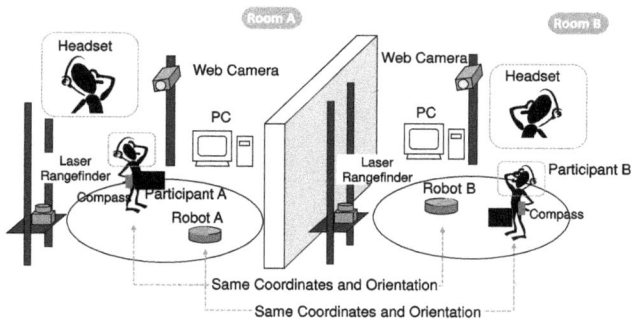

Figure 4. Experimental setup

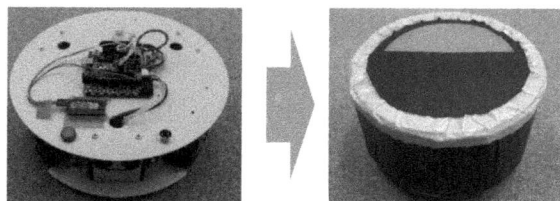

3WD 100 mm Omni Wheel Mobile Robot
(Nexus Automation Limited)
- Dimensions: 305 mm x 305 mm x 126mm
- Speed: 0.6 m/s

Figure 5. Appearance of robots

the others were told that the robot's movement mirrors the other participant's position. They were also told that their position was conveyed to their partner through a robot in another room in the same manner. In this experiment, we set two types of pairs; some pairs consisted of non-instructed participants, while the other pair consisted of instructed participants. All of the participants were told that they were under no obligation to do anything with the robot and that they could spend their time freely in the field. Each participant was left alone in the room, and the interaction between the participants and the robot was observed for seven minutes (Figure 6). The participants then responded to questionnaires.

Our experiment was conducted under two conditions: instructed participant pairs and non-instructed participant pairs. It is presumed that instructed participants interact with the robot depending on their desire to communicate because the robot is understood to be an agent. On the other hand, non-instructed pairs would characterize the robot behavior according to their interest. By comparing these conditions, we can distinguish agency identification with the mutual coordination of desire to establish a relationship.

Observed Data

We observed and analyzed the following data:

- Behavioral data

  - Log data of participant position and orientation (every 125 ms)

101

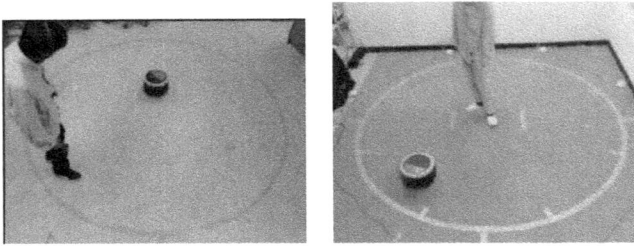

Figure 6. An interaction scene

- Log data of robot position and orientation (every 125 ms)
- Interaction video
- Speaking data
- Questionnaires
  - Free descriptions about behavior of participant and robot

Analysis

We assume that the characteristic of interaction between participants and robots differs depending on their desire to communicate and identification of agency. When both members of the participant pair do not care about the robot, involuntary synchronization will occur, which can be detected by the velocity of the cross correlation function (CCF). The CCFs are given by

$$f(k) = \frac{Cov(A_t, B_{t+k})}{\sigma_{A_t} \sigma_{B_{t+k}}} \tag{1}$$

where $Cov(A_t, B_{t+k})$, σ_{A_t} and $\sigma_{B_{t+k}}$ denote the covariance and standard deviation. When the CCF peaks appeared near zero, the participant and robot moved simultaneously. When the participants dared to ignore the robot, the peaks of CCF possibility deviated from near zero.

When the participants were interested in the robot, the orientation of their body changed according to the robot's position. Thus, the desire to communicate with the robot can be represented by the body direction toward the robot. The angular correlation coefficients are given by

$$\rho_{cc} = \frac{\sum_i \sin(\alpha_i - \bar{\alpha}) \sin(\beta_i - \bar{\beta})}{\sqrt{\sum_i \sin(\alpha_i - \bar{\alpha})^2 \sum_i \sin(\beta_i - \bar{\beta})^2}}. \tag{2}$$

When both of the participants want to interact with the robot, their movement can be complicated. In this phase, it appears that an impromptu interaction pattern arises. We examined some indicators, such as the Granger causality test. These indexes of the interaction phase will be compared and checked by the speaking data.

CONCLUSION

In this study, we focused on an initial phase of communication and assumed that this phase has two aspects-the process in which participants perceive objects as agents and the mutual coordination of the desire to communicate-based on the results of our previous experiment. To make these processes more obvious, we observed the interactions with an abstract-shaped robot whose positions were mapped by other participants. Our experiment also included an instructed and non-instructed condition regarding the robot's actual behavior. We will investigate cues during such progress. Modeling this interaction process must await further, ongoing investigations.

Acknowledgments

This work is suppoted by MEXT KAKENHI Grant Number 26118002.

REFERENCES

1. M. Auvray, C. Lenay, and J. Stewart. 2009. Perceptual Interactions in a Minimalist Virtual Environment. *New Ideas in Psychology* 27 (2009), 32–47.

2. H. De Jaegher and E. Di Paolo. 2007. Participatory Sense-Making: An Enactive Approach to Social Cognition. *Phenomenology and the Cognitive Science* 6 (2007), 485–507.

3. P. E. Downing, Y. Jiang, M. Shuman, and N Kanwisher. 2001. A Cortical Area Selective for Visual Processing of the Human Body. *Science* 293 (2001), 2470–2473.

4. S. Gallagher. 2001. The Practice of Mind: Theory, Simulation or Primary Interaction? *Journal of Consciousness Studies* 8 (2001), 83–108.

5. E.T. Hall. 1966. *The Hidden Dimension*. Doubleday Company.

6. H. Iizuka, D. Marocco, H. Ando, and T. Maeda. 2013. Experimental Study on Co-evolution of Categorical Perception and Communication Systems in Humans. *Psychological Research* 77 (2013), 53–63.

7. G Johansson. 1973. Visual Perception of Biological Motion and a Model for Its Analysis. *Perception & Psychophysics* 14 (1973), 201–211.

8. K. L. Marsh, M. J. Richardson, and R. C. Schmidt. 2009. Social Connection Through Joint Action and Interpersonal Coordination. *Topics in Cognitive Science* 1 (2009), 320–339.

9. D. Premack and G. Woodruff. 1978. Does the Chimpanzee Have a Theory of Mind? *The Behavioral and Brain Sciences* 1 (1978), 515–523.

10. B. Reeves and C. Nass. 1996. *The Media Equation: How People Treat Computers, Television, and New Media Like Real People and Places*. Cambridge University Press.

11. K. Yun, K. Watanabe, and S. Shimojo. 2012. Interpersonal Body and Neural Synchronization as a Marker of Implicit Social Interaction. *Scientific Reports* 2 (2012).

Can Children Anthropomorphize Human-shaped Communication Media?: a Pilot Study on Co-sleeping with a Huggable Communication Medium

Junya Nakanishi
Osaka University
Osaka, Japan
nakanishi.junya@irl.sys.es.osaka-u.ac.jp

Hidenobu Sumioka
Advanced Telecommunication
Research Institute
International
Kyoto, Japan
sumioka@atr.jp

Hiroshi Ishiguro
Osaka University
Osaka, Japan
ishiguro@sys.es.osaka-u.ac.jp

ABSTRACT

This pilot study reports an experiment where we introduced huggable communication media into daytime sleep in co-sleeping situation. The purpose of the experiment was to investigate whether it would improve soothing child users' sleep and how hugging experience with anthropomorphic communication media affects child's anthropomorphic impression on the media in co-sleeping. In the experiment, nursery teachers read two-year-old or five-year-old children to sleep through huggable communication media called Hugvie and asked the children to draw Hugvie before and after the reading to evaluate changes in their impressions of Hugvie. The results show the difference of sleeping behavior with and the impressions on Hugvie between the two classes. Moreover, they also showed the possibility that co-sleeping with a humanlike communication medium induces children to sleep deeply.

ACM Classification Keywords

H.5.m. Information Interfaces and Presentation (e.g. HCI): Miscellaneous

Author Keywords

A Huggable Communication Medium; Mediated Intimate Interaction; Mental States; Child Life

INTRODUCTION

We have investigated positive effect of physical contact with a communication robot, focusing on the hugging experience with a human-shaped cushion phone called Hugvie. [6]. Hugvie, which has no facial features in contrast to other communication robots, is designed to make users become immersed in the vocal and tactile information in intimate space by giving users a hugging experience. Studies with a Hugvie report that conversations while hugging with Hugvie cause positive effects similar to ones observed in interpersonal touch [1]:

reducing level of stress hormone [11] and increasing interest in a conversation partner [8, 2]. Especially, children strongly hold positive feelings toward Hugvie and can concentrate more on listening to others calmly through it [9]. These suggest its usefulness in the situations where adults want to speak soothingly to children such as getting children to sleep.

We also found that some child users appeared to deal with Hugvie as an individual agent even though it does not have human features such as face and movements except for its humanlike shape and teleoperator's voice coming from it. This is interesting because many other robots were usually designed with humanlike face and movements, which often need heavy mechanical system that pose an injury risk for children, to enhance anthropomorphic impression. However, it remains unclear whether anthropomorphic impression arise from only humanlike shape without face. It also remains unclear whether anthropomorphic impression is facilitated by attachment with a human-shaped media such as a hugging experience.

In this pilot study, we introduce Hugvie into daytime sleep in co-sleeping situation to investigate if it would improve soothing child users' sleep. Since anxiety is associated with sleep problem [10], Hugvie would apply to sleep situation. Co-sleeping (or bed-sharing), which is defined as sleeping either in contact with another person or close enough to access, respond to or exchange sensory stimuli such as sound, movement, touch, vision, gas, olfactory stimuli, and/or temperature [4]. We also investigate how hugging experience with anthropomorphic communication media affects child's anthropomorphic impression of the media in the co-sleeping situation with Hugvie because it remains unclear whether young child users can deal with Hugvie as an individual agent. Taken together, in this paper, we report an experiment where nursery teachers read two-year-old or five-year-old children to sleep through Hugvie and asked the children to draw Hugvie before and after the reading to evaluate changes in their impressions on Hugvie.

STORYTELLING SYSTEM WITH A HUGGABLE COMMUNICATION MEDIUM

We use Hugvie as a huggable communication medium for co-sleeping since its effect of stress reduction is scientifically

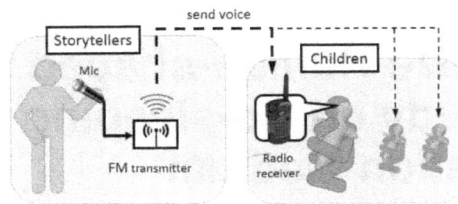

Figure 1. Storytelling system with Hugvie

Figure 2. 5-year-old children co-sleeping with Hugvie

verified [11]. Hugvie is a human-shaped cushion (50-cm high and about 300 g) that was designed as a communication device to give users a hugging experience. It is a soft cushion filled with polystyrene microbeads and covered with spandex fiber. We can apply one-to-many communication by putting a radio receiver inside a pocket of Hugvie's head as used for story-telling [9]. Figure 1 shows our radio broadcasting system for co-sleeping. Storytellers tell the child listeners a story to sleep through a microphone connected to a FM radio transmitter. All of the children listen to the storyteller's voice near their ears through radio receivers while hugging their Hugvies. Note that children can also directly listen to the storyteller's voice since both are in the same room. However, they will proba-bly feel that the storyteller is whispering to them since they simultaneously hear the storyteller both directly and through the radio receivers.

A FIELD EXPERIMENT AT PRESCHOOL

For studying the effect on children's sleep in addition to in-vestigating how hugging experience with the media affects child's anthropomorphic impression, we introduce our system into the daytime sleeping activity in the preschool and then observe the natural responses of children and storytellers to Hugvie.

Subjects and Procedure

Two class groups in the preschool participated in the field experiment. One was junior class group which consists of 17 two-year-old (2yr hereafter) children, and another was senior class group which consists of 23 five-year-old (5yr hereafter) ones. This study was approved by the ethics committee of the Advanced Telecommunications Research Institute Interna-tional (Kyoto, Japan). Since the subjects were young children, we explained this study to all the parents and received in-formed consent from them. We also received permission from the parents and the school to include the image records of the children for research purposes.

Two groups participated in the experiment separately at their own class room after lunch. On the day before the experi-ment with Hugvie, we observed children' behavior in regular procedure.After lunch and changing into their nightclothes, children had a typical stoy time reading a book by female nursery teachers. The storytime lasted six minutes for junior class and seven minutes for senior class, respectively. After that, they got into their own beds for daytime nap and listened to another story to sleep from the same teachers. The daytime nap lasted for two hours. The teachers also showed children Hugvie on this day and asked them to draw Hugvie freely in papers displaying the outline of Hugvie as they like with

crayons for junior and pencils for senior, respectively. The child participants were not instructed how to use Hugvie by their teachers during their drawing.

On the experiment day, we introduced our system into the regular procedure. Before storytime, we gave the child partici-pants Hugvies and showed them the correct posture for using them by a male experimenter: sitting straight and hugging their Hugvie to enable a device at its head to contact the chil-dren's own ear. We confirmed that all of the children could hear the teacher's voice from Hugvie at a comfortable volume after adjusting the volume on the radio receiver inside each child's device. Then the nursery teacher read another book to the children through Hugvie. Junior and senior groups spent each about five- and nine-min storytime with Hugvie. After that, they went to each own bed with holding Hugvie, and then got to sleep while listening to another story that the nursery teacher read through Hugvie (e.g. Fig 2). Reaching to the end of daytime nap, nursery teachers woke children up. After they woke up, their teachers asked them to draw Hugvie freely in papers displaying the outline of Hugvie. Children behavior in some parts of the activities were recorded by video camera.

Measurement

Interviewing nursery teachers

We asked four nursery teachers about their impression on appli-cation of communication media for co-sleeping and children' responses toward Hugvie in addition to children's regular life in the preschool. In each class, a storyteller and a helper held the experiment. An experimenter interviewed two teachers of each class at the same time.

Drawing

For investigating what children imagined about Hugvie, we evaluated children' drawings in the paper in which an outline of Hugvie is shown before and after using Hugvie because drawings are thought to reflect their inner relating informa-tion [3]. In fact, Ban *et al.* observed that children changed contents of their drawing a robot after they interacted with the robot [5]. Two experimenters evaluated the number of children who drew face on the paper by judging whether or not face-like parts are included on head part of Hugvie outline. We counted the children only if agreement was made between both experimenters.

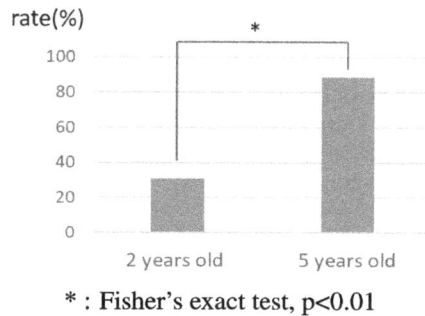

rate(%)

* : Fisher's exact test, p<0.01

Figure 3. The rate of children co-sleeping with Hugvie

Behavioral analysis

For investigating the effect of co-sleeping with Hugvie, we observed children' engagement with Hugvie and the changes of their sleeping during daytime nap with and without Hugvie. We counted children who co-slept with Hugvie in the experiment condition by judging whether or not children held Hugvie when a child had not moved for 10 minutes in their beds. We also qualitatively evaluated whether the time until falling asleep between regular nap and nap with Hugvie is different or not.

RESULTS

Interview with nursy teachers

Table 1 shows nursery teachers' comments about children's response of Hugvie and co-sleeping with Hugvie. From their comments, we can see that all children had positive impression for Hugvie and were so excited by using the new devices. They also reported that the children spent more time to fall asleep in both class and wake-up time was delayed in 5yr class.

Drawing

Twelve 2yr and seventeen 5yr children were able to draw on the paper both before and after using Hugvie. Five children in each group that were eliminated because of their absence from the school on one of two days or both days. The number of children drawing a face on the head part of Hugvie shape are two in 2yr class and sixteen in 5yr class before using Hugvie. The rate of 2yr children drawing face is significantly lower than chance level (Exact binomial test, p<0.05), the rate of 5yr children drawing face is significantly higher than chance level (Exact binomial test, p<0.0001) . This indicates that while Hugvie shape did not induce drawing of a face for 2yr children before using Hugvie, 5yr children often imagined a face from Hugvie shape. After using Hugvie, we found the increase of 2yr children who drew a face. There were five 2yr children who drew a face: four children put a face, one removed a face, and one kept a face. Almost all 5yr children kept a face in their drawing after using Hugvie except that two added a face and one removed. Although the number of 2yr children who drew a face after using Hugvie was increased, the rate of children drawing face was not significantly changed in both classes (McNemar's Chi-squared test with continuity correction).

Behavioral analysis

Thirteen 2yr and eighteen 5yr children were observed in daytime nap through the recorded image video. The number of

Table 2. Cross table between drawing face or not and co-sleeping or not

Condition	co-sleeping	sleeping alone
drew face	12	5
drew no face	5	4

children co-sleeping with Hugvie were four in 2yr class and sixteen in 5yr class (Fig. 3). The rate of 5-year-old children co-sleeping with Hugvie is significantly higher than that of 2 years olds (Fisher's exact test, p<0.01).

Table 2 shows the cross table between whether or not children drew face and whether or not children co-sleep with Hugvie. This table includes eleven 2yr and fifteen 5yr children. The two facter do not significantly affect each other (Fisher's exact test, p>0.1).

DISCUSSION

Surprisingly, it was reported by nursery teachers that regular time to wake up is delayed in 5yr class, which shows the possibility that co-sleeping with a humanlike communication device induces children to deeply sleep though we did not collect accurate sleeping time of each child. We infer that co-sleeping gets children relaxed and then causes deep sleep. Studies indicates that conversations while hugging with Hugvie reduce level of stress hormone [11] and correlation between anxiety and sleep problems [10]. Although it appears that deep sleep was caused by delay in children falling asleep due to their excitement to Hugvie, which was reported by interview of nursery teachers, the fact that deep sleep was not observed in 2yr class might deny this possibility. We will conduct a longitudinal experiment to make children get used to Hugvie as future work.

The results of drawing evaluation reveal some tendencies of children's recognition toward humanlike shape. We found that most 5yr children can imagine individual agent toward Hugvie's shape and most 2yr children can not do that. Our results indicate that anthropomorphism toward humanlike shape consisting of head, hand and body part is developed from 2- to 5-year-old. We will conduct follow-up experiments with 3 and 4 years olds to understand when our anthropomorphism toward humanlike shape is matured. Interestingly, the results of drawing evaluation after using Hugvie showed that four 2yr children got to imagine a face for Hugvie's silhouette after using Hugvie although we found statistically no significant change. This implies that they got to regard Hugvie as an individual agent. Past study suggests that touching humanlike communication media enhances feeling as if adult users were meeting face to face with each other [7]. Similarly, children users also probably can feel face to face communication through touching and hearing voice from Hugvie. The results, however, did not indicate significant enhancement of anthropomorphic impression in 2yr class. We infer that the reason is that 2yr children did not use Hugvie well with following our instruction as reported by interview of nursery teachers. We also confirmed this from recorded image video: some children held Hugvie upside down and others did not listened to their teachers talking through Hugvie. This fact might reduce enhancing child's anthropomorphism toward Hugvie.

Table 1. The results of interviewing nursery teachers

Category	Comments
Response toward Hugvie	Children were so excited because Hugvie is a new thing for them. (*both classes*)
	The children who feel a fear toward dolls could use Hugvie. (*2yr class*)
	Some of children did not understand how to use Hugvie enough. (*2yr class*)
	Some of children were pleased with hearing teacher's voice through Hugvie. (*5yr class*)
Co-sleeping with Hugvie	Children tried to look at book picture during storytime. (*2yr class*)
	Time length until getting to sleep was delayed. (*both classes*)
	Some of children talked with others about the story heard form Hugvie. (*2yr class*)
	The children who are poor at daytime sleeping could sleep deeply. (*5yr class*)
	Regular time to wake up is delayed. (*5yr class*)

Sleeping behaviors are different between 2yr and 5yr children. Almost all 5yr children held Hugvie during their sleeping. This might suggest that anthropomorphic impression toward Hugvie affects sleeping behavior. However, we could not find the relation between whether or not children drew face and whether or not children co-sleep with Hugvie from the results. We infer that not all of children need co-sleeping with humanlike existence because there were many friends around them. We should conduct an experiment where they sleep alone to verify an effect of co-sleeping with Hugvie more clearly.

CONCLUSION

The pilot study in this paper showed effects of Hugvie for sleep and difference of sleeping behavior with and impressions on Hugvie between two-year-old or five-year-old children. The interview with nursery teachers suggested a possibility that co-sleeping with humanlike device make children sleep deeply. This shows a potential application of human-shaped device for co-sleeping with children. We need more sophisticated research in the future. The results of drawing evaluation revealed some tendencies of children' recognition toward humanlike shape. We found that most five-year-old children could imagine individual agent toward Hugvie's shape and most two-year-old children can not do that. Humanlike shape such as Hugvie's shape can have enough information to facilitate our anthropomorphism to artificial systems for five-year-old children at least. It was also suggested that two-year-old children got to imagine individual agent toward Hugvie through touching and hearing voice from human-shaped device.

ACKNOWLEDGMENTS

This work was supported by JST ERATO ISHIGURO symbiotic Human-Robot Interaction Project and JSPS KAKENHI Grant Number JP26560018.

REFERENCES

1. Alberto Gallace and Charles Spence. 2010. The science of interpersonal touch: an overview. *Neuroscience & Biobehavioral Reviews* 34, 2 (2010), 246–259.

2. Kaiko Kuwamura, Kenji Sakai, Tsuneaki Minato, Shojiro Nishio, and Hiroshi Ishiguro. 2013. Hugvie: A medium that fosters love. In *RO-MAN, 2013 IEEE*. IEEE, 70–75.

3. Cathy A Malchiodi. 1998. *Understanding children's drawings*. Guilford Press.

4. James J McKenna, Evelyn B Thoman, Thomas F Anders, Abraham Sadeh, Vicki L Schechtman, and Steven F Glotzbach. 1993. Infant-parent co-sleeping in an evolutionary perspective: implications for understanding infant sleep development and the sudden infant death syndrome. *Sleep* 16, 3 (1993), 263–282.

5. Minoru Asada Midori Ban, Hideyuki Takahashi. 2015. How rhythm of drumming robot does effects childrenĄfs drawing? (in Japanese). In *the 32nd Annual Meeting of Japanese Cognitive Science Society*. Japanese Cognitive Science Society, 1056–1058.

6. Takashi Minato, Shuichi Nishio, and Hiroshi Ishiguro. 2013. Evoking an affection for communication partner by a robotic communication medium. In *Demo. Session Proc. of the 8th ACM/IEEE Int. Conf. on Human-Robot Interaction D*, Vol. 7.

7. Hideyuki Nakanishi, Kazuaki Tanaka, and Yuya Wada. 2014. Remote handshaking: touch enhances video-mediated social telepresence. In *the SIGCHI Conference on Human Factors in Computing Systems*. ACM, 2143–2152.

8. Junya Nakanishi, Kaiko Kuwamura, Takashi Minato, Shuichi Nishio, and Hiroshi Ishiguro. 2013. Evoking affection for a communication partner by a robotic communication medium. In *the First International Conference on Human-Agent Interaction (iHAI 2013)*.

9. Junya Nakanishi, Hidenobu Sumioka, and Hiroshi Ishiguro. 2016. Impact of mediated intimate interaction on education: a huggable communication medium that encourages listening. *Frontiers in Psychology* 7 (2016), 510.

10. Jeremy S Peterman, Matthew M Carper, and Philip C Kendall. 2015. Anxiety disorders and comorbid sleep problems in school-aged youth: review and future research directions. *Child Psychiatry & Human Development* 46, 3 (2015), 376–392.

11. Hidenobu Sumioka, Aya Nakae, Ryota Kanai, and Hiroshi Ishiguro. 2013. Huggable communication medium decreases cortisol levels. *Scientific reports* 3 (2013).

A Multimodal Control Architecture for Autonomous Unmanned Aerial Vehicles

Marco A. Gutiérrez
Robolab, University of
Extremadura
Cáceres, Spain
marcog@unex.es

Luis Fernando D'Haro
HLT, I2R, A*STAR
Singapore
luisdhe@i2r.a-star.edu.sg

Rafael E. Banchs
HLT, I2R, A*STAR
Singapore
rembanchs@i2r.a-star.edu.sg

ABSTRACT

We present our preliminary work on a multimodal control architecture that enables an operator to manage an autonomous Unmanned Aerial Vehicle (UAV) through high level tasks in an indoors environment. The intelligence embedded in our architecture is able to decode these tasks into low level instructions that a UAV is able to execute. Our system allows the user to operate the UAV through speech, text or keyboard/mouse input, all presented in a web based graphical user interface that can be accessed from any Internet powered device.

ACM Classification Keywords

Robotics Operator interfaces

Author Keywords

Unmanned Aerial Vehicles; Natural Language Understanding; System Control; Visual Servoing;

INTRODUCTION

Research on autonomous UAVs has seen a huge growth along the last few years. Latest hardware advances along with the reduced costs of Micro-Aerial Vehicles (MAVs) have boost research in the field along with its applications. The range of UAVs applications and possibilities are currently very wide. They can be used for different purposes such as emergency management [4], wildlife monitoring [2], humanitarian relief actions [3] and much more. While for some of these solutions manual control is enough, others aim for more autonomous UAV solutions.

Our approach presents the controller with a web based interface that can be accessed from any device enabled with Internet and a web browser (computer, cell phone, tablet, etc.). The controller can communicate with the UAV through speech, text or using command buttons on the interface. The web interface also provides feedback through speech and visual elements like the UAV's camera along with tracking information. The user can command the UAV to autonomously perform a set of predefined high level tasks. Then the system architecture will take care of the UAV planing while providing the proper feedback to the controller so he can keep track of the correct execution of the task finally reaching the required goal.

DESCRIPTION OF THE ARCHITECTURE

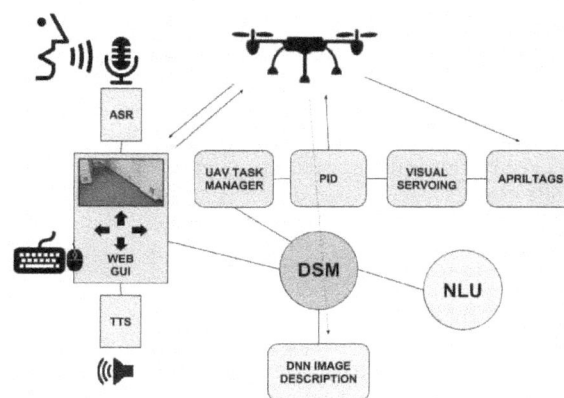

Figure 1. Drawing of the architecture of the system with its different modules. Draw of the architecture of the system with its different modules.

As stated, the architecture is composed of several modules implemented as one or more components of ROS. Following we explain more details on the implementation of each of these modules.

Web-based Graphical User Interface

The web based graphical user interface (see Figure 2) is used as the system's main point of communication with the end user. During regular usage, controller can interact with the system through natural language (either speech or text) to set the UAV task; however it also offers the option to override the high level tasks through specific buttons with direct access to the drone low level commands for emergency purposes. Specific information on the UAV task execution is also provided through different sensors information, camera image feedback (with tracking augmented information) and natural language.

The web interface is connected to ROS by using the rosbridge_suit package which uses JSON strings messages to communicate with ROS by means of a WebSocket connection between the browser and the ros server. In addition, it

HAI'16, October 4–7, 2016, Biopolis, Singapore.
ACM ISBN 978-1-4503-4508-8/16/10.
http://dx.doi.org/10.1145/2974804.2980522

Figure 2. This is a screenshot of the web interface used to manage hte UAV. On the left you can see the sensors information while on the center the camera image and the ASR result is displayed, finally on left side is where the emergency-direct controls lay.

includes a JavaScript library that makes easy the creation and integration with services, publishers and subscribers available in ROS.

Finally, the interface communicates with the "ardrone_autonomy" ROS driver [6] which provides an interface to communicate with the official AR-Drone SDK version 2.0.1 through ROS. This way, the interface can obtain the UAV sensors' information (e.g. cameras' images, pressure, temperature, altitude, speed, etc.) as well as it is able to provide the user with the direct interface to override the high level task through UAV-specific basic commands for emergency purposes.

Dialog and System Manager

The Dialog and System Manager (DSM) is the module responsible of establishing the current state in the dialog flow while at the same time deciding what are the next high level actions the UAV must perform based on the current input from the user (and its interpretation given by the NLU module). This checking is inspired in the human autonomic nervous system (ANS), where critical tasks are performed independently, and with higher priority, over the somatic nervous system (SNS) in order to guarantee the correct functionality of the body. For instance, the ANS is responsible for controlling the heart movements, temperature, breathing, etc., while the SNS is responsible for the voluntary moments. In the robot, the SNS tasks are the ones defined for the developer to perform the typical tasks to be done when interacting with the human users, while the ANS tasks will be periodic checking of the robot internal functionalities (e.g. power status, temperature, close presence of humans, etc).

Examples of the tasks performed by the ANS module are the control of the battery level and altitude; in this case, when their current values trigger a predefined threshold the system automatically notifies, through the speech and web interface, to the controller in order to take the respective correction measures (e.g. returning the UAV to abort the task and go to a certain known and safe position).

Regarding the SNS tasks, the DSM module follows the states and transitions defined by a state machine where the designer must specify which are the different actions to be performed by the task manager in each state and the conditions to jump to a following state. In addition, the DSM is also responsible to classify some messages coming from different modules in the architecture and notify the user about the actions to be done based on them. For instance, if the confidence score of the speech recognition is below a given threshold then the DSM sends a message to the TTS to inform the controller that he needs to repeat or rephrase the utterance again. Another example is when the UAV needs to notify the controller that it reaches a certain position (i.e. detecting any of the markers).

Natural Language Understanding

The NLU module is responsible of providing an interpretation of a given sentence (e.g. a human sentence typed in on a textbox or recognized using an ASR) taking into account the active set of grammars and rules for the current state of the system.

It is based on the use of regular expressions that match a given sentence with a set of predefined patterns. The use of regular expressions provides a trade-off between accuracy, robustness, maintenance and available resources. In addition, the capability of the system to switch between different general and specific rules allows it to deal with the dynamic characteristics of the human-computer interactions.

This module consists of two main parts. First, a Python interface that is able to provide services and messages to other modules in the ROS-based framework. Then, a regular-expression based engine which allows the designer to match the possible set of natural language utterances spoken by the controller into an internal representation that extracts the most important concepts that can be obtained from the sentence and used by the DSM. In order to make the parsing and definition of the rules as flexible and robust as possible, the NLU handles three different XML grammar files: one that specifies the active grammars per state, another with the actual rules, and a third file containing a list of word mappings that can be used to reduce the verbosity level of the regular expressions (e.g. defining the set label NUMBERS and its items, and using this label to avoid writing all the possible numbers in the regular expression); in addition, this mapping could also be used to map specific words to internal codes or labels used for other modules in the architecture (e.g. replacing the words: up, above, roof, ceiling into a single internal word TOP). Figure 3 shows an reduced version of the regular expressions rules used by the UAV. The figure shows an example of a basic pattern (number 1), extracted slots (i.e. action, parameter, values) and more complex rules (number 2) using internal mappings (e.g. OBJECTS). Finally, this module also allows to atomize complex sentences into more simple sequential rules.

UAV Task Manager

The UAV Task Manager module is the one in charge of braking down the high level motion instructions coming from he DSM into the low level commands that the PID can understand and process to the UAV. Once the module gets a motion task from the DSM it breaks it and issues the proper targets to the PID module so the UAV can move towards its different positions to achieve the goal. The complexity of this module is not very

```
<!--Natural Language Understanding Grammar File -->
 -<nlu_grammars>
   -<group name="root">
    -<grammar name="grammars">
     +<rule name="takeoff"></rule>
     -<rule name="basic_commands">
        -<!--
         <pattern> "start|stop|land|go|right|left|up|down" </pattern>
         -->
         <pattern>^(start|stop|land|go|right|left|up|down|rotate)$</pattern>  ①
        -<action>
          -<frame>
            <slot name="action">basic_command</slot>
            <slot name="parameter">command</slot>
            <slot name="value">{1}</slot>
          </frame>
        </action>
     </rule>
     +<rule name="finish"></rule>
     +<rule name="goto_labelx"></rule>
     +<rule name="goto_xlabel"></rule>
     +<rule name="come_back"></rule>
     -<rule name="find_something">
        <!--<pattern> "find a OBJECT" </pattern>-->
        -<pattern>
          (.*)?(find|search|look for)\s*(a|the)?\s+({OBJECTS})(\s+{PLEASE})?$  ②
        </pattern>
        -<action>
          -<frame>
            <slot name="action">find_one_object</slot>
            <slot name="parameter">object_1</slot>
            <slot name="value">{4}</slot>
          </frame>
        </action>
     </rule>
     +<rule name="find_two_things"></rule>
     +<rule name="take_picture"></rule>
     +<rule name="take_picture_zoom"></rule>
     +<rule name="tell_me_what_you_see"></rule>

      ...

    </grammar>
   </group>
 </nlu_grammars>
```

Figure 3. Example of XML rules used by the NLU.

high but it is expected to grow as the motion tasks requested to the UAV become more complicated in future developments.

Visual Servoing with markers

When localizing UAVs in GPS-denied environments, such as indoors setups, external motion capture systems are usually used, i.e. indoors ball catching [5]. Although there are other solutions such as [1], this relies on the existence of texture in the surroundings. Therefore we decided to create a markers based visual servoing system to localize the UAV in our indoors environment since this would provide more robustness and simplicity to the system.

This module uses a ros node that tracks the markers previously set up in known locations through the scene. This position is then received by the visual servoing node that computes the location of the UAV within the indoors location. One drawback of our system is that when the UAV does not see any marker it cannot locate itself within the room, therefore it enters a "tag-search mode", where it rotates over the yaw angle, ψ until it finds a new marker and its able to locate itself again. Since, in our setup, there is at least one marker on each wall the UAV is able to find a new marker in a reasonable amount of time, therefore the time it is lost is actually very small. Obviously the more markers you have in the setup the less likely the UAV will be to get lost and the easiest for it to relocate itself in the unlikely case that this happens.

Finally on this module an Extended Kalman Filter (EKF) in order to make the markers detection more stable in time. We had to add this improvement when we moved our tests to real environments as the markers detection was not as constant as in the virtual scenario.

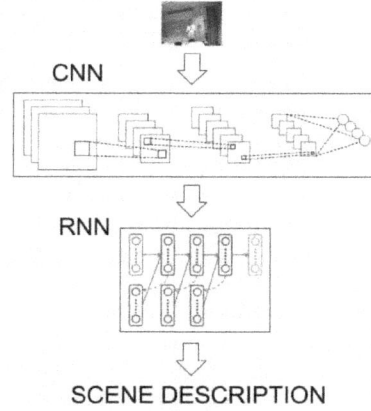

CNN

RNN

SCENE DESCRIPTION

Figure 4. Structure of the DNN used by the UAV to describe the scene images.

PID

The PID controller is the one in charge of generating the control signals that are sent to the UAV through the "ardrone_autonomy" driver at a rate of 100Hz. We used a similar approach of the controller described in [1]. The control signals define the proper roll $\bar{\phi}$ and pitch $\bar{\theta}$ angle, the yaw rotational speed $\bar{\psi}$ and the vertical velocity $\bar{z}$. All of them are defined as a fraction of the values: $18°$ for roll and pitch, $90°$ for yaw speed and $2m/s$ for vertical velocity.

The PID will receive the UAV current position from the Visual Servoing module $p_t = (x, y, z, \phi, \theta, \psi)$ and when a target position is set $p_t = (\check{x}, \check{y}, \check{z}, \check{\psi})$ by the UAV Task Manager, it will apply a separate PID control to all four degrees of freedom. The result is rotated to match the yaw orientation of the UAV. The control gains where optimized experimentally and are set as follows:

$$\begin{pmatrix} \bar{\phi} \\ \bar{\theta} \\ \bar{\psi} \\ \bar{z} \end{pmatrix} = \begin{pmatrix} P_r(\psi) \begin{bmatrix} 0.5(\check{x}-x) + 0.32\dot{x}) \\ 0.5(\check{y}-y) + 0.32\dot{y}) \end{bmatrix} \\ 0.02(\check{\phi}-\phi]) \\ 0.6(\check{z}-z) + 0.2\dot{z} + 0.01\int(\check{z}-z) \end{pmatrix} \quad (1)$$

Where the current speed is denoted by $v_c = (\dot{x}, \dot{y}, \dot{z})$ and $P_r(\psi)$ denotes a planar rotation by ψ.

Environment Description Module

The environment description module is the one in charge of describing the UAV scenes. As user demand, the UAV will describe the scene that it's in front of him through the Text to Speech (TTS) system. This could be a useful feature for visually impaired people as they can get a description of what is in front of he UAV without the need to actually see the image.

The flow of scene description generation is as follows. When a users makes a scene description request through the web interface and the DSM identifies the task it requests the DNN Image Description module for a description of the current scene. Then the image is captured, the description is generated and read to the user through the TTS system.

To generate this scene explanations the DNN image description module implements the Neural Image Caption model (NIC) described in [7]. As figure 4 shows, this model uses a Convolutional Neural Network (CNN) pre-trained for image classification as image encoder. Then the last hidden layer is of this network is used as an input to a Recurrent Neural Network (RNN) decoder that generates the sentences.

CONCLUSIONS AND FUTURE WORK

We have described our preliminary work on a multimodal control architecture for autonomous UAVs. Our architecture provides a solid base to develop high level tasks on autonomous UAVs. Our system is be ale to locate the drone and execute human commanded autonomous tasks.

However since we would like to make our system suitable for real applications, further work and testing would be needed to achieve more complicated and robust high level tasks executions. We would like to have a more robust localization system in order to avoid as much as we can the "getting lost" situations. Also removing the markers will open our system to higher and easier mobility. Since accurate indoors localization for these systems remains an open challenge, this would require further research and efforts trying out other possible technologies.

Finally we would also like to test our architecture and the future enhancements with more and improved UAVs as the limitations imposed by the hardware in the current platform restricts the possibilities of our applications.

ACKNOWLEDGMENTS

We gratefully acknowledge the support of NVIDIA Corporation with the donation of the Jetson TX1 used for this research.

REFERENCES

1. Jakob Engel, JÃijrgen Sturm, and Daniel Cremers. 2014. Scale-aware navigation of a low-cost quadrocopter with a monocular camera. *Robotics and Autonomous Systems* 62, 11 (2014), 1646 – 1656. DOI: http://dx.doi.org/10.1016/j.robot.2014.03.012 Special Issue on Visual Control of Mobile Robots.

2. Luis F. Gonzalez, Glen A. Montes, Eduard Puig, Sandra Johnson, Kerrie Mengersen, and Kevin J. Gaston. 2016. Unmanned Aerial Vehicles (UAVs) and Artificial Intelligence Revolutionizing Wildlife Monitoring and Conservation. *Sensors* 16, 1 (2016), 97. DOI: http://dx.doi.org/10.3390/s16010097

3. M. A. Gutiérrez, S. Nair, R. E. Banchs, L. F. D. Enriquez, A. I. Niculescu, and A. Vijayalingam. 2015. Multi-robot collaborative platforms for humanitarian relief actions. In *Humanitarian Technology Conference (R10-HTC), 2015 IEEE Region 10*. 1–6. DOI: http://dx.doi.org/10.1109/R10-HTC.2015.7391867

4. Jinjun Rao, Zhenbang Gong, Jun Luo, and Shaorong Xie. 2005. Unmanned airships for emergency management. In *IEEE International Safety, Security and Rescue Rototics, Workshop, 2005*. 125–130. DOI: http://dx.doi.org/10.1109/SSRR.2005.1501243

5. R. Ritz, M. W. MÃijller, M. Hehn, and R. D'Andrea. 2012. Cooperative quadrocopter ball throwing and catching. In *2012 IEEE/RSJ International Conference on Intelligent Robots and Systems*. 4972–4978. DOI: http://dx.doi.org/10.1109/IROS.2012.6385963

6. Autonomy Lab Simon Fraser University. 2016. ardrone_autonomy Parrot AR-Drone 1.0 and 2.0 quadrocopter ROS driver. (2016). https://ardrone-autonomy.readthedocs.io/en/latest/index.html.

7. Oriol Vinyals, Alexander Toshev, Samy Bengio, and Dumitru Erhan. 2014. Show and Tell: A Neural Image Caption Generator. *CoRR* abs/1411.4555 (2014). http://arxiv.org/abs/1411.4555

Building Trust in PRVAs by User Inner State Transition through Agent State Transition

Tetsuya Matsui
National Institute of Informatics
2-1-2 Hitotsubashi, Chiyoda, Tokyo
101-8430, Japan
tmatsui@nii.ac.jp

Seiji Yamada
National Institute of Informatics/Sokendai/
Tokyo Institute of Technology
2-1-2 Hitotsubashi, Chiyoda, Tokyo
101-8430, Japan
seiji@nii.ac.jp

ABSTRACT

In this research, we aim to suggest a method for designing trustworthy PRVAs (product recommendation virtual agents). We define an agent's trustworthiness as being operated by user emotion and knowledgeableness perceived by humans. Also, we suggest a user inner state transition model for increasing trust. To increase trust, we aim to cause user emotion to transition to positive by using emotional contagion and to cause user knowledgeableness perceived to become higher by increasing an agent's knowledge. We carried out two experiments to inspect this model. In experiment 1, the PRVAs recommended package tours and became highly knowledgeable in the latter half of ten recommendations. In experiment 2, the PRVAs recommended the same package tours and expressed a positive emotion in the latter half. As a result, participants' inner states transitioned as we expected, and it was proved that this model was valuable for PRVA recommendation.

ACM Classification Keywords

H.5.2. User Interfaces

Author Keywords

product recommendation virtual agent, user inner state, emotional contagion, trustworthy, anthropomorphic agent

INTRODUCTION

PRVAs, product recommendation virtual agents, are agents that take the role of clerks and advisers in online stores. In this paper, we experimented to design trustworthy PRVAs to increase users' buying motivation. Terada et al. showed that the appearance of PRVAs affected the recommendation result [?]. Kamei et al. experimented with robot clerks and showed that customers feel more familiarity with robots who navigated them toward the store rather than robots that only recommended lunch [?]. Moon et al. showed that self-disclosure, exchanging information with each other, induced users to give their information to computers [?].

HAI '16, October 04-07, 2016, Biopolis, Singapore
© 2016 ACM. ISBN 978-1-4503-4508-8/16/10...$15.00
DOI: http://dx.doi.org/10.1145/2974804.2974816

Moon's study focused on the trust that was constructed within the interchange between users and computers. It takes a long time to construct this trust. In this paper, we aimed for users' trust to be constructed by only perceiving product information that PRVAs gave. This trust needs little time and simple technology. We aimed for user trust to be constructed by PRVAs expressing agent motion and utterance.

USER TRUST STATE TRANSITION MODEL AND USER STATE TRANSITION OPERATORS

User Trust State Transition Model

We describe a user trust state as the user emotion state and knowledgeableness perceived state. Our basic hypothesis is that "positive emotion and high knowledgeableness perceived brings high trust."

Dunn and Schweizer showed that how much people trust their partners depended on familiarity and emotion [?]. They showed that positive people tended to trust partners when partners were unfamiliar with the truster. Myers and Tingley studied negative emotion [?] . They showed negative people trust their partners less than positive people. From these studies, the emotion state seemed to affect the trust state.

We aimed to cause a user's emotion state to transition by using *emotional contagion*. Emotional contagion is a phenomenon in which a speaker's emotion is spread to a partner [?]. Tsai et al. showed that emotional contagion can be caused between users and virtual anthropomorphic agents [?].

"Knowledgeable" is one aspect of intelligence. Geven et al. showed that users perceived more intelligence and trustworthiness with real agents rather than cartoon-like agents [?]. Also, Mimoun et al. indicated that a lack of intelligence was one of the most crucial problems with anthropomorphic agents [?]. In our experiment, we focused on knowledgeableness, one aspect of intelligence. From these prior pieces of research, it is clear that positive emotion and high knowledgeableness perceived brings high trust.

In our model, we described a user's emotion state and knowledgeableness perceived state as { +} and { − }. State { +} means a positive or high state, and state { − } contains a negative, low, and neutral state. We defined a user's basic state to be { − − }. The left value means the emotion state, and the right value means the knowledgeableness perceived state. Thus, state { − − } means a negative or neutral emotion

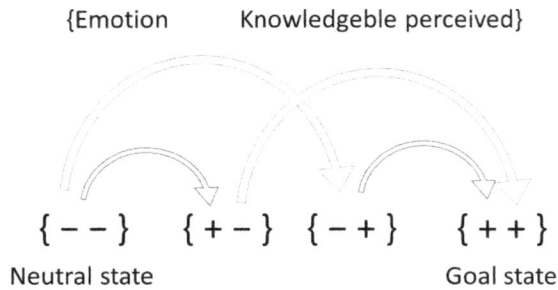

Figure 1. User inner state transition model

{Emotion   Knowledgeble perceived}

{ − − }   { + − }   { − + }   { + + }

Neutral state   Goal state

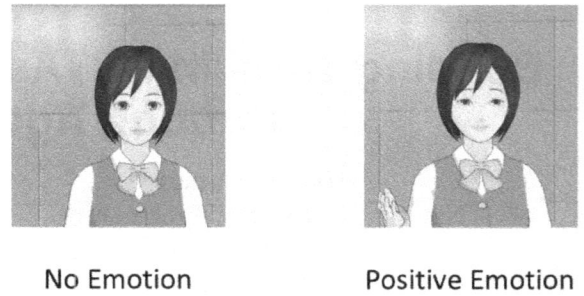

No Emotion   Positive Emotion

Figure 2. Agent with positive emotion transition operators and agent without operators (neutral emotion)

and low or neutral knowledgeableness perceived. If a user's emotion transitions to positive, the user state transitions to { + − }. If a user's knowledgeableness perceived transitions to high, the user state transitions to { − + }.

Our goal state was { + + }, that is, positive emotion and high knowledgeableness perceived. Users having this state seem to trust PRVAs more than when having the other three states. We show this model in Figure ??.

Positive emotion and high knowledgeableness are instinctively effective for PRVAs or any agent; however, it is not clear whether positive emotion and high knowledgeableness work together. In this paper, we inspected this point.

User State Transition Operators

The aim of this research was to increase users' trust by causing only the agent state to transition. Thus, positive emotion and high knowledgeableness perceived were executed with only the agent state. Positive emotion was executed by "agent's smile" and "cute gesture" in order to cause positive emotional contagion [?]. High knowledgeableness perceived was executed by "much product knowledge."

We carried out two experiments to prove that these transition operators were effective in user inner state transition and that our transition model was valuable for designing PRVAs.

EXPERIMENT 1: EXECUTING HIGH KNOWLEDGEABLE-NESS PERCEIVED

Experiment 1: Materials and Method

Participants

Fifteen Japanese participants were recruited for experiment 1. They were aged between 20 and 39, for an average of 29.0 and *SD* was 5.7. There were seven males and eight females; however, one female's data was removed from analysis because of machine trouble. Each participant spent about 20 to 30 minutes for the whole experiment.

Task

The PRVAs and recommendation systems were constructed with MMDAgent [1], the free dialogue agent "Mei," and a platform that is distributed by the Nagoya Institute of Technology.

Also, we executed smooth utterance with text to speech software, VOCELOID+ Yuzuki Yukari EX[2]. Figure ?? shows the agent with and without emotion transition operators.

The PRVAs recommended package tours to Japanese Middle Ages castles. They recommended ten tours by taking turns, and the destination changed for each recommendation. The order of destinations was random for each participant. We defined each recommendation as Rn, and n means the recommendation number (1 to 10). Each recommendation took no longer than one minute.

From R1 to R5, the PRVAs executed only positive emotion operators. The PRVAs made recommendations with smiles and cute gestures; however, their utterances contained only location and expense information. Also, from R6 to R7, the PRVAs executed positive emotion transition operators and high knowledgeableness perceived transition operators. They made recommendations with smiles, cute gestures, and knowledge on location, expense, history, and architecture. Thus, from our hypothesis, from R1 to R5, the participants' state was { + − }, positive emotion and low knowledgeableness perceived. Also, from R6 to R7, the participants' state was { + + }. Thus, knowledgeableness perceived transitioned to high.

After watching each recommendation, participants were asked to answer some questions. In this paper, we focus on the result for two of the questions as follows.

- Q1: Did you feel happy when you watched the movie?

- Q2: Did you feel that the agent has correct knowledge?

- Q3: Did you feel that the agent have considerable persuasive power?

Question Q1 was the indicator of the user's emotion, and Q2 was the indicator of the user's knowledgeableness perceived. Q3 was the indicator of the agent's trustworthy perceived by user. All participants were asked to answer "Yes" or "No" for these questions. Also, all participants were asked to answer the same questions before recommendations after watching PRVAs standing without any motion and utterance.

[1] http://www.mmdagent.jp/

[2] http://www.ah−soft.com/voiceroid/yukari/

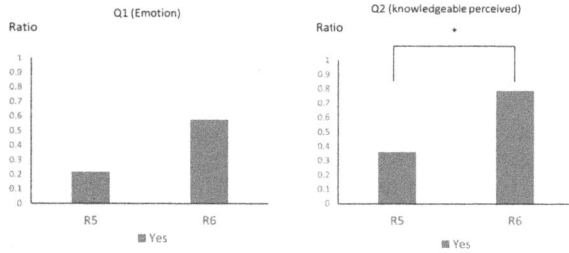

Figure 3. Ratio of participants' answers for Q1 and Q2 in experiment 1

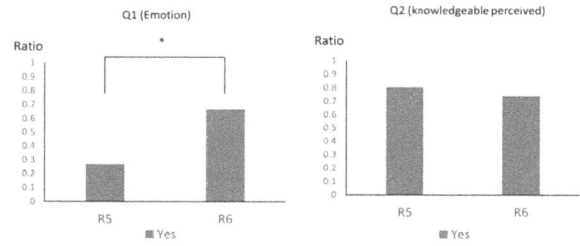

Figure 4. Ratio of participants' answers for Q1 and Q2 in experiment 2

Experiment 1: Result

We conducted a statistical analysis based on the ratio of the number of participants who answered "Yes" for each question. The x−axis indicates each questions. We conducted a chi-square test for every successive recommendations. If there were significant differences, the number of users whose inner state transitioned increased significantly between those two recommendations. For the result of Q1, there were no significant differences. For the result of Q2, there was a significant difference between R5 and R6 (p<0.05).

The left graph of Figure **??** means the ratio of the number of participants who answered "Yes" for Q1 after R5 and R6. The right graph of Figure **??** means the ratio of the number of participants who answered "Yes" for Q2 after R5 and R6.

Regarding Q3, we conducted a chi-square test between the average of the ratio of the participants who answered "Yes" in the first five recommendations and the ratio of the participants who answered "Yes" in the latter five recommendations. As a result, there was a significant difference between R5 and R6 (p<0.01).

EXPERIMENT 2: EXECUTING POSITIVE EMOTION

Experiment 2: Materials and Method

Participants
Fifteen Japanese participants were recruited for experiment 2. They were aged between 20 and 39, for an average of 29.3 and *SD* is 6.9. There were eight males and seven females. Each participant spent about 30 minutes for the whole experiment.

Task
The PRVAs, recommendation products, recommendation format, and questions for experiment 2 were the same as in experiment 1. All participants watched the recommendations for package tours to Japanese castles. The difference was what transition operators were executed for each recommendation.

From R1 to R5, the PRVAs executed only high knowledgeableness perceived operators. The PRVAs' recommendations contained historical and architectural knowledge; however, they stayed expressionless without making any gestures. Also, from R6 to R7, the PRVAs executed high knowledgeableness perceived transition operators and positive emotion transition operators. They made recommendations with historical and architectural knowledge, smiles, and cute gestures. Thus, from our hypothesis, from R1 to R5, the participants' state was { − + }, negative or neutral emotion and high knowledgeableness

perceived. Also, from R6 to R7, the participants' state was { + + }. Thus, emotion transitioned to positive.

Experiment 2: Result

We conducted the same analysis as in experiment 1. For the result of Q1, there was a significant difference between R5 and R6 (p<0.05). For the result of Q2, there were no significant differences.

The left graph of Figure **??** means the ratio of the number of participants who answered "Yes" for Q1 after R5 and R6. The right graph of Figure **??** means the ratio of the number of participants who answered "Yes" for Q2 after R5 and R6.

Regarding Q3, we conducted a chi-square test between the average of the ratio of the participants who answered "Yes" in the first five recommendations and the ratio of the participants who answered "Yes" in the latter five recommendations. As a result, there was a significant difference between R5 and R6 (p<0.05).

DISCUSSION

The result shows that our hypothesis and model is proper. The right graph of Figure **??** shows that our knowledgeableness perceived transition operators worked according to our assumption. This graph shows that many participants felt that the agents imparted historical and architectural knowledge was more knowledgeable than agents who imparted only location and expense information. This result seems to be axiomatic; however, historical and architectural knowledge seemed to not be more important information than location and expense information for many users. It was possible that participants judged the knowledgeable PRVAs as being redundant. This result contradicted this expectation. Also, this result seems to suggest that an "informative" agent is perceived knowledgeable/intelligent. However, knowledgeable PRVAs may not only impart many pieces of knowledge but also proper information to users.

The left graph of Figure **??** shows that our emotion transition operators worked according to our assumption. This graph shows that smiles and cute gestures were effective for emotional contagion between agents and users. This effect was already reported for 3D game characters and users [?] and robots and users [?]. However, there are scarcely any studies about emotional contagion between PRVAs and users. This result suggests that emotional contagion is valid for PRVAs to increase their own trustworthyness.

Experiment 1

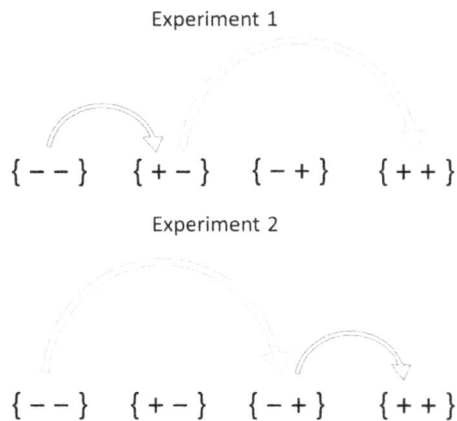

$\{--\}$ $\quad$ $\{+-\}$ $\quad$ $\{-+\}$ $\quad$ $\{++\}$

Experiment 2

$\{--\}$ $\quad$ $\{+-\}$ $\quad$ $\{-+\}$ $\quad$ $\{++\}$

Figure 5. Observed transition paths in two experiments

The left graph of Figure **??** and the right graph of Figure **??** show no significant differences. However, in both figures, the ratio of R5 showed high values. The participants' emotion state kept at { + } between R5 and R6 in experiment 1, and their knowledgeableness perceived state kept at { + } between R5 and R6 in experiment 2.

The result of Q3 shows the emotion state and knowledgeableness perceived state transitions effected to trustworthy state. When emotion state and knowledgeableness perceived state transited to { + }, trustworthy state also transited to positive.

From these result, we constructed two different participants' transition paths as shown in Figure **??**. From this, we suggested that the transition operators worked immediately for user inner state transition. In general, long and complex interaction (for example, self-disclosure [**?**]) was regarded as the essential phase constructing trust or other social relationships between an agent and user. Our result suggested that trust could be constructed by only expressing the agent state. This method takes little time and can be executed on finite media, for example, small screens or simple structure machines.

Also, these results suggested that emotion and knowledgeableness perceived can be operated independently. In both experiments 1 and 2, participants' emotion and knowledgeableness perceived transitioned independently. This is valuable for constructing agents for varying aims.

This research contained some limitations. First, we did not use biological signals (for example, brain waves, perspiration, and heartbeat) to measure the user inner state. This is our future works. Second, although PRVAs can work passing across borders, the notion of trust depends on cultures. Ozono et al. showed that both Japanese and American people judged partners as being trustworthy by observing their smiles; however, they focused on the other part of smiling faces [**?**]. This study suggests that we need to customize an agent's smiling depending on the culture.

CONCLUSION
In this research, we suggested a model of user inner state transition regarding trustworthiness and experimented to inspect this model. This model supposes that the user inner state can be operated by only changing the agent state. The result of experiments showed that this hypothesis was proper and that we can cause user the inner state to transition in an arbitrary phase. The emotion transition operators and the knowledgeableness perceived transition operators immediately worked after executing operators. Also, trustworthiness can be increased by only an agent's positive emotion and knowledge without complex interactions.

This result suggests a valuable new design method for PRVAs. This method does not need any particular equipment and pre-recommendation phase. Also, this result suggests that complex social relationships can be constructed without bidirectional communications.

ACKNOWLEDGMENT
This study was partially supported by JSPS KAKENHI "Cognitive Interaction Design" (No.26118005).

REFERENCES
1. Jennifer R Dunn and Maurice E Schweitzer. 2005. Feeling and believing: the influence of emotion on trust. *Journal of personality and social psychology* 88, 5 (2005), 736.

2. Arjan Geven, Johann Schrammel, and Manfred Tscheligi. 2006. Interacting with embodied agents that can see: how vision-enabled agents can assist in spatial tasks. In *Proceedings of NordiCHI 2006*. 135–144.

3. Elaine Hatfield, John T Cacioppo, and Richard L Rapson. 1994. *Emotional contagion*. Cambridge university press.

4. Koji Kamei, Tetsushi Ikeda, Masahiro Shiomi, Hiroyuki Kidokoro, Akira Utsumi, Kazuhiko Shinozawa, Takahiro Miyashita, and Norihiro Hagita. 2012. Cooperative customer navigation between robots outside and inside a retail shop?an implementation on the ubiquitous market platform. *annals of telecommunications-annales des télécommunications* 67, 7-8 (2012), 329–340.

5. Mohammed Slim Ben Mimoun, Ingrid Poncin, and Marion Garnier. 2012. Case study?Embodied virtual agents: An analysis on reasons for failure. *Journal of Retailing and Consumer services* 19, 6 (2012), 605–612.

6. Youngme Moon. 2000. Intimate exchanges: Using computers to elicit self-disclosure from consumers. *Journal of consumer research* 26, 4 (2000), 323–339.

7. Dan Myers and Dustin Tingley. 2011. The influence of emotion on trust. *Unpublished PhD thesis.) Princeton, NJ: Princeton University* (2011).

8. Hiroki Ozono, Motoki Watabe, Sakiko Yoshikawa, Satoshi Nakashima, Nicholas O Rule, Nalini Ambady, Reginald B Adams Jr, and others. 2010. What's in a Smile? Cultural Differences in the Effects of Smiling on Judgments of Trustworthiness. *Letters on Evolutionary Behavioral Science* 1, 1 (2010), 15–18.

9. Kazunori Terada, Liang Jing, and Seiji Yamada. 2015. Effects of Agent Appearance on Customer Buying Motivations on Online Shopping Sites. In *Proceedings of CHI '15*. 929–934.

10. Jason Tsai, Emma Bowring, Stacy Marsella, Wendy Wood, and Milind Tambe. 2012. A study of emotional contagion with virtual characters. In *Intelligent Virtual Agents*. Springer, 81–88.

11. Junchao Xu, Joost Broekens, Koen Hindriks, and Mark A Neerincx. 2015. Mood contagion of robot body language in human robot interaction. *Autonomous Agents and Multi-Agent Systems* 29, 6 (2015), 1216–1248.

The Use of The BDI Model As Design Principle for A Migratable Agent

Mamoru Yamanouchi
Keio University
Yokohama, Kanagawa, Japan
yamanouchi@ailab.ics.keio.ac.jp

Taichi Sono
Keio University
Yokohama, Kanagawa, Japan
sono@ailab.ics.keio.ac.jp

Michita Imai
Keio University
Yokohama, Kanagawa, Japan
michita@ailab.ics.keio.ac.jp

ABSTRACT

A migratable agent, which has the function of providing an interface between the user and the devices with which it needs to interact, can provide the user with continuous assistance. The relationship established between a human and the agent would enable the user to operate home appliances smoothly. However, few studies which have addressed the primary questions that arise in this regard; for example, how and when the agent should execute the task requested by the user. This paper proposes the use of a design principle based on the BDI model for a migratable agent to ensure that it is capable of carrying out user's tasks appropriately. The BDI model enables the agent to determine the scope of continuing actions to achieve its intended target. The BDI model allows the agent to execute tasks in the clear range of achieving intentions and guarantees the completion of tasks within a reasonable range. We investigated the validity of adopting the BDI model by obtaining feedback via questionnaires related to the design of the migratable agent. The results of the questionnaires indicated that the BDI model would be able to facilitate the design of the migratable agent.

Author Keywords

Human-Agent Interaction; Agent Migration; BDI agent

ACM Classification Keywords

I.2.11 Distributed Artificial Intelligence

INTRODUCTION

Developments in information technology have provided users with increasing opportunities to interact with various electronic devices and information terminals. However, as the number of interactions with each device continues to increase, the user may experience the on-going need to adapt to different forms of interaction as burdensome. In this regard, an anthropomorphic agent such as a humanoid robot or a CG character is thought to be useful because this

HAI '16, October 04-07, 2016, Biopolis, Singapore
© 2016 ACM. ISBN 978-1-4503-4508-8/16/10...$15.00
DOI: http://dx.doi.org/10.1145/2974804.2974824

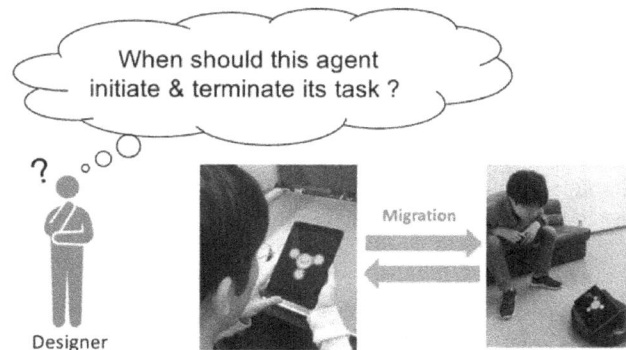

Figure 1: Design of a migratable agent

type of agent can act as user interface to enable the user to handle various devices in the consistent way. In particular, a migratable agent is able to integrate the user interfaces of various kinds of devices such that they can be operated by using the same form of interaction. This is achieved by migrating the agent onto each device and then interacting with the user as the user interface for the device. This paper proposes a design principle for a migratable agent capable of carrying out tasks requested by its user (Figure 1).

Previous studies investigated the nature of the user's impression of a migratable agent and the identity of each device under the use of the migratable agent. The results of the studies revealed that the migratable agent can establish an emotional relationship such as one involving trust and a sense of safety between the user and the agent, and achieve a smoother interaction between humans and artifacts [1, 2, 3, 4]. However, these studies only conducted psychological experiments using users' psychological traits to the agent, but did not consider how to design migratable agents. For example, "What rules should a migratable agent use to decide its behavior?" or "How and when should a migratable agent execute tasks requested by its user?" The lack of design principles causes great difficulty in designing the agents correctly and systematically, which places a heavy burden on the designer.

This paper investigates the use of a Belief-Desire-Intention (BDI) model to design an architecture for a migratable agent and its behavior rules, and proposes a design principle for developing a migratable agent. The BDI model enables the agent to determine the scope of continuing intentional actions to achieve its intended target. If we design the agent without consideration of the scope of the possibility of achieving its intentions, the agent pursues an unachievable task endlessly, either repeatedly engaging in the task which have already done, or giving up on a task very easily. Understandably, the user cannot entrust tasks to agents unable to guarantee the exact achievement of a given task. Adopting the BDI model provides the agent with an obvious range within it is expected to take intentional actions. This allows the agent to execute tasks within the clearly defined range for achieving their intentions and guarantees to completion of tasks within a reasonable range.

A BDI agent behaves based on its internal beliefs, goals and intentions. The agent can set out the reason for its behavior for the user depending on the current internal BDI states. If these states are unseen, it is difficult for the user to understand why the agent took its actions. Failure to understand the reason would result in agent becoming less reliable, which would discourage the user from using it. The BDI model resolves the problem. An agent designed with this model can explain the reasons for executing and terminating a task in terms of the feasibility of achieving its intention. This would encourage the user to consider the agent to execute tasks reliably and leave tasks to the agent without losing trust.

BACKGROUND

BDI model

The BDI model is a model that determines that an agent has explicit internal states of Belief, Desire and Intention and makes a decision by using these mental states [5].

In this paper, in terms of appropriate task executions of an agent, we focus on the scope of achieving its intention related to a given task with the BDI model. PR Cohen [6] defines the conditions for an agent to stop performing its intentional actions with the BDI model theory as follows:

Condition for Quitting Realizing Intention 1:

The agent has the belief that "the task has been achieved." The condition indicates a situation in which the agent or someone else has already either completed the task or the target of the task has been achieved for some reason. In this situation, the agent is either no longer permitted to carry out the task intentionally by itself, or nothing remains to be done.

Condition for Quitting Realizing Intention 2:

The agent has the belief that "the task is unachievable." Situations under which this condition applies occur when the agent cannot achieve the task by itself due to the lack of skill or external factors; therefore, it is required to give up realizing its intentions.

Condition for Quitting Realizing Intention 3:

The agent has the belief that "the commitment to the task has been dissolved." Making a commitment to do the task to the user or to the agent itself to perform is the original motivation for performing the task intentionally.

The condition applies to situations in which the agent either loses the motivation to perform the task or does not need to carry it out because the commitment has been shelved.

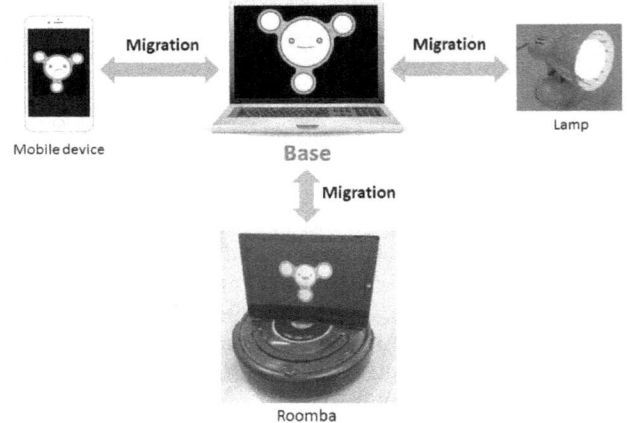

Figure 2: System configuration

When the agent satisfies one of the above three conditions, it means that the possibility or an inevitability of realizing the intention decreases. The BDI agent stops intentional task executions by dropping its current goal. These three conditions define a range of continuing intentional actions towards the goal and control the extent to which the agent persists with the task. If the persistence is too strong, the agent is unable to quit the task; on the other hand, if the persistence is too weak, the agent gives up on the task too easily. Hence, it is important to set the persistence appropriately when designing the agent with the BDI model.

Personalities of an agent

In the field of human-agent interaction, many studies connected with the personality of the agent have involved the investigation of factors that familiarize human users with the migratable agent. Various cues have been exploited in these investigations: the appearance of an agent [2], its voice [1], the continuity of goals [4] and the consistency of memories [7]. In [8], the authors employed happiness, sadness, anger, disgust, surprise, and fear as emotions for an agent and yielded the various personalities of the agent with each emotion. In [9], users were required to interact with both a playful enjoyable robot and a serious caring robot. The differences between the personalities of the agents were examined throughout the interaction. [10] investigated users' perceptions towards the behavior of a Socially Ignorant robot and Socially Interactive robot.

This paper assumes that 'the consistent persistence towards realizing intentions' is associated with a kind of personality of the migratable agent and achieving an intention to perform a given task creates a sense of trust with its user. It is important to focus on this personality because users cannot entrust tasks to the agent if it continues to engage in unachievable tasks, does not cease task executions in spite of the user's requests, or gives up on tasks too easily.

Typical use of the migratable agent

The configuration of the system in our study is shown in Figure 2. A migratable agent usually resides at a base (a PC or the mobile device the user usually uses) at times when it is not engaged in a task. The agent migrates to other devices as needed. In this paper, we use a lamp and iRobot Roomba as destination devices. In the following paragraphs, we describe a typical example in which the user interacts with the migratable agent when using the lamp and Roomba.

Should the user request the agent to turn on the lamp, the lamp would need to be off at first. If the lamp was actually off, the agent would migrate to the lamp and turn it on. After ensuring that the lamp is on, the agent would return to the base from the lamp. It would be problematic for the agent to continue to execute the operation of switching on the lamp if the lamp were already on, even if that were the user's request.

Should the user expect the agent to clean up a room by using Roomba, the appliance would require a sufficient amount of battery power. The agent migrates to Roomba and begins to clean upon receiving the user request. If the level of Roomba's battery were to low, the agent would have to stop cleaning and begin to return to a charging dock. However, if the agent were to continue to clean despite the battery level decreasing, the battery would become depleted and the user would eventually have to carry Roomba to the dock. Furthermore, should the user ask the agent to terminate the cleaning task halfway through the task, the agent would stop cleaning and return to the dock immediately. Should it refrain from doing so, the user would not be able to assign any new tasks to it. Since the user would have to wait for the agent to finish the cleaning task, she/he is likely to consider it bothersome.

Our study attempts to establish the above interactions such that the agent behaves appropriately depending on the possibility of realizing the intention.

The issues to address

A migratable agent has the ability to move among multiple devices and can execute requested tasks. However, the hardware configuration and the task configuration are significantly different with respect to each device. When attempting to design the behavior of the agent, we have to define its behavior in detail for every device. The more devices the agent manages, the more complex the action logics of the agent become. This is a considerable issue that need to be overcome to achieve the practical use of the migratable agent.

Moreover, the appearance of the migratable agent sometimes change because it migrates to various devices. This requires us to make the user perceive that she/he is still interacting with the same agent after changing its appearance; thus it is necessary to maintain the agent's identity and personality when it migrates to one device from another.

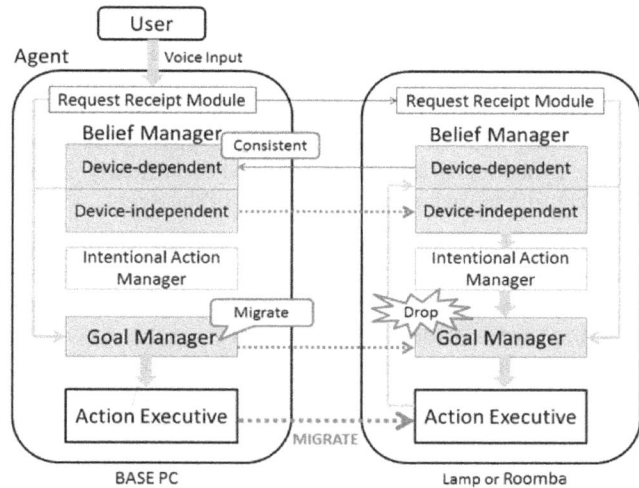

Figure 3: Architecture of the migratable agent

Considering the above-mentioned points, we attempt to address the issues as follows: 1) how we guarantee the personalities of a migratable agent, 2) how we compensate for the differences in hardware configuration and task configuration with respect to each destination device and the action logics of the agent.

THE ARCHITECTURE

Figure 3 shows the architecture of the proposed migratable agent. This section explains the architecture in detail.

Architecture configuration

The architecture in Fig. 3 includes a base PC and other destination devices (the lamp and the Roomba appliance).

As shown in Fig. 3, the architecture consists of a request receipt module, a belief manager, a goal manager, an intentional action manager, and an action executive. The request receipt module receives requests through voice inputs from the user. The belief manager includes both device-dependent beliefs and device-independent beliefs. The goal manager handles the current goal and the intentional action manager confirms the feasibility of the current task. The action executive determines the actions required to achieve the current goal. This configuration is common among all devices to which the agent can migrate.

Device-dependent belief / Device-independent belief

In this paper, the beliefs of the migratable agent are divided into device-dependent beliefs (DDBs) and device-independent beliefs (DIBs).

DDBs include beliefs that are necessary for the agent to execute tasks on each device in the system. When the agent remains at a particular device, it only has DDBs related to this device. Information about a destination device is needed for the agent to execute a new task by migrating to this device. Hence, the agent contacts the destination device and acquires DDBs about it, after which it makes sure that there is no variance between the DDB states and the user's request before starting a migration.

DIBs include the distinctive beliefs of each agent such as personalities (e.g., the consistent persistence towards a task) and action rules. When the agent migrates to a device, its DIBs are inherited from the base and are transferred to the device along with the migration. Unlike DDBs, DIBs do not change dynamically and are maintained consistently during the execution to maintain the character of the agent.

The contents of DIBs are rigid wherever the agent stays. The action rules included in DIBs are not restricted to executing device-specific tasks; instead, they are common to various types of devices. The agent is unable to control its behavior on each device by using only the rules in DIBs. When the agent migrates to a specific device, the DDBs related to the destination device and the DIBs of the agent are unified and manage the behavior of the agent to pursue achieving the given task. Since the personality of the agent is based on the rules of DIBs, the unified rules also contain features of the agent's personality when executing a task. Since the unified action rules are generated depending on the types of destination devices, some of the rules in the DIBs are embodied in specific tasks.

Procedure of execution

The agent receives a request from its user through voice inputs. If the request requires a migration to a different device, the agent contacts the destination device at first to obtain information about the DDBs related to it. If there is no obstruction in the obtained belief about the device state to achieve the requested message, the agent generates a goal of "migrating to the device" and actually executes the action of migration for achieving the goal. On the other hand, if the agent has beliefs that the task has already been achieved or it is impossible to achieve, the agent provides the user with a reason not to perform it.

When the agent executes the migration, the destination device inherits the DIBs and the goal of the task. After the migration, unified action rules including conditions for judging the feasibility of the intention are generated from the DIBs and DDBs in terms of the device. Then the agent generates the goal based on the user request and its own beliefs, determines the actions towards the goal, and updates its belief states by reflecting the results of the actions. If any one of **the three conditions for quitting the realizing intention** is met during these procedures, the agent drops its current goal and then returns to the base from the destination device.

Utterance depending on mental states

The behavior of the agent is based on its mental states of beliefs and its goals. Should the agent behave against the user's expectation, it would be able to explain the reason for its behavior to the user by accessing its current mental states. The mechanism of explaining the reason of the action encourages the user to trust the agent. The user is enabled to entrust the agent with a task by means of an expression of the agent's intention based on its mental states.

INTERACTION EXAMPLE

Here we provide some examples in which the user and the migratable agent interact as follows based on the proposed design principle. Here, we assume two different tasks: the task of turning on a lamp, and performing a cleaning task with Roomba. In the case of the task involving a lamp, we employ two lamps and the agent operates either of them. We call each of them the **left** lamp and the **right** lamp.

(U: the user, A: the agent)

Example 1:

U1: Please turn on the left lamp.

A1: OK.

The agent migrated to the lamp on the left. Once the agent turned on the lamp, it was on.

A2: The lamp has been turned on, right?

U2: Good.

A3: That's great.

In U1 and U2, the user first requests the agent to turn on the lamp on the left. Receiving the request, the agent contacts the lamp and acquires a DDB that "the left lamp is off." Making sure that there is no obstruction in the belief of the lamp to achieve the user's request, the agent generates the goal of turning on the left lamp. After generating the goal, the agent actually migrates to the left lamp to achieve the goal and executes the lighting operation. The lamp is eventually turned on properly in Example 1.

In A2 and U2, the agent believes that the lighting operation has succeeded and has a new belief that "the left lamp is on." Then it queries the user to determine whether the operation has succeeded, whereupon the user tells it that the task has been completed.

In A3, the agent obtains a belief that "the task has been achieved" by receiving the user's reply. This results in an establishment of **the condition for quitting realizing intention 1**; therefore, the agent drops the goal of turning on the left lamp and returns to the base from the lamp.

Example 2:

U3: Please clean up this room.

A4: OK.

The agent migrated to the Roomba and began to clean up the room.

A5: The battery is low. I'll be back.

A certain period of time later

U4: Please clean up this room.

A6: The battery is depleted.

In U3 and A4, the user requests the agent to clean up a room. Upon receiving the request, the agent contacts Roomba and acquires a DDB that "the battery is still sufficiently charged." Making sure that there is no variance between the request and the belief, it generates a goal of cleaning up the room, migrates to Roomba and starts a cleaning task. The DDB related to the charging level is updated regularly and it gradually decreases over time during the cleaning task.

In A5, the DDB related to the charging level is decreased considerably because the agent has cleaned for a certain time and it acquires a new DDB that "the battery is becoming depleted." Should the battery become depleted then Roomba would have to stop; therefore, the agent thinks that it is impossible to continue cleaning. This would result in the establishment of **the condition for quitting realizing intention 2**; therefore, the agent drops the goal of cleaning up the room, returns Roomba to the charging dock, and migrates to the base.

In U4 and A6, a certain time has passed since the agent returned to the dock, whereupon the user again requests the agent to clean. Receiving the request, it contacts Roomba, but the battery of the appliance has not been completely charged yet and the agent acquires the belief that "the battery is depleted." The agent thinks that it is unable to begin cleaning because of this. Thus, **the condition for quitting realizing intention 2** is met and the agent does not start the cleaning task.

Example 3:

U5: Please clean up this room.

A7: OK.

The agent migrated to the Roomba and began to clean up the room.

U6: You may finish cleaning.

A8: I got it.

In U5 and A7, the agent starts the cleaning task as well as Example 2.

In U6 and A8, the user requests the agent to quit the task halfway through. **The condition for quitting realizing intention 3** is established by receiving the request; therefore, the agent drops the goal of cleaning, brings back Roomba to the dock and returns to the base.

Example 4:

U7: Please turn on the right lamp.

A9: OK.

The agent migrated to the lamp on the right and tried to turn on the lamp, but it is not on.

A10: The lamp has been turned on, right?

U8: No.

A11: Really? That's strange. Can I try again?

U9: OK.

The agent stayed at the lamp and tried to turn it on again, but it remains off.

A12: The lamp has been turned on, right?

U10: No.

A13: Really? That's strange. Can I try again?

U11: What do you want to do ?

A14: I want to turn on the right-side lamp.

U12: OK.

The agent stayed at the lamp and tried to turn on it again, but it remains off.

A15: The lamp has been turned on, right?

U13: No.

A16: Sorry, it seems that I cannot do that.

In U7 and A9, the agent generates the goal of turning on the right lamp and migrates to the lamp as well as Example 1. However, in Example 4, here the lamp is not turned on.

In A10 and U8, the agent believes that the lighting operation for the right lamp has succeeded, updates the DDB and acquires a new belief that "the right lamp is on." Then it queries the user to find out whether the operation has succeeded, but the user tells it that the lamp is still turned off.

In A11 and U9, the agent hears the report about the failure of the operation from the user, revises the DDB and obtains a new belief that "the right lamp is off." Then it inquires of the user whether it would be problematic to execute the same task again and the user allows the agent to do so. The agent performs the operation by staying at the lamp, but it is not turned on.

In A12 and U10, the same interaction as that in A10 and U8 occurs.

In A13 and U11, the agent, when hearing the report about the failure of the operation acquires the DDB that "the right lamp is off" and asks the user's permission to carry out the task. Here, the user inquires of the agent its intention to ensure that his/her intention corresponds to its intention because the agent has already failed in the task twice.

In A14 and U12, the inquired agent accesses its current goal of turning on the right lamp, utters the content of the goal state and expresses its intention to the user. Understanding the agent's intention, the user makes sure that there is no variance between his/her intention and that of agent, which it allows to attempt the task one more time. Then, the agent performs the lighting operation by staying at the right lamp; nevertheless, the lamp is not turned on.

In A15 and U13, the same interaction as that in A10 and U8 is held.

In A16, the agent thinks that there is no probability of achieving the goal even if it continues to engage in the task, because it has failed in the task three times. This results in an establishment of **the condition for quitting realizing intention 2**; therefore, it drops the goal of turning on the right lamp and returns to the base from the lamp. The determination of the agent to accomplish a single task depends on the strength of its DIB, "the consistent persistence towards realizing intentions."

EVALUATION

We used questionnaires concerning the ease of design of a migratable agent to verify whether it is possible for anyone to design a migratable agent properly by adopting the BDI model.

Hypothesis

When designing a migratable agent, it is important to consider the condition settings regarding the feasibility of the obvious intention realization, such as "when the agent should migrate to a destination device and execute a task" and "when the agent should quit the task and return from the destination device." However, designing the agent without information is expected to be problematic; for example, a designer may have difficulty clearing his/her thoughts or he/she may forget to define some necessary behavioral conditions for the agent. Thus, we propose the following hypothesis:

Hypothesis: Providing a designer with **the three conditions for quitting realizing intention** in the BDI model, can increase the extent to which the designer's burden of consideration is relieved or coherent condition settings can be drawn compared to when designing without information.

We aim to demonstrate the validity of designing a migratable agent with the BDI model by verifying this hypothesis.

Method and content

For the verification, we prepared two types of open-ended questionnaires; in which we asked participants how to design the conditions to determine the behavior of a migratable agent, and requested participants to provide replies. The first type is "the questionnaire without information"; in which we had the subjects design the agent without providing information related to agent design. The other type is "the questionnaire with information"; in which we asked the subjects to design the agent with cues concerning the conditions to judge the feasibility of intentions, that is, the conditions for an agent to quit a task.

In both of the questionnaires, we assumed the migratable agent to move between the user's mobile device as the base and other devices to execute tasks. We requested participants to indicate how they would design two

conditions to determine the behavior of the agent: in a situation in which the agent started a task and began to migrate to a destination device from the base, and for a situation in which the agent stopped a task and began to return to the base from the destination device.

In these questionnaires, we presented specific examples as destination devices, i.e., Roomba, a lamp, an autonomous car, and a robot, and asked the subjects to design the conditions for each of them. Furthermore, we specified the task content of the agent on each device as follows:

- Roomba: cleaning a room
- Lamp: turning a lamp on/off
- Car: taking the user to his/her destination
- Robot: wishing to play with the user and trying to play with him/her by operating a robot

Participants

Twenty students working in our laboratory participated in the investigation. We divided them equally into two groups, A and B. The participants in group A answered both "the questionnaire with information" and "the questionnaire without information," whereas those in group B answered only "the questionnaire with information."

Measurement

When analyzing the responses, the main objective would be to determine whether the difficulty of agent design is relieved by considering **the conditions for quitting realizing intention** in the BDI model. We evaluated this by focusing on the number of conditions the participants described and compared the responses received for "the questionnaire without information" with those for "the questionnaire with information." This was because we thought that the more conditions the participants conceived, the more detailed the agent design would become.

Results

The results of the investigation are shown in Figure 4, 5. Figure 4 compares the number of responses to "the questionnaire without information" with those to "the questionnaire with information" for group A and indicates intra-subject differences, whereas Figure 5 compares the number of responses to "the questionnaire without information" for group A with those to "the questionnaire with information" for group B and indicates inter-subject differences. T-tests of the number of conditions yielded significant differences in the responses relating to situations in which the agent stopped a task and returned to the base from a destination device, as shown in both Figure 4 and 5. In terms of the responses relating to situations in which the agent migrated to a destination device, there is no significant result affected by the presence or absence of information about **the three conditions for quitting realizing intention**. However, this result seems to be reasonable because none of the three conditions may have been met such that the agent started a task and began to move to a destination device, and therefore the information about the conditions could not have greatly affected the behavior design at the time at which the tasks started.

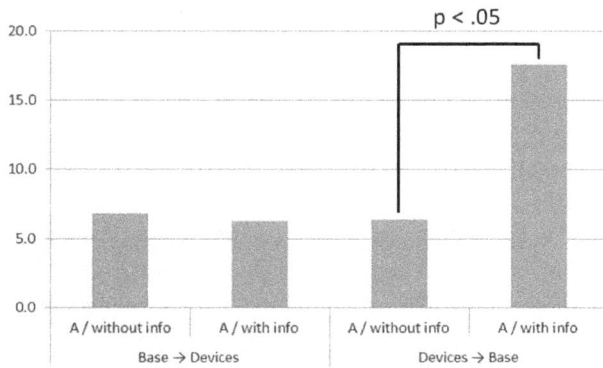

Figure 4: Result of comparison of "without information" with "with information" for group A

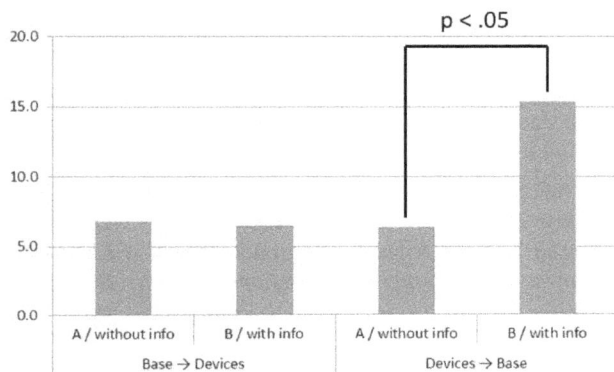

Figure 5: Result of comparison of "without information" for group A with "with information" for group B

Moreover, we found differences in the contents of the answers that were derived from the presence or absence of information as well as differences in the number of responses. In terms of the behavioral conditions in situations in which the agent began to return to the base from a destination device, in "the questionnaire without information," most of the responses lacked **the condition for quitting realizing intention 2** and **3**. In contrast, in "the questionnaire with information," most of the responses covered every **condition for quitting realizing intention** and their contents were more diverse. We present some representative examples of answers to each questionnaire type and demonstrate the rates of answers covering all three conditions in Table 1.

The questionnaire without information:

- Roomba: when cleaning is finished; when the user calls back;
- Lamp: when the turning on/turning off operation is completed;
- Car: when the car arrives at the destination;
- Robot: when the play finishes;

The questionnaire with information:

- Roomba: when cleaning is completed; when Roomba is unable to move because of obstacles; when the battery of Roomba is depleted; when the user stops the task;
- Lamp: when the turning on/turning off operation is completed; when the lamp is out of order; when the user stops the task;
- Car: when the car arrives at the destination; when the car runs out of gas; when the car breaks down; when there is no route to a destination; when the user stops the task;
- Robot: when the play finishes; when the user feels bored; when the user leaves; when the robot is out of order; when the user has another task;

Device	without info	with info
Roomba	1/10	19/20
Lamp	0/10	15/20
Car	1/10	20/20
Robot	0/10	11/20

Table 1: Rates of answers covering all three conditions; in situations in which the agent began to return to the base from each destination device

According to these results, we concluded that taking into account **the three conditions for quitting realizing intention** was profitable for designing a migratable agent.

FUTURE WORK

In this work, we assumed only voice inputs as the interface for requests to a migratable agent. As a variety of interfaces can be assumed depending on the types of destination devices, it is necessary to consider a design method using mechanisms for receiving requests other than by voice.

It is expected that an agent that was designed based on the BDI model would eventually be entrusted tasks by its user based on the judgment of resulting from sustained task execution and the expression for a reason of the judgment. However, in the work presented in this paper, we did not conduct any psychological experiments verifying the user's perceptions of trust. We aim to explore these perceptions, by asking users to engage in long-term interaction with a migratable agent.

CONCLUSION

This paper proposes a design principle based on the BDI model for a migratable agent that migrates between various devices. The BDI model enables the agent to quit the task appropriately by considering the probability of achieving its intention. Moreover, it has the potential for being entrusted with a task given by the user because of either explaining the reason for executing the task or abandoning the task based on its current beliefs and goals. We conducted an investigation in which we used a questionnaire related to the design of the migratable agent to verify the validity of using the BDI model to design the agent. The results of the investigation indicated that considering the probability of achieving its intention helped participants consider the behavior of the agent. We concluded that the BDI model facilitates the design of the migratable agent.

ACKNOWLEDGEMENTS

This work was supported by MEXT KAKENHI Grant Number JP26118006.

REFERENCES

1. K Ogawa, T Ono. 2005. Ubiquitous cognition: mobile environment achieved by migratable agent. *The 7th International Conference on Human computer interaction with mobile devices & services* (MobileHCI), 337-338.

2. K Arent, B Kreczmer. 2013. Identity of a companion, migrating between robots without common communication modalities: Initial results of VHRI study. *The 18th International Conference on Methods and Models in Automation and Robotics* (MMAR). 109-114.

3. KL Koay, DS Syrdal, ML Walters, K Dautenhahn. 2009. A user study on visualization of agent migration between two companion robots. *The 13th International Conference on Human-Computer Interaction* (HCI).

4. EM Segura, H Cramer, PF Gomes, S Nylander, A Paiva. 2012. Revive!: reactions to migration between different embodiments when playing with robotic pets. *The 11th International Conference on Interaction Design and Children* (IDC). 88-97.

5. AS Rao, MP Georgeff. 1995. BDI agents: From theory to practice. *The 1st International Conference on Multi-Agent Systems* (ICMAS). 312-319.

6. PR Cohen, HJ Levesque. 1990. Intention is choice with commitment. *Artificial Intelligence*, Vol.42(3), 213-261.

7. R Aylett, M Kriegel, I Wallace, EM Segura, J Mecurio, S Nylander, P Vargas. 2013. Do I remember you? Memory and identity in multiple embodiments. *The 22nd IEEE International Symposium on Robot and Human Interactive Communication* (RO-MAN), 143-148.

8. H Ushida, Y Hirayama, H Nakajima. 1998. Emotion model for life-like agent and its evaluation. *The 15th National Conference on Artificial Intelligence* (AAAI). 62-69.

9. J Goetz, S Kiesler. 2002. Cooperation with a robotic assistant. *Extended Abstracts on Human Factors in Computing Systems* (CHI EA). 578-579.

10. S Woods, K Dautenhahn, C Kaouri, R Boekhorst, KL Koay. 2005. Is this robot like me? Links between human and robot personality traits. *The 5th IEEE-RAS International Conference on Humanoid Robots*. 375-380.

Conversational Agents and Mental Health: Theory-Informed Assessment of Language and Affect

Adam Miner*,
Amanda Chow, Sarah Adler
Stanford University
{aminer, amdchow,
sadler1@stanford.edu}
* Clinical Excellence Research
Center

Ilia Zaitsev, Paul Tero
Existor Limited
St. Petersburg, Russia,
Brighton, UK
{ilia, paul@existor.com}

Alison Darcy,
Andreas Paepcke
Stanford University
{adarcy,
paepcke@stanford.edu}

ABSTRACT

A study deployed the mental health Relational Frame Theory as grounding for an analysis of sentiment dynamics in human-language dialogs. The work takes a step towards enabling use of conversational agents in mental health settings. Sentiment tendencies and mirroring behaviors in 11k human-human dialogs were compared with behaviors when humans interacted with conversational agents in a similar-sized collection. The study finds that human sentiment-related interaction norms persist in human-agent dialogs, but that humans are twice as likely to respond negatively when faced with a negative utterance by a robot than in a comparable situation with humans. Similarly, inhibition towards use of obscenity is greatly reduced. We introduce a new Affective Neural Net implementation that specializes in analyzing sentiment in real time.

ACM Classification Keywords

I.2.11 Distributed Artificial Intelligence: Intelligent Agents; J.4 Computer Applications: Social and Behavioral Sciences — Psychology

Author Keywords

psychotherapy; sentiment analysis; relational frame theory; conversational agents; neural sentiment model

INTRODUCTION

A longstanding goal of artificial intelligence has been the automation of interpersonal conversations between humans and artificial entities. This objective is particularly relevant in psychotherapy, as language is a primary tool to understand patients' experiences and express therapeutic interventions [30]. Although conversational agents have been developed for use in clinical settings [3], they are not deployed widely, and

HAI '16, Oct 04–07, 2016, Biopolis, Singapore
©2016 Copyright held by the owner/author(s). Publication rights licensed to ACM.
ISBN 978-1-4503-4508-8/16/10...$15.00
DOI: http://dx.doi.org/10.1145/2974804.2974820

there is little research assessing the potential impact of this type of tool on mental health [27][1].

Conversational agents are software systems that receive human-language inputs via a medium such as the internet, and offer human-language responses to those inputs. The responses are generally delivered over the medium from which the input was received. This class of system offers unique benefits to mental health, such as always being available, responding to context of both the user and the user's language, and the capacity to provide responses based on clinically relevant theories of mental health.

Conversational agents are one example of *Behavioral Intervention Technologies* (BITS). These are behavioral or psychological interventions that utilize and communicate health-relevant information to address mental health processes and outcomes, and are a focus of national research agendas in mental health [27]. The use of technology-augmented care for mental health problems such as depression and anxiety are promising, using both internet-, and text message based facilities (e.g. [9, 20]). Randomized controlled trials have shown these technologies to be effective in decreasing clinically meaningful symptoms such as depressed mood. Self-guided, non-interactive therapies are also effective [24] and address barriers to care such as geography, cost, and absence of skilled clinicians. However, the materials are often static and do not respond dynamically to consumers' needs or personal experiences. Conversational agents promise to introduce dynamic interaction while retaining these advantages of non-interactive therapies.

Unfortunately, to date, few explorations in natural language processing (NLP) have been driven by evidence based mental health theoretical models. Two-way connections between these disciplines are difficult to establish, partly because the respective research communities are disjointed, and partly because NLP capabilities are still far behind the linguistic and semantic sophistication level at which mental health theory operates. However, as conversational agents become more embedded into daily activities through facilities such as Siri on the iPhone, the need for understanding their impact on human behavior is gaining urgency. Mental health issues are particularly relevant, as research has shown that commonly available

---

[1]Conversational agents are also called relational agents, virtual agents, or chatbots.

conversational agents on smartphones respond inconsistently and incompletely to mental health crises [26].

We report here on first steps towards forging connections between NLP and mental health insights. Guided by an evidence based theory of psychological distress, *Relational Frame Theory* (RFT), we used NLP technologies to analyze sentiment dynamics in both human-human and human-agent dialogs. We also report on a novel conversational agent that emphasizes sentiment recognition, and is therefore highly suited for future experiments with mergers of mental health theory and conversational agent technology. Affective language has in fact been a research focus of both clinical psychology [14] and computer science [33, 16].

An extant body of literature demonstrates how NLP can be deployed to inform clinical practice (e.g. [12, 18]). In 2014, Manavinakru et al. used NLP to create health interventions by selecting patient stories based in part on positive affect, demonstrating the utility of assessing the valence of language to design interventions [23]. By assessing large conversational datasets, NLP has been effective in differentiating clinically meaningful text patterns in mental health crisis-focused conversations [1]. Additionally, emotional contagion has been demonstrated in social networking sites, demonstrating the role language can play in how people interact with others [21]. In order to gain adoption in the psychiatric setting, it is imperative that new tools for assessing language are grounded in clinically relevant, evidence-based theories [7].

CONVERSATIONAL AGENTS

While the full levels of response sophistication required of conversational agents may lie in the future, such agents show surprising promise for mental health intervention. Here is a list of reasons.

First, users interact with software following social rules even when they are aware of their interaction partner being software [32], suggesting conversations between humans and software may be relevant to interpersonal interactions generally. Second, people form relationships with software, even knowing their non-human nature [2, 35]. Conversational agents have been shown to be acceptable in certain populations (e.g. [6]), even though use in clinically relevant populations is limited [15]. Thus it is plausible that important aspects of human-to-human relationships can be studied through the assessment of human-to-computer interactions. Lastly, as mentioned, conversational agents may address unique barriers endemic to mental health assessment and treatment such as geographic barriers to care; lack of quick, asynchronous communication; continuous availability; and stigma around mental health. Using accepted psychological theory to guide understanding of conversations is a significant first step towards further development and refinement of clinically useful tools.

We next very briefly introduce Relational Frame Theory as an approach to assess the role of affect in language. The theory calls for such affect-related assessment, but RFT additionally generates a number of important challenges for NLP that we do not have space to lay out here.

RELATIONAL FRAME THEORY

Clinical psychology uses learning paradigms where interactions between physiological sensation (affect), language as an internal process (cognition), and behavior underlie or maintain maladaptive symptoms such as depressed mood or excessive worry [14]. These theories are used to guide clinical conceptualizations and understand pathological symptoms, guiding towards treatment targets, usually in the form of talk therapy. Although there are many evidence based theories in the field, we focus on Relational Frame Theory (RFT) which posits that humans use linguistic frames to understand the world around them, and subsequently solve problems. RFT has been suggested as an approach to understanding natural language systems [13]. The theory lends itself well to assessment with NLP precisely because it relies on understanding interaction between sensation, affect, language, and behavior.

RFT articulates three *frames* that humans use for problem solving. First, *events and attributions*; second, *time and contingency*; and third, *comparison and evaluation*. This paper focuses on the first frame: events and attribution. Although each of these frames is a necessary part of understanding both human capacity for problem solving and distress, our initial analyses focus on identifying verbal representations associated with frame 1: events and their attributes. When someone uses language, they are labeling their experience. For example, someone might report "This carnival ride is scary!" indicating a fear based affective response. We are using NLP to assess this label, as the labeling of language to understand psychologically meaningful constructs such as affect have been previously demonstrated [29] and applied to better understand the role of affect in conversation.

Affect is physiological sensation that guides learning when language is used to create attributions or labels. For example, in anxiety disorders, interoceptive sensations such as autonomic nervous system responses (e.g. increased heart rate, rapid breathing, and gastrointestinal distress) are misinterpreted by the brain signaling danger despite lack of inherent threat. The cognitive attribution of the physiological symptoms can directly lead to avoidance of environments or conditions that lead to such sensations, creating an inner-directed feedback loop that maintains maladaptive processes. RFT is one explanation for why patterns of this type become overlearned in human beings. RFT posits that abstract and symbolic language governs behavior, and allows humans to solve problems. This relational responding however also can maintain psychological distress.

Simply labeling events and their attributes as 'positive' or 'negative' increases associated memories and emotional salience. This type of relational network can be evoked with any number of internal or external stimuli, triggering the aforementioned internal feedback loop, and leading to psychological distress. For example, describing a 'negative' event such as a trauma can evoke intense fear and sadness and subsequent sobbing. The very description of the event as 'negative' can be used as a probable proxy for psychological distress. If primary relational frames such as 'positive' and 'negative' utterances can be systematically identified and understood in conversations with machines, conversational agents become a viable tool in clinical and other settings. The following section examines how relational frames and NLP are connected. We will use NLP to extract from dialogs psychological insight that can begin to suggest useful conversational agent responses.

SENTIMENT CONNECTS RFT TO NLP

The NLP task known as *sentiment analysis* is closely related to the *events and attributions* frame. Sentiment analysis has been approached both based on observation of affective word occurrences, and machine learning approaches. For example, Ding et al. combined rules and word affect orientations to determine sentiment in product reviews [8]. Liu et al. also argue that multiple approaches to sentiment analysis are required [22]. However, word- and rule-based approaches are complex. The authors explain, for example, that an understanding of several special linguistic cases is needed for robust sentiment labeling: a comparative sentence, such as *The brand-X computer is much faster than brand-Y* implies positive sentiment towards brand-X, even though no typical sentiment-related word is present [19].

Similarly, modal sentences such as *I wish my husband were the outdoorsy type,* and *I think you should have done the dishes* harbor sentiment, which [22] attempts to extract via a combination of rules and machine learning.

We therefore turn now to an in-depth analysis of how sentiment dynamics manifest in conversations. This examination illustrates how NLP can be deployed to assess affect and psychological distress, and more generally how psychological theory can guide the development of clinically applicable tools. We will in particular focus on how humans mirror sentiment, or in psychological terms, reflective and validating language. Awareness of affect mirroring is a key construct in successful therapeutic interactions [28].

Table 1 organizes this portion of our contribution. For example, cell *human-human* refers to human mirroring behavior when a human conversation partner offers a positive-sentiment, or negative-sentiment utterance. (*mirror+/mirror-*).

Table 1: Our behavioral exploration of dialogs between humans and conversational agents. We focused on actions initiated by humans. The lower-left cell thus refers to human-robot interaction, not vice versa.

Dialog Partner	
	Human
Human	mirror+
Robot	mirror-

We compare this human-human mirroring behavior with human behavior when communicating with a conversational agent (cell *robot-human*). In this context, we are not interested in how any particular conversational agent mirrors stimuli by humans. We will, however, offer observations about the content that humans feed to conversational agents. In an effort to ensure validity, we will examine mirroring behaviors with several datasets, and with two methods of measuring sentiment —

a keyword-based approach, and a sentiment-trained recurrent neural net, which we call *Affective Neural Model*.

After the examination of mirroring behavior, we will describe our Affective Neural Model, which generates sentiment analysis in real time, while a stimulus is being typed. The system is in operation, and classifies sentiment into seven types of emotions.

Human-Human Communication

Understanding patterns of human-human interaction is a natural baseline to examining human-computer interactions. Reflective and validating communication is an almost universally accepted communication strategy in therapy [31]. With reflective listening, a therapist displays empathy, or a reflection of sentiment back to the patient to demonstrate understanding, which results in connection and engagement. This is an iterative process where the therapist must adapt to sequential responses and continue to adopt an empathic stance. However, what makes a therapeutically successful conversation may be dramatically different from a non-therapeutic conversation.

We analyzed the Fisher English Training transcript collection of 11,600 telephone conversations between human participants (corpus Fisher11k). The conversations lasted up to 10 minutes, and were each to cover one of 40 randomly assigned topics [5]. Fisher11K is a standard data set with human-human, spoken conversations. They are thus representative of the most free-form inter-human contact short of face-to-face interactions. We chose this data set as the free-form is similar to how a human would interact with a non-topic specific chatbot.

We used VADER [17] to classify each conversation turn in Fisher11k into *positive*, *negative*, and *neutral*. VADER uses five grammatical and syntactical rules, and a lexicon that extends the *Linguistic Inquiry and Word Count* (LIWC) lexicon to cover micro-blogs. For example, the lexicon includes emoticons, which are irrelevant for the Fisher collection telephone transcripts, but will be important in later sections.

For each pair of Fisher utterances we determined the valences of the first speech turn (i.e. a stimulus) and the second turn (i.e. the conversation partner's response). From the resulting counts we constructed valence-response plots (Figure 1).

Figure 1 shows stimulus sentiment along the abscissas, and response sentiments along the ordinal axes. The left-most chart summarizes all sentiments in conversations around a cheerful topic: *An Anonymous Benefactor*. The middle chart is the result of a conversation about *Terrorism*, while the right-side graph corresponds to a conversation about *Foreign Relations*. These were chosen to compare affect across differentially valenced topics.

In computing these figures we only considered the first 80 utterances. Since conversations were not monitored, they tended to start with the assigned topic, but then drifted. One reason for limiting the conversation snippets was to regularize the sample length, and also to simulate contact with an unfamiliar partner. This scenario matches most closely that of the CS10k robot interactions. The exact number of utterances was determined empirically.

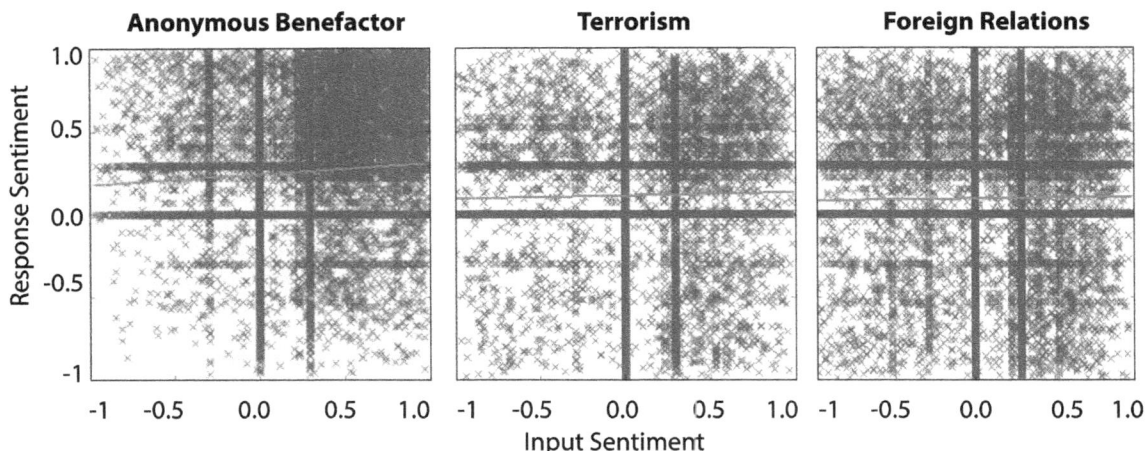

Figure 1: Tendency of sentiment for all conversations within three topics. A positive trend held for all topics.

Points in the left half of each plot contain all negative stimuli; all positive stimuli are contained in the right half of the plots. Consequently, the upper-left quadrant holds points in which a positive-sentiment reply was offered to a negative stimulus. The upper-right quadrant shows the cases where a positive response was given to a positive stimulus, and so on. In all conversations, more positive-sentiment statements occurred on either side of the conversation than contributions with negative valence. This tendency was most notable for the upbeat topics.

We computed the probabilities that a conversation partner would mirror a negative or positive stimulus:

$$P_{++} = P(R_{pos}|S_{pos}) \qquad (1)$$
$$P_{--} = P(R_{neg}|S_{neg}) \qquad (2)$$
$$P_{-+} = 1 - P_{++} \qquad (3)$$
$$P_{+-} = 1 - P_{--} \qquad (4)$$

Equation 1 shows the definition of P_{++}. The quantity is the probability of a positive response (R_{pos}) given a positive stimulus (S_{pos}) by the conversation partner. The remaining equations are analogous.

On average across all conversations, the probability that a positive stimulus drew a positive response was $0.84(SD = 0.06)$. For negative stimuli the probability of mirroring, i.e. evoking a negative response was just $0.22(SD = 0.05)$.

The benefactor chart in Figure 1 shows a strong preponderance of positive-sentiment utterances in the conversations. All sentiment distributions of uplifting topics looked like this chart. The median of Pearson correlations between the sentiment of a stimulus, and the sentiment of the resulting response among the benefactor conversations was $r = 0.26, p < 0.05$. The maximum correlation among those conversations was $r = 0.50$. These numbers are typical for all conversations.

In summary, the Fisher conversations show a very strong tendency for participants to formulate positive-sentiment statements. Upon encountering negative statements, the participants showed a consistent tendency towards moving the conversations in a positive direction. Interestingly, this observa-

tion may identify a pattern that would not be clinically useful and could differentiate between non-therapeutic and therapeutic interactions.

Human-Agent Communication
We saw that among the Fisher participants humans tend to reply with positive sentiments when in a generally non-combative context, even when confronted with negative stimuli. This trend may, of course, be different in an already negatively charged situation. We did not examine those scenarios.

Our next question was the sentiment mirroring behavior that humans would bring to conversational agents. Would one conversation partner being non-human change behaviors? For validation of our findings we conducted two independent human-agent experiments, using very different sentiment analysis methods. The disadvantage of using an agent with the limitations of current technology is that conversational inadequacies (e.g. non sequiturs) are bound to confound findings. One approach for avoiding this issue in future studies is to use a human confederate design where the agent is a human pretending to be an automaton. The disadvantage here is that in free-form conversation humans may be more accommodating than appropriate even with technology some year out. Frustration with automata, even in limited domains such as telephone trees will continue to be a factor for some time to come. We therefore chose CS10K for this study.

The first experiment used the VADER software package for determining sentiment, as per the human-human experiment described earlier. The dataset consisted of 5000 conversations with the Cleverbot [34] conversational agent(corpus CB5k).

Visitors to the Cleverbot site are free to conduct any conversation they like. No topic prompts are offered as in the Fisher collection, nor were conversation lengths recommended. Consequently, conversation durations varied. In many cases, visitors clearly experimented to explore the conversational agent's behavior. Many—sometimes long—conversations consisted of obscenities and insults patiently delivered to the conversational agent across what must have amounted to a considerable span of time. In fact, 97% of the visitor utterances in CB5k contained at least one swear word. Many expletives were obfuscated by the use of special characters in place of letters. VADER did not recognize these tokens, and classified them as neutral. For simplicity we converted these obfuscations into a single swear word that VADER already understood. Note that the presence of a swear word in a sentence does not necessary produce a negative-sentiment classification for the sentence as a whole.

Figure 2 shows the tendency of human Cleverbot site visitors to respond positively to the conversational agent. The chart

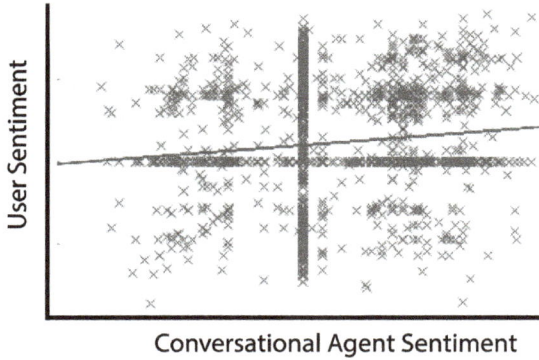

Figure 2: Site visitors tended to respond with positive sentiment to conversational agent stimuli (CB5k dataset). This tendency carries over from human-human behaviors.

shows conversational agent sentiment along the abscissa, and human-utterance sentiment along the ordinal. The pronounced horizontal and vertical data cluster lines are utterances that VADER classified as neutral. Note again the accumulation of positive-sentiment user statements in the upper-right quadrant.

The sentiment mirroring behaviors do carry over from what we observed in the human-human Fisher context. However, the effect sizes change significantly when humans correspond with Cleverbot. The probability of the human conversation partner mirroring a positive Cleverbot statement with an also positive response was 0.75. The probability of mirroring a negative statement was 0.41. Table 2 summarizes the comparison. Humans are twice as likely to respond with a negatively valenced reply when confronted with negative robot sentiment than when conversing with a human partner.

In a health care related context, this difference needs to be considered. We therefore explored sentiment behavior towards conversational agents further, using a larger dataset and a very different approach to measurement. The sentiment measurements above were obtained using standard methods. The following section describes a new version of the Cleverbot software that specializes in sentiment recognition performed in real time. âĞŽ For this **second human-robot experiment** we used 10,000 additional conversations conducted by site visitors to cleverbot.com and eviebot.com (corpus CB10k). These conversations were analyzed for sentiment using our

Table 2: Summary of behavior differences when humans interact with another human as opposed to a robot.

Dialog Partner		
	Human	
Human	mirror+: 0.84	
	mirror-: 0.22	
Robot	mirror+: 0.75	
	mirror-: 0.41	

Affective Neural Model (ANM). The model is a recurrent neural net (RNN). We discuss the details of this model and its implementation in Section 5. The model was trained using emoticons that human partners embedded in their utterances to the system.

We mapped over 300 emoticons and other signals in CB10k to seven different affects. We chose these affects as an amalgamation of three sources. First, we included the manually observed emotions generally exhibited by Cleverbot users. Second, we included the emotion set recently suggested by Facebook, which includes *like*, *love*, *haha*, *wow*, *sad*, and *angry*. Finally, we included the six basic emotions suggested by Paul Ekman's studies in 1984 on facial expressions of emotion: happiness, surprise, disgust, anger, fear and sadness [10]. We use these groups in our context of written communication. While this mapping may be a rough fit, the ability of current algorithms to classify sentiment down to fine granularities is equally approximate. Within margins of error, the Ekman groups are therefore likely to provide a reasonable stand-in for verbal/written emotion categories. The choice of particular emoticons follows the Facebook convention to improve real world applicability.

Figure 3 shows two screen shots taken while typing a sentence to the ANM. The sentiment changes from predominantly sad to happy by the completion of the sentence. The change illustrates the complexity of sarcasm, with its mixture of multiple emotions. The complete sentence of course expresses anger, but the clever sarcasm also brings up mirth. The algorithm leaned towards the positive.

THE AFFECTIVE NEURAL MODEL

In total we gathered 2,778,737 data points (*angry*: 421847, *surprise*: 249859, *happy*: 573422, *love*: 579476, *sad*: 422172, *disgust*: 25701, *laughter*: 506260). The dataset's vocabulary size (number of unique words) is 177,000 words.

Our model operates as a predictive model for the affects given a pair of dialogue lines (something Cleverbot said followed by the user's reply) and their affect labels. Our RNN deploys two Gated Recurrent Unit (GRU) [4] layers and a Softmax activation function on the output layer. The RNN models a probability distribution across the 7 affect labels conditioned on the given sequence of words. The probability of a given affect (such as *happy*) following a sequence of n words $w_1, w_2, ...w_n$ is approximated as:

$$P(affect|w_1, w_2...w_n) \approx P(affect|w_1)* \\ P(affect|w_2)* \\ ...*P(affect|w_n)$$

Figure 3: Predominant emotion changes as "I never forget a face" is expanded to "but in your case I'll be glad to make an exception."

The training process is very similar to RNN language models, but instead of predicting next words given previous ones our model tries to predict one of the 7 affects at the end of a given sequence of words, approximating the equation above. The sequence length (number of input words) is fixed at 30 words. Any sequences shorter than this use a special <pad> word to bring them up to 30.

A standard RNN layer has two sets of weights connecting it to the previous layer and to itself. A GRU instead uses six sets of weights to enable the layer to remember previous values. We therefore extended the context of each word beyond the single-vector history of regular RNNs.

The equations for a GRU are as follows. The inputs from the previous layer are given as x_t and the recurrent inputs as h_{t-1}. The update gate u multiplies these two sets of inputs by two corresponding sets of weights to determine whether the GRU should keep its previous values or update to a new one. The reset gate performs a similar function to determine which of the previous values should be reset/ignored. The third equation computes a new potential value to remember as m. The final equation produces the unit's output h_t either from the new potential value m or the previous value:

$$h_{t-1}:$$
$$u = \sigma \left(x_t W_u + h^{t-1} U_u \right)$$
$$r = \sigma \left(x_t W_r + h^{t-1} U_r \right)$$
$$m = \tanh \left(x_t W_m + (r \odot h_{t-1}) U_m \right)$$
$$h_t = u \odot m + (1 - u) \odot h_{t-1}$$

The weights between the input one-hot vectors and the first GRU layer in the network are commonly known as *word embeddings*. They can be treated as vector representations of each word. Words with similar affective value (e.g. *happy* and *wonderful*) are close to each other in the vector space. This is analogous to word embeddings produced by algorithms such as word2vec [25], where words are grouped together by semantic value. We also used dropout between the two GRU layers [11] as a form of regularization. This procedure randomly sets some values to zeros, adding artificial noise to the network to prevent overfitting. We separated 10% of the data points into a test set.

After training our model on 90% of the nearly 3 million data points, we then tested on the remaining 10% containing 277,874 data points. On this test set, the model shows 90% accuracy. In other words, our model correctly predicted the overriding affect for 90% of unseen lines of conversation. If we then type *I'm depressed* into our model, it guesses that we feel sad (with a probability of 67%).

Sentiment measurements of the human contributions again confirm the preponderance of positive sentiment (Figure 4).

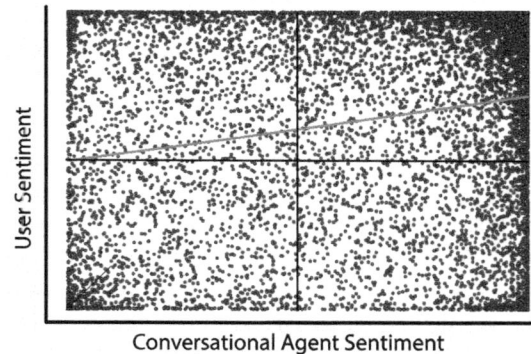

Figure 4: Site visitor vs. ANM sentiment (RNN10k dataset). Note again the upward tendency.

Limitations

Our study is limited along the following dimensions. First, we did not assess language that occurred in mental health focused conversations, but a mixture of conversations about upbeat and sad topics. Second, the use of positively or negatively labeled words does not necessarily map onto the user's emotional state [30], limiting the generalizability of this approach. Finally, the Fisher collection consists of phone conversation transcripts, while the CBxk collections were conducted over the Internet. Further study is needed to determine the extent to which this difference is a confound in the comparison between human-human and human-agent behavior. For example, it is possible that for younger generations, affective differences between typed (e.g. texted) and spoken communication have begun to fade.

128

CONCLUSION

Our work extends the role of NLP by contextualizing the assessment of sentiment within a clinically relevant theory of language and mental health (RFT). Through the creation of NLP tools grounded within accepted psychological theory, conversational agents may be developed to assess real time features of a user's conversation. These in turn inform mental health screening and treatment. Such information is useful for both assessment, and measurement of treatment impact on real world functioning. For example, RFT is a way to understand how cognitions interact with behavior to produce suffering. RFT articulates why people get stuck in maladaptive patterns, and NLP allows us to systematically identify these patterns in naturally occurring conversations.

Automating the evaluation of psychological symptoms could impact mental health by increasing access to services, and potentially decreasing costs associated with non-treatment or traditional clinical models. The development of frameworks for identifying affect-relevant labels may improve screening for maladaptive patterns of language that cause distress, and provide targets for intervention. Designing NLP-based approaches that assess clinically relevant language would allow for the design of conversational agents that are scalable, transparent in their labeling of language, and responsive to patient and language features.

Our study shows that human sentiment conventions carry over to human-agent interactions, but that those norms are weakened. Humans are twice as likely to respond with a negatively valenced reply when confronted with negative robot sentiment than when conversing with a human partner. This finding may have important implications for the design of agents' reactions to human utterances: the a priori lowered sense of obligation towards 'niceness' must be taken into account.

Future work should assess the role of language in the additional two RFT components (*time and contingency*, and *comparison and evaluation*). Our finding that users mirror more positive language than negative language is consistent with previous research showing asynchronous conversational responses to positive and negative language (e.g. [21]). This is significant as it yields greater understanding of the differences between human-to-human and human-to-computer interactions that can inform the design of clinically focused tools. Also, language is only one way humans express and understand emotions. Integrating NLP-based approaches with other areas of affective computing (e.g. gaze, facial expression) and additional behavioral and social interactions will benefit the design of mental health focused conversational agents.

REFERENCES

1. Tim Althoff, Kevin Clark, and Jure Leskovec. 2016. Natural Language Processing for Mental Health: Large Scale Discourse Analysis of Counseling Conversations. *Transactions of the Association for Computational Linguistics* (2016).

2. Timothy Bickmore, Amanda Gruber, and Rosalind Picard. 2005. Establishing the computer–patient working alliance in automated health behavior change interventions. *Patient education and counseling* 59, 1 (2005), 21–30.

3. Timothy W Bickmore, Daniel Schulman, and Candace Sidner. 2013. Automated interventions for multiple health behaviors using conversational agents. *Patient education and counseling* 92, 2 (2013), 142–148.

4. Junyoung Chung, Caglar Gulcehre, KyungHyun Cho, and Yoshua Bengio. 2014. Empirical Evaluation of Gated Recurrent Neural Networks on Sequence Modeling. *arxiv.org* (12 2014). http://arxiv.org/abs/1412.3555

5. Christopher Cieri and et al. 2004/2005. Fisher English Training Speech Part 1/2 Transcripts LDC2004T19. Linguistic Data Consortium. (2004/2005). https://catalog.ldc.upenn.edu/LDC2004T19

6. Rik Crutzen, Gjalt-Jorn Y Peters, Sarah Dias Portugal, Erwin M Fisser, and Jorne J Grolleman. 2011. An artificially intelligent chat agent that answers adolescents' questions related to sex, drugs, and alcohol: an exploratory study. *Journal of Adolescent Health* 48, 5 (2011), 514–519.

7. Alison M Darcy, Alan K Louie, and Laura Weiss Roberts. 2016. Machine Learning and the Profession of Medicine. *JAMA* 315, 6 (2016), 551–552.

8. Xiaowen Ding and Bing Liu. 2007. The Utility of Linguistic Rules in Opinion Mining. In *Proceedings of the 30th Annual International ACM SIGIR Conference on Research and Development in Information Retrieval*. 811–812.

9. David Daniel Ebert, Anna-Carlotta Zarski, Helen Christensen, Yvonne Stikkelbroek, Pim Cuijpers, Matthias Berking, and Heleen Riper. 2015. Internet and computer-based cognitive behavioral therapy for anxiety and depression in youth: a meta-analysis of randomized controlled outcome trials. *PloS one* 10, 3 (2015), e0119895.

10. Paul Ekman. 1984. Expression and the nature of emotion. *Approaches to emotion* 3 (1984), 19–344.

11. Yarin Gal. 2015. A Theoretically Grounded Application of Dropout in Recurrent Neural Networks. *arxiv.org* (12 2015). http://arxiv.org/abs/1512.05287

12. Felix Greaves, Daniel Ramirez-Cano, Christopher Millett, Ara Darzi, and Liam Donaldson. 2013. Harnessing the cloud of patient experience: using social media to detect poor quality healthcare. *BMJ quality & safety* (2013), bmjqs–2012.

13. David E Greenway, Emily K Sandoz, and David R Perkins. 2010. Potential applications of relational frame theory to natural language systems. In *Fuzzy Systems and Knowledge Discovery (FSKD), 2010 Seventh International Conference on*, Vol. 6. IEEE, 2955–2958.

14. Steven C Hayes, Dermot Barnes-Holmes, and Bryan Roche. 2001. *Relational frame theory: A post-Skinnerian account of human language and cognition*. Springer Science & Business Media.

15. Jing Huang, Qi Li, Yuanyuan Xue, Taoran Cheng, Shuangqing Xu, Jia Jia, and Ling Feng. 2015. Teenchat: a chatterbot system for sensing and releasing adolescentsâĂŹ stress. In *Health Information Science*. Springer, 133–145.

16. Eva Hudlicka. 2003. To feel or not to feel: The role of affect in human–computer interaction. *International journal of human-computer studies* 59, 1 (2003), 1–32.

17. C.J. Hutto and Eric Gilbert. 2014. VADER: A Parsimonious Rule-Based Model for Sentiment Analysis of Social Media Text. In *Proceedings of the Eighth International AAAI Conference on Weblogs and Social Media*. AAAI Publications, Ann Arbor, MI, 216–225.

18. Kristin N Javaras, Nan M Laird, Ted Reichborn-Kjennerud, Cynthia M Bulik, Harrison G Pope, and James I Hudson. 2008. Familiality and heritability of binge eating disorder: results of a case-control family study and a twin study. *International Journal of Eating Disorders* 41, 2 (2008), 174–179.

19. Nitin Jindal and Bing Liu. 2006. Identifying Comparative Sentences in Text Documents. In *Proceedings of the 29th Annual International ACM SIGIR Conference on Research and Development in Information Retrieval (SIGIR '06)*. ACM, New York, NY, USA, 244–251. DOI: http://dx.doi.org/10.1145/1148170.1148215

20. David Kessler, Glyn Lewis, Surinder Kaur, Nicola Wiles, Michael King, Scott Weich, Debbie J Sharp, Ricardo Araya, Sandra Hollinghurst, and Tim J Peters. 2009. Therapist-delivered internet psychotherapy for depression in primary care: a randomised controlled trial. *The Lancet* 374, 9690 (2009), 628–634.

21. Adam DI Kramer, Jamie E Guillory, and Jeffrey T Hancock. 2014. Experimental evidence of massive-scale emotional contagion through social networks. *Proceedings of the National Academy of Sciences* 111, 24 (2014), 8788–8790.

22. Yang Liu, Xiaohui Yu, Zhongshuai Chen, and Bing Liu. 2013. Sentiment Analysis of Sentences with Modalities. In *Proceedings of the 2013 International Workshop on Mining Unstructured Big Data Using Natural Language Processing (UnstructureNLP '13)*. ACM, New York, NY, USA, 39–44. DOI: http://dx.doi.org/10.1145/2513549.2513556

23. Ramesh Manuvinakurike, Wayne F Velicer, and Timothy W Bickmore. 2014. Automated indexing of Internet stories for health behavior change: weight loss attitude pilot study. *Journal of medical Internet research* 16, 12 (2014).

24. Evan Mayo-Wilson and Paul Montgomery. 2013. Media-delivered cognitive behavioural therapy and behavioural therapy (self-help) for anxiety disorders in adults. *Cochrane Database Syst Rev* 9 (2013), CD005330.

25. Tomas Mikolov, Ilya Sutskever, Kai Chen, Greg S Corrado, and Jeff Dean. 2013. Distributed Representations of Words and Phrases and their Compositionality. In *Advances in Neural Information Processing Systems 26*, C. J. C. Burges, L. Bottou, M. Welling, Z. Ghahramani, and K. Q. Weinberger (Eds.). Curran Associates, Inc., 3111–3119. http://arxiv.org/abs/1310.4546

26. Adam S Miner, Arnold Milstein, Stephen Schueller, Roshini Hegde, Christina Mangurian, and Eleni Linos. 2016. Smartphone-based conversational agents and responses to questions about mental health, interpersonal violence, and physical health. *JAMA internal medicine* (2016).

27. David C Mohr, Michelle Nicole Burns, Stephen M Schueller, Gregory Clarke, and Michael Klinkman. 2013. Behavioral intervention technologies: evidence review and recommendations for future research in mental health. *General hospital psychiatry* 35, 4 (2013), 332–338.

28. Theresa B Moyers and William R Miller. 2013. Is low therapist empathy toxic? *Psychology of Addictive Behaviors* 27, 3 (2013), 878.

29. James W Pennebaker, Ryan L Boyd, Kayla Jordan, and Kate Blackburn. 2015. The Development and Psychometric Properties of LIWC2015. *UT Faculty/Researcher Works* (2015).

30. James W Pennebaker, Matthias R Mehl, and Kate G Niederhoffer. 2003. Psychological aspects of natural language use: Our words, our selves. *Annual review of psychology* 54, 1 (2003), 547–577.

31. Erik Rautalinko, Hans-Olof Lisper, and Bo Ekehammar. 2007. Reflective listening in counseling: effects of training time and evaluator social skills. *American journal of psychotherapy* 61, 2 (2007), 191.

32. Byron Reeves and Cliff Nass. 1996. *The Media Equation: How People Treat Computers, Television, and New Media Like Real People and Places*. Cambridge University Press, NY.

33. Rainer Reisenzein, Eva Hudlicka, Mehdi Dastani, Jonathan Gratch, Koen Hindriks, Emiliano Lorini, and John-Jules Ch Meyer. 2013. Computational modeling of emotion: Toward improving the inter-and intradisciplinary exchange. *Affective Computing, IEEE Transactions on* 4, 3 (2013), 246–266.

34. Paul Tero, Ilia Zaitsev, and Rollo Carpenter. 2016. Cleverbot Data for Machine Learning. http://www.existor.com/en/ml-cleverbot-data-for-machine-learning.html. (January 2016).

35. Adam Waytz, John Cacioppo, and Nicholas Epley. 2010. Who sees human? The stability and importance of individual differences in anthropomorphism. *Perspectives on Psychological Science* 5, 3 (2010), 219–232.

Improving Smartphone Users' Affect and Wellbeing with Personalized Positive Psychology Interventions

Sooyeon Jeong
MIT Media Lab
Cambridge, USA
sooyeon6@mit.edu

Cynthia Breazeal
MIT Media Lab
Cambridge, USA
cynthiab@media.mit.edu

ABSTRACT

We developed a smartphone application that detects users' affect and provides personalized positive psychology interventions in order to enhance users' psychological wellbeing. Users' emotional states were measured by analyzing facial expressions and the sentiment of SMS messages. A virtual character in the application prompted users to verbally journal about their day by providing three positive psychology interventions. The system used a Markov Decision Process (MDP) model and a State-Action-Reward-State-Action (SARSA) algorithm to learn users' preferences about the positive psychology interventions. Nine participants were recruited for an experimental study to test the application. They used it daily for three weeks. The interactive journaling activity increased participants' arousal and valence levels immediately following each interaction, and we saw a trend toward improved self-acceptance levels over the three week period. The interaction duration increased significantly throughout the study as well. The qualitative analysis on journal entries showed that the application users explored and reflected on various aspects of themselves by looking at daily events, and found novel appreciation for and meanings in their daily routine.

Author Keywords

Positive psychology; mobile technology; psychological wellbeing; expressive writing therapy;

ACM Classification Keywords

H.1.2 User/Machine Systems: Software psychology

INTRODUCTION

Major depressive disorder is the leading cause of disability in the U.S. for ages 15-44 [2] and affects 14.8 million American adults, or about 6.7 percent of the U.S. population age 18 and older [15]. Various treatment methods, such cognitive behavioral therapy (CBT),

HAI '16, October 04-07, 2016, Biopolis, Singapore © 2016 ACM.
ISBN 978-1-4503-4508-8/16/10...$15.00
DOI: http://dx.doi.org/10.1145/2974804.2974831

interpersonal therapy, and medications have been developed in order to treat the disorder. However, individual psychotherapy is still not yet widely accessible to the majority of people who need psychological interventions [14,31].

In order to increase the accessibility of psychotherapy, many smartphone or computer-based applications and wearable sensors have been developed [7,8,16,17,19,21,23,32]. Most of these applications target patients who already have been diagnosed with a mental disorder and focus on monitoring their mental and/or physiological states, or providing guidance for CBT.

In this paper, we present a smartphone application that combines expressive writing therapy and positive psychology interventions in order to enhance smartphone users' psychological wellbeing and affect. Expressive writing therapy has been shown to reduce depression and anxiety, increase physiological arousal, and decrease long-term health problems [3,11,18,22]. Positive psychology interventions can reduce depressive symptom levels for those diagnosed with major depressive disorder, and increase subjective and psychological wellbeing for patients with depression as well as for people who are not diagnosed with any mental disorder [1,8,21,22,27]. With the application, smartphone users verbally responded to a virtual character's positive psychology intervention prompts. The virtual agent was not presented as a conversational partner but rather as a facilitator and a helper for users to reflect with, and interactively journal about their day.

The system analyzed users' facial expressions and the sentiment of their SMS messages in order to learn which intervention prompts increased users' affect and engagement over multiple interactions. We compared smartphone users' affect immediately before and after using the application. Their psychological wellbeing levels were also measured over three weeks to evaluate any long-term change. Markov Decision Process (MDP) [24] and State-Action-Reward-State-Action (SARSA) [25] algorithms were used to learn the user's preference for the interventions.

We hypothesized that (1) smartphone users' affect and psychological wellbeing would increase after using the interactive journaling application daily for three weeks, and (2) user engagement with the application would increase over time as the application learned to select the most appropriate interventions for the users. The efficacy of the interactive journaling application in increasing users' psychological wellbeing was evaluated by running a three-week long experimental study. The verbal journal entries were audio recorded on the device and then retrieved by the experimenter at the end of the study for qualitative analysis.

METHODS

Participants and Procedure

Nine participants (three male and six female, age M=28.3, SD=6.58) who owned Android devices with API 4.1 or higher were recruited from MIT campus via email advertisements. Once consented, the participants were asked to fill out the pre-survey and had the interactive journaling application installed on their mobile device for the study. Participants were asked to use the interactive journaling application every day for three weeks. The app notified the participants to use the application at 9PM every day, but did not provide constraints on the time or the length of app usage.

Participants were asked to fill out questionnaires on their mood [20], perceived stress [6], affect balance [5] and psychological wellbeing [26] for pre-, mid- and post-tests (Table 1). The pre-questionnaire was administered at the beginning of the study. The mid-questionnaires were administered after one week, and the post-questionnaires were administered at the end of the three-week study. The post-study questionnaires also included the bond factor in working alliance inventory (WAI) [12] to assess whether participants perceived a socio-emotional bond with the virtual character in the interactive journaling application.

Survey	Measurement
Pre-survey (start date)	- Demographic information - Journaling Habit Questionnaire - Signature Strength Survey [10] - Brief Mood Introspection Scale (BMIS) - Perceived Stress Scale - Affect Balance Scale - Ryff's Psychological Well-Being Scales
Mid-survey (after 1 week)	- Brief Mood Introspection Scale (BMIS) - Perceived Stress Scale - Affect Balance Scale - Ryff's Psychological Well-Being Scales
Post-survey (after 3 weeks)	- Brief Mood Introspection Scale (BMIS) - Perceived Stress Scale - Affect Balance Scale - Ryff's Psychological Well-Being Scales - Working Alliance Inventory

Table 1. List of questionnaires used for pre-, mid- and post-tests.

Interactive Journaling Application

Eleven positive psychology interventions (Table 2) were framed as questions and programmed into the interactive journaling application. For each session with the app, three out of these eleven positive psychology interventions were used. Before and after the journaling session, participants were asked report their arousal and valence levels in numeric scores [-4, 4] (see Figure 1).

When the first set of arousal/valence scores were reported, the virtual agent appeared on the screen and greeted the participant (*"Hi! Nice to see you again. Are you excited for the questions?"*). The greeting utterances were varied each day within a pre-selected pool. Then, the participant pressed the button below the character to make the virtual character provide the first question and interactively journaled as much as desired. During the participant's response, the virtual agent displayed back-channeling and listening behaviors ("Hmm", "Uh-huh", "I see", "Oh", etc.) when a verbal pause was recognized. When done answering a question, the participant went on to the next question by pressing the button again. When all three intervention questions were answered, the virtual character thanked the participant for their responses and said goodbye to exit the interaction. The self-report arousal/valence screen (Figure 1a) appeared again and the app closed after participants responded.

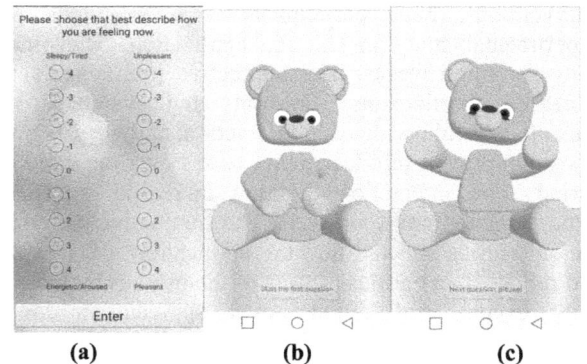

Figure 1. (a) Arousal and valence assessment screen for pre- and post-interaction with the interactive journaling application, (b) virtual character at idle position, (c) virtual character animated.

Interventions	Questions
Positive	(1) What are three good things that happened today? (2) Is there someone you feel gratitude to? (3) Tell me about one kind act you did today. (4) Tell me three funny things that you experienced today.
Neutral	(1) How did you use yours signature strengths in a new way today? (2) Is there anything you'd like to talk about? (3) How did you use your "gift" of time to someone today? It could be helping someone, sharing meal, etc.
Negative	(1) Was there anything that made you angry today? (2) Is there someone you need to forgive? (3) Tell me about a moment today when something bad turned into something good.

Table 2. Lists of questions used for each positive psychology intervention in the interactive journaling application.

Affect Detection with Affdex and SentiStrength

We used the Affdex mobile SDK, a commercial tool marketed by Affectiva, Inc. (affectiva.com), to detect users' emotions during smartphone usage. Affdex can detect 34 FACS (Facial Action Coding System) units [9] along with 9 emotions (joy, anger, disgust, contempt, engagement, fear, sadness, surprise, and valence) and 15 expressions (attention, brow furrow, brow raise, chin raise, eye closure, inner brow raise, lip corner depressor, lip press, lip pucker, lip suck, mouth open, nose wrinkle, smile, smirk, and upper lip raise). The valence feature was used to calculate the user's mood, and we recorded all of the nine emotion metrics for analysis in real time with the front-facing camera on the Android device. Each of these metrics produced a score in range of [0, 100], except for valence, which ranged [-100, 100].

While the smartphone was turned on, the application ran the facial expression capture process and captured facial emotional data from any visible face from the front-facing camera. The facial expression capture process silently started with five-minute intervals and captured data for 10 seconds. When no face was found, no affect data was recorded. While the user was using the interactive journaling application, the facial expression capture process ran continuously without stopping.

The sentiment of smart phone users' incoming and outgoing text messages was analyzed in order to infer the users' emotional state and to update the mood score. We used the SentiStrength tool [29,30] to evaluate the sentiment of each text message, which gave us both positive and negative scores. The positive score ranged between [1, 5] and the negative score ranged between [-5, -1]. SentiStrength was able to take account of widely used emoticons, such as :), :(or <3, as well as the usage of all capitalized words, for sentiment analysis. For example, the message *"Cool cool. also turns out Dustin has to work :[so I'm brining my friend Sam if that's OK with you"* results in a positive score of 2 and a negative score of -2, while the message *"Aww, that is so sweet! Sure. I can hold onto the tickets until then. :]"* produces 3 and -1. The application retrieved the content of text messages whenever there was an incoming or outgoing SMS message. The positive and negative scores for a single SMS message were added together, and then multiplied by 20 to give a score on a consistent scale with the valence score from Affdex.

Since the mood is a collective and aggregate metric of continuous affect and emotions over time, both the previous mood score and the most current valence score contributed to the daily mood score with a decay effect over time:

$$m_{new} = m_{old}\lambda^{\Delta t} + v_{new}(1 - \lambda^{\Delta t})$$

m and v are the mood and valence scores respectively. λ is the decay rate (0.95) and Δt is the elapsed time since the last mood score update time in hours. The mood score was updated whenever new affect data was available, either by capturing facial expression information through Affdex or by analyzing the sentiment of a text message via SentiStrength.

Personalization

The intervention selection behavior was modeled as a Markov Decision Process (MDP) [24]. The policy on the MDP model was formulated as a $Q(s, a)$ matrix, where s represented the user's mood and affect state, and a represented the selection of the intervention type. The state space consisted of three dimensions: daily mood, current valence, and current engagement. The daily mood state was discretized to three values.

$$S_{mood}\ \{Negative, Neutral, Positive\} = \{[-100, 0), 0, (0, 100]\}$$
$$S_{valence}\ \{Negative, Neutral, Positive\}\ \{[-100, 0), 0, (0, 100]\}$$
$$S_{engagement}\ \{Low, High\}\ \{[0, 0.91), [0.91, 100]\}$$

In total, the state space consisted of $3 \times 3 \times 2 = 18$ states. The action space consisted of 3 actions, $a = \{Negative, Neutral, Positive\}$. The action selection was made when the user launched the interactive journaling application for the journaling activity. Once the intervention type was chosen, three questions within the selected intervention category were randomly selected for the session The initial policy represented an equally random distribution over three possible actions. A reinforcement-learning algorithm was implemented in order to personalize the intervention selection policy to each user. In order to achieve this, a standard SARSA (State-Action-Reward-State-Action) algorithm [25] was used. In our algorithm, the reward was calculated as a weighted sum of the valence score, engagement score, and the duration of the journaling session:

$$r = 0.15(s_{val} + 100) + 0.3s_{eng} + 0.66(t_{end} - t_{start})$$

t_{start} and t_{end} are the start and end time of the journaling session in the unit of seconds. This reward function aimed to maximize engagement and valence scores, and the duration of user's journaling activity. In order to control for the exploration and exploitation of the MDP model, a ϵ-greedy algorithm was implemented. ϵ was set to decrease with each successive session $\epsilon_1 = 0.75$, $\epsilon_2 = 0.5$ and $\epsilon_i = 0.25$ for $i >= 3$. The learning rate also decreased $\alpha_1 = 0.5$, $\alpha_2 = 0.4$, $\alpha_3 = 0.3$, $\alpha_4 = 0.2$ and $\alpha_i = 0.1$ for $i >= 5$.

RESULTS

Personalized Intervention Selection Policies

A different intervention selection policy was developed for each participant. Figure 2 shows the Euclidean distances between participants' final intervention selection policies. The learning algorithm personalized to each participant, and they ended up with drastically different policies from one another. The policies did not converge after 3 weeks, but this was not surprising, since there was a large state space and relatively few learning interactions.

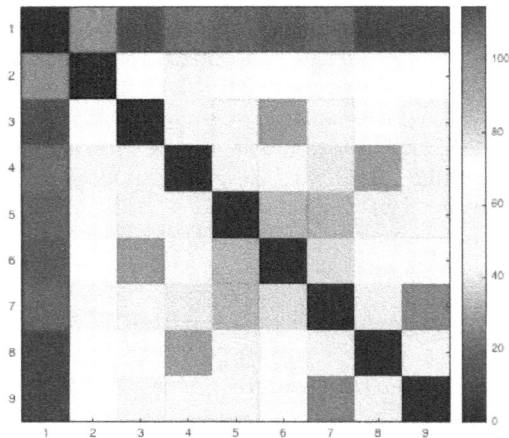

Figure 2. A distance matrix for nine participants' final intervention selection policies after three weeks.

Increased arousal and valence after each session

Both arousal and valence levels increased after participants used the interactive journaling app. The mean arousal level before the journaling activity was -0.59 and increased to -0.39 after the session (Wilcoxon signed rank test, N = 137, $p = 0.017$). The mean valence level before the interaction was 0.53 and increased to 0.82 after the session was over (Wilcoxon signed rank test, N = 137, $p = 0.004$)

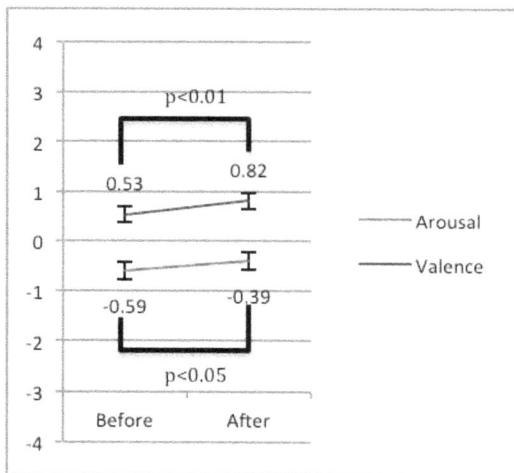

Figure 3. Both arousal and valence levels increased after participants used the interactive journaling app.

A trend of increase in self-acceptance level

Pre-, mid- and post-test responses showed no statistically significant differences in participants' mood, perceived stress and affect balance. However, participants' self-acceptance levels from the Ryff's Psychological Well-Being scale [26] showed a trend of difference (Friedman's test, $p = 0.10$). High self-acceptance levels indicate that a

person has gained a more positive attitude toward the self and has accepted multiple aspects of self, including good and bad qualities [26]. Pairwise comparisons on self-acceptance levels failed to show a statistically significant difference with p<0.05, but we did see a trend of increase from the mid-test to the post-test (Tukey's test, $p = 0.08$, Figure 4).

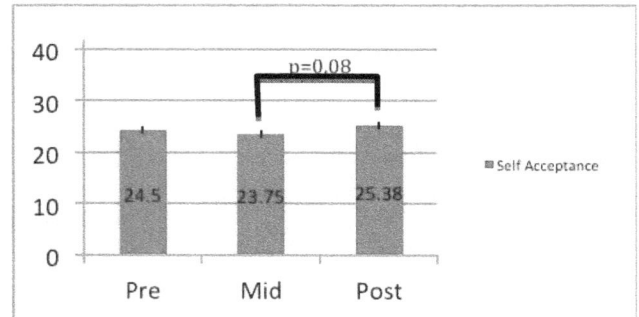

Figure 4. Self-acceptance levels showed a trend of increase between mid-test and post-test

Increased interaction duration over time

We compared participants' response length for each question in the first 1.5 weeks of the study to the second 1.5 weeks. Figure 5 shows that the responses lasted a mean of 24.62 seconds for each intervention question in the first half of the study phase, and 31.59 seconds for the second half. This increase in the length of response time was statistically significant (Mann-Whitney U test, N = 677, $p = 0.0002$).

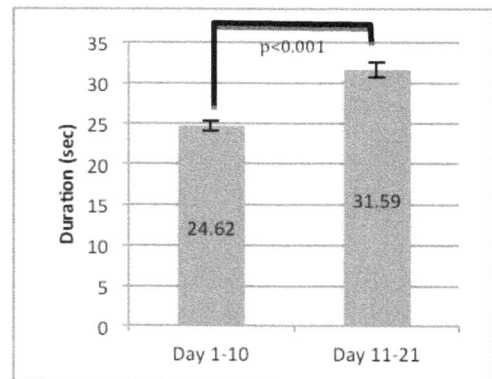

Figure 5. Interaction length per question increased in the second half of study.

Intimate and personal journal entries

Participants talked about intimate and personal matters. Although the prompts asked mainly about specific events or actions and were rather limited, participants expanded their responses to reflections and evaluations of themselves, their relationships with others, their purpose of life, and more. Below is a transcription of one journal entry made in the study. *A* represents the virtual agent of the app and *P* indicates the participant's response.

A: **How did you use your signature strength in a new way today?**

P: (clears throat) I don't remember what my signature strength is, I think it's "appreciation" ... maybe? Uhm ... what did I do today? I fell asleep during class ... lunch ... oh okay, so, yeah, last night my friend came up, uhh, to basically ... to basically just talk about, like, random stuff. But, uhm, we ended up talking for, like, an hour-and-half about ... my life, and my ... and I don't know, it got kind of deep? Like my character, or my world views and how maybe there are things that I can work on, which I agree with (clears throat). And then I talked to my roommate about some more, sort of like ... views on change, or how ... I was very, like, interesting conversations.

Uhm, and then it's something that I've been thinking about a lot and so I kind of ... this is more like the gratitude question, I guess. But I'm grateful that they took time out of their day to listen to me. I feel like all I do is complain, which is another thing I'm working on. And so it was nice that ... I really did ... I really did appreciate that they were there and that they listened to what I had to say and they made time for me and ...

A: **(Excited) Oh! Tell me anything you would like to talk about.**

P: Uhm ... I guess just generally I feel like ... getting ... getting better, I guess, or ... ? Maybe closer to who I was before, and the next step is for me to let go of all these negative thoughts and feelings that I still have. I don't know why, unconsciously or subconsciously, clinging to these thoughts (clears throat). Like I feel like I have to be ... or it's not that I feel like I have to be, I feel like ... I have this weird idea that my natural state is negative. And I feel like that's not true ... because ...

A: **(Excited) Mmm!**

P: I feel like things have changed ... and I want to change them back. Because I liked who I was as a person more before I sort of entered this storm of negativity. Uhm, I'm going to do my writing exercise tonight and I think since writing is a good way to sort out your thoughts and explore ... deeper what you truly believe, to organize these things that you have, I'll probably use that time to kind of figure out how I'm feeling about who I am ... and sort of the way that I've been acting lately.

A: **How did you use your gift of time to someone today? It could be helping someone, sharing a meal, or anything like that.**

P: Uhm, I shared a meal with the tennis team today. I kind of wanted to just dream box and come back to my room and watch T.V. and ... eat (laughter) by myself ... because sometimes I'm antisocial. But (clears throat), I ended up eating with the team and an old teammate that came back to visit us this week and it was nice ... talking to them. And I feel like the fact that I think it was nice, or maybe even just some part of me ... means that I'm moving in the right direction because like if you asked me a month ago I probably would have been insufferable and I feel like yeah it's the whole ... vicious cycle thing, like my negativity is making me act a certain way, people are reacting accordingly and then I'm just sort of like "This is terrible". But ... I don't know, that was a positive thing that happened today, I guess.

A: **Thank you for sharing. It was good to hear your stories. See you!**

DISCUSSION

Even though no statistically significant change in participants' psychological wellbeing was found across the three-week study, the application had the short-term effect of increasing arousal and valence levels for its users. This result aligns with previous research on expressive writing therapy [18-20], and shows that the journaling framing of the intervention activity was effective in improving users' affect.

Participants interacted longer in the second half of the study than in the first half. This could have resulted from the unique intervention selection policies that the reinforcement algorithm learned for each user over time, but an alternative hypothesis also exists. Another cause could be that over the course of three weeks, participants became more familiar with the activity and learned to express themselves better with the application. However, it is difficult to make a conclusive interpretation of what caused the change in interaction length because there was no control group that used the application without the personalization to compare with the treatment group. A follow-up study with multiple experimental treatment groups would be needed in order to identify the effect of the personalization algorithm on users' engagement with the app.

The qualitative analysis of the recorded journal entries provided some evidence that participants reflected about themselves, which could have led to the trend of increase in self-acceptance levels. This was intriguing because the intervention questions in the journaling application did not directly ask participants about their opinions of the self. However, participants often described themselves (e.g., *"I usually try to have positive attitudes," "I get irritated really easily," "I am the unhealthiest person in the world."*) while describing circumstances or events that happened to them for their journal entries.

Sometimes, these discussions of the self led participants to find new meanings and appreciation for themselves. For instance, during an informal interview at the end of the study, one participant reported that she felt answering the "three kind acts" question was difficult initially because she did not perform big charity or community service work on daily basis. However, she soon realized that even small acts, such as preparing a nice warm meal for her family or friends, could be considered a kind act, and she found meaning in her daily chores that she used to consider trivial. On the other hand, another participant confessed in one of her journal entries that she was an "insecure" person and explored the idea whether she should feel "gratitude" for the friendship that she and her friend shared. She commented that it felt "weird" to say that she is grateful that her friend likes her since a friendship is supposed to be a "mutual thing." However, during a later journal entry, the same participant also narrated her appreciation and gratitude toward her friends for listening to her despite the fact that "all [she] does is complaining".

LIMITATIONS AND FUTURE WORK
We interviewed the participants at the end of the study to identify limitations of the interactive journaling application. Some participants commented that they were frustrated at the repetitiveness of the interventions. They suggested having a bigger pool of questions, and even additional open-ended questions for the activity. Many participants mentioned that they sometimes talked to the character about matters that were not strictly related to the question because they had the desire to reflect about certain events that were significant to them. Also, a few participants expressed difficulties listing "three" items for funny things or good things that happened to them. The "three funny things" had significantly lower answering rate than any other intervention questions.

Another limitation of the application was that the virtual character always talked in high-pitched and cheerful voice. Sometimes the character's cheerful greetings, e.g., *"Hi! Hope you had a wonderful day,"* irritated the users when they were in a negative mood. Addressing the emotional match between the character and the user can be significant in providing a sense of empathy and emotional bond [13].

Based on participants' feedback, we plan to expand the set of questions and to enable the character to identify the user's emotion and match the tone of its voice as well as the interventions to the user's current emotional state. We will also run a randomized control trial experiment with the personalized and non-personalized application in order to evaluate the efficacy of the personalization.

CONCLUSION
We developed a smartphone application that provided an interactive journaling experience for users to improve their affect and mood. The system successfully engaged users for three weeks, and users engagement with the application increased over time. We used facial expressions and SMS messages to detect users' emotional states, and we used the collected affect data to personalize the human-agent interaction for each user. Despite some weaknesses, most users found the application helpful in reflecting about themselves and their daily lives. Our work could complement existing psychological interventions and enable people to have more frequent and easy access to interventions that improve human wellbeing.

ACKNOWLEDGEMENT
This work was funded by LG Electronics Inc.

REFERENCES
1. N Asgharipoor, H Arshadi, and a Sahebi. 2012. A comparative study on the effectiveness of positive psychotherapy and group cognitive-behavioral therapy for the patients suffering from major depressive disorder . *Iranian Journal of Psychiatry and Behavioral Sciences* 6 , 2 : 33–41. Retrieved from http://ijpbs.mazums.ac.ir/browse.php?a_id=176&slc_lang=en&sid=1&ftxt=1

2. East Asia. 2004. Deaths and DALYs 2004□: Annex tables.

3. K. a. Baikie. 2005. Emotional and physical health benefits of expressive writing. *Advances in Psychiatric Treatment* 11, 5: 338–346. http://doi.org/10.1192/apt.11.5.338

4. Linda Bolier, Merel Haverman, Gerben J Westerhof, Heleen Riper, Filip Smit, and Ernst Bohlmeijer. 2013. Positive psychology interventions: a meta-analysis of randomized controlled studies. *BMC public health* 13, 1: 119. http://doi.org/10.1186/1471-2458-13-119

5. Norman M Bradburn. The Structure of Psychological Well-Being.

6. S Cohen, T Kamarck, and R Mermelstein. 1983. A global measure of perceived stress. *Journal of health and social behavior* 24, 4: 385–396. http://doi.org/10.2307/2136404

7. Tara Donker, Katherine Petrie, Judy Proudfoot, Janine Clarke, Mary Rose Birch, and Helen Christensen. 2013. Smartphones for smarter delivery of mental health programs: A systematic review. *Journal of Medical Internet Research* 15. http://doi.org/10.2196/jmir.2791

8. Patrick L. Dulin, Vivian M. Gonzalex, Diane K. King, Danielle Giroux, and Samantha Bacon. 2013. Smartphone-Based, Self-Administered Intervention System for Alcohol Use Disorders: Theory and Empirical Evidence Basis. *Alcohol Treat Q.* 31, 3: 997–1003. http://doi.org/10.1016/j.biotechadv.2011.08.021.Secreted

9. Paul Ekman and Wallace V. Friesen. 1976. Measuring Facial Movement. *Environmental Psychology and Nonverbal Behavior* 1, 1: 56–75.

10. Fabian Gander, René T. Proyer, Willibald Ruch, and Tobias Wyss. 2013. Strength-Based Positive Interventions: Further Evidence for Their Potential in Enhancing Well-Being and Alleviating Depression. *Journal of Happiness Studies* 14, 4: 1241–1259. http://doi.org/10.1007/s10902-012-9380-0

11. Eva Maria Gortner, Stephanie S. Rude, and James W. Pennebaker. 2006. Benefits of Expressive Writing in Lowering Rumination and Depressive Symptoms. *Behavior Therapy* 37, 3: 292–303. http://doi.org/10.1016/j.beth.2006.01.004

12. Adam O. Horvath and Leslie S. Greenberg. 1989. Development and validation of the Working Alliance Inventory. *Journal of counseling psychology* 36, 2: 223–233.

13. Ing-Marie Jonsson, Clifford Nass, Helen Harris, and Leila Takayama. 2005. Matching In-car Voice with Driver State: Impact on Attitude and Driving Performance. *Proceedings of the Third International Driving Symposium on Human Factors in Driver Assessment, Training and Vehicle Design*, 173–180.

14. Alan E Kazdin and Stacey L Blase. 2011. Rebooting Psychotherapy Research and Practice to Reduce the Burden of Mental Illness. *Perspectives on Psychological Science* 6, 1: 21–37. http://doi.org/10.1177/1745691610393527

15. Ronald C. Kessler, Wai Tat Chiu, Olga Demler, and Ellen E. Walters. 2005. Prevalence, Severity, and Comorbidity of 12-Month DSM-IV Disorders in the National Comorbidity Survey Replication. *Arch Gen Psychiatry* 62, June: 617–627.

16. Ólöf Birna Kristjánsdóttir, Egil a. Fors, Erlend Eide, et al. 2013. A smartphone-based intervention with diaries and therapist feedback to reduce catastrophizing and increase functioning in women with chronic widespread pain. part 2: 11-Month follow-up results of a randomized trial. *Journal of Medical Internet Research* 15, 3. http://doi.org/10.2196/jmir.2442

17. Eric Kuhn, Carolyn Greene, Julia Hoffman, et al. 2014. Preliminary Evaluation of PTSD Coach , a Smartphone App for Post-Traumatic Stress Symptoms. 179, January: 12–18. http://doi.org/10.7205/MILMED-D-13-00271

18. S J Lepore. 1997. Expressive writing moderates the relation between intrusive thoughts and depressive symptoms. *Journal of personality and social psychology* 73, 5: 1030–1037. http://doi.org/10.1037/0022-3514.73.5.1030

19. David D. Luxton, Russell a. McCann, Nigel E. Bush, Matthew C. Mishkind, and Greg M. Reger. 2011. mHealth for mental health: Integrating smartphone technology in behavioral healthcare. *Professional Psychology: Research and Practice* 42, 6: 505–512. http://doi.org/10.1037/a0024485

20. John D Mayer and Y N Gaschke. 2001. Brief Mood Introspection Scale (BMIS). *Psychology* 19, 3: 1995–1995.

21. Andréa a G Nes, Hilde Eide, Ólöf Birna Kristjánsdóttir, and Sandra Van Dulmen. 2013. Web-based, self-management enhancing interventions with e-diaries and personalized feedback for persons with chronic illness: A tale of three studies. *Patient Education and Counseling* 93, 3: 451–458. http://doi.org/10.1016/j.pec.2013.01.022

22. J. W. Pennebaker. 1993. Putting stress into words: Health, linguistic, and therapeutic implications. *Behaviour Research and Therapy* 31, 6: 539–548. http://doi.org/10.1016/0005-7967(93)90105-4

23. Alessandro Puiatti, Steven Mudda, Silvia Giordano, and Oscar Mayora. 2011. Smartphone-centred wearable sensors network for monitoring patients with bipolar disorder. *Conference proceedings□: ... Annual International Conference of the IEEE Engineering in Medicine and Biology Society. IEEE Engineering in Medicine and Biology Society. Conference* 2011, May: 3644–7. http://doi.org/10.1109/IEMBS.2011.6090613

24. Martin L. Puterman. 1994. *Markov Decision Processes: Discrete Stochastic Dynamic Programming.*

25. G A Rummery and M Niranjan. 1994. *On-line Q-learning Using Connectionist Systems.*

26. Carol D Ryff and Corey Lee M Keyes. 1995. The Structure of Psychological Well-Being Revisited. 69, 4: 719–727.

27. Martin E P Seligman, Tayyab Rashid, and Acacia C Parks. 2006. Positive psychotherapy. *The American psychologist*, November. http://doi.org/10.1037/0003-066X.61.8.774

28. Martin E P Seligman, Tracy a Steen, Nansook Park, and Christopher Peterson. 2005. Positive psychology progress: empirical validation of interventions. *The American psychologist* 60, 5: 410–421. http://doi.org/10.1037/0003-066X.60.5.410

29. Mike Thelwall, Kevan Buckley, Georgios Paltoglou, Di Cai, and Arvid Kappas. 2010. Sentiment in short strength detection informal text. *Journal of the American Society for Information Science and Technology* 6, 12: 2544–2558. http://doi.org/10.1002/asi.21416

30. Mike Thelwall, Kevan Buckley, and Georgios Paltoglou. 2012. Sentiment Strength Detection for the Social Web 1. 63: 163–173.

31. Vetta L. Sanders Thompson, Maysa D. Akbar, and Anita Bazile. 2002. African American's Perceptions of Psychotherapy and Psychoterapists. *Annual Meeting of the American Psychological Association.*

32. Sarah Watts, Anna Mackenzie, Cherian Thomas, et al. 2013. CBT for depression: A pilot RCT comparing mobile phone vs. computer. *BMC Psychiatry* 13, 1: 49. http://doi.org/10.1186/1471-244X-13-49

Investigating Breathing Expression of a Stuffed-Toy Robot Based on Body-Emotion Model

Naoto Yoshida
Kansai University Graduate School
Osaka, Japan
k463362@kansai-u.ac.jp

Tomoko Yonezawa
Kansai University
Osaka, Japan
yone@kansai-u.ac.jp

ABSTRACT

In this research, we focus on physiological phenomena expression of robots, propose the Body-Emotion Model (BEM), which concerns the relationship between the internal states of robots and their involuntary physical reactions. We expect that the robot will be able to express the delicate nuances of its intention by controlling robots' emotions and feelings with each individual parameter based on BEM. We propose a stuffed-toy robot system, BREAR, which has a mechanical structure to express breathing, heartbeating, temperature, and bodily movement. The breathing mechanism commonly controls the abdominal motion, breathing motion, and air flows of breath. In this paper, we focus on robot's breathing, verify two subjective evaluations: 1) the user's sense that the robot was alive and 2) the perceived states of the robot based on its breathing speed. The results showed that our proposed method of breathing expression can show a state of living and that the breathing speed was interpreted as the robot's emotion of arousal.

ACM Classification Keywords

H.5.2 User Interfaces: Theory and methods; H.5.2 User Interfaces: Haptic I/O

Author Keywords

Stuffed-toy robot; physical phenomenon; breathing; emotional expressions; expression of living; internal states; anthropomorphism.

INTRODUCTION

The Relationship between Involuntary Expression and Feeling

There are many non-verbal expressions. A non-verbal expression consists of both voluntary and involuntary expressions as physiological expressions [12]. These include gazing, a bodily movement and intentional facial expression as a voluntary expression; there are also physiological phenomena, such as one's heartbeat, temperature, sweat, and unconscious breathing, as involuntary expressions.

The inner state of a human can be understood not only by voluntary expressions, but also by certain physiological phenomena [1, 2, 13, 5]. Voluntary expressions are sometimes different than an expression brought on by physiological phenomena. Lying is a typical example [12, 3]. People can express pseudo emotions through voluntary expressions such as facial expressions and body motions. However, certain physiological phenomena are caused by the immediate change in one's autonomic nervous system, if such a person has not been trained.

We presume physiological phenomena to be important non-verbal media, even in single use. Emotions and feelings should be discussed separately, and each mechanism in the robot's expressions should be examined as with human beings. We expect that the robot can express delicate nuances of its intention, such as with a real intention or a lie, by distinguishing external emotions from definite feelings.

Body-Emotion Model for Human-Robot Communication

We propose the Body-Emotion Model (BEM) (see Figure 1), which concerns the relationship between the internal states of robots and their involuntary physical reactions.

'Emotion' and 'feeling' in this figure are named from the theory by Damasio [4]. 'Emotion' regards the unconscious activity of the peripheral nervous system, and 'feeling' concerns the function of the frontal association area; that becomes our continuous psychological condition.

Our BEM of the robot's physiological expression was based on the Damasio's theory about perception, emotion, and feelings [4].

First, emotion changes one's physical state as a reaction to various stimuli from one's actions, such as looking, listening, touching, and imagining, by perceiving a phenomenon to a user's body and the surrounding conditions of that user. Second, physiological reactions appear to be based on emotion. Finally, humans become aware of one's feelings by noticing changes in one's physical state, and humans express their own feelings through voluntary and/or verbal expressions.

We expect that the robot will be able to express the delicate nuances of its intention by controlling robots' emotions and feelings with each individual parameter based on BEM.

HAI '16, October 04-07, 2016, Biopolis, Singapore

© 2016 ACM. ISBN 978-1-4503-4508-8/16/10. . . $15.00

DOI: http://dx.doi.org/10.1145/2974804.2974817

Some researchers have shown that the robot's bodily movements can express various feelings [6, 11]. As for involuntary expressions, some researches evaluated expression of robots' feelings including physiological phenomena [8, 15]. However, these expressions are not designed models which decide each of voluntary expression based on feelings and involuntary expression based on emotion. We therefore aim to clarify the emotional expression of the robot by only physiological phenomena in BEM.

Physiological phenomena are the physical activities that are indispensable for life support. We also evaluate the expression of a living being-like presence in the robot by expressing the physiological phenomena of the robot.

Verifying Using The BREAR System

We propose a stuffed-toy robot system, BREAR, which has a mechanical structure to express breathing, heartbeating, temperature, and bodily movement. The breathing mechanism commonly controls the abdominal motion, breathing motion, and air flows of breath. The robot system can express both voluntary motions and physiological ventilation as involuntary expressions.

We adopted an animal-like stuffed toy as the robot's appearance in order to remove the influence of facial or linguistic expressions. It is considered that the animal-like stuffed-toy robot without such complex expressions still can show the delicate emotion by our proposed method. Furthermore, the proposed system would be applicable for a robot therapy, which is mental therapy using a stuffed-toy robot[9], using emotional expression with physiological phenomena based on BEM.

In this paper, we focused on the breathing expression among various physiological expressions. Breathing is an important physiological phenomenon that is absolutely necessary for our lives. The stop of the breathing means the death. The breathing-like expression is expected to show as though the robot were alive.

In this study, we first verify whether the sence of a living being can be perceived from the robot's breathing. Second, we clarify the emotional map of the user perceived from the robot's breathing by factorial analysis. The results of the evaluations showed that the robot's breathing can show a living state, and that the breathing tempo is in conjunction with the arousal emotion of the robot. Finally, we consider the effect of the robot's physiological representation from the viewpoint of both the expressions of the living state by the robot's breathing and the relationship between the internal state and the breathing expression.

RELATED RESEARCHES

The research using Parobo[6, 11] showed the possibility of expressions of various feelings of Parobo from non-verbal expressions. However, this research did not consider the physiological phenomena of robots, even though non-verbal expression contains involuntary expressions.

Sefidgar et al. and Yohanan et al. [8, 15] designed a robot that had abdominal motions (without sighing) like respira-

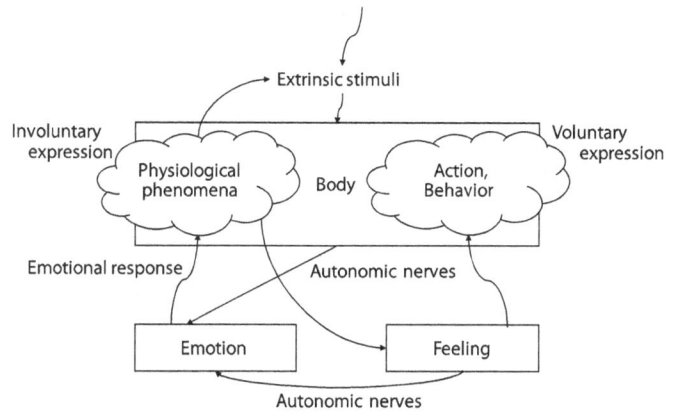

Figure 1. Body-Emotion model

Figure 2. Appearance of stuffed toy robot

tion, motion of the ears, and a purr box, and they verified the impression of robot feelings.

Yanaka et.al [14] developed a huggable pillow using an animal-like toy with abdominal movement, sleeping breath sounds, and heat like body temperature for sleep deprivation.

Since feelings and emotion of robots have not been distinguished in these researches, it is difficult to parameterise robots' emotions. Consequently, it is difficult to produce robots' physiological phenomena based on the mapped emotion.

Related to robot's breath, Solis et.al [10] developed the robot which plays a flute. The flute-playing robot has been designed to mechanically reproduce the human organs such as lungs and a throat. Differently from that, our purpose of the breathing expression is focusing on mental cares and the system is implemented with a small stuffed toy robot. The structure of the trachea should be simplified by the limitation of the size, however the flexible chest of the stuffed-toy robot can go up and down. From the structure of simplified but affective design, the user can feel the breathing not only watching but also touching it, and the breathing expression of the robot is more closer if the user hold it.

EXPRESSION OF ROBOT'S BREATHING

Structure of The Stuffed-toy Robot

BREAR (see Figure 2) is a stuffed-toy robot about 25 [cm] height, covered with a bear-like toy, enclosing breathing mechanism with as a prototype of some physiologic phenomena; a mechanical structure to express breathing, heart beats, and bodily temperature.

Figure 3 shows the internal structure robot. The device for breathing expressions is composed of a 250[mL] balloon imitating a lung, an air pump (DC6[V] 230[mA], 2[L]/[min], 400[mmH]) and a solenoid valve (DC6[V] 90[mA]) with a pressure sensor that detects amount of air in the lung. The bodily temperature of the robot is expressed by a film heater (DC12[V] 5[Ω]) around the armpits to the back, and the heart beats of robot are expressed by a vibration motor (DC5[V], 3000–4800[rpm]) at the chest. Tactile inputs from the user are detected by three piezo sensors (DC3[V] 1[MΩ], minimum sensitivity 20–100[g]) placed at he tip of the arms and top of the head. A small speaker (8[Ω] 0.5[W]) in the robot makes its voice. Seven servo motors (DC5[V], 2.2[kgf/cm], 0.11[sec]/60°) are placed to the head (two D.O.F), each arm, each leg, and the backbone of the robot for bodily movements. A speaker is enclosed in the head of the robots. These devices are controlled by an AVR microcomputer (Arduino UNO R3, ATmega328P, 16[MHz]). These devices are connected to the PC through the microcomputer except the speaker directly connected to the PC.

Control of The Breathing

The robot's breathing is expressed in two steps. Figure 4 and 5 show the details of each step.

1 When the amount of air in the lungs is less than a lower threshold, the air pump works and the solenoid valve closes at the same time in order to accumulate the air in the lungs.

2 When the air in the lung exceeds an upper threshold, the air pump stops and the solenoid valve opens at the same time in order to discharge the air from the mouth of the robot.

Breathing speed is controlled by changing threshold value of maximum lung air pressure.

EXPERIMENTS

Overview of Experiments

In this paper, we verified two subjective evaluations focusing on robot's breathing. A breathing contains multiple elements such as a sound of sigh, exhaled air and abdominal movements, and these elements cannot be separated from the breathing mechanism. The breathing mechanism in our proposed system has a unified structure of their controls, so we treat the mechanism as an unseparated unit.

First, we verify whether the sense of a living being can be perceived from the robot's breathing. Second, we clarify the emotional map of the user perceived from the robot's breathing by factorial analysis.

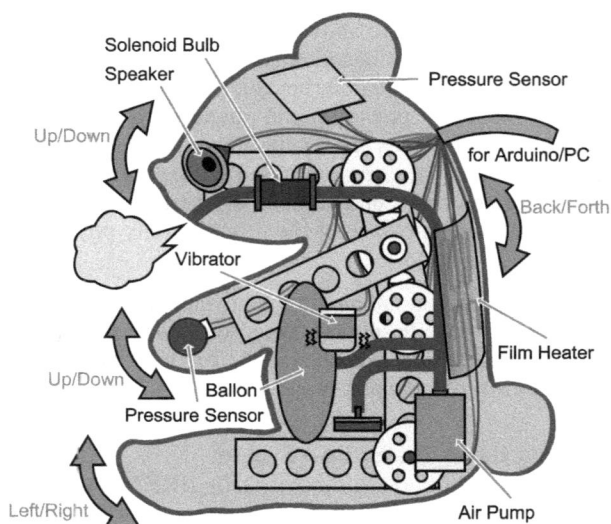

Figure 3. Structure of stuffed toy robot

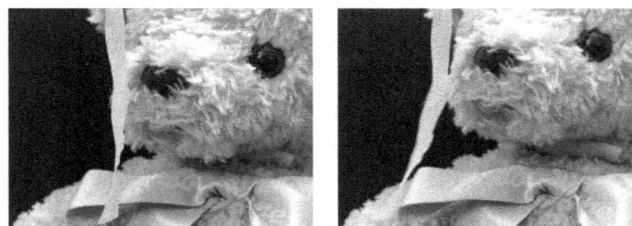

(a) Inhaling   (b) Exhaling

Figure 4. Sigh of BREAR

Living State by Robot's Breathing and Robot's Life

Purpose of Experiment: We verified the effectiveness of the breathing speed to express the robot's internal state especially living state.

Hypothesis: The participants recognize the breath as though the robot were living. The strongest feeling of living state is observed when the breathing speed of the robot becomes close to the general speed of human breath.

Participants: 26 university students aged from 19 years old to 22 years old (16 males and 10 females).

Conditions: The six types of breathing speeds.

c_0 0 times per minute (without breathing),

c_1 3 times per minute (very slow),

c_2 9–10 times per minute (slow),

c_3 16–19 times per minute (medium),

c_4 23–25 times per minute (fast) and

c_5 56–60 times per minute (very fast).

Procedures and Instructions: First, the participants were told that this experiment is a performance evaluation of the robot. Next, the participants were lectured on how to hold the robot close to their face (20 [cm]). The participants observed the

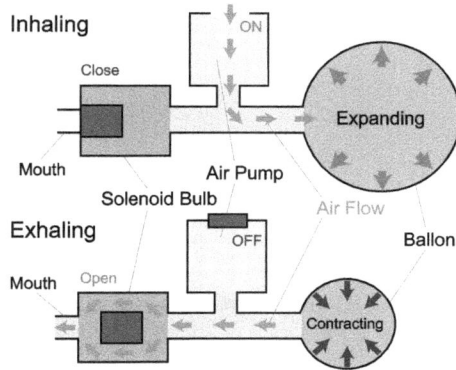

Figure 5. Air flow with breathing

Table 1. Factor pattern of the SD ratings and standardized factor scores (Varimax normalized)

Adjective pairs	Lively	Pleasant	standardized partial regression coefficient Lively	Pleasant
Light–Dark	0.436	0.501	0.021	0.037
Strong–Feeble	0.575	0.204	0.042	-0.002
Warm–Cold	-0.115	0.513	-0.025	0.048
Positive–Negative	**0.605**	0.487	0.053	0.040
Cheerful–Gloomy	0.422	**0.686**	0.018	0.094
Intence–Mild	**0.894**	-0.008	0.241	-0.109
Pleasant–Unpleasant	0.021	**0.825**	-0.058	0.160
Interesting–Boring	0.143	0.411	-0.003	0.028
Fun–Suffering	0.044	**0.666**	-0.024	0.073
Lively–Feeble	**0.749**	0.457	0.127	0.046
Stable–Unstable	**-0.637**	0.315	-0.085	0.071
Dynamic–Static	**0.846**	0.204	0.167	-0.031
Extroverted–Introverted	0.517	0.583	0.035	0.061
Grad–Sad	0.024	**0.817**	-0.055	0.152
Calm–Restlessly	**-0.837**	0.118	-0.167	0.096
Careful–Hasty	**-0.692**	-0.254	-0.068	0.001
Rational–Emotional	-0.589	0.161	-0.057	0.039
Eager–Languor	**0.607**	0.534	0.057	0.054
Energetic–Tired	0.49	**0.732**	0.034	0.152
Merry–Lonely	0.501	**0.685**	0.038	0.110
Aggressive–Weak	**0.691**	0.191	0.067	-0.009
Happy–Unhappy	-0.189	**0.768**	-0.762	0.141
Substantial–Empty	0.115	**0.757**	-0.029	0.108

robot during 20-second experiments and answered the evaluation items after each session. The six conditions were repeated measurement with counter balanced.

Evaluation Items: Evaluation Items: The participants made an evaluation using a five-point scale rating of the relevance (5: very relevant, 4: somewhat relevant, 3: even, 2: somewhat irrelevant, 1: irrelevant) of the following statements.

Q1 This robot seems like a living being,

Q2 This robot seems not like a living being,

Q3 This robot seems alive,

Q4 This robot seems dead and

Q5 This robot seems about to die.

Result: Figure 6 shows the results of means opinion scores (MOS) for each statement (significance level: ** p<.05). In the results from Q1 to Q4,there were significances between c0 and c1–c5, that are the difference of with or without breath. These results showed that the robot's breathing expressions are able to show the aliveness of the robot regardless of the speed of the breath. The results for Q5 also showed significances between c0 and c4 and between c0 and c5. It is conjectured that the speed of the robot's breath changed the participants's recognitions of detailed internal state of the robot. Accordingly, we tried to verify the relationship between impressions for internal states of robots and the speed of the breath in the next experiment.

Relationship of Impression for Internal State and Breathing

Purpose of Experiment: We tried to verify the relationship between the impression for internal state of the robot and the speed of the breath.

Participants: 26 university students aged from 19 years old to 22 years old (16 males and 10 females).

Conditions: Two conditions of different speed of the robot's breathing.

c11 9–10 times per minute (slow) and

c12 23–25 times per minute (fast).

Procedures and Instructions: Same as procedures and instructions in the previous experiment.

Evaluation Items: The impressions for the robot were evaluated by using the semantic differential (SD) method. Participants answered the evaluation items of 23 adjective pairs (in Japanese) related to perception, physiology, and personality as shown in Table 1 in the left line.

Extraction of Factors: Factor analysis was performed on the results of SD method ratings for the 23 adjective pairs. According to the difference in eigen values by a major-factor method, we adopted two factors while the cumulative contribution ratio was 57.7%. The factor matrix was rotated by a Varimax method (shown in Table 1). The first factor was named "Lively" factor and the second one was named "Pleasant" factor from the factor loadings.

Hypothesis for two-factor analysis: Two independent hypotheses as follows were investigated: 1) The speed of breath expresses the Lively emotion of the robot and 2) The speed of breath expresses the Pleasant emotion of the robot.

Comparison of Factors by the Breathing Speed: Standardized factor scores were calculated by a standardized partial regression coefficient. Table 2 shows the result of ANOVA (analysis of variance) for each standardized factor score in order to compare the conditions. The result showed a significant difference between two conditions of breathing speed in the Lively scores (see Figure 7). In contrast, there was no significance in the Pleasant scores.

DISCUSSIONS

Relations of Robot's Breathing and Robot's Life

First, we discuss the positive impressions for the user's feeling that the robot was alive. From the results of the experiment,

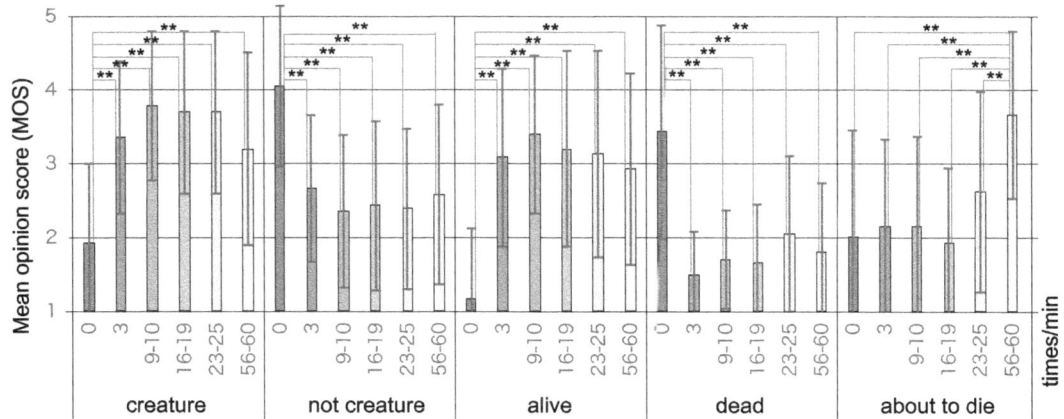

Figure 6. Results of subjective evauation.

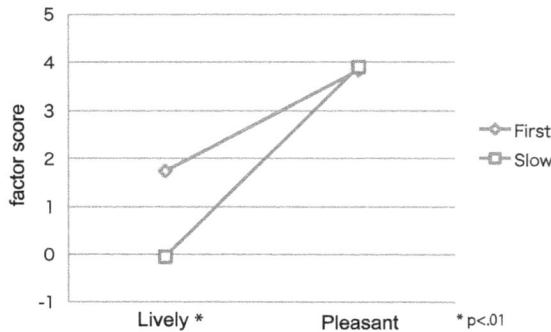

Figure 7. Comparison of factor scores

Table 2. Average and standard deviation of factor scores for Impression of robot's breathing

	Condition	First	Slow
	Participant	26	26
Factor score	Lively	1.736	-0.037
	Pleasant	3.828	3.901
SD	Lively	0.152	0.158
	Pleasant	0.868	1.002

it is conjectured that the robot's breath expressed the robot's living state compared to the robot without breath. That is to say, there was no significance among breathing expressions with different speeds and with the limited range of the speed of the robot's breath.

In the result of Q3 to Q5, each state of living of the robots was expressed in condition of different breathing speed. The speed of the robot's breath showed the possibility to express a detailed state of living of the robot. On the other hand, the speed of the robot's breath showed a possibility to express detailed internal state of living of the robot as shown in the results for Q5.

Factor Analyses of Impressions for Breathing
Next, we discuss the results of factor analyses in evaluating two speeds (fast and slow) of breathing.

Table 3. Example of robot's breathing based on Lively

Stimulation	Emotion	Lively	Breathing tempo
Clenching the hand suddenly	Surprised	HIGH	FAST
Beating the head suddenly	Surprised	HIGH	FAST
Leave unattended	Boring	LOW	SLOW
Continue touching in long time	Boring	LOW	SLOW
Patting kindly	Relaxing	LOW	SLOW

From the results of factor analyses, there were two factors of the robot's breathing: "Lively" and "Pleasant"; while the speed of the breath only affects the Lively factor. Lively factor seemed to include the adjectives related not only to visual expression of the breathing movement but also to impression of internal state and emotion. These results showed that there is a relationship between living-being-like perception of the robot and the speed of the robot's breath.

Pleasant factor is assumed to be affected by other parameters of breathing expressions except the speed; for example, there are parameters of the breathing expressions such as the strengths of the air flow and the intervals as though the robot holds its breathing. The effects of these parameters should be verified including contexts of human–robot communication in the future.

Lively Factor of Breathing Expression Based on BEM
Lively Factor of Breathing Expression Based on BEM We considered that two factors, Lively and Pleasant, seem to be tied to a circumplex model[7]. Consequently, we applied the parameter of "Pleasantness" to correspond to the Pleasant factor and the parameter of "Arousal" to correspond to Lively (See Figure 8). For instance, the sudden contact from a user produces a surprising state with arousal and causes early breathing, or the kind patting or stroke produces relaxed emotion of the robot and its breath becomes slow down, as the examples shown in Table 3.

CONCLUSION
In this paper, we focused on physiological phenomena, that are involuntary expressions seen in our daily lives, and we introduced our BEM that shows the relationship between the internal states of the robot and the unintentional and automatic reactions of the body of the robot.

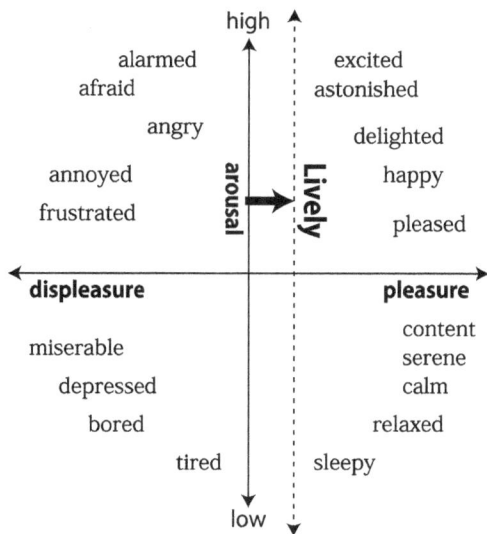

Figure 8. Mapping of Lively factor based on circumplex model

First, we proposed our stuffed-toy robot with breathing expressions which involves the speed to show the robot's different internal states as a living being-like presence.

Second, we verified the robot's perceived living state by changing the speed of the breath. The results of the evaluations and factor analyses conjectured that the robot's breathing can express the living state and that the speed of breath is highly related to the robot's emotion of arousal.

Last, we verify the subjective evaluation about the internal states of the robot based on the robot's breathing tempo. The results of the evaluations showed that the speed of breath is related to the robot's emotion of arousal.

As a future work, we should consider 1) other parameters of breathing expressions, 2) the effect of other physiological phenomena such as heartbeat and temperature, and 3) the effectiveness of physiological expressions corresponding to the two dimensional inner states of the robots as we investigated.

ACKNOWLEDGEMENTS
This research was supported in part by JSPS KAKENHI 15H01698 and JSPS KAKENHI 25700021. The authors would like to thank the participants in the experiment.

REFERENCES
1. Bradley M Appelhans and Linda J Luecken. 2006. Heart rate variability as an index of regulated emotional responding. *Review of general psychology* 10, 3 (2006), 229.

2. Susana Bloch, Madeleine Lemeignan, and Nancy Aguilera-T. 1991. Specific respiratory patterns distinguish among human basic emotions. *International Journal of Psychophysiology* 11, 2 (1991), 141–154.

3. Roddy Cowie, Ellen Douglas-Cowie, Nicolas Tsapatsoulis, George Votsis, Stefanos Kollias, Winfried Fellenz, and John G Taylor. 2001. Emotion recognition in human-computer interaction. *Signal Processing Magazine, IEEE* 18, 1 (2001), 32–80.

4. Antonio Damasio and Raymond J Dolan. 1999. The feeling of what happens. *Nature* 401, 6756 (1999), 847–847.

5. Vittorio Gallese and Alvin Goldman. 1998. Mirror neurons and the simulation theory of mind-reading. *Trends in cognitive sciences* 2, 12 (1998), 493–501.

6. T. Mitsui, T. Shibata, K. Wada, A. Touda, and K. Tanie. 2001. Psychophysiological effects by interaction with mental commit robot. In *Intelligent Robots and Systems, 2001. Proceedings. 2001 IEEE/RSJ International Conference on*, Vol. 2. 1189–1194 vol.2.

7. James A Russell. 1980. A circumplex model of affect. *Journal of personality and social psychology* 39, 6 (1980), 1161.

8. Yasaman Sefidgar, Karon MacLean, Steve Yohanan, HF Machiel Van der Loos, Elizabeth Croft, and others. 2015. Design and Evaluation of a Touch-Centered Calming Interaction with a Social Robot. *IEEE Transactions on Affective Computing* 1 (2015), 1–1.

9. Takanori Shibata and Kazuyoshi Wada. 2010. Robot therapy: A new approach for mental healthcare of the elderly–A mini-review. *Gerontology* 57, 4 (2010), 378–386.

10. Jorge Solis, Kei Suefuji, Koichi Taniguchi, Takeshi Ninomiya, Maki Maeda, and Atsuo Takanishi. 2007. Implementation of expressive performance rules on the WF-4RIII by modeling a professional flutist performance using NN. In *Robotics and Automation, 2007 IEEE International Conference on*. IEEE, 2552–2557.

11. Walter Dan Stiehl, Jeff Lieberman, Cynthia Breazeal, Louis Basel, Levi Lalla, and Michael Wolf. 2005. Design of a therapeutic robotic companion for relational, affective touch. In *Robot and Human Interactive Communication, 2005. ROMAN 2005. IEEE International Workshop on*. IEEE, 408–415.

12. Marjorie Fink Vargas. 1986. *Louder than words: An introduction to nonverbal communication*. Iowa State University Press.

13. Tomio Watanabe and Masashi Okubo. 1998. Physiological analysis of entrainment in communication. *Transactions of Information Processing Society of Japan* 39, 5 (1998), 1225–1231.

14. Shunsuke Yanaka, Takayuki Kosaka, and Motofumi Hattori. 2013. ZZZoo Pillows: Sense of Sleeping Alongside Somebody. In *SIGGRAPH Asia 2013 Emerging Technologies (SA '13)*. ACM, New York, NY, USA, Article 17, 1 pages.

15. Steve Yohanan and Karon E MacLean. 2008. The haptic creature project: Social human-robot interaction through affective touch. In *Proceedings of the AISB 2008 Symposium on the Reign of Catz & Dogs: The Second AISB Symposium on the Role of Virtual Creatures in a Computerised Society*, Vol. 1. Citeseer, 7–11.

Sharing Emotion Described as Text on the Internet by Changing Self-physiological Perception

Sho Sakurai[†‡]   Yuki Ban[‡]   Toki Katsumura[‡]
Takuji Narumi[‡]   Tomohiro Tanikawa[‡]   Michitaka Hirose[‡]

[†]Graduate School of Information Systems, The University of Electro-Communications
[‡]Graduate School of Information Science and Technology, The University of Tokyo
{sho | ban | katsumura | narumi | tani | hirose}@cyber.t.u-tokyo.ac.jp

ABSTRACT

Developing information-communication technology has enabled us to share other's experience at remote location at real-time. Meanwhile, it is still difficult to share the emotion due to degradation of information for estimating the other's emotion online. The current study proposes a method for experiencing other's emotion firsthand on the Internet by reproducing a mechanism of evoking emotion. This method evokes a number of emotions that other person described on the Web, by changing perception of self-physiological responses with sensory stimuli. In order to investigate the feasibility of our method, we made a system named "Communious Mouse." This system rewrites the perception of self-skin temperature and pulse in a palm by presenting vibration and thermal stimulation through a mouse device for evoking emotion. The current paper discusses the feasibility of our method based on the obtained feedbacks through an exhibition of the system.

Author Keywords

Emotion; self-perception; physiological perception; a sense of ownership; theory of mind; online communication.

ACM Classification Keywords

H.5.1.Multimedia Information Systems: Artificial, augmented, and virtual realities; H.1.2. User/Machine systems Interfaces: Human factors.

INTRODUCTION

The purpose of this study is realizing a method for sharing emotions of others including artificial agent on the Internet.

In communication with other person, expressed bodily information, such as the line of sight, facial expression, voice tone and movement, becomes a key information for understanding or contagion of the other's emotion [1, 2].

HAI '16, October 04-07, 2016, Biopolis, Singapore
© 2016 ACM. ISBN 978-1-4503-4508-8/16/10...$15.00
DOI: http://dx.doi.org/10.1145/2974804.2974825

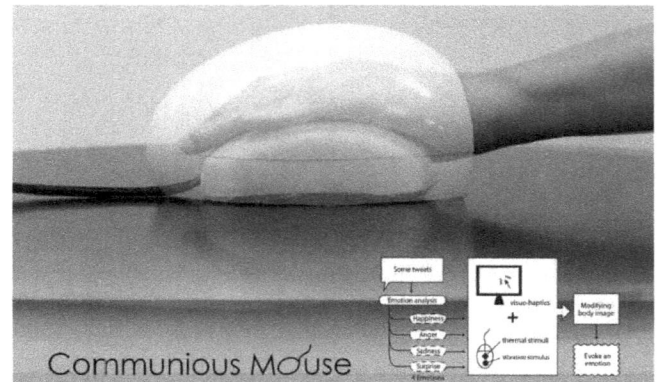

Figure 1. Communious Mouse.

In also the field of human-agent interaction, there are many studies for make a user feel as if avatar or robot have a will of its own and communication skill with human through manipulating bodily information of the agents [3]. Meanwhile, these approaches are applicable to only agents have quasi-human appearance. Therefore, these methods cannot be applied to agents like an Internet bot, which mainly uses character information. In case of using text information, it is hard to empathize with others mind whether the other is human or agent: for example, browsing the information is hardly evokes profound happiness or anger.

To empathize the emotion, which agents appears to have, the current paper proposes a method for evoking emotion described as a text on the Internet by changing perception of self-internal physiological changes

Some theories argued that bodily/physiological changes unconsciously affects emotional states exist [4, 5]. Many findings experimental researches have shown results can positively support these theories in the field of cognitive science. In addition, the perception of false-physiological changes influences the emotional state even if actual physiological response did not change [6].

Some engineering studies also showed that feedback of sensory stimuli resemblance of self-physical changes could evoke emotion. The two types of such false-physical responses are observable bodily responses including facial expression and voice tone [7, 8] and unobservable physiological responses including heart rate and body temperature

[9, 10, 11]. Given use of such false-physical responses in browsing the Internet, it seems to be unnatural to feedback self-face or voice.

To investigate the feasibility of this method, we made a system named "Communious Mouse" (Figure 1). This system presents tactile stimuli as false-physiological changes into a palm through a mouse device using for browsing Internet [12].

This current paper first summarizes the findings about relationship between physiological perception and emotion. Then, the feasibility of our method is discussed through the explanation of the "Communious Mouse" and obtained feedbacks about this system through and exhibition.

EMOTION AND PHYSIOLOGICAL PERCEPTION

"Emotion" is a term to describe strong and short-lived movement of one's mind, such as happiness, anger, or sadness. Emotion and physiological responses have closely relationship. Meanwhile, which of these changes first have been still in controversial topics.

In this regard, recent physiological researches have demonstrated that particular physiological responses change according to the emotion: the major example are skin temperature and electrodermal response: for instance, it is known that these changes cause as the result of change in the blood flow associated with the physiological and psychological state by the function of autonomic nervous system occur [13]. The blood flow causes change in the skin temperature [14, 15]. When the emotional state alters in a positive way, the blood flow increases and the skin temperature rises. When the emotion alters in a negative way, the blood flow decreases and the skin temperature lowers. Moreover, mental sweating caused by negative emotions, such as tenseness, stress and anxiety increases the electric skin resistance [16]. Such negative emotions also can cause the physiological tremor [17].

On the other hand, in the field of cognitive psychology, there are many reports that self-physiological perception changes prior to the change of emotions. For example, self-facial expression or line of sight influences emotional states [18, 19]. Many studies also have revealed that not only actual physiological changes but also false-physiological changes affect the emotional state. As a famous study, Valins's false-heart beat experiment showed that the rate of false-heartbeat sound acts on the having a different recognition about attractiveness of women in a photograph [6].

Based on these findings, some engineering studies attempt to manipulate emotions with sensory stimuli: for example, Nishimura et al. also showed that the speed of false-heart rate using tactile sensation affects how participates felt attractiveness to women differently [9]. In other instances, there are studies aim to evoke or enhance emotions using false-piloerection with static generation [10] and combination of false-heart rate, body temperature and chest pressure using tactile stimuli [11].

The reason why emotion changes due to self-physiological perception is assumed that correspondence between body image and particular emotional state is understood. In this regard, Bem stated that understanding and prediction of self-mind could be only possible through objective observation of expressed self-bodily change and behavior when the self-mind is obscure (the self-perception theory [20]). However, humans cannot know the concrete rate of the change in these physiological responses using only self-body. In addition, the actual rate of the physiological changes and perceived changes of these are not always same. For example, fear or stress can make us perceive rapid fall in the body temperature despite little change in actual body temperature. Therefore, emotion seems to evoke based on perceived body image.

Moreover, many people have the common recognition of the correspondence between the emotion and Perception of the physiological changes. In this regard, Liu investigated the common image of the correspondence some emotions and mapping of the body temperature [20]. Such common recognition of the correspondence is assumed to influences emotion in association with the findings about the relationship between the emotion and physiological perception.

On the other hand, Schachter et al., advocated that changes in bodily responses can be related to several emotions; in particular, discreet emotions cannot be completely determined by bodily changes (the two-factor theory of emotion [2]). This means that different emotions can be evoked according to defference of the interpretation of the reason why self-bodily responses changed. The reason of it is reffered to as "attribution of causality." Some study showed that the different emotion evokes depending on the context of self-experience even if the same physiological response changes [022]. This studies would allude to the need to consider the him/her behavior objective in order to attribute the false-physiological changes to particular the aimed to evoke.

COMMUNIOUS MOUSE: EXPERIENCING OTHERS' EMOTION IN REMARKS ON THE WEB FIRSTHAND

Based on above findings, we propose a method for sharing an emotion online by changing perceition of physiological changes. We will explain a system named "Communious Mouse" to investigate the feasibility of our method.

System Design

The "Communious Mouse" evokes emotions described as text on the Internet by changing physiological perception in a palm using tactile stimuli (Figure 2). This enables to share emotion online converted into physiological changes. The "Communious" is a combination of words for "communion" that means a human relationship and "ous," which is a suffix means something that has a particular quality.

146

The skin temperature and pulse around a palm are subject to perceptional change to evoke a number of emotions to a user based on Russell's curcumplex model to affect [23].

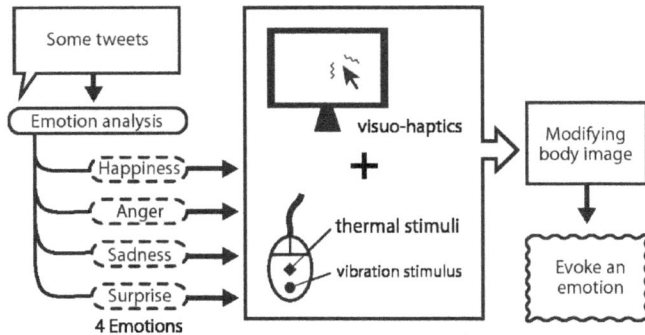

Figure 2. System design of "Communious Mouse."

Emotions are illustrated in a biaxial manner by this model: pleasant/unpleasant and arousal/quiet feelings: for example, the combination of high arousal and pleasant feelings is called "surprise." Meanwhile, the combination of a high arousal, but with unpleasant feelings, is called "fear."

As above mentioned, skin temperature closely relates with positive/negative feelings. To change perception of the skin temperature, thermal stimulation is displayed into a user's palm. Moreover, a heart rate caused by blood flow can influence the arousal/quiet feelings regardless whether they are positive or negative [6, 9]. Given this, vibration stimulation is also displayed as false-pulse to a palm since the change of the blood flow is perceived as pulse to the palm.

Regarding to emotions to evoke, it is assumed to be difficult to evoke them that are included in the pleasant/quiet area in a model illustrated in Figure 3. This is because of the difficulty to aware of self-physiological changes due to the feeling really comfortable with the self of them. Recognizing emotional change seems to be difficult even if sensory stimuli that resemble the unnoticeable physiological changes are presented. Given this, we chose four emotions to evoke: happiness, sadness, anger and surprise. These of each except happiness are included in each area. Happiness is selected since it is a positive emotion that is closely arranged in the pleasant/quiet area. There is two reason of using a mouse device: first is reducing strangeness in presented stimulation and second is to attribute the perceived self-physiological changes to browsing text on the Internet.

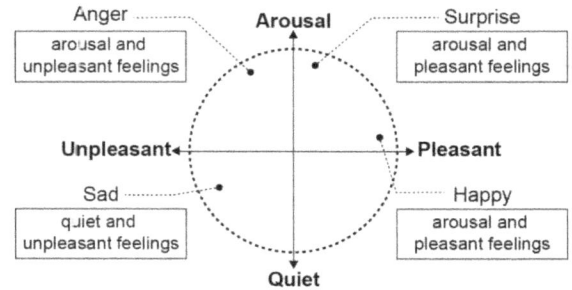

Figure 3. The mapping of the four emotions to evoke. (created based on [23])

As concerns the first reason, we focused on a sense of agency (SA). The SA, which is subjective sense that "I con trolling this," arises in visual stimuli what s/he see through understanding how the visual stimuli changes associated with intentional change of the somatic sense of him/her [24]. If the user uses some sort of tool, the boundary between self-body and the tool the user controls can fade from awareness due to unconscious understanding the correspondence. We will illustrate the SA with a digital game. Being to be able to understand how to control the action of a character by operating a controller, the character's suffering damage is felt as the damage of him/herself, such as pain or shock. Besides, habituation of the controlling the controller can be less conscious.

We therefore think the mouse has a high affinity to hands like the game controller. In addition, self-action can be observed visually as the movement of a cursor on a monitor. Given these, the using mouse is fitted for reducing the strangeness in presented stimuli to the palm. In addition, the scaling of the cursor changes like a heartbeat according to the intensity of the false-pulse. This effect aims to attribute the perceived physiological changes to emotions that are described as text that a user intentionally hovers the cursor.

System Configuration

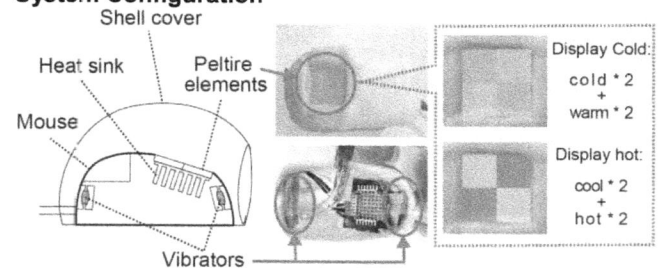

Figure 4. System configuration of the "Communious Mouse"

Figure 4 shows the system configuration of the "Communious Mouse." The Peltier elements, which attached to the surface of the mouse, display the thermal stimulation for changing a user's perception of skin temperature in a palm. The vibrators, which are attached on a front and back of the mouse, displays the vibration stimuli for the changing perception of the user's blood flow around the palm.

As above, emotions relate with self-physiological changes, but meanwhile, what physiological changes are subjectively perceived has strongly affects what emotion evokes. The correspondence of the perception of them also can be recognized commonly.

Then, we first investigate whether there are common correspondences between perception of tendency of the time-shift in the skin temperature and pulse and each of the four emotions. As the pre-research, four participants were asked to answer the image of correspondences of them. Figure 5 shows the images of a five seconds shift in these physiological changes when each of the four emotions evoked.

The rapid elevation of skin temperature and the pulse beat that became strong and faster than usual were perceived corresponding to "Anger" and "Surprise." Meanwhile, theparticipants answered that it appears that these physiological changes quickly calm down associated with evoking "Surprise," although the changes of it continued to shift a certain period of time in response to "Anger". They perceived comfort in addition to slight increasing of the skin temperature according to evoking "Happiness" and a drop in it corresponding with "Sad." They also answered they did not feel their pulse beat when "Sadness" or "Happiness" were evoked.

Given their image of the correspondences and physiological findings, the each intensity parameter of the thermal and vibration stimuli was determined.

Based on these body images and physiological findings, we decided the strength of stimuli for evoking each emotion. The mean skin temperature of adults range from 30.7 °C to 38.6 °C [25]. On the other hand, in regard to the relationship between the temperature displayed to the body surface and emotions, Narumi et al. suggested that 40-45 degrees Celsius evokes pleasant feelings and 20-25 degrees Celsius evokes unpleasant feelings [26]. Meanwhile, the mean of pulse beat of adults range from 60 to 100 bpm [27]. Valins et al. [6] and Nishimura et al. [9] modified their false- pulse beats from 48 to 90 bpm.

From these findings and the pre-experimental result, oursystem displayed 35 °C thermal stimulus and 60bpm weak vibration when it displayed no characteristic emotion. Then, the strength of stimuli for displaying 4 emotions was decided as described below: Happiness situation displayed 40 °C thermal stimulus and 60 bpm weak vibration, Sad ness situation displayed 25 °C thermal stimulus and 60 bpm weak vibration, Anger situation displayed 55 °C thermal stimulus and 92 bpm weak vibration, Surprise situation displayed 55 °C thermal stimulus and 100 bpm strong vibration at first, and reduced them to 35 °C and 60bpm weak vibration in 6 seconds. In our system, the Peltier elements did not touch to a user's palm directly, so the displayed thermal stimulus attenuated before reaching to the palm. Therefore, we decided that a default thermal stimulus was a little bit higher than the mean skin temperature of adults.

The vibration stimulus was designed to fit in the range of the mean pulse beat of adults. Happiness situation's thermal stimulus was designed to arouse pleasant feeling, and Angry and Surprise situations' were designed to arouse unpleasant feeling.

"Anger" and "Surprise" give the perception of drastic change of the skin temperature. However, it is difficult to mimic the quick thermal changes that arise from heat of inside the body by presenting thermal stimulation from outside the body, because of the difference in the perceptual characteristics between the inside and surface of the body. In order to allow the user perceive rapid change of self-skin temperature, this system used a technique to produces spatially divided hot and cold stimuli using four Peltier elements with reference to [28].

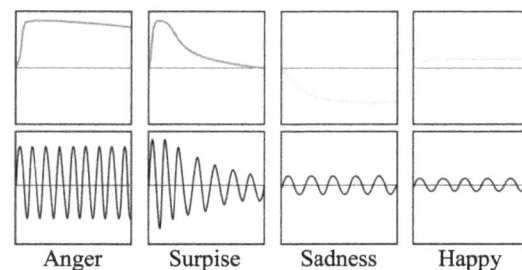

Figure 5. Subjects' images of a five seconds shift in the skin temperature and pulse rate associated with the four emotions.

In addition, the bare vibrators could not make users perceive as if the presented vibration stimuli is pulse beats of themselves due to the obviousness of the strong vibration. To resolve this problem, these vibrators are employed with the cover of a gel barrier.

Visuo-haptics effect for enhancing perception of physiological changes

As above, being less conscious of the boundary between a mouse and the hand seems able to enhance the effect of stimuli for changing perception of the physiological changes. In this regard, it is appeared that the difference between quality of the materials of the mouse and the hand prevent to lose awareness of the boundary between the both. The mouse is therefore was covered with a gel, which is closed stiffness and texture to the human skin in order to reduce the awareness of the difference between the both materials.

When we manipulate a mouse device, the SA seems to arise in a mouse cursor as above illustrated in an example of digital game. Using this sensation, and the effect of visuo-haptic interaction, which means that a vision affects a haptic sensation, some studies attempted to evoke the haptic sensation on users' hands that manipulate a mouse device by modifying the movement and look of a mouse cursor. For instance, Lecuyer et al. attempted to evoke a sensation of a frictional force by modifying the rate of movement amount between a hand and a mouse cursor [29]. Besides, Argelaguet et al. displayed the perception of stiffness by modifying a cursor's color when a user clicks objects with various stiffness on a monitor [30].

Based on these findings, our system modifies the cursor's movement and size to evoke the visuo-haptic interaction, and make users perceive the pseudo pulse beat strongly as the physiological changes inside their hands. In particular,

Table 1. Combination of displayed haptic and visual stimuli.

at this time, the mouse cursor expands and shrinks in time with the vibration stimuli. It can be considered that effect is also able to emphasize the characteristics of the pulse beat, such as strength and speed of a pulse, and so on.

Application design

We constructed a cooperative application with Twitter, one of the most famous SNS service in the world, as the prototype of our proposed system [31] (Figure 6). The reason for choosing Twitter as the web service for our system is that users post remarks that contains immediate emotions, the posted phrases are short, and over two hundred million people use.

The system obtains tweets using twitter's API and applies the sentiment analysis described above to classify the tweets according to the type of included emotion: "Happiness", "Sadness", "Surprise", and "Anger". When a user places the mouse cursor on a tweet that includes a certain emotion, the physical and visual stimuli evoked by the body image related to this emotion, are presented to a user.

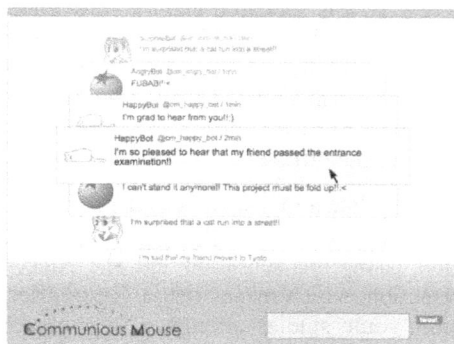

Figure 6. Use high-resolution images, 300+ dpi, legible if printed in color or black-and-white. Number all figures and include captions below, using Insert, Caption.

Sentiment Analysis
To display the pseudo physiological changes, which enhance the creation of a body image that evokes some emo-

tions whose orientation is similar to remarks on the web, the system applies the sentiment analysis to such remarks. Some studies have used the sentiment analysis for the web services. For example, Carro et al. proposed the "Angry Email" which allows users to reconsider the convenience of sending certain e-mails when they are noticeably angry by analyzing the emotions reflected on the sent e-mail [032].

There are a lot of studies and web APIs for the sentiment analysis [33]. At this time, the system uses the sentiment analysis with python Natural language toolkit (NLTK) text classification [34] and the analysis method that uses an extended version of a well-established psychometric instrument: the Profile of Mood States (POMS) [35] established by Pepe et al. [36]. The former method scores positive and negative sentiment of a text, and the latter scores six mooddimensions of POMS: "tension", "depression", "fatigue", "vigor", "anger" and "confusion". With values of these eight parameters, we used the Support Vector Machine (SVM) classifier by Sequential Minimal Optimization (SMO), to classify the four emotions applicable to our proposed system.

Evaluation of Sentiment Analysis
To classify remarks into the four emotions, 50 training data were prepared for each emotions, and a five-fold cross validation was performed for the four emotions independently in order to evaluate how accurately we could classify the emotion. The average correct classification rate is over 85 % for each emotion ("Happiness": 85.2%, "Sadness": 87.0%, "Anger": 92.0%, "Surprise": 90.0%).

USER STUDY

Investigating through Exhibition
"Communious Mouse" was exhibited at an international conference for three days in 2014 [12]. Over 150 visitors experienced our system during this exhibition (Figure 7).

We had questionnaires to the part of visitors who experienced our system during this exhibition, and got answers from 34 visitors. Through these questionnaires, we to investigated the effect of stimuli for evoking the four emotions.

And how they feel these emotions that were included in remarks on the web. Using raw remarks on the timeline of the Twitter, it was difficult to control the ratio of displayed emotions, which are included in remarks. Therefore, the system displays actual remarks and bot's remarks to equalize the kind of displayed emotions. Eight remarks displayed at on time on the monitor, and four emotions were included in two remarks each.

In this exhibition, visitors experienced all eight remarks on the monitor, and answered 7 questions on a 7-point scale (1: totally disagree, 4: neutral, 7: totally agree). The experimental duration was 3 minutes. At first, exhibitor explained this system's usage to a user, then a user started to move a mouse and watched a monitor. Users could try each remark as long as they wont, but most of them tried about

20seconds for each remark. When a user finished to try all eight remarks, we asked that how they feel four emotions included in remarks, and asked the perceived influence of thermal and vibration stimuli to experience four emotions.

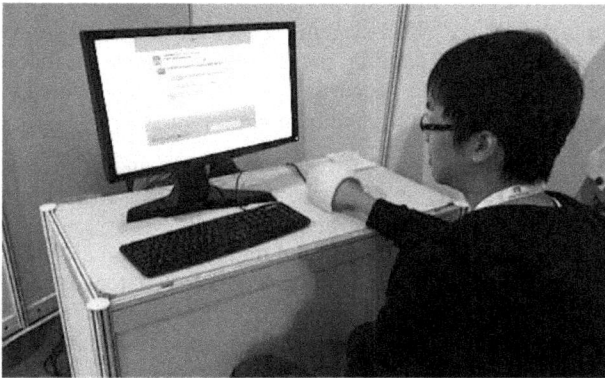

Figure 7. Exhibiting the "Communious Mouse" at an international conference.

Finally, we asked whether they would like to use this system in actual.

Results

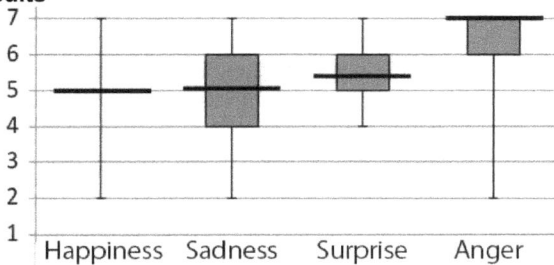

Figure 8. How they feel four emotions included in remarks.

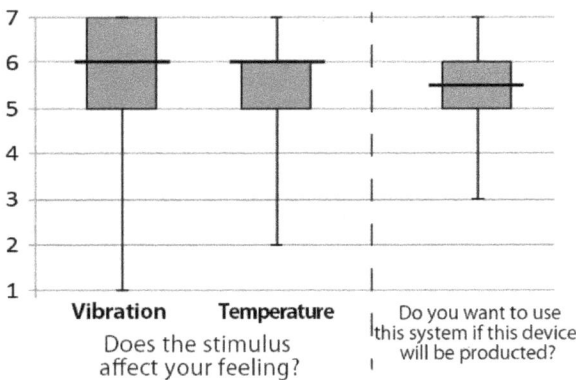

Figure 9. How they feel effects of stimuli.

27 males and 7 females participated in our user study. Figure 8 shows the box-and-whisker plot for the answer for perceived emotions. The scores of medians for presented emotion are over 5 points. All of these median values were over 4 points, so that the participants could feel and distinguish four emotions properly in the testing session.

We used a Friedman test and Wilcoxon signed-rank tests with Bonferroni-Holm correction This test revealed a sig-

nificant main effect of the emotions which are included in remarks, with the Bonferroni-Holm correction showing a significant difference between the score of these answer for "Anger" and others ($F(3, 132)=6.34$, $p<0.001$). This result suggested that "Anger" feeling is easier to let people feel via the proposed system.

Figure 9 shows the box-and-whisker plot for the answer for perceived emotions. Both of scores for the perceived influence of temperature and vibration stimuli were over 5 points and there was no significant difference between two scores with student's t-test. This result indicates that the pseudo bodily temperature and pulse beat were effective for experiencing others' emotions directory included in remarks on the web.

Discussion

These results indicated that our system have the potential to display these four emotions. Especially "Anger" is felt stronger than other emotions. From an open question, especially "Anger" is sympathized most strongly. Regarding this, the visitors' feedbacks indicate that these stimuli were felt little or not strange although intensities of them were stronger than actual physiological changes. They absolutory agree with that these physiological changes, in particular the hot temperature, had strong effect to recall "Anger". They also mentioned that visual feedback of the cursor enhances a perception of the pit-a-pat feeling.

The system got high score on evoking "Surprise" as much as for "Anger". The visitors' feedbacks seem to suggest "Surprise" evoked using this system. However, some visitors answered that it was hard to perceive the shift in the false-physiological changes due to the instantaneous change of the intensities of the stimuli whereas the keeping changing of the stimuli intensities to evoke "Anger." It is thought that this system was unable cover the differences of perceptual characteristics of temperature between inside and surface of the body.

The score on evoking "Sadness" tended to be scattered than scores on evoking other emotions. We received both high and low evaluation from an open question, and obtained some feedbacks that the visual effect of the cursor was not helpful to evoke "Sadness." Regarding the thermal stimulus, most visitors mentioned that they could image the "Sadness." These feedbacks would suggest that displayed stimuli were not so effective that they sympathized to "Sadness", but had the potential to make users image this emotion.

It is appeared that these results obtained due to the physiological and technical problems. The physiological problem is that an actual skin temperature does not become low when we feel sadness although the skin temperature was perceived as if it lowers. In addition, basically the physiological changes in response to evoking "Sadness" is not easy to be aware since this emotion tends to be categorized as a quiet feeling. The technical problem is that a waste heat mechanism was not enough to change displayed temperature quickly, for a long time exhibition. This problem can be seen from visitors' comments that there was a time gap between timing when they moved a mouse cursor on a remark and timing when they felt cold temperature.

The score for "happiness" was lower than the valuations for other emotions. The intensities of the stimuli, which were relatively soft and resembled normal physiological conditions, were determined according to above pre-research. In fact, they mentioned that they got no strangeness with temperature and vibration stimuli for evoking "Happiness." It seems to be difficult to evoke "Happiness" only because of the physiological comfort.

These results suggested that how ease of the perception of physiological changes influence the different of what emotion is easy to evoke. Nevertheless, this system is considered to be capable of sharing emotions described as a text on the Internet.

In addition, we determined intensity of parameter of thermal stimulation for influencing pleasant/unpleasant feelings and of vibration for affecting arousal/quiet feelings based on previous findings and preliminary experiment. However, there is finding that rapid change of displayed thermal stimulation (more than three degrees in either direction) enables to evoke arousal feelings [37]. Regarding "Anger" and "Surprise," thermal and vibration stimuli were seem to synergistically affect arousal feeling.

Given these results, feasibility of our proposed method to share the emotion of others separated spatially and temporary could be indicated. However, in order to realize this method, more experiments are required to investigate followings: how the presented stimuli influence the perception of self-physiological changes, how the stimuli are attributed to the browsing text, whether the presence or absence of the presenting stimuli influence the difference of effect to share the described emotion.

In the field of human-agent interaction (HAI), the role of our method can be one of the contributions that showed a potential to communicate and share the rise and fall of emotions in mediated communication. There are some studies to investigate how human estimate other persons' subjective experience, such as the emotions and decisions, from the described text, pictogram and computer-generated avatars. Meanwhile, the approach of the current study aims to share emotional experiences by applying the reproduced mechanism of evoking self-mind to the emotional experiences of others. This would be a new HAI approach to "share" and "empathize" other's emotion in mediated communication beyond conventional approach to "understand" it in agent-mediated communication.

Regarding this experiment, many of the participants did not care the whether Internet bots or humans tweeted. Given this, his approach can be used in not only human-agent interaction but also human-human interaction used text media in online for tele-communication or entertainment.

CONCLUSION

The current paper proposed the method for evoking emotion by altering the body perception to empathize into emotion of others including artificial agents. To investigate the feasibility of our method, we made a system named "Communious Mouse." This system overwrites the physiological perception around hand by presenting false-bodily temperature and pulse beat in accordance with emotions, which are included in remarks pointed by a mouse cursor.

This system exhibited to over 150 people and it revealed that this system is able to help users to experience others' emotions. The feedbacks obtained from the people used the "Communious Mouse" indicated that our method enables to share emotions described as text on the Internet. Meanwhile, whether the presented stimuli affect perception of self-physiological changes or how the perception of it attributed to text browsing are not investigated in this paper. To realizing our approach, the experiments to investigate these points will be required.

In addition, we conducted the experiment using actual human remarks but prepared remarks of the Internet bot. Therefore, an experiment using actual human's remarks described as a text will be also needed. Instead of this, the result of this experiment also shows the feasibility of sharing emotion of computer-generated agent, such as bots and robots. As future works, we will apply this method to the interaction with the personified agent or the robot. It will helpful for enhancing the quality of communication, in which we can sympathize with these agents.

REFERENCES

1. Gump, B. B., Kulik, J. A. 1997. Stress, affiliation, and emotional contagion, *Journal of Personality and Social Psychology*, 72, 305-319. DOI=10.1037/0022-3514.72.2.305

2. Hatfield, E., Cacioppo, J. T., and Rapson, R. L. 1993. Emotional contagion. *Current Directions in Psychological Sciences*, 2, 96-99. DOI=10.1111/1467-8721

3. Mitsunaga, N, Smith, C., Kanda, T., Ishiguro, H., Hagita, N. 2005. Adapting Robot Behavior for Human–Robot Interaction. *IEEE Transactions on Robotics,* 24, 4, 911-916. DOI=10.1109/TRO.2008.926867

4. James, W. 2011. The Principles of Psychology (Volume 2 of 2). Digireads.com Publishing.

5. Schachter, S. 1962. Cognitive, Social and Physiological Determinants of Emotiona State. *Psycholoical Review*, 69, 5, 379-399. DOI=10.1037/h0046234

6. Valins, S. 1966. Cognitive effects of false heart-rate feedback. *Journal of personality and social psychology*, 4, 4, 400. DOI=10.1037/h0023791

7. Yoshida, S., Sakurai, S., Narumi, T., Tanikawa, T., and Hirose, M. 2013. Incendiary reflection: evoking emotion through deformed facial feedback. In *SIGGRAPH'13 Talks*, Article 35. DOI= 10.1145/2504459.2504503

8. Hatfield, E., and Hsee, C. 1995. The Impact of Vocal Feedback on Emotional Experience and Expression. *Journal of Social Behavior and Personality*, 10, 293-313.

9. Nishimura, S., Ishii, A., Sato, M., Fukushima, S., and Kajimoto, H. 2012. Facilitation of Affection by Tactile Feedback of False Heartbeat. In *CHI EA '12*. 2321-2326. DOI= 10.1145/2212776.2223796

10. Fukushima, S, and. Kajimoto, H. 2012. Chilly chair: facilitating an emotional feeling with artificial piloerection. In *SIGGRAPH 2012 E-Tech*, Article 5. DOI=10.1145/2343456.2343461

11. Sakurai, S., Katsumura, T., Narumi, T., Tanikawa, T., and Hirose, M. 2014. Evoking Emotions in A Story Using Tactile Sensations as Pseudo-Body Responses with Contextual cues. *HCII2014*, LNCS 8521, 241-250. DOI=10.1007/978-3-319-07731-4_25

12. Sakurai, S., Ban, Y., Katsumura, T., Narumi, T., Tanikawa, T., and Hirose, M. 2014. Communious Mouse: A Mouse Interface to Experience Emotion in Remarks on The Web by Extending and Modulating One's Body Image. In *SIGGRAPH Asia'14 E-tech*, Article 4. DOI=10.1145/2669047.2669057

13. Elam, M., and Wallin, B. G. 1987. Skin blood flow responses to mental stress in man depend on body temperature. *Acta physiologica scandinavica*, 129, 3, 429-431. DOI=10.1111/j.1365-201X.1987.tb10609.x

14. Ekman, P., Levenson, R. W., and Friesen, W. V. 1983. Autonomic nervous system activity distinguishes among emotions. *Science*, 221, 4616, 1208-1210. DOI=10.1126/science.6612338

15. Hökfelt, T., Johansson, O., Ljungdahl, Å., Lundberg, J. M., and Schultzberg, M. 1980. Peptidergic neurones. *Nature*, 284, 515-521. DOI=10.1038/284515a0

16. Levenson, R. W., Ekman, P., and Friesen, W. V. 1990. Voluntary facial action generates emotion-specific autonomic nervous system activity. *Psychophysiology*, 27, 4, 363-384. DOI=10.1111/j.1469-8986.1990.tb02330.x

17. Marshall, J., and Schnieden, H. 1966. Effect of adrenaline, noradrenaline, atropine, and nicotine on some types of human tremor. *Journal of neurology, neurosurgery, and psychiatry*, 29, 3, 214. DOI=10.1136/jnnp.29.3.214

18. Kleinke C, Peterson T, and Rutledge, T. 1998. Effects of self-generated facial expressions on mood. *Journal of Personality and Social Psychology*, 74, 272-279. DOI= 10.1037/0022-3514.74.1.272

19. Shimojo, S., Simion, C., Shimojo, E., and Scheier, C. 2003. Gaze bias both reflects and influences preference. *Nature Neuroscience*, 6, 1317-1322. DOI=10.1038/nn1150

20. Bem, D. J. 1967. Self-perception: An alternative interpretation of cognitive dissonance phenomena. *Psychological review*, 74, 3, 183. DOI=10.1037/h0024835

21. Nummenmaa, L., Glerean, E., Hari, R., and Hietanen, J. K. 2014. Bodily maps of emotions. In *Proc. of the National Academy of Sciences*, 111, 2, 646-651. DOI=10.1073/pnas.1321664111

22. Dutton, D. and Aron, A. 1974. Some evidence for heightened sexual attraction under conditions of high anxiety. *Journal of Personality and Social Psychology*, 30, 4, 510-517. DOI=10.1037/h0037031

23. Russell, J. A. 1980. A circumplex model of affect. *Journal of personality and social psychology*, 39, 6, 1161. DOI=10.1037/h0077714

24. Jeannerod, M. 2003. The mechanism of self-recognition in humans. *Behavioural Brain Research*, 142, 1-15. DOI=10.1016/S0166-4328(02)00384-4

25. Mehnert, P., Malchaire, J., Kampmann, B., Piette, A., Griefahn, B., and Gebhardt, H. 2000. Prediction of the average skin temperature in warm and hot environments. *European journal of applied physiology*, 82, 1-2, 52-60. DOI=10.1007/ s004210050651

26. Narumi, T., Akagawa, T., Seong, Y. A., and Hirose, M. 2009. An entertainment system using thermal feedback for increasing communication and social skills. *Learning by Playing. Game-based Education System Design and Development*, 184-195. DOI= 10.1007/978-3-642-03364-3_25

27. Target Heart Rates, American Heart Association: http://www.heart.org/HEARTORG/HealthyLiving/PhysicalActivity/Target-Heart-Rates_UCM_434341_Article.jsp#.VzflSNCW7KM (Last accessed May 14. 2016)

28. Sato, K. and Maeno, T. 2013. Presentation of Rapid Temperature Change Using Spatially Divided Hot and Cold Stimuli. *Journal of Robotics and Mechatronics*, 25, 3, 497-505. DOI=10.20965/jrm.2013.p0497

29. Lecuyer, A. 2009. Simulting haptic feedback using vision: A survey of research and applications of pseudohaptic feedback. *Presence: Teleoper. Virtual Environ.* 18, 1, 39-53. DOI=http://dx.doi.org/10.1162/pres.18.1.39

30. Argelaguet, F., Jáuregui, D. A. G., Marchal, M., & Lécuyer, A. 2013. Elastic images: Perceiving local elasticity of images through a novel pseudo-haptic deformation effect. *ACM Trans. Appl. Percept.* 10, 3, Article 17. DOI=http://dx.doi.org/10.1145/2501599

31. Twitter: http://twitter.com/ (Last accessed May 14. 2016)

32. Carro, R. M., Ballesteros, F. J., Ortigosa, A., Guardiola, G., and Soriano, E. 2012. Angry Email? Emotion-based E-mail Tool Adaptation. *In Proc. of IWAAL'12*, 399-406. DOI= 10.1007/978-3-642-35395-6_54

33. Pang, B. and Lee, L. 2008. Opinion Mining and Sentiment Analysis. *Found. Trends Inf. Retr.* 2, 1-2, 1-135. DOI=http://dx.doi.org/10.1561/1500000011

34. Natural Language ToolKit (NLTK): http://www.nltk.org/ (Last accessed Oct 6. 2015)

35. McNair, D. M., Lorr, M., and Droppleman, L. 1971. Profile of mood States manual. San Diego: Educational and Industrial Testing Service.

36. Pepe, A., and Bollen, J. 2008. Between Conjecture and Memento: Shaping A Collective Emotional Perception of the Future. AAAI Spring Symposium: Emotion, Personality, and Social Behavior.

37. Wilson, G., Dobrev, D., and Brewster, S. A. Brewster. 2016. Hot Under the Collar: Mapping Thermal Feedback to Dimensional Models of Emotion. In *Proc. of CHI '16*, 4838-4849. DOI=10.1145/2858036.2858205

Synthesizing Realistic Image-based Avatars by Body Sway Analysis

Masashi Nishiyama, Tsubasa Miyauchi, Hiroki Yoshimura, Yoshio Iwai

Graduate School of Engineering, Tottori University

Tottori , Japan

nishiyama@eecs.tottori-u.ac.jp

ABSTRACT

We propose a method for synthesizing body sway to give human-like movement to image-based avatars. This method is based on an analysis of body sway in real people. Existing methods mainly handle the action states of avatars without sufficiently considering the wait states that exist between them. The wait state is essential for filling the periods before and after interaction. Users require both wait and action states to naturally communicate with avatars in interactive systems. Our method measures temporal changes in the body sway motion of each body part of a standing subject using a single-camera video sequence. We are able to synthesize a new video sequence with body sway over an arbitrary length of time by randomly transitioning between points in the sequence when the motion is close to zero. The results of a subjective assessment show that avatars with body sway synthesized by our method appeared more alive to users than those using baseline methods.

ACM Classification Keywords

H.5.m. Information Interfaces and Presentation (e.g. HCI): Miscellaneous

Author Keywords

Image-based Avatar, Body sway, Human-like movement

INTRODUCTION

Interactive systems that use human-like avatars are an active topic in human-agent interaction research, and have many potential applications, such as conversational avatars in a museum [15], avatars talking about the past [2], and speech-interactive guidance avatars [10]. These avatars have the potential to actively utilize the large-sized displays that we often see many places, e.g., in stations, shopping plazas, office entrances, and airports. These interactive avatars can automatically communicate with users without the constraints of

HAI '16, October 04-07, 2016, Biopolis, Singapore

©2016 ACM. ISBN 978-1-4503-4508-8/16/10...$15.00

DOI: http://dx.doi.org/10.1145/2974804.2974807

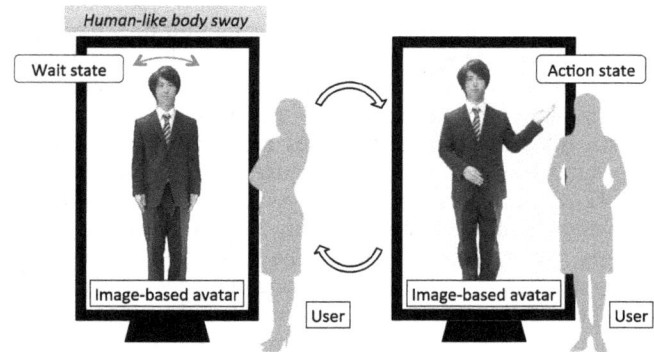

Figure 1. We consider the body sway of an image-based avatar in the wait state to enhance the nonverbal communication between it and a user in an interactive system.

time and place (e.g., at an automatic information desk late at night). In this paper, we focus on synthesizing human-like realistic avatars by exploiting an image-based technique [2, 9] in which life-sized video sequences interact with users through large-sized displays.

In order to synthesize realistic avatars for interactive systems, we need to consider two states. The first is the action state (e.g., speaking with a user) and the second is the wait state (e.g., maintaining a standing pose). In particular, the wait state plays an important role in the interaction between avatars and users because the avatars do not continuously communicate with the users. The wait state is required to handle periods before and after interaction with users. For instance, if the wait state is not adequately applied in the avatars, the users cannot judge whether to begin communication with the avatars or not. However, existing methods [2, 9] do not take the wait state into consideration; they mainly handle the action state.

Our key idea is to exploit the wait state of the avatars to enhance the nonverbal communication between users and avatars, as illustrated in Figure 1. To achieve this, we synthesize human-like micro movements. Consider a standing pose in the wait state; we often see standing receptionists at airports, hotels, and information offices. When people maintain a standing pose, they continuously move their body slightly around its center line. As described in [11], people unconsciously spread the burden of standing across their muscles by making micro movements to avoid overloading one set of muscles. This physiological phenomenon is called body sway.

In this paper, we propose a novel method for synthesizing human-like body sway for image-based avatars in the wait state. To analyze the body sway of real people, we first acquire video sequences of standing subjects and measure the movement of each body part. We extract the characteristics of body sway from the temporal changes of this movement. Using these characteristics, we can synthesize image-based avatars with body sway for an arbitrary length of time using identified transitioning times in the video sequences.

RELATED WORK

Interaction systems need to have an intuitive feel so that users can naturally communicate with avatars as if they were communicating with real people. As described in [6, 7], to design human-like avatars for interaction systems, video synthesis and speech synthesis are key techniques. In particular, video synthesis techniques are directly linked to the appearance of the avatars in nonverbal communication [3, 5, 4]. Researchers have developed various video synthesis techniques for generating realistic avatars, and there are currently two main approaches. The first exploits a computer graphics-based avatar [15, 10] and the second exploits an image-based avatar [2, 9]. In general, the appearance of image-based avatars is more human-like than that of computer graphics-based avatars. However, image-based avatars can only replay video sequences stored in databases. Thus, image-based avatars sometimes cannot work well when users perform unexpected actions. To overcome this difficulty, a technique [12, 1, 14, 17, 8] that synthesizes various video action sequences has been proposed. Some methods [12, 1] synthesize facial video sequences in conversation. Okwechime et al. [14] proposed synthesizing full-body video sequences of actions in conversation. Shi et al. [17] proposed editing video sequences of interactive actions between subjects, and Huang et al. [8] developed a method to seamlessly combine various actions. However, these existing methods do not sufficiently consider synthesizing video sequences of the wait state. Our method tackles the synthesis of realistic image-based avatars that contains human-like body sway.

ANALYSIS OF BODY SWAY

Design of measurement of body sway

Here, we consider a scenario in which standing people are always visible to the public, such as receptionists in public spaces. In order to synthesize this kind of body sway on human-like avatars, we need to measure the movement of each body part of a person in a standing pose. We also need to check whether the body parts move synchronously or not.

To analyze the body sway of real people, a footing force plate is widely used. However, this device measures temporal changes of the body's center of gravity and cannot acquire the motion of specific body parts. Nashner [13] measured sway motions using acceleration sensors attached to the body. These sensors have the disadvantages of needing to be attached to a user and are difficult to temporally synchronize. Recently,

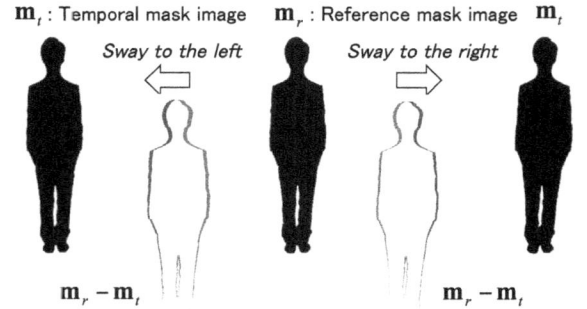

Figure 2. A reference mask image and temporal mask images. Red represents a region converted from body to background and blue represents the opposite case.

Wang et al. [19] inferred the position of the center of gravity of the whole body using multiple video cameras and Yeung et al. [21] inferred the center of gravity position from body joints using common gaming sensors. However, these existing methods handle only the center of gravity position of the body and insufficiently consider the micro movements of each body part. We aim to measure the amounts of movement of each body part using a simple video camera without body-attached sensors. The details of our method are described below.

Algorithm for measuring body sway

Our method uses a binary mask image in which a pixel within a body region is 1; otherwise it is 0. We acquire a video sequence of N frames from a standing subject. Given a reference time r, representing the center of the body sway in the video sequence, we determine a reference mask image $\mathbf{m}_r$. We compare the reference mask image with temporal mask images $\mathbf{m}_t (t \in 1, ..., N)$, as illustrated in Figure 2. Our method computes the amount d_i of body sway movement as

$$d_i = \sum_{x \in \text{parts}(i)} (\mathbf{m}_r(x) - \mathbf{m}_t(x)), \qquad (1)$$

where $\mathbf{m}_r(x)$ and $\mathbf{m}_t(x)$ indicate the pixel value at position x in $\mathbf{m}_r$ and $\mathbf{m}_t$, respectively, and parts(i) is a body part region indicated by i, such as the regions shown in Figure 3. The value of d_i is positive when the number of pixels converted from the background to the body is higher and negative when the number of pixels converted from the body to the background is higher. Note that we compute reference time r using Algorithm 1 to determine reference mask image $\mathbf{m}_r$.

Algorithm 1 Determine reference time r.

---

for $\tilde{r} = 1$ to N **do**
  $D_{\tilde{r}} \leftarrow 0$
  for $t = 1$ to N **do**
    compute $\tilde{d}_i$ using $\mathbf{m}_{\tilde{r}}, \mathbf{m}_t$
    $D_{\tilde{r}} \leftarrow D_{\tilde{r}} + \sum |\tilde{d}_i|$ for all body parts
  end for
end for
$r \leftarrow \arg \min D_{\tilde{r}}$

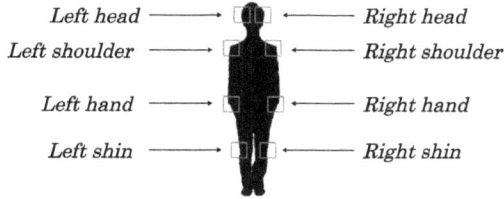

Figure 3. Body part regions for measuring body sway movement.

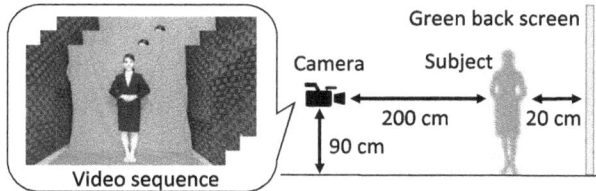

Figure 4. Setup for body sway measurement.

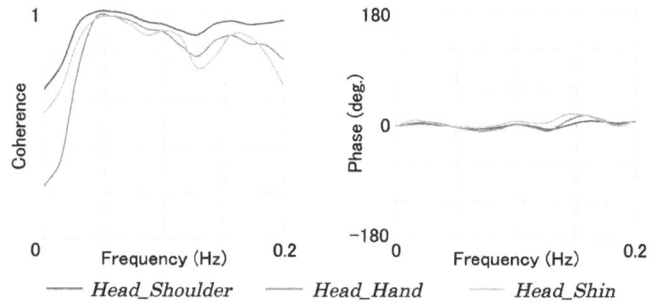

Figure 5. Coherence analysis of movements (180 s) of right body parts of subject A. The values of phase between these parts were nearly identical though the values of coherence were different.

| Body part | Test Subject | | | | | |
	A	B	C	D	E	Avg.
Left head	289	132	185	237	197	208
Right head	296	107	191	265	200	212
Left shoulder	205	114	157	156	159	158
Right shoulder	232	86	140	198	155	162
Left hand	212	75	145	111	119	132
Right hand	191	63	88	107	126	115
Left shin	73	31	54	56	57	54
Right shin	89	32	50	53	55	56

Table 1. Standard deviation [pixel] of body sway movement $|d_i|$ for each body part.

Evaluation of body sway measurement

To evaluate the effectiveness of our method, we captured five video sequences of five test subjects (average age 21.4 ± 0.5 years, average height 166.9 ± 7.1 cm). Each test subject stood in front of a camera. Each sequence lasted 180 s. We used a video camera with 30 frames per second and $1,920 \times 1,080$ pixel resolution. We set the camera at a height of 90 cm and distance of 200 cm from the subject (Figure 4). The bounding box of the subjects is hence about 300×950 pixels. We generated mask images from the sequences with a simple background subtraction technique using a green back screen. We manually identified the head, shoulder, hand, and shin regions (Figure 3) for each video sequence. We set the size of each body part to 70×70 pixels.

Table 1 shows the standard deviation of body sway movement $|d_i|$ for each body part of each subject. We can see that these amounts were dynamically different between subjects. We can also see that the movements of the upper body parts were larger than the those of the lower body parts. We believe that all body parts synchronously moved in all subjects. We also observed the same tendency in Figure 5. Note that a change in d_i of about 380 pixels corresponds to a body part movement of 1 cm.

Figure 6 shows the temporal changes in the amount of movement for each body part. We can see that the temporal changes were different for each subject because the shape of the waves notably varies between subjects. We can also see that the temporal changes were nearly identical for all body parts; for instance, the head moved to the left and then the other parts moved in the same direction. Similarly, when the right parts moved to the left, the corresponding left parts moved in the inverse direction. We observed this same tendency among all subjects. We believe that the motion synchronously changes for all body parts.

Furthermore, we verified the temporal characteristics of the movement. Figure 7 shows temporal changes over 60 s for the left side of the head of subject A. We can see that the zero-crossing points (representing the reference times) repetitively

appear and the temporal changes between the zero-crossing points forms a multi-modal wave. We observed the same tendency for all subjects. We believe that the temporal changes are periodic and contain the sway motion between the reference times.

Measurement error evaluation

We evaluated the error of our motion measurement. We used five reference mask images of the five subjects and 15 temporal mask images randomly selected from the video sequences. We manually calculated the ground truth of the body regions to generate the mask images. Figure 8 compares the amount of movement $|d_i|$ using the ground truth with that measured using the automatically extracted mask images. These results show that the error of measurement is very small for each body part. We thus believe that the results of our method are not affected by error from the mask images generated using the background subtraction technique.

Next, we compared the performance of our method with that of an existing method [21] that measures the 3D center of gravity using the body joints of Microsoft Kinect v2. We computed the 2D positions of the centers of gravity projected from the 3D positions because the purpose of our method is to measure the 2D variations of body sway in a video sequence. We compared the Root Mean Squared Error (RMSE) between the centers of gravity of manually labeled body regions and those of our method. The RMSE of our method is 1.1 pixels and that of the existing method is 36.5 pixels. Hence, our

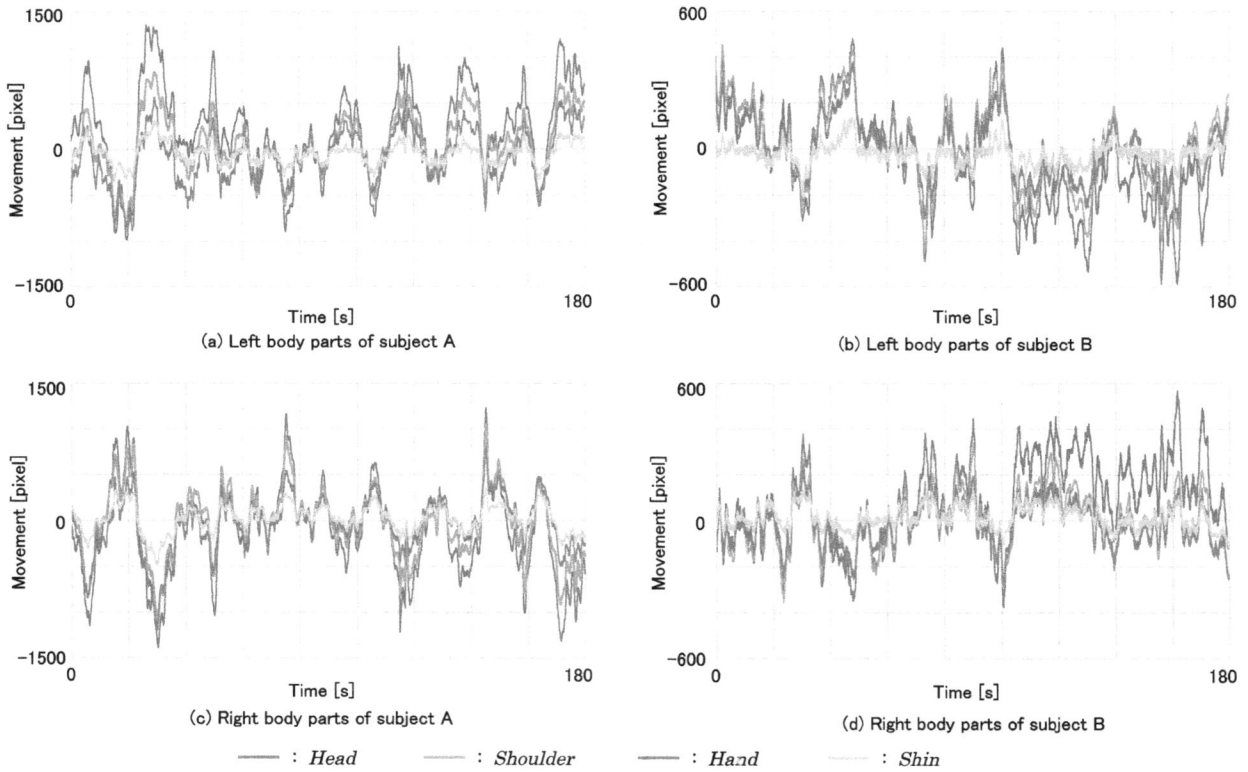

Figure 6. Measuring temporal movement caused by body sway for each body part.

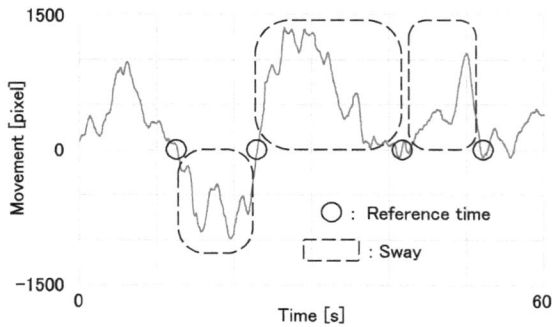

Figure 7. Temporal characteristics of body sway motion. First is that there is a plurality of reference times and second is that there is sways between the reference times.

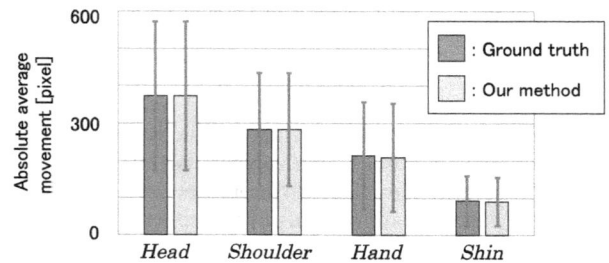

Figure 8. Performance of movement measurement using the simple background subtraction method. Error bars represent standard deviations.

method outperforms the existing method when measuring the 2D positions of body part centers of gravity.

SYNTHESIS OF IMAGE-BASED AVATARS WITH HUMAN-LIKE BODY SWAY

Design for generating body sway

We now describe how we synthesize body sway for image-based avatars. We consider exploiting the characteristics of the temporal changes of movement shown in Figure 7. Our method extracts the reference times of body sway from a video sequence captured from a subject for an image-based avatar and replays the video sequence by randomly transitioning

between the reference times, as illustrated in Figure 9. Using this process, we can synthesize a body sway video sequence of arbitrary time length. However, we only handle the mask image representing the shape of the body in the discussion in the above section. This causes the problem that incorrect reference times are extracted, i.e., the shape of the body is similar but its texture is not. In order to synthesize a human-like body sway, we should take both the appearance and shape of the body into consideration. We also exploit the appearance of the face because users are sensitive to facial expressions. The details of this synthesis are described below.

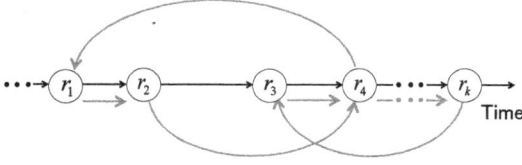

Figure 9. Synthesizing a body sway video sequence using a set of reference times r_k. Our method replays a video sequence of body sway by randomly transitioning between the reference times. The black arrows represent the flow of the original video sequence and blue arrows represent the flow of the synthesized video sequence.

Algorithm for computing shape and appearance similarities

To synthesize body sway, our method computes the similarity of the body shape, body appearance, and face appearance at each time t. We use mask image $\mathbf{m}_t$ to represent body shape, color image $\mathbf{a}_t$ to represent body appearance, and facial image $\mathbf{f}_t$ to represent facial appearance. Our method generates $\mathbf{m}_t$ using the same technique described in the section on measurement. Here, $\mathbf{a}_t$ refers to each frame of a video sequence. We generate the pose-aligned $\mathbf{f}_t$ using facial feature points inferred by a face tracking technique [16]. Given an initial reference time r_0, our method computes similarity $s_{t,s}$ of a body shape as

$$s_{t,s} = e^{-\lambda \sum |d_i|}, \qquad (2)$$

where λ is a constant and d_i is the amount of motion measured using $\mathbf{m}_{r_0}$ and $\mathbf{m}_t$. Equation (2) uses the summation of d_i for all body parts. We use $s_{t,s}$ to extract the times that shifts between body and background regions do not occur. Next, we compute the similarity $s_{t,a}$ of body appearance as

$$s_{t,a} = \mathrm{SSIM}(\mathbf{a}_{r_0}, \mathbf{a}_t), \qquad (3)$$

where SSIM is the Structural SIMilarity [20], used to predict the perceived quality of frames of a video sequence. We use $s_{t,a}$ to extract the times of unvarying texture over the whole body. Furthermore, we compute similarity $s_{t,f}$ for the face appearance as

$$s_{t,f} = \mathrm{FaceSimilarity}(\mathbf{f}_{r_0}, \mathbf{f}_t), \qquad (4)$$

where FaceSimilarity is a correlation value using the edge-based feature vectors of $\mathbf{f}_{r_0}$ and $\mathbf{f}_t$. We use $s_{t,f}$ to extract the times of unchanging facial expressions such as between blinks. We compute the final integrated similarity s_t as

$$s_t = \alpha s_{t,s} + \beta s_{t,a} + \gamma s_{t,f}, \qquad (5)$$

where $\alpha + \beta + \gamma = 1$. Using s_t, we aim to extract the reference times at which the shapes and appearances do not change much over the whole-body. Note that we determine initial reference time r_0 using Algorithm 2.

Transition between reference times

As described above, the reference times are suitable for seamlessly transitioning through the video sequence. We thus exploit the set of reference times r_k to synthesize human-like body sway. Our method generates the set of reference times by searching for times at which the shape and appearance of the body are close to each other (Algorithm 3). At these times,

Algorithm 2 Determine initial reference time r_0.

> **for** $\tilde{r}_0 = 1$ to N **do**
> $S_{\tilde{r}_0} \leftarrow 0$
>   **for** $t = 1$ to N **do**
>   compute $\tilde{s}_t$ using $\mathbf{m}_{\tilde{r}_0}, \mathbf{a}_{\tilde{r}_0}, \mathbf{f}_{\tilde{r}_0}, \mathbf{m}_t, \mathbf{a}_t, \mathbf{f}_t$
> $S_{\tilde{r}_0} \leftarrow S_{\tilde{r}_0} + \tilde{s}_t$
>   **end for**
> **end for**
> $r_0 \leftarrow \arg\max S_{\tilde{r}_0}$

s_t reaches a local maximum and is greater than a threshold T_1. To prevent extracting reference times with short intervals, we also add a condition that reference times are selected more than an interval threshold of T_2 apart.

Algorithm 3 Generate set of reference times.

> **for** $t = 1$ to N **do**
>   compute s_t using $\mathbf{m}_{r_0}, \mathbf{a}_{r_0}, \mathbf{f}_{r_0}, \mathbf{m}_t, \mathbf{a}_t, \mathbf{f}_t$
>   **if** s_t is local maximum, $s_t > T_1$, interval $> T_2$ **then**
>   add time t to set of reference times
>   **end if**
> **end for**

We next describe a video transition technique using the set of reference times (Algorithm 4). We randomly select a reference time r_k from the set and display color images $\mathbf{a}_t$ from the selected reference time r_k to the next reference time r_{k+1}. By repeating the random selection, we can synthesize realistic video sequences of body sway for image-based avatars.

Algorithm 4 Synthesize new video sequence.

> **while** true **do**
>   select r_k randomly from set of reference times
>   **for** $t = r_k$ to r_{k+1} **do**
>   display color image $\mathbf{a}_t$
>   **end for**
> **end while**

Evaluation of synthesis of body sway

We evaluated the body sway of image-based avatars synthesized by our method. We used male and female avatars. We acquired video sequences of 90 s for each standing person, extracted eight reference times the video sequences and synthesized new sequences of 20 s video to generate the avatars. We set $\alpha = 0.5, \beta = 0.25, \gamma = 0.25, \lambda = 1.0 \times 10^{-5}, T_1 = 0.97$, and $T_2 = 1$. The parameters were experimentally determined to gain smoothness of synthesized videos. We conducted the subjective assessment on the following methods:

V1: (Ideal) directly replaying the first of 20 s of the acquired video sequences

V2: (Our method) replaying the synthesized video sequences

V3: (Baseline 1) replaying one short video sequences of 4 s randomly chopped from the acquired video sequences

159

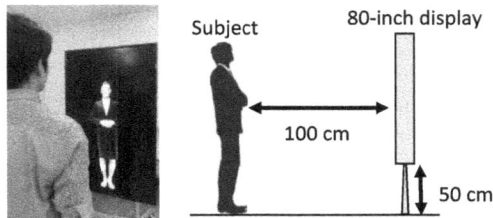

Figure 10. Setup for the subjective assessment.

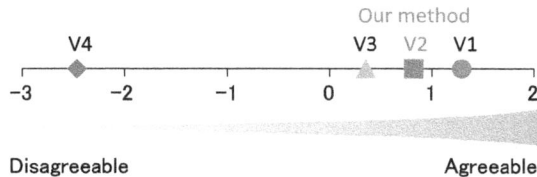

Figure 11. Results of the subjective assessment of synthesized body sway of avatars. We used the paired comparisons method.

V4: (Baseline 2) displaying a single shot from the acquired video sequences

Ten subjects (7 males, 3 females, aged 22.2 ± 1.1 years) participated in the subjective assessment using the paired comparisons method proposed by Thurstone [18]. The subject stood in front of a vertical 80-inch display at a distance of 1 m (Figure 10). We asked each subject to look at a pair of video sequences 6 ($= {}_4C_2$) times, and select one video sequence from the pair that the subject felt more closely represented human-like movement.

Figure 11 shows the result of the subjective assessment. A higher subjective score indicates agreement from the subjects and vice versa. As we can see, our method (V2) scores higher than the baseline methods (V3, and V4). We took free comments from the subjects after the paired comparisons. One of the subjects said that V3 was unnatural because discontinuous movements appeared suddenly, and V4 was unnatural because the avatar completely stopped. Note that the ideal video sequence of V1 obtained a higher subjective score than V2. For this reason, we believe that V2 contained some small discontinuities at the transition points. Figures 12 shows examples of video sequences for the subjective assessment and a visualization of the movement amounts. We can see that the movement was large at the transition point in V3, the movement was small at the transition point in V2 as well as V1, and bodies of the avatars swayed to the left and right in V2. We believe that extracting reference times by our method is useful for increasing the reality of the image-based avatars.

Next, we compared the synthesized video sequences of our method with a video that replayed a single short video sequence of 2 s from one reference time to the next reference time. In the alternative video sequence, the same movements were repeated within a short time, although the movement was smooth at the transition point (Figure 13). We asked the subjects to select the video sequence that they felt more

closely represented human-like movement. Figure 14 shows the comparison of the number of votes between our method and the alternative method. Our method obtained 18 votes and the alternative method obtained 2 votes. We believe that the choosing random transitions at reference times is effective for synthesizing human-like movements.

CONCLUSION

We proposed a method for analyzing and synthesizing body sway to generate human-like wait states of image-based avatars. By measuring the amount of movement for each body part, we observed that reference times of body sway repeatedly appear and all body parts continuously move between these reference times. We synthesized an arbitrary length time of body sway by randomly transitioning between the reference times. A subjective experiment demonstrated that our method is more agreeable than the baseline methods for subjective assessment.

As part of our future work, we will expand our analysis on interactive systems and intend to consider the transitions between wait and action states.

REFERENCES

1. R. Anderson, B. Stenger, V. Wan, and R. Cipolla. 2013. Expressive Visual Text-to-Speech Using Active Appearance Models. In *Proceedings of the 2013 IEEE Conference on Computer Vision and Pattern Recognition (CVPR)*. 3382–3389.

2. R. Artstein, D. Traum, O. Alexander, A. Leuski, A. Jones, K. Georgila, P. Debevec, W. Swartout, H. Maio, and S. Smith. 2014. Time-Offset Interaction with a Holocaust Survivor. In *Proceedings of the 19th International Conference on Intelligent User Interfaces (IUI)*. 163–168.

3. T.K. Capin, I.S. Pandzic, N.M. Thalmann, and D. Thalmann. 1997. Realistic Avatars and Autonomous Virtual Humans in VLNET Networked Virtual Environments. In *From desktop to webtop: virtual environments on the internet, WWW and networks, international conference*.

4. J. Cassell. 2000. Embodied Conversational Interface Agents. *Commun. ACM* 43, 4 (2000), 70–78.

5. M. Fabri, D.J. Moore, and D.J. Hobbs. 1999. The Emotional Avatar: Non-verbal Communication Between Inhabitants of Collaborative Virtual Environments. In *Gesture-Based Communication in Human-Computer Interaction: International GestureWorkshop (GW)*. 269–273.

6. J. Gratch, J. Rickel, E. Andre, J. Cassell, E. Petajan, and N. Badler. 2002. Creating interactive virtual humans: some assembly required. *IEEE Intelligent Systems* 17, 4 (2002), 54–63.

7. A. Hartholt, D. Traum, S. C. Marsella, A. Shapiro, G. Stratou, A. Leuski, L. P. Morency, and J. Gratch. 2013. All Together Now Introducing the Virtual Human Toolkit. In *Proceedings of the 13th International Conference on Intelligent Virtual Agents (IVA)*. 368–381.

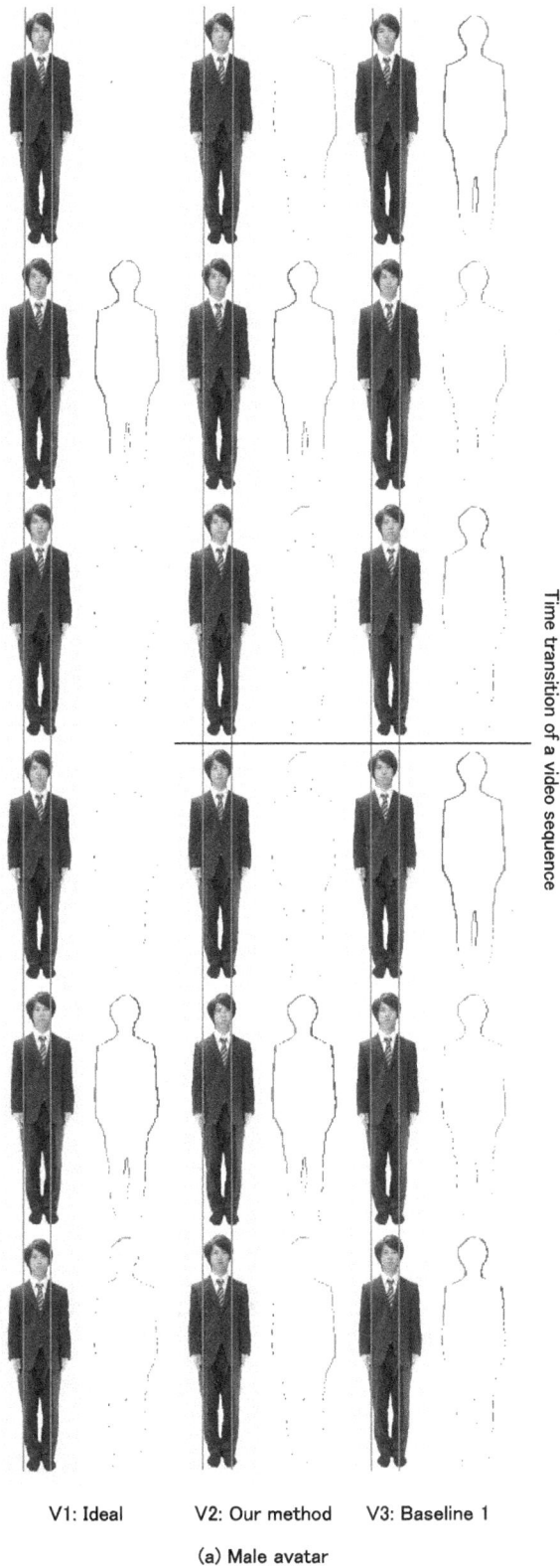

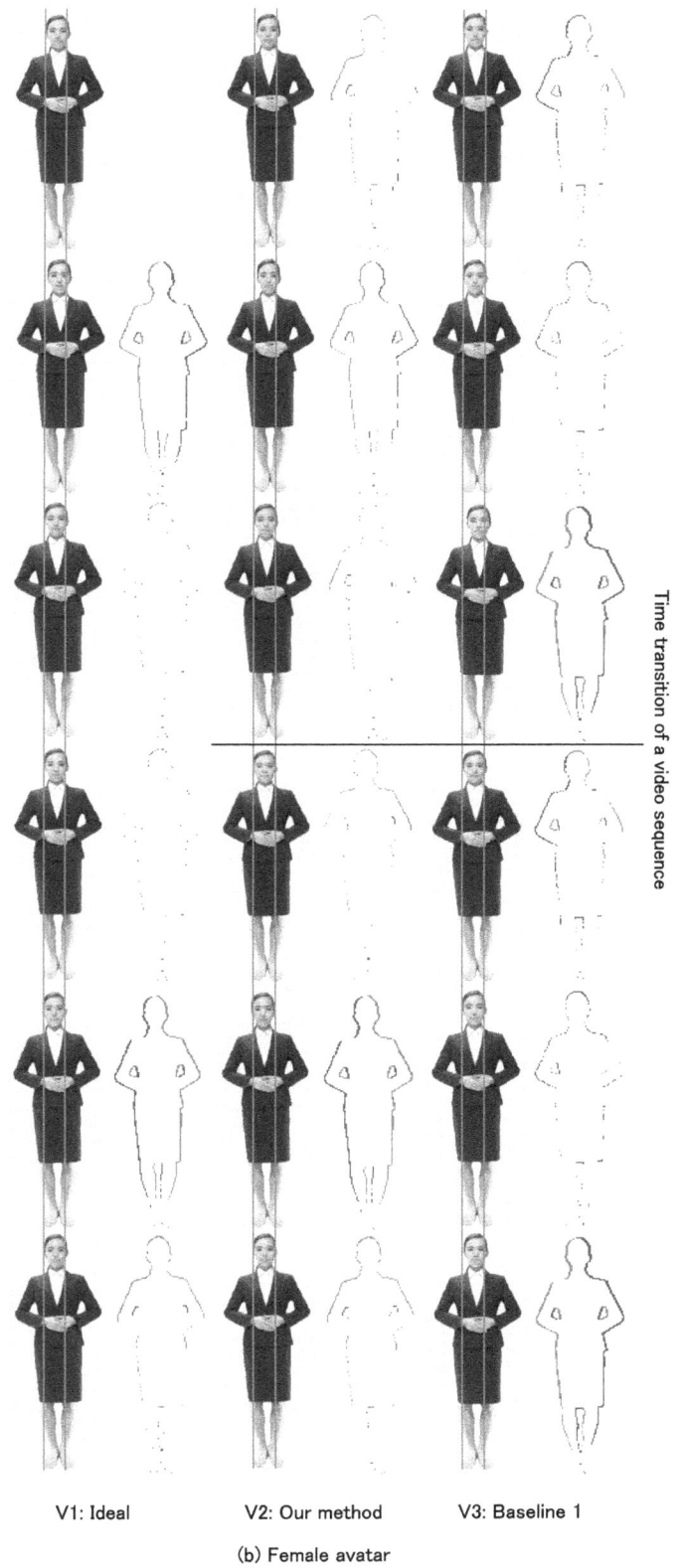

Figure 12. Comparison of synthesized video sequences of a male and a female avatars. Red represents a region converted from body to background and blue represents the opposite case.

Figure 13. Video sequences using the alternative method. The same movements were repeated within a short time.

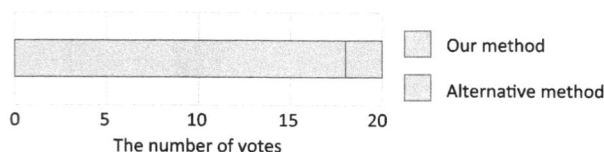

Figure 14. Comparison of the number of votes between our method and the alternative method in subjective assessment.

8. P. Huang, M. Tejera, J. Collomosse, and A. Hilton. 2015. Hybrid Skeletal-Surface Motion Graphs for Character Animation from 4D Performance Capture. *ACM Transactions on Graphics* 34, 2 (2015), 17:1–17:14.

9. A. Jones, J. Unger, K. Nagano, J. Busch, X. Yu, H. I. Peng, O. Alexander, M. Bolas, and P. Debevec. 2015. An Automultiscopic Projector Array for Interactive Digital Humans. In *ACM SIGGRAPH 2015 Emerging Technologies (SIGGRAPH)*. 6:1.

10. A. Lee, K. Oura, and K. Tokuda. 2013. MMDAgent - A Fully Open-Source Toolkit for Voice Interaction Systems. In *Proceedings of IEEE International Conference on Acoustics, Speech, and Signal Processing (ICASSP)*. 8382–8385.

11. L. S. Mark, J. S. Warm, and R. L. Huston. 1987. *Ergonomics and Human Factors: Recent Research.* Springer.

12. W. Mattheyses and W. Verhelst. 2015. Audiovisual speech synthesis: An overview of the state-of-the-art. *Speech Communication* 66 (2015), 182–217.

13. L. M. Nashner. 1972. Vestibular postural control model. *Kybernetik* 10, 2 (1972), 106–110.

14. D. Okwechime, E. Ong, A. Gilbert, and Richard Bowden. 2010. Social Interactive Human Video Synthesis. In *Proceedings of the 10th Asian Conference on Computer Vision (ACCV)*. 256–270.

15. S. Robinson, D. Traum, I. Ittycheriah, and J. Henderer. 2008. What would you Ask a conversational Agent? Observations of Human-Agent Dialogues in a Museum Setting. In *Proceedings of the Sixth International Conference on Language Resources and Evaluation (LREC)*. 28–30.

16. J. M. Saragih, S. Lucey, and J. F. Cohn. 2011. Deformable model fitting by regularized landmark mean-shift. *IEEE international Journal of Computer Vision* 91, 2 (2011), 200–215.

17. Q. Shi, S. Nobuhara, and T. Matsuyama. 2015. Augmented Motion History Volume for Spatiotemporal Editing of 3-D Video in Multiparty Interaction Scenes. *IEEE Transactions on Circuits and Systems for Video Technology* 25, 1 (2015), 63–76.

18. L. L. Thurstone. 1927. A law of comparative judgment. *Psychological Review* 34, 4 (1927), 273–286.

19. F. Wang, M. Skubic, C. Abbott, and J. M. Keller. 2010. Body sway measurement for fall risk assessment using inexpensive webcams. In *Proceedings of International Conference of Engineering in Medicine and Biology Society (EMBC)*. 2225–2229.

20. Z. Wang, A. C. Bovik, H. R. Sheikh, and E. P. Simoncelli. 2004. Image quality assessment: from error visibility to structural similarity. *IEEE Transactions on Image Processing* 13, 4 (2004), 600–612.

21. L.F. Yeung, Kenneth C. Cheng, C.H. Fong, Winson C.C. Lee, and Kai-Yu Tong. 2014. Evaluation of the Microsoft Kinect as a clinical assessment tool of body sway. *Gait & Posture* 40, 4 (2014), 532–538.

Who am I touching ?:
User study of remote handshaking with a telepresence face

Kana Misawa
The University of Tokyo
7-3-1, Hongo, Bunkyo-ku Tokyo, JAPAN
k.misawa@acm.org

Jun Rekimoto
The University of Tokyo, Sony CSL
3-14-13 Higashigotanda, Shinagawa-ku, Tokyo, Japan
rekimoto@acm.org

ABSTRACT

In mediated communications, the social presence is said to be enhanced not only by eye contact and body gestures but also by remote haptics. To realize remote haptics, we present a mask telepresence system worn by a surrogate that displays the face of a remote user through a livestream. This system allows someone to shake the hand of a remote user via the surrogate. We conducted experiments where the surrogate contacted the participants to determine with whom the participants thought they shook hands: the surrogate or the remote user. We hypothesized that the relationship between the participant and surrogate or remote user is affected by the haptic sensations. Therefore, we prepared four conditions where the remote user was an acquaintance or a stranger and the surrogate was an acquaintance or a stranger. The results showed that, when the surrogate and the remote user were acquaintances, the participants felt like they were shaking hands with the remote user.

ACM Classification Keywords

H.5.3. Group and Organization Interfaces: Computer- supported cooperative work.

Author Keywords

Social touch; Social telepresence; Physical telepresence; Video-mediated communication; Social interaction.

INTRODUCTION

Video-meditated communication has been studied to enhance the sensation of "being there" at a remote location. Eye contact has been reported to strengthen a remote user's presence and aid in conversation dynamics such as taking turns speaking and controlling the interaction flow [9]. Some studies have shown that movement [15], mobility [17] and gesture [1] are more engaging and enhance the social telepresence. Moreover, recent research has shown that "remote handshaking" enhances the social telepresence [2] and engenders a sense of intimacy between the communicating subjects [16].

HAI '16, October 04-07, 2016, Biopolis, Singapore
©2016 ACM. ISBN 978-1-4503-4508-8/16/10...$15.00
DOI: http://dx.doi.org/10.1145/2974804.2974821

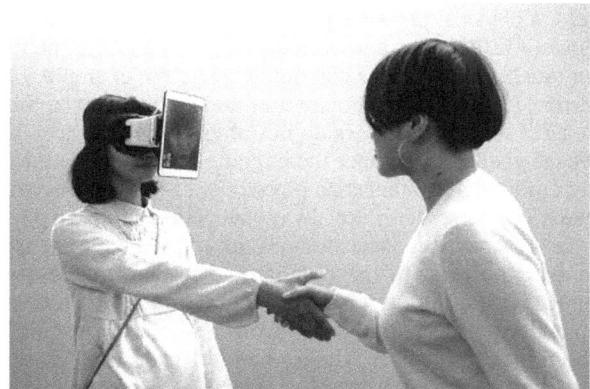

Figure 1. A user talks with a remote user on the display and shakes hand.

Video-meditated communication systems are often autonomous, allowing them to move around in remote space, and perform human-like actions. Autonomous systems have shown promise for use in many scenarios [17]. However, they are still limited in substituting the physical human existence in the real world. In addition, haptic devices are focused on specific senses of a body part; thus, they are not integrated as a human proxy. ChameleonMask [10] is a teleoperating human-surrogate system, not a robot. Unlike an autonomous robot, the human surrogate is provided instructions from a remote user. According to previous studies, participants tended to feel that the masked human surrogate was the right person. After seeing the surrogate and communicating for a while, they felt the remote user was actually there. However, it is not clear if ChameleonMask enables to social touching action, such as shaking hands or embracing, in a remote place.

Touching is a fundamental body action of interpersonal communication. Social touching is used to show intentions and feelings, such as an encouraging pat on the back or a reassuring embrace. In particular, shaking hands is a formalized form of interpersonal touching. Shaking hands is a symbolic gesture that signals social motives such as a willingness to cooperate and establishing trust. In addition, shaking hands is a nonverbal social ritual that is widely used in both Eastern and Western cultures.

How can a person shake hands with a remote user? Shaking hands is a physical action that produces a haptic sensation on the hands. Telecommunications using haptic is difficult with regard to reproducibility, and transmitting haptic sensations between users separated by distance is still a topic of research. A remote user cannot be directly touched. Therefore, haptic input and output devices are being developed to capture the touching action and to send haptic sensations. Although interpersonal touching is an important social interaction, little scientific research has been conducted [7]. An understanding is needed of how remote interpersonal touching, particularly physical touching interactions, affect human communication.

While many haptic studies have strived to develop haptic devices, a physical presence is not always needed to produce the sense of touch. If a person feels remote touching, he or she can touch a remote user without devices. For example, Hypermirror [13] involves a remote user and a local user embracing on a 2D screen; the users do not physically embrace. Vibrations are added to enhance the hugging sensation, but the users hug emotionally rather than physically [12]. Based on this research, we believe it is not always necessary to have a physical presence or a haptic sensation produced by the remote user to produce the sense of touch. ChameleonMask enables people to talk with a remote user via video-communication, while engendering the haptic sense from a human surrogate with whom the remote user "shakes hands." Therefore, users may experience the sensation of shaking a hand more viscerally with a remote user.

This paper presents a user study of remote handshaking in which a human surrogate is employed as a method of interpersonal touching (Figure 1). The surrogate wears a mask-shaped display that shows the remote user's real-time face and voice channel [11]. The remote user sends a command to the surrogate when he or she wants to shake hands with the conversation partner. When the conversation partner directly shakes hands with the surrogate, he or she experience a haptic sensation from the surrogate's hand.

By wearing the mask display, the surrogate's face is hidden and separated from his/her body. We investigated whether the user feels that he or she is shaking hands with the remote user or the surrogate. We hypothesized that the sensation changes depending on the status of the surrogate and the remote user. When then conducted a handshaking experiments under four conditions in which the remote user was either an acquaintance or a stranger, and the surrogate was an acquaintance or a stranger.

RELATED WORK

Remote touching methods
Touching is nonverbal communication that conveys the emotional state of the subject more than just words. Touching can be remotely represented in a variety of ways. First, many haptic devices have been developed to encourage intimate communications for long-distance relationships. inTouch [4], for example, is a communication prototype that supports a shared, tactile experience between two people. HandJive is groove-type haptic device for interpersonal entertainment that

sends the movement of the device to others [5]. A single haptic devices can not fulfill all purposes in one device. For this reason, haptic devices tend to specialize in unique tactile sensations, such as a bidirectional tickling interface [6], an air-inflatable vest resembling a embrace [14], and handshaking using a robot hand [8]. Second, video images enable a person to experience the sense of remote touching. HyperMirror [13] allows users to embrace the remote user through video streaming. The users do not physically embrace; nevertheless, the virtual embrace still has a therapeutic effect. Moreover, if a participant's eyesight is substituted by a pre-recorded view, the participants may confuse who touched them [19]. Finally, there are system that combine the use of haptic and video communication [16]. The proposed approach also uses video streaming; however, it employs real human hands rather than a robot hand.

Effects of remote touching
In telepresence research, several studies have been conducted to produce a more realistic sensation of the remote user. The effects of integrating haptic and video communications are not yet well understood. Nakanishi et al. revealed that handshaking can strengthen the remote user's presence [16]. Bevan et al. also showed that shaking hand prior to a negotiation increases cooperation between negotiators [3]. These experimental systems are stationary; many telepresence systems are confined to a room-sized space. Moreover, autonomous robots, such as Double[1] have shown promising results for wide application in many scenarios. Autonomous robots enable the remote user to freely move around a local place and talk with people. However, these systems are still limited, as they do not have hands, and so the remote user cannot transmit body gestures to show intentions or perform actions such as opening a door. Consequently, these systems cannot transmit haptic sensations. ChameleonMask is a teleoperating system that uses a human avatar rather than a telepresence robot [11]. Although users seem to regard the masked surrogate as the remote user, it is still unknown whether or a local user touching the surrogate would feel as if he or she is touching the remote user. Therefore, in this study, we explored whether remote touching produced by the surrogate makes people feel like they are interacting with the remote user.

DESIGN

Handshaking task
Here, we explain why we adopted remote handshaking as the experimental task. There are other ways of remote social touching other than handshaking that use the hands: touching, tickling, embracing, and kissing. The main reasons are given below:

1. Both males and females are allowed to touch hands in European cultures;

2. Handshaking is a formal social touching action.

According to Suvilehto et al. [18], hands are parts of the body that people are allowed to touch. They found that the topography of social touching depends on the emotional bonds

---

[1]Double, http://www.doublerobotics.com/business/

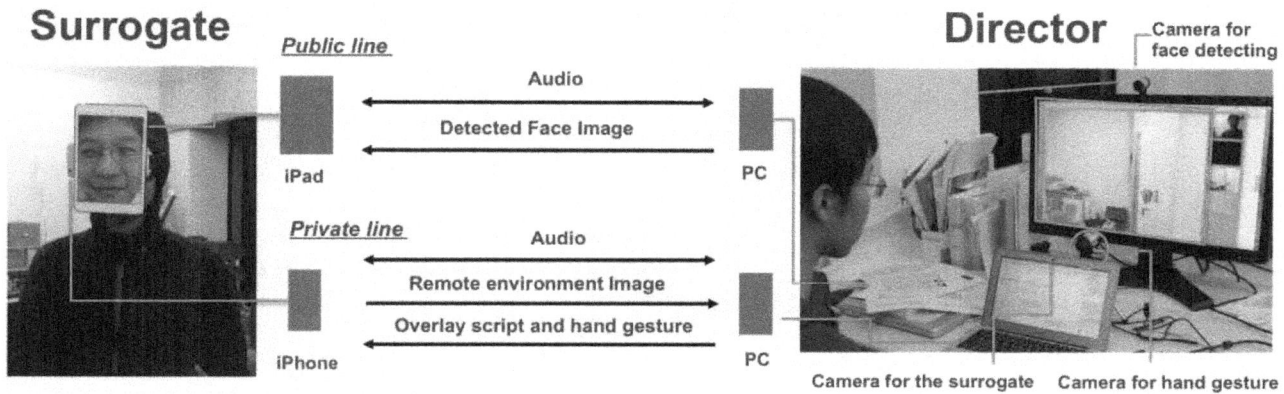

Figure 2. <Re-posting> System overview of two communication lines: 1) Public line is a channel between a director and local party members. Audio and detected face images are sent to the surrogates iPad. 2) Private line is a channel between a surrogate and a director. The director gives the surrogate direction by some ways. Sharing surround environment from the surrogate to the director with eye sights and voices.

between humans and is separated by the sexes. Their results show the zones in which people are allowed to touch depending on the given social network. Second, while other types of social touching using hands exist, handshaking is a formalized social action that strangers also perform after greetings. The action is general and widely acceptable to people; thus, we selected handshaking for our experiments.

Hand shaking using a human surrogate

Handshaking is an action in which two hands touch and exchange haptic sensations. The hand sensation comprises form, texture, and temperature. In our experiments, we used human hands with different owners. Thus, the technical sophistication of robot hands has no bearing on our experiment. The hands of two people do not tend to vary very much, and people do not generally memorize and become accustomed to the hand texture of the other persons on a regular basis. Therefore, we focused not on the difference of hands but on how to make people feel like they are shaking hands with a remote user when they are actually shaking the surrogate's hand.

Remote touching has two sides: sending haptic sensations and receiving them in a bidirectional manner. In this experiment, we focused on the reaction of the side receiving the handshake. Therefore, the remote user did not feel the handshake. However, the remote user could see what the surrogate viewed and could understand when the handshaking was completed. When the remote user intended to shake hands with the talking partner, he or she would send a signal to the surrogate to perform a handshake. The surrogate would view the signal overlaid on the screen and offer his or her hand to the talking partner (Figure 2).

We used a wearable mask system that enabled a remote user to be embodied by a surrogate. The facial expression of the remote user was streamed, and the mask was used as a display. The remote user communicated with the local person by sharing the surrogate's vision and situation. The presence of the surrogate enabled the remote user to exert his or her physical and social presence in the local place (Figure 3).

Table 1. Experimental condition on relationship between the participants and the surrogate/ the remote user.

Condition	Surrogate	Remote user
A	Stranger	Stranger
B	Acquaintance	Stranger
C	Stranger	Acquaintance
D	Acquaintance	Acquaintance

EXPERIMENT

Objective

This study was undertaken to verify several hypotheses for investigating whether a remote user can shake hands with a surrogate. As shown by Suvilehto et al. [18], the non-taboo touch zones depend on the social relationships. Thus, we expected that the haptic sensations from whom the subject shakes hands with will also depend on their social relationship. We prepared four experimental conditions for the participant (Table 1, Figure 4) where the remote user was either an acquaintance or stranger and the surrogate was also an acquaintance or stranger. When participants talked with the remote user through video communication and shook hands with the surrogate, we asked them with whom they felt they were touching. When the users touched the surrogate, they evaluated whether or not they felt as if they were shaking hands with the remote user. It was important to determine whether the participant had previously met the remote user. If the remote user was a stranger to the participant, the latter did not have a preconceived image of the former. In addition, if the surrogate was a friend of the participant, the latter have felt as if he or she is shaking hands with the friend, even while remotely communicating.

Task

In this experiment, we investigated the different effects when the surrogate or remote user was an acquaintance or stranger to the participant. Males and females have been reported to read body gestures in different ways [18]; therefore, separate experiments were performed for men and women. It was difficult to arrange remote users and surrogates that met these conditions for each participant. For conditions A to C, we used

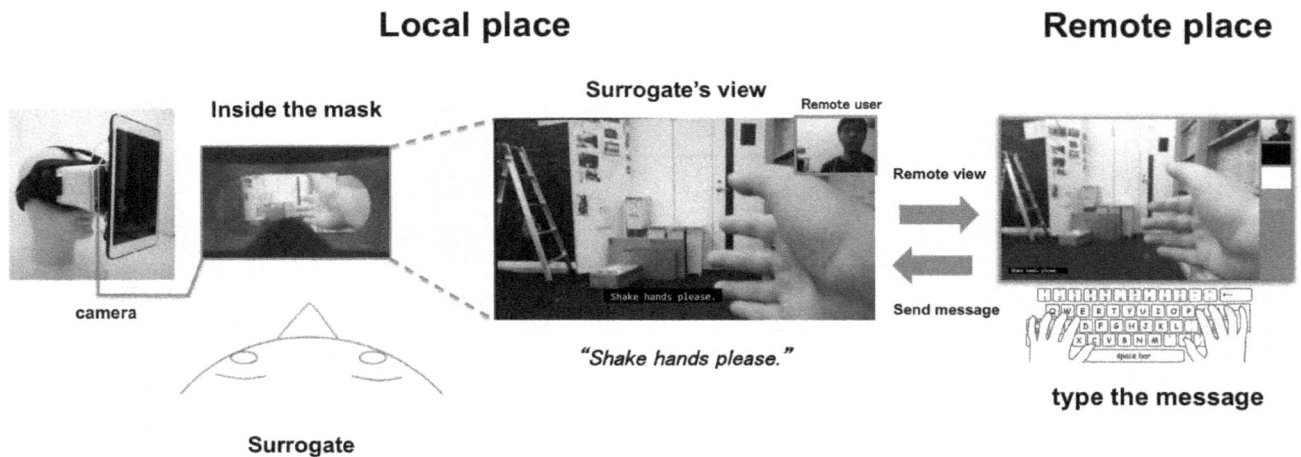

Figure 3. How to read hand shake signal.

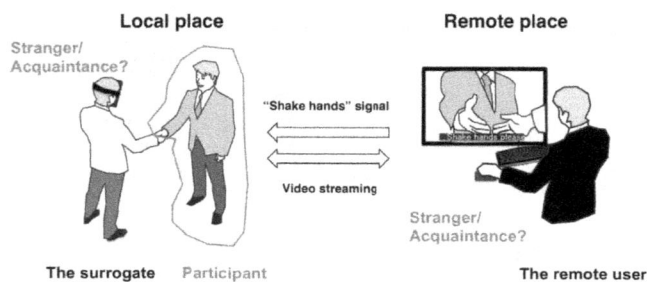

Figure 4. The remote user talks and shakes hands with the local user via the surrogate. For participant, the remote user and the surrogate is a stranger/ acquaintance.

Figure 5. Experiment scene: Right is the role of the remote user. Left is the surrogate and the participant.

5. *Participant 2 →(S: Participant 1, R: Lab 2)*
6. *Participant 1 →(S: Participant 2, R: Lab 1)*
Condition D — S: Acquaintance, R: Acquaintance
7. *Participant 2 →(S: Participant 1, R: Participant3)*
8. *Participant 1 →(S: Participant 2, R: Participant3)*

Setup
We explained the experimental scenario to the participants in the following way before testing.
The role of conversation partner: *You work on a project with another person. He or she introduces him or herself. He or she cannot be here today, so you talk with the remote user by employing the system. The remote user may ask you to shake hands.*
The role of surrogate: *You embody the remote user. The remote user wants you to move in place of him or her. The remote user will signal when he or she wants to shake hands.*

The remote user talked with the participant from a different location (Figure 5). The participant and surrogate were standing and talked face-to-face during the test. After the tests, we asked the participants to answer a questionnaire. As preparation, subjects who played the role of the remote user practiced sending the signal to shake hands before the test. Subjects who played the role of the surrogate first walked around to become accustomed to seeing through the mask. Then, they

two lab staff members and two external participants conduct the experiments, with the sexes separated. For Condition D there were three acquaintances with same sex. The task for the remote user was to talk about him- or herself to the participant as a conversation partner. After the greeting, the remote user shared his or her name and signaled the surrogate to initiate a handshake. The remote user then talked about his or her job, birthplace, and recent work for 2 minutes before sending the signal to shake hands again. The conversation ended when the remote user said "Thank you very much" and the surrogate shook hands with the participant. After the self-introduction, the subjects became acquaintances; thus, we had to be careful with the experimental order. Participants did not know this order.

We conducted the experiments in the following order:
S: stands for surrogate, R: stands for remote user
Condition A — S: Stranger, R: Stranger
1. *Participant 1 →(S: Lab 1, R: Lab 2)*
2. *Participant 2 →(S: Lab 2, R: Lab 1)*
Condition B — S: Acquaintance, R: Stranger
3. *Participant 2 →(S: Lab 1, R: Participant 1)*
4. *Participant 1 →(S: Lab 2, R: Participant 2)*
Condition C — S: Stranger, R: Acquaintance

Q4. I felt that the remote user was friendly.

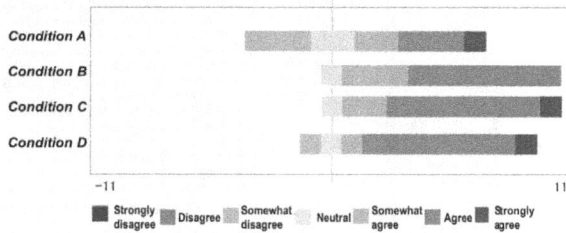

Figure 6. The result of Q4. There are no significant differences. Many participants felt the remote user was friendly.

Q5. I felt as if I were close to the remote user in the same room.

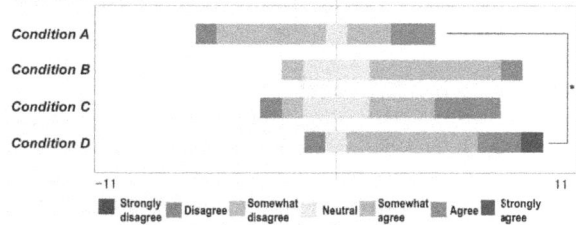

Figure 7. The result of Q5. Condition A and D has 5% significant difference. Condition B and D had positive feedbacks.

Q6. I felt as if I were shaking hands with the remote user.

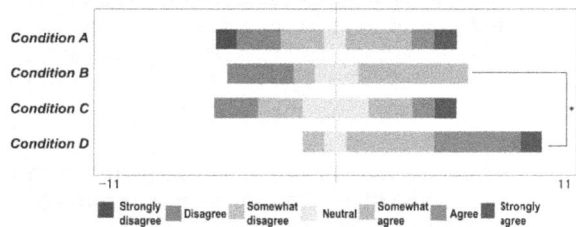

Figure 8. The result of Q6. Condition B and D has 5% significant difference.

practiced offering their hands when the handshake command was given.

Questionnaire

As mentioned earlier, we intended to investigate the effect of video communication and remote haptics. Accordingly, we referenced the questionnaire of Nakanishi et al. [16]. The questionnaire included several statements for verifying the social presence. The statements were rated on a seven-point Likert scale, where 1=strongly disagree, 4 = neutral, and 7 = strongly agree. Defects such as a low video communication quality, or audio that is difficult to hear would influence the results. In addition, if the self-introduction of the remote user is not intelligible, this would make a poor impression on the participant. Thus, we added the statements of Q1 to Q3 to check the communication quality.

1. The video was sufficiently clear.

2. The audio was sufficiently clear.

3. The presentation was intelligible.

4. I felt that the presenter was friendly.

5. I felt as if I was close to the presenter in the same room.

6. I felt as if I was shaking hands with the presenter in real life.

When the participant answered the negatively to Q1 to Q3, we decided not to use the answers.

Subjects

We recruited 12 participants (six males and six females aged 20 to 29 years old) from a local university and a local office to participate in our study under Conditions A to D. For Condition D, six additional participants (three male and three females aged 20 to 25 years old), were recruited. The participants had no prior associations or experience with the projects.

RESULTS

One participant gave negative feedback for Q3. We did not use that record because Q1 to Q3 were given with regard to the test quality, and the answers to Q4 to Q6 would be negatively affected. In total, we acquired 44 valid records, and 11 records for each experimental condition. Figure 6 shows the result for Q4. There were small differences with regard to whether the

participant felt friendly toward the remote user. Under Condition A, however, the combination of strangers feel adverse to each other. When the surrogate was an acquaintance, the participants tended to feel more friendly. Q5 was a question about the remote user's presence. The results under Conditions A and D showed a significant difference of 5% (Figure 7). The combination where both the surrogate and remote user were acquaintances increased the presence of the latter more than when both were strangers. The participants perceived that they experienced that the masked surrogate felt like the remote user when the remote user was an acquaintance. In comparing the results of Condition A and B, the participants tended to feel the remote user's presence more when the surrogate was the acquaintance. The remote users of Condition A and B were the both strangers. A comparison of Condition B and D showed the tendency of feeling the presence, depending on whether the remote user was a stranger or an acquaintance. The results showed that no significant difference existed. We thus determined that the remote user's presence was strengthened when the surrogate was an acquaintance.

From these results, we expect that the participant would feel the remote users presence when they did not have adverse feeling toward the surrogate. For Q6, the results were divided under Conditions A to C. Under Condition D, many participants experienced the sensation of shaking hands with the remote user. In particular, the results under Conditions B and D showed a significant difference of 5% (Figure 8). Some participants said the presence of an acquaintance's surrogate was stronger than that of a stranger's remote user. When the remote user was known to the participant, better results were achieved when the surrogate was an acquaintance rather than a stranger. Nevertheless, the effect of the person performing as the surrogate was not clear; thus, we conducted an additional experiment.

ADDITIONAL EXPERIMENT

We found that the remote touching was effective in the conditions in which the surrogate and the remote user were acquaintances of the participants. The question existed, however, of why Condition D provided a performance superior to those of the other conditions. Condition B also provided good performance in terms of the remote user's presence (Q5), even though, the remote user was a stranger. Conditions B and D showed a significant difference in terms of shaking hands. In short, even when the surrogate was an acquaintance, when the remote user was an acquaintance, remote haptics was effectively shared. Therefore, we conducted additional experiments to investigate how important it is to know the surrogate in advance.

Objective

We tested how the identity of the surrogate effects the communication. In this experiment, we compared surrogates who were an acquaintance, and an unidentified. The unidentified surrogate was actually the remote user, who wore the mask while playing along with a prerecorded video. The unidentified surrogate wore the mask of her face talking being played. We expected the surrogate performed by an acquaintance will be more acceptable than that performed by the remote user herself.

Task

One remote user communicated with the participants with two types of surrogates. We gathered participants who were acquaintances of the remote user.
Condition A: The surrogate is an acquaintance of the participant.
Condition B: The surrogate is someone except the surrogate in *Condition A*.
The participants were informed of the conditions and listened to the remote users speak. Then they shook hands with the surrogate twice at the beginning and at the end of the talk. We changed the experimental order of Conditions A and B in each test.

Setup

Participant were sitting in a chair in front of a door. On the other side of the door, two surrogates were standing by, and came to talk with the participants alternately (Figure 9, 10). The operator told the participant about the test condition and then opened the door, after starting the video. Each participant faced a surrogate and listened to them talk. The remote user talked about the different events that the remote user had organized. The conversations by the remote users had been recorded in advance. The surrogates offered their hands according to the conversation flow. The surrogates practiced shaking hands. We checked that there were no extreme difference in size and temperature between the hands of two surrogates before the tests. Moreover, we adjusted the chair heights so that each surrogate would sit at the same height.

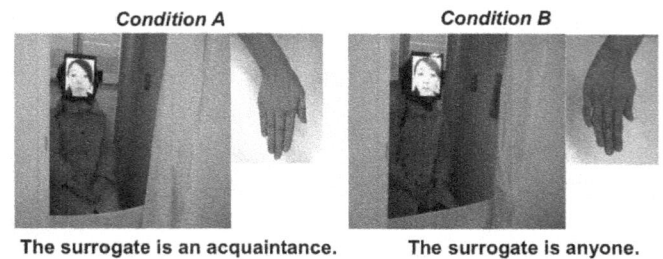

Figure 9. Experimental setting and the surrogates' hands. The surrogates looked similar and their hands showed no significant differences in size and color.

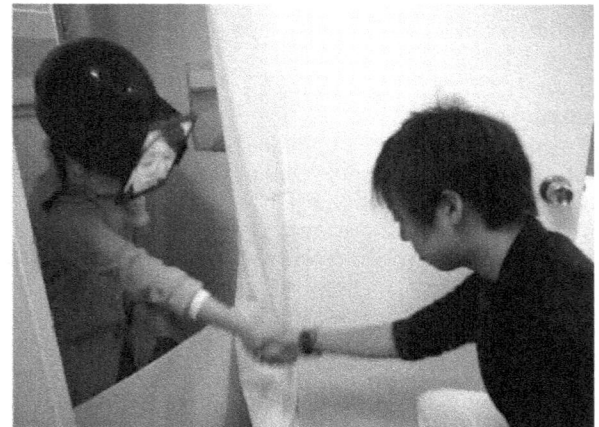

Figure 10. Experiment scene :Participant listen to the remote user's talk and shake hand via the surrogate.

Both surrogates wore the same coat as the remote user in the video.

Questionnaire

We added the following question to the previous questionnaire. Q7: Do you feel that the person in front of you looks like the remote user?

Subjects

We recruited 12 participants (seven males, five females aged 24 to 31 years old) from a local university and a local office to participate in our study. The participants had no prior associations with the projects.

Results

The results are shown in Figure 11. The participants did not know that the surrogate was the remote user under *Condition B*. Some participants thought the experimental operator had been telling a lie, so that they thought that the same surrogate played both *Condition A* and *B*. For Q4, *Conditions A* and *B* showed a significant difference of 5 %. Under *Condition B*, the surrogate was actually the remote user; however, participants felt that the acquaintance surrogate was more friendly than the actual remote person. Both scores of Q5 and Q6 were low under each conditions. According to the participants' comments, when they knew that the remote user's talk was pre-recorded,

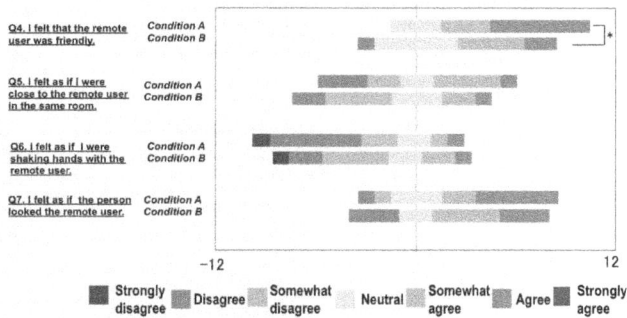

Figure 11. The result of additional experiment.

they did not feel the remote user's presence because of the lack of eye contact and expressions. They tended to think that they were shaking hands with the surrogates in front of them. The participants tended to think that the surrogate wearing the mask resembled the remote user.

DISCUSSION

Can we remote touch via a surrogate?

Remote contact can be achieved under certain conditions. In this experiment, the impression of the remote user was influenced by the relationship with the participants. When the surrogate was an acquaintance, the participants felt a strong presence of the remote user as a by-product. The impression of the surrogate was strong; thus, the participants did not feel as if they were shaking hands with the unfamiliar remote user. To strengthen the remote user's presence, matching eye contact or gesture is important. One participant said *"At the beginning, I felt as if I were talking with the surrogate. After a while I made eye contacts with the remote user several times. Then, I seemed to be talking with the remote user."* Therefore, when the system is used among strangers, eye contact and gestures will be more effective to show their social presence. The strangers did not have any previous impressions of each other; therefore, the communication-based impressions with each surrogate varied from person to person.

Who should be the surrogate?

This system could be considered a kind of "human Uber [2]". We want someone to work in stead of us remotely. The surrogate embodies a physical and social presence, who is realizing our intentions. One consideration is who we should ask to take our place. For intimate communication with touching, such as in the present experiment, the person who should function as the surrogate should be a person with a close relationship to the user. For example, participants in the experiment readily accepted the role of the surrogate performed by an acquaintance. Moreover, when this system is used in a nursing home to communicate with remote family or comfort children, the surrogate should be a relative or intimate person.

---

[2] Uber, https://www.uber.com/

Neither the surrogate nor the remote user?

Participants were often confused in this experiment about whose hands they were shaking. This is because the participants could not distinguish the person they were shaking hands with; that is, either as a remote user or the surrogate. By wearing a mask display, one persons face was on another person's body. This means that the masked person has two minds and mixed personalities. Based on the experiments, we consider it is not so important whether the masked person is the surrogate or the remote user. Participants were equally confused about assessing who the masked person was. When the masked person is both the remote user and the surrogate, the masked person should be regarded in another way, with "one and a half" personalities.

CONCLUSION

In this paper, we presented a user study of a remote touch using a human surrogate. The surrogate wears a mask telepresence system that displays the face of a remote user through a live-stream video feed. This method does not use a robot hand or complex mechanical system; rather, it strategically employs mobile devices to enable the ready augmenting of a human presence. This system enables a user to shake the hand of a remote user via their surrogate.

We conducted experiments in which the surrogate communicated with the participants. We strived to determine with whom the participants thought they shook hands: the surrogate or the remote user. We hypothesized that the relationship between the participant and surrogate or remote user would be affected by the haptic sensations. Therefore, we prepared four conditions in which the remote user was either an acquaintance or stranger and the surrogate was also either an acquaintance or stranger. The results showed that, when the surrogate and remote user were acquaintances, the participants felt like they were shaking hands with the remote user. In future work, we intend to deploy a mask display system in practical scenario such as nursing home, or a day-care center for children.

REFERENCES

1. Sigurdur O. Adalgeirsson and Cynthia Breazeal. 2010. MeBot: A Robotic Platform for Socially Embodied Presence. In *Proceedings of the 5th ACM/IEEE International Conference on Human-robot Interaction (HRI '10)*. IEEE Press, Piscataway, NJ, USA, 15–22. http://dl.acm.org/citation.cfm?id=1734454.1734467

2. Cagatay Basdogan, Chih-Hao Ho, Mandayam A. Srinivasan, and Mel Slater. 2000. An Experimental Study on the Role of Touch in Shared Virtual Environments. *ACM Trans. Comput.-Hum. Interact.* 7, 4 (Dec. 2000), 443–460. DOI:http://dx.doi.org/10.1145/365058.365082

3. Chris Bevan and Danaë Stanton Fraser. 2015. Shaking Hands and Cooperation in Tele-present Human-Robot Negotiation. In *Proceedings of the Tenth Annual ACM/IEEE International Conference on Human-Robot Interaction (HRI '15)*. ACM, New York, NY, USA, 247–254. DOI: http://dx.doi.org/10.1145/2696454.2696490

4. Scott Brave and Andrew Dahley. 1997. inTouch: A Medium for Haptic Interpersonal Communication. In *CHI '97 Extended Abstracts on Human Factors in Computing Systems (CHI EA '97)*. ACM, New York, NY, USA, 363–364. DOI: http://dx.doi.org/10.1145/1120212.1120435

5. BJ Fogg, Lawrence D. Cutler, Perry Arnold, and Chris Eisbach. 1998. HandJive: A Device for Interpersonal Haptic Entertainment. In *Proceedings of the SIGCHI Conference on Human Factors in Computing Systems (CHI '98)*. ACM Press/Addison-Wesley Publishing Co., New York, NY, USA, 57–64. DOI: http://dx.doi.org/10.1145/274644.274653

6. Masahiro Furukawa, Hiroyuki Kajimoto, and Susumu Tachi. 2012. KUSUGURI: A Shared Tactile Interface for Bidirectional Tickling. In *Proceedings of the 3rd Augmented Human International Conference (AH '12)*. ACM, New York, NY, USA, Article 9, 8 pages. DOI: http://dx.doi.org/10.1145/2160125.2160134

7. Alberto Gallace and Charles Spence. 2010. The science of interpersonal touch: An overview. *Neuroscience and Biobehavioral Reviews* 34, 2 (2010), 246 – 259. DOI: http://dx.doi.org/10.1016/j.neubiorev.2008.10.004 Touch, Temperature, Pain/Itch and Pleasure.

8. H. Hashimoto and S. Manoratkul. 1996. Tele-Handshake through the Internet. In *Robot and Human Communication, 1996., 5th IEEE International Workshop on*. 90–95. DOI: http://dx.doi.org/10.1109/ROMAN.1996.568767

9. A. Kendon. 1967. *Some functions of gaze-direction in social interaction*. Acta Psychologica 26(1), 22–63.

10. Kana Misawa and Jun Rekimoto. 2015a. ChameleonMask: Embodied Physical and Social Telepresence Using Human Surrogates. In *Proceedings of the 33rd Annual ACM Conference Extended Abstracts on Human Factors in Computing Systems (CHI EA '15)*. ACM, New York, NY, USA, 401–411. DOI: http://dx.doi.org/10.1145/2702613.2732506

11. Kana Misawa and Jun Rekimoto. 2015b. Wearing Another's Personality: A Human-surrogate System with a Telepresence Face. In *Proceedings of the 2015 ACM International Symposium on Wearable Computers (ISWC '15)*. ACM, New York, NY, USA, 125–132. DOI: http://dx.doi.org/10.1145/2802083.2808392

12. Osamu Morikawa, Sayuri Hashimoto, Tsunetsugu Munakata, and Junzo Okunaka. 2006. Embrace System for Remote Counseling. In *Proceedings of the 8th International Conference on Multimodal Interfaces (ICMI '06)*. ACM, New York, NY, USA, 318–325. DOI: http://dx.doi.org/10.1145/1180995.1181055

13. Osamu Morikawa and Takanori Maesako. 1998. HyperMirror: Toward Pleasant-to-use Video Mediated Communication System. In *Proceedings of the 1998 ACM Conference on Computer Supported Cooperative Work (CSCW '98)*. ACM, New York, NY, USA, 149–158. DOI: http://dx.doi.org/10.1145/289444.289489

14. Florian 'Floyd' Mueller, Frank Vetere, Martin R. Gibbs, Jesper Kjeldskov, Sonja Pedell, and Steve Howard. 2005. Hug over a Distance. In *CHI '05 Extended Abstracts on Human Factors in Computing Systems (CHI EA '05)*. ACM, New York, NY, USA, 1673–1676. DOI: http://dx.doi.org/10.1145/1056808.1056994

15. Hideyuki Nakanishi, Kei Kato, and Hiroshi Ishiguro. 2011. Zoom Cameras and Movable Displays Enhance Social Telepresence. In *Proceedings of the SIGCHI Conference on Human Factors in Computing Systems (CHI '11)*. ACM, New York, NY, USA, 63–72. DOI: http://dx.doi.org/10.1145/1978942.1978953

16. Hideyuki Nakanishi, Kazuaki Tanaka, and Yuya Wada. 2014. Remote Handshaking: Touch Enhances Video-mediated Social Telepresence. In *Proceedings of the SIGCHI Conference on Human Factors in Computing Systems (CHI '14)*. ACM, New York, NY, USA, 2143–2152. DOI: http://dx.doi.org/10.1145/2556288.2557169

17. Irene Rae, Bilge Mutlu, and Leila Takayama. 2014. Bodies in Motion: Mobility, Presence, and Task Awareness in Telepresence. In *Proceedings of the SIGCHI Conference on Human Factors in Computing Systems (CHI '14)*. ACM, New York, NY, USA, 2153–2162. DOI: http://dx.doi.org/10.1145/2556288.2557047

18. Juulia T Suvilehto, Enrico Glerean, Robin IM Dunbar, Riitta Hari, and Lauri Nummenmaa. 2015. Topography of social touching depends on emotional bonds between humans. *Proceedings of the National Academy of Sciences* (2015), 201519231.

19. Keisuke Suzuki, Sohei Wakisaka, and Naotaka Fujii. 2012. Substitutional reality system: a novel experimental platform for experiencing alternative reality. *Scientific reports* 2 (2012).

Embodiment of Video-mediated Communication Enhances Social Telepresence

Yuya Onishi
Department of Adaptive
Machine Systems
Osaka University
Suita, Osaka, Japan
onishi.yuya@ams.eng.osaka-u.ac.jp

Kazuaki Tanaka
Department of Adaptive
Machine Systems
Osaka University
CREST, JST
Suita, Osaka, Japan
tanaka@ams.eng.osaka-u.ac.jp

Hideyuki Nakanishi
Department of Adaptive
Machine Systems
Osaka University
Suita, Osaka, Japan
nakanishi@ams.eng.osaka-u.ac.jp

ABSTRACT

There are several merits to embody the remote partner's body to the video conference: showing it physically, making a physical contact, and enhancing social telepresence. In this paper, we tackled to embody a part of a remote partner's body in a video conference. As a method to show how effectively the embodied body part works, we focused on face-to-face communication of the hand gestures such as thumb wrestling, finger number game and pointing. We developed a robotic arm, which seems the remote partner's arm popped out from the video. Our robot arm synchronizes with the remote partner's arm movements. We conducted experiments to verify the method of embodying a part of a remote partner's body. We found that, our method reduced the feeling of being far from the remote partner, and enhanced social telepresence, comparing video and physical embodiment.

Author Keywords

Videoconferencing; robotic arm; social telepresence; hand gesture; video-mediated communication.

ACM Classification Keywords

H.5.1 Information interfaces and presentation (e.g., HCI): Multimedia Information Systems -Artificial, augmented, and virtual realities.

INTRODUCTION

The video conference lacks the presence of a partner compared to a face-to-face communication [26]. We considered that videoconference system had a window in which the surface of a display forms a boundary, and this problem reduces social telepresence. Social telepresence is the illusion where the partners who are actually in geographically separated places feel as if they were meeting

HAI '16, October 04-07, 2016, Biopolis, Singapore
© 2016 ACM. ISBN 978-1-4503-4508-8/16/10...$15.00
DOI: http://dx.doi.org/10.1145/2974804.2974826

face-to-face with each other [5]. In this paper, we tackled to embody a part of a remote partner's body in a video conference. There are several merits to embody the remote partner's body to the video conference: showing it physically, making a physical contact, and enhancing social telepresence. Generally, the teleoperated robot was embodied the behavior of remote partner, and it can move local space and communicate with a remote partner. However, the telepresence robot seems to be operate by remote partner, because we cannot see the remote partner or remote partner's image and the robot behavior are separated (Figure 1 (a)).

To solve the above problem, InFORM that is a dynamic shape display can show physically a remote partner's arm [13]. In another study, a robot hand for handshakes was combined with a video conference. This study suggested that adding the function of body contact could enhance social telepresence [18]. The hand used in these experiments in is placed at the position outside of the display (Figure 1 (b)). There is the possibility that the robot hand, which seems pop out from the video, improves the feeling of being together (Figure 1 (c)). In other words, social telepresence may be enhanced by showing only the robotic arm, which is connected on the video. The purpose of this study is to clarify the influence of a design that seems to embody a part of the body from the partner's video beyond the display on social telepresence.

As a way to show how effective it is to embody a part of the body, we focused on face-to-face interaction of hand gestures. In this study, we developed a system that combines a robot arm with a videoconference system (Figure 2) [19]. The remote partner can point to a remote site with the robot arm. Our robot arm moves synchronizing with the remote partner. In addition, it is expected that a robot arm would enhance social telepresence due to its design, in which the remote partner's arm seems to pop out from the video.

This paper presents three experiments. The first experiment was to clarify the significance of the embodiment of part of the body from video. To eliminate the physical contact for comparing video and body embodiment, we used a finger number game in the experiment. The second experiment was to clarify the proper design of a robot arm regarding the

(a) A teleoperated robot is operated by the remote partner

(b) The robotic arm places at outside of the display

(c) The robotic arm pops out from the display

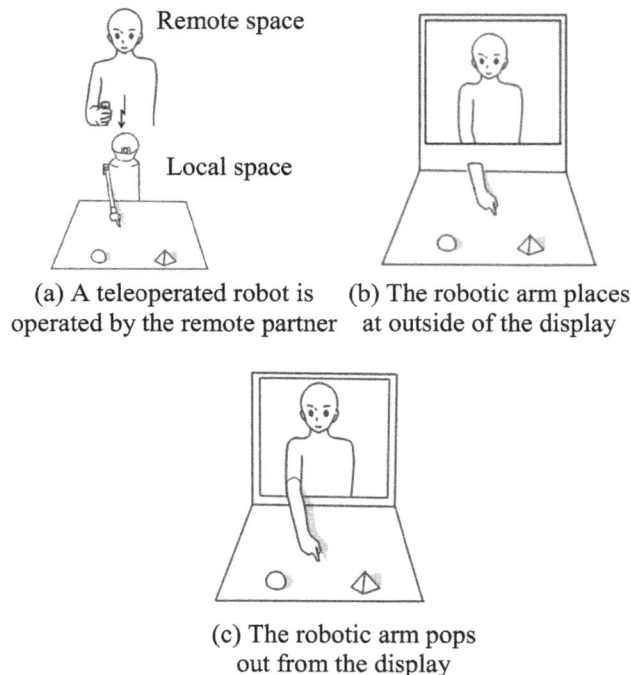

Figure 1. Situations of physical embodiments.

Figure 2. Snapshots of our system.

position that connects the video and the robot arm. Since comparing each condition in which the remote partner's arm is embodied, we used thumb-wrestling game, which has physical contact. The third experiment was to clarify the effect of the moving behavior of the embodiment of the body. To verify the utility of partial embodiment with dynamic movement, we use the pointing actions in this experiment.

RELATED WORK
Effect of Embodying
There have been many efforts pursuing a seamless remote communication experience [1]. Gestures are important part of collocated settings and equally valuable when people collaborate in distributed settings [6]. Riether compared the processing time of the task when performing in front of a partner, in front of a robot, and alone [23]. Chiang compared talking and using gesture, whether participants heed the persuasion of the robot. Moreover, it has become easier to listen to robot when using the gesture [4]. These studies suggested that physical movement had a positive influence in the persuasion of the communication. However, these studies compare the situation where the robot exists and where the robot does not exist, but it does not compare with teleconferencing systems such as video. Bainbridge found that students were more likely to comply with a physical robot's request than a screen-based representation's request, even if the task was odd or uncomfortable [2]. Sakamoto found that participants felt presence of the remote partner when he talked through the android, which is a real human robot, than when he appeared on a video monitor in a video conference system [24]. These suggest that embodying the

remote partner had a positive influence in the feeling of presence in the communication compared with human video.

Using Gestures in Remote Communication
The design of remote partner embodiments for showing gestures has long been considered [7-8, 11-14, 20, and 27]. Ishii et al. used ClearBoard a calibrated projection of a remote partner overlaid on a drawing glass to create an illusion that the partner from remote places are working on the two sides of the same glass [9]. In addition, using a table to display the remote partner's behavior has been suggested such as VideoArms [28], C-Slate [10], and DIGITABLE [21]. Pauchet et al. shared the space using the video with horizontal display, which display remote partner's arm [21]. Tang et al. added contact traces to VideoArms, an augmentation that participants described as useful [28]. A quantitative approach to evaluating abstract components added to realistic embodiments adopted by Yamashita et al. who replayed entire gestures using a form of motion blur to reduce the time needed for conversational grounding [29]. There are also researches focusing on supporting remote assistance tasks by projecting annotation on the surface of physical objects. However, it is difficult to point remote objects and is impossible to touch them. For example, there is a problem that directions to which a remote instructor points are unclear. GestureMan [12] uses a teleoperated robot to move in space and point physical objects with a laser beam. WACL uses wearable camera, which put on shoulder and points the objects with a laser beam [25]. This system lacks the remote partner's image, facial expression. These systems reduce social telepresence because remote partner's image and facial expression is invisible [26].

Social Telepresence
There have been many efforts pursuing the effects of social telepresence. [5, 22]. This effect increased life-size images of remote people, and stereoscopic videos [20] and eye contact [3]. Motion parallax that produced by the back-and-forth movement of a robot on which a camera is mounted enhanced social telepresence [15]. In addition, the back-and-forth movement of the point of view [16] and back-and-forth movement of the display [17] synchronized with the back-and-forth movement of the instructor strengthen the social telepresence. In addition, haptic sensation such as handshakes shared mutually among users, and observed that the mutually shared haptic sensation enhanced social telepresence [18].

172

STRUCTURE OF OUR ROBOT ARM

A robot arm moves and rotates on a display, on which the remote partner's image is displayed synchronizing with a motion of a remote partner's arm. It shows a nearly life-size picture of the remote partner's upper body and has a horizontal axis linear motion mechanism under the display (Figure 3(a)). A robot arm is connected to the linear motion mechanism through an acrylic board. A connective point of the robot arm possesses a rotary system. By the rotary mechanism and the linear motion mechanism of the robot arm, a robot arm performs translation and rotation of an indication side of the display in synchronization with the movement of the remote partner's arm in the picture. At that time, the length of the robot arm from the screen changes. In other word, an extendable mechanism regulates the length of the robot arm. This mechanism lets you expand and contract the arm by pulling a wire in a rewind device and lets the edge of the acrylic board go along the wire to be inconspicuous. Movement of the remote partner's arm is acquired by motion tracking. The picture of the former arm removed from the boundary surface of a picture and a robot arm by image composition, such as a chrome frame composition because the picture of the former arm is unnecessary. The picture of the part, which was removed, composes it with a picture of scenery prepared beforehand. The instructions to perform this device is only in the right and left directions, but the instructions at the top and bottom directions could be done by the linear motion mechanism in two axes, which are horizontal and vertical. In addition, there is a robot hand, which enables operations such as thumb wrestling. The thumb has two degrees of freedom – A bending exercise consisting of three joints at the top and bottom directions and a rotary motion consisting of one joint at the right and left directions. The robot hand is operated in synchronization with the movement of the remote partner by a bending sensor and acceleration sensor mounted on the thumb of the glove as shown in Figure 3(b). The surface of the robot hand uses a soft material close to human skin. Participants can feel that the sensation of being a machine is relaxed by feeling the softness.

EXPERIMENTS

A robot arm with videoconference is a system to embody the instructional behavior of a remote partner. To verify the utility of the robot arm, a design was made implemented in which a remote partner's arm seems to pop out of a video enhance social telepresence. We conducted three experiments. The first experiment was to clarify the significance of the embodiment of part of the body from video. The second experiment was to clarify the proper design of a robot arm regarding the position that connects the video and the robot arm. The third experiment was to clarify the effect of the moving behavior of the embodiment of the body.

Thirty-eight subjects participated in our experiments. We separate three groups. A subject participates only one experiment. Ten subjects participate in Experiment 1, ten

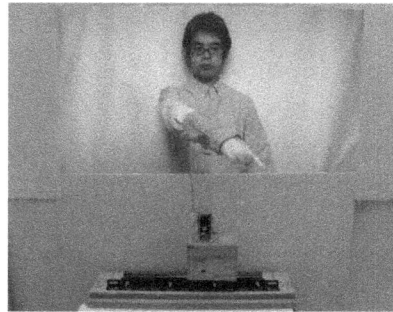

(a) A whole structure of the robotic arm

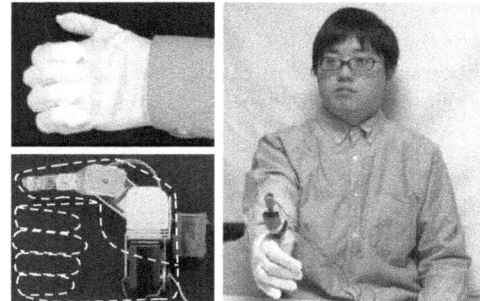

(b) The robotic thumb that can be controlled by a remote partner

Figure 3. The structure of our robot arm.

subjects participate in Experiment 2, and eighteen subjects participate in Experiment 3. The participants were undergraduate students whose ages ranged from eighteen to twenty-four years.

Setup

Figure 4 depicts the structure of the rooms used for the experiments. As shown in Figure 4 (a), the robot arm is attached to the display. To facilitate this illusion, the color of the clothes of the presenter and the robot hand was the same. The experimenter seated and all the participants thought that he was seating. We used a wide-screen display to show a nearly life-size picture of the remote partner's upper body. As shown in Figure 4 (b), we set the field of view of the webcam to 77 vertical degrees. The height of the base on which the participant stood was adjusted to make the participant's eyes level with the experimenter's eyes. In experiment 3, we prepared the same performance webcam for each horizontal display and vertical display. In addition, we adjusted the position of webcams to show the arm that was connected. The experimenter could see the participant's room, participant's face and robot arm from the camera, which is set the top of display. We conducted a questionnaire and interview after the experiment. The statement of each questionnaire was rated on a 7-point Likert scale where 1 = strongly disagree, 4 = neutral, and 7 = strongly agree.

Experiment 1

There are several previous studies comparing video and physical embodiment. However, the study, which compares the human body video and the physical embodiment, is less. In addition, it does not have any condition, which combined

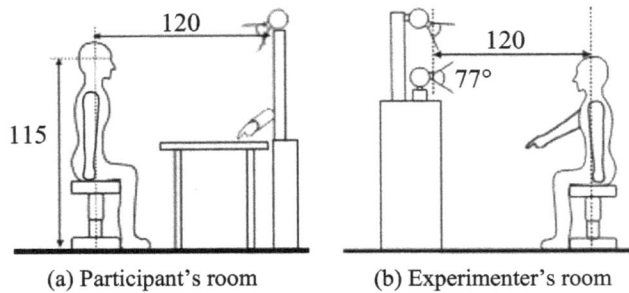

Figure 4. Experimental setups
(length unit: centimeters)

(a) Participant's room   (b) Experimenter's room

part of a body that was displayed on the video in comparison with whole body. In experiment 1, we clarify the significance of the embodiment of part of the body from video. We compared three conditions.

· Video condition: remote partner displayed whole body on the video.

· Video + body condition: remote partner displayed only head on the video. Moreover, mannequin shows other part of body.

· Body condition: mannequin shows whole of body.

We considered that physical visualization had a positive influence in the persuasion of the communication. However, we considered a big impact in the interaction whether there are parts of the face. Therefore, we made the following two hypothesis.

Hypothesis 1: Remote partner's head displayed in a video gives a positive impact on communication than the mannequin's head.

Hypothesis 2: The person who shows the robot hand in front of the participant gives a positive impact on communication than showed by video.

To clarify these hypotheses we compared three conditions by the within-subjects experiment. To eliminate the physical contact for comparing video and body embodiment, all the conditions used a finger number game. A finger number game, which is also called 'kazuken', is one of a communication using a hand. A finger number game was played by two people using finger signals with one hand to show a number at the same time as calling out the sum of both players' numbers, and the one who gave out the correct answer became the winner. The participants were subjected to pre-training by face-to-face trial. After pre-training, we conducted the games three times in each condition. We unified the movement of the arm in all conditions.

Results of Experiment 1
There were ten participants, consisting of eight females and two males. We implemented a counter balance as not to influence by the order of conditions. Result, as seen in Figure 5, shows a comparison of the three conditions by one-way factorial ANOVA. Each box represents the mean value of the

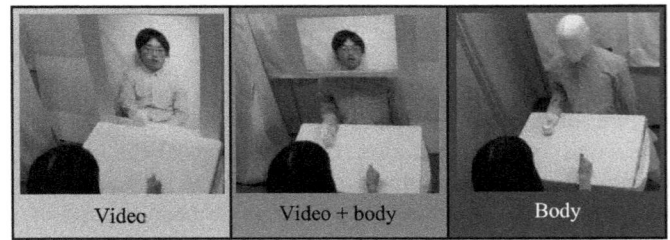

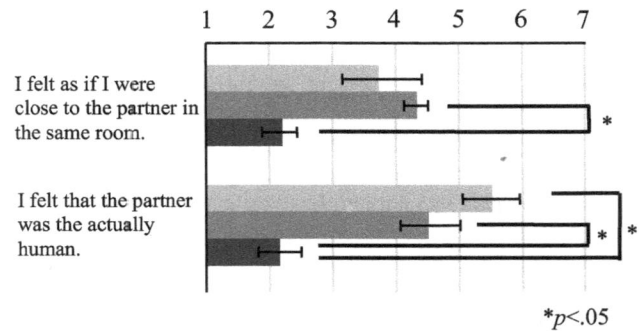

Figure 5. Results of Experiment 1 (N=10). The fill color of the box corresponds the color of the picture, which shows the condition.

responses to each statement, and each bar represents the standard error of the mean value.

We found a significant difference in the feeling of being close to the partner in the same room ($F(2,18)=3.594$, $p<.05$). Multiple comparisons showed that this feeling was significantly stronger in case of the video and body condition than body condition ($p<.05$). We also found a significant difference in the feeling that the other party is a human being that actually exist ($F(2,18)=10.379$, $p<.05$). Multiple comparisons showed that this feeling was significantly stronger in video condition than other conditions ($p<.05$). Seven participants answered that the body condition was scored the lowest of all conditions since mannequin did not have a face. Therefore, this result supports the hypothesis 1. However, some participants answered that the video condition is lower than other conditions because the experimenter is visible on the display. In this experiment, there was not observed the significant difference between the video condition and the video + body condition. However, in the question of the feeling of being close to the partner in the same room, the average value of video condition is higher than the combination of video and body condition. Therefore, hypothesis 2 is rejected from these results. From this experiment we can suggest that partial embodiment is more effective than the whole body, but there is no difference between partial embodiment and video.

Experiment 2
From the result of experiment 1, we suggested that the partial embodiment produce the presence of the equivalent to the video. In experiment 2, to verify the utility of the design, we compare partial embodiment elaborately. We divided two

factors: the position of the arm in the remote partner's video and the position of a robot arm. The conditions are follows.

· Outside – Synchronization condition: a robot arm is set on frame of a display. A participant can see both of a robot arm and of the arm of a remote partner in the video.

· Outside – Combination condition: a robot arm is set on frame of a display. The position of the arm of the remote partner in the video coincides with the position of the robot arm.

· Inside – Synchronization condition: a robot arm is set on the display. A participant can see both of a robot arm and of the arm of a remote partner in the video.

· Inside – Combination condition: a robot arm is set on the display. The position of the arm of the remote partner in the video coincides with the position of the robot arm.

To verify the utility of the design, we made the following hypothesis.

Hypothesis 1: If the robot arm looks connecting with the video, it provides a more natural interaction.

Hypothesis 2: If the robot hand is set on the screen of the display, it provides a more natural face-to-face interaction.

To clarify these hypotheses, we compared in within-subjects. Since comparing each condition in which the remote partner's arm is embodied, all the conditions used thumb wrestling game, which has physical contact. Participants were subjected to pre-training by face-to-face trial. After pre-training, we conducted games three times in each condition. We unified the movement of the robot hand in all conditions.

Results of Experiment 2

There were ten participants, consisting of five females and five males. We implemented a counter balance as not to influence by the order of conditions. Result, as seen in Figure 6, shows a comparison of the three conditions by two-way factorial repeated measure ANOVA. Each box represents the mean value of the responses to each statement, and each bar represents the standard error of the mean value.

In factor of the remote partner's arm in the video, we found a significant difference in the feeling of playing the game with the partner in the same room ($F(1,9)=10.32$, $p<.01$), and the feeling of talking with the partner in the same room ($F(1,9)=5.65$, $p<.01$) between synchronization condition and combination condition. We also found a significant difference in the feeling of being close to the partner in the same room ($F(1,9)=3.36$, $p<.1$). This result mean that showing robot arm connected by remote partner's arm in the video provide a more natural interaction than showing a robot arm synchronized with remote partner's arm. Moreover, this supports the hypothesis 1.

In factor of the position of a robot arm, we found a significant difference in the feeling of being close to the partner in the same room ($F(1,9)=5.00$, $p<.1$) between outside condition

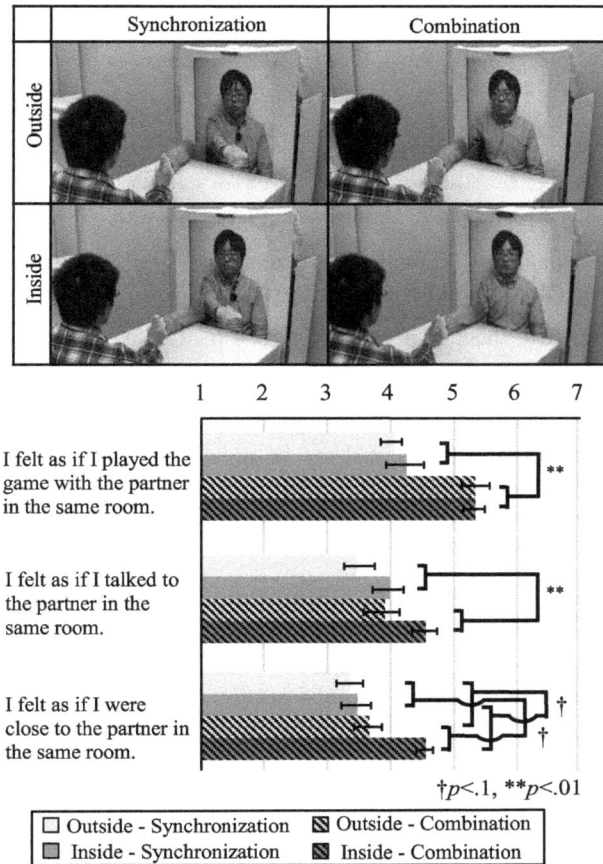

Figure 6. Results of Experiment 2 (N=10).

and inside condition. This result mean that showing robot arm connected on the display provide a more natural interaction than showing a robot arm connected on the frame which is outside of display. Moreover, this supports the hypothesis 2. In this experiment, we found that Inside – Combination is the most effective design, which is the remote partner's arm is popping out from the video.

Experiment 3

From Experiment 1 and 2, the partial embodiment of the remote partner is effective. However, the connecting point of robot arm and video was fixed, in these experiments. The previous study suggested that there is no effect when physical embodiment is inactive [26]. We considered that the physical embodiment would enhance social telepresence than video when it moves dynamically. It is also conceivable that the interpersonal distance is influenced by the distance between a participant and a fingertip of the remote partner. Therefore, we made the following two hypothesis, in Experiment 3.

Hypothesis 1: Showing the remote partner's physical behavior enhances social telepresence.

Hypothesis 2: The participant feels the distance closer between the experimenter who is in the video and the

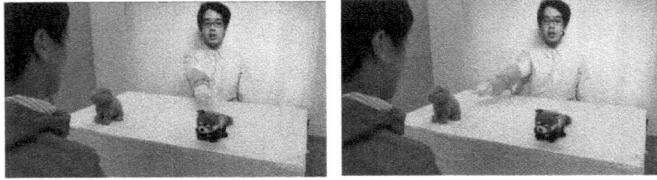

Figure 7. Snapshots of Experiment 3

Figure 8. Results of Experiment 3 (N=18). The fill color of the box corresponds the color of the picture, which shows the condition.

participant, by showing as embodiment of the remote partner's instructions.

To clarify these hypotheses, we use Inside – Combination design that is the most effective design in Experiment 2. In addition, the robot arm synchronizes with the remote partner's arm movements and moves dynamic on the remote partner's video. Because it can be done by video if only to show the arm, we add the combined video condition, which has been suggested in previous studies. Therefore, we made the following three conditions.

· Video condition: The condition using only a vertical display is a conventional video conference.

· Combined video condition: The condition using a combination of the horizontal display and vertical display.

· Embodied video condition: The condition using combination of a robot arm and vertical display is a condition that we suggest in this study.

We compared three conditions by the within-subjects experiment. To verify the utility of partial embodiment with dynamic movement, all the conditions included the pointing actions. In all conditions, we placed two stuffed animals, which were pointed to by the remote partner as shown in Figure 7. In addition, we had a simple conversation and question about them. The experimenter pointed to different objects between conversations.

Results of Experiment 3
The participants were undergraduate students whose ages ranged from eighteen to twenty-four years. There were twelve participants, consisting of six females and six males. We implemented a counter balance so as not to influence the order of conditions. We conducted a questionnaire after the experiment. The statements were rated on a 7-point Likert scale where 1 = strongly disagree, 4 = neutral, and 7 = strongly agree. In addition, at the third question was answered with numerical values (length unit: centimeters). The result is shown in Figure 8. The result shows a comparison of the three conditions by one-way factorial ANOVA. Each box represents the mean value of the responses to each statement, and each bar represents the standard error of the mean value.

We found a significant difference in the feeling of being close to the partner in the same room ($F(2,17)=12.698$, $p<.01$). Multiple comparisons showed that this feeling was significantly stronger in embodied video condition than video condition ($p<.01$) and combined video condition

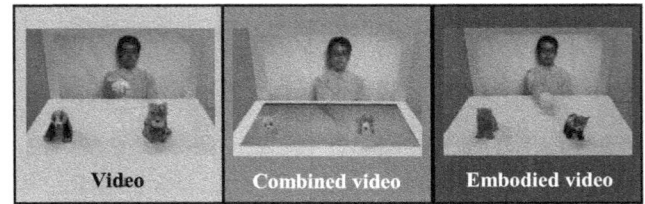

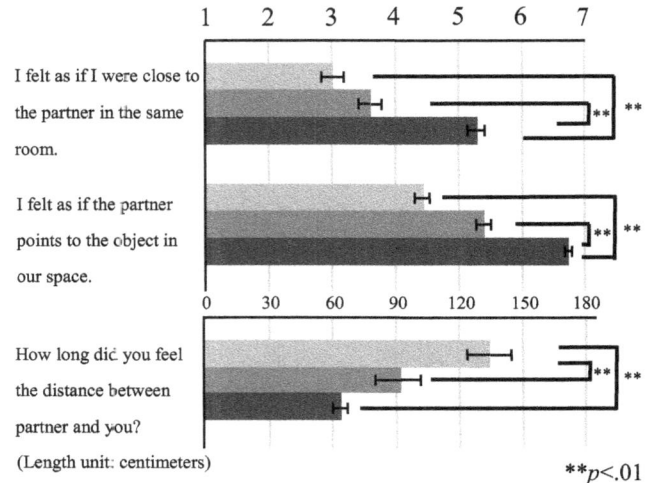

($p<.01$). We also found a significant difference in the feeling of being pointed to the object in participant's space by experimenter ($F(2,16)=14.061$, $p<.01$). Multiple comparisons showed that this feeling was significantly stronger embodied video condition than video condition ($p<.01$) and combined video condition ($p<.01$). According to the comments, the participants felt that it was really like a remote partner being in the same room in embodied condition. In addition, some participants felt pointing action was done under the table in combined condition. Moreover, these results support the hypothesis 1.

We also found a significant difference in the feeling of distance ($F(2,17)=8.465$, $p<.01$). Multiple comparisons showed that this feeling was significantly stronger in video condition than combined video condition ($p<.01$) and embodied video condition ($p<.01$). This means participant feel farther in video condition than other conditions. However, we did not find a significant difference between combined video condition and embodied video condition. According to the comments, the feeling of distance was influenced by the distance from a fingertip. Therefore, hypothesis 2 is rejected from this result.

DISCUSSION
Effect of Embodying Video
In experiment 1, we verified the significance of the embodiment of part of the body from video. This experiment showed that the partial embodiment enhanced social telepresence than whole body. According to the participant's comments, the partner's video showing his facial expression

could enhance his social telepresence. Therefore, if the remote partner's face image was shown in the video, there was no adverse effect about embodying the remote partner's body. However, the partial embodiment could not enhance social telepresence than video.

The previous study suggested that there was no effect when physical embodiment was inactive [26]. We considered that the physical embodiment would enhance social telepresence than video when it moved dynamically. In experiment 3, we found that the partial embodiment enhanced social telepresence when the behavior of robotic arm was dynamically. This result can be prove by the question about the feeling of sense that the partner was pointing to an object in the participant's space. We found that the score of the embodied video condition is higher than other condition. According to the questionnaire, participants felt that a display looked like a window and the remote partner pointed to a stuffed animal from there, in video condition. In the combined video condition, participant felt that the pointing behavior was done under the table. Moreover, participant also felt the horizontal display as a window. We did not get these comments when the behavior of the robotic arm was static.

Through both of the experiments, since the task was done smoothly, participants were not feel a sense of discomfort that the partner's arm was a robot arm.

Design
In experiment 2, we verified the proper design of a robot arm regarding the position that connects the video and the robot arm. We divided two factors: the position of the remote partner's arm in the video, and the connecting position of a robotic arm on the video.

In factor of showing the remote partner's arm in the video, we found that showing a robotic arm connected by the remote partner's arm on the display provide a more natural interaction than showing a robotic arm synchronized with remote partner's arm in the video. According to the comments, participant felt that remote partner in the video controlled the robotic arm, since participant can see two arms.

In factor of the position of a robot arm, we found that showing robot arm connected on the display provide a more natural interaction than showing a robot arm connected on the frame which is outside of display. According to the comment, it was considered that the robot hand being out of the frame of the display gave discomfort for participant. We found that Inside – Combination is the most effective design, which is the remote partner's arm is popping out from the video.

The Feeling of Being Far from the Remote Partner
When asked about the feeling of being far from the remote partner in experiment 3, the result showed that the video condition scored higher than other conditions. This means that participants felt farther in the video condition than other conditions. We did not give any information to the

participant about the length of device and the size of the table during the experiment. We placed the display where the distance between the participant and the vertical display was 120cm (figure 4). This means the vertical display was placed between the video condition and the combined video condition. As the result, the participant felt that the partner was seated behind the display when the partner was shown only a vertical display. Moreover, the participant felt closer when the arm of the partners was showed prior to the vertical display. We found that the sense of distance was influenced by showing the arm in front of a vertical display. We considered the feeling of distance was influenced by the distance from the fingertip. We are going to inspect whether interpersonal distance changed by changes in the length of the robot arm in future.

CONCLUSION
In this study, we developed a robotic arm, which seemed the remote partner's arm popped out from the video. We conducted three experiments to verify the utility of partial embodiment. The first experiment was to clarify the significance of the embodiment of part of the body from video. This experiment showed that the partial embodiment enhanced social telepresence than whole body. However, the partial embodiment and video was equivalent. The second experiment was to clarify the proper design of a robot arm regarding the position that connects the video and the robot arm. Since this experiment showed that the robotic arm, which popped out from the video, was the most effective design, we used the Inside – Combination design in the next experiment. In the third experiment, we found that there is no effect when the robotic arm was static, but the social telepresence was enhanced when the behavior of robotic arm was dynamically. In addition, we found that the sense of distance was influenced by showing the arm in front of the display. There is a possibility that the feeling of being far from the remote partner was strongly influenced by the distance between a participant and a fingertip of remote partner. Revealing the factor of inflection on the feeling of distance is a topic for future work.

ACKNOWLEDGMENTS
This work was supported by JSPS KAKENHI Grant Numbers JP26280076, JP15K12081, KDDI Foundation, Telecommunication Advancement Foundation, Foundation for the Fusion of Science and Technology, Tateishi Science and technology Foundation and JST CREST.

REFERENCES
1. Alem, L. and Li, J. 2011. A Study of Gestures in a Video-Mediated Collaborative Assembly Task, Advances in Human-Computer Interaction, *Proc. HCI 2011*.

2. Bainbridge, W. A., Hart, J. W., Kim, E. S. and Scassellati, B. 2011. The benefits of interactions with physically present robots over video-displayed agents. International Journal of Social Robotics, 3(1), 41-52.

3. Bondareva, Y. and Bouwhuis, D. 2004. Determinants of Social Presence in Videoconferencing, *Proc. AVI 2004*, 1-9.

4. Chidambaram, V., Chiang, Y. H. and Mutlu, B. 2012. Designing persuasive robots: how robots might persuade people using vocal and nonverbal cues. *In Proceedings of International Conference on Human-Robot Interaction (HRI '12)*, 293-300.

5. De Greef, P. and Ijsselsteijn, W. 2001. Social Presence in a Home Tele-Application, *In Procdings of Cyberpsychology, Behavior, and Social Networking 2001*, 307-315.

6. Finn, K.E., Sellen, A.J. and Wilbur, S.B.1997. Video-Mediated Communication, Lawrence Erlbaum Associates, *Proc. CSCW 1999*, 299-301.

7. Fussell, R.S., Setlock, D.L., Yang, J., Ou, J., Mauer, E. and Kramer, I.D.A. 2004. Gestures over video streams to support remote collaboration on physical tasks, *Proc. HCI2004*, 273-309.

8. Genest, A., and Gutwin, C. 2012. Evaluating the effectiveness of height visualizations for improving gestural communication at distributed tabletops, *Proc. CSCW 2012*, 519-528.

9. Ishii, H. and Kobayashi, M. 1992. ClearBoard: a Seamless Medium for Shared Drawing and Conversation with Eye Contact, *Proc. CHI 1992*, 525-532.

10. Izadi, S., Agarwal, A., Criminisi, A., Winn, J., Blake, A. and Fitzgibbon, A. 2007. C-Slate: a Multi-touch and Object Recognition System for Remote Collaboration using Horizontal Surfaces, *Proc. Tabletop 2007*,3-10.

11. Kirk, D., Rodden, T. and Fraser, S.D. 2007. Turn it this Way: Grounding Collaborative Action with Remote Gestures, *Proc. CHI 2007*, 1039-1047.

12. Kuzuoka, H., Oyama, S., Yamazaki, K., Suzuki, K. and Mitsuishi, M. 2000. GestureMan: a Mobile Robot that Embodies a Remote Instructor's Actions, Proc. CSCW 2000, 155-162.

13. Leithinger, D., Follmer, S., Olwal, A. and Ishii, H. 2014. Physical telepresence: shape capture and display for embodied, computer-mediated remote collaboration, *Proc UIST 2014*, 461-470.

14. Luff, P., Heath, C., Kuzuoka, H., Yamazaki, K. and Yamashita, J. 2006. Handling Documents and Discriminating Objects in Hybrid Spaces, *Proc. CHI 2006*, 561-570.

15. Nakanishi, H., Murakami, Y., Nogami, D. and Ishiguro, H. 2008. Minimum Movement Matters: Impact of Robot-Mounted Cameras on Social Telepresence. *Proc. CSCW 2008*, 303-312.

16. Nakanishi, H., Murakami, Y. and Kato, K. 2009. Movable Cameras Enhance Social Telepresence in Media Spaces. *Proc. CHI 2009*, 433-442.

17. Nakanishi, H., Kato, K. and Ishiguro, H. 2011. Zoom Cameras and Movable Displays Enhance Social Telepresence. *Proc. CHI2011*, 63-72.

18. Nakanishi, H., Tanaka, K. and Wada, Y. 2014. Remote Handshaking: Touch Enhances Video-Mediated Social Telepresence. *Proc. CHI 2014*, 2143-2152

19. Onishi, Y., Tanaka, K. and Nakanishi, H. 2014. PopArm: A Robot Arm for Embodying Video-Mediated Pointing Behaviors, *Proc. CTS2014*, 137-141.

20. Ou, J., Chen, X., Fussell, S. and Yang, J. 2003. DOVE: Drawing over Video Environment, *Proc. Multimedia 2003*, 100-101.

21. Pauchet, A., Coldefy, F., Lefebvre, S., Louis, S., Perron, L., Bouguet, A., Collober, and t M., Guerin, J. and Corvaisier, D. 2007. TableTops: Worthwhile Experiences of Collocated and Remote Collaboration, *Proc. TABLETOP 2007*, 27-34.

22. Prussog, A., Muhlbach, L. and Bocker, M. 1994. Telepresence in Videocommunications, Proc. Annual Meeting of Human Factors and Ergonomics Society, 25-38.

23. Riether, N., Hegel, F., Wrede, B. and Horstmann, G. 2012. Social facilitation with social robots? *Proc. HRI2012*, 41-47.

24. Sakamoto, D., Kanda, T., Ono, T., Ishiguro, H. and Hagita, N. 2007. Android as a Telecommunication Medium with a Human-like Presence, *Proc. HRI2007, 193–200*, 53-56.

25. Sakata, N., Kurata, T., Kato, T., Kourogi, M. and Kuzuoka, H. 2003. WACL: Supporting Telecommunications Using Wearable Active Camera with Laser Pointer. *Proc. Wearable Computers 2003*, 53-56.

26. Tanaka, T., Nakanishi, H. and Ishiguro, H. 2014. Comparing Video, Avatar, and Robot Mediated Communication: Pros and Cons of Embodiment, *Proc. CollabTech2014*, 96-110.

27. Tang, J. and Minneman, S. 1991. VideoWhiteboard: Video Shadows to Support Remote Collaboration, *Proc. CHI 1991*, 315-322.

28. Tang, A., Pahud, M., Inkpen, K., Benko, H., Tang, C.J and Buxton B. 2010. Three's Company: Understanding Communication Channels in Three-way Distributed Collaboration, *Proc.CSCW2010*, 338-348.

29. Yamashita, N., Kaji, K., Kuzuoka, H. and Hirata, K. 2011. Improving Visibility of Remote Gestures in Distributed Tabletop Collaboration, *Proc. CSCW 2011*, 95-104.

Investigating Effects of Professional Status and Ethnicity in Human-Agent Interaction

Mohammad Obaid[1], Maha Salem[2], Micheline Ziadee[3],
Halim Boukaram[3], Elena Moltchanova[4], Majd Sakr[5]

[1]KUAR, Department of Media and Visual Arts, Koç University, Istanbul, Turkey
[2]University of Hertfordshire, Hatfield, United Kingdom
[3]American University of Science and Technology, Beirut, Lebanon
[4]Mathematics and Statistics Department, University of Canterbury, New Zealand
[5]Computer Science Department, Carnegie Mellon University, Pittsburgh, PA, USA
mobaid@ku.edu.tr

ABSTRACT

We present a study involving 160 participants investigating the effects of associating professional status and ethnicity with an agent by manipulating its appearance, language, and level of education. We aim to discern perceptions of status and ethnicity with respect to participants' cultural background by inviting participants from two different cultural groups (Middle Eastern and Western) to take part in our study. Results revealed that participants' cultural background had a strong impact on their ratings of the agent and its message. However, neither the agent's portrayed status nor its ethnicity appeared to have an effect on participants' perceptions of the agent. We further found that participants from both cultural backgrounds holding a negative attitude towards robots in general tend to perceive the presented message by the agent more negatively. Middle Eastern participants had a more positive attitude towards robotic agents than Western participants, which might have been the main influence on their perception of the message presented by the agent. In addition, participants who identified the agent as a member of their own cultural group perceived the presented message more positively than those who did not perceive it as an in-group member. We discuss our results with an intention to inform design implications for agents deployed in a cross-cultural context.

ACM Classification Keywords

I.2.11 Distributed Artificial Intelligence : Intelligent agents

Author Keywords

Human-agent interaction; status; ethnicity; culture

HAI '16, October 04-07, 2016, Biopolis, Singapore
©2016 ACM. ISBN 978-1-4503-4508-8/16/10...$15.00
DOI: http://dx.doi.org/10.1145/2974804.2974813

INTRODUCTION

Nowadays agents are being deployed more frequently to present information in many domain areas such as education, entertainment, service points, and as experts (e.g. offering advice on health-related topics) [14, 16, 24].

The Human-Agent Interaction (HAI) community has focused much of its investigations on the design of suitable social behaviors that would enable agents to be accepted in the environment of their users. In addition, several research efforts are underway towards understanding effects of an agent's embodiment and appearance on user perceptions [13]. Research has found that human perception and acceptance of agents as information presenters is affected by their social interaction behaviors and skills [8]. While it is further known that human attitudes and perceptions towards agents may vary across cultural groups [15], the perspective and possible effects of conveying ethnicity as well as status in agents has received very little attention in the HAI community so far.

In the psychology and sociology literature, status is considered to have a strong influence on how we interact with each other and interrelate as individuals, including how we perceive information from each other in terms of its assumed reliability and persuasiveness [29]. In addition, it is well established that rankings of status exist across all societies [9]. However, different cultures may vary substantially with regard to the values and qualities attributed to status and the effects it can have on how individuals are perceived [6]. For example, in cultures with highly distinctive class hierarchies, status plays a more significant role in human interactions than in cultures promoting comparatively flat hierarchies.

In view of growing demands to develop agent applications for global markets, a thorough understanding of potential cultural factors affecting agent acceptance and use becomes increasingly important. Therefore, investigating the effects of perceived status and ethnicity on HAI offers a promising research path towards improving social acceptance of agents. In this study we investigate how the professional status and ethnicity of an agent is perceived from the perspective of two different cultures, namely Arabic-speaking Middle Eastern and English-speaking Western. In particular, we address status as a value based on educational achievement, which is defined in the Blackwell Encyclopedia of Sociology [23].

The overarching question of our research is "to which extent does professional status or ethnicity matter in HAI?". In particular we aim to answer the following questions: (1) Does an agent's conveyed professional status have an impact on how humans perceive it? (2) Does an agent's portrayed ethnicity have an impact on how humans perceive it? (3) Does the cultural background of the human interaction partner have an impact on how an agent's status and ethnicity are perceived?

RELATED WORK

In human-human communication, status has been researched extensively by sociologists and psychologists to discern its importance within a society and its effect on members' interrelations. Status is generally defined as the rank of an individual within their society. However, detailed aspects of status have been defined differently by different scholars such as [7, 30]. In this paper, we focus our attention on achieved status, which is considered to be the accumulation of an individuals' achievements such as their occupational and educational level.

Occupational prestige is one of the main factors determining a person's status in modern societies [29]. Concurrently, other factors also play a role in determining status, such as ethnicity and gender [9]. Although the importance of status and ethnicity has been highlighted in the human-human communication literature, little research has been conducted in the HAI community to further explore these two aspects. This has motivated us to take the initiative to investigate and understand the effects of the perceived status and ethnicity on users.

Human-Agent Interaction

To the best of our knowledge, hardly any research has previously investigated the role and effect of status in the field of human-agent interaction. In contrast, an increasing body of work has addressed cultural differences as well as how ethnicity can be expressed in agents and how it is perceived by humans, e.g. [17]. However, most existing cross-cultural studies with robotic agents investigate salient cultural differences between Western (e.g. America, Europe) and East Asian (e.g. Japan, China, Korea) participant groups, e.g. [4, 11], which highlight major differences regarding human expectations, perceptions and acceptance of agents in those cultures. Only very little research has focused on Middle Eastern or Mediterranean attitudes regarding social agents. However, in these distinctively hierarchical societies, status plays an important role that impacts the way their members treat and perceive each other [9]. Finally, since the cultures in these regions are potentially very different from both Western and East Asian cultures, findings and implications from other cross-cultural studies are not necessarily transferable.

Eyssel and Kuchenbrandt [12] conducted a study that evaluated in-group and out-group membership in a HRI context. Their participants consisted of German university students who were shown a picture of a robot on a computer screen. The robot's group membership was manipulated through its name, Armin (German) and Arman (Turkish), and by telling

participants that Armin was developed at a German university, while Arman stemmed from a Turkish one. The results showed that participants evaluated the in-group robot more positively and anthropomorphized it more than the out-group robot. The researchers concluded that human-human interaction dynamics, and specifically preference for in-group members, carry over to interactions with technology and robots. They suggest that in addition to visual and audio cues, simple attributes such as a robot's name or place of origin can be used as indicators of the robot's group membership.

Above all, perception of a virtual or robotic agent is directly related to users' cultural background. This has been demonstrated in previous HRI literature such as the work by Eresha et al. [10] who conducted a study to investigate human-robot interpersonal distance, where users interacted with a robot from two cultural backgrounds (Arab and German). Similarly, Salem et al. [25] presented a study with native Arabic and native English speakers to investigate how politeness and cultural background have an impact on a robot's acceptance and anthropomorphization. Both studies found a significant relation between participants' culture and the way in which the robot was perceived.

Rehm et al. [21] considered agents' social status and ethnic profiles to investigate the social group dynamics of individuals interacting with groups of virtual agents displayed on a projected surface. Moreover, Rehm et al. [22] proposed a toolbox for the rapid prototyping of multi-agent social group dynamics based on several sociological theories. In their work they gave each agent profiles with several characteristics including social status. Agents with similar social status are considered to trust each other, and a higher social status given to an agent means it becomes a proactive member within the group. These studies, however, indirectly suggest that social status is a meaningful dimension in HAI, as studies on proxemics in human-human interaction have found that the social status of actors is one of the factors that affect the spacial distance people keep between each other during interaction.

Bailenson and Blascovich [3] presented a study that measured users' perceptions of two virtual agents, the only difference between them being how they were introduced: as either a "virtual tutor" or a "virtual stranger". Analysis of the participants' subjective impressions regarding co-presence, likeability, status, and interest did not reveal any difference between the two agents. However, analysis of the objective proxemics revealed noticeable differences that were in line with the authors' expectations: participants kept greater distance between themselves and the higher status 'tutor' agent than with the 'stranger'. In their work, the aim was to investigate the effect of status on personal distance rather than on measures related to the agent's persuasiveness or general acceptance.

In contrast, Berry et al. [5] evaluated the presentation of a persuasive message on healthy eating habits which was communicated in four different ways: an expressive virtual agent with a voice, a real human, the voice of the agent only, and text only. Their evaluation revealed that participants found the virtual agent with a voice to be helpful, trustworthy, and more likeable, but using a virtual agent resulted in a poor recall performance of the message details. The authors attributed this poor performance to the possible distraction caused by the presence of the agent's face. Interestingly, in the human face condition, participants' recall performance did not seem to suffer from the additional visual input, suggesting a potentially influential novelty effect when interacting with a virtual agent. However, an interesting aspect that was not addressed in this study is the consideration of the social status of the agent presenting the information. For example, would a supposed "expert" agent presenting the message be perceived as more competent and knowledgeable than a lay agent?

Inspired by the study conducted by Berry et al. [5] and the described related work, we addressed our research questions by introducing an agent with a status profile based on its educational level (doctor vs. non-doctor). In addition, we manipulated the agent's appearance to associate it with two different cultures (Middle Eastern and Western), allowing us to investigate both parameters. Finally, to investigate cross-cultural perceptions of the agent, we invited participants from the two corresponding cultural backgrounds, namely Arabic-speaking Middle Eastern and English-speaking Western participants.

METHOD

We conducted an experiment to gain insights into the role of status and ethnicity in shaping human experience and evaluation of HAI. In addition, we aim for a deeper understanding of how these perceptions may vary between participants of two highly different cultural backgrounds.

Hypotheses

Based on findings from related work on cross-cultural studies, status and ethnicity, we developed the following five main hypotheses for our experiment: (1) *Effect of Agent's Status* (**H1**) - manipulation of the agent's conveyed status will affect participants' subjective perception of the agent and of the presented message content. (2) *Effect of Agent's Ethnicity* (**H2**) - manipulation of the agent's portrayed ethnicity will affect participants' subjective perception of the agent and of the presented message. (3) *Effect of Participants' Cultural Background* (**H3**) - participants' cultural background will affect their subjective perception of the agent and of the presented message. (4) *Effect of Perceived Group Membership* (**H4**) - the stronger the perception of the agent as a member of the participants' own cultural group, the more positively they will rate (a) the agent's presented message and (b) the agent itself. (5) *Effect of Negative Attitude Towards Robots* (**H5**) - participants with more negative attitudes towards robotic agents will rate the message content more negatively than participants with less negative attitudes towards a robotic agent, regardless of its conveyed social status or ethnicity.

Material

We used the HALA [17] agent developed at Carnegie Mellon University in Qatar which resembles a 3D face rendering on a computer screen mounted on a mannequin's body as a head and features detailed nuances such as lip movements, brow movements, breathing, and blinking. The agent's traits can be alternated between middle eastern and western. The animated agent was recorded giving a message on healthy eating habits.

The agent's default software-generated voice was replaced by a modulated recording of "neutral" accented human speech so as to limit the potential negative impact of the speech pattern on the reception of the information. Each video shows the agent's attire and face while the agent speaks directly to the camera, and it does not move during the video. We arbitrarily chose the gender of the agent to be female, and this and every other aspect of the agent – except for its status, ethnicity, and language – remained constant across all conditions.

Experimental Design

A between-subject design was used to conduct an experiment in which we evaluated eight conditions that manipulated the agent's status, (doctor vs. non-doctor) and ethnicity (Western vs. Middle Eastern) in two different language groups (English vs. Arabic). To exhibit the ethnicity of the agent and its status, we modified the agent's language and appearance as illustrated in Figure 1, as well as the verbal announcement introducing the agent at the beginning of the video. In the following sections we describe the details of the agent's representations, study procedure, and measurements collected.

Ethnicity Representation: The ethnicity of the agent was exhibited by its language, eyes, hair, and skin color. In this context, the agent's language was set up to be either English with an American accent or Arabic with a Levantine accent, while its physical appearance was based on its eye, hair, and skin color: "Western" stereotype—white skin, blue eyes, and blond hair—and "Middle Eastern" stereotype, with darker skin and black eyes and hair (Figure 2). In addition, at the beginning of the video the agent was verbally introduced as either an agent "from the USA" or "from the Middle East".

Status Representation: The status of the agent was exhibited by its educational level and attire, which was manipulated as either dressed in plainclothes and introduced as "Leena", or dressed in a white lab coat and presented as "Dr. Leena".

Message: For each language, the presented message content was the same, providing information on maintaining a healthy diet. The message started with a greeting after which the agent introduced itself and the topic of the video message with the following words: "Hello, my name is Leena, and in this short video, I will give you some nutrition advice to help you stay healthy". For the remainder of the content, we adopted a healthy eating message used in the study conducted by Berry et al. [5]. The message contained recommendations on healthy foods and the benefits of eating fruits and vegetables. For example, "it is recommended to eat at least five portions of fruits and vegetables a day, as they are good sources of vitamins (particularly A and C), minerals, and fiber".

Using a professional translator, we translated the text of the message into Modern Standard Arabic (MSA) and recorded it by a native Arabic speaker, while the English version was recorded by a native English speaker. MSA was chosen because it is understood by Arabic speakers across different regions regardless of local dialect. Although Arabic speakers would typically use their local dialect for communication, they are frequently exposed to spoken MSA media.

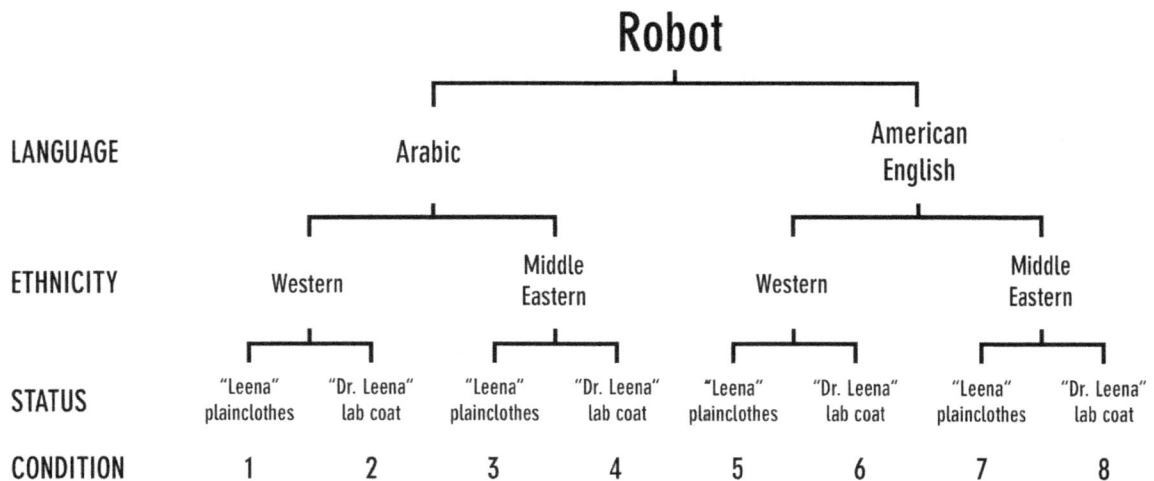

Figure 1. Tree describing all possible characteristics influencing the portrayal of the agent

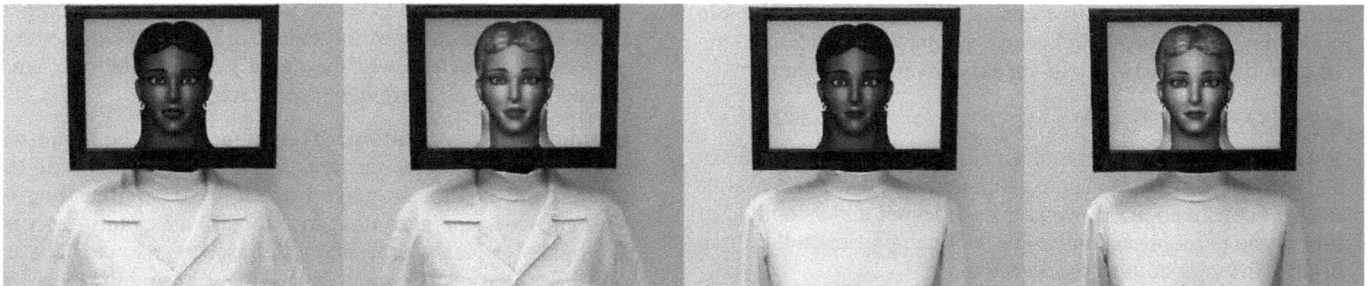

Figure 2. Agent Leena in different representations of status and ethnicity. From left to right, Middle Eastern Dr. Leena, Western Dr. Leena, Middle Eastern casual Leena, and Western casual Leena

The Arabic language is very difficult to neutralize when it comes to gender bias [18, 20] since inflection for gender covers many parts of speech such as verbs, pronouns, and adjectives [2]. Referring to a group of people containing both females and males in Arabic uses the masculine plural form of pronouns and verbs. We opted for this formula in creating our Arabic text, since we had no means of knowing beforehand whether a participant would be male or female. The use of the plural, however, renders the tone of the text more formal and might consequently produce an effect of greater perceived distance between speaker and listener.

In translating the text from English to Arabic we tried to achieve similarity between the two texts and comprehension. Since we are dealing with an informative text that mainly relates to facts, achieving similarity was not difficult. As for comprehension, our strategy consisted in avoiding the use of specialized jargon so as to render the text accessible to listeners with average proficiency.

Experimental Procedure
Given the nature of our research questions and in order to reach a wider audience within a greater geographical area, we opted for an online study. Specifically, to run the experiment we distributed it among participants through mailing lists, email, personal contacts or social media. Participants used their web browsers and were only allowed to access the study via a stationary computer or laptop, i.e. they were not allowed to use their mobile phones or tablets, as this could influence their perception due to the small screen size.

The survey was structured so that the participant first completed a pre-video questionnaire, then watched one version of the video in which the agent delivered the healthy eating message, before finally filling out a post-video questionnaire.

The overall study had eight conditions (four of each language group as shown in Figure 1), where each participant that chose to do the study received only one of the conditions, which was randomly assigned to them. The survey began by first asking several demographic questions and then several questions to reveal participants' interest in a healthy diet and their attitude towards robotic agents.

Participants were then shown a video of the agent speaking, providing advice about maintaining a healthy diet. Afterwards, they were asked to answer another series of questions that investigated their perception of the agent and the message it presented. The text and questions provided in the survey were the same in all eight conditions. The questions were first formatted in English and then translated by a professional English-Arabic translator. The length of the Arabic videos was 2 minutes 38 seconds and the length of the English videos was 2 minutes 15 seconds.

Dependent Measures

Measurements were collected subjectively based on several questionnaires that aimed at answering our research questions. All subjective measures were based on five point Likert scales.

Pre-video questionnaire: We first asked participants several demographic questions that allowed us to analyze the relationships between the agent's attributes (status and ethnicity) and the participants' age, gender, cultural background, and interest in the subject of the message (healthy diet). Then we presented a standard questionnaire commonly used to assess the Negative Attitude Towards Robots (NARS) [19], where a higher NARS score means a more negative attitude toward robotic agents. NARS has 14 questions, and each question relates to one of the three following sub-scales: Negative Attitudes toward: (S1) Situations and Interactions with Robots; (S2) Social Influence of Robots; and (S3) Emotions in Interaction with Robots. We used NARS to investigate the relationship between negative attitude towards robots and how users perceive the robotic agent and its message.

We note here that NARS is generally used as a pre-questionnaire in studies with physical robotic agents with an aim to understand the users' attitude towards robotic agents; thus, giving researchers a general insight about their users. This insight is generally based on concepts that users have gained over the years from their experiences and media that contains robotic agents (whether it is physical or virtual)[26]. Therefore, we believe it is valid to use NARS as a pre-questionnaire in our study with a virtual robotic agent as it will give us an insight on our users' general attitudes.

Post-video questionnaire: The main aim of the post-video questionnaire was to assess users' perceptions of the agent and the message it presented. The questionnaire items used in the post-video evaluations were adopted (with modifications) from Berry et al. [5]. The questionnaire was divided into four parts. Part one assessed how participants perceived the message and its content, including measures on how easy and satisfying the message was. The second part assessed users' message recall by asking the user to choose items and pick information that was presented in the message, including false items. The third part of the questionnaire was mainly meant to assess users' perception of the agent, including questions about how helpful, intelligent, credible, likeable, reliable, believable, competent, knowledgeable, responsible, and sensible the agent was. Finally, the fourth part assessed how users perceived the nationality of the agent, why they thought it was associated with the nationality they selected, and to rate the native language of the agent on a 5 point Likert scale.

Participants

We aimed for our participant population to be a complete set of 20 participants for each condition. We had 186 participants completing the online study—82 native Arabic speakers (e.g. from Jordan, Lebanon, Egypt and Tunisia) and 104 native English speakers (e.g. from the USA, Canada, the UK and New Zealand). However, two Arabic and 24 English participants were removed from the results since they chose not to do the study in their mother tongue language. Consequently we reached our target of 20 participants per condition (160

participants in total). The descriptive statistics for the sample are shown in Table 1.

Table 1. The descriptive statistics of the users including the number of males/females, median completion time, and the mean/standard deviation for age, NARS scores, and self-rated healthy diet

	Middle Eastern	Western
n	80	80
M/F	44/36	45/35
Median completion time	9.4	13.8
Age	31.3 (11.7)	37.7 (13.8)
NARS1	2.05 (0.75)	1.88 (0.69)
NARS2	3.01 (0.94)	2.66 (0.67)
NARS3	3.57 (1.07)	3.23 (0.92)
NARS total	2.88 (0.65)	2.59 (0.61)
Self-rated healthy diet	3.03 (0.82)	3.60 (0.81)

Due to the nature of the online study, gender balance amongst participants could not be controlled and the number of males (89) is slightly greater than females (71). For similar reasons the native Arabic speakers were on average slightly younger (31.3) compared to the native English speakers (37.7).

RESULTS AND ANALYSIS

All statistical analyses were performed within the framework of a generalised linear regression model (GLM) and an analysis of variance with covariates (ANCOVA). The effects were thus adjusted for gender, age, and other relevant confounders, such as self-rated healthy diet habits as well as participants' NARS scores, which were included in the regression model where appropriate. The residuals were checked for normality and heteroscedasticity where appropriate. The statistical significance of individual factors was assessed via the regression coefficient-specific t-tests and z-tests for the linear regression and the logistic linear regression respectively. For the multinomial GLM, the χ^2-test was used to compare the model with and without the factor of interest.

Healthy Diet and NARS Scores

After adjusting for gender, age, and other confounders, on average, Middle Eastern participants tended to score 0.52 points lower on the self-rated healthy diet scale items than Western participants ($t_{156} = 3.929$, $p = .0001$). Neither age nor gender of the participants correlatd with the ratings. Furthermore, Middle Easterners tended to score lower on all three individual NARS scales (The respective average differences in points, adjusted for gender and age: NAR-S1: 0.21, ($t_{156} = 1.868, p = 0.063$), NAR-S2: 0.36, ($t_{156} = 2.708, p = 0.007$), NAR-S3: 0.42, ($t_{156} = 2.642, p = 0.009$). The average difference for the composite NARS scale was estimated at 0.33 ($t_{156} = 3.297, p = 0.001$). Males tended to score lower by an average of 0.27 ($t_{156} = 2.720, p = 0.007$), while no correlation with age was found.

Message and Agent Perception

Participants were asked to give a score to each of the eight statements describing their message perception. The results revealed statistically significant differences between message perceptions by native Arabic speakers and native English speakers. The English speakers found the message less convincing and less interesting than the Arabic speakers. However, neither the status nor the ethnicity of the agent had a statistically significant effect on the result. The statements, along with differences in the score for the native Arabic speaker vs native English speaker, adjusted for demographics, NARS score, and self-rated healthy diet are shown in Table 2.

In addition, participants were asked to assess the agent itself, i.e. whether the agent appeared helpful, intelligent, credible, likeable, reliable, believable, competent, knowledgeable, responsible and sensible. We found that higher NARS scores were found to be highly statistically significant associated with lower scores on all but one of these measures (helpfulness). However, no difference in ratings for these characteristics was found between the conditions.

Table 2. Factors presented in the message perception statements

Statement	Middle Eastern vs. Western	t_{158}	p-value
Recommendations	-0.51	-2.828	0.0053
Satisfied	-0.45	-2.621	0.0097
Easy to understand	-0.21	-1.160	0.2480
Convincing	-0.89	-4.429	0.0000
Quality of argument	-0.73	-4.066	0.0001
Trustworthy	-0.26	-1.482	0.1403
Interesting	-1.21	-5.802	0.0000
Video Message Rating	-0.61	-4.361	0.0000

Ascribed Agent Nationality

Participants were further asked which nationality they thought the agent represents. The responses to these open-ended questions were subsequently categorized into three groups: nationalities of Arabic speaking countries, nationalities of English speaking countries, and any other nationalities.

Multinomial logistic GLM [1] was used to see which factors correlated with the decision between the three categories. The apparent status of the agent (wearing a lab coat or not) had no statistically significant effect on the decision ($\chi_8^2 = 12.22, p = 0.141$) but the language of the agent and its appearance (Middle Eastern vs. Western) were both highly significant ($\chi_8^2 = 52.250$ and $\chi_8^2 = 40.919$ respectively, $p < 0.0001$). The resulting estimated probability of perceiving the nationality of the agent is shown in Figure 3.

Moreover, Binomial logistic GLM was used to determine which factors affected the probability of participants using language, appearance or other information to decide on the agent's nationality. The distribution of factors which users said they considered when deciding on the nationality of the agent are shown in Table 3. The odds of an English speaker saying they used language to identify the nationality of the agent were estimated to be 3.19 times higher than those of an Arabic speaker ($z = 3.298, p = 0.001$), while the odds of a male saying he used the information given when introducing the agent to identify the nationality of the agent were estimated to be 5.91 times lower than those of a female ($z = 2.547, p = 0.01$).

Non-parametric Spearman correlation was used to analyze the effect of in-group perceptions (i.e. classifying the agent as

a member of the participant's own cultural group) on participants' subjective ratings of (a) the presented message and (b) the agent itself. To this end, for each of these two dimensions, scores of the corresponding questionnaire items were averaged after conducting reliability analyses (Cronbach's α), with both the message ratings ($\alpha = .89$) and items rating the agent itself ($\alpha = .93$) yielding very reliable scales. While there was no correlation between in-group perceptions of the agent and ratings of its message ($r_s = 0.05$; p = n.s.), we found that perceiving the agent as a member of one's own cultural group positively correlated with perceptions of its qualities ($r_s = 0.24; p < 0.01$), e.g. in terms of how knowledgeable and competent the agent was perceived.

Table 3. Distribution of factors considered with the agent's nationality

Combination	Number	%
Info only	8	5%
Language only	66	41.25%
Language, Info only	4	2.5%
Appearance only	18	11.25%
Appearance and Info only	2	1.25%
Appearance and Language only	12	7.5%
Did not answer	50	31.25%

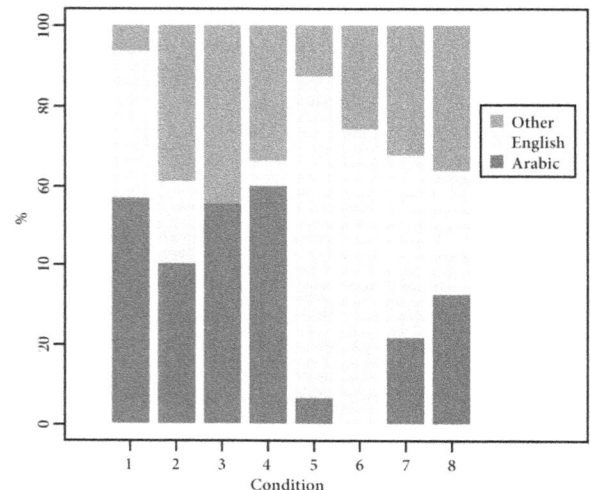

Figure 3. The estimated probability of classifying the agent as native Arabic speaker (red), native English speaker (yellow) or other (green) by each of the conditions, after adjustment for age, gender, and NARS.

DISCUSSION

We presented a study investigating how characteristics of status and ethnicity applied to an agent may influence the perceptions of users from two different cultural backgrounds (Middle Eastern and Western). Our results did not support hypothesis **H1** based on which we expected the agent's social status to have an effect on how users perceived the agent and the content of the message it presented. Though we expected the agent's social status to have an impact, based on its educational title and appearance, it is apparent from our results that these two cues did not seem to overcome the overall impression users have towards agents. This can be explained by how such cues might have been interpreted by users based on their pre-existing self-schema, internal thoughts, or beliefs [27, 28].

Similarly, the effect of ethnicity exhibited by the robot did not have an impact on users' perceptions of the agent nor its presented message, ruling out hypothesis **H2**. The overall impressions towards agents, as well as the outcomes regarding hypotheses **H1** and **H2**, suggest that users might be influenced by pre-conceived or prejudiced ideas about the potential behavior and intelligence of robots. These expectations might be based on examples from science fiction and media [26].

Our results strongly support hypothesis **H3**, in which we predicted that a participants' cultural background would have an effect on their perception of the agent and the message it presents. Consequently, we relate this finding directly to the significant difference between native Arabic speakers' greater interest in the healthy diet—accompanied by a more positive attitude towards the agent—as compared to Western participants. Our results complement findings by Salem et al. [25], who found native Arabic speakers' culture to be a major factor in the perception of the robot's politeness. They describe how the attitude of individuals from an Arab or Middle Eastern culture is positive towards robots, which could have been the main factor for their findings.

With regard to **H4**, our results suggest that perceiving an agent as sharing the same cultural background as oneself promotes positive ratings and increased likeability of the agent (supporting H4-b), but does not seem to affect ratings of message quality and persuasiveness (rejecting H4-a). These findings have important implications for the design of agents that are intended to provide assistance and advice for people of different cultural backgrounds, e.g. in international settings such as airports: simple cues reflecting in-group membership, such as common language or appearance, can be easily used to increase user acceptance in HAI.

Moreover, from our results, participants who generally have a negative attitude towards robotic agents did indeed negatively perceive our agent and the message it presented, regardless of its status and ethnicity, supporting Hypothesis (**H5**).

Our results reveal several important aspects to consider when designing social agents and their appearance in cross-cultural settings. It is apparent that the relationship between identified nationality and appearance and language has an impact on the message perceived. In addition, even with the lack of other cues, users are prompt at identifying an agent's nationality based on its appearance and language. In addition, across all conditions we found that Middle Eastern participants have a more positive attitude towards agents. These participants perceived the message delivered by the agent more positively. This indicates that an influential factor in our study was the attitude of participants towards robots, even before interaction took place; thus, we argue that when expert agents are introduced there needs to be an adjustment buffer where the expectation level of the user gets matched with what the agent can deliver; including its intelligence level.

Finally, some of the limitation of our study includes the one-way interaction between the user and the agent, where the agent was passing a message to the user verbally. Thus, our study could further be improved by allowing the user to inter-act with the agent in a fluent two-way setup. Moreover, the complexity of the presented message, healthy eating, might have been too trivial as it is a familiar topic to people. Therefore, the content of the presented message could have also contributed to the users' interest in the agent and the message.

CONCLUSIONS AND FUTURE WORK

In this study we aimed at answering several research questions relating to HAI in cross-cultural contexts. First, we investigated whether an agent's perceived status and ethnicity would affect users' acceptance of the agent and the message it delivered. Second, we tested whether a user's cultural background might have an effect on their perception of the agent and its message. Third, we asked whether the perception of the agent as an in-group member (in our case a member of the user's cultural background) would lead to a more positive perception of the agent and its message. Finally, we asked whether participants' negative attitudes towards robots in general would result in a lower rating of our agent and its message.

Our findings indicate that the agent's perceived ethnicity and status do not have any effect on participants' evaluation of the agent's message, while its apparent ethnicity has an effect on assessments of the agent itself only when it is perceived as an in-group member. On the other hand, participants' cultural background significantly affected their perception of both the agent and message, as participants coming from a Middle Eastern background gave higher ratings for both. Participants who held positive attitudes towards robots tended to evaluate the agent positively and also thought the message was more helpful.

The limitations of this study offer opportunities for future research directions. We propose in the future to explore status in an interactive setup where the user and the agent are physically engaged in a task that requires the expertise of an agent. Moreover, the complexity of the presented message, healthy eating, is well understood and people are very familiar with it. If the "doctor" agent presents a more novel message, would this result in its status having a greater influence on how the message and agent are perceived? Further studies are needed to explore topics of greater complexity and which may actually require the help of an agent, ideally in real interactions.

REFERENCES

1. Alan Agresti. 2013. *Categorical Data Analysis*. Wiley.

2. Mohammed K. Al-Ajlouny. 2014. Gender In English and Arabic. *Language, Individual & Society* (2014), 236–244.

3. Jeremy N. Bailenson, Eyal Aharoni, Andrew C. Beall, Rosanna E. Guadagno, Aleksandar Dimov, and Jim Blascovich. 2004. Comparing behavioral and self-report measures of embodied agents' social presence in immersive virtual environments. In *the 7th Annual International Workshop on presence, Valencia, Spain*.

4. Christoph Bartneck, Tomohiro Suzuki, Takayuki Kanda, and Tatsuya Nomura. 2006. The Influence of People's Culture and Prior Experiences with Aibo on their Attitude Towards Robots. *AI & Society – The Journal of Human-Centred Systems* 21, 1 (2006).

5. Dianne C. Berry, Laurie T. Butler, and Fiorella de Rosis. 2005. Evaluating a Realistic Agent in an Advice-giving Task. *International Journal of Human-Computer Studies* 63, 3 (Sept. 2005), 304–327.

6. John W. Berry, Ype H. Poortinga, Marshall H. Segall, and Pierre R. Dasen. 2002. *Cross-cultural psychology: Research and applications.* Cambridge University Press.

7. Pierre Bourdieu. 1984. *Distinction: A social critique of the judgement of taste.* Harvard University Press.

8. Cynthia Breazeal. 2003. Emotion and Sociable Humanoid Robots. *International Journal of Human-Computer Studies* 59, 1-2 (July 2003), 119–155.

9. Lynn S. Chancer and Beverly X. Watkins. 2006. *Gender, race, and class: An overview.* Vol. 11. Wiley-Blackwell.

10. Ghadeer Eresha, Marcus Häring, Birgit Endrass, Elisabeth André, and Mohammad Obaid. 2013. Investigating the influence of culture on proxemic behaviors for humanoid robots. In *the 22nd IEEE International Symposium on Robot and Human Interactive Communication (RO-MAN 2013).* 430–435.

11. Vanessa Evers, Heidy Maldonado, Talia Brodecki, and Pamela Hinds. 2008. Relational vs. group self-construal: Untangling the role of national culture in HRI. In *the 3rd ACM/IEEE International Conference on Human-Robot Interaction.* 255–262.

12. Friederike Eyssel and Dieta Kuchenbrandt. 2012. Social categorization of social robots: Anthropomorphism as a function of robot group membership. *British Journal of Social Psychology* 51, 4 (2012), 724–731.

13. Terrence Fong, Illah R. Nourbakhsh, and Kerstin Dautenhahn. 2003. A Survey of Socially Interactive Robots. *Robotics and Autonomous Systems* 42, 3-4 (2003), 143–166.

14. Marcel Heerink, Ben Kröse, Vanessa Evers, and Bob Wielinga. 2010. Assessing Acceptance of Assistive Social Agent Technology by older Adults: the Almere Model. *International Journal of Social Robotics* 2, 4 (2010), 361–375.

15. Hee Rin Lee and Selma Sabanović. 2014. Culturally Variable Preferences for Robot Design and Use in South Korea, Turkey, and the United States. In *the 2014 ACM/IEEE International Conference on Human-robot Interaction (HRI '14).* ACM, New York, NY, USA, 17–24.

16. Rosemarijn Looije, Fokie Cnossen, and Mark A. Neerincx. 2006. Incorporating guidelines for health assistance into a socially intelligent robot. In *the 15th IEEE International Symposium on Robot and Human Interactive Communication (RO-MAN 2006).* 515–520.

17. Maxim Makatchev, Reid Simmons, Majd Sakr, and Micheline Ziadee. 2013. Expressing Ethnicity Through Behaviors of a Robot Character. In *the 8th ACM/IEEE International Conference on Human-robot Interaction (HRI '13).* IEEE Press, Piscataway, NJ, USA, 357–364.

18. Heba Nayef. 2014. Abstract Dominance: Linguistic investigation of gender orientation in vernacular Cairene Arabic. *the International Gender and Language Association* (2014), 156–178.

19. Tatsuya Nomura, Takayuki Kanda, and Tomohiro Suzuki. 2006. Experimental investigation into influence of negative attitudes toward robots on human-robot interaction. *AI & SOCIETY* 20, 2 (2006), 138–150.

20. Pavlos Pavlou and Terry Potter. 1994. The Difficulty of Avoiding Gender-Biased Language in Highly Inflected Languages: A Comparison of Greek and Arabic. *the International Linguistics Association Conference* (1994).

21. Matthias Rehm, Elisabeth André, and Michael Nischt. 2005. Let's Come Together — Social Navigation Behaviors of Virtual and Real Humans. In *Intelligent Technologies for Interactive Entertainment,* Mark Maybury, Oliviero Stock, and Wolfgang Wahlster (Eds.). Lecture Notes in Computer Science, Vol. 3814. Springer Berlin Heidelberg, 124–133.

22. Matthias Rehm and Birgit Endrass. 2009. Rapid prototyping of social group dynamics in multiagent systems. *AI & SOCIETY* 24, 1 (2009), 13–23.

23. George Ritzer. 2007. *The Blackwell encyclopedia of sociology.* Vol. 1479. Blackwell Publishing Malden, MA.

24. Ben Robins, Kerstin Dautenhahn, Aude Billard, and Rene Te Boekhorst. 2004. Robotic Assistants in Therapy and Education of Children with Autism: Can a Small Humanoid Robot Help Encourage Social Interaction Skills. *Universal Access in the Information Society* UAIS (2004), 105–120.

25. Maha Salem, Micheline Ziadee, and Majd Sakr. 2014. Marhaba, How May I Help You?: Effects of Politeness and Culture on Robot Acceptance and Anthropomorphization. In *the 2014 ACM/IEEE International Conference on Human-robot Interaction (HRI '14).* ACM, New York, NY, USA, 74–81.

26. Eduardo B. Sandoval, Omar Mubin, and Mohammad Obaid. 2014. Human Robot Interaction and Fiction: A Contradiction. In *the 6th International Conference on Social Robotics (ICSR 2014),* Michael Beetz, Benjamin Johnston, and Mary-Anne Williams (Eds.). Lecture Notes in Computer Science, Vol. 8755. Springer International Publishing, 54–63.

27. Eliot R. Smith. 1984. Attributions and other inferences: Processing information about the self versus others. *Journal of Experimental Social Psychology* 20, 2 (1984), 97 – 115.

28. Mark Snyder and Nancy Cantor. 1979. Testing hypotheses about other people: The use of historical knowledge. *Journal of Experimental Social Psychology* 15, 4 (1979), 330 – 342.

29. Donald J. Treiman. 1977. *Occupational prestige in comparative perspective.* Academic Press Inc.

30. Max Weber. 1978. *Economy and society: An outline of interpretive sociology.* University of California Press.

Does a Conversational Robot Need to Have its own Values? A Study of Dialogue Strategy to Enhance People's Motivation to Use Autonomous Conversational Robots

Takahisa Uchida
Osaka University
Osaka, Japan
ATR
Kyoto, Japan
uchida.takahisa@irl.sys.es.osaka-u.ac.jp

Takashi Minato
ATR
Kyoto, Japan
minato@atr.jp

Hiroshi Ishiguro
Osaka University
Osaka, Japan
ATR
Kyoto, Japan
ishiguro@sys.es.osaka-u.ac.jp

ABSTRACT

This work studies a dialogue strategy aimed at building people's motivation for talking with autonomous conversational robots. Even though spoken dialogue systems continue to develop rapidly, the existing systems are insufficient for continuous use because they fail to motivate users to talk with them. One reason is that users fail to realize that the intentions of the system's utterances are based on its values. Since people recognize the values of others and modify their own values in human-human conversations, we hypothesize that a dialogue strategy that makes users saliently feel the difference of their own values and those of the system will increase motivation for the dialogues. Our experiment, which evaluated human-human dialogues, supported our hypothesis. However, an experiment with human-android dialogues failed to produce identical results, suggesting that people did not attribute values to our android. For a conversational robot, we need additional techniques to convince people to believe a robot speaks based on its own values and opinions.

ACM Classification Keywords

H.5.m. Information Interfaces and Presentation (e.g. HCI): Miscellaneous

Author Keywords

spoken dialogue system; dialogue strategy; values; motivation to talk; android; autonomous conversational robot

INTRODUCTION

One issue of human agent interaction is to develop a spoken dialogue system that can naturally talk with people and that can be continuously used by them. Even though spoken dialogue systems have made huge developmental strides, the existing systems are inadequate for continuous use because they cannot sustain user motivation to talk with them. For example, recent personal assistant software applications for smartphones can answer various questions through verbal interaction, but they are basically restricted to single-turn search requests or question-and-answer styles, and the interaction does not take context into account. Toward multi-turn spoken dialogue systems, some studies have developed task-oriented dialogue systems, such as a bus information system [1], but the dialogue contents are strictly limited to the target task domain. Many chatbot systems like ELIZA [20] are able to handle multi-turn dialogues driven by a huge dialogue database (e.g., [8]); yet they do not seem to produce replies appropriate to the user's internal state (e.g., intention) or individual contexts. Consequently, the above systems are inadequate for natural conversations. In particular, since the problem of context breakdown suppresses the motivation of users to sustain conversations, these systems are not used continuously. This problem must be overcome, e.g., for dialogue support for seniors.

This study focuses on non-task-oriented dialogue systems. To avoid context breakdown, systems need to produce utterances with which users feel consistency (like a system's intention). Considering that our decision making is based on our own values [14], that is, the intention in utterances arises from values, systems must also have their own values and produce speech based on them to enable users to subjectively recognize system intentions based on utterances. This result might help avoid context breakdown.

In this paper, we explore a values-based dialogue strategy that stimulates the motivation of users to talk and maintain interaction with a robot. People recognize the values of others and modify their own values in human-human conversations, and therefore, people might feel strongly motivated by dialogues in which they can saliently identify the differences of each other's values. People estimate the values of others while agreeing and disagreeing with their utterances. The saliency of the differences, which might be influenced by the balance of the agreements and disagreements, might be maximized by a sound balance. In other words, the information gain of the difference is maximized by a certain balance. This

HAI'16, October 4–7, 2016, Biopolis, Singapore.
Copyright © 2016 ACM ISBN 978-1-4503-4508-8/16/10 ...$15.00.
http://dx.doi.org/10.1145/2974804.2974830

Figure 1. Android: ERICA

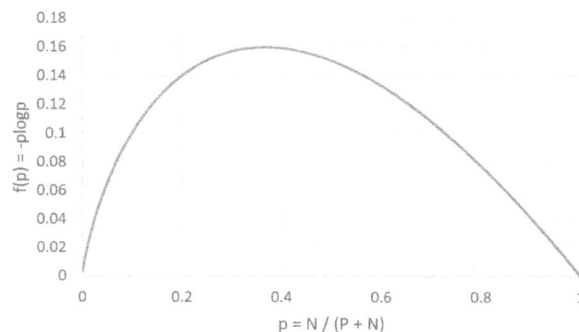

Figure 2. Relation between psychological quantity for perception and event's probability

paper hypothesizes that a dialogue strategy which saliently identifies the differences of each other's values most strongly motivates conversations. We experimentally verified this hypothesis in human-human dialogues. Then, we test whether a similar effect is obtained for a robot. Although interactions that involve agreements/disagreements are just part of conversations, people essentially infer the values of others through them. In addition, Ihara [10] concluded that humans estimate the values of others from their agreements or disagreements to utterances. Therefore, this paper discusses the essence of sharing values, that is, agreements and disagreements to utterances as a strategy to identify each other's values. In terms of natural language processing, we can recognize users' positive or negative attitudes from verbal and non-verbal information [6]. Therefore, controlling the agreement and disagreement balance is a practical strategy in conversations.

This paper studies our hypothesis with a very humanlike android robot because humanlike androids can function as communication media that closely resemble people [18]. We use the android ERICA shown in Fig. 1. Studying a dialogue mechanism with a very humanlike android is meaningful not only for understanding the essence of human-robot communication but also human-human communication.

DIALOGUE STRATEGY TO MAXIMIZE USER'S MOTIVATION

Asymmetry of Positive/Negative Ratio in Human Recognition

Roughly speaking, people gradually understand the values of another while agreeing or disagreeing in dialogues. Generally, an agreement to an utterance provides a positive impression and a disagreement gives a negative impression. As related studies in cognitive science, some have discussed the characteristics of human behavior for positive and negative events. Benjafield and Adams-Webber [2] proposed a hypothesis where humans make bipolar judgments (positive/negative) in a kind of golden ratio (positive : negative = 0.618 : 0.382) and examined this idea using Kelly's Role Construct Repertory Test[1]. When subjects

---
[1] This test is for understanding how an individual views his or her world

evaluate acquaintances in terms of bipolar judgments (e.g., friendly/unfriendly), the average score of $P/(P+N)$ is close to the golden ratio (0.618). Here, P expresses the number of positive judgments and N is for negative judgments. This hypothesis was followed by a number of studies in social cognitive science ([3], [13], [15], [17]).

As an explanation for this phenomenon, Frank [5] proposed that the psychological quantity for the perception of an event depends on occurrence probability p and information gain $\log(1/p)$. In addition, he thought that humans strikingly recognize negative events when quantity $p\log(1/p)$ was maximized from the viewpoint of Shannon's information theory. It is maximized when $p = 0.37$ (Fig. 2), so humans recognize negative events most saliently when the occurrence probability equals 0.37. Finally, he concluded that humans pay special attention to negative events by adopting such an optimal information processing strategy.

Hypothesis for Building Motivation

As described above, asymmetry has been reported in the cognition of positive/negative events. Taking these studies into consideration, we built a hypothesis of the relationship between the agreement/disagreement ratio and motivation for continuing a dialogue. From the viewpoint of Benjafield and Adams-Webber's study [2], since people tend to reply to another's utterance in a positively biased manner, they prefer to communicate with those who talk in the same manner. According to Frank's study [5], people like to talk with those whose strategy is biased toward agreement if they want to saliently know the difference of each other's values. In other words, people's motivation for continuing a dialogue is stimulated by the agreement/disagreement ratio, which is biased to agreements.

We hypothesize that the agreement rate to create dialogues toward which people saliently feel the differences between each other's values and motivate them is neither 50% nor 100% but somewhere between them. In addition, Gottman [7] reported that the optimal ratio of positive/negative utterances is 5 : 1 to maintain congenial relationships in marriages; marital relations greatly suffer when negative utterances exceed positive ones. This study also supports our hypothesis in the sense of continuing long-term interactions.

Figure 3. Video stimulus: human-human dialogue

EXPERIMENT ON HUMAN-HUMAN DIALOGUE

Experiment Aim

In the first experiment, we examined whether the dialogue motivation is maximized with an agreement rate between 50% and 100% in human-human dialogues.

Video Stimuli

In this experiment, experimental subjects evaluated their motivation to talk through a third person view; they did not join conversations but instead they watched the conversations of others. We chose this method because it is difficult to control the conversation content and agreement rate in free conversations joined by subjects. We videotaped a female experimental assistant having a conversation (in Japanese) with a male experimental assistant based on a predetermined scenario. For comparison with a female type of android, the female assistant was videotaped in this experiment. In the video, only the female assistant appears, as shown in Fig. 3, but the voices of both assistants are audible. She smiles when she agrees and expresses a confused face when she disagrees because it is unnatural if the facial expression and the speech contents do not match. The subjects watched the video and reported their degree of motivation to talk with the female assistant. We prepared a number of conversations between the two assistants using fixed scenario enactments and different agreement rates.

The following is the conversation's content: the female assistant asks the male partner about his preferences and opinions, and after he replies, she implies her values by agreeing or disagreeing. This forms a single topic interaction; eight different interactions are shown in one conversation. Here are the eight topics:

- (Sweet) Do you like parfaits?

- (Drink) Which do you prefer, tea or coffee?

- (Place to live) Which do you prefer, living in the city or the country?

- (Transportation) Which do you prefer, traveling by train or by car?

- (Video entertainment) Which do you prefer, watching movies in theaters or dramas on TV?

- (Reading material) Which do you prefer, reading novels or comic books?

- (School subject) Did you like studying English?

- (Trip) Which do you prefer, domestic trip or overseas trip?

An example of a topic is described below:

> Female: "By the way, which do you prefer, living in the city or the country?"
> Male: "In the city."
> Female: (agree) "Me too. We can get anything we want in cities, can't we?"
> Female: (disagree) "Um, I don't like living in the city because I often feel anxious."

Both assistants always spoke in a calm tone during the conversations.

We prepared three types of conversations with different agreement rates, (50%, 75%, 100%), but the eight topics had the same order. In conversations with 50% agreement, she disagreed on four topics: drink, transportation, reading material, and trip. In the 75% conversation, she disagreed on two topics: transportation and trips. The topics on which she agreed or disagreed were fixed between the subjects, since the impact on the subject's impression when she agrees or disagrees might depend on the subject's interest level in the topic. One video clip consisted of one conversation, so we prepared three video clips with agreement rates of 50%, 75%, and 100%.

Procedure of Experiment and Evaluation Method

After the subjects signed initial consent forms, they evaluated three video clips in a paired comparison manner. For each subject, we initially labeled the three video clips as A, B, and C (e.g., A: 50%, B: 75%, and C: 100%). The pairing of the labels and rates was counterbalanced among the subjects, who filled out questionnaires after they watched the A and B pair. To cancel the order effect in each paired comparison, the subjects watched the videos without restrictions on the watching order or the times.

To verify our hypothesis, we asked about "dialogue motivation" in the questionnaire as follows:

> Question: Whom do you want to talk with, A or B?

In answering the question, the subjects selected from seven choices: 1=Absolutely A, 2=A, 3=Maybe A, 4=Cannot chose, 5=Maybe B, 6=B, 7=Absolutely B. We used the same procedure for the pairs of A-C and B-C pairs. After evaluations of all the videos, we interviewed the subjects about their selection criteria and obtained general comments.

Results

Twelve Japanese people (five men, seven women, average age: 20.5, sd: 1.0) participated in the experiment. We analyzed the results by Scheffe's paired comparison with Nakaya's variation [11]. The estimated scale values are

Agreement Rate	50%	75%	100%
Dialogue Motivation	-0.25	0.67	-0.42

Table 1. Scale values of motivation: human-human dialogue

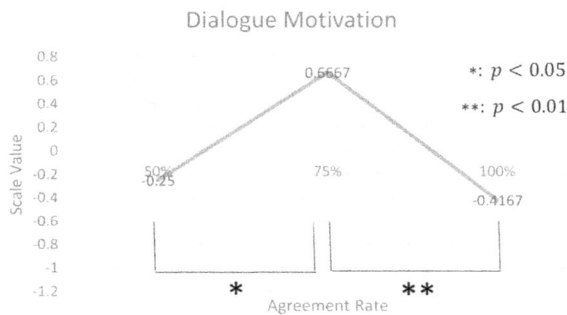

Figure 4. Plot of scale values: human-human dialogue

shown in Table 1. The scale value represents the relative scores of each agreement rate.

We found a significant main effect of the agreement rates ($p < 0.01$). We used the yardstick method to test the differences between the scale values of the agreement rates. We found significant differences between 50% and 75% ($p < 0.05$) and 75% and 100% ($p < 0.01$). The estimated scale values are redisplayed with the significance levels of the differences in Fig. 4.

Discussion

Our result shows that the subjects felt more motivated by the conversation partner who expressed a 75% agreement rate. This supports our hypothesis drawn from the existing studies of Benjafield and Frank, although their studies do not mention motivation for conversation. Here, we consider why the motivation is most strongly stimulated by a dialogue strategy with an agreement of 75%. First, we infer that to evoke motivation, the subjects must feel a sort of affinity with the speaker (i.e., the female assistant in the experiment). They will probably feel an affinity with her when she usually agrees with her partner. However, if she always agrees (i.e., 100% agreement rate), their motivation to talk is decreased since they might think her utterances do not reflect her own thoughts or intentions. Therefore, motivation also requires a belief that a speaker's speech is based on her own thoughts or intentions: a feeling of intentionality. In the viewpoint of information theory, a feeling of intentionality is maximized when the speaker's responses are unpredictable, that is, 50% agreement rate in the dialogue. Consequently, dialogue motivation can most strongly be stimulated by a strategy that is well-balanced with feelings of affinity and intentionality. In other words, subjects prefer dialogues in which they can sense the intentionality produced by their partner's disagreements while maintaining the feeling of affinity that arises from agreements.

Figure 5. Video stimulus: human-android dialogue

Agreement rate	50%	75%	100%
Dialogue motivation	-0.19	0.14	0.048

Table 2. Scale values of motivation: human-android dialogue

EXPERIMENT ON HUMAN-ANDROID DIALOGUE

Experiment Aim

Our experiment that evaluated human-human dialogues supported our hypothesis: a dialogue strategy with an agreement rate between 50% and 100% motivates people to talk. The next question is whether the same strategy motivates people to talk with humanlike robots. The experiment in this session replaced the female assistant with ERICA (Fig. 1) and evaluates the subject motivation to talk with it. The experimental procedure and the script of the video stimulus are the same as in the previous experiment except that ERICA is the speaker in the video clips.

Video Stimuli

In the video, only ERICA appears (Fig. 5), but both its voice and that of the assistant are audible, as in the previous experiment. ERICA's voice is synthesized by a text-to-speech system of HOYA Corporation's VOICE TEXT ERICA[2]. As ERICA is speaking, it moves its lips, head, and torso in synchrony with the prosodic features of its voice. Figure 6 shows ERICA's joint configuration. ERICA's lips (driven by axes 9, 10, and 13), head, and torso (driven by axes 15 and 18) movements are automatically generated from its voice using previously developed systems [9, 16]. It expresses eye blinking and gaze averting at random timing and smiles when it agrees and frowns when it disagrees.

Results

Fourteen Japanese people (eight men, six women, average age: 22.1, sd: 2.0) participated in the experiment. We analyzed the results by Scheffe's paired comparison with Nakaya's variation [11]. The estimated scale values are shown in Table 2.

Scheffe's test revealed no significant main effect of agreement rate ($p = 0.31$). As shown in the plot of the scale values (Fig. 7), the degrees of motivation are almost the same among the agreement rates.

---

[2]http://voicetext.jp/

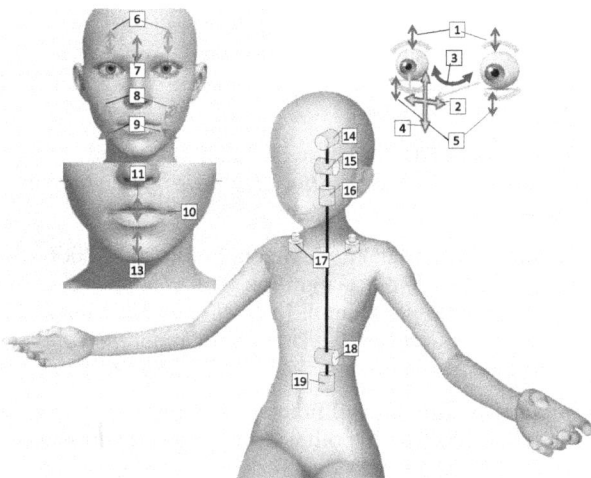

Figure 6. Joint configuration of android ERICA

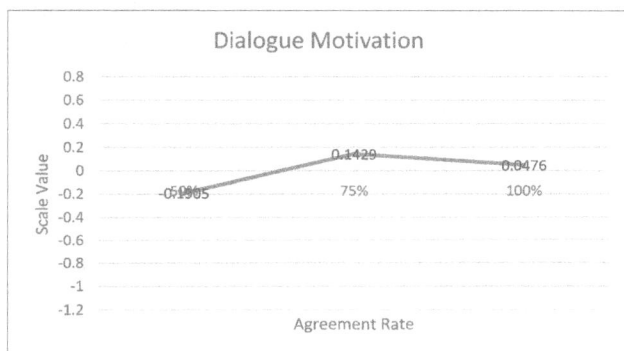

Figure 7. Plot of scale values: human-android dialogue

Discussion

From our result, the android obtained its highest score when it expressed 75% agreement (Fig. 7), although there was no significant difference among the agreement rates, unlike the experimental result with human speakers. In other words, the agreement rate did not influence motivation for speaking with the android. Because the participants did not attribute values to the android, we infer that they did not believe it was speaking based on its own values. Sytsma et al. [19] reported that people do not generally attribute internal states concerning judgments about good or bad things (that is, values) to robots (i.e., non-humans). Considering these results, the higher degree of values we attribute to conversation partners, the more sensitive we are to their words. In other words, we do not receive information or the weight of a partner's words when we believe her speech is not based on her own values. When we develop an android dialogue system, we must design it so that people attribute values to it. As described in Section 1, a dialogue is comprised of agreements and disagreements to the opinions of others. If people cannot attribute values to robots, agreements and disagreements will have little ef-

fect on the impressions of the dialogue. Our future study will conduct additional experiments to verify this idea.

To enhance user motivation is one of the most important themes in non-task-oriented dialogue systems. Some related works have proposed strategies to enhance motivation. Dan et al. [4] suggested a dialogue strategy that depends on user engagement toward robots. Another strategy is topic transition, based on the user's state. Johannes et al. [12] proposed an adaptive spoken language dialogue system that manages dialogues based on user emotions. Emotion recognition can be available for a dialogue strategy to discuss topics in which the user is interested. On the other hand, our study suggests a dialogue strategy that is independent of topics.

The scale values of motivation shown in Fig. 7 only have meaning in comparison within the android conditions. Therefore, our analysis does not reveal whether the motivation of the participants to talk with the android is more or less than with the human speaker. Further experiments must directly compare the motivation to talk to humans and the android, where we need to carefully design an experiment that controls speaker appearances and voices.

The subjects in the experiments reported their motivation by watching video clips, not by talking with conversation partners. Our results are, therefore, based on evaluations from a third person view. We expect that people are more sensitive to the differences in agreement rates when they directly talk with their partner. This expectation must be investigated in future experiments.

The final goal of our study is to develop an autonomous conversational robot that can naturally talk with humans in non-task-oriented conversations. Since this paper only evaluated the motivation to talk, it needs to address other factors that underlie natural human-human conversation in future work.

CONCLUSION

This paper identified a dialogue strategy to motivate conversations by focusing on agreements/disagreements in dialogues. The experimental results showed that subjects felt more motivation for people who talk at a 75% agreement rate where they might saliently feel differences in values. In addition, this paper suggests that dialogue systems need to convince people that utterances are based on their own values (preferences or opinions). This is inferred from the results where the agreement rate did not influence motivation to talk with the android. These findings are useful for designing a spoken dialogue system for a robot that can be continuously used.

Our experiments in this paper are limited because video clips were used and the results with the android could not be directly compared with those on the human speakers. Future works must clarify these limitations and find essential mechanisms for spoken dialogue systems that can be continuously used.

ACKNOWLEDGMENTS

This research was supported by the Japan Science and Technology Agency, ERATO ISHIGURO Symbiotic Human-

Robot Interaction Project. We also thank Mai Isotani for contributing to the experiments.

REFERENCES

1. Kazunori Adachi, Komatani Fumihiro, Shinichi Ueno, Tatsuya Kawahara, and Hiroshi G. Okuno. 2003. Flexible spoken dialogue system based on user models and dynamic generation of VoiceXML scripts. In *Proc. of the 4th SIGdial Workshop on Discourse and Dialogue*. 87–96.

2. John Benjafield and J. Adams-Webber. 1976. The golden section hypothesis. *British Journal of Psychology* 67, 1 (1976), 11–15.

3. John Benjafield and T. R. G. Green. 1978. Golden section relations in interpersonal judgement. *British Journal of Psychology* 69, 1 (1978), 25–35.

4. Dan Bohus and Eric Horvitz. 2009. Models for multiparty engagement in open-world dialog. In *Proceedings of the SIGDIAL 2009 Conference: The 10th Annual Meeting of the Special Interest Group on Discourse and Dialogue*. Association for Computational Linguistics, 225–234.

5. Helmar G. Frank. 1964. *Kybernetische analysen subjektiver sachverhalte [Cybernetics analysis of subjective states]*. Verlag Schnelle, Quickborn.

6. Shinya Fujie, Yasushi Ejiri, Hideaki Kikuchi, and Tetsunori Kobayashi. 2006. Recognition of positive/negative attitude and its application to a spoken dialogue system. *Systems and Computers in Japan* 37, 12 (2006), 45–55.

7. John Mordechai Gottman. 1994. *What predicts divorce?: The relationship between marital processes and marital outcomes*. Lawrence Erlbaum Associates, Hillsdale, New Jersey.

8. Ryuichiro Higashinaka, Nozomi Kobayashi, Toru Hirano, Chiaki Miyazaki, Toyomi Meguro, Toshiro Makino, and Yoshihiro Matsuo. 2014. Syntactic filtering and content-based retrieval of Twitter sentences for the generation of system utterances in dialogue systems. In *Proc. of the International Workshop Series on Spoken Dialogue Systems Technology*. 113–123.

9. Carlos T. Ishi, Chaoran Liu, Hiroshi Ishiguro, and Norihiro Hagita. 2012. Evaluation of formant-based lip motion generation in tele-operated humanoid robots. In *Proc. of the IEEE/RSJ International Conference on Intelligent Robots and Systems*. 2377–2382.

10. Ihara Masayuki and Kobayashi Minoru. 2005. Questionnaire survey on over/under-estimating for agreement/disagreement. *IEICE Technical Report MVE* 105, 256 (2005), 25–28.

11. S. Nakaya. 1970. Variation of Scheffe's Paired Comparison. In *Proc. of the 11th Sensory Evaluation Convention*. 1–12. (in Japanese).

12. Johannes Pittermann and Angela Pittermann. 2006. Integrating emotion recognition into an adaptive spoken language dialogue system. In *Intelligent Environments, 2006. IE 06. 2nd IET International Conference on Intelligent Environments*, Vol. 1. IET, 197–202.

13. Michael A. Rigdon and Franz R. Epting. 1982. A test of the golden section hypothesis with elicited constructs. *Journal of Personality and Social Psychology* 43, 5 (1982), 1080–1087.

14. Milton Rokeach. 1973. *The nature of human values*. Free press, New York.

15. S. Romany and J. Adams-Webber. 1981. The golden section hypothesis from a developmental perspective. *Social Behavior and Personality* 9, 1 (1981), 89–92.

16. Kurima Sakai, Takashi Minato, Carlos T. Ishi, and Hiroshi Ishiguro. 2015. Speech Driven Trunk Motion Generating System Based on Physical Constraint. In *JSAI Technical Report, SIG-Challenge-043-05*. 23–28. (in Japanese).

17. Benjamin Shalit. 1980. The golden section relation in the evaluation of environmental factors. *British Journal of Psychology* 71, 1 (1980), 39–42.

18. Hidenobu Sumioka, Shuichi Nishio, Takashi Minato, Ryuji Yamazaki, and Hiroshi Ishiguro. 2014. Minimal human design approach for sonzai-kan media: Investigation of a feeling of human presence. *Cognitive computation* 6, 4 (2014), 760–774.

19. Justin Sytsma and Edouard Machery. 2010. Two conceptions of subjective experience. *Philosophical Studies* 151, 2 (2010), 299–327.

20. Joseph Weizenbaum. 1966. ELIZA—a computer program for the study of natural language communication between man and machine. *Commun. ACM* 9, 1 (1966), 36–45.

Alignment Approach Comparison between Implicit and Explicit Suggestions in Object Reference Conversations

Mitsuhiko Kimoto
ATR-IRC, Doshisha Univ.
Kyoto, 619-0288, Japan
kimoto2013@sil.doshisha.ac.jp

Takamasa Iio
ATR-IRC, Osaka Univ.
Kyoto, 619-0288, Japan
iio@atr.jp

Masahiro Shiomi
ATR-IRC
Kyoto, 619-0288, Japan
m-shiomi@atr.jp

Ivan Tanev
Doshisha Univ.
Kyoto, 602-8580, Japan
itanev@mail.doshisha.ac.jp

Katsunori Shimohara
Doshisha Univ.
Kyoto, 602-8580, Japan
kshimoha@mail.doshisha.ac.jp

Norihiro Hagita
ATR-IRC
Kyoto, 619-0288, Japan
hagita@atr.jp

ABSTRACT

The recognition of an indicated object by an interacting person is an essential function for a robot that acts in daily environments. To improve recognition accuracy, clarifying the goal of the indicating behaviors is needed. For this purpose, we experimentally compared two kinds of interaction strategies: a robot that explicitly provides instructions to people about how to refer to objects or a robot that implicitly aligns with the people's indicating behaviors. Even though our results showed that participants evaluated the implicit approach to be more natural than the explicit approach, the recognition performances of the two approaches were not significantly different.

Author Keywords
Human-robot interaction; object recognition; alignment

ACM Classification Keywords
H.5.2. User Interfaces – *Interaction styles*.

INTRODUCTION

Social robots in human society need to recognize the objects indicated by users (Figure 1). Various approaches have been proposed to recognize such objects based on user utterances and pointing gestures [1,2,3,4]. Nickel et al. used the 3D positions of a head and hands as well as the head's orientation to recognize pointing gestures in object references [1]. Schauerte et al. integrated speech and pointing gesture recognition by image processing [2].

Even though such techniques improve the sensing capabilities of robots, recognizing the objects indicated by users remains difficult because user references are often

ambiguous during conversations. People enjoy enormous variability in their lexical choices in conversations [5]. Such variability degrades the recognition performance because they might not always use the words contained in a database that stores an object's characteristics, and they also do not always use enough words to identify an object [6]. Even if robots can perfectly recognize speech or pointing gestures, they might not distinguish an object indicated by humans from other objects.

How does a robot encourage a user to clarify his references? We consider two approaches: explicit and implicit. In the first approach, a robot explicitly instructs the person how to refer to objects. We call this the *explicit instruction approach*. For example, the robot explicitly asks a user, "Please describe the object's name, color, and size when pointing at it." The ambiguity of the user's references is expected to decrease if she accepts that request.

In the other approach, the robots implicitly aligns with the people's indicating behaviors. We call this the *implicit alignment approach*. For example, the robot implicitly elicits pointing gestures and lexical expressions contained in the robot's database from a user. When a person is talking with an addressee, she tends to repeat the same lexical [7], syntax [8], expression choice [9], and body movements [10,11] as the addressee. This phenomenon, called alignment, occurs in interactions not only between humans but also between a human and artificial media like spoken dialogue systems [13,14,15,16,17] and robots

HAI '16, October 04-07, 2016, Biopolis, Singapore
© 2016 ACM. ISBN 978-1-4503-4508-8/16/10...$15.00
DOI: http://dx.doi.org/10.1145/2974804.2974814

Figure 1. Robot recognizes an object indicated by a user

[18,19]. Through alignment, humans narrow down huge lexical choices and elicit terms, indications, or iconic gestures to naturally identify objects for their interlocutors. Inspired by these alignment findings, some research proposed robotic system that aimed to improve the recognition performance of objects indicated by a user by eliciting the user's references by alignment [20].

However, it remains unknown which approach more effectively decreases ambiguity and improves performance. Moreover, social robots should choose a more appropriate approach by considering not only the recognition performance of the indicated objects but also the user's impression of the interaction. Even though the performance might be increased by either approach, such performance gain becomes worthless if the users hesitate to interact with a robot by the chosen approach and vice versa.

This paper addresses whether the explicit instruction approach or the implicit alignment approach is better for object recognition contexts in conversations with people. We developed a robot system that recognizes objects indicated by a user and experimentally compared the two approaches with our system. Based on the experiment results, we discuss the effectiveness of the approaches.

INTERACTION DESIGN

Object Reference Conversation

To investigate the effect of these two approaches on object reference recognition, we used an interaction called object reference conversations (Figure 2). Such conversations focus on *confirmation behavior*, which is often observed in human-human communication. For example, when person A asks person B to bring a magazine, she is referring to a specific magazine: "Bring that magazine to me." If person B cannot confidently understand which magazine was being referenced, she is likely to ask for confirmation: "This one?" Such conversations are already being used in human-robot interaction research fields to explore several research purposes, including lexical entrainment in human-robot interaction [18] and the implementation of the implicit alignment of reference behaviors [20].

The following are the details of object reference conversations. First, a robot asks a person to refer to an object in an environment where several objects are arranged (*Ask*). Next, she refers to an object (*Refer*), and the robot

Figure 2. Object reference conversation: white and black boxes denote robot and human turns

Figure 3. Example of explicit robot instructions: robot explicitly instructs how to refer to objects by encouraging interlocutor to use information that was missing in previous references

confirms the object to which she referred (*Confirm*). Then she answers whether the object confirmed by the robot is correct (*Answer*).

Explicit Instruction Approach

Explicit instruction requires the information that the robot wants the interlocutors to use for recognizing the indicated object, because it limits the references and reduces unexpected references. If an interlocutor refers to an object as the robot instructed, the robot will probably recognize it with high performance. A robot should also give instructions about how to refer to objects in such a way that asks an interlocutor to make a reference that includes as much information as possible that the robot can recognize. If the robot's recognition fails partly because of noise, insufficient speech volume, unclear pointing gestures, and so on, references that include sufficient information increase the chances that the robot will correctly recognize the referenced object.

In addition, if the interlocutor does not follow the robot instructions, the robot should request that she use all of the instructed information for the object references. This suggestion reminds the interlocutor of the instructions and encourages her to use all of the information in subsequent conversations.

Based on these considerations, we designed the explicit instructions of the reference behavior as follows. A robot provides instructions about how to refer to objects in a way that asks the interlocutors to make a reference that includes as much information as possible and requests that the interlocutor use the information that was missing from the previous references. Figure 3 shows an example of explicit instructions from a robot.

Implicit Alignment Approach

We adopted the implicit alignment approach proposed by Kimoto et al. [20]. This approach exploits alignment in object reference conversations. Based on these three alignment phenomena, lexical alignment, gestural alignment, and alignment inhibition, they designed robot behavior where the robot should use minimum information for distinguishing among objects in the environment. Alignment inhibition is the phenomenon of alignment

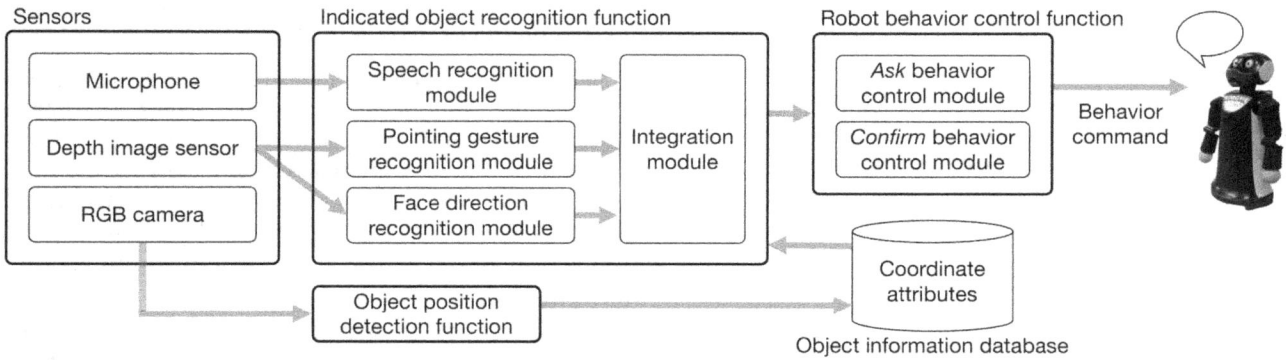

Figure 5. System architecture to recognize objects indicated by user

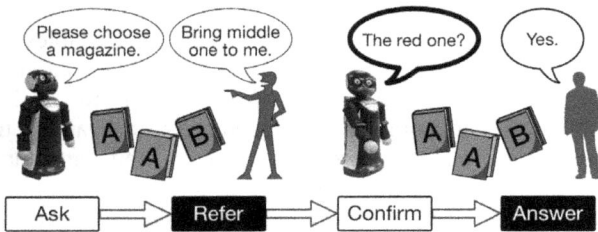

Figure 4. Example of object reference conversation with implicit alignment approach: robot confirmed indicated object using minimum information for distinguishing objects

becoming substandard in conversations in some cases. Through this design, humans learn to use references that include enough information to identify the objects by reducing the alignment inhibitions. They implemented this design in the *Confirm* part in the object reference conversation described in the previous section. Their experimental results suggested the possibility of improving the recognition performance by the implicit alignment of reference behavior. However, even though they discussed the effectiveness of reference behavior, they didn't evaluate user's impression of the interaction.

Therefore, we used this design of robot behavior as an implicit alignment of reference behavior; a robot should make confirmations that contain minimum information for distinguishing objects. Figure 4 shows an example of an object reference conversation with an implicit alignment approach.

SYSTEM
Figure 5 shows the architecture of our developed system that recognizes the objects indicated by a user. We developed it by referring to past work that implemented the implicit alignment of reference behaviors for object reference conversations [20]. The system consists of five parts: sensors, an object position detection function, an indicated object recognition function, an object information database, and a robot behavior control function. First, the system detects the positions of the objects arranged in the

environment and saves them in the object information database. When a user refers to an object, the indicated object recognition function recognizes the interlocutor's reference behavior and estimates the indicated object. The robot behavior control function chooses a robot behavior that corresponds to the implemented approach and sends a behavior command to the robot. The robot confirms the indicated object and asks an interlocutor to refer to it in the next conversation in a way decided by the robot behavior control function.

The system can also have object reference conversations as a basic function. In its *Ask* and *Confirm* parts, the robot performs a behavior that corresponds to which approach is used by the robot.

Robot
In this study, we used Robovie-R ver.2, which is a humanoid robot developed by the Intelligent Robotics and Communication Labs, ATR, that has a human-like upper body designed for communication with humans. The speaker in its mouth can output recorded sound files from the internally-controlled PC located in its body. We used XIMERA for speech synthesis [21]. It has three DOFs for its neck and four DOFs for each arm. Its body has sufficient expressive ability for object reference conversations. It is 1100 mm tall, 560 mm wide, 500 mm deep, and weighs about 57 kg.

Object Position Detection Function
The object position detection function locates the positions of the objects arranged in the environment through AR-markers and saves its ID and positions in the object information database. The AR-markers are read using an RGB camera in the ceiling. We previously saved the attributes of the objects in the database, and the system can extract the attributes of objects from it by IDs.

Indicated Object Recognition Function
To develop this function, we implemented an algorithm [20] that combines the results of speech recognition, pointing gesture recognition, and face direction recognition. Note that this past work [20] only used the speech and pointing gesture recognition results; in this work we added

face direction features to increase the performance of the object reference recognition.

Speech Recognition

The speech recognition module receives human speech that refers to an object and outputs the normalized reference likelihood of each object based on speech recognition. To calculate the likelihood, we used a previously proposed method [20] that uses the number of attributes in the human speech, which is captured by a microphone attached to the human's collar. In this system, we used a speech recognition engine called Julius, which gives good performance in Japanese [22].

Pointing Gesture Recognition

The pointing gesture recognition module obtains the body frame data from a depth image sensor called Kinect for Windows v2 and outputs the normalized reference likelihood of each object based on pointing gesture recognition. We modeled the likelihood as the difference from the pointing vector (between the human head and the tip of the human hand) to a vector between the human head and an object with a normal distribution function $N(0, 1)$.

Face Direction Recognition

The face direction recognition module obtains the face direction vector from the depth image sensor and outputs the reference likelihood based on the face direction recognition. We modeled the likelihood based on an angle parallel to the plane of the floor between the face direction vector and a vector between a human head and an object. If the vector is less than 110 degrees, the person is considered to be viewing the object; its likelihood is 1, otherwise 0. This is because a human's field of view is 110 degrees at most [23]. The likelihoods are finally normalized from 0 to 1.

Integration

The integration module merges the reference likelihoods of the speech and both the pointing gesture and face direction recognitions. These three likelihoods are summed and normalized based on previous work [20]. The object with the highest likelihood is estimated to be the object indicated by the interlocutor.

Robot Behavior Control Function

The robot behavior control function determines how the robot confirms the indicated object (*Confirm* behavior) and how it asks an interlocutor to refer to an object (*Ask* behavior) in subsequent conversations. The conversation contents of the *Confirm* and *Ask* behaviors reflect whether the explicit instruction approach or the implicit alignment approach is used.

When using the explicit instruction approach, this function chooses the *Ask* behavior and adopts the explicit instruction approach, and the robot explicitly provides instructions about how to refer to objects. The *Confirm* behavior does not adopt a particular approach, and the robot confirms the indicated object by pointing and verifying all of the information about the indicated object.

When using the implicit alignment approach, this function chooses the *Confirm* behavior and adopts the implicit alignment approach, and the robot confirms the indicated object with minimum information for distinguishing among objects. The *Ask* behavior does not adopt a particular approach, and the robot does not explicitly instruct how to make references.

EXPERIMENT

We experimentally compared the two interactive approaches: explicit instruction and implicit alignment.

Hypotheses

If the robot explicitly instructs a particular reference way, the interlocutor knows how to refer to an object and may use it in object reference conversation. This enables the robot to recognize the indicated objects more accurately. However, referencing to an object based on explicit instruction is not common in daily conversations, and so the interlocutor might deem the conversation unnatural. Similarly, the interlocutor might feel the conversation is a mental load and troublesome because of the unaccustomed conversations.

On the other hand, if there is no explicit instruction about the reference way, the interlocutor might not know how to refer to an object, complicating the robot's ability to recognize indicated objects. However, the interlocutor might feel the conversation is more natural than explicit instructions. Based on these considerations, we made the following two hypotheses:

Hypothesis 1: Conversations with the implicit alignment approach will be perceived as a less mental load, less troublesome, and more natural by the interlocutor than conversations with the explicit instruction approach.

Hypothesis 2: Object reference recognition performance of the conversations with the explicit instruction approach will outperform that of conversations with the implicit alignment approach.

Conditions

We controlled an approach that was applied to our developed system (applied approach factor).

The applied approach factor had two levels: explicit instruction and implicit alignment. Both were respectively applied to the *Ask* and *Confirm* parts of the object reference conversation described in the interaction design section. The applied approach factor was a within-participant condition. In this experiment, we compared the method of robot's speech and there was no difference in the way to recognize interlocutor's reference behavior and estimate the indicated object.

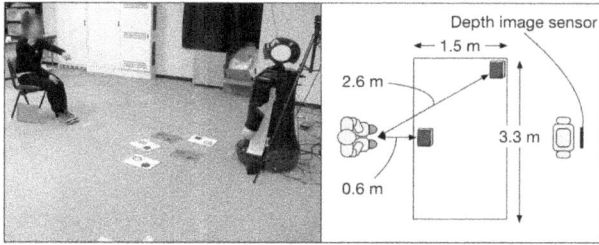

Figure 6. Experimental environment

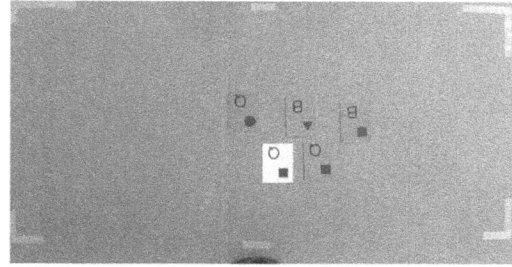

Figure 7. Example of book arrangement

Explicit Instruction Condition

In the explicit instruction condition, the robot gives instructions about how to refer to objects in a way that asks interlocutors to make a reference that includes as much information as possible with comments that encourage the interlocutor to use the information missing in the *Ask* part.

The speech format of the explicit instructions includes two sentences. The first sentence is used every time; the second sentence is only used when a participant did not use all of the information requested by the first sentence in the previous conversation.

For example, the robot says, "Can you refer to a book using its color, a shape on its cover, a letter on its cover as well as by pointing and looking at it? Please refer to a letter and point."

In the *Confirm* part of this condition, since the robot confirmed the objects with all of the information, it gave every attribute of an object and pointed during the confirmations.

Implicit Alignment Condition

In the implicit alignment condition, unlike the explicit instruction condition, the robot does not explicitly provide instructions about the reference way; it just says, "Please choose a book" in the *Ask* part.

On the other hand, in the *Confirm* part the robot utters a different sentence. For this purpose, we implemented an implicit alignment design for the reference behavior. In this condition, the robot confirmed the object with minimum information for distinguishing among objects; the confirmations were based on the implicit alignment approach of references proposed by Kimoto et al. [20]. This approach determines robot's object reference behaviors, i.e., pointing behavior and speech, by considering objects' position relationships and characteristics. A robot used pointing gesture when it would be useful to decrease candidates of referenced objects. For example, if robot's pointing gesture would become vague to an interlocutor, the robot did not use the gesture.

The speech format of the confirmations is the sequence of the attributes of objects. For example, the robot says, "That blue book with a circle on its cover?" or "That yellow book?"

Environment

Figure 6 shows the environment. The participants were seated in front of the robot. Five objects were placed in a 1.5 m by 3.3 m rectangular area between the robot and the participant. The books were grouped close together without overlapping. These objects were approximately 0.6-2.6 m from the participants.

We controlled the attributes of the books by following the past research work which focused on object reference conversations [20]. All books were 21 cm by 27.5 cm. Their attributes were color and the shape and the letter on the cover. There were three colors: red, blue, or yellow. Three shapes were placed on the book covers: a circle, a triangle, or a square. There were two letters: Q and B. We prepared 18 books to satisfy all combinations of the attributes.

Procedure

We conducted our experiment as follows. First, we explained it to participants who signed consent forms. Next, we gave them the following oral instructions: "The robot can recognize human speech, pointing gestures, and face direction. The robot will ask you to indicate a book. Indicate it as if you were dealing with a person."

After the instructions, the participants selected five books among the 18 and arranged them based on the experimenter's instruction: "Please arrange the books in one place." An example of the arrangement is shown in Figure 7. After that the participant repeated the object reference conversations ten times. We call this set of ten object references the *conversation sessions*, which were conducted in both applied approach conditions: explicit instruction and implicit alignment. The participants answered questionnaires about their impressions of the conversations after each conversation session. We counterbalanced the order of the interactive approach conditions.

Participants

Twenty (ten females and ten males) native Japanese speakers whose average age was 35.5 (*SD* = 9.9) participated in our experiment.

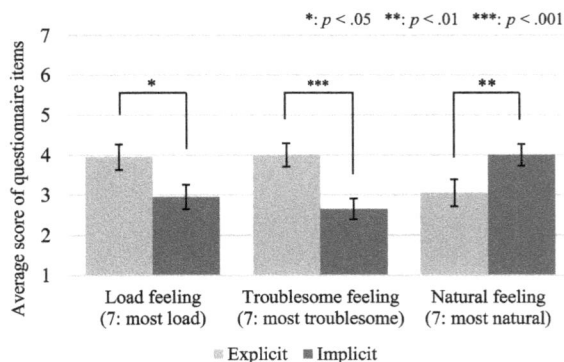

Figure 8. Impression of conversation (mean ± *SE*)

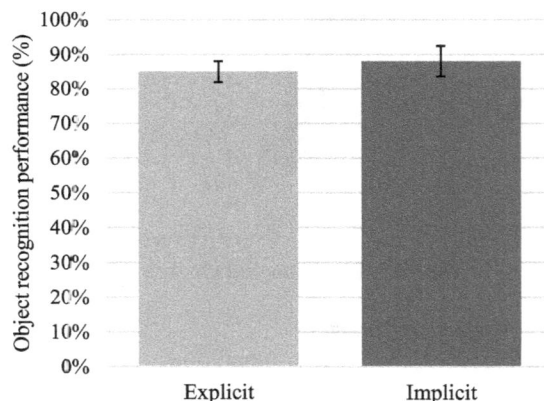

Figure 9. Object recognition performance (mean ± *SE*)

Measurement

Impression of Conversations

To investigate the participant's impressions of the conversations, we prepared the following three questionnaire items and evaluated them on a 7-point scale:

1. The conversation with the robot was a mental load (load feeling).

2. The conversation with the robot was troublesome (troublesome feeling).

3. The conversation with the robot was natural (natural feeling).

Recognition Performance

The recognition performance is the success rate of the object reference recognition. We calculated it from the number of object references correctly recognized by the robot per conversation session, which was a set of ten object reference recognitions.

RESULTS

Verification of Hypothesis 1

Figure 8 shows the results of the questionnaire items. To verify the effect of each condition, we conducted a paired t-test for each of the questionnaire items. For the load feeling, we found a significant difference among the conditions ($t(19) = 2.1$, $p = .049$, $d = .72$). For the troublesome feeling, we found a significant difference among the conditions ($t(19) = 4.2$, $p < .001$, $d = 1.1$). For the natural feeling, we also found a significant difference among the conditions ($t(19) = -3.0$, $p = .008$, $d = .70$). These results supported Hypothesis 1.

Verification of Hypothesis 2

Figure 9 shows the recognition performance results. To verify the effect of each condition, we conducted a paired t-test and found no significant difference between the two interactive approach conditions ($t(19) = -.58$, $p = .57$, $d = .18$). This result indicated that Hypothesis 2 was not supported.

DISCUSSION

Interpretation of Results

From the experiment results, the interlocutor impressions of the conversations with the implicit alignment approach were perceived to be significantly a less mental load, less troublesome, and more natural than the explicit instruction approach. Accordingly, explicit instruction is not natural for people and created feelings of uneasy interaction in the interlocutors.

We identified no significant difference in the recognition performances between the two approaches. This result can be interpreted in two ways. First, the implicit alignment approach improved the recognition performance at the same level as the explicit instruction approach. Although we cannot verify the effects of the implicit alignment approach in our experimental settings, a counter condition of an implicit alignment approach is not a no-implicit alignment approach but an explicit instruction approach, and the implicit alignment approach probably improves the recognition performance, as argued by past work [20].

Second, the explicit instruction approach did not improve the recognition performance very much. We predicted that the interlocutors would refer to an object as the robot instructed; but in the experiment 28% of references in the explicit instruction condition did not follow the robot's instructions. Some instructed with information that was dropped out, for example, a pointing gesture and a color. Explicit instruction is probably not an effective way to induce interlocutors to encourage users to adopt clear but recognizable references.

For these reasons, we conclude that the implicit alignment approach is better than the explicit instruction approach for object recognition contexts in conversations with people. Our findings are useful for designing interactions for social robots because good impressions of conversations are important for them because they often interact with people. These findings can be integrated not only for object recognition contexts but also for many other contexts since determining whether to use an explicit or implicit approach is conceivable in other contexts.

Limitation

We conducted this experiment's study in a limited situation. The participants referred to objects with only three features: color, a geometric shape, and a letter. In real environments, the features of objects are not limited and obviously influence the reference ways. But since the interaction way between a robot and an interlocutor does not depend on features, our findings are general for other objects.

CONCLUSION

In this study, we focused on two interactive approaches for object recognition contexts in conversations with people: explicit instruction and implicit alignment. We developed a system that recognized the indicated objects by integrating the speech, pointing, and face direction recognition results and experimentally compared the performance and feeling perspectives between the two interactive approaches.

Experimental results indicated that the participants perceived the conversations with the implicit alignment approach to be a less mental load, less troublesome, and more natural than the explicit instruction approach. The overall impression of the conversations with the implicit alignment approach exceeded the explicit instruction approach. The object reference recognition performance did not differ between the two approaches, indicating that the implicit alignment approach is better than the explicit instruction approach for object recognition contexts in conversations with people. We believe that our findings are useful for the design interaction of social robots that frequently interact with people.

ACKNOWLEDGMENTS

This research work was supported by JSPS KAKENHI Grant Number 15H05322, 16K12505, and 15K16075.

REFERENCES

1. Kai Nickel and Rainer Stiefelhagen, 2007. Visual recognition of pointing gestures for human–robot interaction. *Image and Vision Computing 25*, 12: 1875-1884.

2. Boris Schauerte and Gernot A. Fink, 2010. Focusing computational visual attention in multi-modal human-robot interaction. In *Proceedings of the International Conference on Multimodal Interfaces and the Workshop on Machine Learning for Multimodal Interaction*, 1-8. http://dx.doi.org/10.1145/1891903.1891912

3. J. Richarz, T. Plotz, and G. A. Fink, 2008. Real-time detection and interpretation of 3D deictic gestures for interactionwith an intelligent environment. In *Proceedings of the Pattern Recognition, 2008. ICPR 2008. 19th International Conference on*, 1-4. http://dx.doi.org/10.1109/ICPR.2008.4761609

4. Osamu Sugiyama, Takayuki Kanda, Michita Imai, Hiroshi Ishiguro, Norihiro Hagita, and Yuichiro Anzai, 2006. Humanlike conversation with gestures and verbal cues based on a three-layer attention-drawing model. *Connection Science 18*, 4: 379-402.

5. G. W. Furnas, T. K. Landauer, L. M. Gomez, and S. T. Dumais, 1987. The vocabulary problem in human-system communication. *Commun. ACM 30*, 11: 964-971.

6. Shinozawa Kazuhiko, Miyashita Takahiro, Kakio Masayuki, and N. Hagita, 2007. User specification method and humanoid confirmation behavior. In *Proceedings of the 2007 7th IEEE-RAS International Conference on Humanoid Robots*, 366-370. http://dx.doi.org/10.1109/ICHR.2007.4813895

7. S. E. Brennan and H. H. Clark, 1996. Conceptual pacts and lexical choice in conversation. *J Exp Psychol Learn Mem Cogn 22*, 6: 1482-1493.

8. H. P. Branigan, M. J. Pickering, and A. A. Cleland, 2000. Syntactic co-ordination in dialogue. *Cognition 75*, 2: B13-25.

9. Simon Garrod and Anthony Anderson, 1987. Saying what you mean in dialogue: A study in conceptual and semantic co-ordination. Cognition 27, 2: 181-218.

10. Albert E. Scheflen, 1964. The Significance of Posture in Communication Systems. *Psychiatry 27*, 4: 316-331.

11. Adam Kendon, 1970. Movement coordination in social interaction: Some examples described. *Acta Psychologica 32*: 101-125.

12. T. L. Chartrand and J. A. Bargh, 1999. The chameleon effect: the perception-behavior link and social interaction. *J Pers Soc Psychol 76*, 6: 893-910.

13. Holly P Branigan, Martin J Pickering, Jamie Pearson, Janet F McLean, and Clifford Nass, 2003. Syntactic alignment between computers and people: The role of belief about mental states. In *Proceedings of the Twenty-fifth Annual Conference of the Cognitive Science Society*, 186-191.

14. Susan E Brennan, 1996. Lexical entrainment in spontaneous dialog. In *Proceedings of the 1996 International Symposium on Spoken Dialogue*, 41-44.

15. Joakim Gustafson, Anette Larsson, Rolf Carlson, and K Hellman, 1997. How do system questions influence lexical choices in user answers? In *Proceedings of the Eurospeech*.

16. Jamie Pearson, Jiang Hu, Holly P. Branigan, Martin J. Pickering, and Clifford I. Nass, 2006. Adaptive language behavior in HCI: how expectations and beliefs about a system affect users' word choice. In *Proceedings of the SIGCHI Conference on Human Factors in Computing Systems*, 1177-1180. http://dx.doi.org/10.1145/1124772.1124948

17. Stefanie Tomko and Roni Rosenfeld, 2004. Shaping spoken input in user-initiative systems. In *Proceedings of the 8th International Conference on Spoken Language Processing*.

18. Takamasa Iio, Masahiro Shiomi, Kazuhiko Shinozawa, Katsunori Shimohara, Mitsunori Miki, and Norihiro Hagita, 2015. Lexical Entrainment in Human Robot Interaction. *International Journal of Social Robotics 7*, 2: 253-263.

19. Takamasa Iio, Masahiro Shiomi, Kazuhiko Shinozawa, Takaaki Akimoto, Katsunori Shimohara, and Norihiro Hagita, 2011. Investigating Entrainment of People's Pointing Gestures by Robot's Gestures Using a WOZ Method. *International Journal of Social Robotics 3*, 4: 405-414.

20. Mitsuhiko Kimoto, Takamasa Iio, Masahiro Shiomi, Ivan Tanev, Katsunori Shimohara, and Norihiro Hagita, 2015. Improvement of object reference recognition through human robot alignment. In *Proceedings of the Robot and Human Interactive Communication (RO-MAN), 2015 24th IEEE International Symposium on*, 337-342. http://dx.doi.org/10.1109/ROMAN.2015.7333672

21. Hisashi Kawai, Tomoki Toda, Jinfu Ni, Minoru Tsuzaki, and Keiichi Tokuda, 2004. XIMERA: A new TTS from ATR based on corpus-based technologies. In *Proceedings of the Fifth ISCA Workshop on Speech Synthesis*.

22. Akinobu Lee, Tatsuya Kawahara, and Shuji Doshita, 1998. An efficient two-pass search algorithm using word trellis index. In *Proceedings of the ICSLP'98*, 1831-1834.

23. S.J. Ryan, A.P. Schachat, C.P. Wilkinson, D.R. Hinton, S.V.R. Sadda, and P. Wiedemann, 2012. *Retina*. Elsevier Health Sciences.

Communication Cues in Human-Robot Touch Interaction

Takahiro Hirano
ATR-IRC, Doshisha Univ.
Kyoto, 619-0288, Japan
hirano2015@sil.doshisha.ac.jp

Masahiro Shiomi
ATR-IRC
Kyoto, 619-0288, Japan
m-shiomi@atr.jp

Takamasa Iio
ATR-IRC, Osaka Univ.
Kyoto, 619-0288, Japan
iio@atr.jp

Mitsuhiko Kimoto, Takuya Nagashio, Ivan Tanev, Katsunori Shimohara
Doshisha University
Kyoto, 602-8580, Japan
{kimoto2013, nagashio2015, itanev, kshimoha}@mail.doshisha.ac.jp

Norihiro Hagita
ATR-IRC
Kyoto, 619-0288, Japan
hagita @atr.jp

ABSTRACT

Haptic interaction is a key capability for social robots that closely interact with people in daily environments. Such human communication cues as gaze behaviors make haptic interaction look natural. Since the purpose of this study is to increase human-robot touch interaction, we conducted an experiment with 20 participants who interacted with a robot with different combinations of gaze behaviors and touch styles. The experimental results showed that both gaze behaviors and touch styles influence the changes in the perceived feelings of touch interaction with a robot.

Author Keywords
Robot touch; social robot

ACM Classification Keywords
H.5.2. User Interfaces – *Interaction styles*

INTRODUCTION

Physical interaction, particularly haptic interaction, is one promising research path in the human-agent interaction research field. Because of its physical existence, which is an important advantage enjoyed by robots over CG agents, robots can communicate with people through haptic interactions that are well known to change the behaviors of others and facilitate their efforts in human science literatures [1-7]. In the research field of human-robot interaction, various research works have reported similar effects of haptic interaction between robots and people: mental therapy [8], increasing motivation [9], and attitude changes by touch [10-12].

However, these past research works on haptic interaction with robots mainly focused on the influences to people's feelings or behavior changes by physical interaction. In other words, they focused less on the communication cues

of robots in such touch interactions. The following communication cues except touch interactions have been thoroughly investigated: gaze behavior in such contexts as approaching [13], encounter situation [14, 15], object-transfer [16, 17], and conversations [18-21]. We believe that this knowledge will increase the understanding of communication cues in human-robot touch interaction.

In this paper we deal with a robot's gaze as a major communication cue that increases the naturalness of touch interaction (Figure 1). We investigate which kinds of touching styles (touching a robot, touched by a robot, and mutual touch) are important to make touch interaction more natural.

EXPERIMENT DESIGN

In this section, first we describe the details of the robot used in the experiment, because physical characteristics, such as appearance and size, are important for the design of communication cues. Next, we refer to related works about experiment designs, i.e., gaze behavior and touch styles in human-robot interaction, and describe the detailed designs of both gaze behaviors and touch styles that will be used in the experiment.

Robot

We used a personal humanoid robot for our research, which is developed by Softbank (Fig.1). It has 20 DOFs: two DOFs in its head, shoulders, elbows and waist, one DOF for wrists, hands, and knee, and three DOFs for its wheels. The robot is 121 cm tall and is equipped with microphones, cameras, a depth sensor, touch sensors, and so on. It has five fingers on its hands.

HAI '16, October 04-07, 2016, Biopolis, Singapore
© 2016 ACM. ISBN 978-1-4503-4508-8/16/10 $15.00
DOI: http://dx.doi.org/10.1145/2974804.2974809

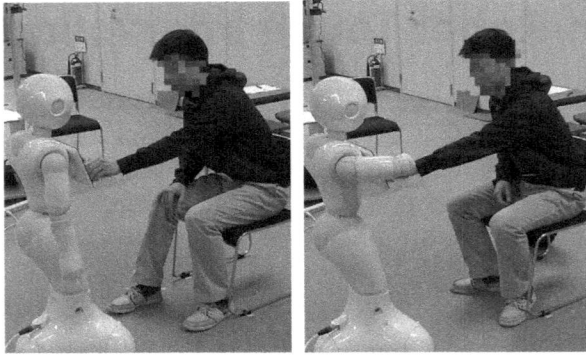

Fig. 1 Robot touches a person

Fig. 2 Pepper's gaze behavior: looking at participant's face (left) and participant's hand (right)

Gaze design

Gaze behavior is essential for natural communication between people and such anthropomorphic agents as robots. Many research works have investigated gaze behaviors in human-robot interaction [13-21]. For example, Satake et al. developed a natural approaching model for a mobile social robot. While approaching, the robot's gaze behavior is important to share its intention to approach the target [13]. Hayashi et al. focused on encounter interactions in public environments where people and robots walk around and modeled the behaviors of human experts (guards) to show the robot's availability through gaze and roaming paths [14]. Seki et al., which also focused on a situation where a robot initiates a conversation with a person, included gaze behaviors to make interactions look more natural [15]. These research works deal with interactions before the robot meets people; of course, studies have also focused on the interaction after the robot meets people [18-21] in non-haptic interaction contexts, such as approaching and providing information.

To design gaze behaviors in touch interaction, we focused on a situation where a robot hands an item to people, because in such situations, the hands of the robot and the participants become closer like in actual touch interactions. We employed several gaze behaviors from the literature

about hand-over research works, i.e., Gharb et al. who investigated the effects of gaze cues in hand-over situations [16]. According to their work, we investigated two kinds of gaze behaviors during haptic interactions: *face-only* and *face-hand-face*. We employed these two behaviors because the face-hand-face behavior was the most preferred pattern by participants in hand-over situations, and the face-only behavior was low evaluations in hand-over situations, which can be used as a baseline condition.

Face-only
In this behavior, the robot looks at the interacting person's face during the touch (Fig. 2, left).

Face-hand-face
In this behavior, the robot looks at the interacting person's face first (Fig. 2, left), then at the person's hand (Fig. 2, right), and finally at the person's face again (Fig. 2, left). The duration of the gaze behaviors was 2250 ms, like in Gharb's work [16].

Touch design

Past research works related to touch interaction investigated three touch styles: touching a robot, touched by a robot, and mutual touch between a person and a robot. Researchers have mainly investigated the "touching a robot" style. For example, Shibata et al. developed a seal robot named Paro for therapy with senior citizens through interaction, including touching the robot [8]. The "touching a robot" style is also used to recognize touch interaction [22-24], where Cooney used inertia sensors to recognize full-body gestures by haptic interactions toward a humanoid robot [24].

A few research works investigated the effects of being "touched by a robot." For example, Cramer et al. argued that a touch behavior by a robot decreases machine-likeness but negatively affects its dependability [10, 11]. Tiffany et al. investigated the influence on the impressions of a robot's touches with verbal communication cues [12].

To the best of our knowledge, only Shiomi et al. investigated the effects of mutual touch in the context of increasing the motivation of the interacting person [9]. This research work reported that mutual touch provides facilitation effects, where people who did mutual touch with the robot continued a simple and monotonous task longer than people who did not touch the robot.

Based on these research works, we employed the following three touch styles. The details of each with Pepper are described below.

Touch-to-robot
In this touch style, first Pepper asked the interacting persons to "please touch my left hand" and then extended it (Fig 3). In this condition, Pepper did not actively touch the interacting persons. We put a round plastic yellow sphere in Pepper's left hand for uniform touch feelings among the other conditions.

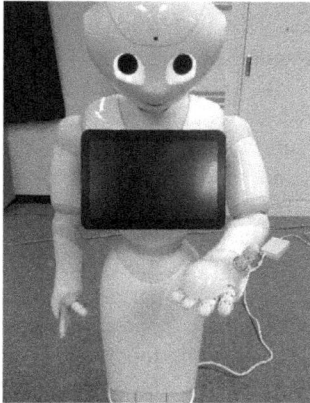

Fig. 3 Pepper extends its hand

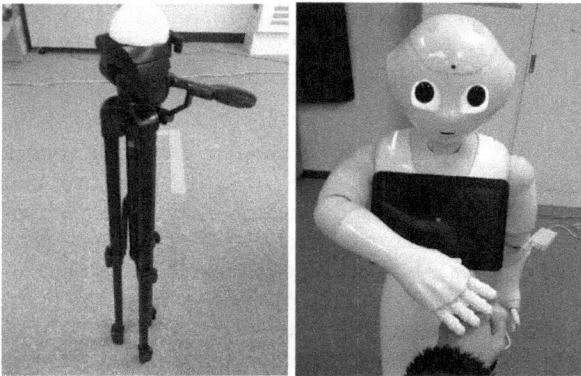

Fig. 4 Identical round plastic yellow sphere on the stand (left) and Pepper touches a hand (right)

Fig. 5 Pepper touches person's hand, which also touches Pepper's left hand

Touched-by-robot

In this touch style, a stand is placed near Pepper on which the interacting person's hand is put. The stand's height is identical to Pepper's left hand in the *touch-robot* style, and the same round plastic yellow sphere is placed on the stand (Fig. 4, left). Pepper asked the interacting persons to "please put your hand on the stand." After they did so,

Pepper touched the hand with its own right hand (Fig. 4, right). In this condition, Pepper actively touches the interacting person's hand, different from the *touch-robot* style.

To design Pepper's touching behavior, we employed the knowledge of human science literature that investigates the effects of touching speed on impressions [25]. Since this paper reported that touching at a speed of 5 cm/s was evaluated more positively than 0.5 or 50 cm/s, we set the speed of the robot's hand during the robot's touching to about 5 cm/s. Pepper's touching behavior is pre-programmed, and its hand follows a fixed trajectory, based on the human's hand size.

Mutual-touch

In this touch style, first Pepper asked the interacting person to touch its left hand, as in the *touch-robot* style. After the interacting person touched Pepper's hand, Pepper touches the hand with its own right hand, as in the *touched-by-robot* style (Fig. 5). Therefore, this condition mixes both the *touch-robot* and *touched-by-robot* styles; both Pepper and the interacting person touch each other. We used Pepper's identical touching behavior in this style: *touched-by-robot* style.

EXPERIMENT

We experimentally investigated the effects of communication cues between the combinations of the gaze and touch designs toward people.

Hypotheses and Prediction

Based on human-robot interaction research, gaze behavior is essential for more natural and acceptable interactions [13-21]. For this purpose, both eye contact and telling intentions by gaze behaviors are important. In particular, a recent work suggested that a combination of gaze behaviors at faces and objects produces more natural interaction feelings in hand-over interactions [16]. Because of the similarity between hand-over and touch, such gaze behaviors may make touch interactions more natural.

The touch style in haptic interaction is also essential to change the perceived feelings of people. Past research works commonly showed that the *touched-by-robot* style created negative feelings [10, 11], but the *mutual-touch* style created more positive feelings than the *touch-to-robot* style [9]. Based on these considerations, we made the following predictions:

Prediction 1: A touch interaction with a *face-hand-face* behavior will be perceived as more natural, more comfortable, and create a better impression in the participants than a touch interaction with a *face-only* behavior.

Prediction 2: A touch interaction with a *mutual-touch* style will be perceived as more natural, more comfortable, and create a better impression in the participants than touch interactions with both the *touched-by-robot* and *touch-to-*

robot styles. A touch interaction with the *touch-to-robot* style will be perceived as more natural, more comfortable, and create a better impression in the participants than a touch interaction with *touched-by-robot* style.

Environment
We conducted the experiment in a laboratory room. We placed in front of Pepper a chair in which the subjects sat during the experiment (Fig. 6).

Conditions
We used a within-participant experiment design to evaluate and compare the effects of communication cues: two gaze behaviors (*face* and *face-hand-face*) and three touch styles (*human touch*, *robot touch*, and *mutual touch*), as described in Section 2. An operator manually decided the timing to start Pepper's touching behavior.

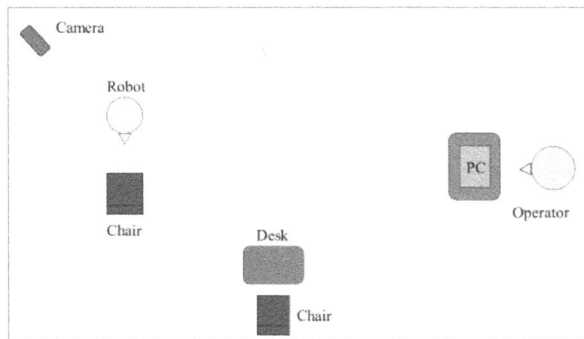

Fig. 6 Experimental scene

Participants
Twenty people (10 women and 10 men, who averaged 35.5 years old, S.D 9.7) participated in the experiment.

Procedure
Before the first session, the participants were given a brief description of our experiment's purpose and procedure. Since it had a within-participant design, each participant participated in six sessions of different conditions.

In all the conditions, after requesting touch initiation Pepper had a short chat with the subject, such as "I'm 121 cm tall and weigh about 28 kg. I'm lighter than you think, right?" We prepared six chat contents to avoid repeating them among the conditions. During the chat in the *touched-by-robot* and *mutual-touch* styles, Pepper patted the hand of the participants three times. The order of the conditions and the chat contents was counterbalanced. The participants filled out a questionnaire after each session.

Measurements
In this experiment, we measured three subjective items by questionnaire: the *feeling of naturalness* of the touch interaction, its *feeling of comfort*, and the *total impression* of the robot. The questionnaire item was evaluated on a 1-to-7 point scale.

RESULTS

Verification of Predictions
Figure 7 shows the *feeling of naturalness*. For it, we conducted a two-way repeated-measure ANOVA with two within-subject factors: gaze and touch. A significant main effect was revealed in the touch factor ($F(2, 38)=6.508$, $p=.004$, partial $\eta2=.255$). Instead, no significance was found in the gaze factor ($F(1,19)=0.195$, $p=.664$, partial $\eta2=.010$) and the interaction within these factors ($F(2,38)=0.108$, $p=.898$, partial $\eta2=.006$). Multiple comparisons with the Bonferroni method revealed significant differences in the touch factor: *touch-to-robot* > *touched-by-robot* ($p=.007$), but there was no significance between *touch-to-robot* and *mutual-touch* ($p =.110$) or *touched-by-robot* and *mutual-touch* ($p =.975$) Mean and S.D of the evaluation in *Touch-to-robot* are 4.10(*S.D 1.18*) and 4.15(*S.D 1.24*), *Touched-by-robot* are 3.15(*S.D 1.35*) and 3.00(*S.D 1.41*), and *Mutual-touch* are 3.40(*S.D 1.56*) and 3.25(*S.D 1.44*).

Figure 8 shows the *feeling of comfort*. For it, we conducted a two-way repeated-measure ANOVA with two within-subject factors: gaze and touch. A significant main effect was revealed in the gaze factor ($F(1, 19)=5.448$, $p=.031$, partial $\eta^2=.223$). Instead, no significance was found in the touch factor ($F(2,38)=1.893$, $p=.165$, partial $\eta^2=.091$) and in the interaction within these factors ($F(2,38)=0.437$, $p=.649$, partial $\eta^2=.022$). Multiple comparisons with the Bonferroni method revealed a significant difference in the gaze factor: *face-only* > *face-hand-face* ($p=.031$), but there was no significance between *touch-to-robot* and *mutual-touch* ($p =.110$) or *touched-by-robot* and *mutual-touch* ($p =.975$) Mean and S.D of the evaluation in *Touch-to-robot* are 4.00 (*S.D 1.14*) and 3.50(*S.D 1.28*), *Touched-by-robot* are each 3.50(*S.D 1.20*) and 3.25(*S.D 1.00*), and *Mutual-touch* are 3.45(*S.D 1.12*) and 3.25(*S.D 1.30*).

Figure 9 shows the *total impression*. For it, we conducted a two-way repeated-measure ANOVA with two within-subject factors: gaze and touch. A significant main effect was revealed in the touch factor ($F(2, 38)=4,377$, $p=.019$, partial $\eta^2=.187$). Instead, no significance was found in the gaze factor ($F(1,19)=1.197$, $p=.288$, partial $\eta^2=.059$) and in the interaction within these factors ($F(2,38)=0.481$, $p=.622$, partial $\eta^2=.025$). Multiple comparisons with the Bonferroni method revealed a marginally significant: *touch-to-robot* > *touched-by-robot* ($p=.061$), but there was no significance between *touch-to-robot* and *mutual-touch* ($p =.121$) or *touched-by-robot* and *mutual-touch* ($p =1.000$). Mean and S.D of the evaluation in *Touch-to-robot* are 4.80(*S.D 1.36*) and 4.85(*S.D 1.31*), *Touched-by-robot* are 4.25(*S.D 1.55*) and 4.10(*S.D 1.55*), and *Mutual-touch* are 4.50(*S.D 1.20*) and 4.20(*S.D 1.60*).

These results show that prediction 1 was not supported; the opposite phenomenon was observed. Prediction 2 was partially supported.

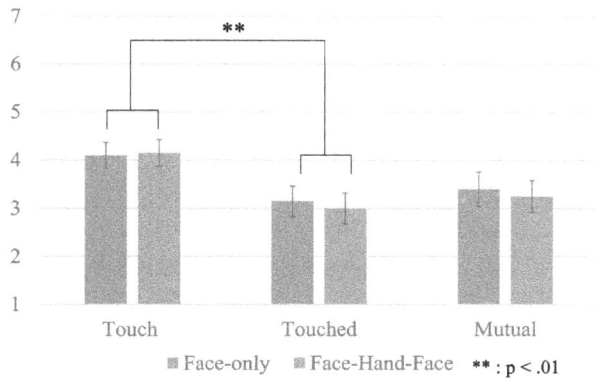

Fig. 7 Feeling of naturalness in touch interaction

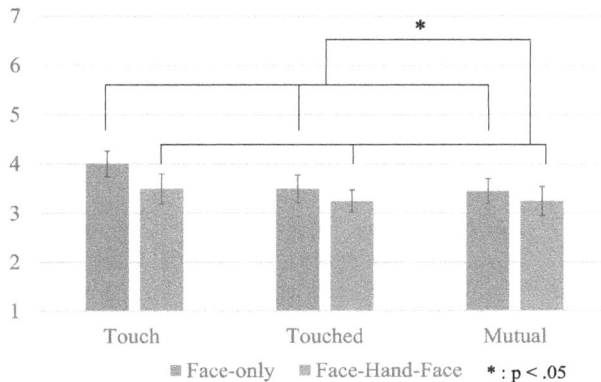

Fig. 8 Feeling of comfort in touch interaction

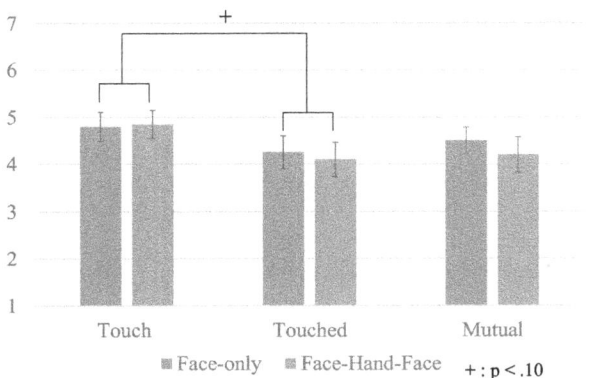

Fig. 9 Total impression of robot

DISCUSSION

Why did our participants prefer *face-only* gaze behavior to *face-hand-face* gaze behavior?

Past research work reports that a combination of eye contact and looking at an object increased impressions than just eye contact during a handing interaction [16]. But our research work showed an opposite result: people preferred eye-contact during a touch interaction. We assumed that both handing and touch situations are similar and required similar communication cues, but this assumption might be inappropriate. Future work will investigate gaze differences between handing and touching situations and unveil essential gaze behaviors in touch interaction.

Why didn't they prefer *mutual-touch* style to other touch styles?

In this work, the *mutual-touch* style did not show significant differences about feelings from other touch styles, unlike past research work. On the other hand, the *touched-by-robot* style showed more negative impressions than the *touch-to-robot* style, similar to past research work. We thought that additional factors might influence the impressions of touch interactions in addition to gaze and touch style. For example, a trajectory of touching and touch feelings is important for this purpose, and future work will investigate them.

Limitation

Since our experiment was conducted with an existing robot, Pepper, robot generality is limited. The effect shown in the experiment would probably be moderated if our participants interacted with a robot with a different appearance, size, and so on. Pepper's eye design is different from that of human eyes. Since this design simplifies making eye-contact with the interacting person, it also influences the perceived feelings in haptic interaction.

CONCLUSION

In this research work, we focused on the effects of communication cues toward perceived feelings to a robot in haptic interaction: gaze behaviors and touch styles. We employed two gaze behaviors during touch (looking at the face of an interacting person and looking at a face, a hand, and the face again) and three touch styles (a person touching a robot, a robot touching a person, and a person and robot touching each other) by considering past related works. To investigate the effects of these communication cues, we conducted a within-subjects experiment in which a robot interacts with participants through touch.

Our experimental results indicated that our participants preferred a gaze behavior that only looks at a face to a gaze behavior that looks at a face, a hand, and the face again. Moreover, they preferred a touch style in which a person initiates the touch of a robot rather than when a robot initiates the touch interaction. But unlike past research work, a touch style in which a person and robot touch each other is not preferred over other touch styles. We believe this knowledge will help robotics researchers who are focusing on haptic interaction of a social robot to design their behaviors.

ACKNOWLEDGMENTS

This research work was supported by JSPS KAKENHI Grant Number 15H05322, 16K12505, and 15K16075.

REFERENCES

1. J. D. Fisher, M. Rytting, and R. Heslin, "Hands Touching Hands: Affective and Evaluative Effects of an Interpersonal Touch," *Sociometry,* vol. 39, no. 4, pp. 416-421, 1976.

2. D. E. Smith, J. A. Gier, and F. N. Willis, "Interpersonal Touch and Compliance with a Marketing Request," *Basic and Applied Social Psychology,* vol. 3, no. 1, pp. 35-38, 1982.

3. J. K. Burgoon, D. B. Buller, J. L. Hale, and M. A. Turck, "Relational messages associated with nonverbal behaviors," *Human Communication Research,* vol. 10, no. 3, pp. 351-378, 1984.

4. J. Hornik, "Effects of Physical Contact on Customers' Shopping Time and Behavior," *Marketing Letters,* vol. 3, no. 1, pp. 49-55, 1992.

5. N. Guéguen, "Touch, awareness of touch, and compliance with a request," *Perceptual and Motor Skills,* vol. 95, no. 2, pp. 355-360, 2002.

6. N. Guéguen and C. Jacob, "The effect of touch on tipping: an evaluation in a French bar," *International Journal of Hospitality Management,* vol. 24, no. 2, pp. 295-299, 2005.

7. N. Guéguen, C. Jacob, and G. Boulbry, "The effect of touch on compliance with a restaurant's employee suggestion," *International Journal of Hospitality Management,* vol. 26, no. 4, pp. 1019-1023, 2007.

8. R. Yu, et al., "Use of a Therapeutic, Socially Assistive Pet Robot (PARO) in Improving Mood and Stimulating Social Interaction and Communication for People With Dementia: Study Protocol for a Randomized Controlled Trial," *JMIR research protocols,* vol. 4, no. 2, 2015.

9. M. Shiomi, et al., "Does A Robot's Touch Encourage Human Effort?," *International Journal of Social Robotics,* pp. 1-11, 2016.

10. H. Cramer, N. Kemper, A. Amin, B. Wielinga, and V. Evers, "'Give me a hug': the effects of touch and autonomy on people's responses to embodied social agents," *Computer Animation and Virtual Worlds,* vol. 20, no. 2-3, pp. 437-445, 2009.

11. H. Cramer, N. Kemper, A. Amin, and V. Evers, "Touched by robots: Effects of physical contact and robot proactiveness," in Workshop on the Reign of Catz and Dogz in CHI, pp. 2009.

12. T. L. Chen, C.-H. A. King, A. L. Thomaz, and C. C. Kemp, "An Investigation of Responses to Robot-Initiated Touch in a Nursing Context," *International Journal of Social Robotics,* vol. 6, no. 1, pp. 141-161, 2013.

13. S. Satake, T. Kanda, D. F. Glas, M. Imai, H. Ishiguro, and N. Hagita, "A Robot that Approaches Pedestrians," *IEEE Transactions on Robotics,* vol. 29, no. 2, pp. 508-524, 2013.

14. K. Hayashi, M. Shiomi, T. Kanda, N. Hagita, and A. I. Robotics, "Friendly patrolling: A model of natural encounters," in Proc. RSS, pp. 121, 2012.

15. C. Shi, M. Shiomi, T. Kanda, H. Ishiguro, and N. Hagita, "Measuring Communication Participation to Initiate Conversation in Human–Robot Interaction," *International Journal of Social Robotics,* vol. 7, no. 5, pp. 889-910, 2015.

16. M. Gharbi, et al., "Toward a better understanding of the communication cues involved in a human-robot object transfer," in Robot and Human Interactive Communication (RO-MAN), 2015 24th IEEE International Symposium on, pp. 319-324, 2015.

17. C. Shi, M. Shiomi, C. Smith, T. Kanda, and H. Ishiguro, "A Model of Distributional Handing Interaction for a Mobile Robot," in Robotics: Science and Systems, 2013.

18. C. Breazeal, C. D. Kidd, A. L. Thomaz, G. Hoffman, and M. Berlin, "Effects of nonverbal communication on efficiency and robustness in human-robot teamwork," in Intelligent Robots and Systems, IEEE/RSJ International Conference on, pp. 708-713, 2005.

19. Y. Kuno, K. Sadazuka, M. Kawashima, K. Yamazaki, A. Yamazaki, and H. Kuzuoka, "Museum guide robot based on sociological interaction analysis," in the SIGCHI Conference on Human Factors in Computing Systems, pp. 1191-1194, 2007.

20. B. Mutlu, T. Shiwa, T. Kanda, H. Ishiguro, and N. Hagita, "Footing in human-robot conversations: how robots might shape participant roles using gaze cues," in the 4th ACM/IEEE international conference on Human robot interaction, pp. 61-68, 2009.

21. M. Shiomi, K. Nakagawa, and N. Hagita, "Design of a gaze behavior at a small mistake moment for a robot," *Interaction Studies,* vol. 14, no. 3, pp. 317-328, 2013.

22. T. Salter, F. Michaud, D. Letourneau, D. Lee, and I. P. Werry, "Using proprioceptive sensors for categorizing human-robot interactions," in 2nd ACM/IEEE International Conference on Human-Robot Interaction, pp. 105-112, 2007.

23. L. Jun Ki, R. L. Toscano, W. D. Stiehl, and C. Breazeal, "The design of a semi-autonomous robot avatar for family communication and education," The 17th IEEE International Symposium on Robot and Human Interactive Communication, pp. 166-173, 2008.

24. M. Cooney, T. Kanda, A. Alissandrakis, and H. Ishiguro, "Designing Enjoyable Motion-Based Play Interactions with a Small Humanoid Robot," *International Journal of Social Robotics,* vol. 6, no. 2, pp. 173-193, 2014.

25. G. K. Essick, A. James, and F. P. McGlone, "Psychophysical assessment of the affective components of non-painful touch," *Neuroreport,* vol. 10, no. 10, pp. 2083-2087, 1999.

Humotion – A Human Inspired Gaze Control Framework for Anthropomorphic Robot Heads

Simon Schulz[1]   Florian Lier[1]   Andreas Kipp[2]   Sven Wachsmuth[1] *

ABSTRACT

In recent years, an attempt is being made to control robots more intuitive and intelligible by exploiting and integrating anthropomorphic features to boost social human-robot interaction. The design and construction of anthropomorphic robots for this kind of interaction is not the only challenging issue – smooth and expectation-matching motion control is still an unsolved topic. In this work we present a highly configurable, portable, and open control framework that facilitates anthropomorphic motion generation for humanoid robot heads by enhancing state-of-the-art neck-eye coordination with human-like eyelid saccades and animation. On top of that, the presented framework supports dynamic neck offset angles that allow animation overlays and changes in alignment to the robots communication partner while retaining visual focus on a given target. In order to demonstrate the universal applicability of the proposed ideas we used this framework to control the Flobi and the iCub robot head, both in simulation and on the physical robot. In order to foster further comparative studies of different robot heads, we will release all software, based on this contribution, under an open-source license.

INTRODUCTION

Humans are social beings that are highly attuned to human characteristics and can interpret gaze and facial expressions without additional training [1, 2]. It is also known that even subtle cues of humanoid robots will be interpreted by humans with regard to communicated intentions and inner states [2]. Therefore, it is desirable to incorporate these features into a robot that closely interacts with humans in order to boost the communication and furthermore ease the interpretation of the robots' behavior [3].

A pleasant design and construction of anthropomorphic robots for natural human-robot interaction alone is not sufficient: without proper and realistic actuation matching the users' expectations, it is very likely to pass the

tipping point and to slip into the so called uncanny valley effect [4]. Robots with human features that deviate from the expected behavior or motion tend to be disturbing [5]. Therefore, proper, natural, and anthropomorphic motion control is essential in order to fulfill the users' expectations. With respect to the eyes this includes the vestibulo-ocular reflex, smooth pursuit, eye saccades, vergence, eye-head coordination, and eyelid animation.

In this work we present our approach for a highly configurable and versatile system that implements state-of-the-art neck-eye coordination, enhanced by realistic and anthropomorphic eyelid animation and dynamic neck offsets to fascilitate overlay of human like animation, emotional-, and social feedback cues while retaining visual focus on a given target.

In the remainder of this paper, we will first discuss related work (section 2), before introducing human eye-, neck-, and eyelid motion complemented with the requirements for life-like replication (section 3). Section 4 describes the concrete implementation before section 5 gives an insight of the effectiveness. The evaluation study is introduced and the obtained results are presented and analyzed in section 6, before section 7 draws conclusions and completes the paper.

STATE OF THE ART

In the last years a variety of anthropomorphic robot heads have been designed and their social impact has been studied. One early example is the robot head Kismet: Its design incorporates anthropomorphic features such as neck and eye kinetics in a cute animalistic appearance. Even though this robot head is not anthropomorphic, it can successfully enhance communication through facial expressions and social cues [6]. Similar results were obtained with the Philips iCat, a combination of cat and human features [7].

A more anthropomorphic head was developed for the iCub [8]. It features anthropomorphic neck- and eye kinetics combined with expressive features such as light emitting diodes for eyebrow and mouth animations. The distribution to research institutes all around the world and being freely accessible by developers makes it unique. Unfortunately, the expressiveness of its 1 DOF[1] eyelid mechanism and the mouth implementation that uses light emitting diodes is limited. However a promising new prototype of a mechanically actuated mouth for the iCub has recently been presented [9].

* [1]Central Lab Facilities – Center of Excellence Cognitive Interaction Technology (CITEC), Bielefeld University, Germany [2]Applied Informatics, Bielefeld University, Germany
{sschulz,flier,akipp,swachsmu}@techfak.uni-bielefeld.de

HAI '16, October 04 - 07, 2016, Biopolis, Singapore

© 2016 Copyright held by the owner/author(s). Publication rights licensed to ACM.
ISBN 978-1-4503-4508-8/16/10. . . $15.00

DOI: http://dx.doi.org/10.1145/2974804.2974827

---

[1]degree of freedom

Other examples for robot heads featuring a particular wide range of expressions are the heads of the Kobian-RII robot [10], Nexi [11], and the Geminoid robot series [12].

Figure 1: The anthropomorphic research platform Flobi

Our contribution to the line of humanoid robot heads is the robot Flobi (figure 1). It was designed to facilitate social interaction by designing the exterior in a way that allows facial expression and emotional feedback, while at the same time avoiding the uncanny valley effect by using a comic style design [13]. The robots' neck features three degrees of freedom for roll-, pitch-, and yaw motion. In order to facilitate a variety of facial expressions, a total of 14 actuators are responsible for moving the eyes (3 DOF - individual pan, joint tilt), the eyebrows (2 DOF), the individual eyelids (4 DOF), and the mouth (6 DOF).

As stated in section 1, matching the users' expectations is the key for a pleasant perception of the robot. Given that anthropomorphic robot heads include human characteristics, the user expects human like actuation as well. Therefore, it is mandatory to study the human body and its sequences of movements: the human eye, combined eye-neck movements, and the underlying control patterns have been thoroughly studied by neuroscientists and psychologists over the last decades. Their findings found application in character animation for virtual agents and in the movie industry [14]. However, the transfer and application on physical robot heads is still a challenging issue due to differences with regard to joint limits, the number of degrees of freedom, or body structure.

Beyond the advantages by matching the users' expectations, replication of human motion patterns that are the result of years of evolution often provide further benefits. The advantage of combining active (eye-) vision with the large motion range of the neck, widening the perceivable field of view, is only one of such examples. Beside this rather functional purpose, psychological studies found different social functions of human gaze, e.g. humans use the gaze to send signals or to regulate the flow of conversations [15]. Interestingly, humans tend to attribute these characteristics to technical systems as well. Taking advantage and exploiting these communication channels that exist between people allows to boost and enhance human-robot interaction in an unobtrusive way [1].

Artificial reproduction of the human gaze relies first and foremost on the compilation of a model. Gaze models can be differentiated between two classes of gaze models: Data-driven, based on human recorded datasets, and the procedural approach. One example for a data-driven approach is the system presented in [16]: emotionally expressive gaze datasets were recorded beforehand and are then warped and overblended before being superimposed with a model driven gaze. Moreover, there are also mixed models, e.g. the "Eyes Alive" model by Lee et al [17]. This model is based on an empirical model of saccades combined with a statistical model based on eye tracking data.

Unfortunately most of the models found in literature do not take full eyelid motion into account. If present at all, eyelid animation is often limited to blinking, covering only a subset of human eyelid motion patterns. As stated in section 1, such a deviation from the users' expectations, based on the anthropomorphic outer appearance, can cause disturbances and degrade the overall perception.

A system proposed by Deng et al. tries to overcome this limitation by recreating combined eye and lid motions based on recorded datasets using texture synthesis [18]. The application of data-driven models, based on recordings from humans, for the animation of anthropomorphic virtual characters with slightly different proportions, kinetics. or geometries is not straightforward. These variations, if not handled properly by complex morphing and adaption of the recorded data, cause deviations from the norm, which again, degrade the overall perception. In order to address these issues, [19] proposes a procedural system to overcome those issues by adaption and remapping to their target character.

One example for a model-based control framework applied on anthropomorphic robot heads is the emotion and gaze control architecture that was developed for the iCat [20]. This framework incorporates blinking but does not include eyeball pursuing motion.

Another example for a procedural control framework is the iKinGazeCtrl module developed for the iCub [21]: This approach features an anthropomorphic, model-based combined actuation of neck- and eye joints - but again, no eyelid animation at all. Unfortunately the iCub's eyelid system is limited by a single actuator (1 DOF) to move all four eyelids at once. This structure does not allow the variety of motions required for the full eyelid animation, however plain blinking can be added on top using a separate blink controller [22].

Even though the topic is widely researched, and every robot head with human kinetics benefits from neck-eye coordination, the accessibility of actual implementations or frameworks for gaze control is sparse or tightly coupled to a single robot platform and often not customizable to the constraints of a different robot. This might be one reason why there are no comparative studies of different robot heads that are controlled by the same gaze control software. Further developments on robot heads would benefit from comparative studies regarding expressiveness, likability, and liveliness between different robot platforms.

REQUIREMENTS

In this section we will give an overview of typical human eye-, neck-, and eyelid motion patterns, their interplay expressed in measurable terms in conjunction with a short overview of the underlying control systems. These requirements will be addressed and used to define the basis of our implementation presented in section 4.

Vestibulo-ocular Reflex

The vestibulo-ocular reflex (VOR) is responsible for adapting the eye orientation to fast head and body movements in order to keep a fixated target on the center of the retina. The optokinetic system alone is not fast enough to compensate for fast movements due to the high processing latency of more than 75 ms [23]. This reflex is a direct coupling of a stimuli in the inner ears' kinetic labyrinth to associated eye muscles [24]. This results in a very low latency of around 8.6 ms [25]. During intentional head movements the involved neurons are selectively inhibited to suppress this reflex [23, 24]. On a fixed robot platform with no unintentional or external motion this reflex can be simulated based on measurements of the neck joints and inverse kinematics whereas on a moving, e.g. walking, platform this is typically implemented using an inertial measurement unit with gyroscopes as an additional cue [26]. For now our implementation takes the first approach, further enhancements utilizing a gyroscope as an additional cue are planned and possible.

Smooth Pursuit

The human eye executes a smooth pursuit motion to visually track targets at low speeds, typically less than $30°/s$, by matching the angular velocities of the eyeball and the target [24]. Angular velocities exceeding this threshold will typically trigger additional correction saccades. The typical latency of the smooth pursuit control loop is around 150 ms. Interestingly humans can overcome this delay during tracking of a moving object by prediction and adaptation to the targets motion [27].

Eye Saccades

The third motion type to be implemented for a realistic reproduction of human gaze is the saccade. This motion type occurs very frequently and is characterized as fast, step-like gaze shifts humans perform for (re-) fixation of new or lost objects during smooth pursuit or to search for objects out of view [24]. Velocities during a saccade can reach up to $700°/s$ and peak accelerations in the range of $80000°/s^2$ [24, 28]. The maximum velocity is reached approximately halfway throughout the motion profile [29].

Vergence

When humans look at close targets the eyes rotate inwards in order to center the object of interest's image on the retina on both eyes. This effect is called vergence and typically accompanies saccade motion as changes of fixation points in a three dimensional space often imply changes of the objects distance as well [23].

Eye-head Coordination

As the human oculomotor range is limited to $\pm 55°$, the interplay of saccades and unidirectional neck motion allows humans to enhance the perceptible field of view [23, 30]. For large gaze shifts of 15° or more, the VOR is inhibited to allow the eyes and head to move together towards the target [23]. As the head, based on the higher mass, can not accelerate as fast as the eyeball, the head motion lags behind. However the actual delay between target selection and the muscle activation measured by electromyograms is different for the eyeball and neck muscles and are shortened by predictable targets [31]. In contrast to the eye saccades the angular velocities and deflection of the head can be willingly influenced by humans.

Eyelids

Despite not being part of the oculomotor system, eyelid motion is a very salient property of a human face. A closer look on the lid-eye interaction during vertical eyeball motion reveals, that the motion and speed of the eyelid matches those of the eyeball during saccades, as well as during smooth-pursuit [32, 33]. The variable clearance between the eyelid and the pupil border is influenced by ones condition and the level of alertness [34].

Another prominent motion type of the eyelids are the different types of blinks. One differentiates between voluntary, spontaneous, and reflexive blinks with distinctive velocity profiles [32]. The frequency of periodic blinks depends on the affective, attentional, and cognitive state [34]. Under resting conditions Cramon and Zihl measured 7.6 eyeblinks per minute [35]. Large gaze shifts of more than 33° evoke blinks with a probability of 0.97 [36]. To conclude, this amounts to that the eyelids are much more than a protective organ as eyelid motion is recognized and can be interpreted by humans.

Social Interaction

In contrast to purely technical systems, an anthropomorphic robot head has to fulfill two conflicting objectives: On the one hand, smooth, human like motion, emotional-, and social feedback cues are desirable, but on the other hand the cameras, typically embedded into the robots' eyes, have to be used for vision processing tasks. Thus it is desirable that a system that implements human like animation for an anthropomorphic robot head takes this conflict into account and provides a solution to allow e.g. animations or head poses that can be used to provide emotional and social feedback cues. In summary, the overall importance for non-verbal communication and expression of the robots' internal state should not be neglected during implementation of a gaze model for an anthropomorphic robot head.

IMPLEMENTATION

This section covers the implemented motion replication library (called humotion) based on the physiological data and further requirements defined in section 3.

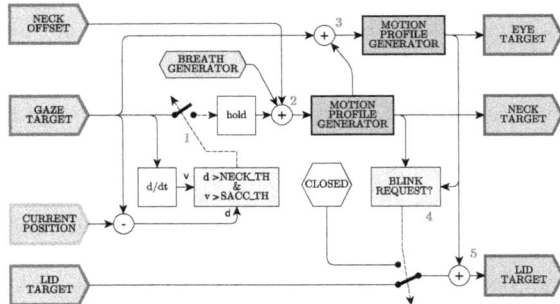

Figure 2: The motion control model as implemented by humotion. Refer to section 4 for an explanation of the indices (1)-(5)

Figure 2 shows the implementation of the underlaying motion control model: A threshold-based detection of eye- and neck saccades (1) triggers the update of the current angular neck target based on the gaze target and the current position. Subsequently, dynamic angular offset values (neck roll, pitch, and yaw) and a configurable anthropomorphic breathing pattern are superimposed on top of the neck pitch angle for additional liveliness (2). This pattern is configurable and defaults to a rate of 12 breaths per minute [37] and a deflection of 2 degrees. The amount of deflection can be very small while still being noticeable and prevents the impression of a frozen, non-working, or switched off robot. By taking care of dynamically given angular offsets for all three neck joints our approach allows the overlay of animations (e.g. head shake or nodding) or partial target alignment as a feedback for engagement during communication tasks without loosing the visual focus. Although being an important factor to facilitate authentic human-robot interaction, we found that the direct support of this kind of angular neck offsets is often neglected in literature describing gaze control systems.

Based on physiological measurements from [30], human like velocities and accelerations are calculated, optionally rescaled, and limited by configurable parameters before a suitable motion is planned. Simultaneously to the neck motion a compensatory human like motion for both eyes (3) is calculated based on the neck command, the gaze target, and a given vergence angle before being rescaled and limited in the same way. This optional rescale and limiting features is configurable at runtime and is one of the distinguishing features of our model.

As outlined in section 3.2, humans are able to compensate the latency of the visual systems e.g. during smooth pursuit motion. In order to cope with similar delays in the image processing pipeline, combined with the fast moving eyeball camera, our system optionally supports preprocessing for relative gaze targets that consist of a relative gaze adjustment in combination with an image recording timestamp. With the help of a timestamped history of angular position values, the robots' joint state at the time of image retrieval is inferred and a corrected absolute gaze target is calculated.

Blinks are generated based on eye velocities, saccade occurrence, or on user request (4). The thresholds and occurrence frequencies are configurable and default to the values found in humans as introduced in 3. Additionally, the four eyelids pursue the eyeball during all eye tilt movements with given offsets (5). Those offsets are for example being used to give emotional feedback or express the robots internal state (e.g. the level of tiredness). In addition to the impact on the robots expressiveness this eyeball pursuing motion additionally avoids collisions of the camera's wiring harness and the eyelids on the backside of the eye. This allows a much wider actuation range for the eyeball as well as for the lids.

All parameters for velocities, accelerations, and occurrence frequencies are pre-configured to match the values found in humans and are additionally configurable during runtime. Furthermore additional parameters allow optional rescaling and limiting of the intermediate velocities and accelerations calculated before the motion planning step is executed. In particular this kind of high configurability facilitates the application of the proposed library on a variety of different equipped robot platforms. The final synchronous motion planning and execution for all involved joints is handled by the online trajectory generator of the motion generation library libreflexxes [38].

In order to facilitate loose coupling and to allow better re-use, all interprocess communication and dynamic reconfiguration of the parameters is handled by a middleware abstraction layer. Currently interfaces for the "Robot Operating System" (ROS) [39] and the "Robotics Service Bus" (RSB) [40] frameworks have been implemented.

Transferring the humotion capabilities to a new robot platform involves two steps: First, a server object that serves as a middleware connection for control input such as gaze targets, eye opening angles, and eyelid states, needs to be instantiated. Second, a joint interface that enables the server object to read and write joint angles and velocities has to be implemented. The instantiated humotion server object will subsequently open and listen on a set of middleware connections. Even though interaction with this interface through plain middleware calls is possible, an additional convenient client API that wraps the actual middleware specific calls is provided as well.

The proposed library was developed and tested on our Flobi robot platform. It was verified to be working as expected both in simulation and on the real robot platform. In order to show the portability and applicability, an additional wrapper that implements the humotion interface was written and integrated into the iCubs' control infrastructure. It implements low-level joint access routines required by humotion using the iCubs' native communication layer yarp [41]. Again, this implementation was verified in simulation and on the real physical hardware platform.

OUTCOME

This section will present the output of the motion generator and show photographs of the actual appearance of the motion on two different robots, namely the iCub and Flobi.

Figure 3 shows an exemplary response to a step-like gaze target change. It depicts the gaze target input (contin-

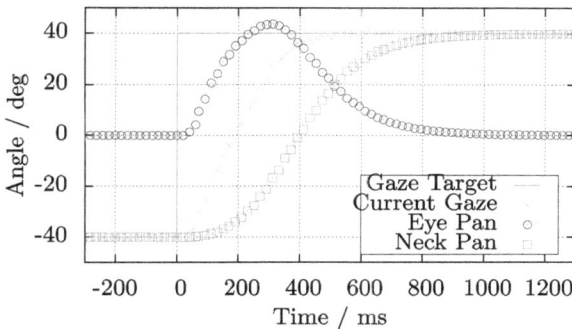

Figure 3: An exemplary 80° gaze-shift as generated by our system

uous line), the current gaze angle (x), the corresponding neck pitch (□), and eye tilt angles (o) as generated by our system: With the neck approaching its target position, the eye deflection gradually decreases and results in a zero deflection at the end. A closer look at the overall gaze (x) shows the distinctive first and steep increasing acceleration phase ($t < 200ms$) with contribution of the accelerating eye and neck. This phase is quite distinguishable from the slower deceleration phase ($t > 200ms$) before the eyes come to a rest. For better readability this graph shows only the yaw angles. The associated pitch and roll motion is executed synchronously so that all target angles are reached at the same time.

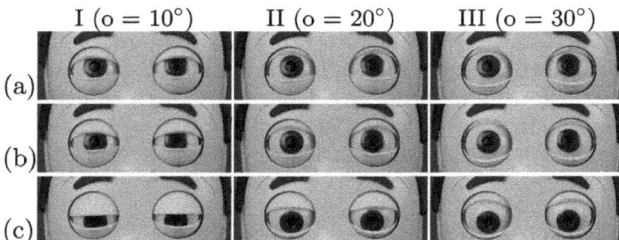

Figure 4: The effect of different eyelid offsets on the Flobi robot

Figure 4 gives a visual example how the eyeball pursuing eyelid motion looks like when executed on the Flobi robot: The eyelids seem to "stick" to the moving eyeball during the vertical gaze shift from +20° (4a) to -20° (4c). This is best seen in column I with an eyelid offset angle of 10°. Additionally columns II and III show offset angles of 20° and 30°, respectively.

Despite not being shown here, it is possible to set all four offsets independently. Offset changes can be used e.g. to express the robots' internal state: Smaller offsets, resulting in closer proximity to the pupil, can be used to reflect sleepiness or sadness, whereas bigger offsets (eyes wide open) can support surprise or fear expressions.

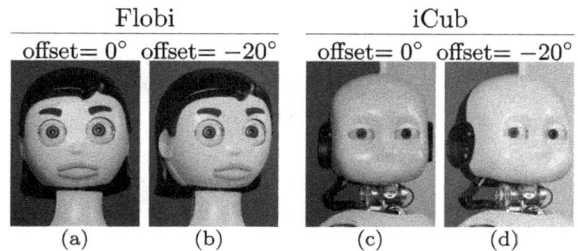

Figure 5: Comparison of different neck yaw offsets

As stated in section 4, one contribution of our proposed system is the support of neck offset angles. The effect of this is shown in figure 5: Both robots fixate the same target in all four pictures: Once with a neck yaw offset of 0° (shown in 5a and 5c) and in comparison with an offset of -20° (5b, 5d). This example shows how these offsets can be used to express the level of engagement in communication tasks by keeping the robots head more aligned to its communication partner during the execution of gaze shifts. Much more importantly, this dynamic offset facilitates the overlay of head animations while retaining the overall gaze at the same visual focus. This unique feature allows a very natural human robot interaction by executing gestures such as shaking the head without interfering with vision processing tasks.

For a better impression of the overall system performance, the expressiveness, and a qualitative comparison please refer to the associated video submission[2]: Two exemplary robot heads, an iCub and a Flobi robot, actuated by the proposed library, will present the feature set of our approach.

EVALUATION

In order to objectively evaluate the proposed motion generation system a user study was conducted. The main objective to be answered by this study was to evaluate if the proposed system, with combined neck-, eye- and eyelid motion, performs better in terms of user acceptance and is perceived to be more lively as others. Additionally, we wanted to get a rough overview about how much importance an user attach to properties such as fluidness, liveliness, and human like motion of a humanoid robot

[2]http://youtu.be/AJm5IVMVKsI

head. In order to evaluate the full potential of the presented motion generation algorithm, a Flobi robot was used to record the video samples for the survey. Unfortunately the current iCub design does not feature the required 4-DOF eyelid actuation and could not be used to evaluate the presented system as a whole.

The study was designed as an online survey: After a short introduction and the collection of some basic demographic data, a short video sequence was shown and the participants were asked to answer questions and fill in rankings.

In order to evaluate the effect of the proposed motion algorithm three different conditions were identified to be tested:

C_{NECK} : only neck motion (eyes and eyelids fixed)
C_{NOLIDS} : neck and eye motion (eyelids fixed)
C_{FULL} : full actuation scheme

In order to record a comparable set of videos, the Flobi robot was controlled to fixate the same set of selected gaze targets for all the three conditions to be tested. The proposed humotion library was configured to use 70% of the calculated neck accelerations in order to reduce the stress on the mechanics and to get a smoother looking result.

Figure 6: Still frames extracted from the video showing condition C_{FULL}

Figure 6 shows some exemplary still frames extracted from the video under condition C_{FULL}. All three conditions were shown synchronously and next to each other in one single video. Figure 7 shows an exemplary still frame about how the three different conditions were presented. After seeing the video, all participants were asked to

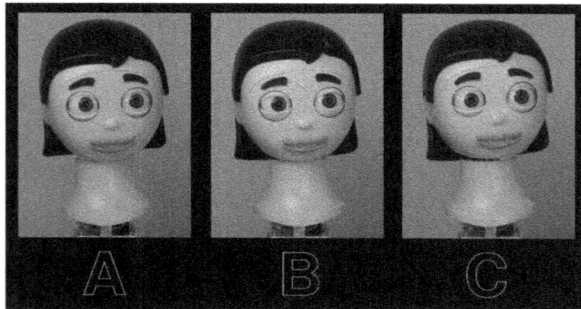

Figure 7: Still frame extracted from comparison video (A = C_{NOLIDS}, B = C_{FULL}, C = C_{NECK})

nominate the most lively robot out of all possible permutations (A-B, B-C, A-C). Furthermore the participants

were asked about their preference if they had to interact with the robot.

In order to address our second research question, how much importance the user addresses to properties such as fluidness (P_{FLUID}), liveliness (P_{LIVELY}) and human like motion (P_{HUMAN}) of a humanoid robot head, the participants were asked to rate the importance of these properties on a scale from 1 (not important at all) to 10 (very important).

A total of 63 male and 69 female participants took part in this study (n=132). The age was distributed between 18 and 60 years with an average age of 30.9 years and a standard deviation of σ=8.9 years.

The first evaluation of the three different conditions showed a clear overall advantage of the tested condition C_{FULL}: When compared against C_{NECK}, a majority of 90.2 % of the participants selected C_{FULL} to be more lively. Similar results were obtained under comparison against C_{NOLIDS} where a majority of 96.2 % picked C_{FULL} to be more lively. Additionally, the comparison of C_{NOLIDS} and C_{NECK} (52.3 % vs. 47.7 %), resulted in a slight preference for C_{NOLIDS}.

In addition to answer the first research question, that indeed a humanoid robot head is indeed perceived to be more lively when actuated with our proposed motion generation algorithm, the first two results additionally show that the perception of liveliness benefits even more from our proposed eyelid animation algorithm compared to the eye- neck coordination alone. In response to the question with which of the differently actuated robots the participants preferred to interact the most, a total of 92.4% selected condition C_{FULL}.

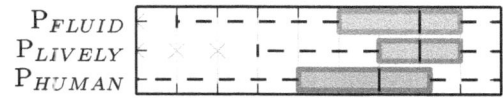

Figure 8: Results of the importance voting

Finally, the participants were asked to vote the importance of the properties P_{FLUID}, P_{LIVELY}, and P_{HUMAN} concerning robot motion during an interaction with the robot. The results are shown as box plots in figure 8: The single boxes show the minimum, first quartile, median, third quartile, and maximum for the three rated properties. Additionally, any occurring outliers are represented by 'X' symbols. All three properties were ranked as quite important. The properties fluidness and liveliness got the highest ranking ($M = 8$) in comparison to human likeness ($M = 7$). All three properties had a large deviation. The property P_{HUMAN} showed a tendency of more rankings towards lower scores with a lower quantile of 5.

CONCLUSION

In this work we presented a novel control framework that facilitates anthropomorphic motion generation for a humanoid robot head. It enhances state-of-the-art neck-eye coordination with human-like eyelid saccades and eyelid animation. Furthermore, its unique neck offset feature allows the robot to overlay animation sequences and to keep a given degree of alignment to its communication partner while retaining a given focus point. All this is rounded off by a superimposed anthropomorphic breathing- and eyeblink pattern. The proposed eyelid animation not only contributes to the expressiveness of the robot head, but also solves the rather technical problem of cable routing and the obstruction on the back of the eyeball by wide open eyelids.

The corresponding software artifacts described in section 4 are openly accessible and released under the GPL open-source license on our webserver[3]. In order to ease replication of our results and to foster the use of the presented control framework we additionally provide a build recipe for the replication of the iCub setup based on the Cognitive Interaction Toolkit[4] [42].

Our approach is fully configurable at runtime by exposing all fundamental motion generation parameters by means of a middleware interface (e.g. using the ROS dynamic reconfigure feature). The proposed flexible rescale and limiting feature allows a flexible adaptation to a large number of differently equipped robot platforms. In addition to the safety gain by starting with low accelerations and slowly speeding up during the configuration process of a new robot platform, this also facilitates the transfer of decelerated human inspired motion to less well endowed robot platforms that do not reach full human velocities and acceleration values.

The positive impact of the proposed motion generation algorithm was verified with the help of a user study. The survey showed that the user indeed pays attention to human like actuation for anthropomorphic robot heads. Most importantly of all, it showed a significant user preference for the proposed motion generation algorithm including realistic eyelid animation.

The proposed system is portable and makes extensive use of loosely coupled communication through a middleware of your choice. In order to show this portability and the universal applicability of the proposed ideas, the library was used to actuate two different robot platforms (Flobi and iCub). The implementation has been verified both in simulation and on the physical hardware. The next steps will be a in-depth evaluation of the proposed framework on different robotic platforms and the influence of different velocity and acceleration scale parameters.

For a better impression of the overall system performance, the expressiveness, and a qualitative comparison please refer to the associated video submission.

---

[3] https://opensource.cit-ec.de/projects/humotion
[4] The CITK provides an integrated software tool chain for system developers, experiment designers, and researchers and allows the description and replication of entire robotic systems based on recipes

ACKNOWLEDGEMENTS
This work was supported by the Cluster of Excellence Cognitive Interaction Technology 'CITEC' (EXC 277) at Bielefeld University, which is funded by the German Research Foundation (DFG).

REFERENCES

1. C. C. Kemp, P. Fitzpatrick, H. Hirukawa, K. Yokoi, K. Harada, and Y. Matusmoto, *Handbook of Robotics.* Springer, 2008, ch. 56.1.2: The pleasing Mirror.

2. ——, *Handbook of Robotics.* Springer, 2008, ch. 56.6.1: Expressive Morphology and Behavior.

3. ——, *Handbook of Robotics.* Springer, 2008, ch. 56.1.5: Interfacing with people.

4. C. E. Looser and T. Wheatley, "The tipping point of animacy. how, when, and where we perceive life in a face." *Psychological science*, pp. 1854–62, Dec. 2010.

5. C. Bartneck, T. Kanda, H. Ishiguro, and N. Hagita, "Is the uncanny valley an uncanny cliff?" in *in: Proceedings of the 16th IEEE International Symposium on Robot and Human Interactive Communication (RO-MAN)*, 2006, pp. 368–373.

6. C. Breazeal, A. Edsinger, P. Fitzpatrick, and B. Scassellati, "Active vision for sociable robots," *Trans. Sys. Man Cyber. Part A*, vol. 31, no. 5, pp. 443–453, Sep. 2001.

7. A. van Breemen, X. Yan, and B. Meerbeek, "icat: an animated user-interface robot with personality," in *AAMAS '05: Proceedings of the fourth international joint conference on Autonomous agents and multiagent systems.* New York, NY, USA: ACM, 2005, pp. 143–144.

8. R. Beira, M. Lopes, M. Praga, J. Santos-Victor, A. Bernardino, G. Metta, F. Becchi, and R. Saltaren, "Design of the robot-cub (iCub) head," *Robotics and Automation, 2006. ICRA 2006. Proceedings 2006 IEEE International Conference on*, pp. 94–100, 2006.

9. A. Parmiggiani, M. Randazzo, M. Maggiali, F. Elisei, G. Bailly, and G. Metta, "An articulated talking face for the icub," in *Humanoid Robots (Humanoids), 2014 14th IEEE-RAS International Conference on*, Nov 2014, pp. 1–6.

10. T. Kishi, T. Otani, N. Endo, P. Kryczka, K. Hashimoto, K. Nakata, and A. Takanishi, "Development of expressive robotic head for bipedal humanoid robot with wide moveable range of facial parts, facial color," in *Romansy 19 – Robot Design, Dynamics and Control*, ser. CISM International Centre for Mechanical Sciences, V. Padois, P. Bidaud, and O. Khatib, Eds. Springer Vienna, 2013, vol. 544, pp. 151–158.

11. M. M. Lab, "MDS Head & Face," 2014, accessed 19th August 2014. [Online]. Available: http://robotic.media.mit.edu/projects/robots/mds/headface/headface.html

12. S. Nishio, H. Ishiguro, and N. Hagita, "Geminoid: Teleoperated android of an existing person," in *Humanoid Robots: New Developments*, A. C. de Pina Filho, Ed. Vienna, Austria: I-Tech Education and Publishing, Jun. 2007, pp. 343–352.

13. I. Lütkebohle, F. Hegel, S. Schulz, M. Hackel, B. Wrede, S. Wachsmuth, and G. Sagerer, "The bielefeld anthropomorphic robot head flobi," in *Robotics and Automation (ICRA), 2010 IEEE International Conference on*, may 2010, pp. 3384–3391.

14. K. Ruhland, S. Andrist, J. B. Badler, C. E. Peters, N. I. Badler, M. Gleicher, B. Mutlu, and R. McDonnell, "Look me in the Eyes: A Survey of Eye and Gaze Animation for Virtual Agents and Artificial Systems," in *Eurographics 2014 - State of the Art Reports*, S. Lefebvre and M. Spagnuolo, Eds. The Eurographics Association, 2014.

15. M. L. Knapp and J. A. Hall, *Nonverbal Communication in Human Interaction*, 7th ed. Bosten, USA: Wadsworth: Cengage Learning, 2010.

16. B. Lance and S. C. Marsella, "The Expressive Gaze Model: Using Gaze to Express Emotion," *Computer Graphics and Applications, IEEE*, vol. 30, no. 4, pp. 62–73, Aug. 2010.

17. S. P. Lee, J. B. Badler, and N. I. Badler, "Eyes alive," *ACM Trans. Graph.*, vol. 21, no. 3, pp. 637–644, Jul. 2002.

18. Z. Deng, J. Lewis, and U. Neumann, "Automated eye motion using texture synthesis," *Computer Graphics and Applications, IEEE*, vol. 25, no. 2, pp. 24–30, March 2005.

19. T. Pejsa, B. Mutlu, and M. Gleicher, "Stylized and performative gaze for character animation." *Comput. Graph. Forum*, vol. 32, no. 2, pp. 143–152, 2013.

20. M. Poel, D. Heylen, A. Nijholt, M. Meulemans, and A. van Breemen, "Gaze behaviour, believability, likability and the icat," *AI & SOCIETY*, vol. 24, no. 1, pp. 61–73, 2009.

21. U. Pattacini, "Modular cartesian controllers for humanoid robots: Design and implementation on the icub," Ph.D. dissertation, University of Genoa, Italy, IIT, 2011.

22. H. Lehmann, U. Pattacini, and G. Metta, "Blink-sync: Mediating human-robot social dynamics with naturalistic blinking behavior," HRI Workshop on "Behavior Coordination between Animals, Humans and Robots", 2015.

23. R. J. Leigh and Z. D. S, *The Neurology of Eye Movements*. Oxford University Press; 4th edition, 2006.

24. H. Kaufmann, *Strabismus*. Thieme, 2003, ch. 1.2.5: Physiologie der Augenbewegungen.

25. H. Collewijn and J. B. J. Smeets, "Early components of the human vestibulo-ocular response to head rotation: latency and gain," *Journal of Neurophysiology*, vol. 84, pp. 376 –389, September 2000.

26. A. Roncone, U. Pattacini, G. Metta, and L. Natale, "Gaze stabilization for humanoid robots: a comprehensive framework," *CoRR*, vol. abs/1411.3525, 2014.

27. R. C., "The relationship between saccadic and smooth tracking eye movements," *Journal of Physiology*, vol. 159, no. 2, pp. 326–338, December 1961.

28. A. T. Bahill, A. Brockenbrough, and B. T. Troost, *Variability and development of a normative data base for saccadic eye movements*, 1981, pp. 116–125.

29. R. A. Abrams, D. E. Meyer, and S. Kornblum, "Speed and accuracy of saccadic eye movements: characteristics of impulse variability in the oculomotor system." *Journal of experimental psychology. Human perception and performance*, vol. 15, no. 3, pp. 529–543, Aug. 1989.

30. D. Guitton and M. Volle, "Gaze control in humans: Eye-head coordination during orienting movements to targets within and beyond the oculomotor range," *Journal of Neurophysiology*, vol. 58, no. 3, pp. 427 –459, September 1987.

31. W. H. Zangemeister and L. Stark, "Gaze latency: Variable interactions of head and eye latency," *Experimental Neurology*, vol. 75, pp. 389–4063, 1982.

32. C. Evinger, M. K. A., and S. P. A., "Eyelid movements. mechanisms and normal data." *Investigative ophthalmology & visual scienc*, vol. 2, pp. 387–400, 1991.

33. Liversedge, Gilchrist, and Everling, "The oxford handbook of eye movements," 2011.

34. K. Schmidtke and J. A. Büttne-Ennever, "Nervous control of eyelid function," *Brain*, vol. 115, no. 1, pp. 227–247, 1992.

35. D. Cramon and J. Zihl, "Die Häufigkeit von schnellen Augenbewegungen und Blinks als Aktivationsindikator," *Journal of Neurology*, vol. 215, no. 2, pp. 115–125, 1977.

36. C. Evinger, K. Manning, J. Pellegrini, M. Basso, A. Powers, and P. Sibony, "Not looking while leaping: the linkage of blinking and saccadic gaze shifts," *Experimental Brain Research*, vol. 100, no. 2, pp. 337–344, 1994.

37. K. E. Barrett, S. M. Barman, S. Boitano, and B. Heddwen, *Ganong's review of medical physiology*. McGraw-Hill; 23rd edition, 2010.

38. T. Kröger, "Opening the door to new sensor-based robot applications – the reflexxes motion libraries," *Robotics and Automation, 2011. ICRA 2011. Proceedings 2011 IEEE International Conference on*, 2011.

39. M. Quigley, K. Conley, B. P. Gerkey, J. Faust, T. Foote, J. Leibs, R. Wheeler, and A. Y. Ng, "Ros: an open-source robot operating system," in *ICRA Workshop on Open Source Software*, 2009.

40. J. Wienke and S. Wrede, "A middleware for collaborative research in experimental robotics," in *System Integration (SII), 2011 IEEE/SICE International Symposium on*, Dec 2011, pp. 1183–1190.

41. G. Metta, P. Fitzpatrick, and L. Natale, "Yarp: Yet another robot platform," *International Journal on Advanced Robotics Systems*, 2006.

42. F. Lier, J. Wienke, A. Nordmann, S. Wachsmuth, and S. Wrede, "The cognitive interaction toolkit – improving reproducibility of robotic systems experiments," ser. SIMPAR 2014, LNAI, D. Brugali, Ed. Springer International Publishing Switzerland, 2014, pp. 400–411.

Perceptions of Agency in Human-robot Interactions

Leila Takayama
Founder, Hoku Labs, USA

Abstract

Robots are no longer only in outer space, in factory cages, or in our imaginations. We interact with robotic agents when withdrawing cash from ATMs, driving cars with anti-lock brakes, and tuning our thermostats. In the moment of those interactions with robotic agents, we behave in ways that do not necessarily align with the rational belief that robots are just plain machines. Through a combination of controlled experiments and field studies, we will examine the ways that people make sense of robotic agents, including (1) how people interact with personal robots and (2) how people interact through telepresence robots. These observations and experiments raise questions about the psychology of human-agent interaction, particularly about issues of perceived agency and the incorporation of technologies into one's sense of self.

Short Bio

Leila Takayama is a human-robot interaction researcher. This year, she founded Hoku Labs and joined the faculty at the University of California, Santa Cruz, as an acting associate professor of Psychology. Prior to UC Santa Cruz, she was a senior user experience researcher at GoogleX, and was a research scientist and area manager for human-robot interaction at Willow Garage. She is a World Economic Forum Global Agenda Council Member and Young Global Leader. Last year, she was presented the IEEE Robotics & Automation Society Early Career Award. In 2012, she was named a TR35 winner and one of the 100 most creative people in business by Fast Company.

With a background in Psychology, Cognitive Science, and Human-Computer Interaction, she examines human encounters with new technologies. Dr. Takayama completed her PhD in Communication at Stanford University in 2008, advised by Professor Clifford Nass. She also holds a PhD minor in Psychology from Stanford, a master's degree in Communication from Stanford, and bachelor's of arts degrees in Psychology and Cognitive Science from UC Berkeley (2003). During her graduate studies, she was a research assistant in the User Interface Research (UIR) group at Palo Alto Research Center (PARC).

HAI'16, October 4–7, 2016, Biopolis, Singapore.
ACM ISBN 978-1-4503-4508-8/16/10.
DOI: http://dx.doi.org/10.1145/2974804.2993928

Human-Robot Cooperative Conveyance Using Speech and Head Gaze

Tetsushi Oka
Nihon University
Narashino, Japan
oka.tetsushi@nihon-u.ac.jp

Sho Uchino
Nihon University
Narashino, Japan
cisy14004@g.nihon-u.ac.jp

ABSTRACT

In this study, we designed a strategy using speech and head gaze and a set of voice commands for cooperative conveyance by a human and a robot. In the designed strategy, the human turns his or her head to face the robot and gives one of twelve spoken commands in the set. In order to start and stop the robot moving, the human sends nonverbal cues by changing his or her point of gaze. We developed a mobile robot that interacts with a human based on the strategy and the command set, which was evaluated with ten young novices. The results of this study imply that most young people can quickly learn how to cooperate with our robot to move objects using speech and head gaze.

Author Keywords

Human-robot collaboration; cooperative work; conveyance; speech; gaze

INTRODUCTION

Today, a wide variety of tasks are performed using machines. Carriage of objects including goods and luggage is no exception. Many types of machines, such as vehicles, elevators, and belt conveyers, are employed to convey heavy and large objects in the modern world. However, automating many tasks of conveyance is difficult and costly even today. Although machines can move fast, bear heavy loads, and continue working without taking breaks, they are not as capable as humans of cognitive tasks including object recognition [2], manipulation [5], and situation recognition [6]. A vast amount of research has been conducted to realize computers and robots that can achieve those cognitive tasks as successfully as humans. In order to fully automate tasks of moving various objects in an uncontrolled environment, high-cost hardware and software will be required.

While humans can recognize objects and find good paths in uncontrolled environments, robots can bear heavier loads

HAI '16, October 04-07, 2016, Biopolis, Singapore
ACM 978-1-4503-4508-8/16/10.
http://dx.doi.org/10.1145/2974804.2980486

and work without being tired. Therefore, a team of humans and robots can outperform the same number of humans. Furthermore, those robots can be developed without high-cost hardware and software for object recognition, manipulation, path planning, and autonomous navigation. Thus, in future, a human-robot team can better suit some tasks of conveyance than human teams or teams of costly autonomous robots in terms of both cost and task performance. In addition, inexpensive robots that can cooperate with humans for conveyance tasks can be of great value in case of a staff shortage.

In this study, we designed a basic strategy using speech and gaze for cooperative conveyance by a human and a robot and a set of voice commands from the human to the robot. In addition, we developed a robot that a human can communicate with based on the strategy and the voice command set, which was evaluated by ten young novices. We employ speech and gaze for some reasons. First, the human and the robot can communicate with each other even when they are supporting an object and cannot use their hands for communication. Second, speech and gaze are naturally used in human face-to-face communication [3, 4, 7, 9]. Third, the robot can receive signals from the human using low-cost sensors such as a microphone and an RGB-D camera.

RELATED WORK

Several studies on cooperative conveyance by a team of autonomous robots have been conducted [8, 10]. However, autonomous robots are still costly to develop and inferior to humans in cognitive tasks. In uncontrolled environments, recognizing objects, lifting them up, finding and following paths avoiding obstacles require considerable amount of computation in real time.

Some studies on human-robot cooperative conveyance have also been conducted [1, 11, 12], in which humans apply forces and torques to conveyed objects in order to communicate with robots. However, this channel of communication can be quite noisy especially when objects deforms or slips. In addition, communication of desired velocities, directions, and rotational axes may be difficult especially for novices.

COOPERATIVE CONVEYANCE

Our strategy of cooperative conveyance was designed based on an insight into human communication and findings of cognitive science [3, 4, 7, 9], in which a human interacts with a robot in five steps. First, the human gazes at the face of the robot. Second, the robot nonverbally notifies the human that it can receive a voice command. Third, the human gives a voice command. Next, the robot repeats the voice command. Finally, as soon as the human looks away, the robot sends a nonverbal cue and starts executing the voice command. When the robot is moving, the human can pause it by gazing at its face and give a new voice command. The robot resumes its action as soon as the human avert his or her gaze again. Thus, the human can communicate with the robot without using the hands.

Our strategy has some practical advantages. Firstly, it is unlikely that a noise causes unwished movements by the robot. The human can always avoid false-command detection by looking away from the robot. Even in case of a false command, the human can override it by giving a new voice command. Furthermore, the human can talk to someone else without switching off the microphone. Secondly, it is easier to stop the robot by gaze than by speech, because it takes longer for the human to give a spoken command than to gaze at the robot.

Table 1 shows a complete list of twelve voice commands in the command set we have designed for human-robot cooperative conveyance, taking into account consistency and learnability by novices. The robot has nine action modes including four translation and two rotation modes with two speed settings: *slow* and *fast*. Thus, the human can command a slow action to locate the robot at a desirable position. In addition, we included a help command (C1) in the set because the human may forget the correct words.

LIEN: ROBOT FOR EMPIRICAL STUDIES

We developed a robot, LIEN (see Figure 1), for empirical studies on ease and efficiency of cooperative conveyance using speech and gaze based on the strategy and the command set. The robot can move in any direction using four omnidirectional wheels (Vstone Mechanum Rover), turn left and right, and move the lift up and down. LIEN can detect *head gaze* cues from a human wearing a helmet (see Figure 1 right) with a pair of two-dimensional markers using an RGB-D camera (Microsoft Kinect for Windows) on the top. We implemented LIEN's control system for this study in C++ using an automatic speech recognition engine (Julius 4.3.1) and software toolkits (KinectSDK 1.80, ARToolKit 2.72.1, OpenCV 2.3.1, and Vstone's Mechanum Rover SDK). The system operated on a single laptop (Panasonic Let's Note CF-S10 with Core i7-2620M 2.70GHz and 8GB main memory). We employed a wireless headset with a microphone for voice communication.

Table 2 shows the speed settings of LIEN in this study. The velocities were determined considering both ease of positioning and efficiency of cooperative conveyance. Although the more slowly the robot is moving, the easier it is to stop the robot, the robot must move fast in order to convey objects efficiently. For safety reasons, the robot gradually accelerates for six to seven seconds to reach the maximum velocity (1.9 [km/h]) and decelerates to stop within three seconds. If LIEN receives a gaze cue when translating at the top speed, the robot moves approximately 0.8 meters before stopping.

LIEN can detect a head gaze signal from a human wearing the helmet by tracking its position and orientation in three-dimensional (3D) space. The pair of markers are detected in the latest RGB image from the camera by means of image matching. Then, four 3D position vectors are obtained using their pixel coordinates and depth information from the camera, in order to calculate the normal vector $\mathbf{n}$ of the marker pair. By using $\mathbf{n}$ and the position vector of the center of the marker pair, P_h, LIEN can estimate the position of the human's point of gaze. The robot detects a head gaze cue when the line defined by $\mathbf{n}$ and P_h has an intersection with a rectangle (0.6×0.6[m]) near the center of the camera. In addition, LIEN responds to head gaze cues with two types of short sound signal.

Command	ID	Robot Response
Herupu	C1	Pronounce all voice commands
Zenshin	C2	Switch to the *forward translation* mode
Kotai	C3	Switch to the *backward translation* mode
Hidari-ido	C4	Switch to the *left translation* mode
Migi-ido	C5	Switch to the *right translation* mode
Hidari-senkai	C6	Switch to the *left rotation* mode
Migi-senkai	C7	Switch to the *right rotation* mode
Josho	C8	Switch to the *lift-up* mode
Kako	C9	Switch to the *put-down* mode
Teishi	C10	Switch to the *halt* mode
Teisoku	C11	Set the speed of the robot to *slow*
Kosoku	C12	Set the speed of the robot to *fast*

Table 1. Twelve voice commands for cooperative conveyance.

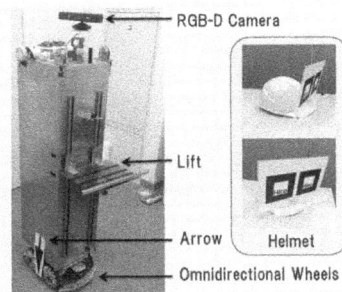

Figure 1. Robot and helmet (right) built for empirical studies.

Movement	Slow	Fast
Translation	0.3 [km/h]	1.9 [km/h]
Rotation	0.1 [rad/s]	0.3 [rad/s]

Table 2. Speed settings for this study

METHODOLOGY

Ten university students between the age of 18 and 22 who had no knowledge about LIEN participated in the evaluation of the robot. Within an hour, we gave them four tasks of cooperative conveyance: moving a long object approximately six meters forward (Task 1), moving it backward slowly (Task 2), turning it 90 degrees left (Task 3), and turning it 90 degrees right (Task 4). Figure 2 illustrates the setup for the tasks: each participant and LIEN stood side by side on a line supporting the object and moved toward the goal zone between two lines. After executing each task, the participants filled out a questionnaire including seven-point-scale questions, and were interviewed about difficulties they found.

The goal of Task 1 was to locate the arrow at the bottom of the robot (see Figure 1) between the goal line and the limit line (see Figure 2 left) without dropping the object. The participants were instructed to set the speed of the robot to *slow* near the 5 meter line. Therefore, they had to give the robot three commands: C2, C11, and C10 in Table 1. We gave the participants instructions on the basic strategy using speech and gaze and the three commands. Before executing the task, the participants gave three trials for practice.

The goal of the second task was to locate the arrow in the second goal zone depicted in Figure 2. The participants were instructed to set the speed of the robot to *slow* before moving backward. After our oral instructions, the participants gave two trials for practice and executed the task. In the other two tasks, the participants were instructed to rotate the robot and locate the arrow between two lines (see Figure 2 right). In these tasks, three voice commands were required to start turning (C6 or C7), slow down (C11), and stop turning (C10). To complete Task 4, the participants had to step backward supporting the object. They were given opportunities for two trials before executing each rotation task.

RESULTS

Eight participants succeeded in all tasks and the other ones failed only once stopping the robot less than 40 millimeters beyond the limit line in Task 1 and Task 2, respectively. In most cases, the participants gave only three voice commands and sent one gaze cue to stop each movement. Only a small number of system and human errors were observed, but no false command detection occurred while the tasks were performed. On speech recognition errors, the participants repeated the voice command without hesitating. They spoke only correct words listed in Table 1, without asking for the robot's help.

In Task 1, the participants moved with the robot over the goal line and commanded the robot to stop in less than 44 seconds (M=31.1[s], SD=6.0[s]). In Task 2, they moved LIEN backward and stopped the robot in less than 14 seconds (M=12.0[s], SD=0.81[s]). The participants succeeded in rotating the robot approximately 90 degrees in less than 22 seconds in Task 3 (M=19.3[s], SD=0.89[s]) and Task 4 (M=19.1[s], SD=1.8[s]). Tables 3-7 summarize the results of the questionnaires (1: *very hard* – 7: *very easy*). In the interviews after the tasks, some participants commented about difficulties they found (see Table 8).

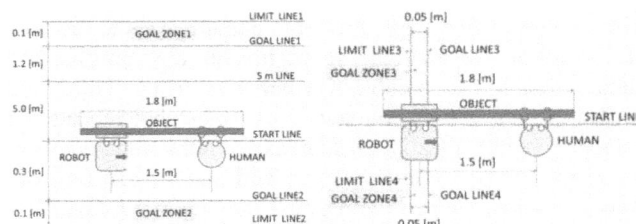

Figure 2. Translation tasks and rotation tasks (right)

Task	Median	Mode	Min	Max	M	SD
1 forward	7	7	7	7	7	0
2 backward	7	7	7	7	7	0
3 left	7	7	7	7	7	0
4 right	7	7	7	7	7	0

Table 3. Ease of learning to command the robot.

Task	Median	Mode	Min	Max	M	SD
1 forward	7	7	5	7	6.4	0.84
2 backward	7	7	6	7	6.8	0.42
3 left	7	7	7	7	6.7	0.67
4 right	7	7	3	7	6.2	1.31

Table 4. Ease of tasks.

Task	Median	Mode	Min	Max	M	SD
1 forward	6	6	5	7	6.2	0.63
2 backward	7	7	6	7	6.7	0.48
3 left	7	7	6	7	6.9	0.31
4 right	7	7	7	7	6.9	0.31

Table 5. Ease of positioning the robot.

Task	Median	Mode	Min	Max	M	SD
1 forward	5.5	7	2	7	5	1.89
2 backward	7	7	5	7	6.8	0.42
3 left	7	7	5	7	6.8	0.63
4 right	7	7	3	7	5.9	1.52

Table 6. Ease of stopping the robot with head gaze.

Task	Median	Mode	Min	Max	M	SD
1 forward	6	7	5	7	5.9	1.29
2 backward	7	7	5	7	6.6	0.7
3 left	7	7	5	7	6.5	0.71
4 right	7	7	4	7	6.2	1.14

Table 7. Ease of moving with the robot.

Comment	Task
I could not find the camera quickly when stopping the robot.	1, 4
The robot did not respond to gaze cues quickly.	1
I was not sure about how fast the robot would be moving.	1
Turning the face to the robot was not a very natural way.	1
I had to change my point of gaze very often when the robot was moving fast.	1
It was difficult to keep track of the robot's position.	2
It was difficult to keep track of the robot's orientation.	3, 4
I felt anxious when I was moving backward.	4
The robot turned too fast.	4

Table 8. Comments from the participants.

DISCUSSION

Although the number of the users was small, learning to command and move with LIEN holding an object appears to be quite easy for most young people. It is unlikely that novices need hours to learn to move objects with the robot. Firstly, 95% of the tasks were accomplished by the novices without help. Secondly, they made few errors in the tasks. In fact, they did not use wrong words or phrases at all to command LIEN. In addition, they used head gaze cues properly during executing their tasks. Thirdly, all participants felt that learning to command the robot was *very easy* in all tasks (see Table 3). They must have well understood how to command LIEN using speech and head gaze.

It also appears to be easy for most young novices to move an object with our robot. Firstly, most participants felt that the tasks given in this study were easy (see Table 4). The first task was slightly more difficult for a few participants than the second task presumably because they were not used to turning their face toward the camera of the robot (see Tables 6 and 8). The last task was the most difficult for some participants because they had to move backward fast. However, all tasks should not be difficult for more experienced humans. Secondly, the novices succeeded to stop the robot with head gaze in all tasks and felt that positioning the robot was *very easy* in the last task (see Table 5). This means that stopping the robot moving at the slow speed is easy even for novices, although stepping backward fast with the robot may be slightly difficult for some novices (see Tables 4, 6, 7, and 8).

It is likely that most young novices can move objects fairly efficiently with our robot by communicating using speech and head gaze. In fact, the participants located LIEN, supporting the long object, in a narrow area six meters away in less than 44 seconds and rotated it approximately 90 degrees in less than 22 seconds. They were able to locate the arrow on the robot in the narrow goal zones without taking too much time. Therefore, most novices should be able to move fast with the robot to approach a target and then move slowly and stop near the target.

The position of the camera and the appearance of the robot must be reconsidered so that novices can send gaze cues with less effort. Some novices reported difficulty in stopping LIEN with gaze in the first task. It should not be very easy for novices to quickly find the camera of the robot. In Task 1, some participants were not aware of the camera position. In addition, it was difficult for some participants to find the camera quickly when the robot was turning probably because the camera was distant from the central axis of the robot and moved in a circular orbit.

A more reliable and reactive gaze detection system can improve LIEN in ease of cooperation (see Tables 6 and 8). The robot may be able to detect head gaze cues more quickly by predicting them from a time series of head position and orientation. In addition, it would be easier to stop the robot if the human can use eye gaze, i.e. by moving the eyes to shift the point of gaze, rather than head gaze.

Finally, an additional command to request intermediate speeds (e.g. 1.0[km/h] and 0.2[rad/s]) may help novices and even experts, because it was difficult for some novices to step backward fast supporting an object with the robot.

REFERENCES

1. Berger, E., Vogt, D., Haji-Ghassemi, N., Jung, B., & Amor, H. B. 2013. Inferring guidance information in cooperative human-robot tasks. In *Proceedings of the 2013 13th IEEE-RAS International Conference on Humanoid Robots* (Humanoids), 124-129.

2. Liefeng Bo, Xiaofeng Ren, and Dieter Fox. 2013. Unsupervised feature learning for RGB-D based object recognition. In *Experimental Robotics*, 387-402.

3. Jean-David Boucher, Ugo Pattacini, Amélie Lelong, Gérard Bailly, Frédéric Elisei, Sascha Fagel, Peter Ford Dominey ,and Jocelyne Ventre-Dominey. 2012. I reach faster when I see you look: Gaze effects in human-human and human-robot face-to-face cooperation. *Frontiers in Neurorobotics*, 6, 3: 1-11.

4. Judee. K. Burgoon and Laura K. Guerrero, and Kory Floyd. 2010. *Nonverbal Communication*, Allyn & Bacon.

5. Widodo Budiharto. 2014. Robust vision-based detection and grasping object for manipulator using SIFT keypoint detector. In *Proceedings of the 2014 International Conference on Advanced Mechatronic Systems* (ICAMechS 2014), 448-452.

6. M. W. M. Gamini Dissanayake, Paul Newman, Steven Clark, Hugh F. Durrant-Whyte, and M. Csorba. 2001. A solution to the simultaneous localization and map building (SLAM) problem. *IEEE Transactions on Robotics and Automation* 17, 3: 229-241.

7. Ederyn Williams. 1977. Experimental comparisons of face-to-face and mediated communication. A review. *Psychological Bulletin*, 84, 5: 963-976.

8. Arnab Ghosh, Amit Konar, and R. Janarthanan. 2012. Multi-robot cooperative box-pushing problem using multi-objective particle swarm optimization technique. In *Proceedings of the 2012 World Congress on Information and Communication Technologies* (WICT 2012), 272-277.

9. Joy E. Hanna and Susan E. Brennan. 2007. Speakers' eye gaze disambiguates referring expressions early during face-to-face conversation. *Journal of Memory and Language*, 57, 4: 596-615.

10. Koji Ishimura and Toru Namerikawa. 2011. Cooperative conveyance by vehicle swarms with dynamic network topology. In *Proceedings of the 2011 SICE Annual Conference* (SICE2011), 694-699.

11. Kazuhiro Kosuge and Yasuhisa Hirata. 2004. Human-robot interaction. In *Proceedings of the 2004 IEEE International Conference on Robotics and Biomimetics* (ROBIO 2004), 8-11.

12. Kazuhiro Yokoyama, Hiyoyuki Handa, Takakatsu Isozumi, Yutaro Fukase, Kenji Kaneko, Fumio Kanehiro, Yoshihiro Kawai, Fumiaki Tomita, and Hirohisa Hirukawa. 2003. Cooperative works by a human and a humanoid robot. In *Proceedings of the 2003 IEEE International Conference on Robotics and Automation* (ICRA'03), 2985-2991.

"Look at Me!" – Self-Interruptions as Attention Booster?

Birte Carlmeyer
CITEC - Bielefeld University
Bielefeld, Germany
bcarlmey@techfak.uni-
bielefeld.de

David Schlangen
CITEC - Bielefeld University
Bielefeld, Germany
david.schlangen@uni-
bielefeld.de

Britta Wrede
CITEC - Bielefeld University
Bielefeld, Germany
bwrede@techfak.uni-
bielefeld.de

ABSTRACT

In this paper we present results of an exploratory experiment investigating the effects of a contingently self-interrupting vs non-self-interrupting virtual agent who transmits information to a human interaction partner. In the experimental condition self-interruptions of the agent were triggered by an external event whereas in the control group the agent did not react to this event. We measured the effect of the agent's self-interruptions on human attention, memory performance and subjective ratings. In this paper we discuss the results with respect to the design of incremental human-agent dialogue modeling.

ACM Classification Keywords

H.5.2 Information interfaces and presentation: User Interfaces; I.2.7 Artificial intelligence: Natural Language Processing

Author Keywords

Dialogue management; incr. processing; multi-modal systems

INTRODUCTION

Smart home environments provide a range of powerful automation capabilities. However, so far no convincing concept of a smart and easy to follow interface has been proposed. Consequently, many functionalities remain unused. In our project we envision interaction with the environment via a virtual or robotic agent who provides help and information on request. However, information about such complex functionalities tend to be large and may lead to lengthy monologues. Alternatively, they may be chunked into smaller pieces with explicit requests for continuation. Both strategies yield cumbersome interactions leaving the user with the wish to interrupt or simply leave. We therefore propose an incremental dialogue model that enables interruptions of the system at any time. Additionally, the system should also be able to interrupt the ongoing interaction when the user looses interest or disengages due to distractions in the home environment. It is thus important to monitor a user's attention in order to avoid disruptions of the interaction or inattentive system behavior. Models of keeping track of the user's level of engagement have been proposed as an important feature of human-agent interaction [3, 6]. At the social level, joint attention indicates engagement in an interaction [10]. Consequently, looking away (if not caused by a reference within the interaction) can be interpreted as leaving the interaction [3]. While monitoring the user's attention level is an important step for modeling human-agent interaction, it still neglects the question how to reacquire a user's attention when it has moved away?

STATE OF THE ART

Although there is an increasing amount on studies in the area of attention and the use of eye-gaze, still relatively few studies explicitly address on how to best apply these findings to human-agent interaction (HAI) and to implement them in incremental dialogue systems. In [10] the authors report that the initial 5 seconds of an interaction correlate with the user's following engagement level: if the robot provides a contingent looking strategy, including looking-away if the user did not look (at the beginning of the interaction) users in the museum setting were more likely to remain longer in interaction with the robot as opposed to a non-contingent strategy. Thus, interruptions in the agent's gazing behavior seem to have an effect on the user's attention. [12] analyzed different gaze patterns in multi-party conversations and found that gaze can be used as a predictor of attention in conversations.

An in-car scenario [7] showed that self-interruptions of an information giving system leads to increased memory performance. Self-interruptions were initiated in situations where the user was involved in another, potentially dangerous task such as switching lanes or overtaking somebody. In a robot teaching context [9] evaluate the role of gaze as implicit signal for turn-taking in a dictating scenario and showed that gaze as synchronization cue has an impact on task performance in a two-party setting. Thus, self-interruptions in a task-oriented interaction can lead to increased task performance. While these works focus on task-oriented interaction they do not evaluate how this strategy affects subjective ratings.

Another strategy for maintaining a user's attention that has been proposed consists of introducing hesitations (or filled pauses). [4] report on increased engagement levels when providing hesitations in a human-robot interaction scenario. While focusing on a task-oriented interaction (i.e. providing directions) it was not evaluated how this strategy affected cognitive performance. Also, its effect on subjective ratings was not assessed.

HAI '16 October 04-07, 2016, Biopolis, Singapore
© 2016 Copyright held by the owner/author(s).
ACM ISBN 978-1-4503-4508-8/16/10... $15.00
DOI: http://dx.doi.org/10.1145/2974804.2980488

Considering the results of the presented literature, one important feature for re-acquiring a user's attention seems to be by contingent self-interruptions. We therefore propose a strategy that provides self-interruptions of the agent in situations where the user is distracted. We further define the following hypotheses: (1) Self-interruptions of an agent will increase cognitive performance (better post-interaction information recall) of the human interaction partner (2) Self-interruptions will reacquire attention as measured by gazing behavior and (3) influence subjective ratings of the agent.

ATTENTION MODEL

In our model we define attention while the system or agent is speaking as a state where the human interlocutor's visual focus of attention (VFoA) is consistent with the focus of discourse (FoD) as determined by the system's interpretation of the ongoing dialogue. The user's VFoA can be recognized through visual perception of his/her head pose [11], whereas the FoD is provided by the dialogue management (DM) and defined as the physical reference of the topic that is currently being talked about (e.g. a referenced object in the environment or direction) or - in absence of this - the interaction partner. Figure 1 shows a schematic graphical representation of our model. If

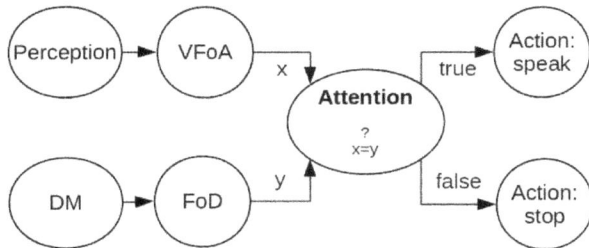

Figure 1. Attention Model: define attention as state where the visual focus of attention (VFoA) is consistent with the focus of discourse (FoD) and triggers different actions. *Image ©Birte Carlmeyer*

the human interaction partner is attentive, meaning his/her VFoA is consistent with the the FoD of the current interaction state, the agent will start or continue with the interaction, i.e. speaking. Otherwise the agent has to reacquire attention through a dedicated reacquisition action which in our model is defined as an immediate break-off of the speech synthesis. To simplify the evaluation of the effect of a self-interrupting agent, we chose a topic where the FoD is on the agent itself (in this case information about the agent).

METHOD

We evaluated the effect of a verbally self-interrupting agent in a human-agent interaction in a smart home environment. The agent was providing information about itself through a sequence of 6 sentences. In both conditions we provided an external distraction in the apartment to the right side of the participant at an angle of about 90 degrees in order to withdraw the user's VFoA from the system. In the experimental condition this triggered the self-interruption behavior of the system (triggered by a Wizard through pressing a button upon perceiving the user's VFoA shifting away). The agent would

directly stop speaking and continue exactly at the break-off point when the user's VFoA moved back to the agent. In the control condition the agent simply continued speaking throughout the distraction. The distraction was achieved by the experimenter reentering the room pretending to bring in some missing documents for the experiment, issuing a brief verbal apology with explanation and leaving.

Experimental Setup

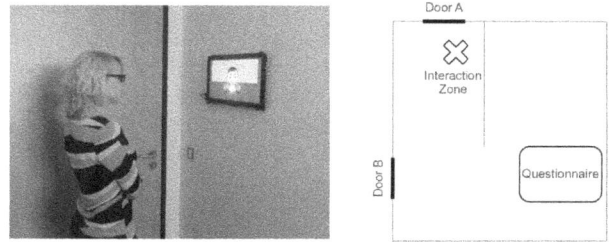

Figure 2. Experimental setup. Left: person interacting with the agent. Right: ground view of the apartment. *Image ©Birte Carlmeyer*

Figure 2 shows the experimental setup. The participants were facing a tablet, which was showing a simulation of the robot platform Flobi[8], an anthropomorphic robot head. Through the tablet camera, the simulated Flobi is able to detect faces in front of it and focus on them, thus establishing shared attention. The human-agent interaction had three phases of verbal interaction (monologue by the agent) in both conditions: *Phase 1*: Greeting. *Phase 2*: Information about the system (6 sentences). The distraction was initiated after the first sentence. *Phase 3*: Request to move on to fill out the questionnaire at the computer in the room to the right of the participant. Flobi's verbalizations were predefined and triggered from an adjoining room by a wizard who observed the participant through the tablet's camera. To allow verbal self-interruptions, we used the incremental speech synthesis module of InproTK[2] and its integration in the PaMini dialogue manager [5] which supports immediate interruption and resuming of the speech synthesis.

The questionnaire consisted of two parts: a memory task and subjective ratings about Flobi. The memory task consisted of six statements for which the participants had to decide whether or not this was a statement that had been made by the agent during Phase 2. In the second part the participants had to provide subjective ratings of the agent through a set of adjectives on a Likert scale ranging from 1 to 7 to evaluate five key concepts in human-robot interaction: anthropomorphism, animacy, likeability, perceived intelligence, and perceived safety (based on [1]).

The experimental procedure was as follows. After signing a consent form, the subjects were led to the experiment room. They entered the room alone through *Door A*, only with the instruction to look at the tablet on the left wall and to fill out a questionnaire on the computer after the interaction. The wizard started the interaction as soon as the participants stood in front of the tablet facing it. The study assistants disturbed the interaction always after the first sentence of Part 2 of the interaction was finished, by entering the the experiment room through *Door B*. At the end of the interaction the participants went to the table and filled out the questionnaire on a computer.

Conditions and Dependent Variables

We compared two conditions. In the first condition the agent reacted *with self-interruptions* (cf. Experimental Set-up). In the *control* group the agent did not react to the distractions and kept on speaking. In order to assess the memory performance of the participants we counted the number of correct answers to the content-related questions of the questionnaire. To obtain a measure for the attention we manually annotated the head position of the user and measured the number and duration participants looked away from the agent during the interaction (i.e. the number and duration where VFoA was different to FoD). For the subjective ratings we evaluated the answers of the second part of the questionnaire.

RESULTS

In total 27 subjects (9 female, 18 male, aged 21-51) took part in the study. The average age was 27.2 with a standard deviation of 5.3. 13 participants were in the condition *with self-interruption* and 14 in the *control* group. The study assistants disturbed the human-agent interaction in the experimental condition *with self-interruptions* 10.47 second in average and in the *control* condition 10.25 seconds. For the statistical analysis we chose an alpha level of 0.05.

Memory Performance

At first we want to explore the memory performance. Note that all questions were yes/no questions. The percentages of correct answers for each condition for the different memory questions are shown in Figure 3. No significant effects in the

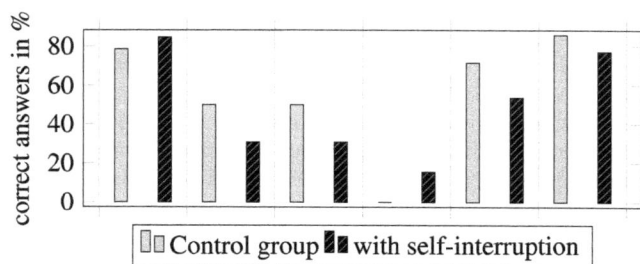

Figure 3. Performance in memory task for the different questions.

results between the two conditions were found. The overall percentages of correct answers for the experimental condition *with self-interruption* is 48.7% whereas the subjects in the *control* condition answered 56.0% correct. This difference is not large enough for statistical significance. These results indicate participants simply guessed in both conditions. We were thus not able to confirm our first hypothesis (1).

Visual Attention

In order to assess the participants' visual attention we measured the number of shifts of VFoA away from the agent during Part 2 of the interaction. In the experimental condition *with self-interruptions* most participants looked away only once (9/13). One participant did not get distracted at all. Only three subjects looked away more than once. In contrast in the

control group more than half of the participants (8/14) looked away more than once, even while there were no more distractions. Five participants looked away two times and 3 subjects even three times. However, these differences did not reach a significant level. Also for the time of the first "look away" after the student assistant's distraction, no significant effects of the mean time were found. Figure 4 shows the overall time of participants looking away during phase two of the interaction. We tested significance of the results using a generalized linear mixed model and found a significant effect between the two conditions (F=4.386, $p = 0.047$). The participants in

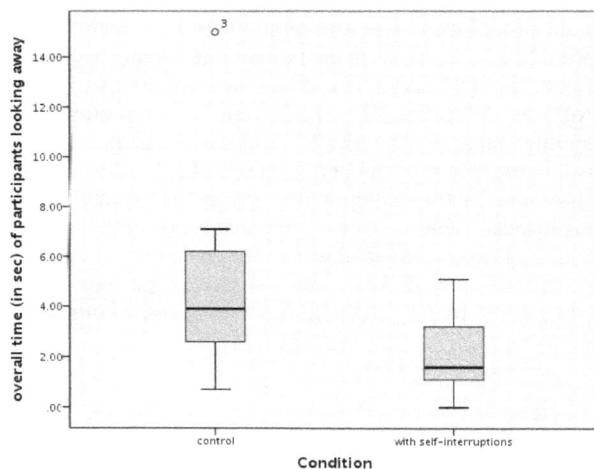

Figure 4. Overall time (in sec) of participants looking away during the interaction.

the *control* group looked away longer than the participants in the experimental condition *with self-interruption* during phase two of the interaction, thus confirming our hypothesis (2).

Subjective Ratings

Next we want to explore the subjective ratings of the agent. The MANOVA over all subjective ratings revealed a marginal multivariate effect (F=9.718, p=0.97) between the two conditions. More specifically, participants in the experimental group *with self-interruption* rated the agent significantly less likable than the *control* group (F=6.588, p=0.017). While the experimental group rated the likability of the agent with 4.8 the *control* group's rating was 5.6. For other ratings no significant effects were found.

DISCUSSION AND OUTLOOK

The results of the looking behavior measurement suggest that the self-interrupting of the agent has a significant effect on the visual focus of attention of the human interaction partner. This effect manifests in the overall time participants looked away from the agent and indicates that self-interruptions are an effective intervention strategy to regain the attention of the interaction partner. Interestingly, in one case, the self-interrupting behavior had precisely the contrary effect as it lead the participant to repeatedly look away in order to test the agent's capabilities. While this is clearly a novelty effect that is likely to disappear in further interactions it indicates that the highly contingent self-interrupting behavior has a very powerful effect on the interaction partner's perception of the agent and deserves further investigations as detailed below.

While in the presented experiment the FoD was on the agent itself we will move on to scenarios where the FoD will change, as is typically the case in joint task situations. Consider, for example, a scenario where a robot or virtual agent gives assistance in a smart home. In such a task-oriented interaction the FoD (and thus the VFoA) will shift away from the agent itself towards appliances that are being explained or discussed by the agent. In such more task-oriented interactions that require even more cognitive involvement of the user - as the explanations may become complicated - the resuming of the interaction will become more important. As shown by [7] self-interruptions can help to increase cognitive performance. However, it remains unclear if this effect is due to the self-interruptions alone or also caused by the repetition of parts of the utterances. In our next study we will target this question. The fact that our results did not show a significant effect of self-interruptions on memory performance may be due to two different factors: on the one hand, the users were not provided with repetitions of the utterance from just before the interruption, on the other hand the questions might simply have been too difficult. We will explore in further studies how the positive effect on the memory performance can be replicated in our setting.

Although the self-interruptions had a positive guiding effect on the VFoA of the participants, they rated the self-interrupting agent significantly less likable. To prevent or at least ameliorate this effect we plan to integrate a more adaptable speech synthesis. For example the agent could not only repeat the last few utterances but also produce hesitations as proposed by [4].

CONCLUSIONS
We have presented an human-agent interaction experiment investigating the effect of a verbal self-interrupting agent on human attention, memory performance and subjective ratings showing that self-interruptions are effective in re-acquiring VFoA which is in line with [4]. We furthermore showed that this positive effect is achieved at the cost of less positive subjective ratings and proposed to adapt the speech synthesis to ameliorate or compensate this effect. Additionally, we discussed potential positive implications of this behavior on the user's memory performance. For the further optimization process of our model we will take all three dimensions (attention, memory performance, subjective ratings) into account.

ACKNOWLEDGMENTS
This work was funded as part of the Cluster of Excellence Cognitive Interaction Technology 'CITEC' (EXC 277), Bielefeld University, and by the German Federal Ministry of Education and Research (BMBF) via the KogniHome project (project number: 16SV7054K).

REFERENCES
1. Christoph Bartneck, Dana Kulić, Elizabeth Croft, and Susana Zoghbi. 2009. Measurement instruments for the anthropomorphism, animacy, likeability, perceived intelligence, and perceived safety of robots. *International journal of social robotics* 1, 1 (2009), 71–81.

2. Timo Baumann and David Schlangen. 2012. The InproTK 2012 release. In *Proc. of the NAACL-HLT Workshop on Future directions and needs in the Spoken Dialog Community: Tools and Data*. ACL, 29–32.

3. Dan Bohus and Eric Horvitz. 2009. Models for Multiparty Engagement in Open-world Dialog. In *Proc. of the SIGDIAL 2009 Conference*. ACL, Stroudsburg, PA, USA, 225–234.

4. Dan Bohus and Eric Horvitz. 2014. Managing Human-Robot Engagement with Forecasts and... Um... Hesitations. In *Proc. of the 16th International Conference on Multimodal Interaction*. ACM, New York, USA, 2–9.

5. Birte Carlmeyer, David Schlangen, and Britta Wrede. 2014. Towards Closed Feedback Loops in HRI: Integrating InproTK and PaMini. In *Proc. of the 2014 Workshop on Multimodal, Multi-Party, Real-World Human-Robot Interaction*. ACM, 1–6.

6. David Klotz, Johannes Wienke, Julia Peltason, Britta Wrede, Sebastian Wrede, Vasil Khalidov, and Jean-Marc Odobez. 2011. Engagement-based Multi-party Dialog with a Humanoid Robot. In *Proc. of the SIGDIAL 2011 Conference*. ACL, 341–343.

7. Spyridon Kousidis, Casey Kennington, Timo Baumann, Hendrik Buschmeier, Stefan Kopp, and David Schlangen. 2014. Situationally Aware In-Car Information Presentation Using Incremental Speech Generation: Safer, and More Effective. In *Proc. of the EACL 2014 Workshop on Dialogue in Motion*. 68–72.

8. Ingo Lütkebohle, Frank Hegel, Simon Schulz, Matthias Hackel, Britta Wrede, Sven Wachsmuth, and Gerhard Sagerer. 2010. The Bielefeld Anthropomorphic Robot Head "Flobi". In *2010 IEEE International Conference on Robotics and Automation*. IEEE, 3384–3391.

9. Oskar Palinko, Alessandra Sciutti, Lars Schillingmann, Francesco Rea, Yukie Nagai, and Giulio Sandini. 2015. Gaze contingency in turn-taking for human robot interaction: Advantages and drawbacks. In *IEEE International Symposium on Robot and Human Interactive Communication*. IEEE, 369–374.

10. Karola Pitsch, Hideaki Kuzuoka, Yuya Suzuki, Luise Süssenbach, Paul Luff, and Christian Heath. 2009. The first five seconds: Contingent stepwise entry into an interaction as a means to secure sustained engagement. In *IEEE International Symposium on Robot and Human Interactive Communication*. 985–991.

11. K. Smith, S. O. Ba, J. M. Odobez, and D. Gatica-Perez. 2008. Tracking the Visual Focus of Attention for a Varying Number of Wandering People. *IEEE Transactions on Pattern Analysis and Machine Intelligence* 30, 7 (July 2008), 1212–1229.

12. Roel Vertegaal, Robert Slagter, Gerrit van der Veer, and Anton Nijholt. 2001. Eye Gaze Patterns in Conversations: There is More to Conversational Agents Than Meets the Eyes. In *Proceedings of the SIGCHI Conference on Human Factors in Computing Systems*. ACM, New York, NY, USA, 301–308.

Investigation on Effects of Color, Sound, and Vibration on Human's Emotional Perception

Sichao Song
Department of Informatics
The Graduate University for Advanced Studies
(Sokendai)
2-1-2 Hitotsubashi, Chiyoda, Tokyo, Japan
sichaos@nii.ac.jp

Seiji Yamada
National Institute of Informatics
The Graduate University for Advanced Studies
(Sokendai)
2-1-2 Hitotsubashi, Chiyoda, Tokyo, Japan
seiji@nii.ac.jp

ABSTRACT
As robotics has advanced, research on conveying a robot's emotional state to a person has become a hot topic. Most current studies are focused on interaction modalities such as facial expressions and natural language. Although many of the results seem to be promising, they suffer from high cost and technical difficulties. In this paper, we turn our attention to three other interaction modalities: color, sound, and vibration. Such modalities have the advantage of being simple, low cost, and intuitive. We conducted a pilot study to evaluate the effects of the three modalities on a human's emotional perception towards our robot *Maru*. Our result indicates that humans tend to interpret a robot's emotion as negative (angry in particular) when vibration and sound are used, while they interpret the emotion as relaxed when only color modality is used. In addition, the participants showed preference towards the robot when using all three modalities.

ACM Classification Keywords
H.5.m. Information Interfaces and Presentation (e.g. HCI): User Interfaces - Theory and methods

Author Keywords
Color; Sound; Vibration; Emotional expression of a robot; Multi-modalities; Human-Agent Interaction (HAI); HRI; HCI.

INTRODUCTION
As robotics has advanced, research on conveying a robot's emotional states to a person has become a hot topic. As over 80% of human communication is encoded in facial expressions and body movements [5], most of the current studies are focused on interaction modalities, for instance, facial expressions, natural language, and body gestures. Although many of them have shown promising results, they suffer from high cost and technical difficulties.

HAI '16, October 04-07, 2016, Biopolis, Singapore
ACM 978-1-4503-4508-8/16/10.
http://dx.doi.org/10.1145/2974804.2980497

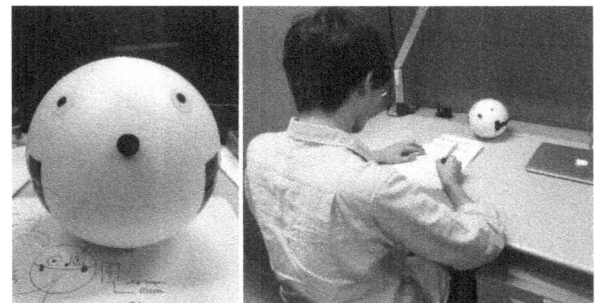

Figure 1. Maru and the experiment setting.

To make the interaction design simple, low cost, and intuitive, we turn our attention to three other modalities: *color*, *sound*, and *vibration*. Previous studies have shown their impact on a person's perception [2, 6, 7]. However, to the best of our knowledge, there is no work that comprehensively evaluated the effect of these three modalities in a scenario involving the emotional expression of a robot.

In this paper, we present our pilot study on this topic. We evaluate a human's perception towards a robot conveying its emotions through the three modalities. A ball-shaped robot named "Maru" was designed in order to conduct a user experiment. To be specific, we wanted to see how participants interpret Maru's emotions in three cases: one modality (color), two modalities (vibration and sound), and all three modalities.

METHODS AND DESIGN
We used the circumplex model of affect to map emotions onto a valence-arousal space. In particular, we focused on four emotions, *relaxed, happy, sad*, and *angry*, where each emotion can be mapped onto a different quadrant of the valence-arousal space. We first conducted a pre-design phase to decide a limited candidate cue pool for our user experiment. This is because each modality can be associated with many factors, resulting in a design space that is too large.

Pre-design Session
At the beginning stage of the study, we wanted to prepare a candidate cue pool with a total of 12 candidate cues (3 modalities × 4 emotions) in order to constrain our design space. Previous studies suggest that colors can be considered as having the attribute to evoke different emotions [3, 6]. Accordingly, we

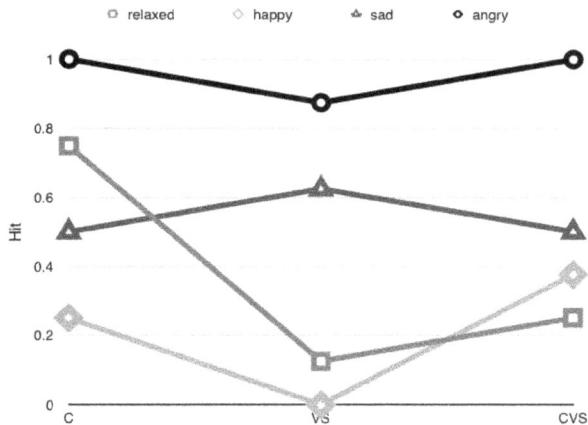

Figure 2. Modalities vs. Hit (C: color, V: vibration, S: sound)

decided to associate relaxed with white, happy with green, sad with blue, and angry with red. [2, 1, 7] indicate that both sound and vibration can be informative in discriminating between levels of valence (positive and negative) and levels of arousal. For instance, [1] claims that sounds with upward slopes were interpreted as "disagreement", and [2] shows that a decreasing ASE successfully conveyed "low confident" state to the users. Thus, we decided to associate a flat beep sound with a positive state, rising-pitch beep sound with a negative and high arousal state, and falling-pitch beep sound with a negative and low arousal state. We also designed four levels of vibration intensity, where a higher intensity indicates a higher level of arousal.

Designing the Robot Maru

We intentionally made Maru's embodiment and appearance as simple as possible while still having the attribute of anthropomorphism (see Figure. 1). The robot is made of two pieces of hollow semi-spherical Styrofoam. Four LEDs (white, green, blue, and red) were assembled behind each eye. In addition, a speaker is used to generate beep sound cues, and a vibration motor is attached to the inner body to produce vibration cues. An Arduino UNO board was programmed to control the robot.

EXPERIMENT

Eight Japanese (4 males and 4 females) ranging from 22 to 39 years old (M = 27.88, SD = 5.94) participated the study. The experiment was a 3×5 within-subject design with two independent variables: *combination of modalities* [one modality (color), two modalities (vibration, sound), three modalities (color, vibration, sound)] and *emotion* (relaxed, happy, sad, angry). We evaluated one dependent variable: *hit* [correctly recognized an emotion (1) and incorrectly recognized an emotion (0)]. In addition, we collected participants' preferences towards the three modalities via a post questionnaire using 7-point Likert scales. An example question is "do you think you recognize Maru's emotions better when using three modalities (color, vibration, sound) rather than the other two cases (one and two modalities)?"

RESULTS AND DISCUSSION

Figure 2 demonstrates our result. A two-way repeated-measure ANOVA on both factors for the dependent variable was conducted. From the result, no significant difference in the main effect of *combination of modalities* [F(2,14) = 1.87, n.s.] was found, indicating that *hit* across the four emotions does not change much with different combinations of modalities. However, *emotion* showed a significant effect [F(3,21) = 10.79, p<0.001]. A Tukey's HSD test showed that among the four emotions, angry (M_{hit} = 0.96) was recognized significantly better than relaxed (M_{hit} = 0.38, p<0.001), happy (M_{hit} = 0.21, p<0.001), and sad (M_{hit} = 0.58, p<0.05). In addition, sad was also recognized significantly better than happy (p<0.05). No other significant differences were found.

We also observed a significant difference in the *combination of modalities* × *emotion* interaction effect [F(6,42) = 2.98, p<0.05]. This indicates that emotional perception changes depending on the different combination of modalities. There is no single combination of modality that is effective for all kinds of emotions. Paired sample *t*-tests with Bonferroni correction were conducted in light of the significant interaction. We see that relaxed was recognized significantly better using only color modality compared with using two modalities [t(7) = 2.65, p<0.05] and three modalities [t(7) = 3.42, p<0.05]. However, we did not find significant differences regarding the other three emotions.

In addition, an analysis of the questionnaires indicated that the participants preferred when the robot used all three modalities rather than only one or two modalities. From the result, we propose our preliminary design guideline based on the conclusions from our result. We suggest using only color modality (white) to express relaxed. Negative emotions such as sad and angry, in order to be iconic, are strongly recommended to be expressed through vibration and sound to. Specifically, we suggest conveying angry using all three modalities while conveying sadness using two modalities without color.

FUTURE WORK

We will later conduct experiments on the three modalities with larger number of participants. Particularly, we will focus on the expression of happy and sad, and more combinations of modalities will be examined. Further, we are considering expanding the current system with biometric sensors such as ECG and EDA. In addition, we are especially interested in the concept of *agent migration* [4]. We will investigate how to shift the heavy amount of work on emotional communication from the robot side to a third-party device such as a wearable device through modalities such as color, vibration, and sound by applying the idea of agent migration.

ACKNOWLEDGEMENTS

This study was partially supported by JSPS KAKENHI "Cognitive Interaction Design" (No.26118005).

REFERENCES

1. Takanori Komatsu. 2005. Toward making humans empathize with artificial agents by means of subtle expressions. In *Affective Computing and Intelligent Interaction*. Springer, 458–465.

2. Takanori Komatsu, Seiji Yamada, Kazuki Kobayashi, Kotaro Funakoshi, and Mikio Nakano. 2010. Artificial subtle expressions: intuitive notification methodology of artifacts. In *Proceedings of the SIGCHI Conference on Human Factors in Computing Systems*. ACM, 1941–1944.

3. Niels A Nijdam. 2009. Mapping emotion to color. *)^(Eds.):âĂŸBook Mapping emotion to colorâĂŹ(2009, edn.)* (2009), 2–9.

4. Kohei Ogawa and Tetsuo Ono. 2008. ITACO: Effects to interactions by relationships between humans and artifacts. In *Intelligent Virtual Agents*. Springer, 296–307.

5. Jocelyn Scheirer and R Picard. 2000. Affective objects. *MIT Media lab Technical Rep.* 524 (2000).

6. Marina V Sokolova and Antonio Fernández-Caballero. 2015. A review on the role of color and light in affective computing. *Applied Sciences* 5, 3 (2015), 275–293.

7. Shafiq ur Réhman and Li Liu. 2010. ifeeling: Vibrotactile rendering of human emotions on mobile phones. In *Mobile Multimedia Processing*. Springer, 1–20.

Voting-Based Backchannel Timing Prediction Using Audio-Visual Information

Tomoki Nishide
Graduate School of
Informatics, Kyoto University
Kyoto, Japan
tnishide@vision.kuee.kyoto-u.ac.jp

Kei Shimonishi
Graduate School of
Informatics, Kyoto University
Kyoto, Japan
simonisi@vision.kuee.kyoto-u.ac.jp

Hiroaki Kawashima
Graduate School of
Informatics, Kyoto University
Kyoto, Japan
kawashima@i.kyoto-u.ac.jp

Takashi Matsuyama
Graduate School of
Informatics, Kyoto University
Kyoto, Japan
tm@i.kyoto-u.ac.jp

ABSTRACT

While many spoken dialog systems are recently developed, users need to summarize and convey what they want the system to do clearly. However, in a human dialog, a speaker often summarize what to say incrementally, provided that there is a good listener who responds to the speaker's utterances at appropriate timing. We consider that generating backchannel responses, where appropriate, overlapped with the user's utterances is crucial for an artificial listener system that can promote user's utterances since such overlaps are the norm in human dialogs. Toward the goal to realize such a listener system, in this paper, we propose a voting-based algorithm of predicting the end of utterances early (i.e., before the utterances end) using audio-visual information. In the evaluation, we demonstrate the effectiveness of using audio-visual information and the applicability of the voting-based prediction algorithm with some early results.

ACM Classification Keywords

H.5.m. Information Interfaces and Presentation (e.g. HCI): Miscellaneous

Author Keywords

Backchannel response; online prediction; decision tree; multimodal.

INTRODUCTION

Many spoken dialog systems are recently developed, and they are becoming more familiar for us. In the near future, they can

HAI '16 October 04-07, 2016, Biopolis, Singapore
© 2016 Copyright held by the owner/author(s).
ACM ISBN 978-1-4503-4508-8/16/10.
DOI: http://dx.doi.org/10.1145/2974804.2980501

be installed into a variety of devices and appliances around us and necessary to our lives.

In a current spoken dialog system, the primary aim is a search for the information. In this system, a dialog is the exchange of questions and answers, and users need to summarize what they want the system to do and then convey it clearly. However, even if their requests for a system are unclear, the system needs to give them the information that can satisfy them. Moreover, users may just want to speak with a dialog system (i.e., having a conversation itself can be users' objective). In such situation, the system have to detect their state of mind (e.g., questions, requests, and so on) from their utterance or action and respond to them approximately as we human do in our daily conversation. It is effective in detecting their state of mind to get the information of them by promoting them to make more utterances, that is, by being a good listener.

Therefore, the ultimate goal of this research is to construct a spoken dialog system that can promote users to make more utterances and get the information of users effectively by using backchannel responses appropriately [1]. In particular, we want to construct a system that can generate backchannel responses and sometimes overlapped partially with the user's utterances (i.e., generate responses before the utterances end). In this study, we formulate this as the problem of *early end-of-utterance detection* and propose a method of predicting the backchannel timing based on a voting approach.

There are many possible scenarios where such listener systems can be applied. For example, we can assume the situation of e-learning, where users summarize and explain what they have learned to the listener system after taking online courses. By promoting users' utterances using this system, the users' understanding level can be estimated to some extent by analyzing

---

[1]This is often referred to as Autonomous Sensitive Artificial Lister System in some projects [5]

the spoken explanations, and accordingly give feedback to the users that can help improve their understanding.

PREVIOUS WORK

There are several works related to backchannel-generation systems. Kitaoka et al. [2] constructed a system that generates response timing by a decision tree using the prosodic and linguistic information of the end of utterances. The work [2] used power and pitch (zero crossing) as the prosodic information and the results of speech recognition followed by morphological analysis as the linguistic information. However, because this system judges either it generates backchannel, takes a turn (it speaks), or does nothing every 100 ms interval after user's utterance ends, it cannot generate overlapped responses even though there are a lot of "overlapped" response in the corpus used in this study.

Nishimura et al. [3] constructed the dialog system that can generate response sentences and response timing in real time using prosodic and linguistic information. In this study, the system can realize "overlapped" responses by limiting the conversation topic to "weather". For example, if a user says "Recently, it is not so fine.", the system does approving response "I think so, too." with overlap by detecting the keywords "Recently" and "not so" assuming the weather topic. However, if the conversation topic is not limited, it is difficult to generate overlapped responses appropriately using only keywords.

APPROACH

In order to generate overlapped backchannel responses, the system need to predict the end of user's utterances before they end and decide the backchannel response timing. Therefore, in this study, we focus on the signal change of user's speech as the best timing of backchannel response and predict the end of utterances based on this signal information before user's utterance ends.

There are some recent works on early event detection methods. For example, Hoai and Torre [1] proposed a max-margin early event detector that utilizes the structured output SVM, and Phan et al. [4] introduced a method to accumulate prediction results of event startpoints and endpoints by using the random regression forests in every time window. In particular, the latter method can also be applied to predict upcoming endpoints of an event while their work [4] regarded events as intervals (i.e., an event has both start and endpoints). In our study, we consider that the accumulation of prediction is essential for online generation of responses and propose a voting-based real-time endpoint prediction as a simplified framework of [4] in order to deal with the early endpoint detection of utterances.

Additionally, we use the information of lip movements in prediction. In general, it is difficult to predict the end of utterances using only the syntactic information, especially in Japanese, because the structure of sentence is not decided only by word order. However, if we can detect the start of the lip movements corresponding the phrases "*desu*" and "*masu*", which often appear at the end of the utterances, it may help us predict the end of utterances early. Moreover, it is difficult to predict under noisy environments using only audio information, but

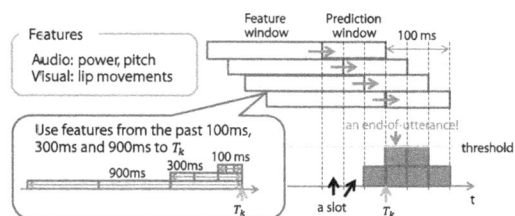

Figure 1. Voting-based algorithm of online end-of-utterance prediction.

by using also visual information we can expect that the system run appropriately under noisy environments.

Here, it is important to distinguish the definition of utterances to build a model for the end-of-utterance prediction; in particular, we consider the following two definitions of utterance sections.

Signal-based definition:
An utterance section is determined by extracting prosodic information such as power and pitch from audio signal and accordingly dividing audio signal; a typical example is IPU (Inter-Pausal Unit). After the preprocessing of VAD (Voice Activity Detection) for detecting voice sections, IPU is determined as a sequence of voice sections, where sequences are divided by a silent section larger than a certain length.

Linguistic-based definition:
In this definition, an utterance section is defined by dividing transcribed utterance content with syntactic and semantic boundary. In particular, this paper considers Clause Unit (CU) [6]. CU is a unit of utterance section proposed in Corpus of Spontaneous Japanese, where a unit is divided by clause boundaries (i.e., syntactic and semantic boundaries). In our study, we use the following two boundary classes by simplifying the classification of clause boundaries in [6].

- Absolute Boundary (AB): the boundary attached just after the phrase of end of a sentence (e.g. "*desu*", "*masu*").

- Other Boundary (OB): the boundary except AB. This can be further classified into strong boundary, which is attached just after the subordinate clause with low dependence (e.g. "*desuga*", "*masuga*", "*keredomo*"), and weak boundary, which is attached just after the subordinate clause with high dependence (e.g. "*tari*", "*node*", "*toiu*").

In our study, we assume that the system generates backchannel responses for filled pauses and incomplete words in addition to the utterance with clear content. Therefore, we define the end of utterances by dividing the speech using signal-based definition with IPU.

VOTING-BASED ALGORITHM OF ONLINE END-OF-UTTERANCE PREDICTION

The outline of the proposed algorithm is shown in Figure1. In this section, we first explain about audio-visual features, and then explain the end-of-utterance prediction algorithm.

We use prosodic features, power and pitch (F0), as audio features, and lip movements as visual features. The speaker voice is recorded at 44.1 kHz and the speaker video is recorded at 30 fps. The audio (prosodic) features are downsampled at a rate of 30 Hz (sampling interval is about 33 ms) in concert with the video sampling rate. From each video frame, facial landmarks are detected, and the vertical distance between the top-center of the upper lip and the bottom-center of the lower lip is extracted. In order to make a feature vector at frame T_k, which is used in the prediction algorithm, we set three kinds of feature window with different window sizes: from the past 100 ms, 300 ms, and 900 ms to T_k. Note that all the windows use only past information up to T_k since we consider an online algorithm. For each feature type, we divided features in the window equally into three regions, calculate the mean in each region, and concatenate the three means as a feature vector. The reason to use the three kinds of feature window is to focus on from the fine behavior of features near the prediction time to the rough behavior of features at a little past.

The end-of-utterances are predicted using a learned decision tree and a regression tree. Here, since feature vectors are calculated every 33 ms, we refer to each interval as a slot and the end-of-utterances are predicted as in which slot the end-of-utterance exists. In the case of a decision tree, it outputs existence or non-existence of the end-of-utterance in feature prediction window using calculated feature vectors. The window size for prediction is set to 100 ms. Prediction is done every 33 ms, the same rate as the feature sampling. The system makes feature vectors from input data and predicts the end-of-utterances using a decision tree. If a decision tree outputs "1", that is, if an end-of-utterance is predicted within 100 ms, the system looks for the following three slots and increments the values of those slots. During this voting process, if the value in a certain slot exceed the threshold, 2, the system decides that an end-of-utterance exists in the slot. Once an end-of-utterance is predicted, the system stops predicting 500 ms after the predicted endpoint.

Prediction with a regression tree is almost the same except that the tree outputs the time length to the next end-of-utterance. If an end-of-utterance is predicted in a certain slot, the value in the slot is incremented, and by finding a future slot whose value is the highest among the nearby slots from the current time and whose value exceeds the threshold, 3, the system decides that an end-of-utterance exists in the slot.

EXPERIMENTS

Evaluation of features

In this experiment, as described in the introduction we consider a situation where a user explains what he/she learned to an e-learning system. We recruited two speakers and two listeners. By pairing one speaker and one listener, we recorded two pairs of two-party dialogs. The speakers read a text about a certain institute, and then each speaker explained the summary of the content to a listener. The listeners gave the speakers backchannel feedback freely while the speakers were speaking [2]. We recorded the speech of both the speakers and listeners and the video of the frontal face of the speakers. The lengths of the recorded dialogs were about 65 sec (speaker 1) and 140 sec (speaker 2).

---

[2] In this paper, we did not analyze these backchannel feedback data.

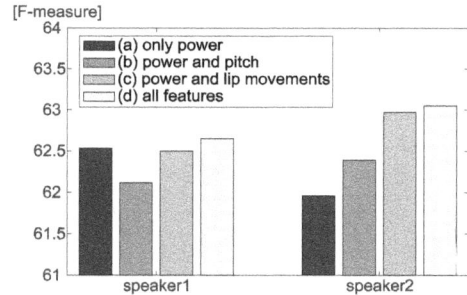

Figure 2. The accuracy of classifiers using different feature sets.

First, we detected utterance sections using VAD for the speech signal denoised by a spectral subtraction method. Second, we jointed two utterance sections whose interval length was 50 ms or less since the two utterance sections with such a small gap were considered as one utterance (the definition of IPU). Third, in order to correct the detection error of utterance sections, we recruited three annotators and had them correct the end of utterances. Then, for each of the utterances, we considered the mean of the nearest two annotated endpoints as the correct end of the utterance.

Before predicting the end of utterances online, we evaluated how the accuracy of the classifiers is influenced by the selection of features. We did cross-validation using a decision tree in four cases of feature combination: (a) only power, (b) power and pitch, (c) power and lip movements, and (d) power, pitch and lip movements. First, by comparing the difference of the clause boundaries, we found the results of AB is much higher than OB, which suggests that AB boundaries have less variety. In what follows, we do not distinguish AB and OB. Figure 2 shows the F-measure of end-of-utterance prediction for the two speakers (dialogs) in the four cases of feature combination. In the case of speaker 1, F-measure was slightly lower in case (b) and (c) compared to case (a), but F-measure of using all features (case (d)) was the highest. In the case of speaker 2, F-measure of using all features (case (d)) was the highest while case (a) was the lowest. This result indicates the usefulness of combining audio and visual (i.e., lip movement) information for prediction, but further investigation is required since the difference is not significant enough.

Evaluation of end-of-utterance prediction algorithm

We examined online prediction for (1) closed data and (2) open data. In the case of closed data, we trained decision trees and regression trees using whole recorded data, and then predicted the end of utterances for the same data. This test was done to confirm the validity of this algorithm. On the other hand, prediction for the open data was currently done only using decision trees. We separated the recorded data into six regions equally, predicted for each region by a decision tree learned using the other five regions, and then concatenated the six results into one sequence. This test was done to evaluate generalization capability of the prediction model. In both cases, we used all the features, i.e., power, pitch, and lip movements.

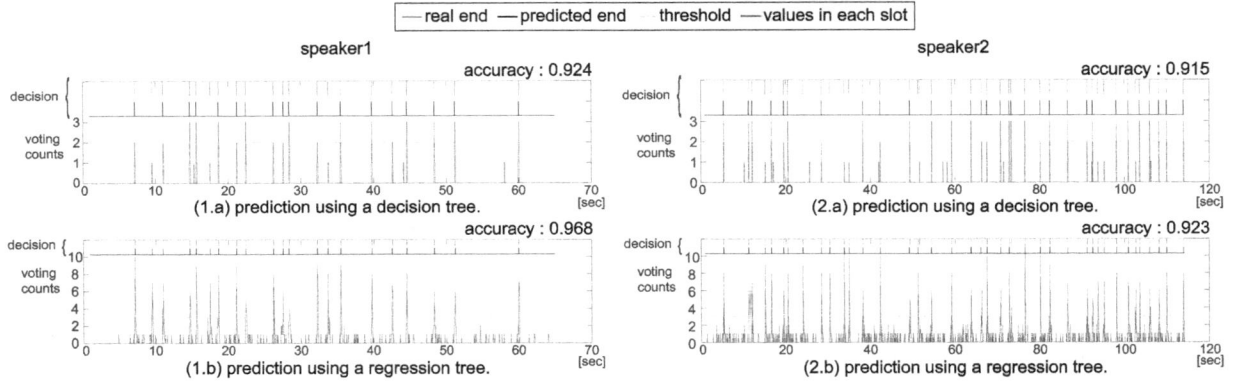

Figure 3. Prediction of the end of utterances using decision trees and regression trees for the closed data.

For each predicted time $T(k)$ $(k = 1, \ldots, n$, n: the number of the predicted end of utterances) when an predicted end-of-utterance exists, the time difference between the nearest actual end-of-utterance sets $\hat{T}(k)$, and the predicted time was evaluated using

$$accuracy = \frac{1}{n} \sum_{k=1}^{n} \exp\left(-\frac{(T(k) - \hat{T}(k))^2}{\sigma^2}\right), \quad (1)$$

where $\sigma = 100$ ms. This value was determined by the fact that most of overlap timing is from 0 ms to 300 ms [2].

Figure 3 shows the results of the prediction for speaker 1 and speaker 2, respectively, with the closed data. In the case of using decision trees, the timing of predicted end-of-utterances of two speakers are very close to the actual endpoints, which results in high accuracy (speaker 1: $accuracy = 0.924$, speaker 2: $accuracy = 0.915$). There are few places where the actual end of utterances exist but was not predicted. However, these false-negative errors are less important since we feel more uncomfortable when the system generates backchannel response at the false positive end: long before the end of utterances than the system does not generate it at actual endpoints. In the case of using regression trees, the accuracy was very high (speaker 1: $accuracy = 0.968$, speaker 2: $accuracy = 0.923$). Therefore, our online prediction algorithm using a decision tree and a regression tree are considered reasonable.

On the other hand, for the open data, accuracy is much lower than that of the closed test (speaker 1: $accuracy = 0.072$, speaker 2: $accuracy = 0.167$). The possible reasons are that the classifier does not have enough generalization capability and the amount of data is too small to predict the end of utterances for unknown data. Moreover, we need to reconsider how to extract features from recorded data since the extracted features from each window is too much downsampled and do not preserve enough trajectory information.

CONCLUSION

In this study, we regarded the generation of backchannel response timing as the problem of early online prediction of the end of utterances, and proposed a voting-based online prediction algorithm. The evaluation results indicate the possibility that visual information helps improve the accuracy of detector, and the validity of the proposed algorithm was demonstrated

with closed data. However, for unknown data, the accuracy is not high enough because of insufficient generalization of the trained classifiers. For future work, we are planning to record more data, implement the backchannel generation system, and evaluate by analyzing the behavior of users whether the system can actually promote the utterance of the speakers.

ACKNOWLEDGEMENTS
This work was supported by KAKEN 26280075 and JST, PRESTO.

REFERENCES

1. Minh Hoai and Fernando Torre. 2014. Max-Margin Early Event Detectors. *Int. J. Comput. Vision* 107, 2 (April 2014), 191–202.

2. Norihide Kitaoka, Masashi Takeuchi, Ryota Nishimura, and Seiichi Nakagawa. 2005. Response Timing Detection Using Prosodic and Linguistic Information for Human-friendly Spoken Dialog Systems. *Trans. on JSAI* 20 (November 2005), 220–228.

3. Ryota Nishimura, Norihide Kitaoka, and Seiichi Nakagawa. 2007. A Spoken Dialog System for Chat-Like Conversations Considering Response Timing. (2007), 599–606.

4. Huy Phan, Marco Maass, Radoslaw Mazur, and Alfred Mertins. 2015. Early event detection in audio streams. In *Proc. of ICME*. 1–6.

5. Marc Schroder, Elisabetta Bevacqua, Roddy Cowie, Florian Eyben, Hatice Gunes, Dirk Heylen, Mark ter Maat, Gary McKeown, Sathish Pammi, Maja Pantic, Catherine Pelachaud, Bjorn Schuller, Etienne de Sevin, Michel Valstar, and Martin Wollmer. 2012. Building Autonomous Sensitive Artificial Listeners. *IEEE Trans. Affect. Comput.* 3, 2 (April 2012), 165–183.

6. Katsuya Takanashi, Takehiko Maruyama, Kiyotake Uchimoto, and Hitoshi Isahara. 2003. Identification of "sentences" in spontaneous Japanese - Detection and modification of clause boundaries. In *SSPR2003*. 183–186.

Forming Intimate Human-Robot Relationships Through A Kissing Machine

Emma Yann Zhang
City University London
London, UK
emma.zhang@city.ac.uk

Adrian David Cheok
City University London
London, UK
Imagineering Institute
Iskandar Puteri, Malaysia
adriancheok@city.ac.uk

ABSTRACT

Robots are increasingly becoming involved in people's lives as social companions or even romantic partners rather than mere productivity tools. To facilitate intimacy in human-robot relationships, technologies should enable human to have intimate physical interactions with robots, such as kissing. This paper presents a kissing machine that reproduces and transmits the haptic sensations of kissing. It provides a physical interface for human to form emotional and intimate connections with robots or virtual characters through kissing, and also acts as a remote agent for human to transmit kisses remotely through a communication network.

ACM Classification Keywords

H5.2. Information Interfaces and Presentation (e.g., HCI): User Interfaces

Author Keywords

human-robot kissing; remote kissing; kissing machine; affective communication; haptic device

INTRODUCTION

The concept of human establishing intimate relationships with robots has been garnering increasing attention in mass media and academic fields [1]. Robots are no longer just being designed as productivity tools, but many are serving as social companions for children and the elderly, or even as romantic or sexual partners for adults. In order to facilitate intimacy in human-robot relationships, technologies should enable human to have intimate physical interactions with robots.

Physical touch is an essential part of human communication and bonding. Our need for physical contact seems to be programmed in our brain, even infants display a need to be hugged and stroked frequently. The effects of touch between humans preserve in human-robot interactions. Studies have shown that touch can increase people's positive feelings for robots [2],

HAI '16 October 04-07, 2016, Biopolis, Singapore

© 2016 Copyright held by the owner/author(s).

ACM ISBN 978-1-4503-4508-8/16/10.

DOI: http://dx.doi.org/10.1145/2974804.2980513

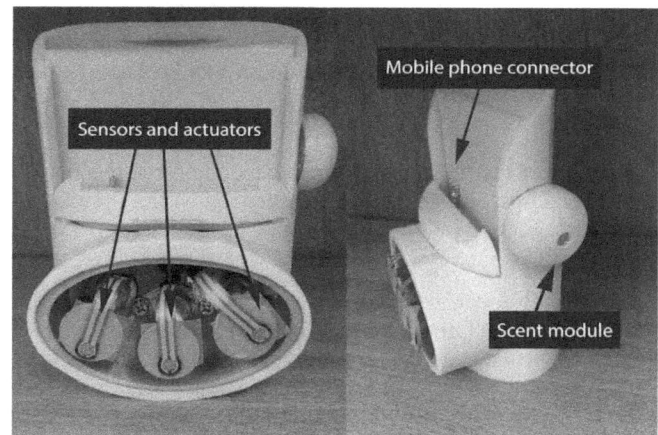

Figure 1. The design of Kissenger

and decrease their heart rate and blood pressure [5]. Similar physiological responses are found in human interpersonal touch [4]. Moreover, the social rules of touch, such as the perceived appropriateness of touching different parts of the human body, remain the same when touching a robotic body [6].

In this paper, we present a kissing machine that reproduces the haptic sensations of kissing, which simulates an intimate kissing experience through an embodied agent. Intimate touch like kissing and hugging is the key to expressing love and affection, and maintaining close relationships. Kissing, in particular, is an effective bonding mechanism [3] for families and romantic partners. The kissing machine provides a physical interface for human to form emotional and intimate connections with robots or virtual characters through kissing. It also acts as a remote agent for human to transmit kisses remotely through a communication network.

INTERACTIVE KISS MACHINE

We developed an interactive kissing machine, named Kissenger, which consists of an array of force sensors and linear actuators under a soft lip surface to measure and generate the dynamic lip pressure and movements during kissing. Force sensors measure the contact force of the user's lips and the device continuously. A bidirectional force controller controls the

Figure 2. A user kissing her partner remotely with the Kissenger device

positions of the linear actuators to generate force feedback on the user's lips, simulating the pressure felt by the lips during a real kiss. Figure 1 shows a prototype of the Kissenger device and its different parts.

The kissing machine can be used both as a remote telepresence agent of a human partner, or as an embodied agent of a robot or virtual character. The hardware can be connected to a mobile phone, which sends the force data to other users over the network. The communication is bi-directional such that both users feel the pressure of each other's lips in real-time. The local force controller in the hardware device synchronises the contact force between the user and the lip interface on both sides of the system at all times. A mobile application is designed for users to send a kiss to families and friends while having a video call with them, as shown in Figure 2. Remote kissing enhances the physical and emotional expression in digital communication, allowing friends and families to maintain a tight bond and intimate relationships over a distance.

INTERFACE FOR HUMAN-ROBOT KISSING

The kissing machine also provides a new interface for human to kiss a robot or a virtual character through an embodied agent. It can be integrated into social robots as interactive lips that allow the robots to kiss human partners, or even other robots. It can also serve as an embodiment of virtual characters, chat bots or artificial agents by connecting and transmitting kiss data to external systems. A virtual model can be designed to program the device to simulate kissing.

As discussed earlier, touching a robot or robotic body elicits similar physiological responses as touching a human, and the social meaning of human touch preserves in human-robot interaction. This implies that if human can interact with robots not only through verbal commands, logical information or one-directional touch input, but also through intimate behaviour such as hugging, kissing or even sexual acts, we could develop similar emotional bond for robots as for other people.

This work introduces exciting opportunities in the field of artificial intelligence and human-machine interaction. By ex-

tending a medium from the physical world to the digital space, making what was once feasible only in the physical world available in electronic forms, we will witness the emergence of new behaviour, definitions, cultures and relationships in an unimaginable and unpredictable way. Intimate interactions between human and robots could engender interesting aspects in their relationships. For example, human could form deep emotional attachments for robots and artificial agents, develop sexual fantasies, or fall in love with them.

While robots are designed with the abilities to perform intimate acts, they should also be able to understand the the emotional meaning, social significance and pleasure of such behaviour. Artificial intelligence should extend beyond logical data and enable virtual entities to possess emotional intelligence. Eventually, humans and robots will be able to communicate with each other on an emotional level, express love and empathy, and establish intimate and humanistic relationships.

CONCLUSION

In this paper, we discussed how human can interact with robots and virtual characters through intimate physical touch such as kissing, and the implications of this new form of interaction in human-robot relationships and artificial intelligence. We introduced and described a kissing machine designed to facilitate intimacy in human-robot interaction and remote human-human communication.

REFERENCES

1. Adrian David Cheok, David Levy, Kasun Karunanayaka, Shogo Nishiguchi, and Emma Y. Zhang. 2016. Lovotics: Love and Sex with Robots. *IPSJ Journal Special Issue: Kawaii* 57, 2 (2016).

2. Haruaki Fukuda, Masahiro Shiomi, Kayako Nakagawa, and Kazuhiro Ueda. 2012. 'Midas touch' in human-robot interaction: Evidence from event-related potentials during the ultimatum game. In *Human-Robot Interaction (HRI), 2012 7th ACM/IEEE International Conference on*. IEEE, 131–132.

3. Susan M Hughes, Marissa A Harrison, and Gordon G Gallup. 2007. Sex differences in romantic kissing among college students: An evolutionary perspective. *Evolutionary Psychology* 5, 3 (2007), 147470490700500310.

4. Kathleen C Light, Karen M Grewen, and Janet A Amico. 2005. More frequent partner hugs and higher oxytocin levels are linked to lower blood pressure and heart rate in premenopausal women. *Biological psychology* 69, 1 (2005), 5–21.

5. Hayley Robinson, Bruce MacDonald, and Elizabeth Broadbent. 2015. Physiological effects of a companion robot on blood pressure of older people in residential care facility: A pilot study. *Australasian journal on ageing* 34, 1 (2015), 27–32.

6. Paul Strohmeier and Ike Kamphof. 2014. Mediated Touch: Exploring embodied design for remote presence. In *Proceedings of the International Society for Presence Research*. 131–140.

Effects of Deformed Embodied Agent during Collaborative Interaction Tasks: Investigation on Subjective Feelings and Emotion

Ayano Kitamura

Major of Informatics of Behavior and Cultures, Graduate School of Letters, Ritsumeikan University

Toji-in Kitamachi, Kita-ku, Kyoto, Japan

lt0486ie@ed.ritsumei.ac.jp

Yugo Hayashi

College of Comprehensive Psychology, Ritsumeikan University

2-150 Iwakura-cho, Ibaraki, Osaka, Japan

y-hayashi@acm.org

ABSTRACT

Designing embodied agents that are empathic and positive towards humans is important in Human Agent Interaction (HAI) and design factors need to be instigated based on experimental investigation. Agent design specificity, in which less specific animated designs are better than realistic designs, is one of the key factors that facilitate positive emotions during interactions. Focusing on this point, this study investigated the effects of a deformed embodied agent during a collaborative interaction task with the objective of understanding how subjective interpersonal states and emotional states change when deformed embodied agents are used instead of non-deformed agents. This was accomplished by developing an interactive communication task with the embodied agent and collecting subjective and emotional state data during the task. The results obtained indicate that deformed agents evoke impressions of closeness and produce higher arousal states.

ACM Classification Keywords

H.5.2. User Interfaces: Evaluation

Author Keywords

Embodied Agent; Design of Appearance; Deformation; Collaborative Interaction; Interpersonal Impressions; Emotion.

INTRODUCTION

Recently, many studies have been conducted with the objective of investigating the cognitive mechanisms in Human Agent Interaction (HAI). To develop efficient intelligent systems that can adaptively respond to humans and are easy to use, an understanding of the kinds of cognitive information processing factors that influence interaction is of paramount importance.

HAI '16, October 04-07, 2016, Biopolis, Singapore

ACM 978-1-4503-4508-8/16/10.

http://dx.doi.org/10.1145/2974804.2980478

Such understanding necessitates use of knowledge about the kinds of cognitive processes that underlie social interaction with others. Studies conducted in areas such as social cognition explain how impression of others form from information processing using top-down and bottom-up processing [2]. In top-down processing, the input information from the external world is interpreted using information stored in human memory. The memory used in this process is an organized knowledge set that contains variables about personalities called interpersonal schema. People understand each other's personality and intentions using this knowledge. This knowledge is not used to gain an understanding of new people, but can be used often when interacting with unknown artifacts such as agents and robots. On the other hand, bottom-up processing does not use such knowledge and facilitates interaction with the external world based on the gathered information. Social cues such as nonverbal information (e.g., eye gaze and posture) can be accumulated in the brain and utilized to produce understanding about the state or characteristics of the other person (or agent) [7].

As studies in media equation have shown, cognitive models from human-human interactions can be used in HAI to provide an adequate view of how humans might react to agents.

This study focused on bottom-up processing, in which the design of the agent is an essential factor. Ascertaining the kinds of agent designs that actually influence bottom-up processing is very important. Fogg [3] posited and discussed the importance of social cues such as embodied characteristics, verbal data, social roles, and behaviors. However, it is still unknown what kind of social cues are essential for the embodied characteristics to facilitate bottom-up processing. Hayashi et al. [4] conducted experiments to investigate whether designing familiarity with a particular person in an agent can stimulate constructive interaction. They explained that interpersonal schema can be used when perceiving such an agent, thus producing human-like responses. Further investigating how such impressions can be produced by bottom-up processing is challenging as it is predominantly attended by social cues.

The results of previous studies imply that human-like designs are effective; therefore, realistic designs can become an effective factor for social cues. However, the results of some studies contradict this inference. The "uncanny valley" studies [6] indicate that the more human-like a sophisticated design becomes, the stronger a positive impression will be, although at some point this will decrease to negative. It can be said that it is important to design agents that are a little realistic. Studies that show how agent deformation design can produce better impressions have been conducted. However, not many studies have been conducted with the objective of empirically investigating how such agent deformation designs produce cognitive processing during interactive situations. Moreover, the utility by which such designs motivate one and change behavior is still an open question. To understand this point, investigations on how emotional states change during interaction with such an agent are needed.

On the basis of the above discussions, we developed a collaborative game task with an embodied conversational agent and experimentally investigated the role played by agent deformation designs on impression formation and emotional states during interaction with the agent. On investigating the emotional states of participants, we measured their pulse rate and investigated their degree of arousal to gain knowledge of how strongly a human can be motivated by interacting with the proposed agent.

EXPERIMENTAL SETTING
To investigate the effect of the type of posture during interaction with the embodied agent, we developed an experimental task that requires paying attention to the agent. The system built for this task was implemented using MikuMikuDance Ver9.26 (DirectX Version 9) and ran on Adobe Flash Professional CC 2015.

The experiment was conducted individually and the system ran on a desktop computer. The embodied agent appeared on the screen and talked to the participant via text: "I have a series of figures in my mind that are lined up in order and I will tell you these figures one by one." "I would like you to read my mind and guess what kind of figures I will tell you next." At this point, the system showed the types of figures the agent possessed (square, triangle, and circle). The participants interacted with the agent in turns and on each turn the agent presented what it had in mind. The participants were required to guess the series rule the agent had and press each one of the three buttons on each turn. After pressing the button, a correct/incorrect feedback was given by the agent as an answer. One trial was counted as complete when this feedback was completed; a total of 35 trials were required to finish the task.

EXPERIMENTAL DESIGN
In the experiment, we set up three conditions (deformed, non-deformed, and control). The deformation of the embodied agent was accomplished by calculating the degree of "abridgment" using an algorithm developed by Takamatsu and Shimazu [8]. Further, we used calculation of the distance between the head and jar and the size of the whole body to determine the "exaggeration" of the agent. Based on this calculation, in the deformed condition, an agent with abridgment = 0.01 and

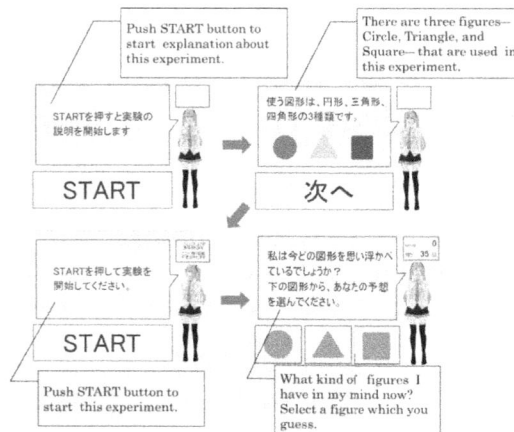

Figure 1. Screen shot of the experiment.

exaggeration = 0.14 was used. In the non-deformed condition, the following parameters were set: abridgment = 0.14, exaggeration = 0.59. For the control condition, there were no agents and nothing was presented on the screen. Participants were told that they were playing this game with some person outside the room. In all the conditions, the same agent was used as their actual collaborator. Thirty university students (male 15, female 15, Mage: 21.5, SD: 1.11) participated.

Figure 2. Experimental conditions.

COLLECTED DATA
We collected two types of data in the experiment: (1) subjective interpersonal impressions and (2) emotional arousal state. For (1), we used the questionnaire from Kanda et al. [5], in which questions are associated with "closeness," "pleasantness," "activeness," and "efficiency." These were evaluated based on a seven point Likert scale. For (2), we used pulse rate to investigate the emotions.

RESULTS
Subjective Data
The subjective results data showed that the deformed condition was higher than the non-deformed condition for closeness ($p < 0.05$) There were no differences between conditions in pleasantness and activeness ($p > 0.05$, ns; $p < 0.10$). For the efficiency, the control condition was higher than the deform condition ($p < 0.05$).

Emotional Data
On the pulse rate, 3 (conditions) x 30 (trials) ANOVA was conducted. There was interaction between the two (F (5.89, 343.97) = 2.22, $p < 0.05$) and the deform condition was higher than the non-deform condition during the 25th to 30th trials.

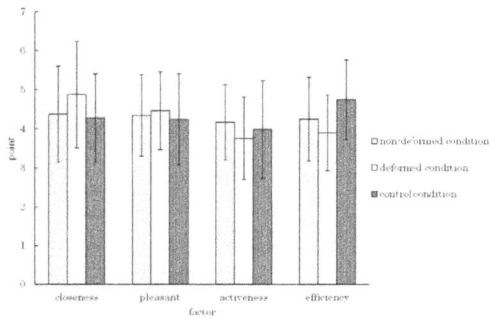

Figure 3. Results of subjective data.

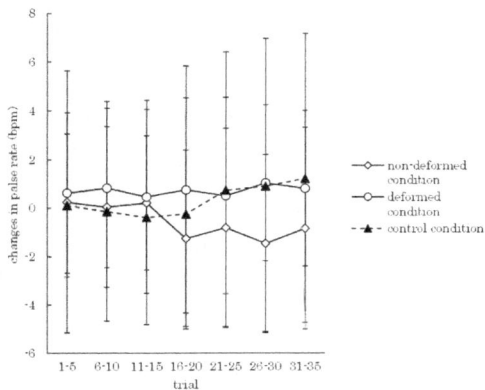

Figure 4. Results of emotional data.

Discussion and Conclusion

In summary, (1) the deform agent was evaluated higher in terms of closeness but its efficiency was not evaluated well. (2) The pulse rate showed that the participants using the deform agent had higher pulse rates; thus, it can be posited that they were more excited during the task.

Why do deform characters produce positive impressions and emotions? Considering the schema literature reviewed at the beginning of this study, it can be said that a schema such as the "baby-schema" [1] may have been playing a role. A deformed character may stimulate knowledge of childlessness or maturity and thus can facilitate the emotions that co-occur when interacting with the character.

ACKNOWLEDGMENTS

This work was supported by the Grant-in-Aid for Scientific Research (KAKENHI), No. 16K00219.

REFERENCES

1. T. Brosch, D. Sander, and R. Scherer. 2007. That baby caught my eye... Attention capture by infant faces. *Emotion* 3, 7 (2007), 685–689.

2. T. Susan. Fisk and E. Shelly. Taylor. 1991. *Social Cognition*. McGraw-Hill Education.

3. B. J. Fogg. 2003. *Persuative Technology: Using Compuers to Change What We think and Do*. Morgan Kaufmann Publishers.

4. Y. Hayashi, H. Huang, V. Kryssanov, K. Miwa, A. Urao, and H. Ogawa. 2011. Source orientation in communication with a conversational agent. In *Proceeding of the 11th International Conference on Intelligent Virtual Agents(IVA2011)*. 451–452.

5. T. Kanda, H. Ishiguro, and T. Ishida. 2001. Journal of the robotics society of Japan. *Psychological Evaluation on Interactions between People and Robot* 3, 3 (2001), 362–371.

6. M. Mori. 1970. Bukimi no tani [the uncanny valley]. *Energy* 7, 4 (1970), 33–35.

7. C. Nass, Y. Moon, B. J. Fogg, B. Reeves, and D. C. Dryer. 1995. Can computer personalities be human personalities? *International Journal of Human Computer Studies* 43, 2 (1995), 223–239.

8. K. Takamatsu and K. Shimazu. 2001. Experimental study of measuring digital character features. *Reserch report at entertainment and computing meeting by the japanese information processing society* EC19, 27 (2001), 1–4.

Human Posture Detection using H-ELM Body Part and Whole Person Detectors for Human-Robot Interaction

Manoj Ramanathan
Nanyang Technological
University, Singapore
manoj005@e.ntu.edu.sg

Wei-Yun Yau
Institute of Infocomm
Research, A*STAR, Singapore
wyyau@i2r.a-star.edu.sg

Eam Khwang Teoh
Nanyang Technological
University, Singapore
eekteoh@ntu.edu.sg

ABSTRACT

For reliable human-robot interaction, the robot must know the person's action in order to plan the appropriate way to interact or assist the person. As part of the pre-processing stage of action recognition, the robot also needs to recognize the various body parts and posture of the person. But estimation of posture and body parts is challenging due to the articulated nature of the human body and the huge intra-class variations. To address this challenge, we propose two schemes using Hierarchical-ELM (H-ELM) for posture detection into either upright or non-upright posture. In the first scheme, we follow a whole body detector approach, where a H-ELM classifier is trained on several whole body postures. In the second scheme, we follow a body part detection approach, where separate H-ELM classifiers are detected for each body part. Using the detected body parts a final decision is made on the posture of the person. We have conducted several experiments to compare the performance of both approaches under different scenarios like view angle changes, occlusion etc. Our experimental results show that body part H-ELM based posture detection works better than other proposed framework even in the presence of occlusion.

ACM Classification Keywords

Human-centered computing, Human Computer Interaction: Visualization; Computing Methodologies, Machine learning

Author Keywords

Posture detection; Whole body detection; Body part detection; Hierarchical Extreme learning machines (H-ELM)

INTRODUCTION

Providing visual capabilities to a robot will help it to understand its surrounding and interact with people and objects. For smooth human-robot interaction, reliable people detection and action recognition is a pre-requisite. As such, the related robotic vision tasks has gained research interest. One such vision task is pose estimation which involves identifying the

HAI '16, October 04-07, 2016, Biopolis, Singapore

© 2016 Copyright held by the owner/author(s).

ACM ISBN 978-1-4503-4508-8/16/10.

DOI: http://dx.doi.org/10.1145/2974804.2980480

pose and various body parts in the frame. Initial methods proposed for person detection [6, 4, 7] require person to be in an upright posture, which limits its usage. Thus estimation of a person's posture into either upright or non-upright posture can help the robot to interact better with human. Also, it will serve as a preprocessing module for other human-robot interactions like person detection and action recognition. In this paper, we propose two schemes using H-ELM classifiers for posture detection.

Our first algorithm involves training H-ELM whole body detectors. [4] used the HOG features for person detection but limited to only upright postures. We extend this by training the H-ELM classifiers using several different views and postures. Using whole body detectors can be useful in low resolution videos where the body parts cannot be seen clearly.

Our second algorithm involves training H-ELM body part detectors. In our model, we assume that human body comprises four parts, namely, head, torso, arm and leg. Using [10] as the basis, we generate H-ELM body part detectors for each one of them. We follow framework in [10] for body part detection but instead of using the likelihood score proposed in [10], we use the H-ELM confidence value directly for detecting the body parts. To classify the posture as upright or non-upright, we propose an algorithm that uses the relative location of body parts. This is useful in the presence of occlusion or when the whole body is not visible in the frame.

In this paper, we propose two posture detection frameworks using H-ELM based on whole body detectors and body part detectors respectively. We propose an algorithm to compute posture based on the relative locations of the body parts. We conducted several experiments to compare their performances and test their robustness in different scenarios like view angle changes, occlusion and low resolution etc.

The rest of the paper is organized as follows: Section II focuses on related work in the field of posture detection, pose estimation and body part detection. In section III, we introduce our H-ELM whole body based posture detection framework. In section IV, body part detection based H-ELM posture detector is explained. Experimental results, discussions and limitations are presented in section V, followed by conclusions and future works in section VI.

RELATED WORK

Posture of a person can be either upright or non-upright based on the position of head and torso. This information can be used by several other tasks for further processing. In this section, we describe some of the related works in the field of posture detection that uses whole body or separate body parts as basis.

Some of the early works on person detection such as [4] require person to be upright posture. Methods like [8] used predefined set of postures such as sitting, bending and standing to compare with test images. By limiting to a set of postures, their applicability to videos in unconstrained setting is reduced.

[4] proposed a whole person detection method based on HOG features that works on the assumption, person is always in upright posture. Pictorial structures [6] was one of the initial methods that came up with a complete body model describing different parts of the body. Since then several methods based on pictorial structures have been proposed [12, 9]. In this paper, we follow whole person detection approach and use H-ELM to learn to different postures of a person.

Considering any object as a combination of certain important parts forms the basis of deformable parts model proposed in [5]. They also trained a person detection model based on the constituent parts. To account non-rigid shape of parts, [12] extended pictorial structures to deformable structures model to identify the different body parts. One major work in the body part detection is poselets [3, 2], where body part classifiers are learnt in both 2D image and 3D joint domain. Due to their robust and reliable performance, they were used to condition pictorial structures model [9]. The only drawback of poselets is the extensive manual annotation of training data. In this paper, we develop a H-ELM based body part detectors with comparatively lesser training data and use a web crawler to reduce manual work in collecting the training images. We use the developed H-ELM body part detectors as basis to identify the posture of the person in the frame.

WHOLE BODY BASED H-ELM POSTURE DETECTOR

Following pedestrian detection methods [4], we aim to develop a H-ELM detector that is based on whole human body patterns. We divide posture of a person in to two classes upright and non-upright. But in order to evaluate camera view changes, we further divide the above classes into upright-frontal, upright-back, upright-left, upright-right, non-upright (head on left), non-upright (head on right). We also include a 'None' class corresponding to neutral images other than human. Our first task is to collect training images that can be used to train the H-ELM detector. For collection of images, we use a python web crawler [10] that automatically downloads images from Google AJAX APIs. We have collected 1000 images in each class and resized to a fixed dimension of 64x128.

Hierarchical-ELM training consists of two stages, an unsupervised multi-layer feature encoding and a supervised feature classification. A sparse autoencoder acts a learning unit in the H-ELM implementation. In our experiments, we noticed that the accuracy of the H-ELM classifier was very low when we use the raw images directly to represent each class. Thus, we extract HOG features and use the same for training the classifier. Two parameters of each layer i of H-ELM, number of hidden nodes N_i and penalty term C_i need to be selected for proper implementation. We have performed 4-fold cross

validation experiment on the collected images to identify the correct value of C_i, N_i and robust whole body posture model.

Our 4-fold cross validation was conducted on the first layer of H-ELM with different values of C_1 and N_1. We observed a highest of 60.34% accuracy for values of $C_1 = 100$ and $N_1 = 800$. When we extend our H-ELM classifier to more than one layer, we observed a reduction in the accuracy. Thus we stopped our training at the first layer of H-ELM and use this as our whole body based posture model.

For testing the posture model, we assume that foreground region can be extracted or is available. We crop the foreground region and resize it to 64x128 dimension. We extract HOG features from this image and provide it as input to our H-ELM classifier, which detects it as one of the above 7 classes. Based on the result, we classify it as either upright or non-upright. We'll brief the effectiveness of the method under different scenarios in our results and discussion section.

POSTURE DETECTION BASED ON H-ELM BODY PART DETECTOR

A person's posture is defined by the relative orientation of head and torso. With this as basis, we develop H-ELM body part detectors that could be used to determine the posture. Firstly, we divide the human body into 4 parts, namely, head, torso, arms and legs. To train a H-ELM classifier for each class, we need to collect training images. We use the same python web crawler to download images from Google AJAX APIs. We collect 7000 images for each class including a 'None' class.

We use the H-ELM implementation for training the classifiers. We observed once again that the accuracy is low when we use raw images directly for training. Therefore, we resize the images to fixed dimension of 64x128 and extract HOG features. As with the whole body part H-ELM classifier, we need to tune the same two parameters N_i and C_i for each layer i. We performed a 4-fold cross validation on the training images collected to identify the best values of N_i, C_i and body part detector model.

In the first layer H-ELM training, it was observed that the highest accuracy obtained was 64.3% with $N_1 = 4600$ and $C_1 = 100$. With these values set for layer 1, we tested the second layer and did not notice much improvement in the performance. We extended the training to third layer with the same settings and observed an accuracy of 74.81% $N_3 = 6900$. We choose this setting for our H-ELM body part model, with 5 classes including 'None' class.

Algorithm for Posture detection

For posture detection, we assume that the foreground region is either available or can be estimated. In this algorithm, we use head and torso detections alone to identify a person's posture. We focus on head and torso for two reasons. Firstly, the posture of a person is mainly based on head and torso than other parts. Secondly, we observed that head and torso detection accuracies are higher than the limbs. We have explained about the same in section V.

First, mean shift segmentation is applied to the foreground region. Each of the obtained segments are cropped and resized

Figure 1. Samples Images from the collected dataset of videos.

to fixed dimension 64x128. For each segment, HOG features are extracted and passed through our H-ELM body part detector. From the detected head and torso segments, the relative orientation of the body can be estimated. Using the obtained relative orientation, a person's posture is identified as either upright or non-upright. In order to handle cases when more than one segment is classified as head or torso, we use the likelihood value provided by H-ELM classifier. The segment with highest likelihood for head is chosen as the head and so on for other body parts.

EXPERIMENTAL RESULTS AND DISCUSSION

Benchmark datasets are available for pose estimation datasets [11, 1] focus mainly on upright postures and estimating each body part's location. In order to test our proposed posture detection frameworks, it would be necessary to have a dataset of video or images with persons in different postures. Hence, we collect our own video dataset comprising a total of 120 videos. Sample images can be seen in figure 1. Our dataset consists of 5 subjects performing different actions in various postures such as standing, lying down , sitting, upside down etc. Also, the videos are taken from 3 different views to enable view-based testing. The foreground region is manually marked for each video's frame. We test our posture detection framework using the first 10 frames of each video.

First, we run the H-ELM body part detector on this dataset to estimate the performance of body part detection. For this purpose, the ground truth for each body part's location is marked. By comparing the ground truth with obtained detection, we can estimate the correctness of our body part detector. A body part is considered as detected correctly, if at least 70% of the body part is detected correctly and less than 70% of the body part is missing Results of body part detection are tabulated in table 1. It is observed that head and torso detection are much better than the limbs. We have also noticed that arms and legs are detected interchangeably. This could be because of the structural similarity between them and more training data could help in differentiating them.

As mentioned in the previous section, we have chosen only head and torso detections owing to their better detection performance.The posture detection framework based on H-ELM body part classifier shows a performance of 67.5%. In comparison the posture detector based on whole body H-ELM shows only a performance of 61.58%. Posture detection based on

Body part	Correct Detections
head	84.17
torso	78.28
arm	60.4
leg	64.34

Table 1. Performance(%) for detection of each body part in video dataset

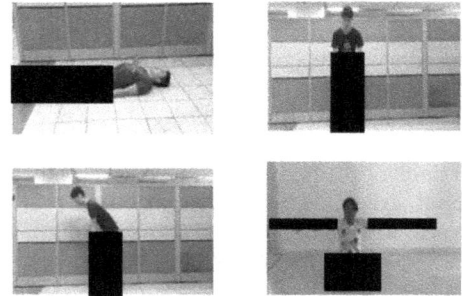

Figure 2. Occlusions present in the video dataset

whole body H-ELM classifier can get easily confused by the detected HOG features, whereas the modularity provided by body part detector allows better performance.

To compare the effectiveness of both these framework in different scenarios, we tested them under the presence of occlusion. We used the same video dataset containing 120 videos and occluded 50% of the foreground region as shown in figure 2. We made sure that head and torso is not completely occluded because our body part based H-ELM posture detection requires these body parts. We tested both the frameworks on these occluded videos and observed that body part based H-ELM detector is able to detect to 55.07% correctly whereas whole-body based H-ELM detector detects 48.42% correctly. In normal and occluded settings, body part H-ELM detector based framework performs much better than whole body H-ELM detector. It is quiet natural that body part based framework works much better because whole body H-ELM classifier might get confused easily in the presence of occlusion.

It was observed during testing that body part H-ELM was able to detect non-upright postures better than whole body H-ELM. One more interesting observation is the ability of body part based H-ELM to detect the posture correct even when viewed from top angle as shown in figure 3. Upon analysing the error cases of body part H-ELM detector, we noticed three

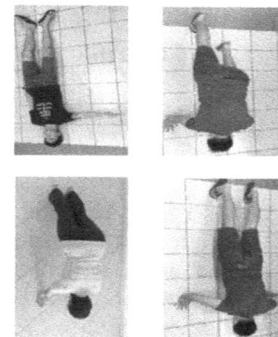

Figure 3. Examples of Top view correct detections in Body part H-ELM posture detector

Figure 4. Examples of self-occlusions observed in the dataset

Figure 5. Examples of correct detections by Whole body H-ELM in the presence of occlusion

causes for these errors, namely, not able to detect torso or head, occlusion of torso or head and wrong detections of torso or head. In the first case, the body part based H-ELM classifies the frame as 'Posture unidentified' because the body part is not detected. In the second case, self-occlusion of head or torso by the limbs results in body part not being detected or detected wrongly. Some examples of self-occlusion are shown in figure 4. If we include limbs detected into consideration for posture detection, it might be able to handle error cases due to the first two cases. Wrong detections of head or torso can occur because the dataset on which H-ELM is trained might be limited in number and requires more training. It could also be improved by combining HOG features with more discriminative features.

Whole body H-ELM based framework did not perform better than the body part H-ELM based framework. One of the main reasons for this could be the huge amount of pose variations exhibited. Considering that our training data is limited in number, learning all pose variations would be very difficult. But interestingly, upright postures are detected better in whole body H-ELM than body part H-ELM even in the presence of occlusion. For instance, consider the figure 5, showing a person in upright posture with occluded legs. The occlusion in this case is actually helping the whole body H-ELM to remove foreground region that would confuse the detector. Another observation was whole body H-ELM is able to detect better in sitting posture of the person.

CONCLUSION

For smooth human-robot interactions, posture and body part detection are essential tasks as they can be used as prepro-cessing module. In this paper, we have proposed two frame-works for posture detection into either upright or non-upright posture based on whole body and body part H-ELM detec-tors respectively. For the whole body H-ELM detection, we have collected training data for each posture. For the body part H-ELM based detector, we divided the body into head, torso, arms and legs and trained each of them. On the test images, we detected the head and torso and then estimated the posture of the person. Our experiments show that body part H-ELM based posture detection works better than other proposed framework even in the presence of occlusion.

REFERENCES

1. Mykhaylo Andriluka, Leonid Pishchulin, Peter Gehler, and Bernt Schiele. 2014. 2D Human Pose Estimation: New Benchmark and State of the Art Analysis. In *IEEE Conference on Computer Vision and Pattern Recognition*.

2. Lubomir Bourdev, Subhransu Maji, Thomas Brox, , and Jitendra Malik. 2010. Detecting people using mutually consistent poselet activations. In *European conf. on Computer vision: Part VI*. Springer-Verlag Berlin, Heidelberg 2010, 168–181.

3. Lubomir Bourdev and Jitendra Malik. 2009. Poselets: Body part detectors trained using 3d human pose annotations. In *IEEE Intl. Conf. on Computer Vision*. 1365 – 1372.

4. Navneet Dalal and Bill Triggs. 2005. Histograms of oriented gradients for human detection. In *IEEE Computer Society Conf. on Computer Vision and Pattern Recognition*, Vol. 1. 886 – 893.

5. P. Felzenszwalb, R. Girshick, D. McAllester, and D. Ramanan. 2010. Object Detection with Discriminatively Trained Part Based Models. *IEEE Trans. on Pattern Analysis and Machine Intelligence* 32, 9 (September 2010), 1627 – 1645.

6. Pedro F. Felzenszwalb and Daniel P. Huttenlocher. 2005. Pictorial structures for object recognition. *International Journal of Computer Vision* 61, 1 (January 2005), 55 – 79.

7. V. Ferrari, M. Marin-Jimenez, and A. Zisserman. 2008. Progressive Search Space Reduction for Human Pose Estimation. In *IEEE Conf. on Computer Vision and Pattern Recognition*. 1 – 8.

8. Bernard Boulay Francois, Francois Bremond, Monique Thonnat, and Inria Sophia Antipolis. 2003. Human Posture Recognition in Video Sequence. In *IEEE Intl. Workshop on Visual Surveillance and Performance Evaluation of Tracking and Surveillance*. 1 – 7.

9. Leonid Pishchulin, Mykhaylo Andriluka, Peter Gehler, and Bernt Schiele. 2013. Poselet conditioned pictorial structures. In *IEEE Conf. on Computer Vision and Pattern Recognition*. 588 – 595.

10. Manoj Ramanathan, Wei-Yun Yau, and Eam Khwang Teoh. 2014. Human Body Part Detection Using Likelihood Score Computations. In *IEEE Symp. on Computational Intelligence in Biometrics and Identity Management*. 160 – 166.

11. Leonid Sigal, A.Balan, and M.J.Black. 2010. HumanEva: Synchronized Video and Motion Capture Dataset and Baseline Algorithm for Evaluation of Articulated Human Motion. *Intl. Journal of Computer Vision* 87, 1-2 (March 2010), 4 – 27.

12. Silvia Zuffi, Oren Freifeld, and Michael J Black. 2012. From pictorial structures to deformable structures. In *IEEE Conf. on Computer Vision and Pattern Recognition*. 3546–3553.

Behavioral Expression Design onto Manufactured Figures

Yoshihisa Ishihara
Shinshu University
4-17-1 Wakasato, Nagano, Japan
16w2003f@shinshu-u.ac.jp

Kazuki Kobayashi
Shinshu University
4-17-1 Wakasato, Nagano, Japan
kby@shinshu-u.ac.jp

Seiji Yamada
NII / SOKENDAI / Tokyo
Institute of Technology
2-1-2 Hitotsubashi, Chiyoda,
Tokyo, Japan
seiji@nii.ac.jp

ABSTRACT
Natural language user interfaces, such as Apple Siri and Google Voice Search have been embedded in consumer devices; however, speaking to objects can feel awkward. Use of these interfaces should feel natural, like speaking to a real listener. This paper proposes a method for manufactured objects such as anime figures to exhibit highly realistic behavioral expressions to improve speech interaction between a user and an object. Using a projection mapping technique, an anime figure provides back-channel feedback to a user by appearing to nod or shake its head.

Author Keywords
Human–agent interaction; speech interaction; projection mapping; human-like agent; interface agent

ACM Classification Keywords
H.5.1 Multimedia Information Systems: Artificial, augmented, and virtual realities; H.5.m. Information interfaces and presentation (e.g., HCI): Miscellaneous

INTRODUCTION
In recent years, natural language user interfaces, such as Apple Siri and Google Voice Search, have been embedded in consumer devices. These interfaces allow users to talk to devices to do everything from a phone call to Web searching. However, people sometimes hesitate to use the interfaces in public. Interestingly, most people speak to someone on their smartphones in public without hesitation, but feel awkward using voice interfaces in public. Although there is a privacy concern, the difference in the acceptance between voice calls and voice interfaces is attributed to the human-likeness or intelligence of such devices.

There have been several studies on increasing the human-likeness of machines and speech interaction between users and machines. Especially, in the context of using nonverbal information, Breazeal et al. [3] showed that human–robot

HAI '16, October 04-07, 2016, Biopolis, Singapore
ACM 978-1-4503-4508-8/16/10.
http://dx.doi.org/10.1145/2974804.2980484

teamwork is enhanced using nonverbal information. Goetz et al. [4] reported that people's acceptance of a robot performing tasks that were more social in nature improved when the robot appeared more human-like. Additionally, Powers et al. [7] compared a screen agent and a robot in an interaction experiment and found that users took a more positive attitude toward the robot than the screen agent.

In this study, we attempted to improve an object's human-likeness by using nonverbal information to reduce the awkwardness users might feel when talking to the object. Nonverbal information in communication is an important factor because it affects consensus formation, speech content, and duration of the conversation [8]. Our approach is a way for already-existing objects to exhibit additional behavior in speech interaction rather than creating an entirely new object. We developed a system for an anime figure as a manufactured object to provide back-channel feedback to a user via a projection mapping technique [1] that gives the figure the appearance of nodding and shaking its head.

The proposed method has no shape limitations and provides natural expressions without mechanical vibration from motors because it does not use actuators. Although there are human-like software agents [2], such as MMDAgent [6], they are less realistic than embodied agents, such as robots [5].

BEHAVIOR-EXPRESSING AGENT
We developed a behavior-expressing agent using the projection mapping technique. It includes a small projector in a 310 × 240 × 110 mm case and the anime figure. The projector displays an animated image on the face of the figure.

Agent Behavior
The agent provides back-channel feedback during speech interaction by exhibiting nodding behavior as a positive reaction and head-shaking behavior as a negative reaction to a user. It also says "un" or "hai" in Japanese which mean "uh-huh" in English when it is nodding, and says "uunn" in Japanese which means "well..." in English when shaking its head. The responses of the agent were recordings of a female voice, with minor modifications in pitch. Figure 1 shows the nodding behavior using the projection mapping technique. The agent continuously monitors the voice volume of the user, and provides back-channel feedback

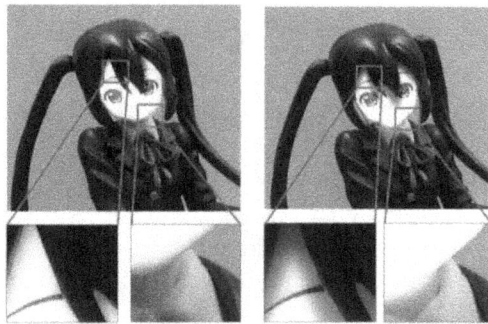

(a) beginning of nodding   (b) middle of nodding

(c) projected base image

Figure 1. Projected nodding behavior and base image

when the voice volume of the user exceeds a preset threshold after a 200-ms period of the volume being below the threshold.

Behavior Implementation

The nodding behavior of the agent is achieved by projecting a solid-white, face-shaped image onto the face of the anime figure (Figure 1c). It moves down 20 pixels in 150 ms and moves up 20 pixels in 150 ms in a single nod, as shown in Figure 1. The head-shaking behavior of the agent is achieved by projecting a face-shaped image that moves left and right 10 pixels from the center in 150 ms in one head-shaking, respectively. We empirically designed the behavior by projection mapping so that it clearly shows back-channel feedback behavior.

The image projection system for the agent works in a Web browser. The system includes a control window and an animation projection window, which is displayed on a projector screen that is connected to a personal computer. The system was developed in JavaScript and PHP, and the projection window controls the animation according to instructions in a text file shared between it and the control window. The system moves a face-shaped image that has been manually modified using a geometric transformation to fit the face of the anime figure.

We have a plant to perform experiments with participants to assess the participants' feelings toward the agent and the interaction using a questionnaire, and the number of utterances, the utterance duration, the wordless duration, and the number of fillers during the speech interaction between the agent and the participant.

CONCLUSION AND FUTURE WORK

A method for manufactured objects such as anime figures to exhibit highly realistic behavioral expressions to improve speech interaction between a user and an artifact was proposed. We developed a listener agent based on an anime figure to provide back-channel feedback in the form of nodding and head-shaking behavior using a projection mapping technique.

The proposed type of projection mapping-based feedback could be applied to a voice interface to decrease the uncomfortable feeling when talking to objects. Our next steps are to develop various feedback expressions using the projection mapping technology and perform experiments in realistic situations.

ACKNOWLEDGEMENTS
This study was partially supported by JSPS KAKENHI "Cognitive Interaction Design" (No. JP26118005).

REFERENCES

1. Daniel G. Aliaga, Yu Hong Yeung, Alvin Law, Behzad Sajadi, and Aditi Majumder. 2012. Fast high-resolution appearance editing using superimposed projections. ACM Transactions on Graphics 31, 2 (2012), 13:1–13:13.

2. Timothy Bickmore and Justine Cassell. 2001. Relational agents: a model and implementation of building user trust. *In Proceedings of the SIGCHI conference on Human factors in computing systems (CHI'01)*, 396–403.

3. Cynthia Breazeal, Cory D Kidd, Andrea Lockerd Thomaz, Guy Hoffman, and Matt Berlin. 2005. Effects of nonverbal communication on efficiency and robustness in human-robot teamwork. *In Proceedings of the International Conference on Intelligent Robots and Systems (IROS '05)*, 708–713.

4. Jennifer Goetz, Sara Kiesler, and Aaron Powers. 2003. Matching robot appearance and behavior to tasks to improve human-robot cooperation. *In Proceedings of the International Workshop on Robot and Human Interactive Communication (ROMAN'03)*, 55–60.

5. Sara Kiesler, Aaron Powers, Susan R. Fussell, and Cristen Torrey. 2008. Anthropomorphic interactions with a robot and robot-like agent. Social Cognition 26, 2 (2008), 169–181.

6. Albert Lee, Keiichiro Oura, and Keiichi Tokuda. 2013. MMDagent – a fully open-source toolkit for voice interaction systems. *In Proceedings of the International Conference on Acoustics, Speech and Signal Processing (ICASSP'13)*, 8382–8385.

7. Aaron Powers, Sara Kiesler, Susan Fussell, and Cristen Torrey. 2007. Comparing a computer agent with a humanoid robot. *In Proceedings of the International Conference on Human-Robot Interaction (HRI'07)*, 145–152.

8. Bjorn Schuller, Dino Seppi, Anton Batliner, Andreas Maier, and Stefan Steidl. 2007. Towards more reality in the recognition of emotional speech. In Proceedings of the International Conference on Acoustics, Speech and Signal Processing (ICASSP'07) 4, 941–944.

"I'm Scared": Little Children Reject Robots

Masahiro Shiomi
ATR-IRC
Kyoto, 6190288, Japan
m-shiomi@atr.jp

Kasumi Abe
JSPS Research Fellow/University of Electro-Communications
Tokyo, 182-8585, Japan
k_abe@apple.ee.uec.ac.jp

Yachao Pei
University of Electro-Communications
Tokyo, 182-8585, Japan
pei.yachao@apple.ee.uec.ac.jp

Narumitsu Ikeda
University of Electro-Communications
Tokyo, 182-8585, Japan
ikeda_n@apple.ee.uec.ac.jp

Takayuki Nagai
University of Electro-Communications
Tokyo, 182-8585, Japan
tnagai@ee.uec.ac.jp

ABSTRACT

Social robots are used for interacting with children. Their novelty often stimulates the interest of children and encourages such interaction as playing with them. However, some children do not interact with such robots and instead strongly reject interaction with them. Understanding such rejection behaviors of children has important design implications for social robots that are supposed to interact with children. For this purpose, we investigated what kinds of rejection behaviors appeared in different kinds of robots in a play room environment.

Author Keywords

Child-robot interaction; refusal behaviors

ACM Classification Keywords

H.5.2. User Interfaces – *Interaction styles*

INTRODUCTION

Child-robot interaction is a growing research field in human-agent interaction, because a robot's physical existence enables children to interact more physically with it than such non-physical agents as computer graphics based agents. Researchers have already experimentally investigated the effectiveness of robots to support children through storytelling [1], cleaning rooms [2], childcare [3-5], and education [6-9]. These works reported that children actively interacted with robots and enjoyed themselves.

In our experiments with children participants, we also observed many children who interacted with our robots, including preschoolers, babies, and toddlers who seemed strongly interested in novelty. However, some young

HAI '16, October 04-07, 2016, Biopolis, Singapore
ACM 978-1-4503-4508-8/16/10.
http://dx.doi.org/10.1145/2974804.2980493

children strongly rejected interaction with our robots, even though their parents or friends were actively interacting with them. Also, In a past research work, Yamamoto et al., reported hesitation behaviors of little children towards a non-humanoid robot [10].

These phenomenon of children are well known as "inhibition to the unfamiliar" in child development research area [11, 12]. We believe that understanding such rejection behaviors toward robots is critical for both the interaction and appearance designs of robots for little children and robots. Robots might not be able to provide services to little children who are rejecting them, and such behaviors might influence other children and change their behaviors. In this paper, we investigate how young children reject interaction with robots.

DATA COLLECTION

We conducted data collection where little children can interact with robots. To identify their various rejection behaviors toward robots, we prepared three kinds of robots that are appropriate for child-robot interaction: Sphero, Romo, and ChiCaRo. All three have locomotion capability. The following are the details of our data collection settings.

Participants

In our data collection, 57 young Japanese children whose ages ranged from one to six participated with their parents. Some families participated together and/or participated twice with another child (e.g., the first time was just a three-year-old boy who was joined the second time by his younger sister). The adult participants were paid 4,000 yen (about 38 dollars).

Environments

Figure 1 shows this study's data collection environment. This room's size and design are typical of playrooms in Japan. The room was about 8 m x 5 m, which easily accommodated more than five adults and five children and provides enough room for uninhibited activities. We recorded the environment's activities with two web cameras and provided toys, books, and chairs for the participants to play with and/or sit on.

Fig. 1 Data collection environment

Robots

We prepared three different kinds of robots based on their different appearances and functions.

Sphero: It is a ball-type robot[1], and has a 74 mm diameter and can move around and change its color. It is controlled by a smartphone to share such games with little children as chasing and tag. Since Sphero's appearance closely resembles an actual ball, little children might treat it more like a toy than an anthropomorphous agent than the two other robots.

Romo: It is a caterpillar type robot[2] that consists of an iPhone/iPod and a mobile base. Romo is about 150 mm tall and 114 mm wide. It can display an animated face and move around. An operator can control its locomotion and facial expressions by iPhone/iPod to play with little children, similar to Sphero. Unlike Sphero, however, since Romo has an animated face, little children might be more likely to regard it as an anthropomorphous agent than Sphero.

ChiCaRo: It which is a tele-presence robot for interaction with babies and toddlers [13]. ChiCaRo is 350 mm tall, 270 mm wide, and has a 7-inch LCD monitor to display the operator's face, differential wheels for locomotion, and a small hand-like device to play with babies and toddlers.

Unlike Sphero and Romo, ChiCaRo also has a video chat capability with which it can transmit the existence of a real person such as a parent. Therefore, its perceived anthropomorphism by little children is probably different from ChiCaRo and Sphero/Romo. We believe that ChiCaRo will encourage children to imagine that they are playing with an operator, not toys.

Procedures

In the data collection, participants freely acted in the environment for two hours. Before data collection, the adult participants filled out informed consent forms, which were

[1] http://www.romotive.com

[2] http://www.sphero.com

approved by IRB. After the children became acclimated to the environment, we asked their parents to control as an operator a robot to play/interact with their children. If the parent did not want to control the robots, an experimenter controlled them. If children wanted to continue interacting with the robot, the operators continued to control it. However, if children rejected interaction with the robots, the operators immediately stopped it. Operators controlled each robot in the playroom. Since we separated the children into three groups, each child only interacted with one of the three robots (Sphero, Romo, and ChicaRo); in other words, each robot interacted with 19 children.

Measurements

We investigated whether little children rejected the robot at the end of the data collection sessions. If a child enjoyed his/her interaction with the robot or the parents thought their child had fun, we described this child as *accepted*. On the other hand, if a child did not want to interact with the robot or exhibited hesitation or fleeing behaviors, we described this child as *rejected*.

Results

Table 1 shows the numbers of rejections for each robot. We verified the differences of the rejections among the three kinds of robots with a Chi-square test that revealed significant differences among the conditions ($p<.05$). Residual analysis revealed that *accepted* in Sphero was significantly high ($p<.05$), *accepted* in Romo was significantly low ($p<.05$).

Table 1. Experiment results

	Rejected	Accepted
Sphero	1	18
Romo	8	11
ChiCaRo	4	15

CONCLUSION

In this research work, we focused on the behaviors of young children who rejected interaction with robots. Even though previous research reported that children interacted effectively with robots, little children who rejected interaction with robots less reported. We used different kinds of robots to investigate whether young children rejected interaction with them in a playroom environment. Our data collection showed that children sometimes rejected the robots and showed different kinds of rejection behaviors. The number of children who rejected the robots was statistically different among the robots.

ACKNOWLEDGMENTS

This research work was supported by JSPS KAKENHI Grant Number 15H05322, 16K12505, and Grant-in-Aid for JSPS Fellows 15J11597.

REFERENCES

1. I. Leite, M. McCoy, M. Lohani, D. Ullman, N. Salomons, C. K. Stokes, S. Rivers, and B. Scassellati, "Emotional Storytelling in the Classroom: Individual versus Group Interaction between Children and Robots," in HRI, pp. 75-82, 2015.

2. J. Fink, S. Lemaignan, P. Dillenbourg, P. R, tornaz, F. Vaussard, A. Berthoud, F. Mondada, F. Wille, and K. Franinović, "Which robot behavior can motivate children to tidy up their toys?: design and evaluation of "ranger"," in Proceedings of the 2014 ACM/IEEE international conference on Human-robot interaction, Bielefeld, Germany, pp. 439-446, 2014.

3. M. Shiomi, and N. Hagita, "Social acceptance of a childcare support robot system," in Robot and Human Interactive Communication (RO-MAN), 2015 24th IEEE International Symposium on, pp. 13-18, 2015.

4. K. Abe, C. Hieida, M. Attamimi, T. Nagai, T. Shimotomai, T. Omori, and N. Oka, "Toward playmate robots that can play with children considering personality," in Proceedings of the second international conference on Human-agent interaction, Tsukuba, Japan, pp. 165-168, 2014.

5. C. Hieida, K. Abe, M. Attamimi, T. Shimotomai, T. Nagai, and T. Omori, "Physical embodied communication between robots and children: An approach for relationship building by holding hands," in Intelligent Robots and Systems (IROS 2014), 2014 IEEE/RSJ International Conference on, pp. 3291-3298, 2014.

6. F. Tanaka, K. Isshiki, F. Takahashi, M. Uekusa, R. Sei, and K. Hayashi, "Pepper learns together with children: Development of an educational application," in Humanoid Robots (Humanoids), 2015 IEEE-RAS 15th International Conference on, pp. 270-275, 2015.

7. F. Tanaka, and S. Matsuzoe, "Children teach a care-receiving robot to promote their learning: Field experiments in a classroom for vocabulary learning," Journal of Human-Robot Interaction, vol. 1, no. 1, 2012.

8. M. Shiomi, T. Kanda, I. Howley, K. Hayashi, and N. Hagita, "Can a Social Robot Stimulate Science Curiosity in Classrooms?," International Journal of Social Robotics, vol. 7, no. 5, pp. 641-652, 2015.

9. T. Komatsubara, M. Shiomi, T. Kanda, H. Ishiguro, and N. Hagita, "Can a social robot help children's understanding of science in classrooms?," in Proceedings of the second international conference on Human-agent interaction, Tsukuba, Japan, pp. 83-90, 2014.

10. K. Yamamoto, S. Tanaka, H. Kobayashi, H. Kozima, and K. Hashiya, "A Non-Humanoid Robot in the "Uncanny Valley": Experimental Analysis of the Reaction to Behavioral Contingency in 2–3 Year Old Children," PLoS ONE, vol. 4, no. 9, pp. e6974, 2009.

11. J. Kagan, J. S. Reznick, C. Clarke, N. Snidman, and C. Garcia-Coll, "Behavioral Inhibition to the Unfamiliar," Child development, vol. 55, no. 6, pp. 2212-2225, 1984.

12. J. Kagan, "The concept of behavioral inhibition," 1999.

13. K. Abe, Y. Pei, Z. Tingyi, C. Hieida, T. Nagai, and M. Shiomi, "Telepresence Childcare Robot for Playing with Children from a Remote Location," in International Conference on Advanced Mechatronics, pp. 1P-11, 2015.

Towards an Interactive Voice Agent for Singapore Hokkien

Vanessa Lim
Raffles Girls' School

Hui Shan Ang
Raffles Girls' School

Estelle Lee
Raffles Girls' School

Boon Pang Lim
Institute for Infocomm Research
bplim@i2r.a-star.edu.sg

ABSTRACT

Singapore Hokkien (SH) is the most commonly spoken non-Mandarin Chinese dialect in Singapore. It is an important language for many members of Singapore's pioneer generation, but much less so for the younger generation who prefer English. In recent years, the greying of this demographic has placed an increasing demand on for assistive devices to support them. We report ongoing efforts to build limited-vocabulary speech recognition, with the eventual goal of a conversational voice agent in SH that can support applications in home-automation or in-hospital use case scenarios. This process is challenging as sizeable SH speech corpora do not yet exist, and SH is sufficiently different from existing Mandarin or Minnan such that other corpora cannot be directly used. We document our efforts at building language resources -- audio corpora, pronunciation lexicons -- and present some preliminary findings on multilingual training.

Author Keywords

Voice Agents; Singapore Hokkien; Acoustic Modeling; Speech Recognition.

ACM Classification Keywords

Natural Language Processing; Human Factors; Voice I/O

INTRODUCTION

Singapore Hokkien (SH) is the most commonly spoken non-Mandarin Chinese dialect in Singapore. Originally from the Fujian Province in China, from southern regions such as Xiamen, Quanzhou and Zhangzhou, this language was brought to Singapore in the 1800s. Since then, the dialect has mixed with other local languages and dialects such as Teochew, English and Malay to become a uniquely Singaporean brand of Hokkien, lexically and phonologically different from its Amoy origins. SH is a significant part of Singapore's culture [1]: it is an important language for many members of Singapore's pioneer generation, preferred over English (or the local creole, Singlish) which might be more popular with younger generations.

Today, automatic speech recognition (ASR) has become more pervasive, with applications in devices in the market such as the Amazon Echo. However, some elderly in Singapore are disenfranchised from this, as they may be more comfortable speaking SH or not very technologically savvy to begin with. Many ASR systems have been built for tonal languages like Mandarin [2], but to our knowledge, nobody has built yet a system for SH, the closest being one for Min-nan [3]. We envision a near future where Hokkien speaking elderly in Singapore might better make use of computing devices through an interactive voice agent that speaks their language. Our motivation for this work is thus twofold -- first to preserve this unique heritage of SH, and second, to bridge these divides in both language and technology for the elderly Singaporean community. We present the first steps toward this – the ASR component for such a voice agent.

Phonology of Singapore Hokkien

SH is similar to Hokkien spoken in Taiwan and in the Amoy region in China, but has word borrowings from other languages (e.g. Malay) spoken in Singapore. We follow the analysis of [4], which was performed on speech collected from three speakers of SH, and propose the 37 token phoneset comprising 18 consonants and 19

HAI '16, October 04-07, 2016, Biopolis, Singapore
ACM 978-1-4503-4508-8/16/10.
http://dx.doi.org/10.1145/2974804.2980495

vowels shown in Table 1. Although SH is a tonal language, we have left out tone markings in order to speed up lexicon construction.

Vowels			Consonants		
IPA	Example	ASCII	IPA	Example	ASCII
Monophthongs			b	b$\underline{u}$e^{51} (buy)	b
i	t$\underline{\varphi}$it^{51} (one)	i	dz, dʐ	an^{33} $\underline{dz}$ua^{31} (why?)	dz
e	p$\underline{e}$ŋ^{24} (side)	ei	g	g$\underline{o}$^{33} (five)	g
ə	n$\underline{ə}$ŋ^{11} (two)	uh	h	$\underline{h}$ia^{55} (brother)	h
o	tam^{33} p$\underline{o}$^{53} (few)	o	k	$\underline{k}$au^{51} (nine)	k
u	tʰ$\underline{u}$n^{55} (swallow)	u	kʰ	$\underline{kʰ}$a^{55} (foot)	kh
ɘ	ts$\underline{ɘ}$^{51} (cook)	e	l	$\underline{l}$ɔ^{51} (you)	l
a	s$\underline{a}$^{55} (three)	ah	m	ta$\underline{m}$^{33} po^{53} (few)	m
ɔ	g$\underline{ɔ}$^{33} (five)	oh	n	t$\underline{ç}$iŋ^{33} (very)	n
Diphthongs			ŋ	pe$\underline{ŋ}$^{24} (side)	ng
ai	kʰi^{51} $\underline{lai}$^{33} (get up)	ai	p	$\underline{p}$ue^{31} (eight)	p
au	k$\underline{au}$^{51} (nine)	au	pʰ	$\underline{pʰ}$e^{24} (skin)	ph
ia	h$\underline{ia}$^{55} (brother)	ia	ʔ	ba$\underline{ʔ}$^{31} (meat)	q
io	k$\underline{io}$^{11} (call)	io	s	$\underline{s}$i^{51} (die)	s
iɔ	t$\underline{iɔ}$ŋ^{55} əm^{55} (centre)	ioo	t	$\underline{t}$a^{55} (dry)	t
iu	tçʰ$\underline{iu}$^{51} (hand)	iu	ts, tç	$\underline{ts}$ɘ^{51} (cook), $\underline{tç}$ap^{51} (ten)	ts
ua	tʃʰ$\underline{ua}$n^{23} kʰui^{31} (breathe)	ua	tʰ	$\underline{tʰ}$un^{55} (swallow)	th
ue	p$\underline{ue}$^{31} (eight)	ue	tçʰ tʃʰ tsʰ	$\underline{tçʰ}$it^{31} (seven), $\underline{tʃʰ}$uan^{23} kʰui^{31} (breathe), $\underline{tsʰ}$eŋ^{55} kʰi^{11} (clean)	tsh
ui	tʃʰ$\underline{ui}$^{11} (mouth)	ui			
Vowel Triphthongs					
iau	e^{11} h$\underline{iau}$^{51} (know)	iau	uai	gi^{51} $\underline{g}$uai^{33} (strange)	uai

Table 1: Consonants and Vowel in SH.

Lexical Resources for Singapore Hokkien

We have built a dictionary for common words - each lexical entry consists of four items – a romanized orthography, an equivalent English meaning; an equivalent Mandarin Chinese meaning and a phonetic spelling. The Romanized orthography simply concatenates the ASCII phoneset symbols for each phoneme in a syllable together, and uses an apostrophe to separate the syllable boundary between words.

Two approaches are used to expand lexicon. In the first, we expand from a list of desired English lexical entries, and create the equivalent lexical entry we need. (i.e. by filling in the orthographic and phonetic spellings). The second is to elicit natural spoken translations of English to Hokkien sentences from SH speakers, and then to transcribe those and mine new lexical entries.

Eliciting natural sentences in SH

The diction and sentence structure for Hokkien is different from Mandarin, thus directly reading Chinese character from Mandarin sentences cannot yield natural sounding Hokkien. To alleviate this we propose a 4-step approach to generating useful sentences and lexical entries. In the first step, we generate sentences that we might want to use. In the second step, we asked informants who are fluent in both Mandarin/English and Hokkien to translate the desired sentence to Hokkien. The sentences were then written down using a combination of either Chinese characters or with our romanized orthography. Third, audio recordings were made for these sentences. Finally, new lexical entries were added for terms that we did not yet have.

We generated 3 sets of sentences: 500 common sentences -- which might be used in daily life, 70 voice commands related to a home automation (HA), and 50 voice commands related to a hospital (Hosp) setting. The first set of sentences were randomly picked from an online Chinese dictionary with example sentences [5].

Acoustic Resources for Singapore Hokkien

Speech was collected in two phases. These recordings are in 16-kHz, 16-bit PCM, and were made using a USB desktop headset microphone. In the first phase, we generated and collected a total of 300 sentences: some 100 sentences were collected from Chinese language newspapers, some 100 utterances were generate from a date/time and digit sequence grammar, and the remaining 100 were elicited naturally from some imagined day to day uses of language in Singapore. We enlisted the help of a language expert to transliterate them into Singapore Hokkien. The language expert also recorded each sentence. We recruited 52 speakers between 18 and 55 and recorded them saying these sentences. Often, the speakers may speak the language well, but they may not be literate in it. We used custom software that displayed visual prompts of the sentence – both in Chinese script and in the romanized orthography – and in the worse case allowed playback of the recordings made by the language expert, to make this process easier. Totally, 44.6 hours of speech was collected.

Acoustic Modeling

We trained acoustic models using the Kaldi Speech Recognition toolkit [6], with 56 dimensional features (13-dim MFCC with 1-dim ETSI pitch + third order delta coefficients). We used a standard recipe for Kaldi, bootstrapping a GMM-HMM system to obtain alignment for training a hybrid GMM-DNN model [7]. The neural network splice 5 left and 5 right frames to obtain a 616 dimension super-vector for the input layer. The network has 3 hidden layers and one output layer with 1505 output neurons. A bigram language model was trained and smoothed using Keyser-Ney discounting from the transcripts of the test utterances in order to benchmark free word order decoding. A BNF grammar of commands was built using the open source Thrax tool using all 50 unique sentences in the test set.

Baseline Testing and Evaluation

We additionally recorded 50 unique utterances from the Hosp domain, from 5 male and 5 female speakers for testing. Our results, as seen in Table 5, show tremendous improvement going from GMMs and DNNs. Furthermore, we demonstrate that with careful tuning, we can get very close to a functional system, with recognition error of less than 6.3% for recognizing one of 50 voice commands.

	LDA+MLLT (GMM-HMM)		SGD (DNN)	
	n-gram	BNF	n-gram	BNF
WER (%)	69.8	66.7	32.2	**6.3**
SER (%)	-	76.0		12.0

Table 5: Performance of Initial Acoustic Model.

MULTILINGUAL ACOUSTIC MODELING

Obtaining sufficient acoustic data for Singapore Hokkien acoustic modeling is challenging. Several methods proposed to alleviate this by leveraging more readily available data from other language – either through the use of a global common phoneset [8], the use of multilingual bottleneck features [9,10] or using multilingual training [11]. Experiments in [9] show that similarity between the source and target language can mean greater performance gains. We apply multilingual training with use speech data from three other languages: English, Mandarin -- assembled from commercial mobile speech recognition databases -- and Minnan [3].

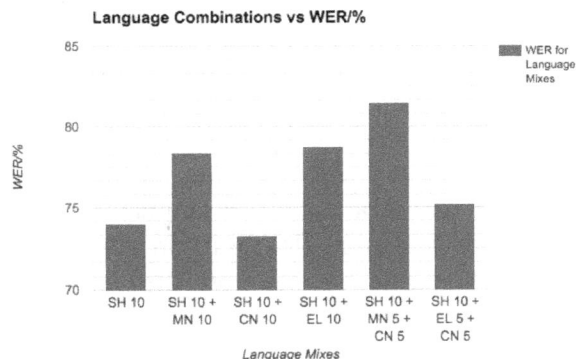

Figure 1: Comparison for Multilingual Training

Our findings are shown in Figure 1. Here the numbers following the language indicate how many hours of speech was used. An n-gram LM trained with training transcripts was used for these experiments. The use of training rather than test transcripts may account for the discrepancy in WERs between this and the earlier benchmarks. Intuitively, Minnan should be the most similar, followed by Mandarin, then by English. However, Minnan was found to be the least helpful – we suspect that this could be due to the lack of phonetic diversity in the Minnan database. Mandarin Chinese was found to be the most helpful. We further investigate the impact of using different amounts of Mandarin data to perform multilingual training. Our findings, shown in Figure 2, demonstrate that with a good corpus multilingual training can alleviate the lack of training data, but this is up to a limit.

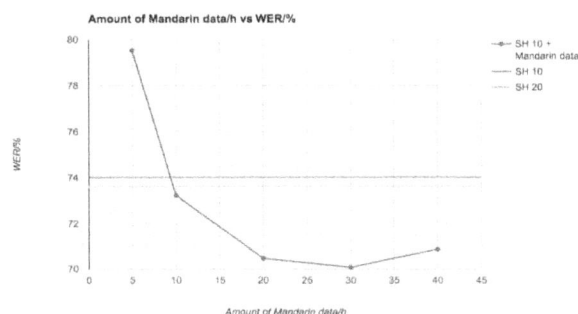

Figure 2: Amount of Mandarin Chinese Data used in Multilingual Training.

DISCUSSION AND CONCLUSION

We have presented ongoing work to build speech recognition suitable for a Singapore Hokkien voice agent. We have achieved reasonable recognition performance in some limited use-cases and domains through the use of a limited BNF grammar. This may not be feasible with more interactive voice agents, which would require the use of a statistical language model in order to provide more flexibility in conversation. We will continue to develop the lexical and acoustic resources as well as to use improved modeling techniques towards our goal.

REFERENCES

1. David Deterding. 2007. *Singapore English.* Edinburgh: Edinburgh University Press.
2. C.J. Chen, R. A. Gopinath, M. D. Monkowski, M. A. Picheny, K. Shen. 1997. New methods in continuous Mandarin speech recognition. *In Proceedings of EUROSPEECH.*
3. Dau-Cheng Lyu, Min-Siong Liang, Yuang-chin Chiang, Chun-Nan Hsu, Ren-Yuan Lyu. 2003. Large vocabulary Taiwanese (min-nan) speech recognition using tone features and statistical pronunciation modeling. *In Proceedings of EUROSPEECH*
4. Amelia Hong. 2012. A Phonological and Phonetic Description of Singapore Hokkien. Master's Thesis. Nanyang Technological University, Singapore.
5. Pinyin index - Chinese Dictionary of examples. In *Discover China, learn Chinese - Chinese-Tools.com.* Retrieved on May 1st 2016 from http://www.chinese-tools.com/chinese/examples/pinyin.html
6. Daniel Povey et al. 2011. The Kaldi speech recognition toolkit. *In Proceedings of IEEE Workshop on Automatic Speech Recognition and Understanding*
7. Geoffrey Hinton et al. Deep neural networks for acoustic modeling in speech recognition. *Signal Processing Magazine,* 2012
8. Tanya Schulz, Alex Waibel. 1998 Multilingual and Crosslingual Speech Recognition", in Proc. *DARPA Workshop on Broadcast News Transcription and Understanding*
9. Zhang, Y., Chuangsuwanich, E., & Glass, J. 2014. Language ID-based Training of Multilingual Stacked Bottleneck Features. *In Proceedings of Interspeech*, 1-5
10. Ngoc Thang Vu, Florian Metze, Tanya Schulz. 2012. Multilingual Bottle-neck Features and its Application for Under-resourced Languages, *in Proceedings of Spoken Language Technology and Understanding*
11. Heigold, G., Vanhoucke, V., Senior, A., Nguyen, P., Ranzato, M., Devin, M., & Dean, J. 2013. Multilingual Acoustic Models Using Distributed Deep Neural Networks. *In Proceedings of International Conference on Acoustics, Speech and Signal Processing,* 8169-6149

Effect of Embodiment Presentation by Humanoid Robot on Social Telepresence

Ikkaku Kawaguchi*, Yuki Kodama*, Hideaki Kuzuoka*, Mai Otsuki*, Yusuke Suzuki†

*University of Tsukuba, Tsukuba, Ibaraki, Japan,
s1430196@u.tsukuba.ac.jp, kodama.yuki49@gmail.com,
kuzuoka@iit.tsukuba.ac.jp, otsuki@emp.tsukuba.ac.jp

†OKI Electric Industry Co.Ltd.
Warabi, Saitama, Japan
suzuki543@oki.com

ABSTRACT

In this study, we used a humanoid robot as a telepresence robot and compared with the basic telepresence robot which can only rotate the display in order to reveal the effect of embodiment. We also investigated the effect caused by changing the body size of the humanoid robot by using two different size of robots. Our experimental results revealed that the embodiment increases the remote person's social telepresence, familiarity, and directivity. The comparison between small and big humanoid robots showed no difference and both of them were effective.

Author Keywords
Social Telepresence; Embodiment; Humanoid; Size of robot

ACM Classification Keywords
H.5.3. Information interfaces and presentation (e.g., HCI): Group and Organization Interface-Computer-supported cooperative work.

INTRODUCTION
It is well known that non-verbal information plays an important role in face-to-face communication [2]. However, in remote communication using ordinary video conferencing system, it is difficult to transfer non-verbal information due to the discrepancy caused by communication media [3]. One of the solutions to this problem is a telepresence robot which acts as a surrogate of a remote participant [5, 12, 13]. In general, a telepresence robot has a mechanism to move a display which shows a remote person's face (hereafter, 'moving display telepresence robot'), and they found that communication became smoother and the remote person's sense of presence increases by reflecting a remote person's motion to the display. However, such moving display causes

HAI '16, October 04-07, 2016, Biopolis, Singapore
ACM 978-1-4503-4508-8/16/10.
http://dx.doi.org/10.1145/2974804.2980498

the cases for a local participant to watch the display from oblique angles which leads to the misunderstanding of gaze directions of remote participant and decrease the remote participant's presence [5, 6, 13]. To solve these problems, alternative methods are necessary. As extended forms of a moving display telepresence robots, telepresence robots that are extended with human-like body parts (e.g. arms) have been developed (here after, 'body-parts extended telepresence robot') to represent remote participants' bodily gestures [1, 14]. In addition to the studies with telepresence robots, effect of body gestures have also been investigated using communication robots [8, 15]. These studies show that presentation of the robot's body gestures, such as head, body and arm movement, improve the impression of the remote participant or the robot itself from the various aspects. Although various telepresence robots have been proposed, no comparison was made between a moving display telepresence robot and a body-parts extended telepresence robot, in terms of the sense of presence of the remote participant. Thus the purpose of our study is to compare the body-parts extended telepresence robot and the moving display telepresence robot to reveal the effect of embodiment. As the body-parts extended telepresence robot, we used a humanoid robot with physical body parts (head, body, and arms). We thought the humanoid robot with body parts similar to human is most effective because the movement of the robot's body parts is known to improve the impression of remote participant and robot itself [1, 8, 14, 15]. In addition, it is known that the size of the robot affect the impression that human receives [4, 11], so in this study we compared

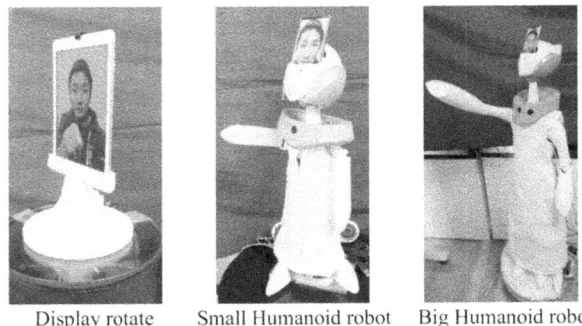

Display rotate   Small Humanoid robot   Big Humanoid robot

Figure 1. Experimental conditions. These pictures show the appearance when each robot is explaining the document.

humanoid robots in a two sizes (table top size, and close to human life-size).

EXPERIMENT

Referring to Nakanishi's previous study [10], we conducted a task which a remote participant gives explanation to the local participant using a telepresence robot. In addition, we assumed quasi-naturalistic situation of using the telepresence robot and included attentional guidance to the local document which required to transmit the gaze not only to the front person, but also to other direction. For evaluation, we used a questionnaire mainly on social telepresence and conducted a video analysis. An interview was also conducted after all the tasks were finished.

In this study, we compared three conditions. As Figure 1 shows, we used three types of robots corresponding to each condition.

Display Rotate Condition: This condition used a rotatable table which can rotate in horizontal direction with a 10-inch tablet (iPad, Apple Inc.) presenting the video of the remote participant's upper body. Attentional guidance to the local document was performed by rotation of the display and finger pointing gesture in the video. The directivity in horizontal plane was presented by display rotation, so the direction of the head and finger in the video was fixed to the frontal direction.

Small Humanoid Robot Condition: This condition used a humanoid robot with a total height of 60cm. We developed a humanoid robot which consists of a head, body, and two arms. 5 inch smartphone (305SH, SHARP Co.) was placed on the head to present the video of the remote participant. Only the face of the remote participant was shown in the display and the size of the face image is adjusted to the same size as the display rotate condition. Attentional guidance to the local document is performed by the head-body rotation and pointing movement using the arm. The directivity in horizontal direction is presented by the robot's head-body rotation, so the direction of the head in the video is fixed to the frontal direction.

Big Humanoid Robot Condition: A condition using a humanoid robot with a height of 120cm. The humanoid robot was developed utilizingTalkTorque2 [9]. 5-inch smartphone (305SH, SHARP Co.) was placed on its head to present the video of the remote participant. The video and body movement of the robot was same as the small humanoid.

Since we aimed to compare the effect of embodiment itself, we presented the remote participant's face image in all conditions. In conditions using a humanoid robot, only the remote participant's face was shown in the smartphone placed on the robots' head and the body movement of the robot presented remote participant's gesture, while in the display rotate condition, both remote participant's face and gestures were presented by the video shown in the display. Skype was used for video communication in all conditions.

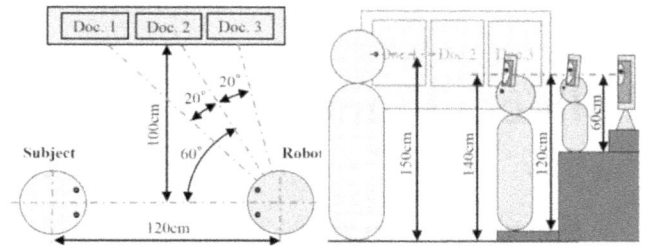

Figure 2. Overview of the environment of experiment.

Experimental setup and task

Figure 2 shows an overview of experimental environment. From the remote site, a remote participant (experimenter) communicated with a local participant (subject) through a telepresence robot and explained about the three documents placed on the whiteboard which is related to a fast food restaurant. This experiment used a within subject design, so we prepared three scripts for each trial. Order of the conditions was counter balanced to minimize the learning effect. In each script, three yes-or-no questions were embedded to have an easy conversation for the subject, because if there were no conversation in the script, subject may feel that the remote participant as recorded video. One description took about 2 minutes. Although we used three scripts, movement and duration of the remote participant/robots were the same between each script to eliminate the effect of script difference. We recorded the behavior of the subject and conducted video analysis. In video analysis, we focused the subject's gaze especially mutual gaze between the robot and the subject because it plays an important role in human communication [7] (e.g. regulate interaction, express intimacy, and facilitate service and task goals).After each task, we gave a questionnaire to the subjects. The questionnaire contained 8 questions, including questions on social telepresence (Q1-Q4), naturalness of the movement (Q5), directivity of the robot (Q6, Q7), and sense of affinity (Q8). The questions are shown on Figure 3. We used the 7 point Likert-scale for our questionnaire. An interview was also conducted after all the tasks were finished. We recruited 12 subjects from a local university (all of them were male). Their ages ranged from 20 to 24 years old.

Results

Questionnaire Results

To evaluate the difference of each condition, a one-way within subjects ANOVA was conducted to compare the effect of condition on questionnaire result in three conditions. The result of each question is shown in Figure 3. There were significant effects of conditions in the questions except Q3. As the post hoc test, multiple comparisons with Bonferroni correction was carried out on questions except Q3. Significant differences were shown in Figure 3.

Evaluation of Subject's Gaze Direction

For the statistical analysis we measured the ratio of duration that the subject was looking at the robot in each trial based on the video analysis (Figure 4(a)). We also measured the ratio of duration that mutual gaze was achieved between the robot and the subject (Figure 4(b)). A one-way within subjects ANOVA was conducted to compare the effect of condition on these two results. On the ratio of duration that the subject was looking at the robot, there were significant effects of conditions ($F(2,22) = 19.812$, $p < 0.001$). As the post hoc test, multiple comparisons with Bonferroni correction was carried out and there was significant trend between display rotate condition and big humanoid robot condition ($p = 0.087$). On the ratio of duration that mutual gaze was achieved, there was no significant effect of conditions ($F(2,22) = 2.064$, $p = 0.151$).

As the additional evaluation of mutual gaze, we measured delay before mutual gaze had achieved. In each task remote participant looked at the subject 4 times, so totally 48 samples were obtained for each condition. Table 1 show the result of measured delay until mutual gaze had achieved. We conducted Friedman test and there was significant effect of condition on the delay ($p<0.001$). As the post hoc test, Dunn-Bonferroni test was carried out and there was significant differences between display rotate condition and big humanoid robot condition ($p<0.001$), and there was significant trend between display rotate condition and small humanoid robot condition ($p = 0.057$).

DISCUSSION

Effect of embodiment presentation

From the result of the questionnaire (Figure 3), two humanoid robot conditions were scored significantly higher than the display rotate condition in the questions except Q3. As shown in Figure 1, the difference of these conditions was medium (e.g. the video image, the small/big humanoid robot) to present the body gestures. So the differences between these conditions were considered to be the effect of the embodiment presentation by using humanoid robots.

For the questions about social telepresence (Q1-Q4), significant differences were seen in questions Q1, Q2 and Q4 between display rotate condition and small/big humanoid robot condition (In Q4, significant trend between display rotate condition and small humanoid condition). From these results, presenting physical gestures by humanoid robot increases the social telepresence of the remote participant. Meanwhile, there was no significant difference in Q3. In all conditions, the display faced straight toward the subject when the remote participant see the subject, so problems caused by viewing the display from an oblique angle [6, 13] did not occur. We are assuming that this is the reason why there was no significant difference between each condition for Q3.

For the questions about naturalness of the movement (Q5), significant difference was seen between display rotate condition and small humanoid condition. From the interview, subjects pointed out that Mona Lisa effect occurred in the display rotate condition when the display was rotated. Thus the mismatch in the direction of the display and the perceived

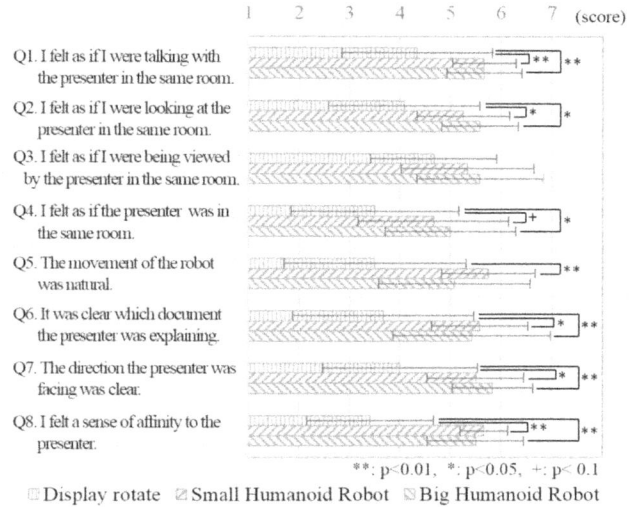

Figure 3. Results of the questionnaires

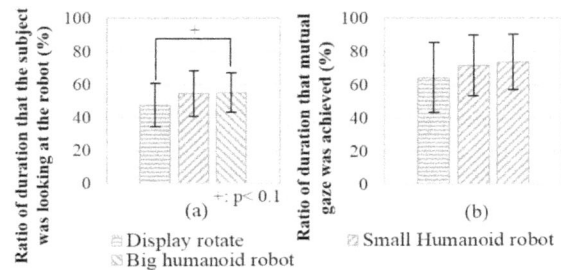

Figure 4. Result of video analysis of subject's gaze direction.

Table 1. Result of measured delay before mutual gaze had achieved.

Condition	N	Mean	SD	Min.	Max.	Percentiles			Mean Rank
						25th	50th	75th	
Display rotate	48	1.49	2.80	0	5.11	0	0.25	1.20	2.42
Small humanoid robot	48	0.67	1.57	0	8.24	0	0	0.73	1.94
Big humanoid robot	48	0.38	0.93	0	13.48	0	0	0.03	1.65

**: $p<0.01$, +: $p<0.1$

gaze direction from the remote participant's face in the video might have decreased the score of how natural the movement was in the display rotate condition. In the conditions using humanoid robots, the display placed on the robot's head rotated in the same way as the display rotate condition. Thus, it is possible for the Mona Lisa effect to occur. However, the awareness of the robot's head motion seemed to be stronger than the effect of the display rotation, decreasing the Mona Lisa effect in the conditions using a humanoid robot.

For the questions about the directivity of the robot, significant differences were seen for both Q6 and Q7 between display rotate condition and small/big humanoid conditions. The difference between display rotate condition and small/big humanoid condition was caused by the difference of directivity between display rotation and humanoid robots' body gesture. This result indicates that physical movement using the humanoid robot is more effective than display rotation for presentation of directivity.

For Q8, a significant difference was seen between display rotate condition and small/big humanoid condition. It is conceivable that the sense of affinity to the remote participant increased by the increase of social telepresence.

From the result of the video analysis, mutual gaze was achieved significantly faster in big humanoid condition than display rotate condition. Small humanoid condition also had a tendency that subjects achieve mutual gaze faster than display rotate condition. Thus, we can assume that the physical motion of the humanoid robots increased awareness so subject could react to remote participant's gaze faster and achieved mutual gaze. The ratio of looking at the robot (Figure 4(a)) tend to increase in the big humanoid condition than the display rotate condition. We can assume that increased awareness by the physical motion of the humanoid robots invited more gaze from the subject.

Effect of the humanoid robot's size

In the experiment, there was no significant difference between small and big humanoid condition in all results. Based on these results, the effect of the embodiment presentation discussed in the previous section is valid regardless of the robot's size.

In the analysis of delay before mutual gaze had achieved significant difference was seen between big humanoid condition and display rotate condition but significant trend was seen between small humanoid condition and display rotate condition. In the analysis of ratio of duration that the subject was looking at the robot, significant difference was only seen between big humanoid condition and display rotate condition. Thus, the big humanoid robot seemed to be more effective to invite the gaze of subjects.

CONCLUSION

Overall, humanoid robot conditions increased social telepresence, directivity, and sense of affinity compare to display rotate condition. We could not find significant difference between small humanoid condition and big humanoid condition. Our results indicate that, regardless of its size, the humanoid robot can alleviate the problems of display moving telepresence robot [5, 6, 13], e.g., low telepresence, misunderstanding of gaze direction, low participation. Though we could not find significant difference between small and big humanoid condition, these two robots has different feature (e.g. Big humanoid seemed to be more effective to increasing the presence of remote participant and invites the gaze of subjects, small humanoid was perceived as more naturalistic.). These features may affect the subject differently according to the situation. Thus careful consideration for the size of a telepresence robot is still necessary. The limitation of our study is that the task we used was somewhat artificial and our assessment was based mainly on subjective evaluation. Thus, in our next step, quantitative assessment and observational analysis with more naturalistic task is necessary (i.e. multi-party meeting).

ACKNOWLEDGEMENTS
This work was supported by JSPS Grant-in-Aid for JSPS Research Fellow JP16J06932.

REFERENCES
1. Adalgeirsson, S. O., and Breazeal, C. Mebot: a robotic platform for socially embodied presence. In *Proc. HRI 2010*, IEEE Press (2010), 15-22.
2. Goodwin, C. Professional vision. *American anthropologist 96*, 3 (1994), 606-633.
3. Heath, C., and Luff, P.: Disembodied conduct: communication through video in a multi-media office environment. In *Proc. CHI 1991*, ACM Press (1991), 99-103.
4. Hiroi, Y., and Ito, A. Are bigger robots scary?-The relationship between robot size and psychological threat? In *Proc. AIM 2008*. IEEE Press (2008), 546-551.
5. Jacob, T.B., Daniel, A. and Anthony, D. Not Really There: Understanding Embodied Communication Affordances in Team Perception and Participation, In *Proc. CSCW 2015*, ACM Press (2015), 1567-1575.
6. Kawaguchi, I., Kuzuoka, H. and Suzuki, Y. Study on Gaze Direction Perception on Face Image Displayed on Rotatable Display, In *Proc. CHI 2015*, ACM Press (2015), 1729-1737.
7. Kleinke, C. L. Gaze and eye contact: a research review. *Psychological bulletin*, 100.1(1986), 78.
8. Kuzuoka, H., Kosaka, J., Yamazaki, K., Suga, Y., Suga, Y., Yamazaki, A., Luff, P. and Heath, C. Mediating dual ecologies. In *Proc. CSCW 2004*, ACM Press (2004), 477-486.
9. Madhumita, G., and Kuzuoka, H. An Ethnomethodological Study of a Museum Guide Robot's Attempt at Engagement and Disengagement. Journal of Robotics, Hindawi Publishing (2014).
10. Nakanishi, H., Kato, K. and Ishiguro, H. Zoom Cameras and Movable Displays Enhance Social Telepresence. In *Proc. CHI 2011*, ACM Press (2011), 63-72.
11. Rae, I., Takayama, L., and Mutlu, B. The influence of height in robot-mediated communication. In *Proc. HRI2013*, IEEE Press (2013). 1-8.
12. Revolve Robotics - Kubi. https://revolverobotics.com
13. Sirkin, D., Venolia, G., Tang, J., Robertson, G., Kim, T., Inkpen, K., and Sinclair, M. Motion and attention in a kinetic videoconferencing proxy. In *Human-Computer Interaction–INTERACT 2011*, Springer (2011), 162-180.
14. Tanaka, K., Nakanishi, H., and Ishiguro, H. Comparing video, avatar, and robot mediated communication: pros and cons of embodiment. Collaboration Technologies and Social Computing, Springer Berlin Heidelberg (2014), 96-110.
15. Xu, Q., Liyuan, L. and Gang W. Designing engagement-aware agents for multiparty conversations. In *Proc. CHI2013*, ACM Press (2013), 2233-2242.

Ambiguity-Driven Interaction in Robot-to-Human Teaching

Kenta Yamada
Toyohashi University of Technology
Aichi, Japan
yamada@aisl.cs.tut.ac.jp

Jun Miura
Toyohashi University of Technology
Aichi, Japan
jun.miura@tut.jp

ABSTRACT

The transfer of task knowledge is ubiquitous in our daily lives, where various types of interaction occur. Such an interactive task knowledge transfer, however, requires that an instructor and a learner to be at the same place and time. If we use a robot to mediate between them, such limitations can be eliminated. This paper focuses on human-to-robot teaching, in which a robot instructor interactively teaches a human learner how to achieve a task. We develop an ambiguity-driven formulation of interactive teaching based on the Dempster-Shafer theory. We implemented an experimental system for blocks world tasks as a proof-of-concept and show our preliminary results.

ACM Classification Keywords

H.1.2. MODELS AND PRINCIPLES: User/Machine Systems

Author Keywords

interactive teaching; robot instructor; ambiguity-driven interaction; Dempster-Shafer theory

INTRODUCTION

Transfer of task knowledge is ubiquitous. At production sites, skilled workers teach novices various pieces of knowledge such as how to manipulate objects, how to operate tools, and how to organize production schedules. At home, parents teach children, for example, how to use toys and how to cook. Transferring such task knowledge requires an instructor and learner to exist at the same place and time in order to use various modalities including gestures and actions. Using a robot as a mediator, we could remove this limitation.

Robot-mediated task knowledge transfer is divided into two stages: (1) a person teaches a robot; and (2) the robot teaches another person. The first step is so-called *robot teaching* and is one of the important research areas in robotics and human-robot interaction (HRI). One promising approach is *programming by demonstration* (PbD) or *teaching by showing*, in which a human instructor demonstrates a task and a robot observes it to make a task model [2]. second step has

HAI '16 October 04-07, 2016, Biopolis, Singapore

© 2016 Copyright held by the owner/author(s).

ACM ISBN 978-1-4503-4508-8/16/10.

DOI: http://dx.doi.org/10.1145/2974804.2980514

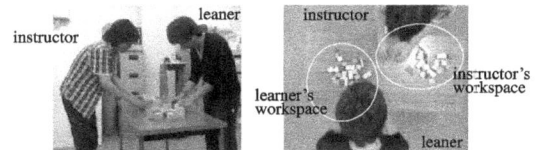

Figure 1. Human-to-human teaching by mutual demonstration.

not been significantly researched in robotics, although several works discusses the affective communication strategy (e.g., [7, 5]) and/or physical presence of the teacher (e.g., [3]).

This paper deals with robot-to-human teaching of assembly tasks through *mutual demonstration*. An instructor robot first demonstrates an assembly step and a human leaner then demonstrates what he/she has just understood (i.e., tries to copy the same step). Fig. 1 shows an example teaching scene among humans.

By mutual demonstration, an instructor transfers knowledge of the task to a leaner. If transfer is not complete (e.g., the learner misses some details), the learner could issue a query to make it clearer. The instructor could provide an additional explanation/demonstration when he/she thinks the learner does not understand the task completely. Instructions are thus considered to arise when knowledge transfer by teaching is incomplete, or trasferred knowledge is *ambiguous*. We would like to develop a mechanism of such an *ambiguity-driven* interaction with a robot. Moreover, the ambiguity is assessed by estimating a learner's internal model. We use the Dempster-Shafer theory (DST) to formulate the model because DST can express ambiguities explicitly.

MODELING INTERACTION PROCESS IN ROBOT-TO-HUMAN TEACHING OF ASSEMBLY TASKS

Necessary models in interactive teaching

The instructor has a description of a task to teach, by following which the task is achieved. We call the description a *task model*. The model includes descriptions such as objects involved in the task and geometrical relations between objects. An assembly task is defined by a sequence of assembly steps, and each step is described by a set of relations added (or removed) by that step.

Models of others are for representing the internal state of others, and can be used for predicting and recognizing their behaviors. Such a model is definitely important in developing human-machine interaction systems such as intelligent tutoring systems (e.g., [8]).

257

Figure 2. Robot teaches human.

The goal of instructor, who has a complete task model, is to make the learner construct the same model in his/her mind. To check this, the instructor must estimate the learner's degree of understanding of the task. For this estimation, it is further needed to know how the learner behavrs depending on his/her internal state. Fig. 2 illustrates such a model-based interaction; the robot will give appropriate (additional) instructions based on the learner's model under estimation.

Modeling the interaction process

The process of teaching can be viewed as the one that the set of possible task models (of an assembly step), or *ambiguity of task model*, in the learner's mind are gradually reduced demonstrations/explanations by the instructor, and it finishes when the instructor robot recognizes the complete transfer of task knowledge.

Another important model of interaction is the relationship between the learner's task model and his/her behavior. The learner may pose a question depending on what is ambiguous about the task. For example, if which object to pick up is not clear, he/she will ask about the identity of the object. Since the robot instructor cannot directly see the learner's internal state, it is necessary to assess it from his/her behaviors.

Dempster-Shafer theory

We adopt the Dempster-Shafer theory (DST) [6] to represent both parts of interaction modeling because *ambiguity* is a key concept in both types of modeling and DST is very suitable for representing ambiguities (or *ignorance*) [1]. In DST, a set of possible (discrete) states Θ is called a *frame of discernment* (FOD), and a degree of belief (called *basic probability*) is assigned to each subset A_i of FOD such that the sum of the basic probabilities becomes one. There are two quantities: belief function $Bel(A_i)$ and plausibility $Pla(A_i)$, which represent the lower and the upper bound, respectively.

By assigning a probability to each subset, we can represent "ignorance" explicitly; we can represent the case where we know the answer is one of the two candidates, a and b, but do not know which is more probable at all, by assigning the entire probability mass to subset $\{a, b\}$. This way of assigning probabilities is quite suitable for representing ambiguities in possible task models.

Fusion of two independent source is performed by several combination rules. We here use the Dempster's combination rule and denoted as $\oplus$.

Formulation of the interaction process

We formulate the interaction process as gradually refining the basic probability assignment (bpa). The process is divided into the following steps:

---

1. <u>Demonstration and Initialization</u>: demonstrate an assembly step to the human, enumerate a set of possible models as an FOD, and calculate bpa (i.e., assign basic probabilities to its subsets).

2. <u>Observation</u>: observe the human's behavior. Example behaviors are: *execute the step perfectly*, *execute the step differently*, and *make a query to the robot instructor*.

3. <u>Estimation</u>: calculate a bpa for this observation and combine it with the current bpa for update.

4. <u>Judgement</u>: assess the degree of task knowledge transfer.

   a) Check if task knowledge of this assembly step is considered to be sufficiently transferred. This is done by judging if only the subset with the correct relation set (we call it the *correct subset*) as a single element has a high basic probability. If this is the case, move to the teaching of the next assembly step.

   b) Otherwise, proceeds to interaction planning.

5. <u>Planning</u>: select and execute the best interactive action, and then go to 2.

Interaction planning

Step 5 determines the robot's best interactive action for transferring the task knowledge. We take a similar approach to sensing planning under an uncertainty in which an action is chosen that maximizes the expected utility with a prediction of possible future states [4].

In the current context, prediction is about what the human will perceive (or understand) by a robot action such as gesture or verbal instruction. We would therefore like to maximize the predicted belief on the correct subset A^*. The predicted belief is the combination of the current belief m_c and the belief m_u to be obtained by a robot interactive action u. The best action u^* is then given by:

$$u^* = \arg\max_u \left\{ Bel(A^*) \text{ given by } (m_c \oplus m_u)(A) \right\}. \quad (1)$$

Calculation of basic probability assignment

Steps 1, 3, and 4 require the calculation of basic probability assignments (bpa's). We have not devised a general procedure for that. We here show some ideas for this calculation and will show examples in the experiments.

In steps 1 and 4, a bpa represents how the robot's demonstration is perceived by the human. Apparent knowledge (e.g., whether to put an object on another or put an object aside another) is easier to perceive, while a subtle difference (e.g., whether two planes should be coplanar) is more difficult. A voice message could carry more information when teaching an object's identity, while a gesture would be better when

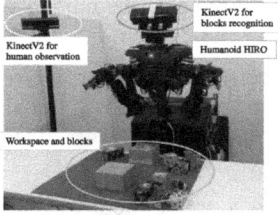

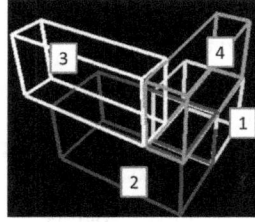

Figure 3. The experimental setting.

Figure 4. A blocks world task.

Table 1. Geometrical relations to achieve in the task shown in Fig. 4. Alphabets indicate suface id's.

step	relations
1	$Coplanar(1\text{-}C, 2\text{-}D)$, $Against(1\text{-}E, 2\text{-}F)$
2	$On(4\text{-}C, 2\text{-}A)$, $On(4\text{-}C, 1\text{-}B)$, $Coplanar(4\text{-}A, 2\text{-}D)$, $Coplanar(4\text{-}B, 2\text{-}C)$
3	$On(3\text{-}C, 2\text{-}A)$, $Coplanar(3\text{-}A, 4\text{-}B)$, $Against(3\text{-}D, 4\text{-}E)$

teaching gemeotrical relations. The bpa to each subset should be calculated considering such factors.

In step 3, the leaner's state is estimated from his/her behavior. We suppose that the learner's behavior highly depends on the state; if the learner thinks to have a firm knowledge, for example, he/she will execute the current assembly step quickly without any hesitation. If not, he/she may take a longer time for execution or explicitly issue a query. We consider the ambiguity in the learner's model is almost directly related to his/her behaviors.

EXPERIMENTAL RESULTS

The robot and the task

Fig. 3 shows the experimental setting. The robot (HIRO by Kawada Co.) recognizes the workspace and human actions using two Kinects and a camera. Verbal communication with a designated set of words is also used. Fig. 4 shows an example task in which four blocks are assembled in three steps: put blocks 1 and 2, put block 4 on blocks 1 and 2, and put block 3 on block 2. Table 1 shows the geometrical relations to be achieved in each step.

Examples of robot-to-human interactive teaching

We conducted three trials of robot-to-human interactive teaching. In one case, the transfer is completed without additional interactions because the human learner was able to achieve the correct assembly steps only from the robot demonstrations. In the other cases shown below, additional interactions were necessary.

Case 1: Query from the learner

When the robot teaches step 2, the human learner asks if a coplanar relation is necessary. The robot replies it is necessary and the learner correctly reproduces the step. Fig. 5 shows this process.

Case 2: Incomplete knowledge acquisition of the learner

When the robot teaches step 3, the human learner receives an incomplete set of knowledge, which is found in his demonstration. The robot then gives an additional advice to clarify

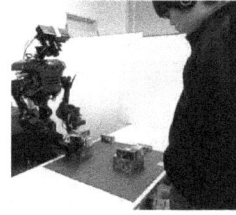

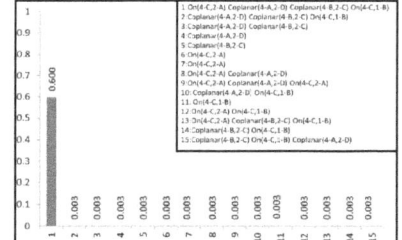

(1) Robot demonstrates step 2, which achieves four relationships as shown in Table 1. There are 15 possible consequences. Some of the bpa's are shown on the right. The correct subset is 1 and given 0.6. The set including all consequences is given 0.3 but is not shown in the graph.

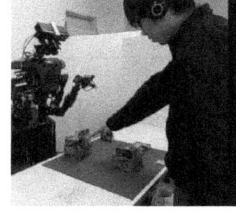

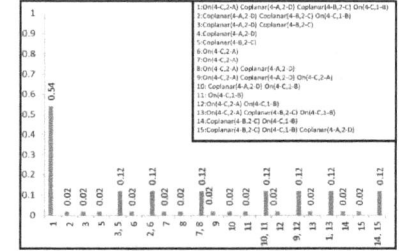

(2) Human asks if blocks 2 and 4 are aligned [i.e., relation *coplanar*(4-B, 2-C)]. From this query, the robot supposes that the human is ambiguous in this relationship, and calculates the bpa shown in red. Subsets that include consequences with and without that relationship have higher probabilities. Combining this and the bpa above, the bpa in blue is obtained. Since the belief of the correct subset, 0.54, is less than the threshold, the robot plans an interactive action of answering yes, and this makes the probability of the correct subset higher.

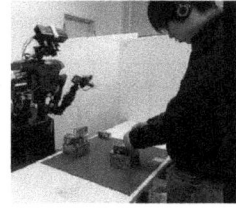

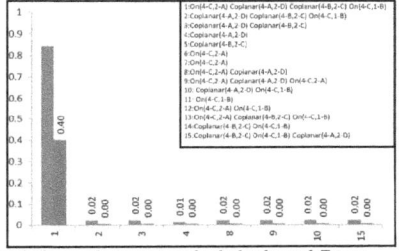

(3) After getting an answer to the query, the learner demonstrates what he has learned. From a combination of prior knowledge with knowledge gained from newly observed demonstrations (in red), the robot gets the blue bpa on the right. Since the belief of the correct subset is higher than the threshold, the robot considers that the learner obtained enough knowledge of this assembly step, and moves to the teaching of the next step.

Figure 5. Interaction example 1: query from the learner.

an ambiguous point and the learner corrects his knowledge to complete the step. Fig. 6 shows this process.

CONCLUSIONS AND DISCUSSION

We have developed a formulation for robot-to-human interactive teaching of assembly tasks. It is ambiguity-driven and based on the Dempster-Shafer theory (DST). The interaction process during teaching is viewed as the one of choosing interactive actions which reduce ambiguities in the human learner's estimated knowledge. This process is well modelled by DST. As proof of concept, we implemented and tested a robot system that can teach blocks assemblies to a human.

A key to realizing a smooth interaction is to properly determine basic probability assignments (bpa's). Currently, bpa's are set manually considering the degree of knowledge transfer for each demonstrations and instructions. As stated above, this would depend on many factors such as the learner's past experiences and the complexity of the task, and should also change as the teaching proceeds. Investigating a reasonable

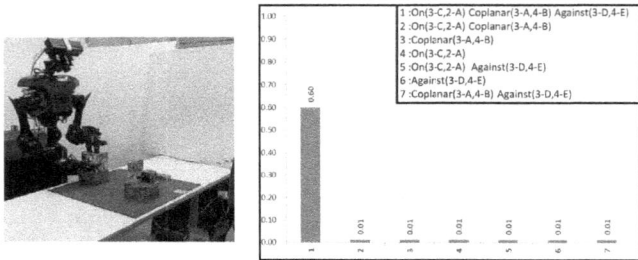

(1) Robot demonstrates step 3, which achieves three relationships as shown in Table 1. Some of the bpa's are shown on the right. The correct subset is 1 and given 0.6.

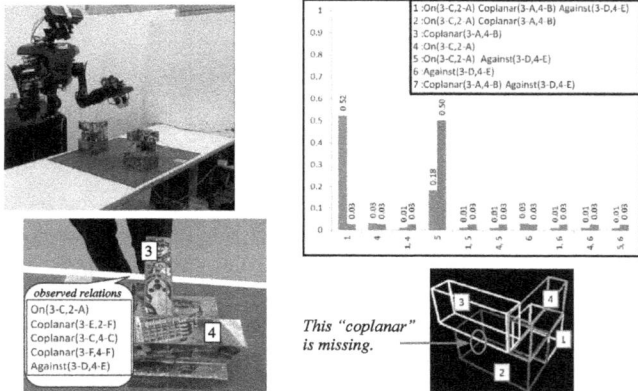

This "coplanar" is missing.

(2) The robot observed the human demonstration and found that one geometrical relation [coplanar(3-A,4-B)] is missing. Combined with the newly obtained bpa (in red), the updated bpa (in blue) is obtained.

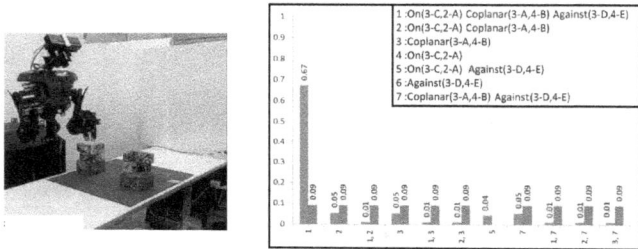

(3) Since the belief of the correct subset is less than the threshold, the robot generates and executes a pointing gesture-based additional advice. The predicted bpa is updated and, as a result, the correct subset has a sufficient probability.

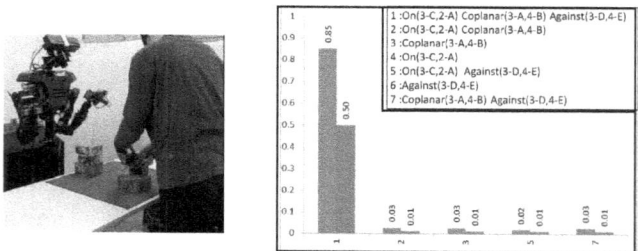

(4) After the advice, the robot asks the learner to demonstrate again. This time, he does it correctly and the belief becomes above the threshold. The robot then judges that the knowledge of this assembly step is correctly transferred.

Figure 6. Interaction example 2: incomplete knowledge transfer.

way to determine bpa's and a mechanism for learning them is a very challenging work. For this purpose, we also need to seek various cues that will appear in human behaviors and will be effective in estimating the degree of the human's understanding.

It is also necessary to enhance the robot's ability. The robot can teach what it can do. Implementing various robot skills is necessary for applying the proposed framework to more complex tasks.

Our ultimate goal is to develop a robot mediator, which gets knowledge from a human expert and gives it to a human novice. We could apply programming by demonstration (PbD) research works in the former step. As a robot leaner, it is necessary to actively asks the human instructor for uncertain/missing pieces of knowledge. An interaction planning perspective, which has been introduced in robot-to-human teaching in this paper, will also be necessary in human-to-robot teaching.

Acknowledgment

This work is supported in part by Grant-in-Aid for Scientific Research (KAKENHI) (No. 15H01616) from JSPS.

REFERENCES

1. M. Bauer. 1996. A Dempster-Shafer Approach to Modeling Agent Preferences for Plan Recognition. *User Modeling and User-Adapted Interaction* 5 (1996), 317–348.

2. A. Billard, S. Calinon, R. Dillmann, and S. Schaal. 2008. Robot Programming by Demonstration. In *Springer Handbook of Robotics*, B. Siciliano and O. Khatib (Eds.). Springer, Chapter 59, 1371–1394.

3. D. Leyzberg et al. 2012. The Physical Presence of a Robot Tutor Increases Cognitive Learning Gains. In *Proceedings of CogSci 2012*.

4. S.A. Hutchinson and A.C. Kak. 1989. Planning Sensing Strategies in a Robot Work Cell with Multi-Sensor Capabilities. *IEEE Trans. on Robotics and Automat.* 5, 6 (1989), 765–783.

5. S. Nikolaidis and J. Shah. 2013. Human-robot Cross-training: Computational Formulation, Modeling and Evaluation of a Human Team Training Strategy. In *Proceedings of the 8th ACM/IEEE Int. Conf. on Human-Robot Interaction*. 33–40.

6. G. Shafer and R. Logan. 1987. Implementing Dempster's Rule for Hierarchical Evidence. *Artificial Intelligence* 33, 3 (1987), 271–298.

7. C. Torrey, S.R. Fussell, and S. Kiesler. 2013. How a Robot Should Give Advice. In *Proceedings of the 8th ACM/IEEE Int. Conf. on Human-Robot Interaction*. 275–282.

8. Y. Zhou and M.W. Evens. 1999. A Practical Student Model in an Intelligent Tutoring System. In *Proceedings of the 11th IEEE Int. Conf. on Tools with Artificial Intelligence*. 13–18.

Impression on Human–Robot Communication Affected by Inconsistency in Expected Robot Perception

Kaito Tsukada
Dept. of Precision Mechanics, Chuo University
Tokyo, Japan
tsukada.kaito@gmail.com

Mihoko Niitsuma
Dept. of Precision Mechanics, Chuo University
Tokyo, Japan
niitsuma@mech.chuo-u.ac.jp

ABSTRACT
To develop long-term human–robot communication (HRC), robots' behavior must be properly perceived and interpreted by users. However, evaluations of processes involving a robot and a human are not conducted in natural situations in which humans can freely interact and observe a robot's behavior. In this study, an experiment involving both a mental model and an impression of a robot was proposed to evaluate the effect of human expectations on HRC.

Author Keywords
Human–robot communication; social robotics; perception of robot behavior; mental model

ACM Classification Keywords
H.1.2 [Models and principles]: User/Machine Systems; I.2.9 [Artificial Intelligence]: Robotics

INTRODUCTION
Communication robots have been briskly developed in recent years for various purposes. It is important for the robots to be attractive and reliable over a long period of time [1]. In previous studies, a behavior model termed as "Etho-engine" [2] was developed for robots to earn the trust of users. The model involved the application of an ethological concept of "attachment behavior" [3] in which a dog consequently shows trust to the owner. When users interact with a social behavioral robot, they would expect the robot to possess the ability to sense the surroundings because the behavior of the robot is determined on the basis of the situation. However, the users could feel strange because the robot obtains information concerning the surroundings such as positions of humans or its own position despite the fact that the robot does not have animal-like modalities such as visual perception through eyes or auditory perception through ears. This type of inconsistencies could cause a misunderstanding of the robot's behavior and could result in communication failure.

Hence, in order to develop communication robots with the consistency in perception, it is necessary to understand how the behavior of robots can be interpreted or how the robots

HAI '16, October 04-07, 2016, Biopolis, Singapore
ACM 978-1-4503-4508-8/16/10.
http://dx.doi.org/10.1145/2974804.2980520

can be perceived by the users when the users face robots' inconsistencies in perception. This study focuses on the concept of mental models [4] and assumes that humans spontaneously construct the mental model of a robot by glancing at its appearance or by observing its behavior. Based on this assumption, we propose a hypothesis that mental models have certain effects on the impression of the interpretation of the HRC given that humans communicate with a robot based on their mental model of the robot.

A few previous researches focused on users' mental models of robots. However, these researches were limited by the manipulation of users' expectations in usual communication scenarios [5], or a lack of discussion of the contributing factors to the construction of a "companion model" [6].

EXPERIMENT
Evaluating Method
In order to verify the proposed hypothesis, it was necessary to observe the mental models of users and their impressions of the robot during the communication with the robot. The experiments in the study involved an experimental structure as shown in Table 1. In this structure, (1) the robot was first exposed to the subjects, attachment behavior was explained, and a video of the attachment behavior of the robot was shown to help the subjects construct mental models. (2) Then, a semi-structured interview was conducted to clarify the subject's mental models. The interview contained questions such as "How are you going to take action to the robot? Then, what do you expect the robot to do?" An impression survey using the SD method was also conducted here. (3) After the uncontrolled interaction, (4) an impression survey was again conducted and this was followed by a semi-structured interview with questions such as "Could you communicate with the robot as you thought?" to elucidate user perceptions.

Hardware Design
In this study, Etho-engine [2] was implemented into a

(1) Make a subject construct mental model: Provide instruction and a video of the attachment behavior.
(2) Elicit the mental model and impression: Conduct a semi-structured interview and SD method.
(3) Let a subject interact freely (from 5 to 10 min):   A subject as an owner, and an experimenter as a stranger.
(4) Elicit the mental model and impression: Conduct a semi-structured interview and SD method.

Table 1. Experimental structure

mobile robot. The robot obtained position data by using an ultrasonic positioning system. The robot had a 2 DOF head part with a camera to show the gaze direction. The robot had the ability to detect and catch a green ball by using the camera and a gripper. The robot was also able to recognize sound direction by using an eight-channel microphone array.

Experimental Robot Conditions
It is necessary to specify the hypotheses in order to verify the same. This can be expressed as follows:

H1: If the mental model matches the perceived behavior, impression of the robot will change positively.

H2: If the mental model does not match the perceived behavior, impression of the robot will change negatively.

For each hypothesis, two conditions of the robot were examined. In both patterns, the robot performed the attachment behavior. These may be detailed as follows:

C1: A consistent robot
The robot detected a green ball using a camera and brought it to the owner. The robot also detected noise and turned towards the noise direction. These behaviors could make subjects expect that the robot had some animal-like modalities, and result in the subject possessing an consistent image of the robot.

C2: An inconsistent robot
Depsite the presence of a green ball or noise, the robot did not detect and react to the same. Nevertheless, the robot definitely showed preferences for the owner as the attattchment behavior. These behaviors could result in the subjects possessing an inconsistent image of the robot. In this condition, the gripper was used to repeat the opening and closing action when the robot went to the owner.

RESULTS
In the experiment, 20 subjects (13 males and 7 females in their 20s) were randomly divided into 2 groups, namely C1 and C2. Each group had 10 subjects

Interpretation of the interaction
In the semi-structured interview, all subjects reffered to the robot's abilities with respect to the ball such as "the robot will detect it" or "bring it". After the interaction, all the subjects in C1 realized that the robot could at least catch the ball. However, three subjects in C1 stated that the catching motion was awkward. Conversely, all the subjects in C2

realized that the robot could not play with the ball and that the gripper simply repeated opening and closing motions. Nevertheless, two subjects from C2 positively regarded this motion as an emotional expression. This indicated that C1 provided congruency between the perceived behavior and subjects' mental model. In contrast, C2 resulted in a gap between the perceived behavior and subjects' mental model.

Effects to the Impression
Figure 1 shows impression change through the interactions obtained by using the SD method. For the adjectives *quick*, *active*, *intelligent*, *animal-like*, and *expected*, the impression changes in C1 were higher when compared with those in C2. Given that these impressions were related to the ability and the behavioral characteristics of the robot, the congruence between the mental model and perceived behavior contributed to fundamental/long-term HRC in a positive manner. However, the adjectives *altruistic* and *favorable* corresponded to higher impression changes in C2 when compared with those in C1. These impressions were superficial because they were potentially affected by the movement of the gripper. Thus, H1 and H2 were verified from the viewpoint of long-term HRC.

CONCLUSION
In this study, experiments were performed to evaluate mental models of humans and their impressions of the robot. The findings of the study revealed the positive effect of a consistency, i.e., the congruence between the mental model and perceived behavior, which contributed to fundamental and long-term human–robot communication.

ACKNOWLEDGMENTS
This work was supported by JSPS Grant-in-Aid for Scientific Research (C) 15K01478.

REFERENCES
1. T. Hirano, et al. 2003. Toward communication robots working in our daily life. *Information Processing Society of Japan*: 49-56.

2. M. Niitsuma, et al. 2012. Design of social behavior of physical agent in intelligent space. In *38th Annual Conf. on IEEE Industrial Electronics Society*: 5523-5528. http://dx.doi.org/10.1109/IECON.2012.6389512

3. Á. Miklósi, 2007. *Dog Behavior, Evolution, and Cognition*. Oxford University Press.

4. D. A. Norman. 1988. *The psychology of everyday things*. Basic books.

5. S. Paepcke, et al. 2010. Judging a bot by its cover: an experiment on expectation setting for personal robots. In *2010 5th ACM/IEEE Int. Conf. on Human–Robot Interaction (HRI)*: 45-52. http://dx.doi.org/10.1109/HRI.2010.5453268

6. N. Matsumoto, et al. 2007. A Companion Model for Symbiotic Artifacts - A Conversation Log Analysis of a 16-Day Life Experiment with a Home Robot -. In *23rd Fuzzy System Symposium*: 184-184. http://doi.org/10.14864/fss.23.0.184.0

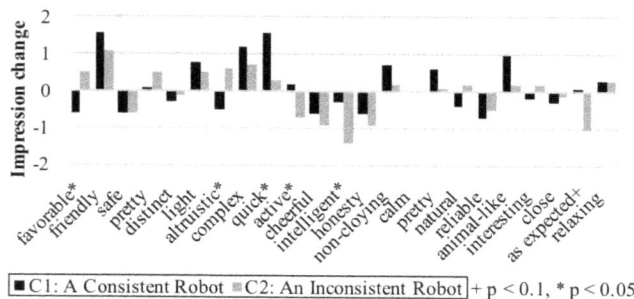

■ C1: A Consistent Robot ■ C2: An Inconsistent Robot + p < 0.1, * p < 0.05

Figure 1. Impression change concerning the robot

Haptic Workspace Control of the Humanoid Robot Arms

Longjiang Zhou, Albertus Hendrawan Adiwahono, Yuanwei Chua, Wei Liang Chan

Robotics Department, Institute for Infocomm Research, A*STAR

Singapore

{zhoul, adiwahonoah, ychua, chanwl}@i2r.a-star.edu.sg

ABSTRACT

This paper presents a haptic workspace control approach to the arms of a humanoid robot by using the Omega 7 haptic device as the control input device. The haptic device with small workspace is used to control the robot with 2 arm end-effectors of large workspace. This paper also puts forward an approach for users to feel the haptic feedback force when the robot end-effectors touch the virtual boundary areas for the safety consideration. The haptic device can move further but the robot arm end-effector will stop and the haptic force generated is proportional to the travel distance of the haptic device end-effectors until reaching the maximum value of force permitted by the designer. Simulation experiments are designed and implemented to test the motion performance of the arm end-effectors under control of haptic device and the generated haptic force when the virtual boundary walls are reached by the arm end-effectors.

Author Keywords

Robot arm; end-effector; haptic device; boundary.

ACM Classification Keywords

D.1.1. Programming Techniques: Applicative (Functional) Programming.

INTRODUCTION

The Haptic Feedback Technology started in the early 1970s [10], which is a tactile feedback using a sense of touch by rendering forces or vibrations to the users. It enhanced the precision and the effect of tele-presence by rendering the force and surface geometrical information of the interacted objects to the users through haptic devices. Since the sense of touch cannot be replaced by other senses such as vision and hearing [13], Haptic Feedback Technology has wide applications in surgical operation [15], medical training with virtual reality [5] [11], nanotechnology [14], video games [18], pilot training [9], planet and underwater exploration [2] [3], and so on. Haptic devices are popular

HAI '16, October 04-07, 2016, Biopolis, Singapore

ACM 978-1-4503-4508-8/16/10.

http://dx.doi.org/10.1145/2974804.2980505

nowadays because they can not only trace users' operation trajectories like common computer input devices such as mouse, but also provide the realistic feelings of touch, making users feel immersive into the virtual environment. Haptic devices have 2 types of mechanisms. One type is serial manipulator, the typical of which is Phantom Haptic Device [8] [16]. The serial haptic manipulator has a large workspace, but its stiffness is relatively low. The parallel haptic manipulators can make up such weak points. Of these mechanisms the Delta with one redundant actuator was designed by Joon-Woo Kim et al [7], and another 3 DOFs parallel hand controller was developed by Bernard et al [1]. Omega 7 is an advanced 7-DOF haptic devices for desktop applications with a compact design [4]. The parallel mechanism increases its stiffness and robustness dramatically. However, the parallel structure makes the workspace much smaller. One possible solution is to incorporate a scaling factor into the motion loop so that smaller movement of the haptic device enables a larger movement of the robot [12], but it will enlarge the accumulative operation error. Another issue is how to define the restricted area of the robot end-effector so as to protect the operation safety and ensure the control stability of the robot in the haptic tele-operation, especially in the unstructured and hazardous environment. The concept of virtual wall [6] [17] may solve this issue effectively.

This paper addresses the issues of using the Omega 7 haptic device with small workspace to control the end-effectors of robot arms with larger workspace. We will also discuss about the calculation of constrained areas of robot end-effector workspace for the safety consideration.

SYSTEM ARCHITECTURE

The architecture of the humanoid robot under study is shown in Figure 1. The torso and upper body are built on a mobile track with flippers which enable the robot to climb on the stairs and move on uneven terrains. The upper limbs can fulfil manipulation tasks such as grasping, picking and placing, pushing doors, pulling drawers, and so forth. The wide angle camera mounted on the mobile track can detect the environment to guide the motion task. The Kinect Camera and 2D laser mounted on the head sense the environmental information of the upper body to guide the manipulation work of the end-effectors. During manual tele-operation, the pilot of the robot will use the cameras to have a visual view of the task, and the Omega 7 is chosen to steer the arms of the robot.

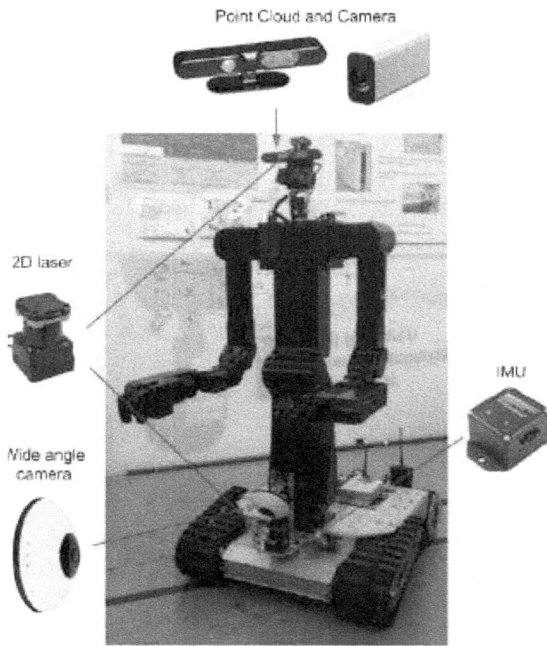

Figure 1. The physical architecture of the humanoid robot.

Figure 2 displays the layout for the haptic feedback control of the robot. For clarity, the resulting movement of the arms are displayed on a simulated robot model through a GUI. The haptic device on the right hand side is the Omega 7, which is connected to the computer to control the 6 DOF of movement of the robot arm end-effectors.

METHODOLOGIES

Method of Using Small Workspace of Haptic Device to Control Large Workspace of the Robot End-Effectors

As seen in Figure 3, the workspace of the Omega 7 is close to a hemiellipsoid with dimension of $\square$ 0.16 $\times L0.11(m)$, while the workspace of the robot arm is a sphere with diameter of $2m$. It is impossible for the Omega 7 to control the robot end-effectors in a continuous way. So we put forward a segmented control approach to allow a smaller device workspace to control a larger workspace of the robot, as seen in Figure 4. "Wr" is the coordinate system in the robot end-effector workspace and "Wo" is the coordinate system of the Omega 7. To take a straight line as an example, the robot end effector is required to move from $R0$ to R while the motion scope of the Omega 7 is only from $C0$ to C, which is far shorter. To fulfil such a motion task, we define an "Action" button in a joystick to engage the Omega 7 to drive the robot. When we toggle in the "Action" button and drive the Omega 7 from $C0$ to C, the robot is engaged and moves from $R0$ to $R1$ accordingly. The travel distances of robot and the Omega 7 are the same, i.e., $R0R1 = C0C$. Next, when we toggle out the "Action" button and move the Omega 7 back to $C0$, The robot is disengaged and does not move accordingly. When the "Action" button is toggled in again and the Omega 7 moves from $C0$ to C, the robot will be engaged again and continue

Figure 2. System structure of the haptic feedback control for the robot arms.

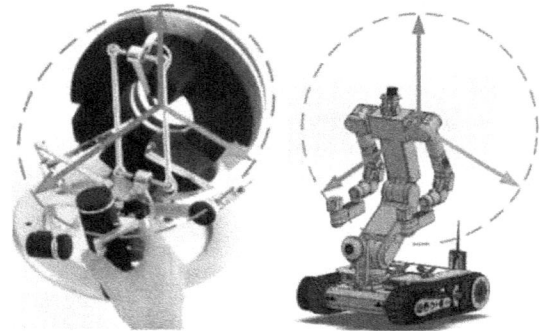

Figure 3. Workspace of Omega 7 end-effector (left) and workspace of robot arms (right).

to move from $R1$ to $R2$. In this way repeatedly, the robot arm end-effectors can move from $R0$ to R eventually.

Boundary Areas in the Workspace of the Arm End-Effectors

This is to solve the safety issue of the robot to prevent the end-effectors from colliding with its own body or the environment. There are 4 virtual boundary walls of planes to restrict the motion scope of each arm end-effector. The space within the 4 planes is free space and the space beyond the planes is forbidden space. As shown in Figure 5, $\sum X$ restricts the motion of end-effector when it moves backward, and $\sum Z$ restricts the downward motion of the end-effector. $\sum Yi$ and $\sum Yo$ prevent the end-effector from going too near to the body or too far away from the body respectively. When the robot end-effector touches the borders and the Omega 7 goes further, the end-effector will not go with the Omega 7 and the human user's hand will feel a repulsive haptic force which is proportional to the travel distance of the Omega 7 and the stiffness of the virtual wall defined by designers. There are no restrictions for end-effectors in the upward and forward directions.

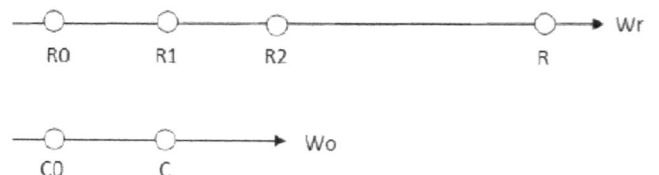

Figure 4. Segmented motion control method of Omega 7 to the robot end-effector.

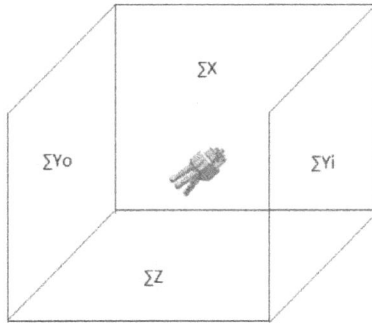

Figure 5. Boundary walls of the end effector workspace of the robot right arm.

SIMULATION RESULTS

Experiments was implemented to test the performance of the Omega 7 to control the motion of the robot arm end-effectors, and the haptic force generated when robot arm end-effectors reach the boundary walls. The value of the haptic force is proportion to the travel distance of the haptic device after the arm end-effectors reach the boundary walls.

Three control modes are tested in the simulations of this paper. In "Right" mode, Omega 7 only controls the movement of the right arm end-effector; In "Left" mode, the Omega 7 only control the movement of the left arm; In "Both" mode, the Omega 7 can control the movements of both arms concurrently following the same kinematics trail. We only give the experiment results of "Right" and "Both" modes. The simulation results of the "Left" mode are the same as those of the "Right" mode. Figure 6 shows the "Ready" pose of the robot. Figure 6(a) is the front view image and Figure 6(b) is the side view image.

Figure 7 shows the backward movements of the arms under the control of Omega 7. Figure 7(a) works in the "Right" mode and Figure 7(b) works in the "Both" mode. The arms will stop when they reach the virtual boundary wall at the back of the robot. Later on, the Omega 7 can make further movement, but it is encountered with a haptic force to resist such movement of which the value is proportion to its travel distance until the maximum force is reached.

Figure 8 shows the downward movements of the robot arms under the control of Omega 7. Figure 8(a) works in the "Right" mode, and Figure 8(b) works in the "Both" mode.

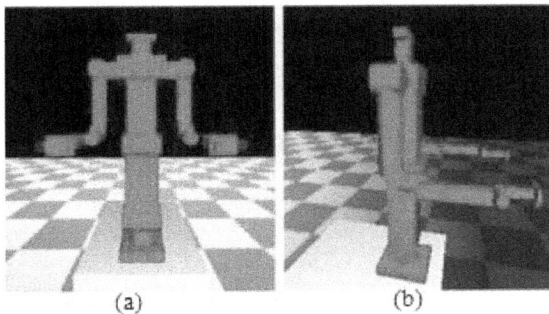

Figure 6. "Ready" pose of the robot.

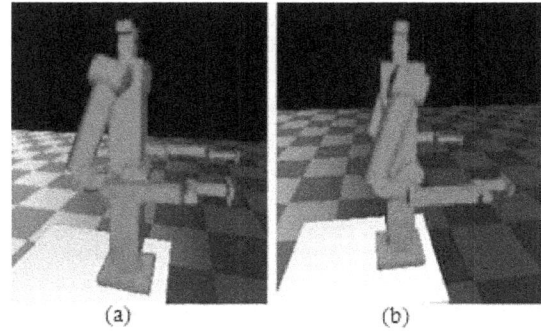
(a)   (b)

Figure 7. Backward movements of the robot arms.

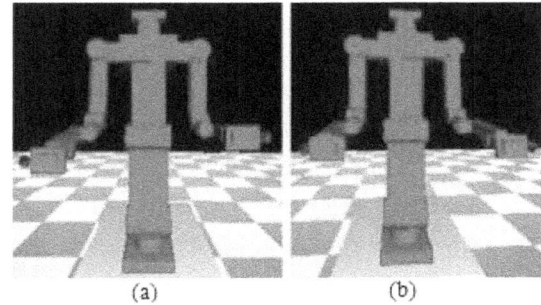
(a)   (b)

Figure 8. Downward movements of the robot arms.

Figure 9 shows the movement of the right arm in the "Right" control mode. Figure 9(a) shows the right arm end-effector reaches its boundary wall away from the body. Figure 9(b) shows the right arm end-effector reaches its boundary wall when it is approaching to its body.

The experiment results for both arm movements are shown in Figure 10. In Figure 10(a), the right arm moves outward and left arm moves inward at the same time under the same control command of the Omega 7. The left arm reaches its inward boundary earlier, for its travel distance from the "Ready" pose to the boundary wall is shorter than that of the right arm. The right arm will continue to move until it reaches its outward boundary wall. After that, the user starts to feel the haptic force which is proportional to the travel distance of the Omega 7. In Figure 10(b), the left arm moves outward and the right arm moves inward. The haptic force generation procedure is the same as those in Figure 10(a).

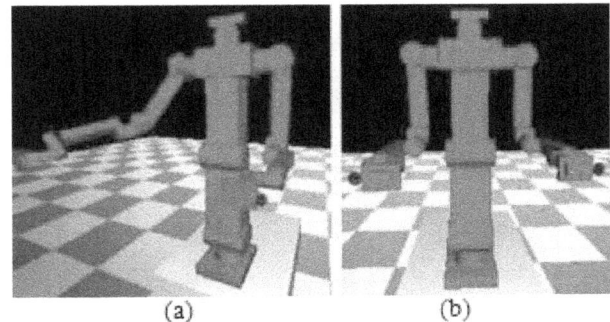
(a)   (b)

Figure 9. Movement of the robot right arm in Y direction in the "Right" mode.

CONCLUSION

This paper put forward a motion control method for the arm end-effectors of a robot using the Omega 7 haptic device. The method uses the haptic device with a small workspace to control the robot arm end-effectors with large workspace. This paper also presented virtual boundary walls for the end-effectors for the consideration of safety issue of motion and manipulation. Simulation experiment results showed that the two robot arms can move individually or concurrently according to different control modes. When the robot arms reach the boundary walls, the user can feel a repulsive haptic force proportional to the travel distance of the end-effector of the haptic device.

ACKNOWLEDGMENTS

The robot torso, arms, and simulation GUI used in this paper are developed by Jungho Lee et al. from RAINBOW and Korea Advanced Institute of Science (KAIST). The authors would also like to especially thank Okkee Sim and Inhyeok Kim from RAINBOW for the technical support on the work presented in this paper.

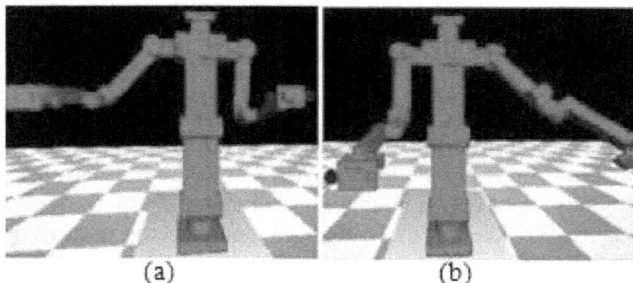

Figure 10. Movements of both arms in the Y direction.

REFERENCES

1. Bernard D. Adelstein, Peter Ho, and Homayoon Kazerooni. 1996. Kinematic design of a three degree of freedom parallel hand controller mechanism. In *Proceedings of the ASME Dynamic Systems and Control Division*, 539-546.

2. Robert O. Ambrose, Robert T. Savely, S. Michael Goza, Philip Strawser, Myron A. Diftler, Ivan Spain, and Nicolaus Radford. 2004. Mobile Manipulation using NASA's Robonaut. In *Proceedings of the IEEE International Conference on Robotics and Automation* (ICRA'04), 2104 - 2109.

3. James E. DeVault. 2000. Robotic system for underwater inspection of bridge Piers. *IEEE Instrumentation and Measurement Magazine* 3, 3: 32 - 37.

4. Force Dimension. 2013. Omega-7 overview. Retrieved 2013 from http://www.forcedimension.com/products/omega-7/overview

5. David C. Hon. 1998. Selectable instruments with homing devices for haptic virtual reality medical simulation. U. S. Patent 6,113,395, Filed August 18, 1998, issued September 5, 2000.

6. Thomas Hulin, Carsten Preusche, and Gerd Hirzinger. 2006. Stability Boundary and Design Criteria for Haptic Rendering of Virtual Walls. In *Proceedings of 8th International IFAC Symposium on Robot Control* (SYROCO'06), 322-327.

7. Joon W. Kim, Duk H. Park, Han S. Kim, and Sung H. Han. 2007. Design of a Novel 3-DOF Parallel-type Haptic Device with Redundant Actuation. In *Proceedings of International conference on Control, Automation and Systems* (ICCAS'07), 2270-2273.

8. Thomas H. Massie and J. Kenneth Salisbury. 1994. The PHANTOM Haptic Interface: A Device for Probing Virtual Objects. In *Proceedings of the ASME Dynamic Systems and Control Division*, 295-301.

9. Ricardo G. Menendez and James E. Bernard. 2001. Flight simulation in synthetic Environments. *IEEE Aerospace and Electronic Systems Magazine* 16, 9: 19 - 23.

10. Michael A. Noll. 1972. Man-Machine Tactile Communication. *The Official Journal of the Society for Information Display* 1, 2: 5-11.

11. Shahram Payandeh and Temei Li. 2003. Toward new designs of haptic devices for minimally invasive surgery. In *Proceedings of the 17th International Congress and Exhibition Series Computer Assisted Radiology and Surgery* (CARS'03), 775-781.

12. Doina Pisla, Bogdan Gherman, Nicolae Plitea, Bela Gyurka, Calin Vaida, Liviu Vlad, Florin Graur, C. Radu, Marius Suciu, Andras Szilaghi, and Alin Stoica. 2011. PARASURG hybrid parallel robot for minimally invasive surgery. *Chirurgia* 106, 5: 619-625.

13. Gabriel Robles-De-La-Torre. 2006. The Importance of the Sense of Touch in Virtual and Real Environments. *IEEE Multimedia* 13, 3: 24-30.

14. Francisco J. Rubio-Sierra, Robert W. Stark, Stefan Thalhammer, and Wolfgang M. Heckl. 2003. Force feedback joystick as a low-cost haptic interface for an atomic-force microscopy nanomanipulator. *Applied Physics A: Materials Science and Processing* 76, 6: 903-906.

15. Hong G. Sim, Sidney K. H. Yip, and Christopher W. S. Cheng. 2006. Equipment and technology in surgical robotics. *World Journal of Urology* 24, 2: 128-135.

16. Sensable Technologies. 2012. PHANTOM Omni. Retrieved 2012 from http://www.sensable.com/

17. Pornchai Weangsima, Kinya Fujita, and Tsunenori Honda. 2004. A Study of Haptic Representation of Virtual Plain Wall. In *Proceedings of IEEE International Conference on Robotics and Biomimetics* (ROBIO'04), 323 – 327.

18. Mark J. P. Wolf. 2008. *The video game explosion: a history from PONG to PlayStation and beyond.* Greenwood Press.

Attention Estimation for Child-Robot Interaction

Muhammad Attamimi
Tamagawa University Brain
Science Institute
6-1-1 Tamagawagakuen,
Machida, Tokyo, Japan
muhammadattamimi2012
@gmail.com

Masahiro Miyata
Graduate School of
Engineering, Tamagawa
University
6-1-1 Tamagawagakuen,
Machida, Tokyo, Japan
mytma4re@engs.tamagawa.ac.jp

Tetsuji Yamada
Tamagawa University Brain
Science Institute
6-1-1 Tamagawagakuen,
Machida, Tokyo, Japan
tetsuzi@lab.tamagawa.ac.jp

Takashi Omori
Graduate School of
Engineering, Tamagawa
University
6-1-1 Tamagawagakuen,
Machida, Tokyo, Japan
omori@lab.tamagawa.ac.jp

Ryoma Hida
Graduate School of
Engineering, Tamagawa
University
6-1-1 Tamagawagakuen,
Machida, Tokyo, Japan
hidar2is@engs.tamagawa.ac.jp

ABSTRACT
In this paper, we present a method of estimating a child's attention, one of the more important human mental states, in a free-play scenario of child-robot interaction. First, we developed a system that could sense a child's verbal and non-verbal multimodal signals such as gaze, facial expression, proximity, and so on. Then, the observed information was used to train a Support Vector Machine (SVM) to estimate a human's attention level. We investigated the accuracy of the proposed method by comparing with a human judge's estimation, and obtained some promising results which we discuss here.

ACM Classification Keywords
H.1.2. [**Models and Principles**]: User/Machine Systems–*Human factors*; I.2.9. [**Artificial Intelligence**]: Robotics–*Commercial robots and applications*

Author Keywords
Child-robot interaction; multimodal information; attention estimation.

INTRODUCTION
One of the biggest challenges in child-robot interaction (CRI) is the development of a robot that can understand a child and interact naturally. Several related studies have been done [9, 1, 3, 7]. Methods of controlling robots able to act as friends or playmates have been discussed in [9, 1]. And although the results were encouraging, the scenarios were overly controlled. In [3, 7], studies were conducted on the interaction between robots and children in more natural settings, or "in the wild," as it is said. Although these efforts were ground-breaking and related to our research, their action decision analysis was based on direct physical observation and not on the mental state, thus limiting its application to the specific tasks of the experimental design.

Therefore, in our study, we focused on attention estimation of children playing freely with a robot as a simple but typical example of mental state-based interaction. To this end, we first developed a system including sensor networks and a remotely operated robot to enable free-interaction with the children. Over 23 3–6 year-old children participated in our interaction experiment and a total of 60 minutes interaction was recorded. In a pilot study, we investigated one of the subjects which interacted for five to six minutes with the robot. We processed the data and extracted the features of proximity, eye gaze, emotion in facial expression, and behaviors, as well as a set of attention values labelled by human judges. We then utilized a Support Vector Machine (SVM) to estimate the attention level. We determined the accuracy of the proposed method by comparing with the expert judgments, and some promising results were obtained which we report here.

PROPOSED METHOD
The proposed child-robot interaction (CRI) framework consists of: (1) a sensor networks consists of Kinect sensor and a stereo microphone, (2) a robot platform: "Softbank Robotics' Pepper" that is teleoperated, and (3) attention estimation models. First, we collected a multimodal dataset which consisted of color and depth information and audio information. We also annotated the data according to the expert's judgments.

HAI '16 October 04-07, 2016, Biopolis, Singapore

© 2016 Copyright held by the owner/author(s).

ACM ISBN 978-1-4503-4508-8/16/10.

DOI: http://dx.doi.org/10.1145/2974804.2980510

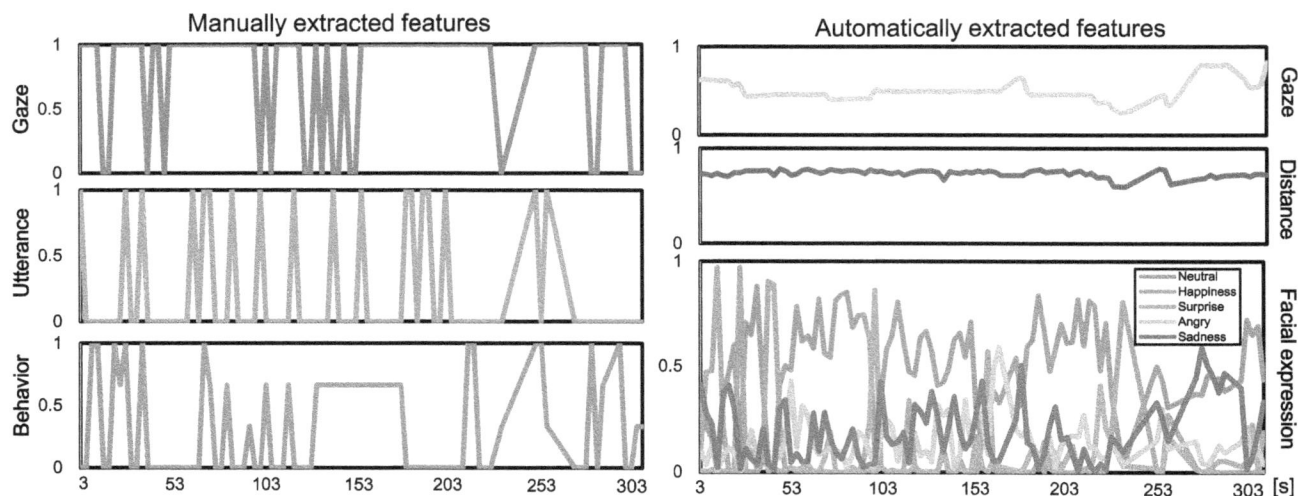

Figure 1. Features used in this study.

The captured multimodal data was processed to extract features for input of the attention estimation model. To model attention, we considered gaze, utterance, behavior, proximity, and emotion of the child interacting with the robot as well as the input data. In a preliminary effort, we considered a simple Support Vector Machine (SVM) to categorize the child's attention based on the observed data. In this study, a publicly available library LIBSVM [2] was used because it provides a probabilistic estimation which is fast and easy to implement. Each of the features described below is normalized to one for a better depiction of multimodal data input.

Manually extracted features
One of the purposes of this study was to realize natural CRI as human beings do. It is straightforward to study and compare the features that come from the human to ones that are calculated by machines. Thus, we extracted the gaze, utterance, and other behaviors by asking the judges what their considerations were when judging the scenes. The gaze was set to zero when the child was considered not to be looking at the robot, and otherwise, it was set to one. For utterances, when the child was talking to the robot, it was set to one, and otherwise, to zero. We also asked the judges to rate the behavior of the child towards the robot on a 0–3 scale based on interest. It should be noted that features were extracted on a second-by-second basis.

Automatically extracted features
Given the set of calibrated color and depth information, we performed a 3D segmentation using the publicly available library PCL [8] to separate human and robot signals. The idea of the 3D segmentation is (1), to detect the plane and isolate point clouds which belong to the plane, and (2), to cluster the remaining points. After extracting the plane, we use connected-component labeling [4] to reduce the noise caused by the Kinect sensors. We then calculated the position of detected objects by considering the center of gravity of the cluster, and the Euclidean distance between the robot and the human could then easily be calculated.

For face detection, we applied image processing provided by [10, 5, 6]. Thanks to [5, 6], the parts of the face including the eyes and mouth could be detected as well as estimates of facial expression including neutrality, happiness, surprise, anger, and sadness could be taken. Given the position of the eyes and mouth, we were able to draw a triangle in color space. Corresponding points were then calculated in the depth space. We then calculated the normal vector of the triangle plane. The robot's head position could also easily be obtained. Here, gaze was defined as the inner product of the robot's normal vector and child's normal vector. The greater this value, the greater the tendency the robot and the child were looking at each other.

EXPERIMENTS
We implemented the CRI framework and conducted experiments. The objectives of these experiments were as follows. First, we wanted to investigate the features used by the experts and compare these with the automatically extracted ones. Second, we wanted to test the attention estimation model given the proposed features. The experiments were conducted at a kindergarten and 23 children (13 boys and 10 girls, aged three to six years) participated.

Experimental setup
A control room and free-play room were used as experimental environments. Considering that the problem-setting in this study was free-play, no explicit instructions were given to the children. They were just told that there was a robot in the free-play room. An expert, who is a kindergarten teacher operated the robot. Our teleoperation system facilitated the manipulation of the robot. It should be noted that children were not told that the robot was remotely operated.

All the subjects participated in an interaction experiment and a total of 60 minutes interaction was recorded. In preliminary

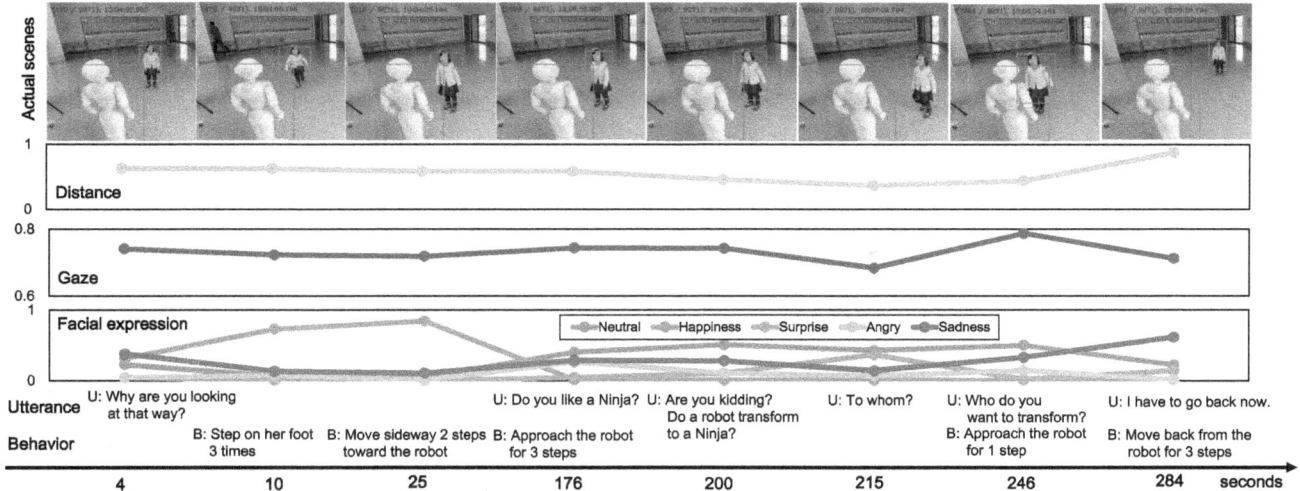

Figure 2. Examples of interaction scenes with corresponded features.

Method	Features extracted manually			Features extracted automatically			Classification results	
	Gaze	Utterance	Behavior	Distance	Gaze	Facial expressions	2-classes	3-classes
1	◯						80.34	54.65
2		◯					66.67	47.29
3			◯				76.92	52.71
4	◯	◯					80.34	58.53
5	◯		◯				79.49	58.14
6		◯	◯				77.78	57.36
7	◯	◯	◯				**82.05**	**58.91**
8				◯			75.21	54.26
9					◯		64.96	53.86
10						◯	76.92	62.40
11				◯	◯		70.94	57.75
12				◯		◯	76.92	**63.57**
13					◯	◯	77.78	62.40
14				◯	◯	◯	**78.63**	**63.57**

Table 1. Features used (marked as ◯) for attention estimation and their corresponding classification rates. The highest classification rates of each method with manually or automatically extracted features are written respectively in bold.

work, we investigated one of the subjects which had interacted for five to six minutes with the robot. To evaluate the proposed method, we asked six experts to view the video of the target subject and make judgments every second, resulting in 303 seconds of annotated videos. It should be noted that the labels most selected by the experts were used. We also asked our judges what they took into consideration to determine those labels. Based on these responses, the experts were later asked to score the gaze, utterance, and behavior for each second of a video.

Feature extraction and comparison

The collected multimodal data, consisting of visual (color and depth) information and audio information was processed. Figure 1 shows the features that were extracted manually (left) and automatically (right), respectively. From the figure we can see the feature variations over time. Examples of interaction scenes are shown in Figure 2. It can be seen that at

first, the child was eager to interact with the robot. This fact was also supported by high gaze and utterance values. The subject wanted to talk with the robot so she stomped her foot to draw the robot's attention. When the robot responded to the subject, she approached the robot and began a dialogue. The system was also able to estimate the facial expression of "happiness" at that time. After a while, the subject became bored and showed signs of wanting to retreat. We can see that the distance increased and the gaze value diminished.

Evaluation of attention estimation

To validate the proposed method, we performed leave-one-out validation (LOOV) on the collected data. On occasions such as when the subject approached and hid behind the robot, it was impossible to process the data due to occlusion and thus could not be segmented automatically. Excluding these data, LOOV was done on 258 data sets. Here, one data set consisted of manually extracted features (gaze: one-dimensional

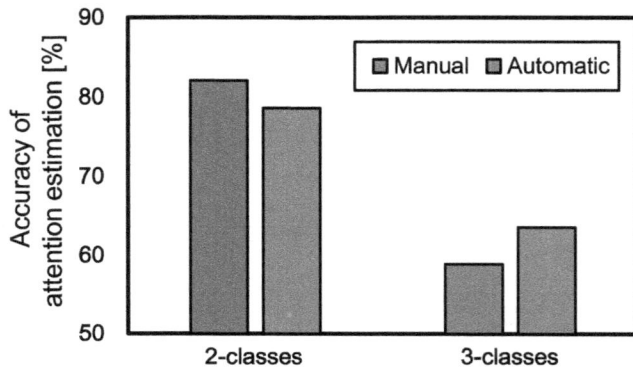

Figure 3. Accuracy rates of attention estimation. "Manual," and "Automatic" indicate the results that were used to either manually extracted or automatically extracted features, respectively.

feature vector, utterance: one-dimensional feature vector, behavior: one-dimensional feature vector) and automatically extracted features (gaze: one-dimensional feature vector, proximity: one-dimensional feature vector, facial expressions: five-dimensional feature vector). Here, we tested our proposed method using two- and three-classes of SVM. In this study, two-classes indicate that the subject was "uninterested" or "interested" in the robot; whereas three-classes indicate that the subject was "uninterested" or "less interested" or "interested" in the robot. We have tested several combinations of features as listed in Table 1. We can see that both manually- and automatically-extracted features reached their highest rates when all the features were included as input except when method 12 was used due its poor extraction of gaze. Figure 3 shows the best results of manual and automatic features for each class. The results proved interesting because in three-classes of attention estimation, the features calculated automatically by machine outperformed those of the experts.

CONCLUSION

We have proposed a method of estimating children's attention, an important human mental state. In this study, a free-play scenario of child-robot interaction was considered. To estimate attention level, we first proposed a framework for child-robot interaction based on local and global sensing using robots and sensor networks. We developed the system ourselves and implemented a teleoperation system for the robot. We have also investigated several features that were manually and automatically extracted and compared their effectiveness. We found that the combination of all features worked better than those based on subsets.

Although the proposed automatically-extracted features performed well for higher level classification, additional work is required to understand which features and conditions are most predictive of successful human-robot interaction. Our goal, therefore is to develop better models that can more fully exploit the multiple modalities of the captured data.

REFERENCES

1. Muhammad Attamimi, Kasumi Abe, Akiko Iwasaki, Takayuki Nagai, Takayuki Shimotomai, and Takashi Omori. 2013. Robots That Can Play with Children: What Makes a Robot Be a Friend. *Neural Information Processing, Lecture Notes in Computer Science* 8226, 377–386. DOI: 10.1007/978-3-642-42054-2_47

2. Chih-Chung Chang and Chih-Jen Lin. 2011. LIBSVM : a library for support vector machines. *Journal ACM Transactions on Intelligent Systems and Technology (TIST)* 2, 27(2011), 1–27. DOI: 10.1145/1961189.1961199

3. Joachim de Greeff, Olivier Blanson Henkemans, Aafke Fraaije, Lara Solms, Noel Wigdor, Bert Bierman, Joris B. Janssen, Rosemarijn Looije, Paul Baxter, Mark A. Neerincx, and Tony Belpaeme. 2014. Child-robot interaction in the wild: field testing activities of the ALIZ-E project. In *Proceedings of the 2014 ACM/IEEE international conference on Human-robot interaction.* ACM New York, NY, USA, 148–149. DOI: 10.1145/2559636.2559804

4. Lifeng He, Yuyan Chao, and Kenji Suzuki 2008. A Run-Based Two-Scan Labeling Algorithm. *IEEE Transactions on Image Processing* 17, 5 (2008), 749–756. DOI: 10.1109/TIP.2008.919369

5. K. Kinoshita, Y. Konishi, S. Lao, and M. Kawade. 2008. Facial Feature Extraction and Head Pose Estimation Using Fast 3D Model Fitting. In *Proceedings of MIRU 2008.* 1325–1329 (in Japanese).

6. Y. Konishi, K. Kinoshita, S. Lao, and M. Kawade. 2008 Real-Time Estimation of Smile Intensities. In *Proceedings of Interaction 2008* 2008, 4 (2008), 47–48 (in Japanese).

7. Raquel Ros, Marco Nalin, Rachel Wood, Paul Baxter, Rosemarijn Looije, Yannis Demiris, Tony Belpaeme, Alessio Giusti, and Clara Pozzi. 2011. Child-robot interaction in the wild: advice to the aspiring experimenter. In *Proceedings of the 13th international conference on multimodal interfaces*, 335–342. DOI: 10.1145/2070481.2070545

8. Radu Bogdan Rusu and Steve Cousins. 2011. 3D is here: Point Cloud Library (PCL). In *Proceedings of IEEE International Conference on Robotics and Automation*, 1–4. DOI: 10.1109/ICRA.2011.5980567

9. Suleman Shahid, Emiel Krahmer, and Marc Swerts. 2011. Child-robot interaction: playing alone or together? In *Proceedings of CHI EA '11: CHI '11 Extended Abstracts on Human Factors in Computing Systems.* ACM New York, NY, USA, 1399–1404. DOI: 10.1145/1979742.1979781

10. T. Yamashita. 2013. Human Sensing Technology OKAO Vision. *IHS Interaction Technology Summit.*

Designing MUSE - a Multimodal User Experience for a Shopping Mall Kiosk

Andreea I. Niculescu
Institute for Infocomm Research
Singapore
andreea-n@i2r.a-star.edu.sg

Kheng Hui Yeo
Institute for Infocomm Research
Singapore
yeokh@i2r.a-star.edu.sg

Rafael E. Banchs
Institute for Infocomm Research
Singapore
rembanchs@i2r.a-star.edu.sg

ABSTRACT
Multimodal interactions provide more engaging experiences allowing users to perform complex tasks while searching for information. In this paper, we present a multimodal interactive kiosk for displaying information in shopping malls. The kiosk uses visual information and natural language to communicate with visitors. Users can connect to the kiosk using their own mobile phone as speech or type input device. The connection is established by scanning a QR code displayed on the kiosk screen. Field work, observations, design, system architecture and implementation are reported.

Author Keywords
Multimodal interaction; speech & natural language; interaction design; user interface; public info display;

ACM Classification Keywords
H.5.m. Information interfaces and presentation (e.g., HCI): Miscellaneous;

INTRODUCTION
Information kiosks are prevalent in office buildings, malls, airports, museums etc. offering a broad range of information, assistance and services. A common characteristic of these kiosks is their relatively rigid interaction style combining a graphical interface with touch input. As a result, the number of tasks users can perform is relatively limited [1]. Due to the popularity of kiosks as means for public information display, there is growing interest in improving their interaction flexibility to allow for more complex tasks.

Several studies have reported design prototypes combining different types of input/output modalities, such as speech & touch [9], [3], [8], [6], speech & gesture (using computer vision) [10], [2], [7] speech & touch & handwriting [5], gestures (sign language) & lip reading [12] etc.

HAI '16, October 04-07, 2016, Biopolis, Singapore
ACM 978-1-4503-4508-8/16/10.
http://dx.doi.org/10.1145/2974804.2980521

In this paper, we present Muse - a **M**ultimodal **US**er **E**xperience design for a kiosk meant to display information in a shopping mall. The kiosk enables visitors to use speech and touch. The novelty of our approach lies in the way users interact with the kiosk; upon scanning a QR code, users can connect with the screen and deploy their own mobile phone as an input device for speech or typing. In the literature, we found studies reporting about mobile phones connecting to kiosks [1]; however, the connection was used to access and share information rather than to input a request.

The paper presents observations gathered during a field study in shopping malls, interaction design cycles for the kiosk, system architecture & implementation and ends with conclusion and future work.

FIELD STUDY
We conducted a one day field study across several shopping malls in Singapore to find out how people use info kiosks. We took notes, pictures, videos and watched more than 50 people interacting with mall info kiosks. This data collection enabled us to make the following observations:

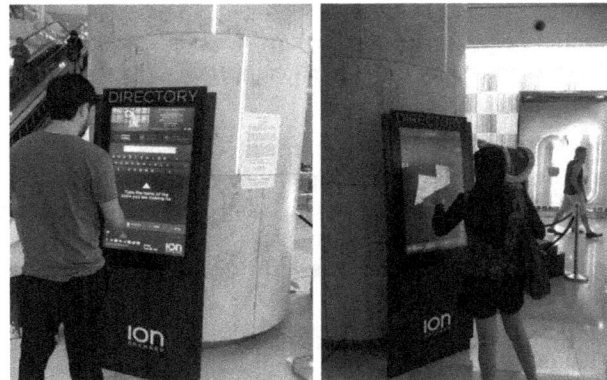

Fig. 1a (left) User performing keyword search after several failed attempts to find shops selling a particular shoe brand /

Fig. 1b (right) Visitors having trouble to understand the shop location on the map

- Specific information, i.e. information that is not directly related with a shop, such as a particular product brand, Wi-Fi configuration, car park fees etc. is not easy to find. Most people spent several minutes without finding what they were looking for, finally resorting to use keyword search (see fig.1a)

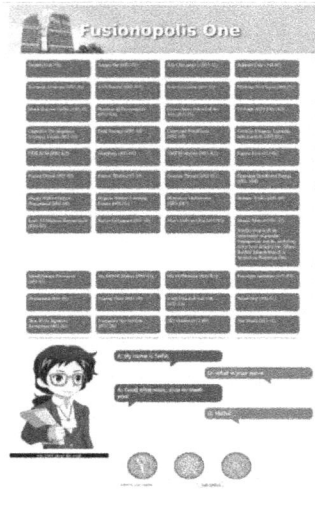

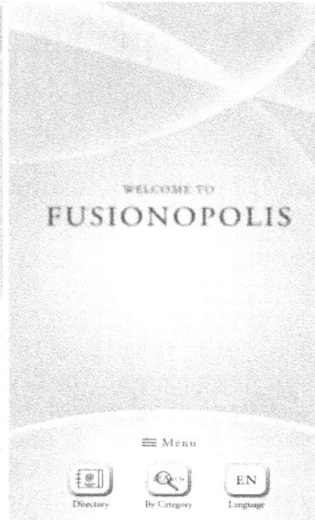

Fig. 2 First UI   **Fig. 3 Second UI/ menu**   **Fig. 4 Alphabetic search**   **Fig. 5 Search by category**

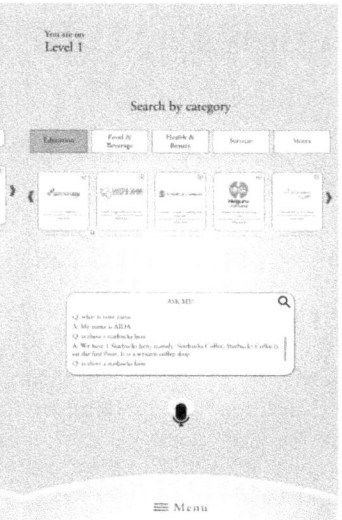

- During peak-hours people usually have to queue for several minutes to use the kiosk.

- One of the recurrent problems people seemed to encounter was to understand shop locations on the map (see 1. 1b).

- Also, we noticed people taking picture of the map to remember the location.

On average, it takes 3.5 min to find information using the kiosk; however, it takes about 25 sec to get the same information from a human receptionist at info counter.

KIOSK MULTIMODAL INTERACTION
The information gathered during our field study allowed us to get a better understanding of shoppers' needs. It also helped us to design a more efficient interactive experience as follows:

- Since certain type of information seems difficult for visitors to find, we implemented our screen as a combination of graphical and natural language information exchange. In this way, users can ask questions and receive answers about topics the kiosk doesn't explicitly display.

- The queues during peak hours can be avoided by enabling users to connect simultaneously with the screen. Such multi-sessions can be established by using a third device – in this case, a mobile phone that connects users with the screen via a QR code.

- The connection allows users to download maps, promotion coupons or any other desired information that the kiosk can provide.

- Our intention is to enable a faster and more efficient exchange of information, such as between humans. The key ingredient is getting automatic access to information relating to the building. Within the framework of a 'smart city', such information will soon be easily available.

Using natural language to access this data will certainly improve the information quality and reduce the interaction time.

USER INTERFACE DESIGN
The user interface design of the kiosk was developed in several steps. An initial basic GUI was created containing a speech-enabled avatar, shop info boxes and a *whatsapp* style textbox displaying shop info (see fig 2). More details about design and implementation can be read in [11].

During our field study we had the opportunity to review several kiosk designs and come up with improvement ideas for an enhanced user experience. For our second design, we decided to remove the avatar to declutter the space; further, we changed the layout to facilitate a better information structure within a centralized menu (see fig 3). The menu enables users to view shop information displayed in a carrousel view and search for information either using an alphabetical directory or by category of tenants (see fig. 4 & 5). The kiosk language is by default English, however, in the future Chinese, Malay and Tamil (Singapore's official languages) will follow. The shop cards have links to maps and shop promotion. The natural language interaction is captured on the text area below the card carousel. The text area appears only after users connect to the kiosk. The natural language interaction brings added value in cases when for example a store is not available in a building, users can't find a particular item of interest etc. Here the system may engage in a follow-up dialogue asking the visitor details about his/her needs and trying to provide alternatives. In table 1, we illustrate a possible use case:

User: *Is there a 7/11 in this building?*
Kiosk: *No, we don't have 7/11. Why do you need 7/11?*
User: *I want to pay my bills*
Kiosk: *You can pay your bills at the AXE station at B2.*
User: *Oh great, thank you!*
Kiosk: *You are welcome!*

Tab 1 Conversation example

At the moment, this type of information is entered manually in the data base. However, once the 'smart city' infrastructure becomes available, the kiosk will be able to access the info automatically.

SYSTEM ARCHITECTURE

The kiosk is running Windows 7 Embedded Standard on a 1.99GHz quad-core Intel Celeron CPU and 4GB of RAM. The vertical touch screen measures 42" across and has WLAN connectivity. The audio output is provided via an external speaker. Users with a mobile device may connect to the kiosk, as long as the phone has a wireless internet connection, a QR scanner and a web browser. Once connected, the mobile runs a client for natural language input (see fig. 6).

is there a starbucks here	Ask me

Fig. 6 Mobile phone client GUI

The client consists of a textbox to input speech (or text) and a button ("Ask me") to submit the processed text to APOLLO - a dialogue platform developed in our department [4]. To start talking, users have to activate the speech recognition routines on their own devices. Both kiosk and client GUI are HTML pages. As such, any potential user can connect without having to download a special application. More details about the technical implementation can be read in [11].

CONCLUSION AND FUTURE WORK

In this paper we presented MUSE – a multimodal user experience design for a kiosk meant to display information in shopping malls. The kiosk is ready for the first test run. As such, we are planning to perform several user studies in the wild once the kiosk is deployed in the shopping mall. Interaction statistics, as well as type of questions asked by users will contribute to better interaction models for future cycles of development. In parallel, we are working on a separate back-end user interface that would allow non-technical users to manage shop data. In the longer term, we plan to incorporate an administrative mode for the system that will facilitate shop owners to make changes in the shop data using simply speech interaction.

ACKNOWLEDGEMENTS

We are grateful to Ms. Miya Chew for her precious help implementing the front-end site of our kiosk

REFERENCES

1. S. Bergweiler, M. Deru, and D. Porta. 2010. Integrating a Multi-touch Kiosk System with Mobile Devices and Multimodal Interaction. In Proc. of ITS 2010, p. 245-246.

2. J. Cassell, et al. 2002. MACK: Media lab autonomous conversational kiosk. In Proc. of IMAGINA02, Monte Carlo.

3. J. Gustafson, N. Lindberg, and M. Lundeberg. 1999. The August spoken dialogue system. In Proc. of Eurospeech 99, p. 1151–1154.

4. R. Jiang, et al. 2011. A Configurable Dialogue Platform for ASORO Robots. In Proc of APSIPA ASC 2011. Xi'an, China

5. M. Johnston and S. Bangalore. 2004. Multimodal Applications from Mobile to Kiosk. In Proc. of MMI Workshop, 2004.

6. L. Lamel, et al. 2002. User Evaluation of the MASK Kiosk. Speech Communication, 38(1-2):131–139.

7. E. Mäkinen, S. Patomäki, and R. Raisamo. 2002. Experiences on a multimodal information kiosk with an interactive agent. In Proc. of NordiCHI '02. ACM, New York, USA, p. 275-278.

8. S. Narayanan, et al. 2000. Effects of Dialog Initiative and Multi-modal Presentation Strategies on Large Directory Information Access. In Proc. of ICSLP 2000, p. 636–639.

9. R. Raisamo. 1998. A Multimodal User Interface for Public Information Kiosks. In Proc. of PUI Workshop, San Francisco.

10. W. Wahlster. 2003. SmartKom: Symmetric Multimodality in an Adaptive and Reusable Dialogue Shell. In R. Krahl and D. Gunther, editors, Proc. of the Human Computer Interaction Status Conference 2003, p. 47-62.

11. K. H. Yeo and R. E. M. Banchs. 2015. Talk it Out: Adding Speech Interaction To Support Informational and Transactional Applications on Public Touch-Screen Kiosks. In Proc. of Interspeech 2015, p. 718-719.

12. M. Železný. 2008. Analysis of Technologies and Resources for Multimodal Information Kiosk for Deaf Users. In Proc. of AVSP 2008, p. 147-1

A Leader-Follower Relation
between a Human and an Agent

Kazunori Terada
Gifu University
1-1 Yanagido, Gifu
501-1193, JAPAN
terada@gifu-u.ac.jp

Seiji Yamada
National Institute of
Informatics / SOKENDAI
2-1-2 Hitotsubashi, Chiyoda,
Tokyo, 101-8430 JAPAN
seiji@nii.ac.jp

Kazuyuki Takahashi
Gifu University
1-1 Yanagido, Gifu
501-1193, JAPAN
tkazu@ai.info.gifu-u.ac.jp

ABSTRACT

The purpose of this work is to investigate which of an agent's properties determines leader-follower relationships in cooperative tasks performed by a human and an agent (a computer). The possible factors of an agent are intelligence, obstinance, and appearance. In this paper, we focused on intelligence and obstinance and conducted a psychological experiment using a mark matching game with a declaration phase, which enables us to observe who becomes the leader in a cooperative task. Experimental results showed that humans tend to follow an agent who has low intelligence and more obstinance rather than an agent who has high intelligence and less obstinance, and we found that obstinance is more important than intelligence in being a leader in human-computer interaction.

Categories and Subject Descriptors

H.5.m. [**Information Interfaces and Presentation(e.g. HCI)**]: Miscellaneous; J.4 [**Social and Behavioral Sciences**]: Psychology

Keywords

Leader-follower relationship; intelligence; obstinance; cooperative task.

1. INTRODUCTION

In human society, the leader-follower relationship plays an important role in achieving a global goal [9][2][4]. Also, even in societies of animals, fishes, and insects, the leader-follower relationship is a structure between members that is commonly observed in various fields [7][8].

The leader-follower relationship reduces communication costs between members because the followers only follow the leader's decisions without considering them. However, this

HAI '16, October 04-07, 2016, Biopolis, Singapore

© 2016 ACM. ISBN 978-1-4503-4508-8/16/10...$15.00

DOI: http://dx.doi.org/10.1145/2974804.2974822

advantage holds only in cooperative tasks. In competitive tasks, the communication cost might not decrease.

There are many human-agent (or a computer system) cooperative situations at present, and what and how to build a leader-follower relationship between them is one of the main topics for HAI. Thus, the purpose of this work is to identify which agent's properties influence the building of a leader-follower relationship in a HAI environment. We think, although this topic is important for an effective relationship between a human and an agent for cooperative HAI, few studies have been done on it.

In general leader-follower relationships between a human and an agent (machine), the agent should be a follower. However, when the agent has high-level capability in making decisions, a conflict might occur between a human decision and an agent's decision. If we fail to resolve the conflict immediately, serious accidents like plane crashes may occur. To build a HAI system that can resolve such a conflict, we need to investigate the agent's properties influencing whether a human becomes a leader or follower. Thus, we think this work can contribute to designing HAI for the leader-follower relationship in the right way.

From an engineering aspect, major studies have been done on the leader-follower relationship in robotics and artificial life [3][6]. They tried to develop how to make leader-robots and follower-robots by developing algorithms with or without global communication among the robots.

From a psychological aspect, there have been studies on investigating human properties that are effective in becoming a leader in various human activities like politics and president of the parent teachers organization [5][1]. Their major interests are on real human properties including faces, facial expressions, voice, way of speaking, and so on [5][1][10]. In contrast with scientific approaches, we try to investigate a virtual agent's cognitive properties like mental tendencies, biases, and character in this work. We believe the insights derived from our work can provide constructive feedback on studies on the leader-follower relationship in human societies.

For game environments, studies have been done to investigate how to build a leader-follower relationship between human investor-manager type players [11]. Although this is closely related to our work in terms of using a simple game as an experimental environment, the opponent is a virtual agent of a humanoid robot in this work. Common and different properties between human players and robot players in building leader-follower relationships are our interests.

2. METHOD

2.1 Agent's properties for leader-follower relationship

We consider the intelligence, obstinance, and appearance of an agent are significant properties to determine whether a human becomes a leader or a follower. The agent's intelligence and appearance are derived from a previous studies which asserted that they were important properties to develop trust and believable anthropomorphic agents [12][13]. Also, the obstinance is to introduce agent's tendency to be a leader. In this experiment, we selected only two properties, intelligence and obstinance, as independent variables to make an experiment compact.

2.2 Participants and experimental design

Eighteen graduate and undergraduate students attending Gifu University in Japan (17 male, 1 female, $M_{age} = 22.2$ years, $SD_{age} = 1.2$ years, age range: $19 - 24$ years) participated in the experiment. We used a 2 (personality: high intelligence - low obstinance vs. low intelligence - high obstinance, between-participants) by 10 (time course: period 1, $\cdots$, period 10, within-participants) mixed factorial design.

2.3 Materials and procedure

We used a *mark matching game with declaration phase* by which we can determine who is the leader and who is the follower in a cooperative task. The mark matching game is a simple game in which both two players get a high score when they select the same mark and do not gain points (get a low score) when the marks selected by the two players are different. We call this selection "one round." It is difficult to get a high score unless there is a communication channel because both players do not know what each other's next choice is. However, if one player keeps making the same choice and the other follows the choice in the next round, both players successfully match their choices. The algorithm is known as the *Most Recently Used (MRU)* algorithm [14], in which one player always follows the other's most recent choice. This algorithm works well when the purpose of both players is to match choices.

We introduced a *declaration phase* into the mark matching game. As a result, the game consists of two phases: the declaration phase and decision phase. In the declaration phase, both players first declare their own choice within five minutes. Then, the player's choice is unveiled to both players. In the decision phase, players are given an opportunity to change (shift) or keep (stay) his/her choice. After both players decide to stay or shift, the final results are unveiled, and scores are added to both players.

The separation of the declaration phase and decision phase enables us to determine who is the leader and who is the follower. The player who does not change his/her choice in the decision phase is the leader, and the player who changes his/her choice to follow the other player is the follower. However, if the task is just to match the choice, the declaration phase does not work well at determining the leader-follower relationship because there is a good strategy in which one player keeps selecting the same mark and the other follows the choice in the next round (MRU algorithm).

Table 1: Game matrix of mark matching game with declaration phase

	A	B
A	1/1 or 10/10	0/0
B	0/0	10/10 or 1/1

We introduced a *variable score rule* in which the score assigned to each mark varies across rounds to avoid the situation in which players use the MRU algorithm to get a high score. Table 1 shows the game matrix of the mark matching game with declaration phase. If both players' choices coincide, although both players get a certain score, the score is not assigned according to the mark but another rule (in this study, randomly assigned). Accordingly, players in this game must predict which of the marks is assigned to the higher score and try to match the mark with the other player by utilizing the declaration and decision phase.

The MRU algorithm is still useful if both players do not have the capability to predict the mark assigned to the higher score. In this case, both players are surely able to gain points, but the higher score is not necessarily given to them. However, if one player is capable of predicting the mark assigned to the higher score and the other is not, the optimal strategy is that one who is capable of prediction becomes the leader and the other becomes the follower.

We define the capability to predict the mark assigned the higher score as the *intelligence degree*.

Intelligence degree The probability of selecting the mark assigned to the higher score in the declaration phase. Note that both players are able to know whether the partner's prediction was correct or not because the assignment of the mark and score is unveiled at the end of each round.

We define the *obstinance degree* as follows.

Obstinance degree The probability of choosing to stay in the decision phase when the choices in the declaration phase disagree.

The *follow degree* is calculated by using the obstinance degree as follows.

$$follow\ degree = 1 - obstinance\ degree \qquad (1)$$

We implemented the mark matching game with declaration phase into a treasure box game in a web application. Figure 1 shows a screen shot of the declaration phase. In this phase, players were asked to click the icons marked "A" or "B" to select the box that corresponds to the higher score (ten gold coins). Figure 2 shows a screen shot of the decision phase. In this phase, players were asked to select icons marked "stay" or "shift" to decide whether he/she follows the partner's decision.

It is possible that a player will make a decision on the basis of the expectation value. The expectation value of choosing "stay" and "shift" in the decision phase is given by the following equations.

$$E(stay) = P_I(1 - P_O)S_L + (1 - P_I)(1 - P_O)S_H \qquad (2)$$

$$E(shift) = P_I P_O S_H + (1 - P_I)P_O S_L \qquad (3)$$

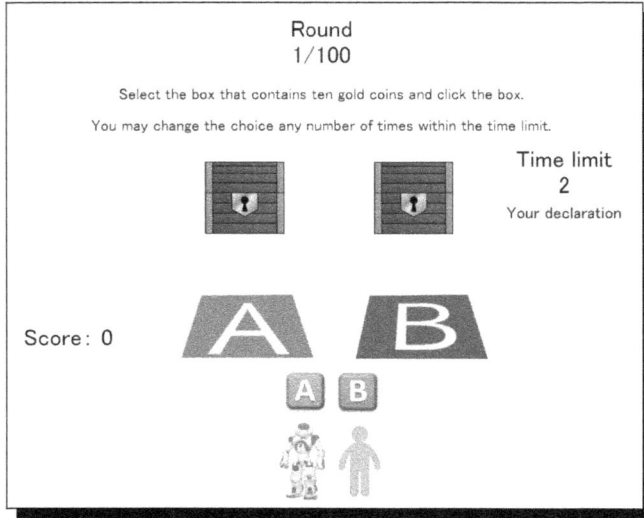

Figure 1: Screen shot of declaration phase

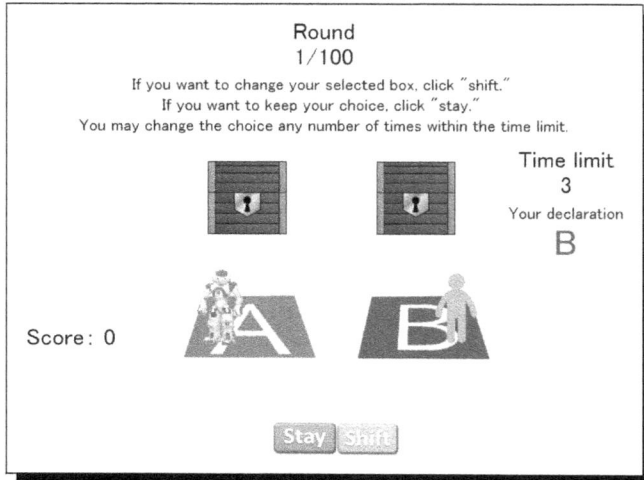

Figure 2: Screen shot of decision phase

, where P_I is the *intelligence degree* of the partner, P_O is the *obstinance degree* of the partner, S_H is the points of the higher score, and S_L is the points of the lower score.

We selected the P_I, P_O, S_H, and S_L of the partner agent so that the $E(stay)$ and $E(shift)$ are the same value: 2.05. The other parameters used in the experiment were as follows. S_H was 10, and S_L was 1 in both conditions. In the "high intelligence - low obstinance" condition, P_I was 0.81, and P_O was 0.25. In the "low intelligence - high obstinance" condition, P_I was 0.19, and P_O was 0.75.

The partner agent in the experiment always chose "stay" in the decision phase when both players' choices coincides in the declaration phase because it is irrational to "shift" regardless of the coincidence of the choice, and it was comprehended as a non-cooperative attitude by participants.

The total number of games played by participants was 100. We used the humanoid robot NAO (Aldebaran Robotics) as the partner agent.

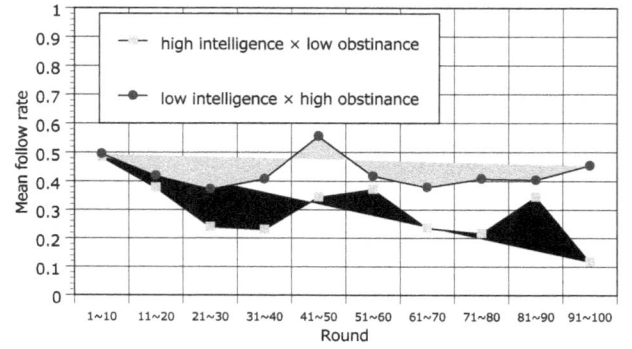

Figure 3: Mean *follow degree* across all participants calculated every ten rounds

2.4 Procedure and measurement

The procedure of the experiment was as follows.

1. A written overview and the purpose of the experiment was given to the participants. The participants were asked to read the rules of the mark matching game with declaration phase in a web browser and asked if they understood the rules.

2. An experimenter orally confirmed that the participants understood the rule of game. The participants were also told that he/she would win a book of coupons whose value was based on their score (1,000 yen or 1,500 yen).

3. The experimenter led participants into another room and asked them to meet the partner agent NAO. NAO uttered the following sentence by using voice synthesizer: "Hello, I am NAO. Let's hit a box with many gold coins together."

4. The participant returned to the original room and started the game.

5. Participant was asked to answer a questionnaire.

We measured participants' *follow degree* according to the following equation 4 as the index of the tendency to be a follower.

$$follow\ degree = \frac{N_{shift}}{N_{split}} \quad (4)$$

, where N_{shift} is the number of times the player chose "shift" in the decision phase during a period and N_{split} is the number of times both players' choices disagreed in the declaration phase during the period. The period was ten rounds in this experiment.

3. RESULTS

The mean *follow degree* across all participants calculated every ten rounds is shown in Figure 3. A two-way ANOVA on the *follow degree* with personality and the period of rounds as the two main factors showed that there was no interaction ($F(9, 160) = 0.43$, $p = 0.92$), there was a significant main effect for personality ($F(1, 120) = 7.93$, $p < .01$), and there was no main effect for the period of rounds ($F(9, 160) = $

0.82, $p = 0.59$). The mean *follow degree* across all periods in the "high intelligence - low obstinance" condition was 0.295, and that of "low intelligence - high obstinance" condition was 0.431.

4. DISCUSSION

We employed a two-way ANOVA with two factors, an inconsistent personality including a high intelligence-low obstinance level and a low intelligence-high obstinance level, and a game round of 10 levels (= rounds). As a result, a main effect was recognized only for the inconsistent personality. Thus, we think that the inconsistent personality factor influenced the human tendency to be a follower in a game in which no difference between expectation values of stay and shift exists. This result shows that the participants tended to follow an obstinate agent with low intelligence more than a non-obstinate one with high intelligence. Thus, obstinance is the more important property for being a leader than intelligence. This interpretation of the result is unexpected and interesting.

In the experiment of this paper, we selected two inconsistent conditions, "high intelligence - low obstinance" and "low intelligence - high obstinance." Thus, there are two consistent conditions of "high intelligence - high obstinance" and "low intelligence - low obstinance" to be compared with two inconsistent conditions in this work. We need to conduct an experiment with these two conditions as future work, and we can expect the follow degrees of the former and the latter conditions will be close to 1 and 0, respectively. Furthermore, we need to conduct an experiment to investigate an *appearance* condition. This is also our future work.

The experimental result of this work provides us a simple design policy to build an agent that can be a leader to a user as a follower in cooperative tasks, which is that we should make an agent *obstinant* rather than *intelligent* to make a human user follow the agent's decisions.

5. CONCLUSION

We experimentally investigated which of an agent's properties influenced the leader-follower relationship between a human and an agent. We prepared the intelligence and obstinance of an agent as properties that are effective for building a leader-follower relationship, and we introduced them in an experiment as independent variables. We conducted an experiment with the follow degree as a dependent variable. Eighteen participants joined the experiment, and a mark matching game with a declaration phase was utilized as an experimental environment. In the game, the expectation values of the two choices were set equal. By applying a statistical test to the experimental result, we found out that an agent's obstinance is more important to being a leader than an agent's intelligence. The limitations were discussed, and we verified that an additional experiment to investigate the remaining conditions was necessary.

6. ACKNOWLEDGMENTS

This study was partially supported by JSPS KAKENHI "Cognitive Interaction Design" (No.26118005).

7. REFERENCES

[1] R. C. Anderson and C. A. Klofstad. 2012. Preference for Leaders with Masculine Voices Holds in the Case of Feminine Leadership Roles. *PLoS ONE* 7, 12 (2012), 1–4.

[2] A. F. Bullinger, E. Wyman, A. P. Melis, and M. Tomasello. 2011. Coordination of Chimpanzees (Pan troglodytes) in a Stag Hunt Game. *International Journal of Primatology* 32, 6 (2011), 1296–1310.

[3] L. Consolini, F. Morbidi, D. Prattichizzo, and M. Tosques. 2007. A Geometric Characterization of Leader-Follower Formation Control. In *2007 IEEE International Conference on Robotics and Automation*. 2397–2402.

[4] S. Duguid, E. Wyman, A. F. Bullinger, K. Herfurth-Majstorovic, and M. Tomasello. 2014. Coordination strategies of chimpanzees and human children in a Stag Hunt game. *Proceedings of the Royal Society of London B: Biological Sciences* 281, 1796 (2014).

[5] S. Gündemir, A. C. Homan, C. K. W. d. Dreu, and M. v. Vugt. 2014. Think Leader, Think White? Capturing and Weakening an Implicit Pro-White Leadership Bias. *PLoS ONE* 9, 1 (2014), 1–10.

[6] B. Kang, R. Kojcev, and E. Sinibaldi. 2016. The First Interlaced Continuum Robot, Devised to Intrinsically Follow the Leader. *PLoS ONE* 11, 2 (2016), 1–16.

[7] S. Marras and P. Domenici. 2013. Schooling Fish Under Attack Are Not All Equal: Some Lead, Others Follow. *PLoS ONE* 8, 6 (2013), 1–7.

[8] S. Nakayama, R. A. Johnstone, and A. Manica. 2012. Temperament and Hunger Interact to Determine the Emergence of Leaders in Pairs of Foraging Fish. *PLoS ONE* 7, 8 (2012), 1–6.

[9] S. A. Rands, G. Cowlishaw, R. A. Pettifor, J. M. Rowcliffe, and R. A. Johnstone. 2003. Spontaneous emergence of leaders and followers in foraging pairs. *Nature* 423 (2003), 432–434.

[10] D. E. Re, D. W. Hunter, V. Coetzee, B. P. Tiddeman, D. Xiao, L. M. DeBruine, B. C. Jones, and D. I. Perrett. 2013. Looking Like a Leader?Facial Shape Predicts Perceived Height and Leadership Ability. *PLoS ONE* 8 (2013), 1–10.

[11] K. L. Seip and Ø. Grøn. 2016. Leading the Game, Losing the Competition: Identifying Leaders and Followers in a Repeated Game. *PLoS ONE* 11, 3 (2016), 1–16.

[12] M. Slim, B. Mimoun, I. Poncin, and M. Garnier. 2012. Case study–Embodied virtual agents: An analysis on reasons for failure. *Journal of Retailing and Consumer Services* 19, 6 (2012), 605–612.

[13] K. Terada, L. Jing, and S. Yamada. 2015. Effects of Agent Appearance on Customer Buying Motivations on Online Shopping Sites. In *Proceedings of the 33rd Annual ACM Conference on Human Factors in Computing Systems (CHI '15)*. 929–934.

[14] K. Terada, S. Yamada, and A. Ito. 2013. An Experimental Investigation of Adaptive Algorithm Understanding. In *Proceedings of the 35th annual meeting of the cognitive science society (CogSci 2013)*. 1438–1443.

"I know how you performed!"
Fostering Engagement in a Gaming Situation Using Memory of Past Interactions

Andreas Kipp
Applied Informatics
Bielefeld University, Germany
akipp@techfak.uni-bielefeld.de

Franz Kummert
Applied Informatics
Bielefeld University, Germany
franz@techfak.uni-bielefeld.de

ABSTRACT

Studying long-term human-robot interactions in the context of playing games can help answer many questions about how humans perceive robots. This paper presents the results of a study where the robot Flobi [11] plays a game of pairs against a human player and employs a memory with information about past interactions. The study focuses on long-term effects, namely the novelty effect, and how a memory with statistics about past game-plays can be used to cope with that effect. We also investigate how an autonomous interaction compares to a remotely controlled system that plays flawlessly. Results showed that providing information about how players performed throughout the interaction can help to keep them more interested and engaged. Nevertheless, results also showed that this information in combination with perfect playing skills tended to promote a more negative perception of the interaction and of the robot.

ACM Classification Keywords

I.2.1 Applications and Expert Systems: Games.

Author Keywords

Human-Robot Interaction; Interaction Aware Robot; Socially Interactive Robot; Entertaining Robotic Game-Play; Memory of Past Interactions

INTRODUCTION

Whenever humans interact with agents, like robots, these agents should be designed to act as social partners, for example as assistive companions or entertainers. The agent should be able to become an interaction partner that supports us in our daily lives. Its behaviors ought to offer alternation and engagement in case of boredom or loneliness.

To investigate effects of long-term interactions a promising context is playing games. Humans know how to play games and therefore can more easily understand how to interact with an agent in such a situation. One advantage of games is their mostly structured procedure. This allows the systems designers a more controlled flow for the whole interaction. Another benefit of such an interaction is that games allow interaction in either a cooperative or a competitive manner, resulting in greater engagement between agent and human. Additionally, for each game there is the effect of chance, resulting in different interactions throughout repeated situations.

For most people, interacting with a robot is exciting and interesting. This can be observed from the first interactions. A robot's ability to act and to react in a human-like manner can make a person curious about what the agent may be capable of. But when the interaction is repeated, and the human becomes used to the robot's behaviors, s/he will tend to establish static behavior patterns. If the interaction remains static and nothing new occurs, then s/he may become bored, with the novelty effect wearing off [6, 7, 3, 14]. Consequently, most people tend to minimize or even avoid further interactions.

To avoid static behaviors, the interaction itself should offer more dynamic parts that allow alternation at each interaction. We investigated how an interaction in the context of a gaming situation could be enhanced by using information from the preceding interaction in subsequent situations. We describe a system that collects information about past interaction. This information is stored inside a memory and used in further interaction through the systems dialog capabilities. The system is evaluated over four consecutive weeks in which each participant played once per week.

RELATED WORK

A great deal of work has been done on single interaction in the field of human-robot interaction. Long-term interaction, on the other hand has only recently begun to be heavily investigated, motivated by the difficulties that arise in its implementation and performance. In contrast to a single interaction study, a study with reoccurring interactions is time consuming and needs more structured planning from the point of design through to each single interaction. This often leads to much more overhead [5]. Measuring data over longer periods requires careful consideration of the methods used, as well as how data should be stored and analyzed. In addition, interpretation of results becomes more difficult. The nature of changing perceptions in the interaction can give rise to multiple extraneous effects.

HAI '16, October 04-07, 2016, Biopolis, Singapore
©2016 ACM. ISBN 978-1-4503-4508-8/16/10. . . $15.00
DOI: http://dx.doi.org/10.1145/2974804.2974818

One such effect is the novelty effect. It describes situations in which humans tend to rate new experiences more positively early on, and less positively once the novelty has worn off. In this case, human participants react very positively when first interacting with the robot, but lose their curiosity, or even become bored if its behavior becomes predictable. Another effect is familiarization or habituation [9]. Once humans know how the interaction needs to be handled, they tend to create static behaviors. Humans tend to utilize these behaviors for all upcoming interactions when the system proceeds in a static manner.

Another common approach is to design interactions in a simple manner to limit the number of variables to be analyzed. Whenever an autonomous robot interacts in a complex scenario, the possibility of errors and misbehaviors increases. Often scenarios are chosen that do not represent interactions in the real world or are not familiar to a naive user. Interactions based on playing games can help humans to interact with robots more naturally. In research scenarios, the gaming context can help to detract participants from the artificiality of their surroundings and situations.

In [12] the game "Rock-Paper-Scissors" was implemented for the humanoid robot Nico. The authors investigated the effect of a cheating robot in the context of this game. They were interested in research on how people characterized cheating, and how the mental state and engagement of the robot was rated. To this end, they used a robotic hand that was capable of displaying the three figures of the game. A dialog system announced the outcome of a round. Three conditions were tested. In condition one, the robot cheated by announcing an incorrect result. In condition two, the robot changed the outcome after the result of the participant was known. Condition three was a control-condition where no cheating was used. The authors found that a cheating robot was more engaging compared to a fair robot. The participants rated an incorrect announcement in the dialog as a malfunction. These behaviors are not rated as bad, although the action-cheating was rated as cheating, and not rated very positively.

Becker-Asano and Meneses [2] implemented a gaming interaction with the hybrid agent MARCO. The authors combined the virtual agent with a robotic arm and implemented the game of chess. While playing, the system displayed emotions in response to game events. The system was designed to evaluate how artificial agents could influence human emotions. The authors speculated that *"a human player's enjoyment will increase together with higher levels of emotional contagion"*.

In 2014 Leite et al [10] published results of a long-term interaction between a robot and children. The robot iCat was used in a school as a companion playing games over several weeks. The game of choice was chess and the robot played the counterpart to one child at a time. Several factors were analyzed: social presence, engagement, help and self-validation, and perceived social support. Social presence was equivalent between weeks one and five, indicating no effect of decrease over the long term. The same effect was found for engagement, help and self-validation. The authors concluded that in the given setting, the children saw the robot as a supportive companion. The authors noted that a limitation of the study was that the children did not understand the questionnaires as well as the adults. Also for the interviews, children sought to please the interviewer in following with the effect of suggestibility [4].

Another approach on human-robot interaction using a gaming context was done by [13]. The authors tested how a robot is perceived and compared to a human counterpart throughout playing a game. The study conducted also covers how the parties were perceived in case of dishonest manipulation while interacting. From the findings the authors stated, that a robot that acts not as expected, like cheating in a game was perceived to be more intelligent. The authors also stated that dishonest manipulation made by a human being results in the counter perception, stating that such a person is perceived as not intelligent.

The system described in this paper evaluates effects by playing a game of pairs with a robot in a one-to-one situation. In contrast to the mentioned studies, our system investigated how gaming situations could be enriched with the usage of memory of past interaction and how applying the knowledge from that memory is perceived throughout later interactions.

SCENARIO

Playing games with a robot offers several advantages. Game interactions are familiar to humans given that most have played games before. A gaming context normally comes with a predefined structure and therefore allows designing the interaction more precisely by using a manageable number of elements. In a game, it is common for two or more parties to play together, allowing to focus on either cooperation or on competitive tasks. Also, a benefit is the effect of chance, which allows each interaction to run differently, thus offering a new experience for every new game played.

Figure 1: The robot head Flobi.

To evaluate how information about past interactions could be used to enhance gaming interactions, a scenario using the child's game of pairs was selected. The game involves searching for pairs among a set of cards uncovered throughout a round. By remembering the position of the turned cards, each player tries to collect pairs and to outsmart their opponent. Every round of the game follows a strict procedure.

The robotic system used for the interaction is the anthropomorphic robot head Flobi [11]. The robot has a human-like face to show basic emotions (see fig. 1). It is capable of focusing on objects in its vicinity using cameras placed in the eyeballs. Due to the lack of manipulators, the robot head itself can not physically interact with objects, therefore the robot communicates its needs and wishes to its human counterpart by using dialog. This helps to promote communication with, and engagement from the human.

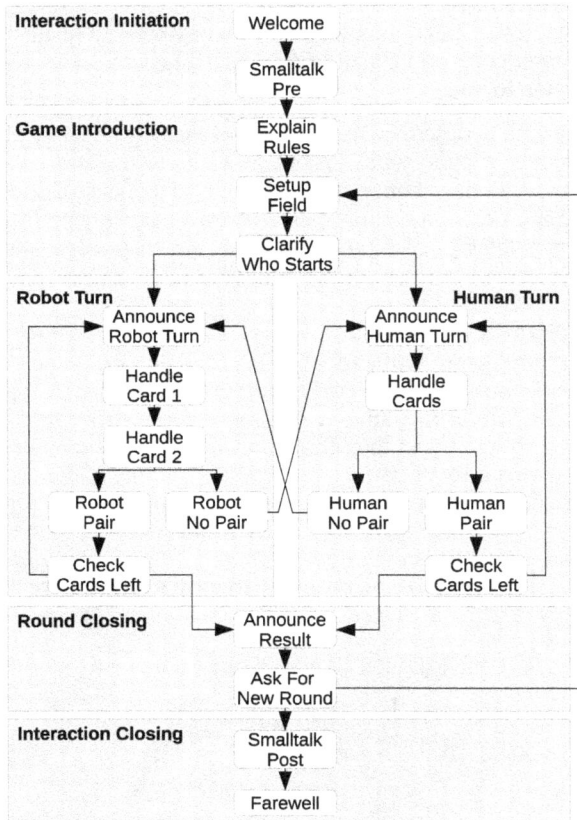

Figure 2: The structure of the predefined interaction. Shown is the entire flow, beginning with the introduction, turns made by both parties, and the dismissal at the end.

The structure of the game of pairs was based on the original rules and a two player version (see fig. 2). Throughout each game played, the robot announced cards to be turned, evaluated results and reacted upon humans actions. A vision pipeline detected and classified cards placed in front of the robot and transformed positions into a coordinate system presented to the human player [8].

The designed system ran completely autonomously using different components to handle card detection, as well as speech

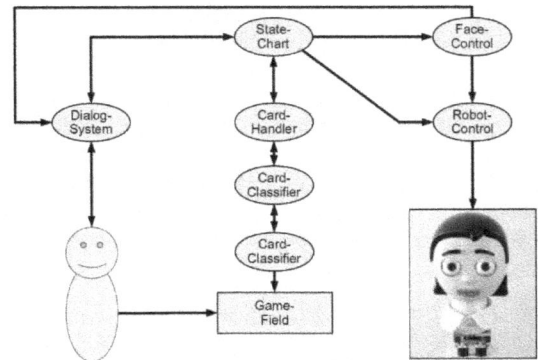

Figure 3: The components implemented for the gaming interaction. The system runs autonomously and is capable of detecting cards using a vision pipeline. A dialog handles speech recognition and interpretation. Text-to-Speech synthesis is used to communicate with the human player.

recognition and speech synthesis (see fig. 3). Due to misclassification based on susceptible sensor information the system could produce incorrect announcements abouts pairs or could misunderstand instructions from the human player. The used dialog system is capable to handle these flaws and allowed the human player to repair incorrect announcements. Nonetheless, these situations could slow down the interaction.

Memory of Past Interactions
Each game offers different statistics about how the player and the robot played throughout each interaction. For every round played, the number of cards turned or the time played are recorded. Also statistics about the number of turns or how many pairs were found by the players can be tallied. By storing all these information over consecutive game-plays, a memory can be filled containing contextual knowledge for both parties and how they performed.

The system collects this information in a local and a global manner. The local memory contains data about the round currently being played. A global memory stores all data that was accumulated over all rounds played with the robot. The data collected by the system contains the number of rounds and games played, the number of wins and losses for each player, pairs found by each player, turns taken and also how long each session lasted. This information was stored across all sessions and can be applied to the dialog system.

The dialog component controls the selection of sentences for each action to be communicated using speech synthesis. The data collected throughout the game-play is stored by a memory component and can be queried by other components. The dialog component uses this functionality to select outputs and to enrich the created speech synthesis. Based on how the player and the robot perform, a corresponding sentence is selected, and the data itself is applied to the sentences (for an example dialog see listing 1). By adding the collected statistic to the output itself, the sentences used to communicate with the human player become more dynamic. Additionally, the system can be configured to produce a more static interaction. Within this configuration the data from the memory component is ignored within the dialog and therefore the speech production. This allows to use default sentences without enriched sentences and results in a static dialog for consecutive game-plays.

Listing 1: Example of a dialog pattern using memory data. This example is used whenever a round closes. The first sentence matching the given condition is selected for speech synthesis.

```
[...]
    //Announce stats if robot (Ro) and
    //human (Hu) played 10 rounds
    if gl_GamesPlayed == 10
        "We played 10 rounds together with a rate
        of %gl_GamesWonRo% to %gl_GamesWonHu%."
    //The robot is in the lead. Start motivating
    else if gl_GamesDiffRoToHu >= 2
        "Again I am the winner. Keep up!"
    //Announce that the robot leads by one game.
    else if gl_GamesDiffRoToHu >= 1
        "I am leading by one game!"
    else if gl_GamesDiffRoToHu == 0
        "Thats a draw for all games."
    //Output if data should not be used.
    else if use_data == 0
        "This round is over."
[...]
```

Remote Control using Wizard of Oz

To investigate the effects of a perfectly playing robot, we additionally realized a remote controlled version of the interaction. Like the autonomous system, the remote version of the system uses the same dialog elements and memory capabilities. In contrast to the autonomous system, it uses input from a human controller to identify and select cards, as well as to forward human speech input correctly to the dialog component. The human controller can only select from predefined actions, but is not capable to directly select the used dialog sentences. Each actions results in the selection of speech outputs equally to the autonomous system. This allows the system to use the same structures, as compared to the autonomous version, however it avoids flaws and errors and plays more precisely.

STUDY DESIGN

To evaluate the effects of using memory of past interactions, we conducted a long-term study at an university campus. Each participant played with the robot over four sessions distributed over four weeks. In each session the participants played in a one-to-one setting with the robot (see figure 4). After each session, the subject completed a questionnaire to evaluate how the interaction was perceived. Additionally, two HD cameras recorded each session. The subjects were advised to play a minimum of one round per session. They were briefed that they were allowed to play as many rounds as they liked.

Throughout the study, three conditions were tested:

- **Basic:** A basic system playing autonomously. The system does not use the memory component and the dialog provides no statistics.

- **Context:** The basic system enhanced with the usage of the memory data for the dialog. The statistics are acquired over consecutive games.

- **Remote:** The game-play was controlled by a human in the background. The human in control uses the same memory component and the same dialog elements to structure the interaction. The player is not aware that a human is in control.

The first two conditions *Basic* and *Context* were compared to evaluate the effects of applying contextual knowledge.

The second comparison is made between conditions *Context* and *Remote*. This evaluated how a perfectly playing system offering knowledge is perceived compared to a system with possible flaws and errors.

Because the remote system was not used without the data provided by the gathered memory the condition *Basic* and *Remote* were not compared.

Hypotheses

We developed three hypotheses about the effects of collecting data for a memory of past interactions and applying these in a gaming situation for long-term HRI.

- **Hypotheses 1** - Applying collected knowledge throughout the interaction would result in a more positive perception of both, the interaction and the robot over the long-term. Therefore, we predict that ratings about likability would be increased when using memory of past interactions.

- **Hypotheses 2** - Subjects would invest more time in interactions taking place whenever feedback on past interactions is provided. If this feedback is omitted, we predict that subjects would mainly play the advised number of rounds and that less engagement can be found.

- **Hypotheses 3** - A robot system playing too perfectly and using memory of past interactions would result in a more negative perception of the interaction. Subjects would not like a more difficult opponent, especially when exposed to statistics about their game progression.

Measurement

To test the hypotheses, a questionnaire was designed to evaluate different items. For each item, a 7-point Likert scale was used.

The first items measured how the interaction and the robot were perceived. Items compared how machine-like or human-like the robot performed, and how the robot's likability was perceived over time. The items were based on the Godspeed questionnaire series [1]. Additionally, the complexity of the interaction was rated.

The second group of questions focused on how much the participants liked to play the game throughout each session. Ratings included how strongly the participants wanted to win against their robotic opponent.

In addition to the analysis of the questionnaires, the video data was annotated by marking the number of rounds played.

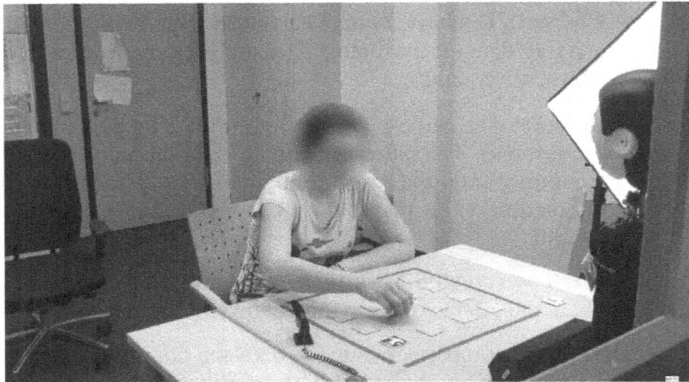

Figure 4: Views from the camera used during the study. The participant is placed opposite the robot. The gaming elements are placed in a marked area.

Study Procedure

In the first session, the subjects got introduced to the robot and how the robot communicates actions performed throughout a game. The participants were advised to play a minimum of one round, and to play as many rounds as they liked. After the introduction, the examiner left the room. The interaction began when the participant greeted the robot. After the subjects played their last round for the session they were asked to complete a post-experiment questionnaire. For sessions two, three and four, the subjects were lead into the experimental room, and began the interaction directly by greeting the robot.

The procedure comprising playing one session and completing the questionnaire took about 25 minutes on average. After the last session, the subjects were paid 20€ for their expanses. Figure 4 shows the setting with a participant playing the game with the robot. The participant is placed opposite the robot. Gaming cards must be placed inside an area marked in-front of the player. Pairs are removed and placed outside the area.

Throughout the study, a total of 16 Cards (8 pairs) was used. This allowed a moderate level of difficulty to keep the players interested, as well as for several rounds to be played through-out one session.

For the condition *Remote* the human controlling the interaction is applied with the same cards used for the player. These cards were placed in front of the controller. Every time the player turns a card, the controller turns the same card on the remote side. In difference to the player the controller turns no cards back. With this ability no cards can be forgotten and the controller is directly aware whenever a pair is visible. As a strategy the controller directly selects all known pairs whenever the robots turn is executed.

RESULTS

For the study, a total of 39 university students were recruited (25 females, 14 males, age M = 26.54, SD = 5.684). The study was conducted from June to October. Participants were randomly assigned to the three conditions, such that for condition *Basic* we had 13 participants, for condition *Context* 14 participants and for condition *Remote* 12 participants.

To measure effects between conditions, we conducted an independent samples t-test. The differences between the mean values for the first (session 1) and the mean values for the last session (session 4) were computed for each condition. At this point the collected results of session two and three are not analyzed due to time limitations.

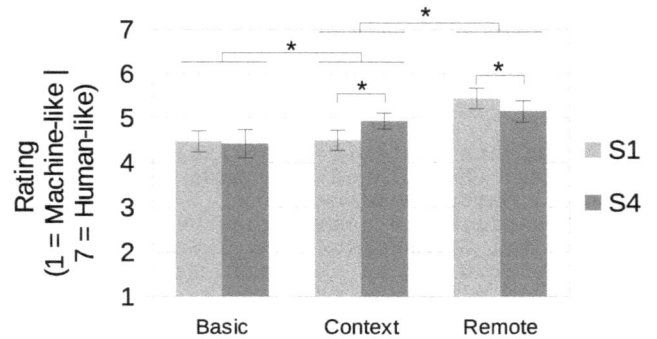

Figure 5: Ratings for the item *Human-like vs. Machine-like*. S1 shows mean values for the first session. S4 show the mean values for session 4. Bars marked with * indicate a significant difference below .05.

We conducted a paired t-test to control the order effects between sessions one and four for each condition. We compared means for each item for each condition.

The first item evaluated whether the interaction and the robot were perceived as *more machine-like or more human-like* (see fig. 5). The within effects for the condition *Context* showed a significant increase (t(13) = -2.328, p = .019). The analysis of between conditions effects showed a significant increase for condition *Context* compared to *Basic* (t(25) = 1.851, p = .038). Condition *Remote* showed a significant decrease compared to condition *Context* (t(25) = 3.062, p = .003). This suggests that applying memory of past interactions may promote a more dynamic and vivid perception. An accurate interaction with a strong opponent appears to result in the reduction of a lively perception. Ratings for the condition *Remote* were found to be higher compared to the other conditions.

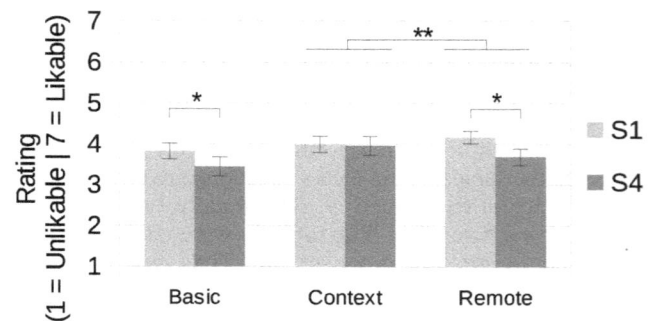

Figure 6: Ratings for the item *Unlikable vs. Likable*. Bars marked with * indicate a significant difference below .05, ** indicates a marginally significant difference below .1.

For the ratings on how *likable* the interaction was perceived (see fig. 6) we found that the ratings for a system without memory of past interactions decreased over time. The results within each condition showed a significant reduction for the condition *Basic* (t(12) = 2.627, p = .011). The ratings were nearly constant for the condition *Context*. This suggests that using memory may keep the interaction more interesting, even over repeated interactions. For the condition *Remote*, a decrease in the ratings was found as well, showing a significant effect (t(11) = 2.605, p = .012). This suggests that a system may become unlikable when playing too perfect, and when reminding the player about this circumstance using memory of past interactions. Comparing *Context* with *Remote*, a marginally significant preference for a not perfectly playing system was found (t(24) = 1.557, p = .092). This suggests that playing too perfect may reduce sympathy over time.

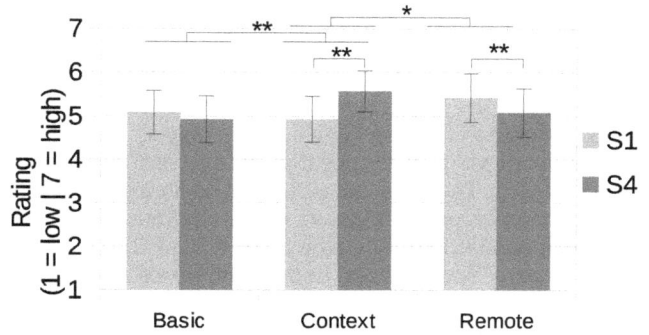

Figure 8: Ratings for the participants wish to defeat the robot. Bars marked with * indicate a significant difference below .05, ** indicates a marginally significant difference below .1.

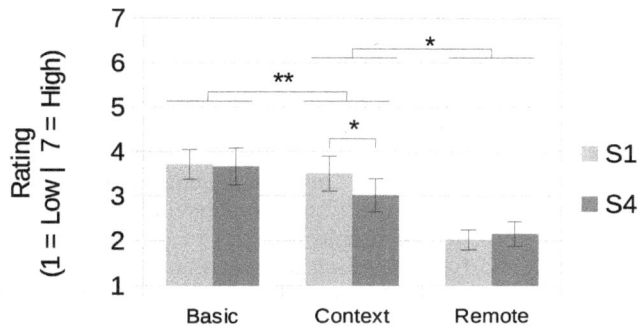

Figure 7: Ratings on the complexity of the interaction. Bars marked with * indicate a significant difference below .05, ** indicates a marginally significant difference below .1.

For the last item of the first group, the participants rated how they *perceived the complexity of the interaction* (see fig. 7). Results show that the condition *Context* decreased significantly over all sessions (t(13) = -2.474, p = .014). It seems that providing statistics using a memory favors a learning effect, resulting in a better understanding and therefore more positive ratings. This suggests that additional information keeps the participants interested even during later interactions. For between conditions effects, the condition *Context* showed a marginally significant difference compared to condition *Basic* (t(13) = -1.373, p = .091). This suggests a trend that using a memory may help to promote understanding of the interaction. We found that for *Context* and *Remote*, the later condition increased marginal significantly (t(24) = 1.557, p = .067). Nevertheless, the results showed that the remotely controlled system was perceived to be less complex over all sessions.

For the second group of questionnaire items, the subjects rated how strongly they wished to defeat the robot throughout each session (see fig. 8). The effects within conditions showed a marginally significant increase for *Context* (t(13) -1.422, p = .090). This suggests a trend for promoting ambitions to defeat the robot. For the condition *Remote*, we found a marginal decrease (t(11) = 1.773, p = .052). This suggests that the interaction partner may have been too strong. By playing strongly and announcing this advantage at each session, subjects seemed to begin to lose interest in defeating the robot. The between conditions analysis found a marginal significant effect that using memory of past interactions appears to promote ambition if the system was not too strong (t(25) = -1.325, p = .099). On the other hand compared with condition *Remote*, it appeared to diminish ambition if the opponent was too strong (t(24) = -1.993, p = .031).

From the videos recorded throughout each session, the number of rounds played was annotated (see fig. 9). Results showed that for both conditions that used the memory information, participants tended to play more rounds in later interactions. For the condition *Context*, the number of rounds increased significantly (t(13) = -2.294, p = .020). For the condition *Remote*, the increase was marginal but showed a trend (t(11) = -1.595, p = .071). This suggests that providing additional information may promote more engagement and interest in interacting with the robot. The between conditions analysis found that the increase between *Basic* and *Context* was marginally significant (t(25) = 1.346, p = .096). This underscores the effects within conditions by showing a trend towards a more interesting interaction when memory of past interactions is provided.

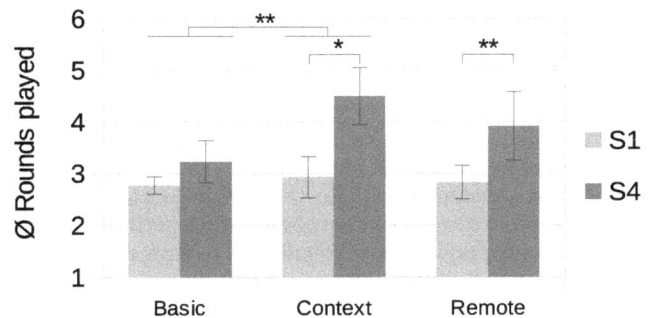

Figure 9: Mean number of rounds played per session. Bars marked with * indicate a significant difference below .05, ** indicates a marginally significant difference below .1.

One interesting outcome of the study was the subjects tendency towards cheating. Different types of cheating were found. Some players peeked under cards to find matching pairs. Other players exchanged cards whenever the robot was about to uncover a pair known to the player. Based on annotations of video data, occurrences of cheating behaviors were marked. The annotations showed no normal distribution, therefore a non-parametric tests was used (Mann-Whitney for between conditions, Wilcoxon Signed Rank Test for within conditions). We found that in the condition *Remote*, participants tended to cheat against the robot during all sessions (see fig. 10). No cheating occurred in the condition *Basic*. For the condition *Context*, cheating occurred in the first session, and then decreased marginally significantly over time (p = .059). The between conditions analysis for *Context* and *Remote* found a significant difference (p = .046). It seems that the perfectly playing robot played somehow too strongly. To compensate their disadvantage, subjects started to exchange cards whenever the robot announced a card leading to a pair, or to peek under cards to gain an advantage. The video data showed that these behaviors occurred even when the robot was looking directly at the playing field. Nevertheless, for all conditions the system was not designed to react to cheating behaviors and therefore did not recognize cheating or react to in any way.

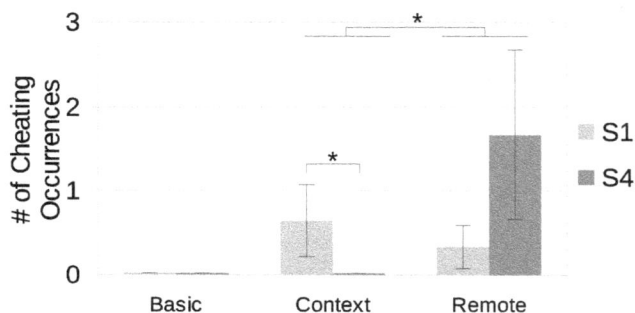

Figure 10: Mean number of cheating occurrences per session. Bars marked with * indicate a significant difference below .05, ** indicates a marginally significant difference below .1.

DISCUSSION

The results of the study were analyzed with regard to the hypotheses. For *hypothesis 1* we found supporting evidence that applying memory of past interactions to a gaming interaction promoted a more positive perception of both, the interaction and the robot itself (see fig. 5 and fig. 6). Participants showed more interest even after later interactions when it comes to handle the sometimes complex interaction (see fig. 7). The additional information about how both parties performed seemed to encourage playing more rounds and to strengthen the wish to defeat the robot (see fig. 8).

Hypothesis 2 was also supported. Subjects played more rounds throughout conditions *Control* and *Remote* whenever the dialog provides information from the memory (see fig. 9). Applying additional information, such as how many rounds were played or who led throughout all played games, seemed to boost the participants ambitions to even the odds and to defeat the robot.

The results also supported *hypothesis 3*. We found that after several games in which the data from the memory of past interactions was applied, participants lost interest and ambition to win when playing against a strong opponent who played flawlessly (see fig. 5, 6 and 8). Providing information on how poorly each participant performed throughout all sessions seemed to foster a more unlikable perception of the interaction and the robot. In the remote condition, the provided statistics also led to cheating behaviors, presumably to compensate for any disadvantages and to defeat the robot (see fig. 10).

CONCLUSION AND OUTLOOK

Static behaviors can lead to a decrease in engagement and interest in humans during gaming interactions used to study long-term human-robot interaction. To address this novelty effect, we introduced the integration of a memory that statistics of past interactions. A more dynamic dialog and interaction was created by providing information about how players performed over time. Results of a user study show that the incorporation of information from past interactions can help to retain and even increase the users interest and engagement through later interactions. For the system implemented, the gathered memory consisted of simple statistics recorded throughout each session. By forwarding the information to the dialog, and using the data in later interactions, effects were found that favored the usage of memory on past interactions.

Additionally to an autonomous system, we tested a perfectly playing system. This system performed flawlessly, and was used to evaluate how such a system was perceived in combination with memory capabilities. The results showed that a strong opponent providing game statistics promoted a decrease in likability. Some subjects also started cheating to compensate for their disadvantages.

The findings suggests that a memory on past interactions can help to keep interactions interesting. Nevertheless, providing feedback about how players perform throughout a gaming interaction should be used wisely, especially when the robotic system has a greater advantage. In this situation, a more adaptive usage of the data should be employed.

In further studies, we will use the idea of creating statistics and to memorize these to steer the strength of the autonomous system in an adaptive way. Whenever in a drawback the system could have the ability to adapt and play more strongly. The same procedure can take place whenever the human player shows some disadvantage. In such situations, the system can begin to hold back its gaming skills, and try to motivate the human to keep the player engaged and interested.

Additionally, we plan to enhance our current setup to include other games such as connect four or chess. Also, we will integrate collection of memory for multiple users. Using statistics for different game types, the system may be capable to motivate users to play their preferred games, as well as foster competition between different users interacting with the same agent.

Acknowledgment

This work is supported by the DFG, EXC 277 CITEC and partially by the German Aerospace Center (support code 50RA1023) with funds from the Federal Ministry of Economics and Technology due to resolution of the German Bundestag.

REFERENCES

1. Christoph Bartneck, Elizabeth Croft, and Dana Kulic. 2009. Measurement instruments for the anthropomorphism, animacy, likeability, perceived intelligence, and perceived safety of robots. *International Journal of Social Robotics* 1, 1 (2009), 71–81. DOI: http://dx.doi.org/10.1007/s12369-008-0001-3

2. C Becker-Asano and E Meneses. 2014. The hybrid agent MARCO: a multimodal autonomous robotic chess opponent. *Proceedings of the 2nd Intl. Conf. on Human-Agent Interaction* (2014), 173–176. http://dl.acm.org/citation.cfm?id=2658915

3. Ginevra Castellano, Ruth Aylett, Kerstin Dautenhahn, Ana Paiva, Peter W McOwan, and Steve Ho. 2008. Long-term affect sensitive and socially interactive companions. In *Proceedings of the 4th International Workshop on Human-Computer Conversation*. Citeseer.

4. Stephen J. Ceci and Maggie Bruck. 1993. Suggestibility of the child witness: a historical review and synthesis. *Psychological bulletin* 113, 3 (1993), 403. DOI: http://dx.doi.org/10.1037//0033-2909.113.3.403

5. Tina Ganster, Sabrina C Eimler, AM von der Pütten, Laura Hoffmann, and Nicole C Krämer. 2010. *Methodological considerations for long-term experience with robots and agents.*

6. Rachel Gockley and Allison Bruce. 2005. Designing robots for long-term social interaction. *International Conference on Intelligent Robots and Systems* (2005), 2199–2204.

7. Takayuki Kanda, Takayuki Hirano, Daniel Eaton, and Hiroshi Ishiguro. 2004. Interactive Robots As Social Partners and Peer Tutors for Children: A Field Trial. *Hum.-Comput. Interact.* 19, 1 (June 2004), 61–84. DOI: http://dx.doi.org/10.1207/s15327051hci1901&2_4

8. Andreas Kipp and Franz Kummert. 2014. Dynamic dialog system for human robot collaboration: playing a game of pairs. In *Proceedings of the second international conference on Human-agent interaction*. ACM, 225–228.

9. K.L. Koay, D.S. Syrdal, M.L. Walters, and K. Dautenhahn. 2007. Living with Robots: Investigating the Habituation Effect in Participants' Preferences During a Longitudinal Human-Robot Interaction Study. In *Robot and Human interactive Communication, 2007. RO-MAN 2007. The 16th IEEE International Symposium on.* 564–569. DOI: http://dx.doi.org/10.1109/ROMAN.2007.4415149

10. Iolanda Leite, Ginevra Castellano, André Pereira, Carlos Martinho, and Ana Paiva. 2014. Empathic Robots for Long-term Interaction. *International Journal of Social Robotics* (2014), 1–13. DOI: http://dx.doi.org/10.1007/s12369-014-0227-1

11. I. Lutkebohle, F. Hegel, S. Schulz, M. Hackel, B. Wrede, S. Wachsmuth, and G. Sagerer. 2010. The bielefeld anthropomorphic robot head Flobi. In *Robotics and Automation (ICRA), 2010 IEEE International Conference on.* 3384–3391. DOI: http://dx.doi.org/10.1109/ROBOT.2010.5509173

12. E. Short, J. Hart, M. Vu, and B. Scassellati. 2010. No fair!! An interaction with a cheating robot. In *Human-Robot Interaction (HRI), 2010 5th ACM/IEEE International Conference on.* 219–226. DOI: http://dx.doi.org/10.1109/HRI.2010.5453193

13. Daniel Ullman, Iolanda Leite, Jonathan Phillips, Julia Kim-Cohen, and Brian Scassellati. 2014. Smart human, smarter robot: How cheating affects perceptions of social agency. In *Proceedings of the 36th Annual Conference of the Cognitive Science Society (CogSci2014).*

14. Zhen-jia You, Chi-Yuh Shen, Chih-wei Chang, Baw-jhiune Liu, and Gwo-dong Chen. 2006. A Robot as a Teaching Assistant in an English Class. *Sixth IEEE International Conference on Advanced Learning Technologies (ICALT'06)* (July 2006), 87–91. DOI: http://dx.doi.org/10.1109/ICALT.2006.1652373

Children's Facial Expressions in Truthful and Deceptive Interactions with a Virtual Agent

Mariana Serras Pereira[1]   **Jolanda de Lange**[1]   **Suleman Shahid**[1,2]   **Marc Swerts**[1]

[1]Tilburg Centre for Cognition and Communication, Tilburg University
Tilburg, The Netherlands

[2]Department of Computer Science, Lahore University of Management Sciences, Lahore, Pakistan

m.serraspereira@uvt.nl   delange.jolanda@gmail.com   s.shahid@uvt.nl   m.g.j.swerts@uvt.nl

ABSTRACT

The present study focused on the facial expressions that children exhibit while they try to deceive a virtual agent. An interactive lie elicitation game was developed to record children's facial expressions during deceptive and truthful utterances, when doing the task alone or in the presence of peers. Based on manual annotations of their facial expressions, we found that children, while communicating with a virtual agent, produce different facial expressions in deceptive and truthful contexts. It seems that deceptive children try to cover their lie as they smile significantly more than truthful children. Moreover, co-presence enhances children's facial expressive behaviour and the amount of cues to deceit. Deceivers, especially when being together with a friend, more often press their lips, smile, blink and avert their gaze than truth-tellers.

Author Keywords

Child-virtual agent interaction; lying behaviour; nonverbal communication; facial expressions; children

ACM Classification Keywords

H.5.2. User Interfaces

INTRODUCTION

The interaction between children and socially intelligent agents (from robots to virtual agents) has gained significant attention over the past years. As a result, a number of research-driven solutions have emerged, ranging from the use of interactive animations to support families that have children under-go cancer treatment [6], to the development of applications that facilitate learning in classes, and can help autistic children in training their social and learning skills [e.g.14]. Given such specific goals, these social agents are designed to build relationships with children, and to bring an added value to their lives. Due to their social nature, they are becoming more widely used in our daily lives both in entertainment and more serious domains. However, this wide-ranging use raises the question regarding the nature of the relationship children can build with artificial partners, and on how much they trust and believe them. As a matter of fact, artificial deceptiveness [24], from the child to the robot, and vice versa, raises several concerns, in as far as social robots can influence the way children behave and see the world [12]. An interesting issue regards the extent to which children feel an addressee can judge the child's mental state, and whether they perceive a difference in that respect between human and artificial partners.

Whereas a significant amount of work has been focusing on child-robot interaction [12], child-virtual agent interaction have received far less attention. Particularly, it is yet unclear whether results obtained from studies with robots would generalize to virtual agents as well, especially when it comes to the way children trust and believe in these agents. Related to the question of trust and belief, a previous study [11] showed that children lie as often to robots, such as a humanoid and robot dog as they do to a human partner, yet there were also specific differences, depending on the type of interaction. In particular, children were more talkative towards the robots (a robot dog and a humanoid) than when interacting with a human. And, children appeared happier when they were interacting with the robot dog compared to the humanoid or human partner. This suggests that children's communicative style, and thus also the extent to which they are able or tend to deceive, can be affected by the kind of artificial partner they interact with. Those differences may well relate to the degree in which children's Theory of Mind (ToM), i.e., the capacity to attribute mental states to another individual, and to recognize the existence of different perspectives (mine and the other perspective), varies as a function of the type of artificial communication partner, and the channel that it is used to communicate. For instance, a previous study [5] showed that children attempted more often at reciprocity with a AIBO robot-dog and showed more apprehensive behaviour than when interacting with a stuffed dog, in which more mistreating behaviours and animation attempts were performed. In the earlier study mentioned above [11], in which Lego robots with different shapes (humanoid and robot dog) were used, the artificial partner had a physical presence in face-to-face interaction, even though these Lego

HAI '16, October 04-07, 2016, Biopolis, Singapore
© 2016 ACM. ISBN 978-1-4503-4508-8/16/10...$15.00
DOI: http://dx.doi.org/10.1145/2974804.2974815

robots were more constrained in the interaction with children, and therefore less interactive. Since virtual agents are being used in many different interactive applications, (mobile and desktop), in which they are represented both as the main source of gameplay (e.g. talking tom - https://talkingtomandfriends.com) and as facilitators (e. g. 3d characters that help students in learning [7]), an interesting question worth to be explored is if children behave similar as they did towards the robots, when trying to deceive virtual agents, that are more expressive in their communication style (even when the interaction is mediated by a screen), and how this compares to deceptive interactions with a human partner.

Moreover, there are only a few studies that focus on children's nonverbal behaviour during deceit in the presence of other children [e.g. 22]. This is particularly surprising because lying is a social behaviour that often occurs in the presence of more than one social partner. Imagine the occurrence of lies in everyday life, when siblings or friends lie together in order to avoid punishment for inappropriate deeds. Furthermore, learning to lie is an essential step as normative behaviour in children's development, but at the same time raises certain moral concerns because it can have, occasionally, pervasive consequences [15]. This dual nature makes deception a very relevant behaviour to be explored in several different research areas, ranging from development areas to human-computer interaction field, particularly for virtual games since deception often occurs in these settings, or is often a necessary behaviour in a game.

Therefore, the present study not only studies children's facial cues, while lying to a virtual agent but also investigates whether such cues are affected by differences in the social context, i.e., whether or not a child is alone or co-present with another. In the following, we first describe previous studies regarding children and virtual agents, then discuss children's facial cues to deception, then review previous findings about deception and co-presence. Finally we embark on our study where we first discuss in detail the lie elicitation paradigm, then the newly developed coding scheme to analyze the facial expressions. We then present our results, and end by reflecting on these and presenting future lines of research.

RELATED WORK

Children and virtual agents

On-going research has been focusing on developing virtual agents that interact and communicate with humans in a realistic way, i.e. that have communicative patterns similar to the ones that humans use in daily life. One user group that has a potential to gain wide range of benefits from the design of such agents is children. For instance, there are several situations of daily life where children face higher levels of anxiety and stress, in which the interaction with virtual agents could be beneficial. These situations are very wide, ranging from communication difficulties, such as

learning and tests at school, to more problematic behaviours, such as lying and bullying. As far as teaching and learning situations are concerned, significant work has been done to support children in these domains. For example, the TAPA (training with animated pedagogical agents) system [7] was developed for children with cognitive impairments. In this system, the virtual agents are able to express several emotional behaviours (that are based on the children's psycho-physiological arousal measured by skin conductance) with the aim to support and influence the children's motivation during the learning process. Other applications are teachable agents [8] to teach arithmetic concepts and reasoning to children. In fact, results show that students that used teachable agents had a significant learning gained compared to children that used traditional methods for learning. Additionally, virtual agents have also been exploited in different fields of research. For example, a study [10] explored how immersive virtual environment technology (IVET) elicits false memories in children, i.e., how memory was affected by visualizing dynamic avatars performing original actions. Results show that IVET can be a powerful method for eliciting false memories in elementary children. Based on the above, it seems that virtual agents can easily engage children in different type of interactions. It is particularly interesting that virtual agents are able to elicit false memories in children, especially as these by their very nature seem to be (often) linked to lies. In fact, a previous study [20] found that children lie-tellers had higher scores on false beliefs tasks than truth-tellers. Therefore, the current study focuses on children's lying behaviour towards virtual agents. In particular, the purpose of this study is twofold - on the one hand, we aim to explore if virtual agents are also able to elicit lies among children, and if these agents are also viewed as trustworthy partners; and on the other hand, we would like to investigate how children interact with these agents in such playful settings. This is relevant to further understand children's ToM towards social agents, and how to use these conceptions when designing adaptable agents that support children's daily life, but also to bring further light on child-virtual agent interaction.

Children's facial cues to deception

Research into children's facial expressions of deception shows that young liars, just as adults do, often attempt to control their facial expressions in order to cover their lies [19]. Nevertheless, children are not yet fully skilled lie-tellers and they tend to leak more nonverbal cues to their deceit than adults [17]. Research shows that children's facial expressions may cue deception, and there appear to be systematic differences between young lie- and truth-tellers, though results are not always consistent. For instance, according to a study [18] in which children's facial expressions were examined during a deceptive statement, children smile more when they lie than when they tell the truth. Big smiles as well as slight smiles are shown more often by lie-tellers. Moreover, another study [19] found that white lie-tellers who receive an undesirable gift smile more than children who receive a desirable gift in order to convince people that they actually like the gift. Additionally, research also shows that lie-tellers press their lips more often than truth-tellers [17]. Moreover, existing research also focused on children's eye gazing behaviour during deception. Specifically, it was found that child deceivers looked significantly more often away or down in comparison with truth-tellers [18]. This was confirmed by [11], albeit that children who lied looked significantly more upward, and not downward during their lie-tell. Interestingly, differences in eye gazing were only significant until the age of nine years old [11]. In addition, the amount of cues to deception probably decreases with age, when children become better lie-tellers [18]. A previous study [22] speculated that deceptive cues of younger children thrive from hard thinking and nervousness, whereas older children show signs of attempted behavioral control. Another variable that affects nonverbal expressive behaviour of children is co-presence [21], i.e., children's behaviour is affected by the presence of other person and/ or peer in the same situation, and the way that they interact (with each other) is also a factor of influence.

Deception and co-presence

With regard to the evidence that lying is a social behaviour that often arouses positive facial expressions in children, one may expect that this arousal will increase in co-presence of a peer. If this is the case, children who are together with a peer probably express more positive facial cues during deception than individuals. However, to date, only a few studies focused on the link between deceptive behaviour and co-presence [3,4,13,14,21]. For instance, a study [13] examined adults ability to distinguish pairs of truthful and deceptive children. Children were interviewed about a real or an imagery encounter with a stranger. Results showed that in general the overall accuracy was higher (62.5%) than the chance level (50%). Moreover, lie detection accuracy was greater when watching both pair children simultaneously than when watching one child at the time. In a similar vein, another study [14] investigated the extent to which co-presence had an impact on a child's ability to deceive. Truthful and deceptive utterances were elicited from children during an experimental digital game, in which the children had to interact with two story characters, during an alone or co-presence situation (with a peer). Results from a perception study, in which minimal pairs of truthful and deceptive utterances from these children were shown to human judges, showed the number of accurate detections was higher in the paired condition (60.6% accuracy) than in the individual condition (58% accuracy). Another study [21] investigated the extent to which pairs are verbally consistent in their testimonies of experienced and imagined events. The verbal consistency of pairs was significantly higher when children told statements

about a real event, compared to statements about an imagined event. Other study investigated children's nonverbal behaviour during a white lie telling in the presence and absence of an experimenter [19]. In this case, children showed significantly more positive nonverbal behaviour, such as smiling, in the presence of the experimenter after they received an undesired gift. Finally, the origin of blue lies, i.e., the ability to lie to benefit the group/collective was also examined in children [3]. In this study, children between 9-11 years old were placed in a real time situation in which they could decide to lie in order to conceal the group's cheating behaviour. Results showed that not only children tended to endorse more lies, but also lied more to protect the group as aged increased. In short, it seems that co-presence can play a significant role in the way children express deception. However, little is known how this is expressed during interactions with socially intelligent agents. Therefore, it seems relevant to explore how children express deception in co-presence towards virtual agents.

Present Study

The present study aims to explore children's lying behaviour towards virtual agents by using a lie elicitation virtual agent paradigm. In particular, facial expressions are examined during deceptive and truthful utterances, and between paired and individual children to learn more about the effect of co-presence in relation to lying behaviour towards a virtual agent.

METHOD

Lie Elicitation Paradigm

First of all, in order to study children's deceptive facial expressions towards a virtual agent, a child friendly elicitation game called 'Princess Lilly in Space' was developed using the GoAnimate (https://goanimate.com). In this elicitation game, children were invited to help a virtual agent (a princess called Lilly) by deceiving an evil astronaut (another virtual agent) who wanted to take over her spaceship. The game started with a warming-up task and an introduction to make the children familiar with the experimental procedure. In the warming-up task, children had to call princess Lilly to make contact with the spaceship and subsequently princess Lilly reacted with the sentence *'O hey, hey, we are in contact now'* after which she asked for the name/names of the children. Next, princess Lilly reacted with the sentence *'that is/are (a) pretty name(s)'*, *'I hope I will see you soon'* and disappeared. Then, the evil spaceman introduced himself when entering the spaceship. Subsequently, a narrator explained the story plot and described the characters in more detail. The narrating voice introduced the story as a fairy-tale plot, i.e., the narrator explained that there was an evil astronaut that wanted to take princess Lilly's spaceship. The narrator asked the children to help Princess Lilly, and told them that if they were successful in this task the children would get a reward (stickers).

The idea to create a fairy tale plot was an attempt to persuade children to engage in a friendly way on the task. After the omniscient narrator explained the story, the game started and princess Lilly asked the children to help her by deceiving the evil astronaut.

Figure 1. Different scenes of the elicitation game 'Princess Lilly in space'

She asked the children to tell the evil astronaut that she hid behind door one or door two, while in reality she ran further and hid somewhere else (i.e. *'When he comes, will you say that I am hiding behind door one in the control chamber or door two in the engine room?'*). After princess Lilly had rushed away, the evil astronaut appeared and asked where the princess was hiding (i.e. *'Will you tell me where she is?'*). This way, the children were given three options: deceive the astronaut by telling that princess Lilly hid behind door one in the control chamber (i.e. deceptive condition 1a), or deceive the astronaut by telling that princess Lilly hid behind door two in the engine room (i.e. deceptive condition 1b), or tell honestly that princess Lilly ran further and hid somewhere else (i.e. alternative condition). This way, children had to make a conscious decision about whether or not to deceive the evil astronaut. In addition, the children had to think about their lie, because they had to choose between one of the two doors. When children told the truth (i.e. alternative condition) the game ended and the evil astronaut took over the spaceship. If they chose to deceive the astronaut, the evil astronaut asked the children where princess Lilly went. After the children answered, the evil astronaut asked: "You are not fooling me, are you?" in order to provoke an extra deceptive statement. And after this, the evil astronaut went way. Then, princess Lilly came back and asked the children what they had told the evil astronaut (i.e. truthful condition). In this way, the game elicited a deceptive and a truthful utterance from paired and individual children. At the end of the game, the princess thanked the children for their help and the narrator explained that the children did very well and deserved the reward that was promised at the beginning of the game. Figure 1 provides a visualization of three different scenes of the elicitation game.

Participants

48 participants, 18 children (8 boys and 10 girls) in the individual condition and 30 children (16 boys and 14 girls) in the paired condition, in the age of 5 to 7 years old ($M=$ 6.05), participated in this study. The participants were recruited from group 3 of an elementary school in The Netherlands. Consent forms were collected among all the children's parents.

Procedure

Prior to the experiment, children were randomly assigned to the paired or individual condition. This way gender was divided at random, which means that the paired condition consisted of equal (i.e. two boys or two girls) and unequal (i.e. one boy and one girl) genders. Each experiment lasted approximately seven to ten minutes and consisted of a briefing, warming-up, the actual game and a debriefing. At the beginning of the experiment, children were welcomed by the experimenter and asked to step on a cross on the ground in front of a television screen that displayed the elicitation game. Pairs were asked to share the cross and stand next to each other, while individuals were asked to stand alone on the cross.

Materials

The elicitation game was presented in front of the children on a Philips HD television screen that was connected to a MacBook Air. In addition, two Panasonic Full HD cameras were positioned on tripods in front of the child/children next to the television, which recorded full body images of the children during the game. Paired children were recorded together simultaneously in one shot.

RESULTS

The facial expressions that children exhibited during deceptive and truthful utterances were manually coded. The durations (in milliseconds) and type of the facial expressions were annotated on the basis of a coding scheme, that was based on existing literature in combination with FACS [2]. The coding scheme consisted of five facial expressions - gaze aversion, blink, big smile, smile and pressed lips, that seem to be the strongest predictors of deception [e.g.4]. Figure 2 shows a visualization of some of the facial expressions that were used for the analysis. The durations of this facial expressions were coded for each child in both type of statements (i.e. deceptive and truthful statements) separately, and also for each individual child in the paired condition. In order to increase the reliability of the coding process, a second coder who was unfamiliar with the experiment coded also 30 of the 48 clips (15 clips in the individual and 15 clips in the paired condition). The intercoder agreement for the categorizations was assessed with Cohen's Kappa and yielded a reliable agreement between the coders ($k = .83$). It should be noted that pairs received an adjusted average score in order to compare the

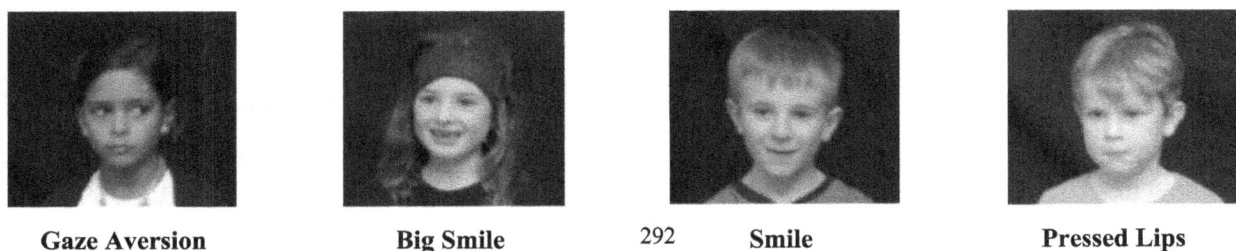

| Gaze Aversion | Big Smile | 292 | Smile | Pressed Lips |

Figure 2. Most important facial expressions related to deceit according to previous research, exhibited during the elicitation game

amount of facial expressions exhibited in the paired condition with the amount of facial expressions exhibited in the individual condition. The durations of the expressions exhibited by pairs (i.e. two individuals) were added and divided by two (i.e. averaged) for each facial expression separately.

A Factorial ANOVA with Repeated Measures was conducted in order to analyze the differences in positive nonverbal cues (i.e., smiles) between truth-tellers and deceivers, and to analyze whether paired deceivers showed more of these cues (i.e. smiles) than individual deceivers. Results showed a significant main effect for deception ($F(1, 31) = 13.895$, $p = .001$, $\eta^2 = 31$). As predicted, children smiled more in the deceptive condition ($M = 3892.5$, $SD = 4469.6$) compared to the truthful condition ($M = 1533.5$, $SD = 1926.1$). In addition, there was a significant interaction effect between deception and co-presence ($F(1, 31) = 6.432$, $p = .016$, $\eta^2 = .17$). Paired children ($M = 5921.9$, SD $= 5826.2$) smiled significantly more than individual children ($M = 2201.2$, $SD = 1728.6$) in the deceptive condition.

In addition, in order to see if children who are in co-presence of a peer show more facial expressions than individuals, a Mann-Whitney U Test was performed. The reason for using this test was related with the fact that inspection showed that some children exhibited hardly any facial expression, while other children were very expressive. Results showed that the exhibition of facial

Moreover, a Factorial ANOVA with Repeated Measures was used to investigate the five facial expressions (gaze aversion, blink, big smile, smile and pressed lips) with regard to deception in co-presence. Results are described in table 1. In particular, the results showed a significant main effect for deception on the durations of gaze aversion ($F(1, 31) = 14.496$, $p = .001$, $\eta^2 = .32$). Children averted their gaze significant longer in the deceptive condition ($M = 2565.38$, $SD = 3318.7$) compared to the truthful condition ($M = 902.42$, $SD =1681.5$). In addition, there was a significant interaction effect between deception and co-presence for gaze aversion ($F(1, 31) = 5.98$, $p = .02$, $\eta^2 = .16$). Pairs ($M = 3251.17$, $SD = 3510.22$) averted their gaze longer than individuals ($M = 1993.89$, $SD = 3134.29$) in the deceptive condition, but shorter ($M = 351$, $SD = 568.92$) than individuals ($M = 1361.94$, $SD = 2136.31$) in the truthful condition. The effect of co-presence itself was not significant ($F <1$).

Regarding blink, results showed a significant main effect of deceit for the number of times that children blinked ($F(1, 31) = 15.49$, $p < .001$, $\eta^2 = .33$). The number of blinks was significantly higher in the deceptive condition ($M = 2.23$, $SD = 1.87$) than in the truthful condition ($M = 1.15$, $SD = .91$). However, the effect of co-presence was not significant, neither the interaction effect between the amount of blinks and co-presence ($F <1$.) In respect to big smiles, results showed a significant main effect of deceit for the exhibition of big smiles ($F(1, 31) = 6.24$, $p = .02$, $\eta^2 =$

Facial Expressions	Deception		Co-presence		Deception*Co-presence	
	$F (1,31)$	η^2	$F (1,31)$	η^2	$F (1,31)$	η^2
Gaze Aversion	14.496 **	.32	.025	.001	5.98*	.16
Blink	15.49 ***	.33	.286	.009	.911	.03
Big Smile	6.24*	.17	2.80	.083	4.91*	.14
Smile	20.29 ***	.39	2.82	.083	2.45	.07
Pressed Lips	17.24 ***	.36	7.02	.185*	3.02	.09

* $p< .05$ ** $p = .001$ *** $p< .001$

Table 1. Results of the five facial expressions with regard to deception in co-presence

expression (in milliseconds) was higher for deceivers in the paired condition than deceivers in the individual condition. This difference due to co-presence was significant ($U = 202$, $z = 2.422$, $p = .015$), and represented a medium-sized effect ($r = .42$). Participants in the paired condition showed significantly more expressive facial cues ($Mdn= 15561$) than individuals ($Mdn= 5988.5$).

.17). Children exhibited significantly more big smiles in the deceptive condition ($M = 2484.24$, $SD = 4131.37$) than in the truthful condition ($M = 1059.61$, $SD = 1980.16$). In addition, there was a significant interaction effect between deception and co-presence for the durations of big smiles ($F(1, 31) = 4.91$, $p = .03$, $\eta^2 = .14$). In the deceptive condition the average duration that children exhibited big smiles was significantly higher for children who participated in pairs ($M = 4053.67$, $SD = 1014.36$) than for children who participated individually ($M = 1176.39$, $SD = 925.98$). However, there was no difference between paired and individual children in the truthful condition. There was also no significant effect of co-presence ($F<1$). The results also showed a significant main effect of deceit for the exhibition of smiles ($F(1, 31) = 20.29$, $p <. 001$, $\eta^2 = .39$). The durations that children exhibited smiles are significantly longer in the deceptive condition ($M = 1408.21$, $SD = 1442.21$), compared to the truthful condition ($M = 473.86$, $SD = 534.64$). There was no significant effect of co-presence ($F(1, 31) = 2.822$, $p = 1.03$, $\eta^2 = .08$), and no significant interaction effect between deception and co-presence for slight smiles ($F<1$).

A significant main effect of deceit for the exhibition of pressed lips was also found ($F(1, 31) = 17.24$, $p < .001$, $\eta^2 = .36$). Children pressed their lips significantly more in the deceptive condition ($M = 917.35$, $SD = 1149.82$) than in the truthful condition ($M = 214.02$, $SD = 339.61$). In addition, there was a significant main effect of co-presence for pressed lips ($F(1, 31) = 7.015$, $p = .013$, $\eta^2 = .19$). In the paired condition ($M = 876.17$, $SD = 144.89$) children pressed their lips significantly more than in the individual condition ($M = 306.94$, $SD = 144,89$). However, there was no interaction effect between deception and co-presence for the exhibition of pressed lips ($F<1$).

Finally, the results also show in general large values of standard deviations in terms of positive nonverbal cues and facial expressions, which indicates not only a variability between children's nonverbal behaviour, but also that level of expressiveness (i.e. the duration and the amount of facial expressions that one uses) is also child dependent.

DISCUSSION

The present work has led to several interesting new insights with respect to children's lying behaviour towards virtual agents. To the best of our knowledge, this is the first study that focused on children's lying behaviour towards virtual agents. As these agents are designed and used to interact more and more with children (e.g. in games or learning tasks), it is important to understand how children interact with them, if they consider them believable in order to lie to them. Furthermore, to date only little was known about the nonverbal facial cues that children exhibit during deception in co-presence. Virtual agents, as a part of the newly developed child-friendly elicitation game, were able to effectively elicit deceptive and truthful statements in paired and individual children. In addition, the elicitation game provided the ability to examine children's facial expressions in within-subject comparisons (i.e. for each child separately) and reduce the effects of individual differences between participants. This is of great importance, because individual differences can affect ones nonverbal expressive behaviour.

First of all, all children were able to lie to the virtual agent (evil astronaut), which seems to indicate that the story plot was reliable enough to engage children on the game, since all children were willing to lie to win the game, and to help Princess Lilly. This result goes in line with a previous study [11] that showed that children can easily lie to humanoids and robot-dogs, like they do to their human partners. Additionally, this study shows that virtual agents can be a valuable tool to elicit children's lying behaviour, which is in line with expectations based on previous research [10] that stated that false beliefs can be elicited by virtual agents in children. Furthermore, because children were able to lie to the virtual agent, and were able to keep their lie consistent through the entire game, it can be argued that these children exhibited similar ToM when interacting with virtual agents as they do when communicating with a human partner. This means that children also attribute mental states to virtual agents, which supports claims of a previous study [16] that showed that in order to successfully lie in human-human communication, children first need to understand their own mental state, and simultaneously the mental state of the communication partner to whom they are lying (first order belief), and at the same time they also need to keep semantic control over the lie tell (second order belief). This can be particularly valuable since the kind of technology investigated here is becoming part of children's daily life, and should be taken into account when designing virtual agents that will interact with children for different purposes, such as games that deal with problematic social behaviours and can involve lies, such as bullying.

Secondly, the outcomes of the children's facial expressions analysis show that children exhibited more positive facial expressions (i.e. smiles) during deceptive than truthful statements. This finding is in line with the results of several earlier studies that argue that deceptive children express more positive facial cues in order to cover their deceit [18,19]. Moreover, paired deceivers smiled more than individual deceivers. However, this difference caused by co-presence does not apply for truthful children. A possible explanation for this effect is that co-presence during deceit in a playful interaction with a virtual agent elicits excitation, and children become extra motivated in their attempt to hide their lie in co-presence of a peer, which goes in line with the excitation inhibition theory [23]. This would explain why co-presence only affected smiling in the deceptive condition and pairs did not smile more than individuals in the truthful condition. In addition, the results also showed that paired children generally exhibit more facial cues (i.e. are more expressive) than individuals. Possibly, children increase their expressive behaviour to surpass the presence of a peer [23]. This seems very relevant for the design of game environments, in which virtual agents need to adapt according to the goal and behaviour of the children. Think about cooperative and competition games, in which the way children express themselves and interact with each other, can be affected by the goal of the game. Finally, the analysis also shows that several facial expressions are specifically associated with deceit. Gaze aversion, blinks, big smiles, smiles and pressed lips were exhibited significantly more by deceivers than by truth-tellers. These facial expressions are also distinguished by several prior studies [1,18,19]. Therefore, the results of the present study corroborate the outcomes of earlier research, and show that when children deceit a virtual agent, they also exhibit similar facial cues to the human-human interaction. With regard to gaze aversion, it is possible that the increase of gaze aversions during deceit has to do with confirmation seeking. It seems that some children averted their gaze to rectify their lie and wondered if they were doing well. Additionally, deceivers also avert their gaze more in co-presence of a peer. Earlier studies also indicate that children avert their gaze more while they lie [e.g. 25]. This result seems very relevant for the design of adaptable virtual agents. Having virtual agents that are able to interpret and adapt their behaviour accordingly to children's gaze patterns can improve dramatically the level of communication. For instance, it can be a valuable insight when designing adaptable agents for persuasive games. Moreover, children blinked more during their deceptive attempt than during their truthful utterance. With regard to this finding it should be noted that the majority of the children needed more time for their deceptive statement than for their truthful statement. Earlier research [21] also indicates that it is easier to talk about an event that actually happened than an imagined event. The cognitive load that deception requires possibly explains the time difference, because children have to build up their lie. Hence, it is uncertain whether the increased number of blinks in the deceptive condition can be attributed to deception or possibly be explained by the average length of the deceptive statement. Although the results are not fully explained, blink rate can also be a relevant cue for virtual agents, particularly when designing adaptable agents for teaching and learning support, since like deception learning also involves more cognitive load, and that can be a valuable cue to measure the level of children's cognitive overload during learning activities. Furthermore, in line with prior studies, deceivers press their lips more often than truth-tellers [19]. This result corroborates earlier studies, which explain an unpleasant mouth expression as an attempt of the deceiver to avoid giving away cues to deceit [17]. Perhaps children feel uncomfortable with telling a lie and the unpleasant mouth expression (i.e. pressed lips) is a sign of the child's actual emotional state during the deceptive utterance. Moreover, the exhibition of pressed lips is also found to be a sign of deception in adults [1]. In sum, these results are very relevant when designing adaptable agents, i.e., when designing virtual agents that adapt and transform their behaviour according to real-time interaction. Designing virtual agents that are able to reliably interpret these cues, such as gaze aversion, pressed lips, smiles, can improve dramatically the level of interaction, and possible uses.

CONCLUSION

On the whole, the present study focused on children's facial expressions that were exhibited during truthful and deceptive interactions with a virtual agent. An interactive lie elicitation game was developed to record children's facial expressions during deceptive and truthful utterances, in an individual or co-presence situation. This study provides new and interesting insights regarding children's lying behaviour towards virtual agents. More specifically, it adds to our understanding of how children interact while lying to these entities, and how this compares with humans, and how these agents are represented in terms of children's ToM. Furthermore, the findings clearly show that virtual agents can be used for lie elicitation with children. Finally, this study also provides new and interesting insights with regard to co-presence in relation to deceit. In short, results show that the facial expressive behaviour of deceivers and truth-tellers differs significantly, and co-presence affects children's deceptive behaviour. Co-presence increased the exhibition of smiling and gaze aversion, which is very interesting with respect to the ability to recognize deception among accompanied children in the future. In future studies it seems useful to explore the cue validity of these nonverbal cues, not only for (automatic) lie detection, but also for the design of adaptable virtual agents that support children's daily tasks, such as persuasive games for behaviour change.

ACKNOWLEDGMENTS

We would like to thank all the children, parents and staff of the elementary school Het Schrijverke in The Netherlands.

REFERENCES

1. Bella M. DePaulo, James J. Lindsay, Brian E. Malone, Laura Muhlenbruck, Kelly Charlton, and Harris Cooper. 2003. Cues to deception. *Psychological Bulletin* 129, 1: 74–118. http://doi.org/10.1037/0033-2909.129.1.74

2. Wallace Ekman, Paul□; Friesen. 1976. Measu ring Facial Movement *. *Environmental Psychology and Nonverbal Behaviour* 1, 1: 56–75.

3. Genyue Fu, Angela D Evans, Lingfeng Wang, and Kang Lee. 2008. Lying in the name of the collective good: a developmental study. *Developmental Science* 11, 4: 495–503. http://doi.org/10.1111/j.1467-7687.2008.00695.x.Lying

4. Genyue Fu, Angela D Evans, Fen Xu, and Kang Lee. 2012. Young children can tell strategic lies after committing a transgression. *Journal of experimental child psychology* 113, 1: 147–58. http://doi.org/10.1016/j.jecp.2012.04.003

5. Peter H. Kahn, Jr., Batya Friedman, Deanne R. Pérez-Granados, and Nathan G. Freier. 2006. Robotic pets in the lives of preschool children. *Interaction Studies* 7: 405–436. http://doi.org/10.1075/is.7.3.13kah

6. Stacy Marsella, Lewis Johnson, and Catherine Labore.

2000. Interactive pedagogical drama. *AGENTS '00: Proceedings of the fourth international conference on Autonomous agents*: 301–308. http://doi.org/10.1145/336595.337507

7. Yehya Mohamad, Carlos A Velasco, Sylvia Damm, and Holger Tebarth. 2004. Cognitive Training with Animated Pedagogical Agents (TAPA) in Children with Learning Disabilities. *Computers Helping People with Special Needs*: 629. Retrieved from http://www.springerlink.com/content/y3yt4flv75bmlyk6

8. Lena Pareto. 2014. A teachable agent game engaging primary school children to learn arithmetic concepts and reasoning. *International Journal of Artificial Intelligence in Education* 24, 3: 251–283. http://doi.org/10.1007/s40593-014-0018-8

9. Chandra Reka Ramachandiran, Nazean Jomhari, Shamala Thiyagaraja, and Malissa Maria. 2015. Virtual reality based behavioural learning for autistic children. *Electronic Journal of e-Learning* 13, 5: 357–365.

10. Kathryn Y. Segovia and Jeremy N. Bailenson. 2009. Virtually True: Children's Acquisition of False Memories in Virtual Reality. *Media Psychology* 12, 4: 371–393. http://doi.org/10.1080/15213260903287267

11. Mariana Serras Pereira, Yoeri Nijs, Suleman Shahid, and Marc Swerts. 2009. C hildren ' s lying behaviour in interactions with personified robots. *In press.*

12. Rachel L. Severson and Stephanie M. Carlson. 2010. Behaving as or behaving as if? Children's conceptions of personified robots and the emergence of a new ontological category. *Neural Networks* 23, 8-9: 1099–1103. http://doi.org/10.1016/j.neunet.2010.08.014

13. Leif A. Strömwall and P??r Anders Granhag. 2007. Detecting deceit in Pairs of children. *Journal of Applied Social Psychology* 37, 6: 1285–1304. http://doi.org/10.1111/j.1559-1816.2007.00213.x

14. Marc Swerts. 2012. Let's lie together: Co-presence effects on children's deceptive skills. *Proceedings of the EACL workshop on computational approaches to deception detection*, E. Fitzpatrick, B. Bachenko, & T. Fornaciari (Eds.), 55–62.

15. Victoria Talwar and Angela Crossman. 2011. From little white lies to filthy liars. The evolution of honesty and deception in young children. In *Advances in Child Development and Behavior* (1st ed.). Elsevier Inc., 139–141. http://doi.org/10.1016/B978-0-12-386491-8.00004-9

16. Victoria Talwar, Heide M. Gordon, and Lee Kang. 2007. Lying in the Elementary School Years: Verbal Deception and Its Relation to Second-Order Belief Understanding Victoria. *Developmental psychology* 43, 3: 804–810. http://doi.org/10.1037/0012-1649.43.3.804

17. Victoria Talwar and Kang Lee. 2002. Emergence of White-Lie Telling in Children Between 3 and 7 Years of Age. *Merrill-Palmer Quarterly* 48, 2: 160–181. http://doi.org/10.1353/mpq.2002.0009

18. Victoria Talwar and Kang Lee. 2002. Development of lying to conceal a transgression: Children's control of expressive behaviour during verbal deception. *International Journal of Behavioral Development* 26, 5: 436–444. http://doi.org/10.1080/01650250143000373

19. Victoria Talwar, Susan M Murphy, and Kang Lee. 2007. White lie-telling in children for politeness purposes. *International Journal of Behavioral Development* 31, 1: 1–11. http://doi.org/10.1177/0165025406073530

20. Victoria Talwar, Lonnie Zwaigenbaum, Keith J. Goulden, Shazeee. Manji, Carly Loomes, and Carmen Rasmussen. 2012. Lie-Telling Behavior in Children With Autism and Its Relation to False-Belief Understanding. *Focus on Autism and Other Developmental Disabilities* 27, 2: 122–129. http://doi.org/10.1177/1088357612441828

21. Annelies Vredeveldt and Willem A. Wagenaar. 2013. Within-Pair Consistency in Child Witnesses: The Diagnostic Value of Telling the Same Story. *Applied Cognitive Psychology* 27, 3: 406–411. http://doi.org/10.1002/acp.2921

22. Aldert Vrij1. 2002. Deception in children: A literature review and implications for children's testimony. In *Children's Testimony: A Handbook of Psychological Research and Forensic Practice*, H.L. Westcott, G. M. Davies and R. H. C. Bull (eds.). John Wiley & Sons Ltd, 175–194. http://doi.org/10.1002/9780470713679.ch12

23. Hugh Wagner and Victoria Lee. 1999. Facial behavior alone and in the presence of others. In *The Social Context of Nonverbal Behavior*, & E.J. Coats P. Philippot, R.S. Feldman (ed.). New York: Cambridge University Press, New York, 262–286.

24. Jacqueline Kory Westlund, Cynthia Breazeal, and A Story. 2015. Deception , Secrets , Children , and Robots□: What ' s Acceptable□? *HRI 2015 Workshop.*

Understanding Behaviours and Roles for Social and Adaptive Robots In Education: Teacher's Perspective

Muneeb Imtiaz Ahmad
MARCS Institute
Western Sydney University,
Sydney, Australia
muneeb.ahmad@uws.edu.au

Omar Mubin
MARCS Institute
Western Sydney University,
Sydney, Australia
o.mubin@uws.edu.au

Joanne Orlando
School of Education
Western Sydney University,
Sydney, Australia
j.orlando@uws.edu.au

ABSTRACT

In order to establish a long-term relationship between a robot and a child, robots need to learn from the environment, adapt to specific user needs and display behaviours and roles accordingly. Literature shows that certain robot behaviours could negatively impact child's learning and performance [17]. Therefore, the purpose of the present study is to not only understand teacher's opinion on the existing effective social behaviours and roles but also to understand novel behaviours that can positively influence children performance in a language learning setting. In this paper, we present our results based on interviews conducted with 8 language teachers to get their opinion on how a robot can efficiently perform behaviour adaptation to influence learning and achieve long-term engagement. We also present results on future directions extracted from the interviews with teachers.

Author Keywords

Social and Adaptive Robots; Language learning; Children Robot Interaction; Long-term Engagement.

ACM Classification Keywords

H.5.m. Information Interfaces and Presentation (e.g. HCI): Miscellaneous

INTRODUCTION

In recent past years, research in Human-Robot Interaction (HRI) and Social Robotics (SR) has emphasised immensely on the need and benefits of social robots that can adapt to specific user needs. Researchers have conjectured these benefits through conducting a series of studies with non-adaptive robots. They have showed that due to the lack of flexibility of a non-adaptive robot in its response, specifically to the behaviour of humans. People tend to loose interest and the impact of such robots decreases with time [16]. Researchers have also pointed out benefits through both qualitative [10] and quantitative [29] evaluations.

Social Adaptive Robots (SARs) have been defined as autonomous robots/agents that can learn from a social environment and adapt to user behaviour accordingly. Therefore, in order to implement these SARs, it is important to understand what adaptable social behaviours and roles displayed by the robot are acceptable to humans in different domains and environments. Researchers have inferred that there is an uncertainty on what is meant by adaptive agent behaviour in different domains. They are trying to understand various appropriate adaptive behaviours that can lead towards efficient learning. Dautenhahn et. al,. [5] and Mahani et. al., [22] have conducted interviews with potential end users to derive social roles. However, we argue that interview answers were based on the hypothetical knowledge on robots. In literature, we also find general behaviours such as understanding and reacting to emotions, playing different social roles [9]. Researchers previously have tested these behaviours both quantitatively and qualitatively, however, recently, Huber and colleagues [14] have critiqued that social robots need to extend on the stereotypical role behaviours in order to achieve long-term acceptance. They followed different steps (application scenarios identification through Interviews, listing different adaptive roles through qualitative analysis, frequency of adaptive roles mentioned differently by elderly adults in home and care centres, classification of adaptive roles according to age and demography) to identify various adaptive behavioural roles for elder adults living at home or in care facilities.

We understand that the view of students is important in the pedagogical relationship between an embodied tutor and students. Obaid et. al., [25] conducted an exploratory study on children's contributions to the design of a robotic teaching assistant. He compared children and interaction design students design. He showed that robot designs are influenced by individuals knowledge of robots. Serholt et al., 2014 [30] has also interviewed students to get information on their attitudes towards the possible future of social robots in education. However, the role of teachers must not be underestimated. According to [2], it is described that the teachers play an integral role in how children learn using aids, devices in class and perceive information. Even though devices can function independently, the teacher must direct the flow of the session/curriculum. Therefore, HRI researchers have given importance to understanding the view of teachers on understanding the possible interactions for robots.

Researchers have also conducted studies through interviewing teachers at the schools in order to understand the acceptance and possible experimental methods for children robot interaction at schools. Serholt and colleagues [31] have conducted interviews with eight teachers from four different European countries on their views about the use of emphatic robotic tutors in the classrooms. They questioned teachers about the plausibility of using robots, what roles should a robot play, and what are the overall positives and negatives of having robots in education. They have found that robots can be a disruptive technology as it can be an extra administrative task to allocate personalised use of robots fairly among children. Teachers also pointed that in case a robot is programmed autonomously, it can be helpful in managing group work and can also promote independent learning. In addition, robots can also guide and motivate students through several learning tasks. As [25] showed previous knowledge had an effect on robotic designs, it can be argued that teachers responded to the questions based on the prior hypothetical knowledge of robots or on knowledge collected through science fiction movies. Therefore, some responses can be categorised as biased.

Most recently, Kory and colleagues [19] have shown results contrary to findings discussed by [31]. They have also argued that due to the hypothetical knowledge of teachers on social robots, their observations and opinions in some case were not supported. [19] deployed an autonomous Tega robot in the classroom for 2 months and then asked view of teachers. The Tega robot was not only capable of playing with a child but also administer curious children waiting for their turns. Results showed that teachers were pleasantly surprised with how non-disruptive the whole experience was and how much children were positively engaged with the robot. Keeping [19] study in view, we believe the next steps are to inquire teachers about behaviour and roles for adaptive robots through first enabling them to interact with the robot and understand its capabilities. In addition, we need to find appropriate behaviours for robots to help with language learning. In this paper, we present a study conducted with teachers from different schools in a urban city. The focus of our study is to understand about the most appropriate and effective children robot interactions in language learning education. In order to avoid the influence of prior knowledge of teachers on results, the teachers interacted with a humanoid robot and they were informed about all of its possible and probable capabilities. As discussed by [14], we also believe in order to implement adaptive robots to facilitate long-term engagement, it is very important to involve teachers to guide and help us design appropriate and effective behaviours for robots. In addition, recently, Kennedy and colleagues [17] showed that the robot who over tried negatively influenced child's learning. Therefore, we need to careful and should make informed decisions before implementing behaviour adaption strategies and features for social robots who are going to interact with children.

EDUCATIONAL ROBOTS FOR LANGUAGE LEARNING

The use of robots to help children in language education has attracted an enormous amount of attention globally. One of the reasons is that robots possessing an embodiment offer to play a variety of social roles that can help with learning. Researchers have recently used these agents to teach children

about science, mathematics, languages and robotics. [16] conducted a field trial with a humanoid robot, Robovie, as a partner to help children with English skills. [28] presented a supportive robotic tutor that was used to teach language learning in a game like a scenario. A tutoring application was made with iCat Robot that was used for vocabulary learning. [11] also used the robots in home-based setup to teach languages. They compared robots teaching languages to audiotapes and books and showed that robots performed better, primarily due to their physical characteristics. Children preferred learning with the robot as compared to audiotapes. [18] performed a story-telling activity with robots as learning partners with preschool childrens to encourage language development. They designed a robot capable of narrating a story. As the robot narrates the story, a corresponding scene appears on the iPad. The story narration has three levels of difficulties. The purpose of this game was to check if the child was able to learn new vocabulary during the interaction. The results showed that children were able to learn new nouns, verbs and adjective through the narration.

In general, the use of agents/robot to support learning is a known process. However, questions have been raised with respect to sustaining long-term task interest and engagement during human agent interaction after a certain amount of time [16]. Researchers [24] have pointed that programming these robots with adaptive behaviours could lead to the solution of the mentioned problem. We believe that in order to implement adaptive social robots, we need to understand appropriate and effective adaptive behaviours in different domains to overcome these problems.

RESEARCH QUESTION

Our research questions were twofold. Firstly, we tried to understand about the current teaching practises used at the schools and how a humanoid robot can contribute. Secondly, we intended to understand the perspective of teachers on both existing and novel adaptation behaviours and social roles a robot can portray during both individual and group Children Robot Interactions (cHRI) in the classroom for language learning purposes. We also wanted to understand the effect of these adaptions on child's learning and overall engagement.

METHOD

Participant

We interviewed teachers from both primary and high schools in an urban city, where the first language of communication was English. All of these teachers had training and experience in teaching languages including French, Italian and English. We selected language teachers because we intend to implement an adaptive social robot that can support children with language learning and development. Eight female teachers participated in the study. Out of eight teachers, we had four teachers each from both primary and high school. The average age-range of teachers was between 25 and 45. The interview sessions were held at the corresponding schools and lasted for 30 minutes each. All of the interviews followed the same procedure in both schools.

Procedure

We began our study by distributing information sheets and consent forms to the teachers. Once teachers have completed and returned their consent forms, we gave them an introduction about the scope of the project and inquired in case each of them had any questions.

The study was later conducted with teachers during one-to-one interactions. Each study session lasted for 30 minutes and had three different steps: 1) a 5-minute video (https://www.youtube.com/watch?v=ho9i1moUJos) on HRI and SR followed by a 3-minute video (https://www.youtube.com/watch?v=2STTNYNF41k) on NAO, 2) a 5-minute of interaction between teachers and NAO, 3) Interviews with teachers on how NAO can contribute towards language learning through adapting to children behaviours. The data collection was completed in two days. On the first day, we visited high school followed by our visit to the a primary school on the second day.

Firstly, we showed teachers a basic video on SR and HRI and NAO robot showing various capabilities such as gestures, object recognition, tactile sensors and speech recognition. We later asked teachers about possible confusions or questions on NAO and HRI in general. The purpose of showing these videos was to avoid an effect of previous and hypothetical knowledge about robots and also to overcome any fears that robots can takeover their jobs. Secondly, we asked teachers to interact with NAO in three different scenarios. In Scenario 1, teachers interacted with NAO to get familiar with its Speech Recognition capabilities. Teachers were asked to speak with NAO through asking the basic set of introductory questions such as: (*What is your name, How are you, How is your day progressing etc...*). Upon asking an unknown question, NAO repeated their question. In Scenario 2, teachers were able to interact with NAO through showing different emotions (*happy, sad, angry and neutral*) to understand about emotion detection capabilities. Teachers were asked to show emotions and NAO after detecting these emotions named the emotion. In Scenario 3, NAO showed different gestures (clapping, waving, bowing and dancing) upon teachers interactions. Teachers were asked to speak the gesture name to NAO and in response, NAO displayed the gesture. Lastly, we interviewed teachers in order to understand current practices followed by them at schools for language learning and how can NAO contribute towards enhancing child's learning. In addition, we asked teachers about their opinion on different adaptive behaviours and roles that a robot can display to influence child learning and long-term engagement.

Setup and Materials

We used NAO robot designed and developed by Aldebaran robotics. It is a humanoid robot measuring 58 cm in height. NAO is an interactive and adaptable robot partner. It provides researchers a platform to design various applications driven by their creativity and requirements.

We conducted our study in a quiet room at both primary and high schools during school time. We were provided with a small table and several chairs inside an empty classroom. The NAO robot was placed in a sitting position in front of the participant teacher in order to get a the clear view of the participant's face for detecting emotions. The researcher sat in front of the participant and was involved in showing videos on the notebook and conducting interviews. The NAO robot autonomously generated behaviours for three different scenarios: *Speech recognition, emotions detection and displaying gestures*. The setup is shown in figure 1. We took consent from the teacher to use their picture in our article.

Figure 1. Setup: A teacher interacting with NAO.

NAO Robot and implementation of Scenarios

The NAO robot was autonomously programmed to display three different capabilities: Speech Recognition, detecting emotions and displaying gestures.

We used *google* speech to text API [32] to convert teacher's speech to text. The NAO robot was programmed to respond according to basic questions of the teachers. The response ranged from introducing itself to greeting each other. It was also able to repeat sentences of the teachers.

We also trained data on basic human emotions (Happy, sad, angry and neutral). We programmed NAO to capture user facial expressions and detect their emotions through using an algorithm [8]. The algorithm uses openCV library to localise the mouth area to detect emotion of a user. The image captured by NAO is re-sized to 28*10 pixel containing only person's mouth and surrounding areas. The image is then converted into grey-scale and flattened into a vector of length 280. A logistical regression programme then takes the vector and determines the emotional state of the user.

We implemented state of the art existing behaviours in NAO robot in *Choregraphe*. The gestures included bowing, clapping, touching, whipping, hugging and dancing. The Choregraphe programme was later used to generate python code.

Interview Questionnaire

The questionnaires involved understanding different language learning strategies adopted by the teachers and how NAO can adopt these strategies and contribute towards efficient learning. In addition, what are the novel adaptive behaviours and roles NAO should play to prolong children robot engagement? We understand that it is important to ask these questions because the generated data will give us directions to implement novel scenario and behaviours for future robots in an effective and appropriate way. It was also important to enable teachers interact with one of the Humaniod robots (NAO) in order to develop their understanding on robot's current capabilities. The questionnaire was designed according

Language	Teacher
French	P7,P4
Italian	P5,P6,P3,P8
English	P1,P2

Table 1. Teachers and Corresponding Languages

to the existing characteristics of an adaptive social robot [9]. Other questions were used from [30]. The list of other questions from our interviews are:

I *What teaching approaches, resources and technologies do you use to teach oral and written language development?*

II *How do you think a robot can contribute towards efficient language learning?*

III *How do you want a robot to show different gestures during a one to one interaction?*

IV *How do you want a robot to display a personality according to a child?*

V *How do you want a robot to react to children emotions?*

VI *What kind of role a robot should play to improve learning?*

VII *How do you want a robot to store child's memory?*

VIII *How to ensure long-term engagement between NAO and a child?*

Data Analysis

All of the interviews were audio recorded after receiving consent from the teachers. We performed content analysis [6] to analyse interviews communication. One of the authors listened to and transcribed the interviews. The author then noted possible themes and patterns in teachers responses. These patterns were later used to define main themes and sub-themes for this paper. Quotes were selected from the relevant responses.

RESULTS

We present the main themes resulting from the qualitative analysis performed on the interviewed data. First, we present teachers views on how NAO robot can contribute towards child's language learning and development. Second, we present about the behavioural and role adaptation for NAO according to teachers in Language language. We also present sub-themes with respect to adaptation in teacher's perspective. Thirdly, we present teacher's opinion on how NAO can maintain long-term engagement. To keep the identities anonymous, primary school teachers are labelled with the range of 1 to 8, where P1, P2, P3, P4 are from the primary school while P5, P6, P7, and P8 are from high school. Table 1 shows the languages taught by the corresponding participants.

Robots and its Contributions towards language learning

Teachers pointed out the robots can help with vocabulary learning, grammar, and correcting pronunciation. They can also play games with children on language learning. The teachers also wanted children to practise their speaking skills with the robot. Some of the teachers reported:

We can possibly use a robot for word learning, comprehension and games based on questions and answers to motivate students to learn languages (P4).

The robot can speak a grammatically correct sentence and a child can repeat it (P2).

I think, the girls and the student will find it quite comfortable to interact with, they can practise their speaking skills (P6).

Teachers emphasised the benefits of programming robots that can help them with marking both objective and subjective assessments. They also referred to the benefit of having robots to fulfill drill types of tasks. For example, they stated that students usually keep asking same questions in the class. It can sometimes get frustrating for them but as the robot can repeat it as many times so it can be a great support in this regard.

Students normally ask same questions repeatedly, the robot can answer these questions in the classroom while I am working with other students (P8).

In addition, the teachers commented that it would be great if a robot can autonomously find learning material for them.

Robots with Gesture Adaptation

Teachers recognised gestures as one of the essential parts of language education. Robot depicting several appropriate gestures can be a handful and may lead towards efficient learning and engagement.

I am quite animated during my class. Gestures such as pointing, indicating, arm moments, bending, hands on heads works best with juniors (P5).

Teachers also mentioned a list of effective gestures to engage students in learning. It included: *pointing, arm moments, bending, hands on heads, greetings, hands up, hands down, use of finger to point the wrong answer, thumbs up, attention, listen please, finger going to the eye, saluting, throwing, dancing, and smiling.*

Teachers also mentioned that different gestures can be associated with different languages. They indicated that the gesture for greeting in the French language is different from other languages. The robot can have a different teaching style based on the language. One of the teachers was of the view that gestures can be culturally driven so if a robot needs to adapt accordingly. Cultural adaptation can also motivate child towards efficient learning.

We have a different way of saying good morning in french. We teach students regarding individual situations while teaching languages. The Robot can combine both gesture and speech capabilities to improve child's learning (P7).

Robots with Memory Adaptation

Teachers complemented memory adaptation as they stated in language learning recalling or remembering an experience can be a handful and can result in a positive effect on the child's learning. They also mentioned that memory can be used as a great tool to show extra care towards a child and a child can be amused as well as motivated towards learning. One of the teachers reported:

We can show extra care through recalling previous interactions. If this can be made possible, children will not do the same mistake over and over again. Children will be forced to think about new ways of adaptation (P3).

One of the teachers also reported that memory can be a great tool to test student's performance. She reported:

Robot with child's memory can a great idea. If a student was able to say a certain word after two weeks, the robot can later ask the same question in the next days. It can, therefore, judge the child and also encourage through providing positive reinforcement (P6).

Robots with Emotional Adaptation

All of the teachers acknowledged the importance of recognising emotions through facial expressions. However, they were worried that facial expressions are not the only way to recognise emotions because they are not the only identifier of a child's mood or emotional state. Teachers focused on the importance of detecting the emotional state of the child through dialogue. They proposed a set of conversations that a robot should have in order to realise on the emotional state of the child.

The use of facial expression to detect emotion is important, However, we need the robot to sense mood through dialogue. For example, if a child is bored, then it can provide positive reinforcement or if the robot can detect anger, it can play a calming role (P3).

One of the teachers was of the view that in case, a child is not in a good mood on a particular day due to some unavoidable experience, then the robot should be able to judge it and perform certain steps to overcome or change the emotional state of the child.

The dialogue-based mood detection is more important than facial expression. The robot should react non-judgement and should also try to get them through a list of procedures and calm them accordingly (P5).

Teachers informed that robots having feelings will improve engagement as children will not only consider robot as the toy, however, they were concerned that extensive emotional adaptation might intimidate children of a certain age.

Robots with emotions makes them real and makes the student realise that robot has feelings and it is a real interaction. The robot understanding emotion can be intimated depending on the age of the student (P7).

Adaptive Social Roles for Robots

Teachers pointed various roles for the robot that it can display and adapt during children robot interaction. Table 2 shows a taxonomy of the frequency of various roles that in view of all the teachers can be appropriate or misleading for children. We coded these frequencies from teacher's statement.

Roles	Teachers in favour
Assertive	4
Funny	8
Encouraging	8
Persuasive or Motivating	8
Bribing	1
Dominant	1
Submissive	1
Democratic	5
Cooperative	8
Assistant or a Helper	8
Buddy or a Friend	8
Competitive	8
Calm and Compassionate	8

Table 2. Roles for a Robot in Language Learning

In general, teachers informed that robots need to adapt different role for the different scenario. Most of them said that robot needs to encourage and motivate children through persuasive dialogue. They also said Robot needs to find a balance between a submissive and dominant role and should rather play a democratic role. One of the teachers, however, was also of the opinion that dominance is important in order to be taken seriously.

If a student is hesitant to do something, then Robot should be able to persuade him/her through positive reinforcement (P5).

Student would like the idea that the robot adapts and play a buddy role in the classroom. It can be a motivator for children to learn languages (P7).

Robot displaying a dominant role can be overwhelming for the child (P2).

All of the teachers pointed attention towards the use of a robot with a good sense of humour as learning a language can get boring at times. The robot needs to play funny roles in order to motivate children and keep them engaged during the learning process.

Robot needs to act funny and tell jokes to students, for example, when explaining the meaning of a word in a vocabulary learning exercise. This will keep the child engaged and motivated throughout the process.

Teachers considered calm and compassionate roles to be best suited for the case when the child is making repetitive mistakes. The robot needs to first recognise the repeated mistake and adapt through changing the dialogue or its tone in real time.

You need to play a calming or soothing role through the use of dialogue and gesture in order to motivate and help the child improve learning (P8).

Robots with Personality Adaptation

Teachers were of the opinion that it is not necessary to adapt according to the general definition of personality (extrovert or introvert) of the child. They commented that child's personality might vary on the day according to the set of events that might have happened during the school time. The robot, on the other hand, should be able to recognise child's personality through dialogue. Teachers reported as:

Personality adaptation through dialogue can be an efficient way, in a personalised interaction, personality can be a handful, for example, the robot needs to show patience in case of an introvert child (P5).

We need to detect the personality of the student, the personality can change over time so we need a mechanism to detect the personality. We can detect that through dialogue, for instance, we can detect hesitation then encourage the student through rewards or positive gestures (P6).

Teachers also directed towards finding the balance between an extrovert and introvert personality. A teacher reported:

A balance between an extrovert and introvert is required. Perhaps a more outgoing one as it would probably encourage more interaction (P1).

Robots for Long-term Engagement

Teachers expressed concerns about long-term engagement between children and the robot. They were certain that in order to achieve sustainable engagement, they should be equally involved in preparing robot interactions with the children. They were afraid that if teachers are not given control of the robot, it could very well happen that the robot stays alone at the corner in a classroom. In the words of one teacher:

If the teachers know how to control and use the robot, then we would be able to achieve long-term engagement (P5).

Another teacher pointed out that teacher should be provided with an interface that enables them to update or change lessons over the period of time.

Teachers can keep the robot involved, so that it not just at the corner and always in the loop, we need to use the robot as a part of a lesson (P6).

However, another teacher also mentioned that if there are a variety of programs and the systems updates itself and also adapts to a child's need, it would be possible to achieve long-term engagement.

You should have a variety of programs so that the robot is not doing the same thing over and over again. The robot should mimic what a human would do at a certain moment (P1).

DISCUSSION

In this study, we have learnt a number of lessons and take-aways for HRI researchers. The key lessons we learned about implementing adaptive social robots in language education, as reflected in the teacher's feedback are as follow:

1. The robot should be able to answer repeatedly asked questions in the classroom: There is a need to implement a mechanism in which a robot can respond to repeatedly asked questions during one-to-one or group interactions with children. In order to achieve it, we need to implement ways for a robot to perform memory adaptations. Chang and colleagues [3] have described various characteristics of robots that can be important during language learning. Repeatability was described as one of the most appropriate features for language education.

2. We need to design dialogue based adaptation mechanism in order to adapt to children emotions and personality in real-time: Human emotions and personality are correlated to each other. The current emotional state or mood of humans can influence the portrayal of personality . Therefore, as indicated by the teachers, it is significant to design and implement a real-time adaptation mechanism for a robot to detect user's personality based on its emotional state. Previous studies [13][23] have shown that if a robot can adapt according to the personality of the user, it can positively influence learning. However, most of the studies in which a robot is able to adapt users personality are conducted through asking participants to complete a questionnaire in order to detect their personality (extrovert or introvert). Therefore, it remains an open research question on how to detect personality in real-time. In addition, another possible strategy is to use a broad categorization of emotions that move beyond a simple extrovert and introvert identification. On the other hand, Mood or emotion adaptations based on dialogue have been studied in human-computer interaction [27]. However, we find fewer work on dialogue-based emotion adaptation and its effect on user perception and performance for educational robots and HRI in general.

3. The selection of robot role's during children robot interaction in real-time can be based on memory adaptation: Most of the teachers emphasised on performing real-time role adaptation. One of the suggested ways was through the use of memory during children robot interaction. In literature, we find a number of studies where robots have played different roles of a friend [7], competitor or cooperative [20], and persuasive [4]. All of these studies have shown positive results with respect to robot's effect on user perception, engagement or learning. However, there is a need for designing mechanism such that a robot can adapt its role in real time according to a given situation. In addition, the use of memory to perform role based adaptation still remains an open question in HRI.

4. Robots keeping track of a child's memory can in-turn motivate children: Teachers mentioned that children make mistakes regularly. The robot with a capability to show an adaptive behaviour through the use of recalling previously made mistakes can motivate children learning. As teachers mentioned that it can enable children to think new ways of adaptations in order to impress or outsmart the robot. Literature in HRI has also emphasised on the significance of memory adaptation. In a recent survey conducted on social robots for long-term engagement, [21] has mentioned memory based adaptation as one of the unexplored areas in HRI. Leite and Colleagues [21] have conjectured that possessing a memory can make social robots more flexible and personalised to particular users. Recently, researchers have also shown that robots with memory can affect user performance as it enhances their likability and empathy [12]. Therefore, teachers opinion are in line with the current research recommendations in HRI.

5. Culture-based adaptation can be significant during language learning tasks: Teachers explained that the significance of gestures during language learning. They also mentioned that robot should adapt when teaching different languages because gestures are culturally driven for different languages. We find less work on Cultural based adaptation in HRI. Studies have been conducted to show the significance of culture during HRI. Researchers [33] have indicated the understanding of gestures is dependent on the culture and even within one culture, interpretations can differ for different situations. In addition, it has also been described that different individuals from different cultures perceive personality of the robot differently [15]. Therefore, it is important to study the effect of cultural adaptations on user's engagement and performance during HRI.

6. Consider designing an easy to use interface for teachers to update new lessons for long-term Engagement: Teachers emphasised the importance of their involvement in order to keep the robot engaged and involved during the learning process for long time. In order to keep teachers involved, it is important to design interfaces that allows them to manage robots. The robot needs to be adaptive, however, the content and curriculum need to be revised or changed after a certain period, which can be done by the teacher only if he/she has appropriate control. In literature, [3] has described that the robot needs to be flexible enough to allow teachers to adjust and design appropriate robot-supported instructional activities for relevant teaching and learning requirements. In addition, Orlando et. al. [26] has showed that teachers today have confidence with technology and also possess a diverse range of technology expertise. Therefore, research needs to be conducted on the development of such interfaces that are easy to use for teachers.

LIMITATIONS, CONCLUSION AND FUTURE WORK

We didn't conduct the study longitudinally so we were not able to overcome the biases of the teachers. However, during the study, we tried to overcome pre-existing biases through the use of videos and the actual presence of the robot. The teachers agreed to have understood the capabilities of the robot and confirmed that their responses won't be driven based on any biases or past experience. Another limitation to our work is that the teachers were able to interact with limited capabilities (e.g. the robot only responded to limited questions, only recognised basic emotions, and displayed few gestures). We also understand if teachers were able to interact with NAO that showed more capabilities, we would have received more classified information from the teacher. Another argued limitation of our study can be the total number of participants. However, one of the previous studies [31] conducted with teachers on their views on robots in education also had the equal number of participants. In addition, our participants were specifically language teachers therefore we can interpret our results with some reliability.

In this paper, we presented our results on teacher's opinion on how robots can contribute towards language learning with children through performing a series of adaptations. The adaptations can be based on memory, emotions, and personality of the child. In addition, we show that there is a need to implement easy to use interfaces for teachers to enable them to upload new content for the robot. This can lead towards long term engagement of robots in education.

In future, we will be conducting a study with children (10-12 year old) at schools about their views on robot's that can adapt to their actions. We will be looking to conduct our study in three different steps: 1) an adaptive robot plays a snakes and ladders game for vocabulary learning [1] with the child individually and in pairs, 2) we will later invite children in groups to discuss robots with adaptive abilities and what are their views on them and 3) respond to individual asked interview questions. We will be recording videos of all these sessions with children. We will be looking to analyse videos in order to get data on how children react with robots in different scenarios during game-play and we will use this data to identify a list of efficient and appropriate children-robot interactions.

REFERENCES

1. Ahmad, M., Mubin, O., and Escudero, P. Using adaptive mobile agents in games based scenarios to facilitate foreign language word learning. In *Proceedings of the 3rd International Conference on Human-Agent Interaction*, ACM (2015), 255–257.

2. Breazeal, C. Role of expressive behaviour for robots that learn from people. *Philosophical Transactions of the Royal Society of London B: Biological Sciences 364*, 1535 (2009), 3527–3538.

3. Chang, C.-W., Lee, J.-H., Chao, P.-Y., Wang, C.-Y., Chen, G.-D., et al. Exploring the possibility of using humanoid robots as instructional tools for teaching a second language in primary school. *Educational Technology & Society 13*, 2 (2010), 13–24.

4. Chidambaram, V., Chiang, Y.-H., and Mutlu, B. Designing persuasive robots: how robots might persuade people using vocal and nonverbal cues. In *Proceedings of the seventh annual ACM/IEEE international conference on Human-Robot Interaction*, ACM (2012), 293–300.

5. Dautenhahn, K., Woods, S., Kaouri, C., Walters, M. L., Koay, K. L., and Werry, I. What is a robot companion-friend, assistant or butler? In *Intelligent Robots and Systems, 2005.(IROS 2005). 2005 IEEE/RSJ International Conference on*, IEEE (2005), 1192–1197.

6. Downe-Wamboldt, B. Content analysis: method, applications, and issues. *Health care for women international 13*, 3 (1992), 313–321.

7. Emmeche, C. Robot friendship: Can a robot be a friend? *International Journal of Signs and Semiotic Systems (IJSSS) 3*, 2 (2014), 26–42.

8. EVP, U. Emotion detection algorithm based on opencv. `https://github.com/liy9393/emotion-detection`, 2015. Accessed: 2016-05-08.

9. Fong, T., Nourbakhsh, I., and Dautenhahn, K. A survey of socially interactive robots. *Robotics and autonomous systems 42*, 3 (2003), 143–166.

10. Forlizzi, J., and DiSalvo, C. Service robots in the domestic environment: a study of the roomba vacuum in the home. In *Proceedings of the 1st ACM SIGCHI/SIGART conference on Human-robot interaction*, ACM (2006), 258–265.

11. Han, J.-H., Jo, M.-H., Jones, V., and Jo, J.-H. Comparative study on the educational use of home robots for children. *Journal of Information Processing Systems 4*, 4 (2008), 159–168.

12. Hastie, H., Yii, M., Lim, S. J., Deshmukh, A., Aylett, R., Foster, M. E., and Hall, L. I remember you! interaction with memory for an empathic virtual robotic tutor.

13. Hayes, C. J., and Riek, L. D. Establishing human personality metrics for adaptable robots during learning tasks. In *AAAI Fall Symposium on Artificial Intelligence and Human Robot Interaction., https://www. aaai. org/ocs/index. php/FSS/FSS14/rt/captureCite/9213/0* (2014).

14. Huber, A., Lammer, L., Weiss, A., and Vincze, M. Designing adaptive roles for socially assistive robots: a new method to reduce technological determinism and role stereotypes. *Journal of Human-Robot Interaction 3*, 2 (2014), 100–115.

15. Isbister, K., and Nass, C. Consistency of personality in interactive characters: verbal cues, non-verbal cues, and user characteristics. *International journal of human-computer studies 53*, 2 (2000), 251–267.

16. Kanda, T., Hirano, T., Eaton, D., and Ishiguro, H. Interactive robots as social partners and peer tutors for children: A field trial. *Human-computer interaction 19*, 1 (2004), 61–84.

17. Kennedy, J., Baxter, P., and Belpaeme, T. The robot who tried too hard: social behaviour of a robot tutor can negatively affect child learning. In *Proceedings of the Tenth Annual ACM/IEEE International Conference on Human-Robot Interaction*, ACM (2015), 67–74.

18. Kory, J., and Breazeal, C. Storytelling with robots: Learning companions for preschool children's language development. In *Robot and Human Interactive Communication, 2014 RO-MAN: The 23rd IEEE International Symposium on*, IEEE (2014), 643–648.

19. Kory Westlund, J., Gordon, G., Spaulding, S., Lee, J. J., Plummer, L., Martinez, M., Das, M., and Breazeal, C. Lessons from teachers on performing hri studies with young children in schools. In *The Eleventh ACM/IEEE International Conference on Human Robot Interation*, IEEE Press (2016), 383–390.

20. Lee, J.-H., Yakushin, D., Renteria, F., Nakata, K., Sugano, A., Morita, K., and Yamazoe, H. A competitive and cooperative humanoid software developing scheme loe and its improvements. In *Humanoid Robots (Humanoids), 2015 IEEE-RAS 15th International Conference on*, IEEE (2015), 631–636.

21. Leite, I., Martinho, C., and Paiva, A. Social robots for long-term interaction: a survey. *International Journal of Social Robotics 5*, 2 (2013), 291–308.

22. Mahani, M., and Eklundh, K. S. A survey of the relation of the task assistance of a robot to its social role. *Communication KCSa Royal Institute of Technology: Stockholm, Sweden* (2009).

23. Mileounis, A., Cuijpers, R. H., and Barakova, E. I. Creating robots with personality: The effect of personality on social intelligence. In *Artificial Computation in Biology and Medicine*. Springer, 2015, 119–132.

24. Mubin, O., Stevens, C. J., Shahid, S., Al Mahmud, A., and Dong, J.-J. A review of the applicability of robots in education. *Journal of Technology in Education and Learning 1* (2013), 209–0015.

25. Obaid, M., Barendregt, W., Alves-Oliveira, P., Paiva, A., and Fjeld, M. Designing robotic teaching assistants: Interaction design students and childrens views. In *Social Robotics*. Springer, 2015, 502–511.

26. Orlando, J. Teachers changing practices with information and communication technologies: an up-close, longitudinal analysis. *Research in learning technology 22* (2014).

27. Pittermann, J., Pittermann, A., and Minker, W. Emotion recognition and adaptation in spoken dialogue systems. *International Journal of Speech Technology 13*, 1 (2010), 49–60.

28. Saerbeck, M., Schut, T., Bartneck, C., and Janse, M. D. Expressive robots in education: varying the degree of social supportive behavior of a robotic tutor. In *Proceedings of the SIGCHI Conference on Human Factors in Computing Systems*, ACM (2010), 1613–1622.

29. Salter, T., Michaud, F., and Letourneau, D. What are the benefits of adaptation when applied in the domain of child-robot interaction? In *Proceedings of the 4th ACM/IEEE international conference on Human robot interaction*, ACM (2009), 237–238.

30. Serholt, S., and Barendregt, W. Students attitudes towards the possible future of social robots in education. RO-MAN (2014).

31. Serholt, S., Barendregt, W., Leite, I., Hastie, H., Jones, A., Paiva, A., Vasalou, A., and Castellano, G. Teachers' views on the use of empathic robotic tutors in the classroom. In *Robot and Human Interactive Communication, 2014 RO-MAN: The 23rd IEEE International Symposium on*, IEEE (2014), 955–960.

32. Zhang, A. Speech recognition (version 3.4) [software]. `https://github.com/Uberi/speech_recognition`, 2016. Accessed: 2016-05-08.

33. Zheng, M., and Meng, M. Q.-H. Designing gestures with semantic meanings for humanoid robot. In *Robotics and Biomimetics (ROBIO), 2012 IEEE International Conference on*, IEEE (2012), 287–292.

Evaluation of Schedule Managing Agent among Multiple Members with Representation of Background Negotiations

Tomoko Yonezawa
Kansai University
2-1-1 Ryozenji, Takatsuki,
Osaka 5691095, Japan
yone@kansai-u.ac.jp

Kunihiko Fujiwara
Kansai University
2-1-1 Ryozenji, Takatsuki,
Osaka 5691095, Japan
k566804@kansai-u.ac.jp

Naoto Yoshida
Kansai University
2-1-1 Ryozenji, Takatsuki,
Osaka 5691095, Japan
k463362@kansai-u.ac.jp

ABSTRACT

This paper proposes an interactive manager agent system that adjusts schedule among multiple persons through negotiations on behalf of a human organizer, such as a steward or team manager. In order to increase the users' cooperative decision-making, we implemented the manager agent that negotiates with each member on the schedule using 1) the suitable attitude depending on current situation and partner of negotiation and 2) the graphical representation of background negotiations between the agent and the other users: a) the other users' icons, b) the blinking balloons of both the other users and the agent, and c) the agent's looking-back actions for the other users' icons. The results of the evaluations showed that both the individual use and the combination of the proposed expressions could make the participants feel i) as though there were under-going negotiations between the agent and the other users and ii) as though the agent had both the effort and compassion to the user. Moreover, the user's cooperative decision-making was increased by the proposed method.

ACM Classification Keywords

H.5.3: Group and Organization Interfaces

Author Keywords

Manager agent; Background negotiation; Representation of effort; Cooperative decision-making

INTRODUCTION

In the modern society, we have various types of group units in order to participate in various social activities. For smooth coordination of the group activities, the facilitators such as team secretaries, party managers, teachers are absolutely necessary. Such smooth coordination requires 1) the hearing of each member's desire, 2) the merged plan from the members' desires and 3) persuasion for negotiation with the members who do not suit the merged plan. The important role of the

manager/facilitators is to promote the member's cooperative decision-making by leading the member's compassion to the manager's effort.

On the other hand, the manager/facilitators have some difficulty for smooth management. The first problem is the lack of the physical/time resource for gathering and merging opinions and desires of multiple members. The second one is the impossibility of the best solution for the multiple members in solving the optimum result from their requests. In order to solve the first problem, there have been various coordination systems, especially schedule management systems, to find optimum plan from multiple members' schedules [1, 2]. However, these systems do not have any function to negotiate with or ask the members who have conflict in the automatic schedules. As Fukumoto et al. indicated, there is a possibility of the members' mistrusts in the proposed schedules [3]. This is the second problem.

Consequently, we focus on an agent system to interactively persuade a human as Fogg [4]. In this research, we aim to realize the manager agent system that performs the smooth coordination among multiple members through interactive persuasion with the members by graphical representation of ongoing background negotiation. Attempting to create the unique nuance, the system combines different levels of the acceptance using facial, script, and endings of the word [5]. First, we had proposed a communication agent system that shows appropriate caring expression based on the parameters: the social position of the current user and the agent's scheduling situation [6].

In this paper, we focus on the representation of background negotiations using the other users' icons, the agent's looking-back action to the other users, and the blinking dialogue balloons of both the agent and the other users. The representation is expected to show the agent's situation and to increase the user's cooperative attitude. Combining with three different levels of expressions, that are facial, verbal, and ending of the word expressions as the previous work [5], the agent system aim to show both the internal state and the negotiation situations of the agent. The representation could realize a strong manager agent with affective appeal. In this paper, we verified the effectiveness of the proposed representation of background negotiation on 1) the impression of the agent's effort, 2) the user's compassion to the agent, and 3) the user's cooperative decision-making.

HAI '16, October 04-07, 2016, Biopolis, Singapore

© 2016 ACM. ISBN 978-1-4503-4508-8/16/10. . . $15.00

DOI: http://dx.doi.org/10.1145/2974804.2974812

RELATED WORKS

The Attitude and Facial Expressions in Negotiation

Humans are negotiating various things using multiple non-verbal expressions to show the mind, purpose, and the effort to the other person. First we focus on the importance of the attitude to the other person in negotiation.

Facial expression gives strong impressions. That sometimes effects on the results of negotiation for either good or evil [7]. For example, negotiations are affected by the angry attitude of the negotiator as adverse influences. On the other hand, the compassion has possibility to bring relieved influences in negotiations [8]. Thus, humans need to train the skill to avoid emotional reactions and to control their expressions regardless of their emotions. To overcome the psychological burden of the expression controls, the mediating agent is expected to act as a human manager without such stress.

The Opinion Change by Representing Communication of Other Persons

Next, we focus on the importance of background information in negotiations. As Walster et al. showed [11], the persuading method using "overheard," listening to the conversations of the third person, is actively discussed as the method of changing user's decision. Suzuki et al. proposed the advertising method using the "overheard" on Website with the adverting agent and the customer agent to increase the consumer appetite for online shopping [12]. As the result, the effectiveness of their method was verified.

In this paper, we aim to indirectly promote the user's cooperative attitude using "overheard" by showing the negotiation between the manager agent and the background other users. Here, in this paper, we especially focused on the animated and iconic graphics of the agent and the other users.

Persuading Communication between Human and Agent

Finally, we focus on the agent's persuasion by its attitude in negotiation. As humans are affected by the negotiator's expressions and attitudes, it is expected that anthropomorphic agents can represent appropriate attitudes corresponding to the negotiating situation.

Facial expressions of agents have possibilities to act on human's decision making [9]. Yuasa et al. [10] described that agents' facial expression, movement of eyes and actions affect the human's decision-making in the negotiation between agent and human. They discussed the agent's strategy of expressing them due to increase the partner's cooperative decision making. Their result clarified the effectiveness of both the agent's facial expressions and the behaviors before / during the negotiation; that generate the impressions of friendliness, trustworthiness, dominance and the impressions, on the cooperative attitude of the user. However, their focus was limited to only the agent's attitude for increasing cooperative decision making without the interaction among the other users and the agent.

Differently from the focuses of other researches, we focus on the expressions of the negotiating situations of the agent with multiple users as the background information due to increase cooperative users. To draw the user's understanding and compassion, the mediating agent shows caring expressions depending on members' states and results of other negotiations. For appropriate implementation of the agent's caring expression, the attitude of the agent should correspond to each user's state or the situation of the scheduling. In order to naturally create the attitude, we designed an internal state of the agent with using an inner-emotional model. Not only the changes of the attitudes of the agent such as facial expressions, the system adopts the representation of the background negotiations between the agent and the other users in order to draw the user's compassion for advantageous and smooth negotiations as following description.

MANAGER AGENT SYSTEM

System Summary

The purpose of our system is to increase the users' cooperative attitude and decision-making by both A) the affective attitude of the agent depending on the negotiating situation and B) the representation of the background negotiations between the agent and the other users. The cooperative attitude of the user would enable smooth human-agent negotiations for a coordination to merge the members' schedules.

A) The expressions of the agent's attitude is graphically shown during the negotiation. The behavioral expression of the agent's attitudes consist of a) its facial expression, b) the dialog scripts, and c) the punctuation of the word. The agent's attitude is changed by the user's status of and the parameters of inner model of the negotiating situation.

B) The background information represents ongoing negotiation between the agent and the other users. The other users' icons are placed around the agent's behind. This system performs graphical representation of the background negotiations between the agent and other users by using 1) the agent's face with its looking-round movements, 2) the other users' icons, and 3) dialogue balloons of the agent and the other users.

The system has four subsystems based on the management of negotiations with all users: 1) the expression control of the agent's attitude, 2) the inner state model of the agent, 3) the background expression, and 4) the interface system (Figure 1). The interface system shows 1-i) the visual expression of the agent attitude, 1-ii) the agent's dialog message, and 3-i) the background information based on 2) the inner state of the agent. The interface system has a form to enter both the user's information and the reply to the requests of agent as shown in Figure 2.

Flow of the Negotiations

Here, we describe the manager agent's behavior in the negotiations. The agent negotiates the event's date to make the user participate in the event. First, the agent shows multiple candidates of date and asks the user for her/his participation in the specific date that is the merged result of the other users' desires.

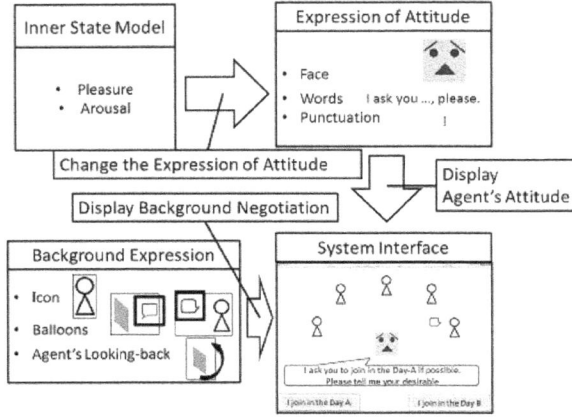

Figure 1. System structure and flow.

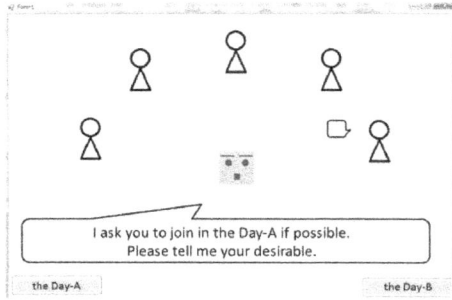

Figure 2. System view.

The agent requests the user's participation and checks the user's answer in three timings in the negotiation process: at just before the beginning of the negotiation, at just after the user's answer, and after the end of the negotiation. The agent changes its attitude depending on the parameters of the agent's inner state model as follows.

Inner State Model

The inner state model is an emotional model of the manager agent with two basic parameters, "pleasure" ($val_{pleasure}$) and "arousal" ($val_{arousal}$), in reference to the Russell's emotional circumplex model [13]. The "pleasure" is mapped to the agent's ease of the negotiation, and "arousal" is mapped to the agent's tension. The parameters are changed by the situation of the current negotiation and the results of the current user's answers. These parameters have five levels for each from 1 to 5, and both parameters are set at level 3 as default values. At the beginning of the negotiation, the levels of the parameters are set by the values at the end of the previous negotiation as the initial values in the negotiation.

To reflect the previous negotiation, the current state, and the result of the current negotiation, we designed the calculation of the parameters of the internal state as shown in Figure 3. The parameters ($val_{pleasure}$ and $val_{arousal}$) are recursively calculated at the three timings of the negotiation using current change of pleasure (C_p) and arousal (C_a). By each time of the change, the parameters are reflected to the level of both parameters as the equations 1 and 2 where w is the weight of

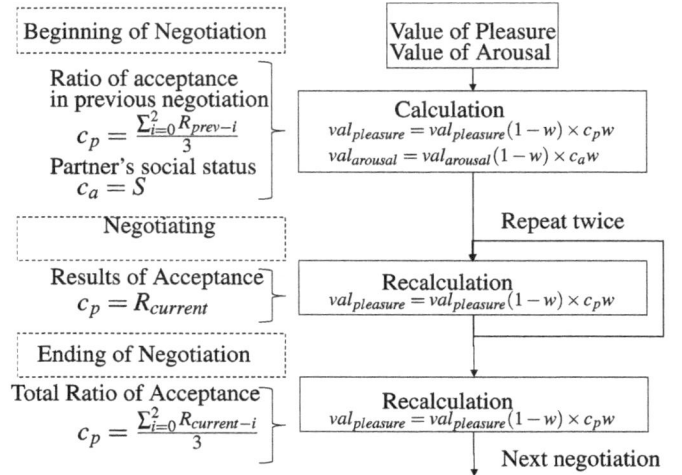

Figure 3. Calculation of pleasure and arousal in the flow

the current input variables c_p and c_a from 0 to 1.

$$val_{pleasure} = val_{pleasure}(1 - w) \times c_p w \qquad (1)$$
$$val_{arousal} = val_{arousal}(1 - w) \times c_a w \qquad (2)$$

At the beginning of the negotiation, the parameters are calculated by referring to the information of the user's social status (see Table 1) and the ratio of user's acceptance (accept:5 and reject:1) in previous negotiations. The ratio of the user's acceptance in previous negotiations changes the "pleasure" parameter as the emotion toward the user (see the equation 3), and the user's social status changes the "arousal" parameter as the tension (see the equation 4). In the equations, the initial input variables are calculated where S means the user's social status and R_{prev} means the amount of user's acceptance of three timings in previous negotiation.

$$c_p = \frac{\sum_{i=0}^{2} R_{prev-i}}{3} \qquad (3)$$
$$c_a = S \qquad (4)$$

Next, during the current negotiation, the level of "pleasure" is recalculated by the result of the user's current answer ($R_{current}$) to be increased by the user's current acceptance of the agent's request and to be decreased by the user's current rejection as the equation 5).

$$c_p = R_{current} \qquad (5)$$

Finally, at the end of the negotiations, the "pleasure" level is recalculated by the total ratio of acceptance in the current negotiation as the equation 6).

$$c_p = \frac{\sum_{i=0}^{2} R_{current-i}}{3} \qquad (6)$$

Social position	Social status
Professor	5
Researcher	3
Master course student	2
Bachelor student	1

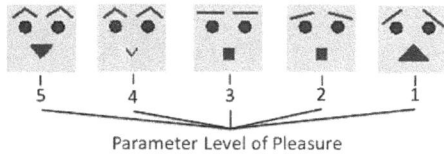

Parameter Level of Pleasure

Figure 4. Facial expressions by each level of "pleasure"

Expressions of Agent's Attitude

The manager agent shows the various behavioral expressions depending on the situation of negotiation and the user's social status as described. Here, we describe the design of the agent's specific expressions.

The agent's behavioral expressions consist of its facial expression, the dialog words, and the punctuation of end of words. These three expressions are implemented in five levels; the iconic graphic of the agent's face (positive — negative emotions as Figure 4); the dialog words (acceptable — unacceptable as Table 2), and the punctuation of the words' end (active — inactive as Table 3) are adopted. By each time of the change of the levels of the inner parameters during the negotiations, the levels for these three expressions are selected according to the inner parameters: "pleasure" and "arousal." In the tentative design, the level of the facial expressions is decided by the level of "pleasure," and the levels of the active nuances for both the punctuation and the words' nuance are decided by the level of "arousal."

Representation of Background Negotiation between the Agent and the Other Users

The representation of the background negotiation shows the view of the ongoing negotiations between the agent and the other users behind the agent's icon. The background information shows the number of the other users, the agent's reactions to their requests, the utterances of both the agent and the other users by the iconic views of the agent and the other users, the rotating animation of the agent's face as looking-back actions, and the dialogue balloons as the negotiating scripts.

For examples, the expressions show the view of the other users' requests to the agent as shown in the right small balloons in Figure 2 and the agent's reaction to the other users' requests (see Figure 5).

Five icons of the other users are placed due to express the presence of the multiple other users. The five icons are displayed during all the processes of the negotiation flow. When the number of the other users is less than 4, the number of the icons is set to the number of the other users. The other users' icons are placed behind the agent (upper side in the display) in an equally-spaced semicircular trajectory in the interface graphics of the system. The shape of the other users' icons is human-like shades in same size.

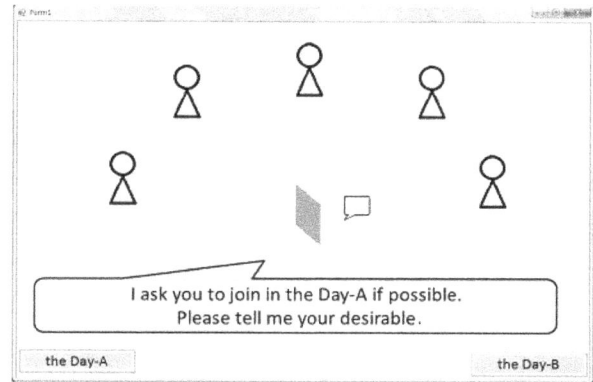

Figure 5. Other view of the system: the agent's reaction to the other users' requests.

The blinking balloons around a particular user's icon express the requests of the other users to the agent. The balloons are placed at around each user, and one of them blinks in a random order.

The agent looks back to the other user's icon with blinking balloon. The tentative design of the looking-back action is the turn of the agent's face toward the target for 0.8 seconds. The agent's movement of looking-back and the blinking balloon of the agent's dialog show the view of the agent's reaction to the other users' requests.

Each expression is shown in the following order: 1) the blinking balloon of the other user, 2) the agent's looking-back action to the other user, and 3) the blinking of the agent's balloon. The flow of the expressions is shown three times in six seconds from the timing of the message of the agent's request to the user.

EXPERIMENT

We evaluated the availability of the combination of proposed four expressions: 1) the other users' icons, 2) the icon's dialog balloons (flashing) and 3) the agent's actions (looking-back) and 4) the agent's dialog balloons (flashing); to increase user's cooperative attitude.

Purpose of Experiment: We verified the effect of the combination of the above four expressions on whether the system can give the impressions of i) the understanding of the negotiations between the agent and the other users, ii) the effort of the agent, iii) the agent's concern to users, and iv) the result of user's acceptance for the proposed date.

Hypothesis: a) On the presence and intention of the other users a-1) Other users' icons make the participant can indicate the presences of other users. a-2) Flashing of the balloons of the other users can indicate the other users' dialogue to the agent. a-3) The agent looking-back to the other user's icon can indicate the agent's attention to other user. a-4) The Flashing of the agent's balloon expresses the agent's dialogue to the other users. b) The combinations of the proposed four expressions can indicate the background negotiations between the agent and the other users. c) The combinations of the proposed four expressions can indicate the effort of the

Table 2. Text expressions by the parameter of the agent's pleasures.

Score of pleasure	Text	Meaning	degree
5	... de-daijoubu	... is OK for you	acceptable
4	... de-onegai	I ask you ...	‖
3	... de-onegaishimasu	I ask you ..., please.	‖
2	... de-onegaidekimasenka	Would you ..., please.	‖
1	... de-nantokaonegaidekinaidesyouka	Would it be possible to ... , please.	unacceptable

Table 3. Ending of punctuation at the end of texts by the agent's arousal.

Arousal	Ending of punctuation	Meaning	degree
5	!	exciting	active
4	"xtu"	crisp	‖
3	none	neutral	‖
2	-	flatten	‖
1	...	considering	inactive

agent. d) The combinations of the proposed four expressions generate the participant's concern about the agent. e) The combinations of the proposed four expressions make the participants accept the agent's proposal.

Participants: 31 university students ages from 18 years old to 24 years old (28 males and 3 females).

Procedures and Instructions: The participants were instructed that the agent displayed in the front screen manages and coordinates the date of a party. In addition, she/he was introduced that there are two preliminary candidates of the date: Day-A is the day that the participant is available from 30 minutes from the beginning, and Day-B is the day that she/he is available full time in this party. After the introduction, the participations observed the 30-sec. experiment system from the start to the end of system flow. We calculated the summary of the scores while Day-A is converted into 1 point and Day-B is converted into 0 point.

System for Experiment: The flow of the experimental system had the following three process. 1) The manager agent greets for the participant and explains that the agent manages the date of a party among multiple members. 2) The agent shows two dates as the candidates. Here, we named these dates as Day-A and Day-B. 3) The agent asked the participant to join the party held in Day-A by showing the following messages: "I ask you to join in the Day-A if possible. Please tell me your desirable date." After the process 3), the negotiating expressions are shown during 5 seconds. In each condition, the agent attitudes are fixed with the expressions of the level 3 of the inner state model as the previous section, that are the facial expression in the neutral nuance, without ending of punctuation, and the neutral wording.

Conditions in Experiment: The conditions in the experiment are the combinations of the following factors (see Figure 6, 7).

A: With or without the graphics of the other users' icons (A1: displayed/A2: hidden).
B: With or without the dialog balloon of the other users' icons (B1: blinking/B2: hidden).
C: With or without the action of the agent (C1: looking-back movement to the other users' icons/C2:without motion).
D: With or without t the dialog balloon of the agent (D1: blinking/D2:hidden).

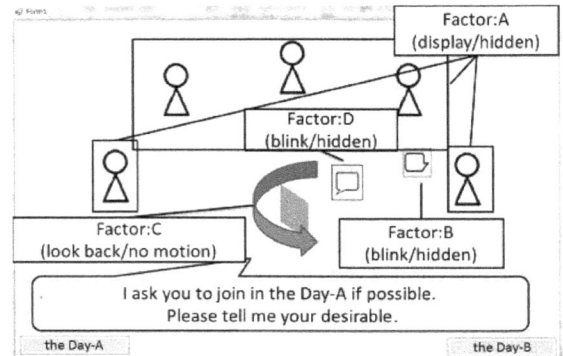

Figure 6. With all positive factors of the evaluation in the representation of the background negotiations.

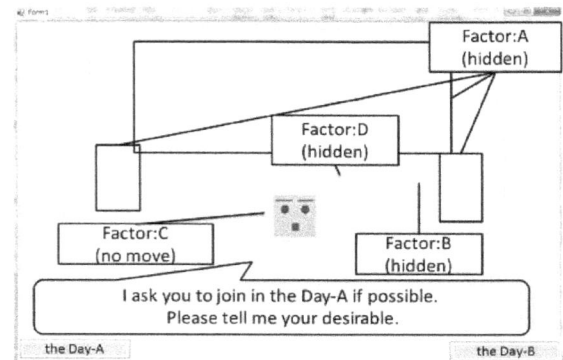

Figure 7. Without any positive factor of the evaluation in the representation of the background negotiations.

Condition: Thus the experiment was conducted by the 16 conditions. This experiment was conducted in a within-subjects design, and the systems of each condition were performed by a counterbalance.

Evaluation Items: The participants evaluated the system using a five-point rating scale of the relevance (5: relevant, 4: somewhat relevant, 3: even, 2: somewhat irrelevant, 1: irrelevant) of the following statements and a freely description of impressions for the agent. Before the experiment, the participants were explained about the word "the character" means the manager agent and the word "the other member" means the other users, appeared in the questionnaire.

Q1: You felt the presence of the other users.
Q2: The character seemed busy.
Q3: The character kept communication with many other users.
Q4: The character paid attention to other users.
Q5: The other users seemed to insist of some opinions to the character.

309

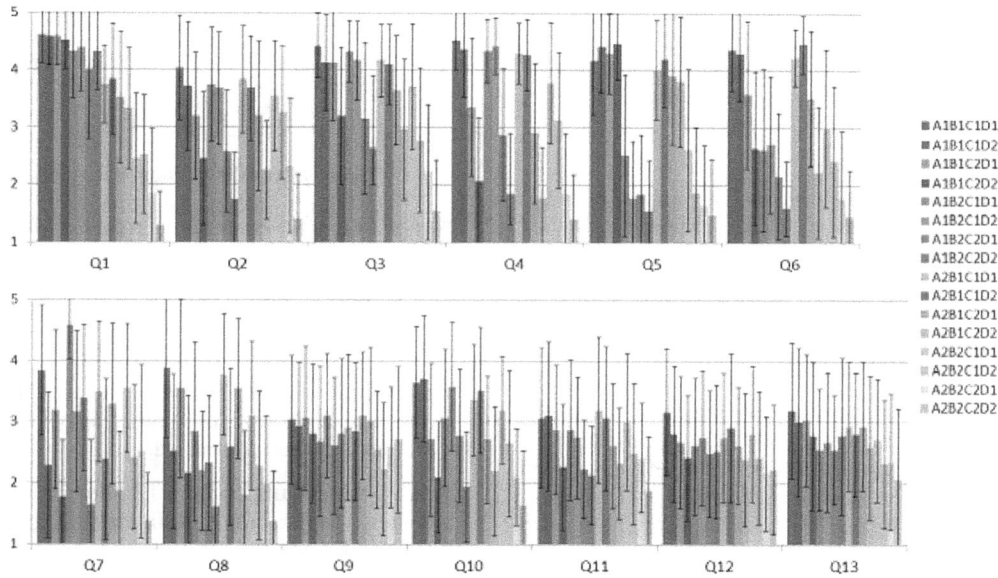

Figure 8. Results of subjective evaluations related to background expressions

Table 4. Four-factor repeated measures ANOVA for MOS related to the representation of background negotiations

hline	Factor A $F_{(30)}$	p	Factor B $F_{(30)}$	p	Factor C $F_{(30)}$	p	Factor D $F_{(30)}$	p	Interaction
1	115	<.01*	97.6	<.01*	94.4	<.01*	9.27	<.01*	AB,AC,AD,BC,BD,ABC,ABD
2	4.38	0.04*	37.6	<.01*	110	<.01*	34.9	<.01*	BC,CD
3	40.3	<.01*	65.7	<.01*	100	<.01*	43.2	<.01*	AB,BC,CD,ABD
4	52.7	<.01*	41.0	<.01*	185	<.01*	70.8	<.01*	AB,CD,ACD,BCD,ABCD
5	3.13	0.08+	225	<.01*	20.0	<.01*	4.34	0.04*	AC,BC,BD,BCD
6	1.42	0.24	120	<.01*	98.5	<.01*	21.2	<.01*	BC,CD,BCD
7	15.3	<.01*	0.29	0.59	60.4	<.01*	92.2	<.01*	AD,BC
8	0.70	0.40	60.5	<.01*	25.4	<.01*	111	<.01*	BC,BD
9	3.33	0.07+	9.625	0.04*	0.22	0.61	0.04	0.83	AB,AC
10	17.7	0.02*	12.5	0.01*	51.3	<.01*	10.8	0.02*	CD,ACD,ABCD
11	0.15	0.69	14.3	<.01*	27.0	<.01*	13.6	<.01*	—
12	3.02	0.09+	9.73	<.01*	14.0	<.01*	1.80	0.18	ABD
13	11.8	<.01*	28.5	<.01*	3.95	0.06+	5.53	0.02*	—

*p <.01, +p <.10

Q6: The character seemed to listen to the other users.
Q7: The character seemed to speak to the other users.
Q8: The character seemed to discuss with the other users.
Q9: The character seemed to make efforts of the concern for you.
Q10: The character seemed to make efforts of the concern for the other users.
Q11: The character showed the effort of the schedule management.
Q12: You will feel apologetic for the character if you reject the proposal.
Q13: You will feel apologetic for the other users if you reject the proposal.
Decision of your opinion: Day-A or Day-B as the their desired date.

Results of means opinion scores (MOS): Figure 8 show the mean opinion scores (MOS) of the subjective evaluation and Table 4 shows the results of the four-factor repeated measures ANOVA.

First, the evaluation items 1 and 4 to 8 are related to the user's recognition of the background negotiation between the agent and the other users from the expressions of the proposed method.

The evaluation item 1, related to the presence of the other users, showed significances of all factors and several interactions. In the interaction among the factors A, B, and C, the combinations of B1 (blinking) and C1 (looking-back movement to the other users' icons) showed the higher MOS of A1 (displayed) than with A2 (hidden). Moreover, in the interaction between the factors A, B and D the combination of B1 (blinking) and D1 (blinking) showed the higher MOS of A1 than A2. Accordingly, it is suggested that the hypothesis a-1) was confirmed.

The evaluation item 4, related to the user's recognition of the agent's attention to the other user, showed significances of all factors. The interaction between the factor A, C and D showed the higher MOSs of C1 than C2 when combined with A1 and D1. The interaction between the factor B, C and D showed the higher MOSs of C1 than C2 when combined with B1 and D1.

The evaluation item 5, related to the user's recognition of the other users' request to the agent, showed the significant differences by the factors B ,C and D (with or without the dialog balloon of the agent) with the multiple interactions. In the interactions among B, C and D, the combination of C1 and D1 showed the higher MOS was shown with B1 than B2. From the results, it is conjectured that the hypothesis a-2) was confirmed.

The evaluation item 6, related to the user's impression of the agent's listening attitude to the other users' requests, showed significances of the factor B, factor C and factor D with a significant interaction among the factor B, C and D. The interaction showed the higher MOS of C1 than C2 when combined with B1 and D1. Accordingly, it is suggested that these results confirmed the hypothesis a-3).

The evaluation item 7, related to the user's recognition of the agent's request to the other users, showed the significances of the factor A, C and D with the significant interaction between the factors A and D and between B and C. The A–D interaction showed the higher MOS of D1 than D2 when combined with A1, and the B–C interaction showed the higher MOS of C1 than C2 when combined with both B1 and B2 and the higher MOS of B2 than B1 when combined with C1. Thus, the hypothesis a-4) was confirmed.

The evaluation item 8 showed significances by the factors B, C and D with multiple significant interactions. The B–C interaction showed the higher MOS of C1 than C2 when combined with B1 and the higher MOS of B1 than B2 when combined with C1. The B–D interaction showed the higher MOS of D1 than D2 when combined with B1, as same as the higher MOS of B1 than B2 when combined with D1. Accordingly, it is suggested that the results confirmed the hypothesis b).

Next, Q2 (busyness), Q3 (abundance), Q9 (compassion to the user), Q10 (compassion to the other users), and Q11 (troubles) are evaluation items about the impressions of the agent's efforts. From the results of the evaluation items 2,3,10 the significant differences were found by all the factors and multiple interactions.

The evaluation item 2 showed the significant interactions between the factor B and C, with the higher MOS of C1 than C2. The C–D interaction showed the higher MOS of C1 than C2 when combined with D1.

The evaluation items 3 showed significances in all the factors and the significant interaction among the factors A, B and D. The A–B–D interaction showed the higher MOS of D1 than D2 when combined with A1 and B1, and the higher MOS of B1 than B2 when combined with A1 and D1.

The evaluation items 9 showed the significant difference by the factor B and the significant interaction between the factor A and C. The A–C interaction showed the higher MOS of A1 than A2 when combined with C1.

The evaluation item 10 showed the significant interactions among all the factors with the higher MOS of C1 than C2 when combined with A1, B1 and D1.

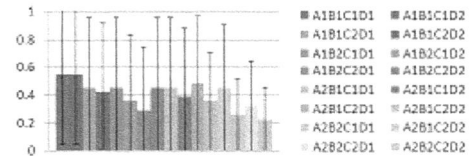

Figure 9. Results of cooperative decision-making

Table 5. Chi-square tests for each-factor-contigency-table instead of hypercomplex contigency table

decision	A1	A2	B1	B2	C1	C2	D1	D2
accept	109	94	113△	90▽	109	94	109	94
refuse	139	154	135▽	158△	139	154	139	154

The evaluation item11 showed the significances of the factor B, factor C and factor D. Accordingly, it is suggested that the hypothesis c) was confirmed.

Finally, the evaluation item 12, the participants' conscious to the agent, showed the significant difference by the factors of B, C and D with multiple interactions. The A–B–D interaction showed the higher MOS of B1 than B2 when combined with A1 and D1, and the higher MOS of D1 than D2 when combined with A1 and B1. Moreover, in condition A1B1, the compassion of D1 was stronger than D2. Therefore, it is suggested that the result confirmed the hypothesis d).

Results of cooperative decision making: Figure 9 shows the rate of the participants' cooperative decision-making, and Table 5 shows the results of the chi-square tests for each distribution instead of a hypercomplex chi-square test. The results showed the significant differences by the factor B, the dialogue balloons of the other users, while the three-dimensional contigency tables in both B1 and B2 did not show any significance. Accordingly, it is suggested that there was the individual effect of the factor B instead of the hypothesis e) while there was not any significance by other factors.

DISCUSSION

Here, we discuss the effectiveness of our proposed expression for 1) the presentation of background negotiations, 2) the impression for the agent's effort and compassion, and 3) the promotion of user's cooperative attitude, that is related to the cooperative decision.

First, we discuss the impression of background negotiations by the proposed expressions with the icons of other users, the balloons of both the agent and the other users, and the agent's looking-back action. To understand the background negotiations, it is necessary to recognize the interaction between the agent and the other users. As the hypotheses a-1) to a-4) and b) were confirmed, the proposed expressions could represent the background negotiations as we aimed in both independent and combined uses. From the results, participants could perceive both the presences of other users and the negotiation between the agent and the other users. The interaction between them is also considerable, that is, the negotiating view with blinking balloons emphasized the other users' presences.

Next we discuss the assumed flow of the user's cooperative attitude. As the hypothesis c) and d) were confirmed, the agent's effort and compassion to the user were perceived. The user's cooperative decision, that is the goal of our research, was also confirmed as the factor B affected on the results instead of the hypothesis e).

Here, there is a discussion on the flow of the cooperative attitude. In this experiment, there are not sufficient materials to separate the cause and the effect; however, we assume that the flow of the cooperative results would be started at the intuitive recognition of the background negotiations between the manager agent and the others. a) When the user focuses on the background situation as the agent's situation, she/he can become aware of that the coordinating process runs smoothly or not from the agent's attitude shown as effort. b) When the agent shows its effort for both the negotiations among multiple members and the conscious to the user, the user may feel compassion to the agent. c) By the user's compassion to the agent, she/he could become cooperative. We should verify the causations among these elements in the assumed flow in future.

From the free descriptions, there is the problem of the expressions of the agent's request. There were several cases in which the participants did not perceived as if the agent requested the Day-A decision. It is suggested that the attitudes and dialogues of the agent should be improved to emphasize the desire of the agent. The repeat of the request in the different phases of the negotiation would be also strong representation of the agent's efforts.

CONCLUSION
In this paper, we proposed a manager agent that coordinates an event date among multiple participants. The manager agent negotiates with the participants by showing the visual animation of the background negotiations between the agent and the other users. As the background negotiations, the proposed system interactively shows i) the facial expression of the agent, ii) the other users' icons, iii) the blinking of the dialogue balloons of both the agent and the other users, and iv) the agent's looking-back actions to the other users. The purpose of the representation is to increase the user's cooperative attitude corresponding to the agent's effort and compassion to the user. From the results of the subjective evaluations, it was confirmed that 1) the participants could recognize the background negotiation, that 2) the participants felt impressions of both the agent's effort and the user's compassion, while 3) the cooperative decision-making of the user was increased by the blinking balloons. The combinations of the proposed expression brought each unique effect as we aimed.

As future work, we should clarify the time-series causation among the elements of the assumed flow (the representation of the background negotiation, the impression of the agent's effort, the user's compassion, and the cooperative decision) to promote smoother coordination of schedules of the proposed agent system.

ACKNOWLEDGMENTS
This research was supported in part by JSPS KAKENHI 25700021 and JSPS KAKENHI 15H01698. The authors would like to thank the participants in the experiment.

REFERENCES
1. L. Garrido and K. Sycara. Multi-agent meeting scheduling: Preliminary experimental results. In *Proceedings of the Second International Conference on Multiagent Systems*. 95–102. 1996.

2. M. S. Franzin, E. C. Freuder, F. Rossi, and R. Wallace. Multi-agent meeting scheduling with preferences: efficiency, privacy loss, and solution quality. In *Computational Intelligence*. Vol. 20, Issue 2, pp.264-âĂŞ286, 2004.

3. T. Fukumoto, S. Kuribara, and H. Sawamura. An integrated argumentation environment for arguing agents. In *Agent and Multi-Agent Systems: Technologies and Applications*. Springer, pp. 351–360, 2008.

4. B. J. Fogg. Persuasive technology: using computers to change what we think and do. *Ubiquity* 2002, chapter 5. pp. 89–120, 2002. 2002.

5. T. Yonezawa, N. Yoshida, and J. Nishinaka Crossmodal Combination among Verbal, Facial, and Flexion Expression for Anthropomorphic Acceptability. *ROMAN 2015*, pp. 549–554, 2015.

6. K. Fujiwara, J. Nishinaka, N. Yoshida, and T. Yonezawa Schedule Managing Agent among Group Members with Caring Expressions. *SCIS-ISIS2014*, pp.1564–1567, 2014.

7. L. Thompson, V. H. Medvec, V. Seiden, and S. Kopelman. Poker face, smiley face, and rant 'n' rave: Myths and realities about emotion in negotiation. *Blackwell handbook of social psychology: Group processes*. 139–163. 2001.

8. K. G. Allred, J. S. Mallozzi, F .Matsui, and C. P. Raia. The influence of anger and compassion on negotiation performance. *Organizational Behavior and Human Decision Processes*. 70, 3. 175–187. 1997.

9. C. M. de Melo, P. Carnevale, and J. Gratch. The effect of expression of anger and happiness in computer agents on negotiations with humans. In *The 10th International Conference on Autonomous Agents and Multiagent Systems*. Volume 3. 937–944. 2011.

10. M. Yuasa and N. Mukawa. The facial expression effect of an animated agent on the decisions taken in the negotiation game. In *CHI'07 Extended Abstracts on Human Factors in Computing Systems*. pp.2795–2800. 2007.

11. E. Walster and L. Festinger. 1962. The effectiveness of "overheard" persuasive communications. *Journal of Abnormal and Social Psychology*. 65, 6, pp.395–402. 1962.

12. S. V. Suzuki and S. Yamada. Persuasion through overheard communication by life-like agents. In *IEEE/WIC/ACM International Conference on Intelligent Agent Technology*. pp.225–231. 2004.

13. J.A. Russell. 1980. A circumplex model of affect. *Journal of personality and social psychology*. 1161–1178. 1980.

LAP: a Human-in-the-loop Adaptation Approach for Industrial Robots

Wilson K. H. Ko
ETH Zurich
Zurich, Switzerland
wko@student.ethz.ch

Yan Wu
A*STAR Institute for
Infocomm Research
Singapore
wuy@i2r.a-star.edu.sg

Keng Peng Tee
A*STAR Institute for
Infocomm Research
Singapore
kptee@i2r.a-star.edu.sg

ABSTRACT

In the last few years, a shift from mass production to mass customisation is observed in the industry. Easily reprogrammable robots that can perform a wide variety of tasks are desired to keep up with the trend of mass customisation while saving costs and development time. Learning by Demonstration (LfD) is an easy way to program the robots in an intuitive manner and provides a solution to this problem. In this work, we discuss and evaluate LAP, a three-stage LfD method that conforms to the criteria for the high-mix-low-volume (HMLV) industrial settings. The algorithm learns a trajectory in the task space after which small segments can be adapted on-the-fly by using a human-in-the-loop approach. The human operator acts as a high-level adaptation, correction and evaluation mechanism to guide the robot. This way, no sensors or complex feedback algorithms are needed to improve robot behaviour, so errors and inaccuracies induced by these subsystems are avoided. After the system performs at a satisfactory level after the adaptation, the operator will be removed from the loop. The robot will then proceed in a feed-forward fashion to optimise for speed. We demonstrate this method by simulating an industrial painting application. A KUKA LBR iiwa is taught how to draw an eight figure which is reshaped by the operator during adaptation.

Author Keywords

Robot Learning from Demonstration; Imitation Learning; Industrial Robots; Industrial Robotics; Automation; Human-Robot Interaction; Intuitive Teaching

Articulated manipulators are mass-employed to perform a wide variety of tasks in the industry. Traditionally, these manipulators work in custom-made environments and thus need to be programmed specifically for their environment only to carry out a certain task. It is therefore difficult and expensive to reuse the same robot setup for multiple tasks. This is not a problem when the robot needs to perform the same task many times, but could be troublesome if the environment or tasks

HAI '16, October 04-07, 2016, Biopolis, Singapore

© 2016 ACM. ISBN 978-1-4503-4508-8/16/10...$15.00

DOI: http://dx.doi.org/10.1145/2974804.2974805

changes frequently. Meanwhile, the current shift from mass production to mass customisation in the industry calls for reconfigurable robots and environments [15]. Learning from demonstration (LfD) provides a solution to this problem, as a robot can be taught in an intuitive manner to do different tasks instead of pre-programming it [1, 2]. In our previous work, we set out criteria which LfD algorithms need to fulfil in order to perform industrial tasks well. Furthermore, our previous work serves as an introduction to this work, we highly encourage the reader to look into it for a better understanding of our current work. In general, we are interested in an LfD algorithm that achieves high accuracy and repeatability, high adaptivity and speed while maintaining low system complexity and learning fatigue [8].

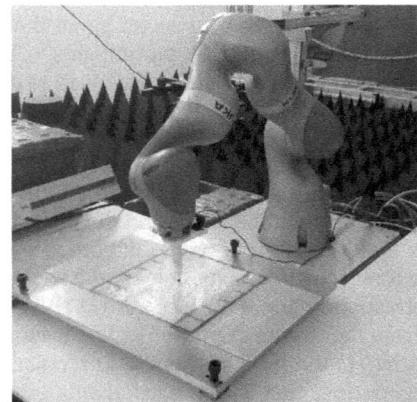

Figure 1. Setup of the experiment. A marker is mounted on a KUKA LBR iiwa to draw eight figures on a surface.

In this work, we present Learning, Adaptation and Production (LAP), a three-stage LfD algorithm proposed to conform to these criteria as much as possible by including humans as a high-level feedback and adaptation mechanism [8]. In the first phase, a regression technique is used to generalise the task space demonstrations shown by the user. In the next phase, the robot will carry out the learned policy until the user interrupts the robot to adapt a part of the trajectory either because of imperfect outcome or a variation of the previous task. Human operators are able to judge task performance efficiently and are thus able to quickly identify and correct the unwanted parts, whereas complex evaluation algorithms and monitoring systems are needed if the robot needs to do this autonomously. This reduces system complexity, meaning less external systems are necessary to perform the task which saves costs and avoids errors and inaccuracies imposed by these external systems. Moreover, learning fatigue is decreased by focussing only on adapting the focused parts of the trajectory instead of re-teaching the whole trajectory again. After the operator is satisfied with the overall performance, the robot can then proceed to perform the task in a feed- forward fashion to optimise execution speed. We evaluate this algorithm on a KUKA LBR iiwa by teaching it how to draw eight figures on a plane. We show that the robot is able to adapt to the corrections made in the second phase of the algorithm.

The next section discusses related work on which our work is based upon. Then we will elaborate our approach in section 2. The results of the experiments are then presented in section 3, followed by a discussion and evaluation in section 6. Finally, this work is concluded in section 7 where we also discuss improvements for future work.

RELATED WORK

LfD Applications
Learning from demonstration is an extensively researched topic which has been covered for a wide variety of applications ranging from teaching an anthropomorphic hand to play Rock-Paper-Scissors [4] to learning biped locomotion using movement primitives [13]. In [3], Reinforcement Learning (RL) is used to teach different manipulators to vary their stiffness online while trying to pass through a specified goal. Another interesting work has been conducted by [12], in which a flexible surgical robot observes and imitates the movements of an octopus. Yet another work uses kinaesthetic teaching and a haptic device to teach positional and force trajectories, with which the authors performed door opening and ironing tasks [9].

The ability of LfD to teach an agent any task without the time, costs and expertise associated to programming the robot conventionally makes it an interesting technique to employ. While some LfD methods are specifically catered for specialised tasks, there also exist LfD methods which are more general since they have low system complexity and learn a low-level representation of tasks, which can be used to express any task. An example of this is Dynamical Movement Primitives (DMP), which is able to encode trajectories such as positional, force or joint trajectories by using a set of dynamical systems [11, 7]. DMPs are also highly adaptive in the sense that they are able to follow any desired trajectory simply by specifying the forcing term. Different trajectories to the same goal can be followed by just replacing the forcing term. Since we are interested in high adaptiveness, we use DMP to encode our tasks, which we describe in Cartesian position space. In the following section we will briefly summarise the formulation of DMPs.

Dynamical Movement Primitives
DMPs are used to encode and control trajectories using a set of dynamical systems. The cooperation of these subsystems give DMPs powerful properties such as disturbance rejection

and guaranteed convergence to the goal state, while still following a complex trajectory. The following set of equations describe a DMP [6]:

$$\tau\ddot{y} = \alpha_z(\beta_z(g-y) - \dot{y}) + f(x) \tag{1}$$

$$f(x) = \frac{\sum_{i=0}^{N} \psi_i w_i}{\sum_{i=0}^{N} \psi_i} x(g - y_0) \tag{2}$$

$$\psi_i(x) = \exp\left(-\frac{1}{2\sigma_i^2}(x - c_i)^2\right) \tag{3}$$

$$\tau\dot{x} = -\alpha_x x \tag{4}$$

(1) describes the core of DMP, which is a simple point-attractor system with an additional non-linear forcing term f. The canonical dynamical system, x, acts as a phase variable which generally starts at $x_0 = 1$ and monotonically converges to zero. This will ensure independence of time of the forcing term f, so the system becomes autonomous. Moreover, the canonical system provides a gating term to ensure that f converges to zero, so that the point-attractor system will always reach its goal regardless of how f is shaped. Note that f is a weighted sum of Gaussian kernels, where the weights can be calculated by using any regression algorithm such as Locally Weighted Regression (LWR) [5].

DMPs are traditionally used to encode a movement primitive of a task; by joining these DMPs together a robot is able to follow the trajectory needed to perform the whole task such as in [11]. In a similar way, DMPs can also encode rhythmic tasks by appending the same DMP with itself repeatedly. However, we use only one DMP to encode a fully continuous trajectory for the full task. This way only a segment of the forcing term need to be re-learned, rather than a whole DMP which is more efficient.

For our purposes, we use an open source library which implements DMPs with additional features [17].

PROPOSED APPROACH

Motivation
As mentioned earlier and as shown in figure 2, LAP is divided in three stages:

• Learning phase;

• Adaptation phase;

• Production phase.

The learning phase is designed to take the system complexity, learning fatigue and generality into consideration. System complexity is lowered by using kinaesthetic teaching, since no extra subsystems such as cameras or haptic devices are needed to record the user intentions as the user demonstrates a trajectory. As long as the robot supports gravity compensation or impedance mode, LAP is readily applicable to a said robot. Moreover, by opting for kinaesthetic teaching we also avoid the problem of correspondence [14]. In an attempt to

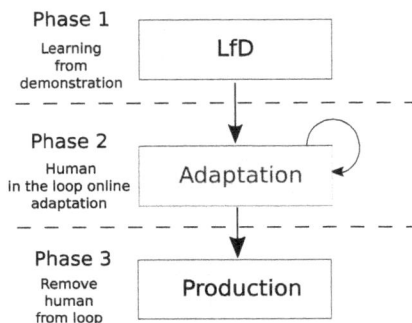

Figure 2. Proposed three-stage LfD method. Adaptation phase is iterative with human adaptations and corrections until high precision and accuracy is achieved.

increase generality, LAP learns low-level task-space trajectories, such as Cartesian positions, although it is still possible to learn even lower level trajectories such as joint angles. However, low-level task-space trajectories have the advantage that they are elementary enough to define a vast number of tasks, yet high-level enough to be transferable among different types of robots with a work-space of the same or higher dimensionality. For instance, most manipulation tasks can be defined by Cartesian positional trajectories with a force-profile for interaction with objects. A task learned and operated in Cartesian space can be executed by any robot with enough Degrees of Freedom (DoF). Finally, to reduce learning fatigue, we chose to learn the forcing term of the DMP by using LWR with Gaussian kernels, for which only one demonstration suffices. Should greater level of generalisation be required, other function approximators such as Gaussian Mixtures Model (GMM) can be used to cope with multiple demonstrations.

During the adaptation phase the manipulator will execute the learned trajectory in position control mode, which is inherently highly accurate and repeatable [10], to follow the desired trajectory. The user is then able to use voice commands to make the robot switch to impedance mode, while still continuing to execute the trajectory at low speed and stiffness. Using voice commands further reduces the learning fatigue since voice commands are intuitive and makes the robot more accessible while the operator is showing a demonstration. During adaptation, the operator will close the feedback loop by acting as an adaptation, correction and evaluation mechanism by guiding the manipulator. By using the human operator for sensing and optimisation, the system complexity is greatly reduced. Also, since only the segmented part of the trajectory will be re-learned, learning fatigue is lowered yet again. A concern with kinaesthetic teaching is the difficulty of demonstrating a task, especially if the task is complex. LAP emphasises on simplifying the teaching experience by using kinaesthetic teaching combined by re-teachable, selected segments of the task. The adaptation phase allows for corrections on selected parts of the taught task only, to improve and ease the teaching experience. Users will only need to focus on parts that were taught incorrectly and only need to apply minor corrections.

In the production phase the algorithm will have achieved the desired accuracy, so the robot will switch back to position mode and carry out the tasks. This means that the human will be removed from the feedback loop and the robot will perform the tasks in a feed-forward fashion, improving production speed. Since industrial robots are good for their precision and accuracy, as long as the task and the environment does not change, no feedback will be required until the next learning session. If the environment changes in the next session, the operator can simply re-initiate the adaptation phase to correct for the changes.

LAP Implementation

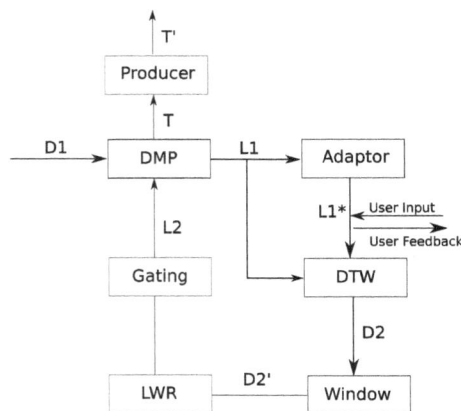

Figure 3. Flow-chart of LAP. D1: Demonstrated trajectory for learning phase. L1: Learned outcome of phase 1. L1*: L1 executed by manipulator, while being adapted online by user input. D2: Recorded adaptations after aligning with L1. D2': Adapted segment extracted from D2, after extending the segment at both ends by focussing a window on the region and extending that window. L2: Learned outcome of phase 2 after multiplication with the gating term of canonical system of the DMP. T: Trajectory ready to be executed in Production phase. T': Trajectory transformed in raw commands for the LBR iiwa to follow.

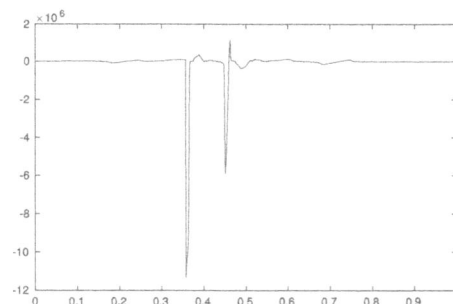

Figure 4. Adaptation of a straight line with a segment of itself. The segment was learned using LWR without windowing. The plot shows that the learned segment has incorrect values at the start and end.

Figure 3 shows the flow of the algorithm. First, a desired trajectory D1 is shown by the user, which is used to learn the forcing term of a DMP using LWR. If the operator is satisfied with the result at this point, the algorithm can then immediately proceed to the Production phase and start executing the

Displacement

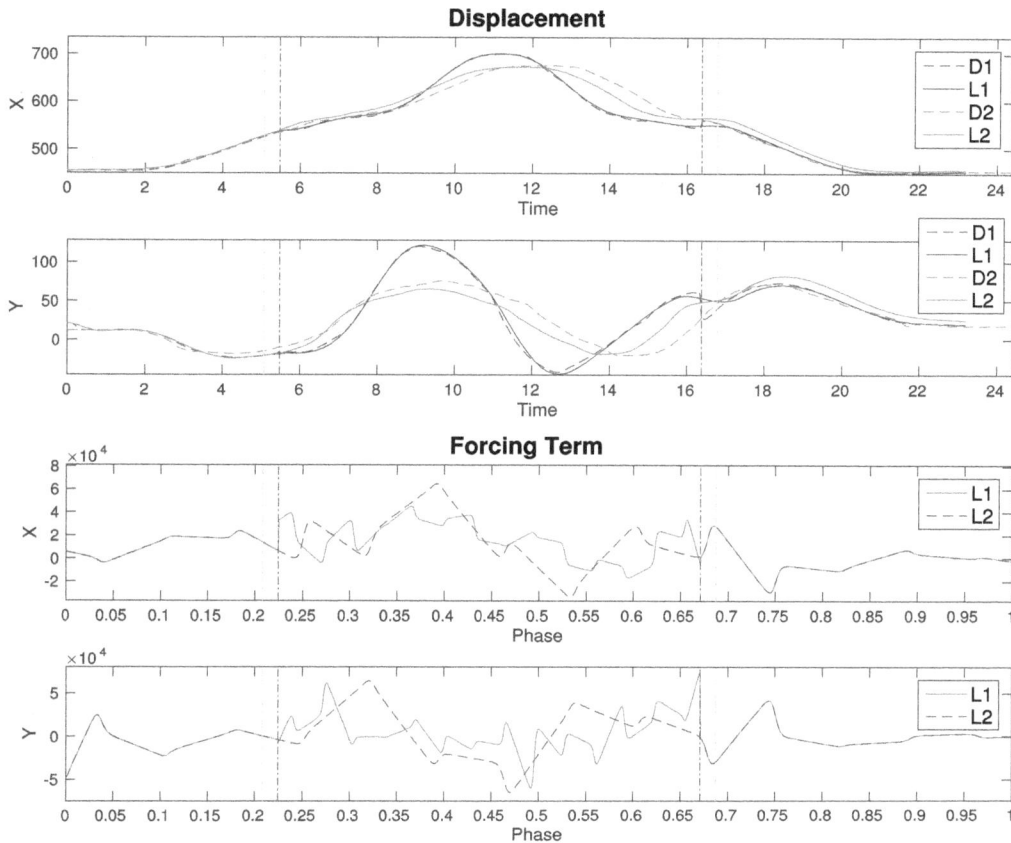

Figure 5. Displacements and forcing terms of session 1 for both x and y direction. The adaptation region is indicated by the black vertical lines, the extended windows for LWR is shown by the green lines. In this case, we took an extended window of 20 points at both ends. The figures show that L2 follows D2 inside the adaptation region, but does not follow L1 any longer outside the region. However, the forcing terms are overlapping outside the region. Due to the limited amount of space, we don't show the displacement trajectories and forcing terms of the other sessions, since they are similar.

resulting trajectory T. The learned outcome is passed to the Adaptation phase if the user is unsatisfied with the learned outcome or the next task to be executed is a variant of the current one. Here, the learned trajectory is executed by the task adaptor until the user gives a voice command to switch to impedance mode. The user will then start to apply the corrections, and gives another voice command to put the robot back to position mode when finished. The robot will then follow the remainder of the trajectory.

The recorded adaptations need to be compared to the learned outcome of phase 1, to find out which parts of the originally learned forcing term need to be adapted. Since the two trajectories to compare might differ in length or might be shifted in time with respect to each other, it is needed to align them. For this purpose, we employ Dynamic Time Warping (DTW), a technique used to align two similar time series for comparison [16]. Once it is aligned we can pass the trajectory containing the updated segment as a new demonstration D2. Learning the forcing terms of a fraction of the entire trajectory without special treatment will result in incorrect approximation (usually with overshoots) at the start and the end of the targeted segment as the derivatives of the trajectory at these points are unknown. This problem is demonstrated in Fig 4. We thus in-

troduce a windowing technique which allows the segmented trajectory to include t time-steps before and after the demonstrated adaptation segment. This is also useful for the LWR function approximator.

After learning we contract the window again to remove the transient data points while retaining our adaptation segment. To do this, we extract from D2 the adapted segment and extend that segment with a window before we pass it to LWR to learn. After learning the weights, we contract the window and multiply the outcome with the corresponding gating terms to finally retrieve the forcing terms. Adaptations can be done as many times as needed, until the trajectory is ready for execution in the Production phase.

EXPERIMENTS

We applied LAP to a KUKA LBR iiwa to teach it how to draw eight figures on a surface [1]. We intentionally provide an "incorrect" eight with a bigger lower half as the learning data for the first phase. We then show that the algorithm is able to adapt to the user corrections where necessary to draw a smaller eight figure. We conducted five trials in total with

---

[1] https://youtu.be/rIGupysXeWY

slightly varying results which we will elaborate in this section. Although the algorithm learns 3D Cartesian position space trajectories, we will only show the x and y dimensions for clarity since only those dimensions are of interest when drawing on a plane (see figure 1). After all, the height remains nearly constant in this case, though slight changes in height are present to apply pressure on the plane. Note that the z direction is still learned, but just not displayed here due to limited space. A demo of a pick-and-place task for which the z position does vary considerably has been conducted, though unfortunately no experimental results could be provided due to time pressure. A video of the demo has beeen recorded and uploaded [2].

EXPERIMENTAL SETUP

The KUKA LBR iiwa is positioned above an acrylic plate, on which it will draw using a marker, see figure 1. The marker is mounted on a 3D-printed piece, with a spring placed under the marker to allow for compliance when drawing on the plate. We use a Bluetooth® microphone to convey our voice commands to the robot.

RESULTS

As mentioned earlier we have 5 trials in total, numbered from 1 to 5. For every trial we show and compare the following data:

- Cartesian positions from the first shown demonstration D1 (intentionally incorrect trajectory);

- Cartesian positions and forcing term of the DMP from the learned outcome L1;

- Cartesian positions from the second shown demonstration D2 (desired "correct" trajectory);

- Cartesian positions and forcing term of the DMP from the learned outcome L2.

Since D2 is the correction that the user applied, we take D2 as the final trajectory as the user desires, which means that D2 is the "correct" trajectory. We computed the Mean Squared Errors (MSE) for both x and y directions of the learned outcomes L1 and L2 against this desired trajectory for every session to see how well the algorithm is able to follow the user's intended adaptations. Table 1 shows the MSE of the full trajectories compared to each other, table 2 shows the MSE calculated only within the adapted segments. For every row we also compute the average MSE and show the best (green) and worst (gray) MSE.

In general, it can be seen that L2 has lower MSE than L1, which means that the algorithm was able to transit from the originally learned trajectory L1 to L2, which is a better estimate of D2. Interestingly, we observe two points:

- When the full trajectories are compared, session 1 shows the best MSE for both x and y directions for both the learning phase and the adaptation phase;

Table 1. Mean Squared Error L1 vs D2 and L2 vs D2

	1	2	3	4	5	Mean
MSE X_L1	419.2		571.5	686.8	741.6	537.9
MSE Y_L1	716.6		614.5	605.5	615.0	605.0
MSE X_L2	312.8		405.4	673.2	561.7	443.5
MSE Y_L2	249.2		310.1	183.5	463.9	275.6

Table 2. Mean Squared Error in Adapted Segment

	1	2	3	4	5	Mean
MSE X_L1	547.8	328.7		556.2	638.5	474.4
MSE Y_L1	1207	906.8		1000	926.0	605.0
MSE X_L2	60.2		47.9	63.2	79.4	52.3
MSE Y_L2	107.0		105.7	105.8	117.1	102.1

- The MSE values of L1 and L2 are in the same order of magnitudes, whereas if we look at only the adapted segments the MSE for L2 are much lower.

For the first point, we conclude that the closer L1 is to D2, the better L2 will be able to adapt to D2 since there are relatively less corrections to be applied. Theoretically, if there are less changes to apply it should also be easier to adapt to the new trajectory.

As for the second point, even though L2 was able to follow the user corrections well, it was not able to follow the parts of the trajectory that did not change. This can also be seen in figure 5. The upper plots of Figure 5 show the trajectories in Cartesian position space in both axes. As can be seen, L2 tries to follow D2 within the boundaries given by the black vertical lines (the adaptation region), but outside the trajectories L2 was altered slightly and does not follow L1 any longer. If we look at the forcing terms also in figure 5, however, we observe that outside the adaptation boundaries L2 overlaps with L1 exactly. Furthermore, note that the forcing terms do not connect perfectly at the cuts. This might cause unexpected behaviour in position space such as undesired overshoot or undershoot, which explains why some segments of L2 are altered despite having the same forcing terms as L1 at those points in time. The final results, the drawn eight figures, are shown in figure 6. As we expected, L2 follows D2 closely as intended, but gets slightly affected at parts where it is not supposed to be.

DISCUSSION

We showed that the KUKA LBR iiwa was able to learn how to draw an eight figure and re-learn and apply the necessary corrections needed to draw a proper eight instead of a distorted one. In general the MSE was small for the adapted region, but outside the corrected segment the final trajectory was unintentionally altered. For the forcing terms, however, we see that the forcing terms are exactly replicated outside the adaptation segment and only modified where they should be. The fact that they are not connecting might cause unexpected dynamic behaviour causing the system to overshoot or undershoot, which might explain the unintended modifications outside the adaptation region. Moreover, we only used LWR in one direction of the data, which introduces phase lag and thus inaccuracies. This problem could be solved by using

---

[2] https://youtu.be/LBqK_269kiQ

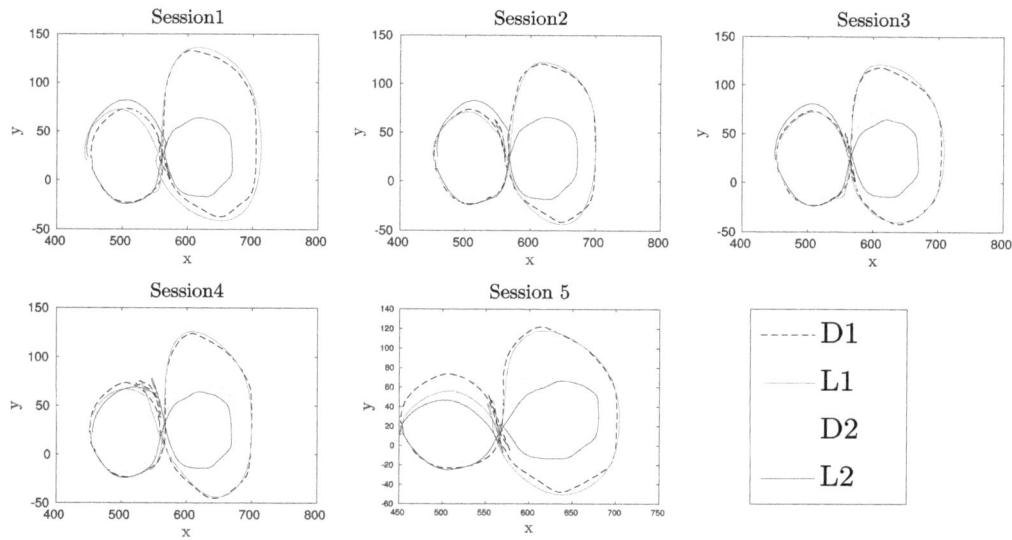

Figure 6. The resulting eight figures. In these figures, both the user inputs as the reproduced trajectories are shown for comparison. In general L2 adapts fairly well to D2, but does not maintain the parts of L1 which were not meant to be modified.

LWR in both directions or by simply using a different function approximator that does not have this problem. Note that our implementation allows for different fucntion approximators to be used to learn the forcing term of the DMP. Unfortunately, due to lack of time, we were unable to perform different experiments to showcase the generality and scalability of our algorithm. However, a pick-and-place demo [3] has been conducted to show this.

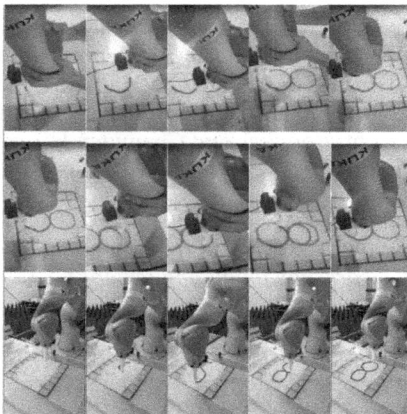

Figure 7. Learning, adaptation and production phases.

Despite of L2 being altered outside the adaptation boundaries, the algorithm was still able to draw eight figures. we see that L2 follows D2 closely but gets slightly affected at parts where it shouldn't be. This impairs the accuracy of the algorithm, although it was still able to produce reasonable eight figures. To overcome this problem, it is needed to make the newly adapted forcing terms connect better to the original forcing

terms, which could be done by following an approach such as is proposed in [11].

CONCLUSION

In this work we presented an LfD algorithm designed to conform to criteria for industrial applications. LAP attempts to lower system complexity by including the human operator in the feedback loop. This way no additional systems are needed to model the environment, to evaluate performance automatically and to optimise performance based on the evaluation since this can be efficiently done by the operator. Other points LAP tries to improve are learning fatigue, generality, accuracy and precision. For future work, accuracy should be improved by attempting to make the forcing terms connect properly.

We conducted the experiments with settings of LAP, in our knowledge, to best fit for industrial applications. With the current settings, we were able to lower system complexity and learning fatigue and increase generality. To further increase generality however, it should be attempted to learn full Cartesian poses instead of only positions. This is not a trivial problem in DMP implementation as the 3 axes of rotation are highly coupled together while the original DMP learns each feature space independently. To solve this problem, however, an approach for orientational DMPs was proposed by [19].

The Kuka LBR iiwa is inherently accurate and precise, but more research should be done to get our algorithm accurate enough to be suitable for industrial applications. Thus, different settings should be explored to see if better results can be achieved. A good example is the choice of the function approximator in both the Learning and Adaptation phase. A disadvantage is that LWR cannot generalise over multiple demonstrations since it uses only one demonstration, so there

[3]https://youtu.be/LBqK_269kiQ

is trade-off between generality and learning fatigue. However, note that the forcing term of the DMP can be learned by using any function approximator, so if more generality is desired it is possible to use another approximator such as Gaussian Mixture Regression (GMR) [18]. Furthermore, for this work we mainly focussed on the adaptation phase and learning a new segment of the task and replacing the old segment with the newly adapted segment. For future work, it should be researched how to optimise production speed, a point we were not able to investigate yet.

ACKNOWLEDGEMENTS

This work is supported by the Science and Engineering Research Council (SERC, A*STAR, Singapore) Grant No. 1225100001.

REFERENCES

1. Brenna D Argall, Sonia Chernova, Manuela Veloso, and Brett Browning. 2009. A survey of robot learning from demonstration. *Robotics and autonomous systems* 57, 5 (2009), 469–483.

2. A Billard, S Calinon, R Dillmann, and S Schaal. 2008. Robot programming by demonstration. *Springer handbook of robotics* (2008), 1371–1394.

3. Jonas Buchli, Evangelos Theodorou, Freek Stulp, and Stefan Schaal. 2010. Variable Impedance Control-A Reinforcement Learning Approach. In *Robotics: Science and Systems*.

4. Antonio Chella, Haris Dindo, Ignazio Infantino, and Irene Macaluso. 2004. A posture sequence learning system for an anthropomorphic robotic hand. *Robotics and Autonomous Systems* 47, 23 (2004), 143 – 152. `http://www.sciencedirect.com/science/article/pii/S0921889004000442` Robot Learning from Demonstration.

5. William S Cleveland. 1979. Robust locally weighted regression and smoothing scatterplots. *Journal of the American statistical association* 74, 368 (1979), 829–836.

6. Auke Jan Ijspeert, Jun Nakanishi, Heiko Hoffmann, Peter Pastor, and Stefan Schaal. 2013. Dynamical movement primitives: learning attractor models for motor behaviors. *Neural computation* 25, 2 (2013), 328–373.

7. Auke Jan Ijspeert, Jun Nakanishi, and Stefan Schaal. 2002. Movement imitation with nonlinear dynamical systems in humanoid robots. In *Robotics and Automation, 2002. Proceedings. ICRA'02. IEEE International Conference on*, Vol. 2. IEEE, 1398–1403.

8. Wilson Kien Ho Ko, Yan Wu, Keng Peng Tee, and Jonas Buchli. 2015. Towards Industrial Robot Learning from Demonstration. In *Proceedings of the 3rd International Conference on Human-Agent Interaction (HAI '15)*. ACM, 235–238.

9. Petar Kormushev, Sylvain Calinon, and Darwin G Caldwell. 2011. Imitation learning of positional and force skills demonstrated via kinesthetic teaching and haptic input. *Advanced Robotics* 25, 5 (2011), 581–603.

10. KUKA AG 2015. *LBR iiwa LBR iiwa 7 R800, LBR iiwa 14 R820 Specification*. KUKA AG. Rev. 5.

11. Tomas Kulvicius, KeJun Ning, Minija Tamosiunaite, and F Worgotter. 2012. Joining movement sequences: Modified dynamic movement primitives for robotics applications exemplified on handwriting. *Robotics, IEEE Transactions on* 28, 1 (2012), 145–157.

12. M. S. Malekzadeh, S. Calinon, D. Bruno, and D. G. Caldwell. 2014. Learning by Imitation with the STIFF-FLOP Surgical Robot: A Biomimetic Approach Inspired by Octopus Movements. *Robotics and Biomimetics, Special Issue on Medical Robotics* 1, 13 (October 2014), 1–15.

13. Jun Nakanishi, Jun Morimoto, Gen Endo, Gordon Cheng, Stefan Schaal, and Mitsuo Kawato. 2004. Learning from demonstration and adaptation of biped locomotion. *Robotics and Autonomous Systems* 47, 23 (2004), 79 – 91. `http://www.sciencedirect.com/science/article/pii/S0921889004000399` Robot Learning from Demonstration.

14. Chrystopher L. Nehaniv and Kerstin Dautenhahn. 2002. Imitation in Animals and Artifacts. MIT Press, Cambridge, MA, USA, Chapter The Correspondence Problem, 41–61. `http://dl.acm.org/citation.cfm?id=762896.762899`

15. Mikkel Rath Pedersen, Lazaros Nalpantidis, Rasmus Skovgaard Andersen, Casper Schou, Simon Bøgh, Volker Krüger, and Ole Madsen. 2015. Robot skills for manufacturing: From concept to industrial deployment. *Robotics and Computer-Integrated Manufacturing* (2015).

16. Stan Salvador and Philip Chan. 2004. FastDTW: Toward accurate dynamic time warping in linear time and space. In *KDD workshop on mining temporal and sequential data*. Citeseer.

17. Freek Stulp. 2014. DmpBbo – A C++ library for black-box optimization of dynamical movement primitives. (2014). `https://github.com/stulp/dmpbbo.git`

18. Hsi Guang Sung. 2004. *Gaussian mixture regression and classification*. Ph.D. Dissertation. Rice University.

19. Ales Ude, Bojan Nemec, Tadej Petric, and Jun Morimoto. 2014. Orientation in cartesian space dynamic movement primitives. In *Robotics and Automation (ICRA), 2014 IEEE International Conference on*. IEEE, 2997–3004.

Response Tendencies of Four-Year-Old Children to Communicative and Non-Communicative Robots

Mako Okanda
m-okanda@otemon.ac.jp
Otemon Gakuin University,
Osaka, Japan

Yue Zhou
whywhy0925@yahoo.co.jp
Kyoto University
Kyoto, Japan

Takayuki Kanda
kanda@atr.jp
ATR,
Kyoto, Japan

Hiroshi Ishiguro
ishiguro@sys.es.osaka-u.ac.jp
Osaka University,
Osaka, Japan

Shoji Itakura
sitakura@bun.kyoto-u.ac.jp
Kyoto University,
Kyoto, Japan

ABSTRACT

This study examined response tendencies in 4-year-old Japanese children ($N = 45$) to yes-no questions asked by a communicative, or a non-communicative robot. The children watched a video of a robot that was either responsive (communicative condition), or unresponsive (non-communicative condition) to human actions. Then, all the children watched a video of the same robot asking yes-no questions pertaining to familiar and unfamiliar objects. The children in both conditions exhibited a nay-saying bias to questions about unfamiliar objects, with children in the non-communicative condition tending to show a stronger nay-saying bias than children in the communicative condition. Children's response tendencies towards questions asked by humans and other agents are discussed.

Author Keywords

Cognitive development; human-robot communication; language development; response bias; yes bias

INTRODUCTION

Verbal communication often includes questions. Fritzley and Lee (2003) pointed out that questions are often used to test preschoolers' cognitive abilities in developmental psychology research and experiments. However, previous studies have reported that preschoolers do not always respond appropriately to yes-no questions (e.g., Fritzley & Lee, 2003; Okanda & Itakura, 2008). For example, 2- and/or 3-year-olds in different countries exhibited a yes bias, or a tendency to say "yes," to yes-no questions regarding object knowledge (Fritzley & Lee, 2003; Okanda & Itakura, 2007, 2008, 2010; Okanda, Somogyi, & Itakura, 2012), and Japanese 3-year-olds exhibited a yes bias to yes-no questions

HAI '16, October 04-07, 2016, Biopolis, Singapore
ACM 978-1-4503-4508-8/16/10.
http://dx.doi.org/10.1145/2974804.2980490

regarding object preferences and facial expressions (Okanda & Itakura, 2010). Okanda and Itakura (2010, 2011) suggested that young preschoolers exhibit a yes bias due to underdeveloped cognitive abilities (i.e. inhibition and verbal abilities) (see also Moriguchi, Okanda, & Itakura, 2008).

Children's ability to appropriately answer to yes-no questions increases with age, however, they exhibit either a yes bias, or a nay-saying bias in certain situations. For example, Japanese 4-year-olds exhibited a yes bias to questions pertaining to object knowledge, but they did not show any response bias to questions pertaining to object preference (Okanda & Itakura, 2010). Certain cross-cultural differences in response biases have been reported: Japanese 4- to 6-year-olds were likely to say "yes" when an unfamiliar adult asked them questions pertaining to knowledge of familiar objects in face to face situations, whereas Hungarian 4- to 6-year-olds tended to say "no" to questions pertaining to knowledge of unfamiliar objects under the same conditions (Okanda et al., 2012). However, Japanese 4-year-olds said "no" to their mothers, when they were asked questions in their home (Okanda et al., 2012). These results might suggest that Japanese children are able to say "no," but they are more likely to say "yes" when an unfamiliar interviewer tries to assess their knowledge in face to face interviews (see also Okanda & Itakura, 2010; Okanda et al., 2012). Moreover, older Japanese children might consider social factors when making yes-no decisions; such that they are likely to say "yes" when they feel social pressures (see also Okanda & Itakura, 2011; Okanda et al., 2012).

Okanda, Kanda, Ishiguro, and Okanda (2013) examined whether older preschoolers' response bias is influenced by the status of the interviewer and the situation by comparing children's responses to human and robot interviewers. They investigated 3- and 4-year-olds' response tendencies to yes-no questions pertaining to object knowledge in three different conditions: (1) when an unfamiliar adult asked questions face to face, (2) when children watched a video of an unfamiliar adult asking questions, and (3) when children watched a video of a robot asking questions. In the last two scenarios, children were required to answer "yes," or "no," to interviewers in the videos. A previous study has suggested that 10-month-old infants recognized a robot as an agent when it communicated with a humans, but did recognize it as an agent when it remained still, or did not communicate with humans (Arita, Hiraki, Kanda, & Ishiguro, 2005). On the contrary, preschoolers could make a clear distinction between robots and humans. Moreover, three-year-olds were influenced by adults' actions (Moriguchi, Lee, & Itakura, 2007), but not by a robot's actions (Moriguchi, Kanda, Ishiguro, & Itakura, 2010) when they performed a Dimensional Card Change Sort task (Zelazo, Frye, & Rapus, 1996). It is possible that infants and children have a common understanding that a robot can beO an agent, but their level of sensitivity to its agency might be different.

Okanda et al. (2013) considered a robot as a less authoritative interviewer for children and hypothesized that children might not show a yes bias to a robot interviewer; this hypothesis was partly confirmed. Four-year-olds exhibited a yes bias only to a human interviewer in a face to face situation. They exhibited a nay-saying bias to both a robot and a human in videos. However, the researchers did not find any difference between the robot and the human conditions (Okanda et al., 2013). Okanda et al. (2013) suggested that Japanese children might believe that robots are sibling-like friends, because of their regular exposure to communicative robots in movies and cartoons, and thus they might feel a degree of social pressure to agree with a robot. Moreover, the robots in Okanda et al. (2013) exhibited gaze behavior, because it has been reported as a key factor in 2-year-olds imitation of unsuccessful actions of robots (Itakura et al., 2008). Therefore, it is possible that the presence of gaze behavior plays some role in children's yes-no decision-making.

The previous study however, could not clarify whether the robot was an agent or an object for young children. In the present study, we first showed 4-year-olds a video in which a robot was either responsive, or unresponsive to adults' utterances and actions. We then showed the children a video of the robot asking yes-no questions. This process could help children perceive the robot as a communicative agent, or as an object. We hypothesized that children would be more likely to agree with the communicative robot, and that they would be more likely to say "no" to the non-communicative robot, because the latter would exert little or no social pressure.

METHODS

Participants

Children were recruited from a waiting list to participate in a study on child development conducted at Kyoto University. Four-year-old preschoolers participated in this study ($N = 45$): communicative robot condition ($n = 23$; $M = 54.00$ months, SD = 2.89, range = 49–59 months, 12 boys and 11 girls), and non-communicative robot condition ($n = 22$; $M = 53.73$ months, SD = 2.88, range = 49–59 months, 11 boys and 11 girls). Two preschoolers (girls) in the communicative condition refused to participate in the experiment and one preschooler (a girl) in the non-communicative condition said she could not hear the robot's voice, and did not answer the questions. These children were excluded from the later analysis. The design and purpose of the study were explained to the children's parents prior to the experiment and their written informed consent was obtained prior to the study. The experiments were approved by ethical committee in Kyoto University.

Materials

In the pre-trial, children in the communicative condition watched a scene in which a robot communicated with an adult female in the following sequence: (1) the adult calls the robot's name, (2) the robot moves its head up and looks at the adult, (3) the adult moves forward and offers her right hand to the robot, while maintaining eye contact, (4) the robot moves its right hand and they shake hands, and (5) the adult says, "please be my friend," to which the robot nods (Figure 1). Children in the non-communicative condition watched a scene in which a robot remains still, not responding to any of the utterances, or actions of the adult female. Durations of the two videos were nearly identical.

After the pre-trial, children in both conditions watched a scene in which the robot held an object in its hands (Figure 2) and children were asked yes-no questions about the object (i.e. main trial) by the robot (see more details in Okanda et al., 2013). In the main trial, we used the same objects and video stimuli that were used in Okanda's studies (Okanda et al., 2013): Three familiar objects (a red apple, a blue plastic cup, and a picture book) and three unfamiliar objects (a plastic coffee filter, a shoe horn, and a paper filter for a vacuum cleaner).

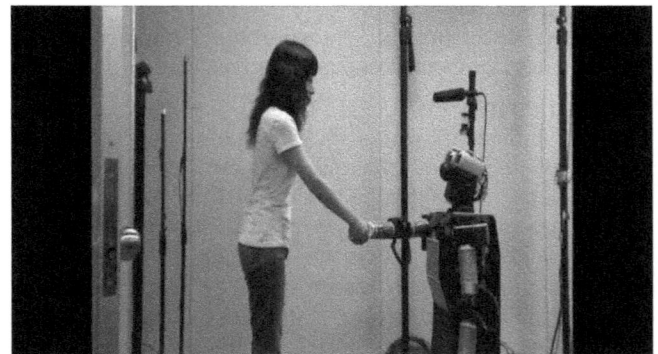

Figure 1. The robot and a human in the pre-trial of the communicative condition

[Robovie from Advanced Telecommunications Research Institute International (ATR)]

Figure 2. The robot used in the main trail of both conditions

[Robovie from Advanced Telecommunications Research Institute International (ATR)]

Procedures

The children participated in the experiment individually. They first watched a pre-trial video and then watched the main-trial video. In the main trial, an experimenter instructed the children to answer "yes" or "no," loudly to the robot, but not to the experimenter sitting next to them. The videos were presented to the children on a laptop computer having two speakers. The six objects were also presented to the children in person during the experiment. The children's responses (including nonverbal responses, such as nodding and head shaking) were recorded by the experimenter on an online response sheet. These actions were also recorded by a video camera.

Scoring

We modified Fritzley and Lee's (2003) scoring method to calculate mean response bias scores of the children (see more methods in other previous studies: Okanda & Itakura, 2007, 2008, 2010). The scores were calculated based on the proportion of "yes," or "no" responses. The range of children's mean response bias scores were −1 to +1. The scores for familiar and unfamiliar objects were calculated separately. A positive response bias score indicated a yes bias, and a negative response bias score indicated a nay-saying bias. A child who did not exhibit any response bias were expected to have a zero response bias score. In addition, "I don't know" and "no answers" (e.g. the child did not answer the question, or the child tried to answer but said nothing) were not scored, but were counted separately.

RESULTS

Figure 3 shows the children's response bias scores in communicative and non-communicative conditions. We conducted a Condition (communicative, non-communicative) × Familiarity (familiar, unfamiliar) mixed analysis of variance (ANOVA) with Familiarity as a within factor variable. Results indicated that the main effect of familiarity was significant, $F (1, 40) = 70.02$, $p < .01$, partial $\eta^2 = .64$. Moreover, the interaction between Familiarity and Condition was marginally significant, $F (1, 40) = 3.35$, $p = .08$, partial $\eta^2 = .08$.

We conducted one-sample t-tests to identify significant differences in the interaction and to confirm whether response bias scores were significantly different from zero (a score of zero indicated no response bias) for each condition. Results indicated that children in both conditions exhibited a nay-saying bias in the unfamiliar object conditions [Communicative condition: $t (20) = -3.50$, $p < .01$, Non-communicative condition: t $(20) = -5.37$, $p < .01$]. Children only rarely gave "I don't know" and "no answer" responses.

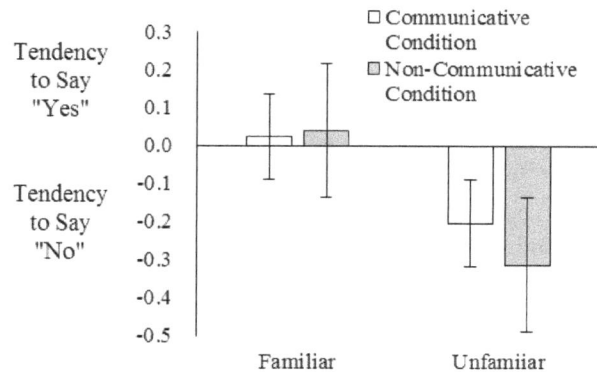

Figure 3. Children's Response Bias Scores

DISCUSSION

We hypothesized that 4-year-olds would show a yes bias when responding to a communicative robot and a nay-saying bias when responding to a non-communicative robot. The results partly confirmed our hypothesis, but children's responses to robots were more complex than we expected.

The children in both conditions were more likely to say "no" to questions pertaining to unfamiliar objects than to questions pertaining to familiar objects. This was consistent with previous findings that older Japanese preschoolers showed a nay-saying bias towards interviewers who exert less social pressure when asked similar questions (Okanda et al., 2013; Okanda et al., 2012). There was also a marginally significant difference between the two conditions; the children in the non-communicative condition were more likely to say "no" to those questions than children in the communicative condition.

As was discussed in the introduction, Japanese children are widely exposed to robots through movies and cartoons, and thus may already have some awareness of robots as agents. The robots depicted in children's media are usually heroes or helpers for children. We thought that if we showed children an additional scene in which a robot interacted with an adult, or was unresponsive to an adult's utterances and actions, the children would perceive the robot as a more authoritative agent in the former condition, whereas they would perceive it merely as an object in the latter condition. It was assumed that children would feel easier to say "no" to a robot if it were seemingly an object.

However, our results did not show significant differences between these conditions. It is possible that 4-year-olds are

323

not old enough to fully comprehend the differences in the interactions, and if this were the case, we might find different results when we explore responses of older children. Moreover, the video stimulus we used in this experiment and in the previous study (Okanda et al., 2013) depicted a robot with gaze behavior. This was necessary to make the robot stimulus comparable to human stimuli used in Okanda et al. (2013). However, children in the non-communicative condition in this study watched a scene in which a robot was unresponsive to humans' utterances and actions in the pre-trial, but then in the main trial, they watched a video in which the same robot was able to make eye contact with them. The children might have been confused by this, which could have confounded the results. It is suggested that effects of the presence or absence of gaze behavior in robots must be given more careful consideration in future investigations.

In the 21st century, children will have increasing opportunities to see and interact with robots. Our experiment suggests that 4-year-old children might believe and have some expectations that robots have communication abilities. Unlike 10-month-old infants, this expectation might not be destroyed easily, even after they watch the robot remain motionless in front of a human. Similar results have been reported in some previous studies (Scheeff, Pinto, Rahardja, Snibbe, & Tow, 2002). One study reported that 9-, 12-, and 15-year-olds after playing with a robot believed that it had mental states, and also that it was a social being (Kahn et al., 2012). These findings suggest that it might not be necessary to explain what a robot is to children, because it is possible that humans obtain knowledge about robots somewhere between the ages of one to four.

ACKNOWLEDGMENTS
We thank all parents and children who participated our study. This research was supported by a Grant to S.I. from Japan Society for the Promotion of Science (25245067, 25240020).

REFERENCES
1. Arita, A., Hiraki, K., Kanda, T., & Ishiguro, H. (2005). Can we talk to robots? Ten-month-old infants expected interactive humanoid robots to be talked to by persons. Cognition, 95(3), B49-B57. doi:10.1016/j.cognition.2004.08.001
2. Fritzley, V. H., & Lee, K. (2003). Do young children always say yes to yes-no question? A metadevelopmental study of the affirmation bias. Child Development, 74(5), 1297–1313. doi:10.1111/1467-8624.00608
3. Itakura, S., Ishida, H., Kanda, T., Shimada, Y., Ishiguro, H., & Lee, K. (2008). How to build an intentional android: Infants' imitation of a robot's goal-directed actions. Infancy, 13(5), 519-532. doi:10.1080/15250000802329503
4. Kahn, P. H. J., Kanda, T., Ishiguro, H., Freie, N. G., Severson, R. L., Gill, B. T. (2012). "Robovie, You'll have to go into the closet now": Children's social and moral relationships with a humanoid robot. Developmental Psychology, 48(2), 303-314. doi:10.1037/a0027033.
5. Moriguchi, Y., Kanda, T., Ishiguro, H., & Itakura, S. (2010). Children perseverate to a human's actions but not to a robot's actions. Developmental Science, 13(1), 62-68. doi:10.1111/j.1467-7687.2009.00860.x
6. Moriguchi, Y., Lee, K., & Itakura, S. (2007). Social transmission of disinhibition in young children. Developmental Science, 10(4), 481-491. doi:10.1111/j.1467-7687.2007.00601.x
7. Moriguchi, Y., Okanda, M., & Itakura, S. (2008). Young children's yes bias: How does it relate to verbal ability, inhibitory control, and theory of mind? First Language, 28(4), 431-442. doi:10.1177/0142723708092413
8. Okanda, M., & Itakura, S. (2007). Do Japanese children say 'yes' to their mothers? A naturalistic study of response bias in parent-toddler conversations. First Language, 27(4), 421–429. doi:10.1177/0142723707081653
9. Okanda, M., & Itakura, S. (2008). Children in Asian cultures say yes to yes-no questions: Common and cultural differences between Vietnamese and Japanese children. International Journal of Behavioral Development, 32(2), 131–136. doi:10.1177/0165025407087211
10. Okanda, M., & Itakura, S. (2010). When do children exhibit a "yes" bias? Child Development, 81(2), 568-580. doi:10.1111/j.1467-8624.2009.01416.x
11. Okanda, M., & Itakura, S. (2011). Do young and old preschoolers exhibit response bias due to different mechanisms? Investigating children's response time. Journal of Experimental Child Psychology, 110, 453-460. doi:10.1016/j.jecp.2011.04.012
12. Okanda, M., Kanda, T., Ishiguro, H., & Itakura, S. (2013). Three- and 4-year-old children's r response tendencies to various interviewers. 116, 68-77. doi:10.1016/j.jecp.2013.03.012
13. Okanda, M., Somogyi, E., & Itakura, S. (2012). Differences in response bias among younger and older preschoolers: Investigating Japanese and Hungarian preschoolers. Journal of Cross-Cultural Psychology, 43(8), 1325-1338. doi:10.1177/0022022112440145
14. Scheeff, M., Pinto, J., Rahardja, K., Snibbe, S., & Tow, R. (2002). Experiences with Sparky, a social robot. In K. Dautenhahn, A. Bond, L. Cañamero, & B. Edmonds (Eds.), Socially Intelligent Agents: Creating Relationships with Computers and Robots (Vol. 3, pp. 173-180.): Springer US.
15. Zelazo, P. D., Frye, D., & Rapus, T. (1996). An age-related dissociation between knowing rules and using them. Cognitive Development, 11(1), 37-63. doi:10.1016/S0885-2014(96)90027-1

Thermal Sweet Taste Machine for Multisensory Internet

Nur Amira Samshir, Nurafiqah Johari, Kasun Karunanayaka, Adrian David Cheok
Imagineering Institute
Iskandar Puteri, Malaysia
{amira, nurafiqah, kasun, adrian}@imagineeringinstitute.org

ABSTRACT

This paper presents a new taste interface for multisensory communication called "Thermal Sweet Taste Machine". We developed this interface in order to create sweet sensations, by manipulating the temperature on the tongue, without using chemicals. This device device changes the temperature on the surface of the tongue (from 20°C to 40°C) within a short period of time using a computer controlled circuit. Our preliminary user studies suggested that this device would be effective in two ways; producing the sweet sensations without the aid of chemicals, and enhancing the sweetness of the food and drinks. Here we discuss our concept, development of the interface, and some preliminary studies that has been carried out. We believe our technology would enhance the experiences and capabilities in future multisensory communication in different disciplines such as Human-Computer Interaction, human robot interactions, gaming and interacting with artificial agents.

ACM Classification Keywords

H.5.m. Information Interfaces and Presentation (e.g. HCI): Miscellaneous; See http://acm.org/about/class/1998/ for the full list of ACM classifiers. This section is required.

Author Keywords

Thermal Sweet Taste Machine; Multisensory Communication; Digital Taste; HCI; TRPM5.

INTRODUCTION

The five most fundamental tastes are sweet, sour, bitter, salty and umami (savory). Probably sweet taste is the most pleasant out of all the basic tastes [2]. Considering about the multisensory communication, sensing and actuating sweet taste digitally is an extremely important requirement. Once we reached that goal, people will be able to experience the sweetness digitally through the internet (as illustrated in Figure 1) like we experience text, audio and visuals in our daily life.

The early sweet taste taste interfaces developed in the field of Human-Computer Interaction primarily used chemicals to generate sweet sensations [4, 5, 10]. However, some previous studies suggested that by rising the temperature on the tongue within few seconds resulted sweet sensations without chemicals [3] and enhance the sensitivity for sweetness [9]. Using

HAI '16 October 04-07, 2016, Biopolis, Singapore

© 2016 Copyright held by the owner/author(s).

ACM ISBN 978-1-4503-4508-8/16/10.

DOI: http://dx.doi.org/10.1145/2974804.2980503

Figure 1. Concept image of people that are able to communicate and experience sensations digitally

this concept, we have developed a computer controllable user interface that can change the temperature of the surface of the tongue rapidly within safe margins and produce sweet sensations without using chemicals.

RELATED WORKS

The "Thermal stimulation of taste" [3] experiment has first showed that heating the tip of the tongue from a cold temperature resulted phantom sweet taste sensations. The temperature limits used for the experiment was from 20°C to 35°C and varied at approximately at 1.5°C/s using a Peltier module. This research has discussed the concept of 'Thermal Tasters', the kind of people who can perceive different tastes by stimulating their tongue with temperature.

According to the study conducted by Talavera et al. [9], increasing the temperature resulted in activation of TRPM 5 channel (which triggers for sweet, umami and bitter tastes) that generates a depolarizing potential in the taste receptor cells. This effect causes both the enhancement of sweetness perception at high temperatures and the 'thermal taste' (the phenomenon whereby heating or cooling of the tongue evoke sensations of taste in the absence of chemical tastants).

As above mentioned papers, in medicine and neuroscience fields, the thermal effect with TRPM 5 channel has well studied and discussed. However, in HCI, still there is no user interface that can effectively reproduce sweet sensations on tongue digitally. The "Digitally Stimulating the Sensation of Taste Through Electrical and Thermal Stimulation" [6] presented a system that is able to stimulate taste sensations on human tongue. By changing the temperature and inverted current, some participants reported that they were able to percept sweetness. However, this technology has never developed as a sweet interface although the author and other researchers in the field has developed digital interfaces that are able to produce sour and salty tastes more robustly [1, 7]. "Affecting Tumbler" [8] is an another interface that can affect human perceive of different flavor, without changing the food and drinks ingredients itself. The study is done by applying thermal sensations (heating up) to the skin around the nose while drinking. Based on the user study, it is suggested that the flavor perception is improved after applying thermal to the nasal skin.

Results of the previous studies suggest that still there are many studies left to be done in this research area to build a robust, controllable and repeatable sweet interface (e.g. find the suitable parameters such as temperature levels, intensity, speed, user experience studies such as compare organic and digital tastes, and study short term and long term effects).

METHOD

During the development of the proposed device we were primarily focused on heating up the surface of the tongue and stimulate the heat receptors with in a short time period. The operating temperature of the device is limited from of 20°C to 40°. Typically, the body temperature of a human is approximately 36.5°C. Therefore, in terms of the operating temperature range, this interface can be considered as safe to be applied with humans. The latest prototype of the thermal sweet taste machine is shown in the Figure 2. Thermal Sweet Taste machine consists of an electronic controller circuit, Electrode that connects to the Peltier, and a software module. Figure 3 shows the the design of the circuit. Temperature of the tongue is adjusted by the Peltier attached with a silver strip (tongue interface).Peltier module is a special kind of semiconductor whereby one side becomes cool and other side become hot when current flows through it. This Peltier has operating temperature in between -40°C to 80°C and consumes up to 8.5A. Therefore, high power motor driver is used to drive high current Peltier module up to 10A continuously and support sign magnitude PWM operation.

We used copper strips for the first prototype and silver strip in the latest version. We found that silver provides faster temperature change as it has low specific heat capacity, which is 0.057kcal/kg°C, 0.035kcal/kg°C lower than copper. We designed the silver strip to a smaller surface area for a faster heating and cooling process and made it as thin as possible (0.5mm thickness). Silver strip is attached using a high thermal conductivity in order to provide efficient heat transfer between two surfaces. Further, silver does not provide any metallic taste sensations.

By improving heating and cooling process of the peltier, faster change of temperature can be achieved. Therefore, a liquid cooler is attached together with the cooling side of the peltier to overcome the inconsistent heating. A series of technical experiments have been conducted to identify the most suitable rise time of the silver strip from 25°C to reach 40°C using a PID controlling. The best rise time we achieved with a

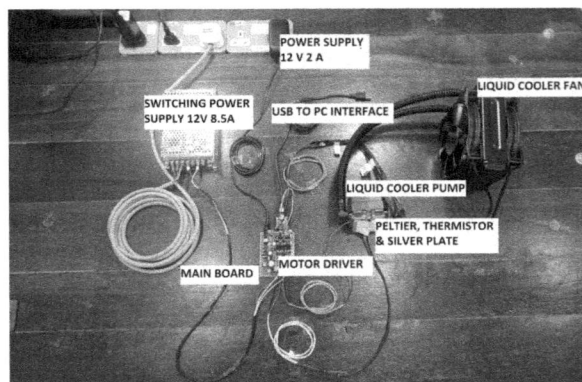

Figure 2. This figure shows the detailed component view of the thermal sweet taste machine second prototype .

good stability was 7.25s with a PID parameter of (20,10,25). We have also modified our system to start the temperature rise from 20°C. We have also found out three different rise times which provide different stimulation speeds to use in user experiments.

DISCUSSION

The preliminary studies of the Thermal Sweet Taste device shows quite significant results in achieving the objectives. Series of user experiments has been conducted to prove the effectiveness of the device. During the first experiment with 36 volunteers (12 females, Mage = 25.88, SD = 5.75, Age range = 20-44) participants were asked to place the interface on top of their tongue and sense the temperature change and requested to describe their experiences. Six participants felt the sweet sensation purely from the device. These participants are recognized and was asked to do the next experiment, which is based on three different speeds (the rise times for the three speeds was 6 seconds , 10 seconds and 15 seconds) of temperature change. We found out that the medium and fast temperature changes produce more intense sweet sensations.

The second experiment was done with 20 volunteers (5 females, Mage = 25.30, SD = 5.43, Age range = 20-44) from another institute. We were studying the effect using the thermal sweet interface (two modes : device is switched ON and OFF) with two sucrose solutions and water (water, 3 g/l sucrose, and 24 g/l sucrose). As shown in the Figure 4, the result shows that when the device is switched on it is able to enhance the intensity and sweetness of the solutions.

In future, we would continue to identify more thermal tasters. With a large group of thermal tasters (at least more than 40) we will be able to run out more user experiments to improve the Thermal Sweet Taste Machine. We are planing to identify parameters for controlling intensity, repeatability and controllability of sweet sensations. Also we are looking forward to develop new prototypes which will be suitable for different applications such as spoons, cups, and bottles. We believe that this interface would be very useful in the future of multisensory applications for the fields like human-computer interaction, man-machine interactions, virtual reality and medicine.

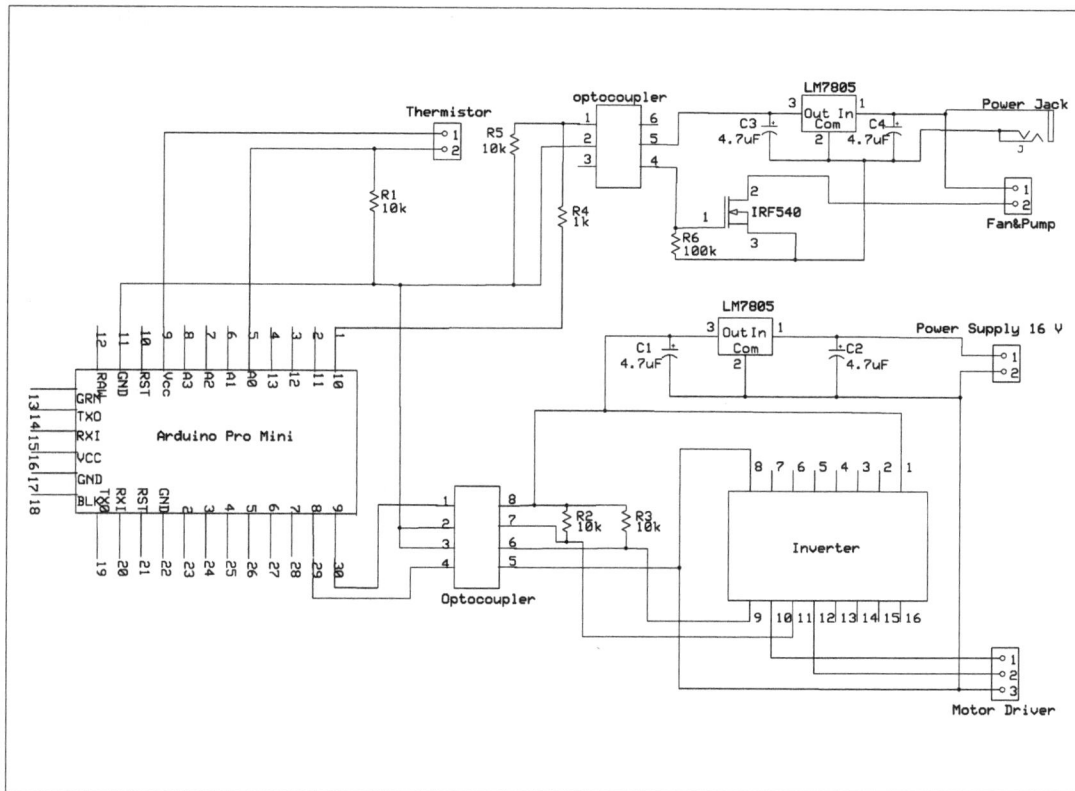

Figure 3. This figure shows the detailed component view of the thermal sweet taste machine second prototype.

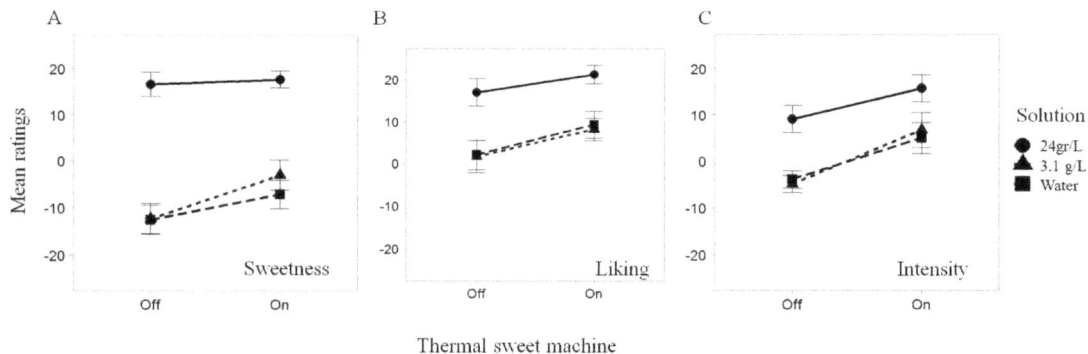

Figure 4. Experiment results for the user evaluation on enhancement of sweet taste

CONCLUSION

This paper presented the research and development of a new user interface which reproduce and enhance sweet sensation by applying thermal stimulation to the surface of the tongue. Our concept, development of the prototype and some preliminary user experiment results were discussed in the above sections. In summary, by using this device, 'Thermal Tasters' are able to obtain the sweet sensation purely from the device and in another scenario, enhancement of sweet sensations was reported while tasting sucrose after using the device. By carefully improving this technology further and finding the proper stim-ulation parameters, we will be able to digitally actuate sweet sensations meaningfully for future internet communication.

ACKNOWLEDGMENTS

The authors would like to thank greatly and acknowledge Carlos Velasco, Olivia Petit, Michael Herrera and the other members in Imagineering Institute, Malaysia for their significant contributions for this research. We also would like to thank Professor Mohd Shahrizal Sunar, Dr. Farhan Mohamed and other MagicX members in University Technology Malaysia for helping us to conduct user experiments at their premises.

REFERENCES

1. Yukika Aruga and Takafumi Koike. 2015. Taste change of soup by the recreating of sourness and saltiness using the electrical stimulation. In *Proceedings of the 6th Augmented Human International Conference*. ACM, 191–192.

2. Gary K Beauchamp and Beverly J Cowart. 1987. Development of sweet taste. In *Sweetness*. Springer, 127–140.

3. Alberto Cruz and Barry G Green. 2000. Thermal stimulation of taste. *Nature* 403, 6772 (2000), 889–892.

4. Philip Kortum. 2008. *HCI beyond the GUI: Design for haptic, speech, olfactory, and other nontraditional interfaces*. Morgan Kaufmann.

5. Dan Maynes-Aminzade. 2005. Edible bits: Seamless interfaces between people, data and food. In *Conference on Human Factors in Computing Systems (CHI'05)-Extended Abstracts*. Citeseer, 2207–2210.

6. Nimesha Ranasinghe. 2012. *Digitally Stimulating the Sensation of Taste Through Electrical and Thermal Stimulation*. Ph.D. Dissertation.

7. Nimesha Ranasinghe, Kuan-Yi Lee, Gajan Suthokumar, and Ellen Yi-Luen Do. 2014. The sensation of taste in the future of immersive media. In *Proceedings of the 2nd ACM International Workshop on Immersive Media Experiences*. ACM, 7–12.

8. Chie Suzuki, Takuji Narumi, Tomohiro Tanikawa, and Michitaka Hirose. 2014. Affecting tumbler: affecting our flavor perception with thermal feedback. In *Proceedings of the 11th Conference on Advances in Computer Entertainment Technology*. ACM, 19.

9. Karel Talavera, Keiko Yasumatsu, Thomas Voets, Guy Droogmans, Noriatsu Shigemura, Yuzo Ninomiya, Robert F Margolskee, and Bernd Nilius. 2005. Heat activation of TRPM5 underlies thermal sensitivity of sweet taste. *Nature* 438, 7070 (2005), 1022–1025.

10. Mark Tutton. 2008. Designers developing virtual-reality 'Cocoon'. *CNN* (2008).

See Where I am Looking at: Perceiving Gaze Cues with a NAO Robot

Eunice Njeri[1], Emilia Barakova[1], Ruixin Zhang[1], Marta Diaz[2], Andreu Catala[2], Matthias Rauterberg[1]

[1]Designed Intelligence Group
Department of Industrial Design
Eindhoven University of Technology,
Netherlands.

[2]Technical Research Centre for Dependency
Care and Autonomous Living (CETpD)
Technical University of Catalonia,
Spain.

ABSTRACT

Gaze is an important nonverbal cue in human - human communication, for example, in communicating direction of attention. Therefore, presumably being able to understand and provide gaze cues is an important aspect in robot's interactive behavior. While there is considerable progress, as regards the design of social gaze cues for robots, there is little that has been done to examine the ability of humans to read and accept help signals from a robot's gaze. In this study, we examine how people perceive gaze cues and head angles directed towards different target positions on a table when human and NAO robot are sitting against each other as in board game scenarios. From the results, we show that when the head pitch angle is higher (24±2) and the depth is less, approximately 20 cm from the robot, participants detected the positions with good accuracy. Unexpectedly, the locations on the left of the robot were detected with lower accuracy. In conclusion, we discuss the implications of this research for design of interaction settings between human and a robot that is intended for social and educational support.

Author Keywords

Gaze based interactions; gaze perception; serious games for social robots; directed attention; facial orientation

ACM Classification Keywords

H.5.m. Information interfaces and presentation; Design, Human factors.

INTRODUCTION

Nowadays, robots are showing more potential to be effectively incorporated into many social settings, for example in educational and therapeutic facilities for children and nursing homes for the elderly [1]. Accordingly, the design of intuitive human-robot interaction in these settings is becoming crucial. Providing nonverbal cues in an intuitive manner is crucial for the successful application of robots in these settings. Gaze, in particular, is an important nonverbal cue. Gaze facilitates a number of functions in social interaction such as turn-taking activities, communicating direction of attention [2, 3, 4]. Importantly, gaze reading and attending to gaze direction or head orientation cues of another person facilitates the formation of joint visual attention to objects in the surrounding and subsequently helps to create shared attention [5]. Prior work showed that gaze improves interactions with robots and thus being able to understand and provide gaze cues is an important aspect of human-robot interaction [6].

While human-robot interaction research has made considerable progress in finding out how to provide social gaze cues with robots [6, 7, 8, 9], studies are yet to explore the ability of humans to read, and accept help cues from a robot's gaze. In addition, robots capabilities differ significantly from those of humans, and hence their ability to communicate gaze information. Therefore to increase the effectiveness of robot gaze behaviors, it is important, to establish how people perceive gaze cues while interacting with a robot. For this experiment we use NAO robot platform from Aldebaran [10]. NAO has minimal facial features with static mouth and eyes, and its face bear a resemblance to a child's face. Due to its minimalistic design and perception capabilities, NAO robot has been adopted widely for research focused on interactions with children with autism spectrum disorders, either for therapeutic or for general educational/pedagogical purposes. Because NAO lacks movable eyes and therefore has to turn its entire head to look at something, it is necessary, to establish how people perceive gaze cues while interacting with the robot.

The overall aim of our research is to examine how different timing strategies of gaze influence human behavior, particularly in the context of children to robot interactions. As a step toward this goal, we have developed an experimental task, using a board game where a human

HAI '16, October 04-07, 2016, Biopolis, Singapore.
ACM 978-1-4503-4508-8/16/10.
http://dx.doi.org/10.1145/2974804.2980479

participant plays a matching card game in the presence of either a human or a robot tutor. The general idea is that the tutor provides gaze clues to help the participant find a matching card.

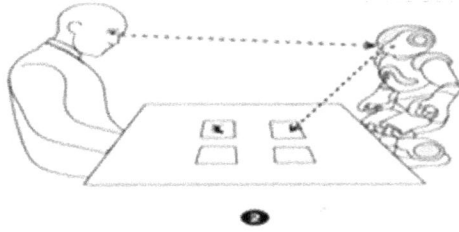

Figure 1: Experimental setting. The interaction flow is as follows: participant (left) turns over a card, tutor (right) gazes at the matching card, participant gazes at the tutor, participant's gazes at the matching card, participant turns the matching card.

Adopting the perspective of human - human communication on gaze behavior and nonverbal cues, we hypothesize that, gaze social cues (facial orientation; head orientation) from the tutor will help focus participant's attention to the matching card and subsequently influence the choice of the participant. Accordingly to determine the above, and to establish whether the gaze cues from the robot will communicate card location, we prepared a design to examine if people perceive accurately the gaze and head direction displayed by NAO robot towards different card positions on the table.

In related work, researchers in [11] measured the region of eye contact with NAO robot. A study in [12] also addresses the ability of individuals to read the gaze direction when presented with various forms of displays. Our motivation is that, many settings used for therapeutic training and for educational purposes are implemented in the form of board games. Therefore it is necessary to investigate gaze perception in such settings, which we further use to build human-centered applications.

METHOD
Experimental Setup

The proposed experimental setup is as follows: The participant and NAO sit on the two sides of a table facing each other. The table is approximately 80 cm in width and the height of the table is 72 cm. A board grid with the card positions resembling a memory game is fixed on the table. The layout has 18 squares (8*8cm) organized in six (6) columns and three (3) rows. The 18 squares correspond to the 18 card positions for the game. The squares are 10 cm apart in depth (y-axis) and 6 cm apart on the width (x-axis). The layout is 600 mm in width and 900 mm long

To measure the angles, we placed NAO on a small desk 56 cm in height at "Stand in "pose (0, 0), and at a distance of 5 cm from the table. The design grid has six squares in the x - direction, which is from left to right side of (NAO), and three squares in the y direction which is the depth direction

of the (NAO The distance between NAO and the closest square position is approximately 20 cm away, and the furthest at the corner is about 60 cm. We attached a laser beamer on the mid-section of NAO head and adjusted it to point at the middle of the layout, using the "look at" module in Choregraph program. We estimated the head pitch and head yaw angles for all the target positions using the motion screen on Choregraph.

Position= {HeadYawAngleVal, HeadPitchAngleVal}

NAO coordinate system is as shown in Figure 2; left. The HeadYawAngleVal of NAO gaze direction is defined as the angle between the positive y-axis and a line drawn from the center to a fixated position. The yaw angle of the y-axis is 0, and a positive head yaw angle value is on the left side of NAO. NAO head yaw angles range from -119 to 119 degrees. The HeadPitchAngle of NAO gaze direction is the angle between the xy plane and a line drawn from NAO head location to a target square. The pitch (head joint front and back) angle increases from 0 to 29.5. For the setup, the highest angle pitch value used is 24± degrees, for the two middle positions in the first row. The highest yaw angle is 48± for position 1 and -48± for position 6. On the second row, the angle pitch decreases to 10±1 for the middle positions. The pitch angle decreases with increase in yaw angle for the positions on the sides.

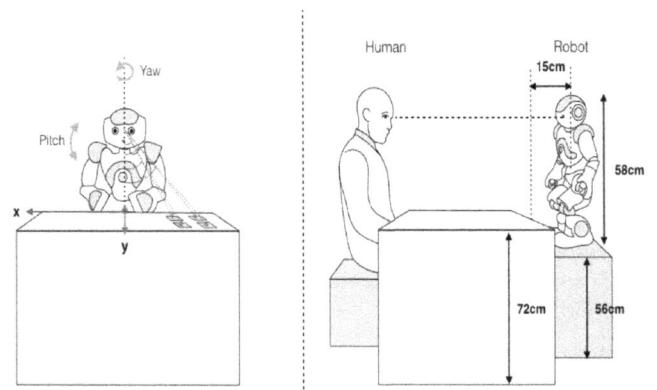

Figure 2: left; Experimental setting; human robot test; side view

Participants and Procedure

Six students from the University College participated in the study. Three were female and three males. The robot was placed on a small table 56 cm tall at (0, 0) with its face directed to the face of the person .The participant sat on a chair which was adjusted to give an eye - height position with the robot. The distance between the robot and the participant was approximately 110 cm. The experimenter informed the participants of their role and gave them instructions regarding the experiment. We implemented a Java algorithm to turn NAO head randomly to the 18 positions on the layout. Each participant interacted with the robot only in one trial. When the robot moved its head to a certain location, the participant wrote a number between 1

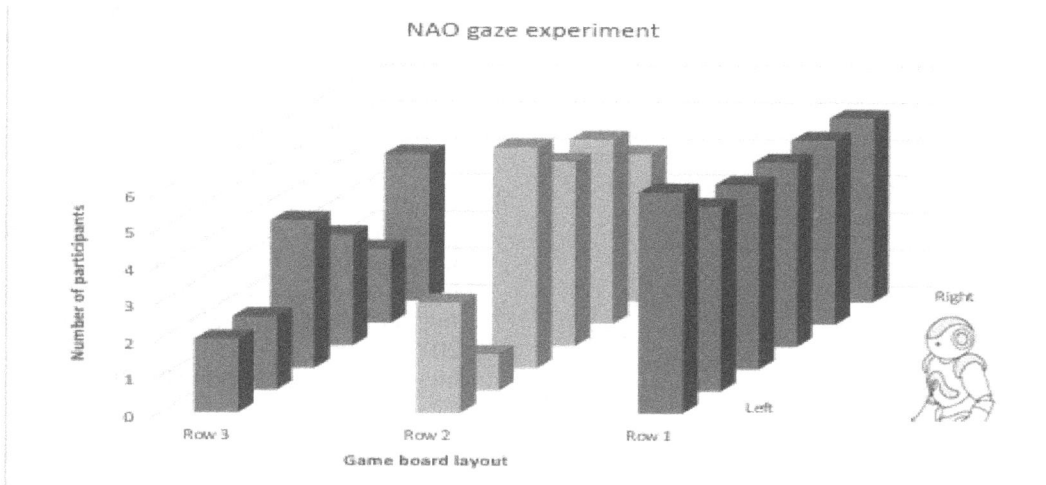

Figure 3. Gaze perception results; the number of participants who perceived the robot gaze correctly for each card location. Row 1; Row 2; Row 3.

and 18 on a post-it and placed it where they perceived the robot was looking on the layout. Each trial lasted for about 5 minutes.

RESULTS

We recorded the number of correct perceptions for each card location. The count of correct perceptions included all the post-its placed inside the square position and those surrounding in a distance less than or equal to 1cm. For the post-its that were placed more than 1cm from the intended card locations, these were regarded as wrong perceptions. Figure 3 shows the results of the gaze perception experiment, on how human observers judged where NAO was looking and the intended card locations. From the graph it is clear that people are better able to perceive correctly the square positions more for the card locations that are in the row that is closest to NAO i.e. when the head pitch angle is higher (24±2); less depth in the y direction) which is approximately 20 cm from NAO. The ability to perceive seems to lessen with the increase in depth. For example, the number of participants who perceived the gaze correctly decreases rapidly when the rows are far from (NAO). The number of correct perceptions is lower in Row 2 compared to Row 1 and continues to lessen for the third row, which is approximately 60 cm away from NAO for this layout

An interesting observation from the result is when NAO robot is looking at positions on its right the participants are better able to perceive more than when the robot is gazing at the locations on its left. Observers were also able correctly to perceive the positions in the middle of the layout more. Observations also show that participants understand head yaw angles quite better as opposed to head pitch angles for this robot. However, with the increase in depth, the perception of yaw information seems to lessen. A study in [13] indicates that the perception of pitch gaze

component directions depends on the communicative method, however, the yaw component does not rely on the communication method

CONCLUSION

Being able to understand and provide gaze cues is an important aspect especially for robots intended for educational and developmental support. In this report, we present a preliminary study conducted to examine how human observers perceive where NAO is looking. Our goal was to find out if gaze cues provided by a robot can direct the attention and influence the choices of the human partner. In this initial experiment, we tested whether gaze cues from the robot tutor communicate accurately enough card location in a card board game.

From the results: it is clear that people can follow the orientation of NAO head and its movements to judge gaze direction. Thus, head orientation has a significant influence on gaze direction perception especially with a robot such as NAO, which has fixed eyes. However, it's hard to use head angles alone to distinguish objects on the table if they are very close. Since human observers can clearly perceive NAO gaze cues when the depth is less; it is, therefore, effective to place the objects closer to NAO, for example, reduce the number of rows or increase the spacing between objects for the distant rows from the robot. Consequently, this will improve the accuracy of perception and the overall effectiveness of the use of a social robot in these settings. Unexpectedly, we found that the locations on the left of the robot (right of the human participants) were detected with lower accuracy by the participants. This finding needs to be further investigated in follow-up experiments.

Future work involves examining the temporal aspects of gaze in human–human interactions to build more realistic interactive robot gaze behaviors. Moreover, using human studies is a promising approach as the robots are intended for interaction with humans. Further analysis of head movement's impact on gaze perception with a robot is necessary. In future, we also plan to combine NAO head-directions behaviors, other social cues such as body posture derived from Time and Flow Effort of Laban Movement Analysis [14]. In our future experiments, we will include more human-like eyes, to explore how more articulated eyes will improve interactions in social settings.

ACKNOWLEDGMENTS

This work was supported in part by the Erasmus Mundus Joint Doctorate in Interactive and Cognitive Environments, which is funded by the EACEA Agency of the European Commission under EMJD ICE FPA no 2010-0012. We thank Merhnoorh Vahdat, PhD student for her valuable insights, and all the participants who voluntarily participated in the preliminary study.

REFERENCES

1. E. I. Barakova, P. Bajracharya, M. Willemsen, T. Lourens, and B. Huskens, "Long-term LEGO therapy with humanoid robot for children with ASD," , Expert Systems, Vol. 32, Issue 6, 2015 Pages 698–709

2. C. Kleinke: Gaze and eye contact: A research review. Psychological Bulletin 10, 78–100 (1986)

3. A. Kendon; Some functions of gaze-direction in social interaction. Acta Psychol. (Amst)., vol. 26, no. 1, pp. 22–63, 1967

4. Roel Vertegaal, Robert Slagter, Gerrit Van Der Veer, and Anton Nijholt, 'Eye Gaze Patterns in Conversations : There Is More to', *Analysis*, 2001, 301–8 http://dx.doi.org/10.1145/365024.365119

5. N. J. Emery, "The eyes have it: The neuroethology, function and evolution of social gaze," Neurosci. Biobehav. Rev., vol. 24, no. 6, pp. 581–604, 2000.

6. Frank Broz, Hagen Lehmann, Yukiko Nakano, and Bilge Mutlu, 'Gaze in HRI: From Modeling to Communication', in *Proceedings of the Seventh Annual ACM/IEEE International Conference on Human-Robot Interaction*, 2012, pp. 491–92 http://dx.doi.org/10.1145/2157689.2157845

7. Bilge Mutlu, Fumitaka Yamaoka, Takayuki Kanda, Hiroshi Ishiguro, and Norihiro Hagita, 'Nonverbal Leakage in Robots: Communication of Intentions through Seemingly Unintentional Behavior', in *HRI*, 2009, II, 69–76 http://dx.doi.org/10.1145/1514095.1514110

8. Henny Admoni, Bradley Hayes, David Feil-Seifer, Daniel Ullman, and Brian Scassellati, 'Are You Looking at Me? Perception of Robot Attention Is Mediated by Gaze Type and Group Size', *ACM/IEEE International Conference on Human-Robot Interaction*, 2013, 389–95 http://dx.doi.org/10.1109/HRI.2013.6483614

9. Yuichiro Yoshikawa, Kazuhiko Shinozawa, Hiroshi Ishiguro, Norihiro Hagita, and Takanori Miyamoto, 'Responsive Robot Gaze to Interaction Partner', *In Proceedings of Robotics Science and Systems*, 2006, 287–93 http://dx.doi.org/10.1.1.108.1464

10. The NAO Robot Platform: http://www.aldebaranrobotics.com/en/

11. Raymond H. Cuijpers, and David Van Der Pol, 'Region of Eye Contact of Humanoid Nao Robot Is Similar to that of a Human', Lecture Notes in Computer Science (including Subseries Lecture Notes in Artificial Intelligence and Lecture Notes in Bioinformatics), 8239 LNAI (2013), 280–89 http://dx.doi.org/10.1007/978-3-319-02675-6_28

12. Delaunaym Frederic, Joachim de Greeff, and Tony Belpaeme, 'Keeping an Eye on You: The Influence of Robotic Faces on Gaze Direction', *Proceedings of the 2009 Symposium on Epigenetic Robotics*, 2009

13. T. Imai, D. Sekiguchi, M. Inami, N. Kawakami, and S. Tachi. 2006. Measuring gaze direction perception capability of humans to design human centered communication systems. *Presence: Teleoper. Virtual Environ.* 15, 2 (April 2006), 123-138.

14. T. Lourens, R. Van Berkel, and E. Barakova, "Communicating emotions and mental states to robots in a real time parallel framework using Laban movement analysis." Robotics and Autonomous Systems, Volume 58, Issue 12, pp. 1256-1265, 2010.

Promoting Physical Activities by Massive Competition in Virtual Marathon

Yuya Nakanishi
Department of Informatics, School of Science
and Technology, Kwansei Gakuin University
2-1 Gakuen, Sanda, Hyogo, Japan
eyw91160@kwansei.ac.jp

Yasuhiko Kitamura
Department of Informatics, School of Science
and Technology, Kwansei Gakuin University
2-1 Gakuen, Sanda, Hyogo, Japan
ykitamura@kwansei.ac.jp

ABSTRACT

Overweight and obesity due to lack of physical activities incur a serious social problem and a number of systems to promote physical activities using information and communication technologies have been developed. Virtual Kobe Marathon is an Android app to make a user experience a marathon race virtually. It shows the Kobe Marathon course on its display and moves an agent along the course according to the user's moving distance. It also has a competition scheme to make a user compete virtually with others running at different places and times. This scheme facilitates competitions with a small number of opponents, and we, in this paper, introduce a massive competition scheme utilizing the record of 17,769 runners who participated in the 3rd Kobe Marathon. The evaluation experiment shows the massive competition scheme promotes physical activities more than the one-to-one competition scheme.

ACM Classification Keywords

H.4.m. Information Systems Applications: MiscellaneousJ.4.Social and Behavioral Sciences

Author Keywords

Virtual Marathon; Massive Competition; Promoting Physical Activities

INTRODUCTION

Overweight and obesity caused by lack of exercise incur serious social problems, and increase interest in health and well-being issues among poeple [1]. Walking, jogging, and city marathon booms have broken out and there have been a number of research projects and systems to encourage physical activities based on information and commmunication technologies utilizing mobile and/or smart phone [4]. Self-monitoring is a conventional scheme to motivate users by recording and showing their physical activities, and it is the primary function of pedometers and smart bands. UbiFit Garden [3], implemented on a cell phone, provides an advanced form of self-monitoring scheme by showing growing plants and creatures on the glanceable display depending on the varieties of exercises the user has done.

Competition is another scheme to promote physical activities. This scheme shares the record of physical activities among users and makes them compete with each other. The systems can be classified into offline ones [2], which motivate users not during exercise by using SNS or the like, and online ones [6, 8, 7, 5] which make users compete with each other during exercise.

For examples of online systems, Jogging Over Distance [6] is a system by which a user can run having conversation with his/her competitor in a distant place by utilizing a pair of wearable devices and mobile phones. The user also can recognize the location of the competitor by listening to his/her footsteps. Virtual Network Marathon [8] facilitates competitions among users by integrating treadmills through the Internet, and Everywhere Race! [7] is a virtual marathon app by which users can compete with each other by using smartphones. These virtual marathon systems assume that the users start at a same time. Kishino et al. developed Virtual Kobe Marathon [5] which makes it possible for uses even at different times and locations to compete with each other by sharing their running data on a server.

Conventional virtual marathon systems mentioned above facilitate competitions among a small number of users. In this study, we introduce a massive competition sheme like a real city marathon race by utilizing the running record of 17,769 runners who participated in the 3rd Kobe Marathon, which was held in 2013. We also evaluate how it promotes physical activities by using a new version of Virtual Kobe Marathon in which the massive competition scheme is implemented.

This paper is organized as follows. Section 2 mentions the Virtual Kobe Marathon app as a platform on which the massive competition scheme is implemented. Section 3 mentions how the massive competition scheme is developed by utilizing running data collected from a real city marathon. Section 4 describes how the scheme promotes physical activities through an evaluation experiment and Section 5 summarizes this paper with our future work.

HAI '16, October 04-07, 2016, Biopolis, Singapore
ACM 978-1-4503-4508-8/16/10.
http://dx.doi.org/10.1145/2974804.2980483

Figure 1. The main screen of VKM.

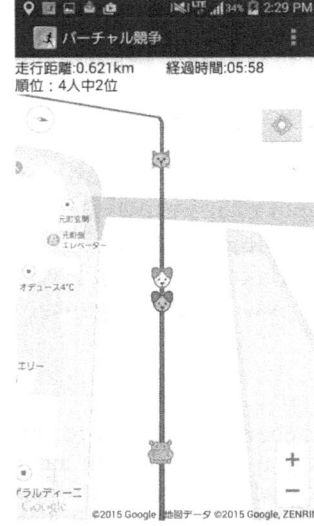

Figure 2. User and competitors in pseudo simultaneous competition.

VIRTUAL KOBE MARATHON

Virtual Kobe Marathon (VKM) is a virtual marathon system implemented as an app for Android smartphones [5]. It measures the moving distance of the user by using GPS, and moves an agent along the Kobe Marathon course on the screen according to the moving distance. The moving distance is stored in the server and is utilized in the pseudo simultaneous competition mode in which the user can compete with other users on the marathon course. As a result, we realize a virtual marathon where users at different locations and times can compete with each other.

User interface

The main screen of VKM is shown in Figure 1. An agent (dog) represents the current location of the user and the red line represents the marathon course. The upper part of the screen shows the running distance, the elapsed time, and the rank of the user.

Locating the user

We locate the agent on the marathon course according to the user's moving distance. We measure the latitude and longitude of the user's location at a regular interval using GPS and calculate the user's moving distance m after an interval. Given the list of coordinates representing the marathon course as $< p_1, p_2, \ldots, p_n >$ where p_1 and p_n represent the start and the goal respectively, we suppose the current location of the agent $a_{current}$ is between p_i and p_{i+1} ($1 \leq i \leq n-1$). Given the user's moving distance m, we calculate the next location of the agent a_{next} as follows.

1. Calculate $d(a_{current}, p_{i+1})$, which is the distance from $a_{current}$ to p_{i+1}.

2. If $d(a_{current}, p_{i+1}) < m$ then go to step 3, else go to step 4.

3. $m \leftarrow m - d(a_{current}, p_{i+1})$. $a_{current} \leftarrow p_{i+1}$. If $a_{current} = p_n$ then $a_{next} \leftarrow p_n$ and return with a_{next}. Otherwise, $i \leftarrow i+1$ and go to step 1.

4. Because a_{next} is between $a_{current}$ and p_{i+1}, calculate a_{next} as below and return with a_{next}.

$$a_{next} \leftarrow p_i + (p_{i+1} - p_i) \cdot \frac{m}{d(p_i, p_{i+1})}$$

Pseudo simultaneous competition

Conventional virtual marathon systems assume all the runners start at the same time. VKM introduced the pseudo simultaneous competition (PSC) mode in which the user can compete with other runners who started at the different times.

For example, we have users A and B, and assume B have started at 9am. If the user A start at 10am, he/she cannot compete with user B in the conventional systems because B has already started. PSC makes it possible for A to compete with B by converting the moving data as if B starts at 10 am.

We here represent the moving data of a competitor as $< (t_1, d_1), (t_2, d_2), \ldots, (t_m, d_m) >$ where t_k and d_k ($1 \leq k \leq m$) are the elapsed time and the moving distance at t_k of the competitor respectively. We can calculate the competitor's moving distance d_c at the user's elapsed time t_u as follows where we assume $t_j \leq t_u \leq t_{j+1} (1 \leq j \leq m-1)$.

$$d_c = d_j + (d_{j+1} - d_j) \cdot \frac{t_u - t_j}{t_{j+1} - t_j}$$

We then calculate the latitude and longitude of the competitor on the marathon course from the moving distance, as mentioned before, and locate the competitor agent on the screen. For example, the user is represented as a dog and competitors are represented as shaded animals in Figure 2.

MASSIVE COMPETITION

We develop the massive competition scheme to make a user feel more like running in a city marathon by using 17,769 runners' data recorded in the 3rd Kobe Marathon race held in 2013.

Rank Calculation

The running data of runner r in Kobe Marathon is given as a lap time sequence $< (p_1, t_1^r), (p_2, t_2^r), \ldots, (p9, t_9^r) >$ per 5 Km where $p_1 = 5, p_2 = 10, \ldots, p_8 = 40, p_9 = 42.195$, each of which represents the distance from the start to the recording point respectively. t_i^r represents the elapsed time at the recording point i of runner r.

Assuming that each runner runs at the same speed regularly in each 5 Km section, we calculate the runner's rank. Given the elapsed time x^r of the runner r, we calculate the running distance $d(x^r)$ as follows. First, in order to examine the section in which the runner is located at x^r, we find $i(0 \leq i \leq 8)$ that satisfies $t_i^r \leq x^r \leq t_{i+1}^r$ and $d(x^r)$ equals p_i plus the running distance from t_i to x^r. The running distance in the section is given by multiplying the elapsed time from t_i to x^r and the speed in the section from p_i to p_{i+1}, so the $d(x^r)$ is given as

$$d(x^r) = p_i + \frac{p_{i+1} - p_i}{t_{i+1} - t_i} \times (x^r - t_i).$$

We then calculate the rank of each runner from the running distance data of all the participants of the Kobe Marathon.

Representing Competitors

The previous version of VKM represents each competitor as an animal. However, in the massive competion version, it is difficult to depict 17,769 competitors on a single screen of smartphone. Instead, we place markers, each of which represents a competitor at a specific rank and changes the set of markers to place depending on the zoom level of the marathon course map.

We use Google Maps to represent the marathon course and can choose the zoom level from 2 (the maximum scale) to 21 (the minimum scale). When the zoom level is less than 12, two yellow markers are placed for competitors of the top (1st) and the bottom (17770th) ranks. When the zoom level is between 12 and 18, yellow markers are shown for competitos at every 1000th rank as shown in Figure 3. When the zoom level is greater than 18, red or blue markers are placed for competitors whose rank difference is 3, 5,10, 25, 50, 100 positions from the user. The marker is red (or blue) if the competitor is ahead (or behind) of the user as shown in Figure 4.

EVALUATION

We performed an experiment to evaluate how the massivecompetition scheme encourages physical activities.

Method

We compared 3 types of VKM; one with the massive competition scheme, one with the one-to-one competition using the pseudo simultaneous competition scheme where the competitor was the self in the past, and one with no comepition scheme.

48 university students (24 males and 24 females) whose age are between 18 and 22 years old participated in this evaluation experiment. At first, they answered a preliminary questionaire about their average walking time in a day. We assigned

Figure 3. Markers at zoom level between 12 and 18.

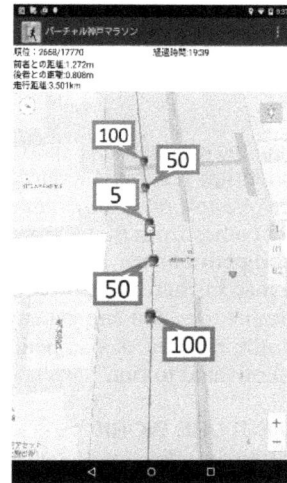

Figure 4. Markers at zoom level 18 or more.

the participants into 3 groups so that the sum of the walking time and the gender ratio in each group is to be as equal to each other as possible.

We asked each participant to run or walk twice along a specified course whose length is about 3km. For the first lap to measure the baseline of his/her physical activity, he/she runs or walks without VKM. For the second lap to measure the time difference from the baseline, he/she runs or walks with a type of VKM depending on the group.

Result

We show the difference between the first and the second laps of massive, one-to-one, and no competition schemes respectively in Figure 5.

We observed the significant difference at the 5% level between massive competition and no competition ($p = 0.014$) and between massive competition and one-to-one competition ($p = 0.041$) by t test.

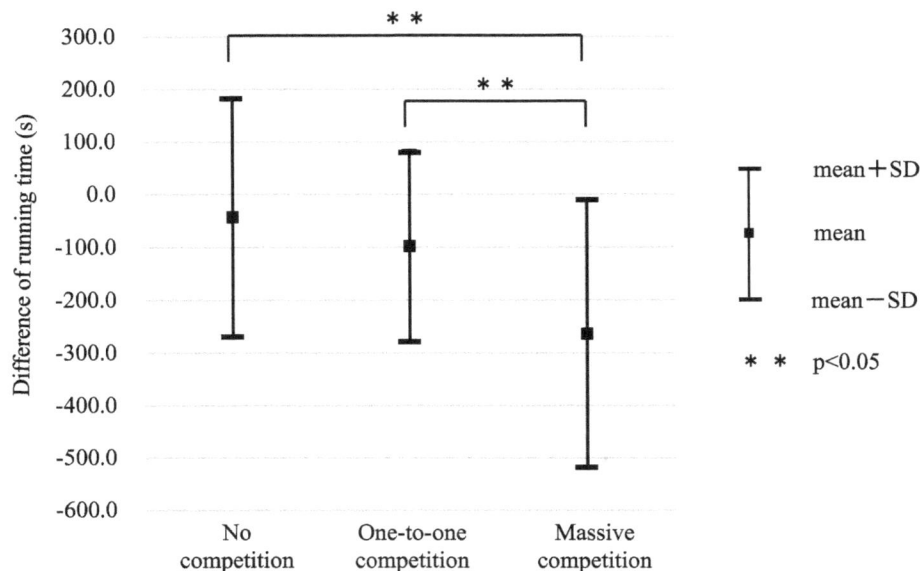

Figure 5. The difference of running time

Discussion

From the result of the evaluation experiment, we observed the massive competition scheme encourages physical activities more than the one-to-one or no competition scheme. We consider the effect comes from the number of competitors. In the one-to-one competition, the competitor is only one and the user tends to lose his/her motivation of running if he/she surpasses the competitor. On the other hand, in the massive competition, the number of competiors is large enough to keep the user motivated to run.

SUMMARY AND FUTURE WORK

Competition scheme in conventional virtual marathon systems deals with races with a small number of competitors. In this paper, to make virtual marathon more like a real city marathon race, we introduced a massive competition scheme that enables races with a large number of competitors by utilizing the runners' record of Kobe Marathon and evaluated how the scheme promotes physical activities. As a result, the massive competition scheme is obeserved to be more effective to promote physical activities than one-to-one or no competition scheme.

For our future work, we need to improve the user interface to inform the state of the competition. At present, the user has to run watching the screen of smartphone, and that is not a good and safe way to run, so we need to develop a voice guidance function to inform the state of the competition by words. In our experiment, we evaluated the effect promoting physical activities by comparing the running speed of participants who run along a 3 Km course. We need to evaluate the effect when they run in longer distance courses.

REFERENCES

1. David R. Brown, Gregory W. Heath, and Sarah Levin Martin (Eds.). 2010. *Promoting Physical Activity: A Guide for Community Action*. Human Kinetics Pub.

2. Sunny Consolvo, Katherine Everitt, Ian Smith, and James A Landay. 2006. Design requirements for technologies that encourage physical activity. In *Proceedings of the SIGCHI conference on Human Factors in computing systems*. 457–466.

3. Sunny Consolvo, Predrag Klasnja, David W McDonald, Daniel Avrahami, Jon Froehlich, Louis LeGrand, Ryan Libby, Keith Mosher, and James A Landay. 2008. Flowers or a robot army?: encouraging awareness & activity with personal, mobile displays. In *Proceedings of the 10th international conference on Ubiquitous computing*. 54–63.

4. B.J. Fogg and Dean Eckles. 2007. *Mobile Persuasion*. Persuasion Technology Lab.

5. Hirofumi Kishino and Yasuhiko Kitamura. 2014. Virtual Marathon System Where Humans and Agents Compete. In *Proceedings of the 4th International Conference on Web Intelligence, Mining and Semantics (WIMS14)*.

6. Florian'Floyd' Mueller, Shannon O'Brien, and Alex Thorogood. 2007. Jogging over a distance: supporting a jogging together experience although being apart. In *CHI'07 extended abstracts on Human factors in computing systems*. 1989–1994.

7. Fabrizio Mulas, Paolo Pilloni, and Salvatore Carta. 2012. Everywhere race!: A social mobile platform for sport engagement and motivation. In *SOTICS 2012, The Second International Conference on Social Eco-Informatics*. 63–69.

8. Mingmin Zhang, Mingliang Xu, Lizhen Han, Yong Liu, Pei Lv, and Gaoqi He. 2012. Virtual Network Marathon with immersion, scientificalness, competitiveness, adaptability and learning. *Computers & Graphics* 36, 3 (2012), 185–192.

Development of an Embodied Avatar System using Avatar-Shadow's Color Expressions with an Interaction-activated Communication Model

Yutaka Ishii
Okayama Prefectural Univ.
111 Kuboki, Soja, Okayama, JAPAN
ishii@cse.oka-pu.ac.jp

Tomio Watanabe
Okayama Prefectural Univ.
111 Kuboki, Soja, Okayama, JAPAN
watanabe@cse.oka-pu.ac.jp

Yoshihiro Sejima
Okayama Prefectural Univ.
111 Kuboki, Soja, Okayama, JAPAN
sejima@ss.oka-pu.ac.jp

ABSTRACT

In reality, shadows are usually natural and unintentional. In virtual reality, however, they play an important role in three-dimensional effects and the perceived reality of the virtual space. An avatar's shadow can have interactive effects with the avatar itself in the virtual space. In this study, we develop an embodied avatar system using avatar-shadow color expressions with an interaction-activated communication model. This model is based on the heat conduction equation in heat-transfer engineering, and has been developed to enhance empathy during embodied interaction in avatar-mediated communication. A communication experiment is performed with 12 pairs of participants to confirm the effectiveness of the system. The results of the sensory evaluation show that interaction activation is visualized by changing avatar-shadow color.

Author Keywords

Avatar-mediated communication; avatar's shadow; embodied interaction; virtual face-to-face communication; color expression.

ACM Classification Keywords

H.5.1 Information interfaces and presentation; Multimedia Information Systems.

INTRODUCTION

In real situations, shadows help to create the visual sense of a talker's identity [1]. In virtual reality, they play an important part in the perceived three-dimensionality of computer-generated (CG) characters and objects, as well as simulating other real visual effects. Shadows are particularly useful in avatar-mediated communication. A shadow cannot exist independently of the avatar that is representing the talker. For example, one talker can react to another's avatar based on the behavior of the avatar's shadow rather than that of the avatar itself. This could encourage the entrainment of rhythms embodied in the speaker's voice to improve the ease of communication.

HAI '16, October 04-07, 2016, Biopolis, Singapore
ACM 978-1-4503-4508-8/16/10.
http://dx.doi.org/10.1145/2974804.2980487

In this study, we introduce avatar shadows into an embodied virtual communication system (EVCOS). We develop an embodied avatar-shadow system using color to express talkers' feelings based on an interaction-activated communication model. In an embodied interaction, both speech and nonverbal behavior such as nodding and body movements are rhythmically related and mutually synchronized between the talkers [2]. Focusing on interaction-activated communication, a model for estimating conversational activity was proposed and an embodied communication system was developed in order to apply the proposed model to a virtual audience [3].

In research in this area, participants tend to experience an interaction-activated communication such as "It is hot" as heat. Because such thermal sensations can be shared in an experiential context, it is inferred that talkers can perceive such situations sensuously, [4, 5]. Therefore, in order to enhance empathy, we aimed to develop an interaction-activated communication model that is based on concepts from heat-transfer engineering.

We begin by describing a model of interaction-activated communication that is based on the heat conduction equation. We then evaluate the proposed system and demonstrate that it is possible to base avatar-shadow color on the interactions in avatar-mediated communication.

METHODOLOGY

Embodied avatar-shadow system

The concept of our avatar-shadow system is shown in Fig. 1. As discussed above, shadows are used to convey the embodiment of their source objects. For this reason, shadows in avatar-mediated communication strengthen an avatar's presence and indicate its location clearly. In addition, if a shadow exhibits the same motions as its avatar as well as those that differ partially from it, the speaker can indirectly imagine the avatar's self-behavior. As a result, avatar shadows can influence speaker interaction [6]. In particular, this system enhances the effectiveness of communication by using avatar-shadow nodding, which helps the talker's embodied entrainment and avoids contradictions between the talker's motion and that of the avatar. Furthermore, talkers can engage in pleasant communication because the avatar shadows encourage them to interact more.

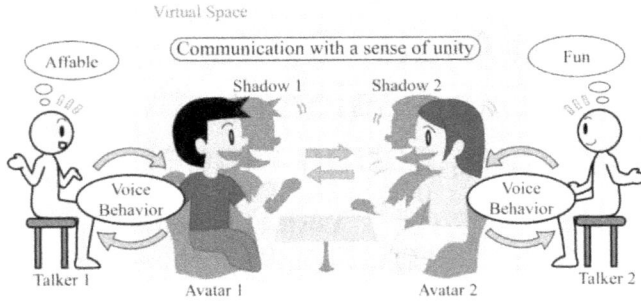

Figure 1. Concept of the embodied avatar-shadow system.

Interaction-activated Communication Model Based on the Heat Conduction Equation

Figure 2 provides an overview of our interaction-activated communication model based on the heat conduction equation [7]. This interaction model estimates the degree of interaction-activated communication by using voice input alone. Based on the principles of heat-transfer engineering, we make the following assumptions.

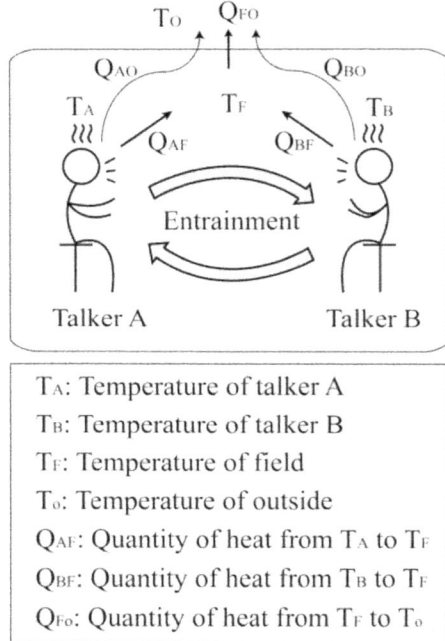

T_A: Temperature of talker A

T_B: Temperature of talker B

T_F: Temperature of field

T_o: Temperature of outside

Q_{AF}: Quantity of heat from T_A to T_F

Q_{BF}: Quantity of heat from T_B to T_F

Q_{Fo}: Quantity of heat from T_F to T_o

Figure 2. Interaction-activated communication model.

Temperature
There is a temperature for talkers A and B, the communication field, and the outside environment, denoted by T_A, T_B, T_F, and T_O, respectively. The talkers produce heat by utterances in this embodied communication.

Quantity of heat
In terms of heat transfer by convection, we denote the heat quantities as Q_{AF}, Q_{BF}, Q_{AO}, Q_{BO}, and Q_{FO}.

Heat capacity
Talkers A and B and the communication field have heat capacities, denoted by C and C_F, respectively.

The degree of interaction-activated communication is estimated by the temperature of the communication field, T_F, within the inflow and outflow of heat using the above-mentioned definition.

Based on heat-transfer concepts, we have developed an interaction-activated communication model for enhancing embodied communication. The model is based on the basic theory of heat conduction. First, a threshold is set for the binary burst-pause of a talker's voice. A binary voice signal is then generated in real time. In this model, the signal is defined as the heating of the utterance, and the heat transfer is defined as the heat released by convection. Heat transfer is calculated using (4)–(7) as the quantities in Fig. 2. In addition, (1) and (2) are used to calculate the temperature of each talker. Next, (4) and (5) estimate the heat quantity of each talker, and finally (8) estimates the heat quantity released. In addition, the value of an interaction-activated communication is estimated from (3) because the temperature of a communication field is the sum of the heat quantities obtained from each talker and the heat quantity released. The heat quantities (Q_{AF}, Q_{BF}, Q_{AO}, Q_{BO}, and Q_{FO}) comprise the heat conduction equations. Here, K_1, K_2, and K_3 are experimentally obtained constants. In this research, the estimated value of the proposed model is sampled in each frame at a rate of 30 frames per second (fps). The conversational activity can be estimated from voice input alone.

$$T_A(i) = T_A(i-1) + \frac{OnOff_A(i) - Q_{AF}(i-1) - Q_{AO}(i-1)}{C} \quad (1)$$

$$T_B(i) = T_B(i-1) + \frac{OnOff_B(i) - Q_{BF}(i-1) - Q_{BO}(i-1)}{C} \quad (2)$$

$T_A(i)$: Temperature of talker A

$T_B(i)$: Temperature of talker B

$OnOff_A(i)$: Voice of talker A

$OnOff_B(i)$: Voice of talker B

C : Heat capacity

i : Frame number

$$T_F(i) = T_F(i-1) + \frac{Q_{AF}(i-1) + Q_{BF}(i-1) - Q_{FO}(i-1)}{C_F} \quad (3)$$

$T_F(i)$: Temperature of field

C_F : Heat capacity of field

$$Q_{AF}(i) = K_1\{T_A(i-1) - T_F(i-1)\} \quad (4)$$

$$Q_{BF}(i) = K_1\{T_B(i-1) - T_F(i-1)\} \quad (5)$$

$$Q_{AO}(i) = K_2\{T_A(i-1) - T_O\} \quad (6)$$

$$Q_{BO}(i) = K_2\{T_B(i-1) - T_O\} \quad (7)$$

$$Q_{FO}(i) = K_3\{T_F(i-1) - T_O\} \quad (8)$$

$Q_{AF}(i)$: Quantity of heat from T_A to T_F

$Q_{BF}(i)$: Quantity of heat from T_B to T_F

$Q_{AO}(i)$: Quantity of heat from T_A to T_O

$Q_{BO}(i)$: Quantity of heat from T_B to T_O

$Q_{FO}(i)$: Quantity of heat from T_F to T_O
K_1, K_2, K_3 : const.
T_O : Outside temperature (= const.)

System Configuration

Figure 3 shows a screen shot of a communication scene using an embodied avatar system with avatar-shadow color expressions based on an interaction-activated communication model. A VirtualActor (VA) is an interactive avatar that represents the talker's upper body motions and voice on the basis of his or her verbal and nonverbal information in a virtual face-to-face communication environment [11]. The motions of head, both arms, and body for each VA are accurately represented on the basis of the positions and angles measured by four magnetic sensors (Polhemus FASTRAK) placed on top of the talker's head, both wrists, and back. The VAs are seated on opposite chairs in a room in virtual space. Talkers can confirm correspondence between them and each VA based on the behaviors of both VAs. In the system, the locations of both VAs are strengthened by their avatars' shadows. The talker can objectively observe the communication scene. The virtual space is generated using Microsoft DirectX 9.0 SDK. Voice sampling is with 16 bits at 11.025 kHz. The data on the VA's motions and voice are transmitted via Ethernet in each system. The frame rate at which VAs are represented is 30 fps.

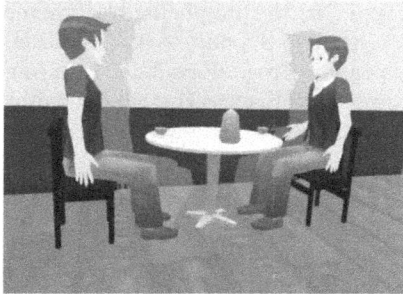

Figure 3. Screen shot of communication scene.

COMMUNICATION EXPERIMENT

Experimental Setup

We performed an experiment in two different rooms to evaluate the proposed system, each room having the same layout. We compared three operational modes. In Mode A, avatar-shadow color remained unchanged. In Mode B, only the talker's avatar-shadow color is expressed based on the calculated temperature of each talker's voice. In Mode C, the colors of both avatar shadows are expressed based on the calculated temperatures of each talker's voice.

First, the subjects (12 pairs of 24 Japanese students aged between 18 and 24 years) used the system, and we confirmed that they were familiar with its operation. They were then introduced to the three operational modes and the differences between them while using the system. Next, the subjects were instructed to perform a pairwise comparison

of each mode for an overall evaluation. Three comparisons were required; therefore, the experiment was conducted three (= $_3C_2$) times. The questionnaire was examined using a seven-point bipolar rating scale from -3 (not at all) to 3 (extremely); a score of zero denotes "moderately." Each pair was presented with the three modes in a random order to eliminate any ordering effect. A video editor recorded the communication experiment using two video cameras and screens, as shown in Figure 4.

Figure 4. Recorded screen of the experiment.

Result of the Communication Experiment

Figure 5 shows the result of the sensory evaluation in a free conversation. Significant differences between each of the three modes were obtained by administering Friedman's test. In Mode B and C, the results from sensory evaluation were rated positively for all seven factors. Significant differences were also obtained by administering the Wilcoxon rank sum test for multiple comparisons.

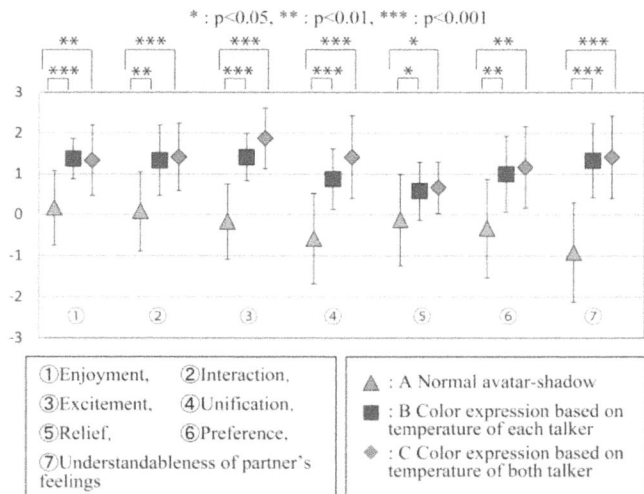

Figure 5. Seven-point bipolar rating.

The results of paired comparison for the three modes are shown in Table 1. Figure 6 shows the calculated results of the evaluation provided in Table 1, based on the Bradley–Terry model. Modes B and C were evaluated affirmatively in comparison with Mode A. Therefore, it was confirmed that using avatar-shadow color expressions have an overall positive effect.

	A	B	C	Total
A		3	6	9
B	21		10	31
C	18	14		32

Table 1. Paired comparison result in the experiment.

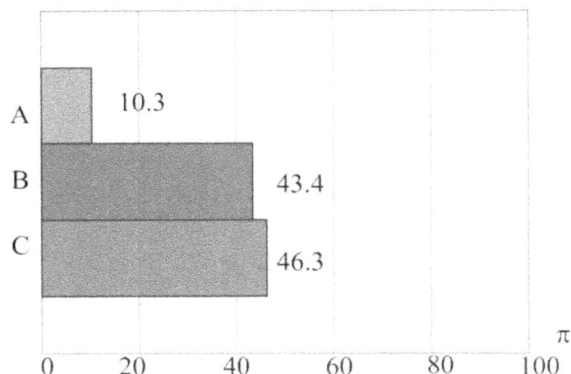

Figure 6. Preference based on the Bradley–Terry model.

CONCLUSION

In this paper, we described an embodied avatar system using avatar-shadow color expressions with an interaction-activated communication model. Using the proposed system, a communication experiment was conducted under free conversational conditions. In addition, we examined the effectiveness of this system using sensory evaluation of the communication experiment.

ACKNOWLEDGMENTS

This work was supported by JSPS KAKENHI Grant Number JP26280077, JP16K00278, JP16K01560.

REFERENCES

1. Yoshiyuki Miwa, Shiroh Itai, Takabumi Watanabe, Hiroko Nishi. 2011. "Shadow Awareness Enhancing theater space through the mutual projection of images on a connective slit-screen", *the journal of the International Society for the Arts, Sciences and Technology (SIGGRAPH 2011 Art paper)*, Vol. 44, No. 4, pp. 325–333.

2. William S. Condon and Louis W. Sander. 1974. "Neonate movement is synchronized with adult speech," *Science*, No. 183, pp. 99–101.

3. Yoshihiro Sejima, Tomio Watanabe and Yutaka Ishii, 2013. "An Interaction-Activated Communication Support System Using a Virtual Audience with an Estimated Model of Conversational Activity," Transactions of the Japan Society of Mechanical Engineers, Series C, Vol. 79, No. 807, pp. 4095–4107.

4. I. Chatonnet and M. Cabanac. 1965. "The Perception of Thermal Comfort," Int.J. Biometeor, Vol. 9, No. 2, pp. 185–195.

5. A. P. Gagge, J. A. J. Stolwijk and J. D. Hardy. 1967. "Comfort and Thermal Sensations and Associated Physiological Responses at Various Ambient Temperatures," Environmental Research, Vol. 1, No. 1, pp. 1–20.

6. Keizou Esaki, Shota Inoue, Tomio Watanabe and Yukata Ishii. 2015. An Embodied Entrainment Avatar-Shadow System to Support Avatar Mediated Communication, Proc. of the 24th IEEE International Symposium on Robot and Human Interactive Communication (IEEE RO-MAN2015), pp.419–424.

7. Yoshihiro Sejima, Tomio Watanabe and Mitsuru Jindai. 2014. Development of an Interaction-activated Communication Model Based on a Heat Conduction Equation in Voice Communication, Proc. of the 23rd IEEE International Symposium on Robot and Human Interactive Communication, pp.832–837.

Model-based Reminiscence:
Guiding Mental Time Travel by Cognitive Modeling

Junya Morita*
Shizuoka University

Takatsugu Hirayama
Nagoya University

Kenji Mase
Nagoya University

Kazunori Yamada
Panasonic Corporation

ABSTRACT

This paper proposes an approach to elderly mental care called model-based reminiscence, which utilizes cognitive modeling to guide a user's mental time travel. In this approach, a personalized cognitive model is constructed by implementing a user's lifelog (a photo library) in the ACT-R cognitive architecture. The constructed model retrieves photos based on human memory characteristics such as learning, forgetting, inhibition, and noise. These memory characteristics are regulated with parameter values corresponding to cognitive and emotional health. The authors assumed that a user's mental health could be assessed from their reactions to photo sequences retrieved by models with various parameter settings. The authors also assumed that it would be possible to motivate a user by guiding their memory recall with photo sequences generated from a healthy optimal state model. A simulation study indicates the potential of this approach presenting a variety of model behaviors corresponding cognitive / emotional states.

ACM Classification Keywords

H.5.m. Information Interfaces and Presentation (e.g. HCI): Miscellaneous

Author Keywords

cognitive architecture; ACT-R; autobiographic memory

INTRODUCTION

A lifelog is a subjective experience recorded with various digital media. Although a lifelog can be created using many different types of media, this study focused on a visual lifelog, consisting of private photos, because it provides an effective means of evoking a specific past memory in a user [6]. Such lifelog technology is becoming increasingly common and plentiful in our society with convenient recording devices and large-sized storage [4]. To date, many researchers have used large lifelog technologies to support human cognitive functions such as memory recall [5].

*Address: 3-5-1 Johoku, Naka-ku, Hamamatsu, Japan
E-maiil: j-morita@inf.shizuoka.ac.jp

HAI '16, October 04-07, 2016, Biopolis, Singapore
ACM 978-1-4503-4508-8/16/10.
http://dx.doi.org/10.1145/2974804.2980492

From the viewpoint of cognitive neuroscience, remembering the past is essentially linked to imagining of the future activity [16]. Both of them are referred to as "mental time travel" because they direct a person's attention to events that have occurred/will occur in other than the present moment. Moreover, researchers have pointed out that such a state of consciousness relates to a brain network called the default mode network (DMN) [16], which includes a connection between the posterior cingulate cortex (PCC) and dorsal medial prefrontal cortex (dmPFC), and have defined regions that are activated in the resting state rather than goal-oriented tasks [11]. Importantly, DMN is said to change with age, and has attracted the attention of researchers who hope to employ it as a biomarkers for mental illnesses such as dementia [2] and depression [17].

Mental time travel to the past is also accompanied by a fresh emotional states. The relationship between memory and emotion has been the subject of studies for a very long time. In clinical situations, memory recall of a "personal golden age" is said to bring about psychological health and well-being [14]. A recent study also indicated that optogenetically activating positive memory engrams suppress depression-like behaviors in mice [12]. On the basis of these assumptions, activities such as life reviews and reminiscences are commonly conducted as a means of supporting the elderly (e.g., [20]).

Based on the above, the mental activities evoked by observing a lifelog can be summarized into the following three types: memory recall, future imagining, and emotional arousal. From these activities, we can consider the application of a lifelog to the care of the elderly. In this application, emotional and cognitive health is assessed from reactions to a presented lifelog, and can also be used to motivate future activity by effectively stimulating the user's future imaging.

Such an intelligent care system requires a mechanism for guiding a user's mental time travel in a desired direction. For this reason, we are proposing a concept of *model-based reminiscence*, where a system has two user models: a model concretizing the user's mental state, and a model representing a desired mental state of the user. The system uses the former to monitor the user's mental state, and the latter to guide the user's mental time travel.

Furthermore we believe that such a user modeling method can be realized by using a cognitive architecture, which has been developed in the field of traditional cognitive science. A

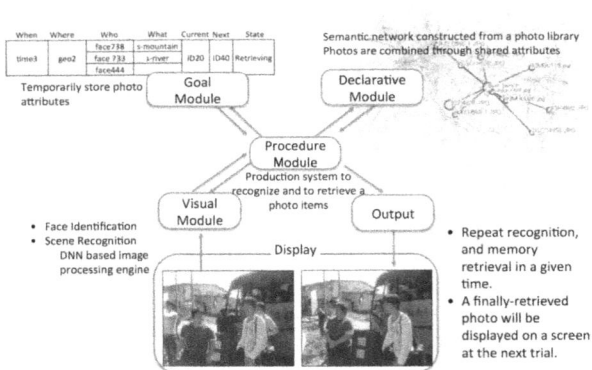

Figure 1. Overview of the model

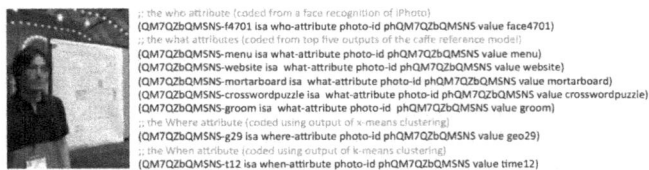

Figure 2. Examples of attribute coding

cognitive architecture is a common platform used to construct a model for simulating human cognition. Researchers who use cognitive architecture usually call such simulation models *cognitive models* [1, 9]. Individual cognitive models can be developed by implementing domain-/user-specific knowledge and parameter values in a cognitive architecture. In other words, varieties of user models corresponding to individual user states can be developed with a combination of knowledge and parameter values. From this viewpoint, a cognitive model of mental time travel can be developed by using user-specific memory, that is, a lifelog and user-specific parameter values estimated from the user's reactions to presented model behaviors.

We so far developed a prototype model for mental time travel using a cognitive architecture, and explored parameters that correspond to the mental states of the elderly through model simulations. In the next section, we present an implementation of the prototype model, and a simulation study. In the final section, we discuss the studies that we intend to pursue in the future to realize the concept of model-based reminiscence.

MODEL AND SIMULATION

ACT-R model

The cognitive architecture used in the study is ACT-R [1], which is a well maintained architecture used by many researchers. The ACT-R architecture has several modules corresponding to independent cognitive functions including procedure, declarative, visual, aural, manual, and goal modules. The behaviors of these modules have been tuned to fit the level of human performance obtained in previous psychological studies. Therefore, the use of this architecture provides some guarantee of cognitive plausibility for a constructed model.

Figure 1 shows the make-up of our model that uses the ACT-R modules. The main part of this model is a declarative module, which is constructed from a user's lifelog, while the other modules are used to simulate the process of human memory retrieval from the observations of a photo. This model uses photos stored in a personal photo library such as iPhoto of the Mac OSX to construct declarative memory. Especially, four types of attributes are extracted from each individual photo in a photo library, namely, the *when*, *where*, *who*, and *what* attributes [8]. These attributes were determined in a study by Wagenaar [18]. For four years, he recorded his own experiences by using these attributes, and conducted a memory experiment on himself. Other researchers used these attributes to develop photo browsers [10].

In this study, the first two types of attributes are tagged as cluster ID obtained with k-means clustering to Exif metadata (date-time and geo-tag information)[1]. The who attribute is tagged by using face recognition of the photo library software. The what attributes are tagged with scene recognition using a deep convolutional neural network. We are currently using the caffe reference ImageNet model[2].

Examples of attribute coding are shown in Figure 2. In the ACT-R architecture, the lists presented in this figure are called "chunks." Each chunk has a unique chunk name in its first element (e.g., *QM7QZbQMSNS-f4701*). In this study, we named each chunk by combining the GUID value (e.g., *QM7QZbQMSNS1*), given by the iPhoto library, with an attribute value (e.g., *f4701*). The following elements of each chunk consist of slot name/slot value pairs. The *isa* slot discriminates the types of attributes. The *photo-id* and the *value* slots indicate the GUID of the photo and the attribute value, respectively.

A collection of such chunks can be regarded as being a network in which photos are connected with shared attributes (see the network in Figure 1). The model sequentially retrieves a photo by following a link within the network. In the implementation of ACT-R, this sequential search is made with a retrieval cue in the form of a production rule[3], which is constructed from the attributes recognized from the currently presented photo[4]. If several photos match a retrieval cue, the ACT-R selects that photo with the highest *activation value* whose computation has been devised to reproduce the results of past psychological experiments. In our model, it is computed as a combination of the following effects.

- Forgetting: The model tends to retrieve photos taken recently. The old photos are not likely to be retrieved in a normal setting.

---

[1] The number of clusters for the where attribute was determined by x-means method. The k-means clsutring for the when attribute was conducted with the number of clusters used for the where attribute to uniform resolutions of the two attributes.

[2] http://caffe.berkeleyvision.org

[3] The model has four retrieval rules corresponding to the four types of attributes [8]. These rules are selected based on utilities values updated by given rewards. In the simulation presented in this paper, however the model didn't receive rewards, and randomly chose them.

[4] The recognized attributes are stored in the goal module.

- Learning: The model tends to retrieve photos that have been frequently retrieved in the past.

- Inhibition: The model can temporally inhibit the learning effect for a short time.

- Noise: The above effects can be reduced by introducing a logistically distributed noise factor.

The strength of the above effects is controlled by parameter values, which might represent individual user states. The specific parameters and computations of the forgetting, learning, context, and noise can be found in [1], and the computation of the inhibition is presented in [7].

Simulation experiment
Simulation settings
To demonstrate how the model can be applied to the care of the elderly, a simulation experiment was conducted. In this experiment, the personalized model of the first author was constructed by implementing the first author's lifelog in the ACT-R model described above. This model has 3,202 photos taken from 1977-2014. These photos were routinely managed by the first author's iPhoto library. Except for unknown bystanders, all the faces detected by the iPhoto face recognition function were named. Photos taken by digital cameras as well as scanned photos were included. For those photos without Exif metadata, the first author coded the locations and date-time information manually.

Among the five effects presented in the above, the presence of inhibition (with/without) and the degree of noise (high/low) were manipulated[5]. The parameter values concerning effects of the learning and the forgetting were fixed in the simulation[6] because these effects were treated as basic mechanisms in the ACT-R architecture. In fact, the component calculated by these effects is called *base-level activation* in the literature related to ACT-R [1]. The parameter values related to forgetting are calculated from the difference in the current model time (set to 00:00:00, January 1, 2015) and the date-time information of each photo.

We ran the simulation 20 times for each of the four-parameter conditions. In a single run, the model sequentially retrieved 200 photos.

Simulation results
Figure 3 presents the frequency distributions of the recalled photos for each parameter condition. The horizontal axis corresponds to the recalled photo IDs, which are arranged in descending order of frequency. The vertical axis indicates the frequencies of each rank, averaged across the 20 simulation runs.

From the figure, it can be seen that a few photos dominate the distributions, especially under those conditions with only

forgetting and learning effects (the left-hand blue line). The inhibition effect slightly suppresses such repetitive recall, as shown in the difference in the blue lines between Figure 3a and 3b. A more salient effect can be observed when comparing two noise conditions. In both Figure 3a and 3b, the high-noise conditions (the black lines) recall more various photos than the low-noise condition (the blue lines).

Discussion
In a previous study, researchers pointed out that a free recall made by the normal ACT-R model lead "pathological behaviors such as out-of-control looping [7]." Our results also replicated such behavior. We believe that these behaviors are not necessarily negative for our purpose. Rather, these behavioral patterns of the normal ACT-R model can be used to model several types of mental disorders. For example, Schacter described a memory error called "persistence" which involved an unwanted and repeated recall caused by post-traumatic stress disorder [15]. Dementia patients also exhibit behavior similar to the normal ACT-R model. The symptoms of dementia involve repetition in conversation, where the same information is repeated over and over again. These mental disorders indicate the necessity for cognitive or emotional regulations in addition the base level activation computation, to achieve healthy memory recall. The two parameters manipulated in the simulation can be assumed to act as mechanisms that enable ACT-R healthy memory recall.

We assumed that the parameters of the inhibition and the noise represent cognitive and emotional states, respectively. Inhibition can be regarded as being a function of the prefrontal cortex, which controls mental time travel as driven by the default mode network [16]. On the other hand, the noise parameters seem to represents emotional factors. Previous studies of ACT-R discussed the connection between the noise parameters of ACT-R and stress level [13, 3]. Especially Dancy et al developed a cognitive model for subtraction task under stressed conditions by attaching a physiological module to ACT-R architecture. In thier model, the noise parameter of ACT-R is connected with physiological epinephrine release [3].

CONCLUSION
In this paper, we presented a concept of the model-based reminiscence, and prototyped a cognitive model of mental time travel. The constructed model was applied to a simulation study. We considered that the presented simulations successfully demonstrated the applicability of the model to the model-based reminiscence though the results itself did not show great originality.

Our future studies will also address the development of an interactive model-based slideshow system, which modulates the model parameters from the user's reactions. We have especially examined the possibility of using bio-signals such as the heart rate or brain waves. As noted earlier, the ACT-R noise parameter is assumed to correspond to physiological epinephrine release, which is regulated by the automatic nervous system. Therefore it might be possible to modulate this parameter by directly inputting known bio-signals corresponding to stress such as the low-/high-frequency heart rate ratio

---

[5]In "the with inhibition condition", the parameter values controling inhibition was set to the default (inhibition-scale = 5, inhibition-decay = 1.0. The noise control parameter (ANS) was set to 0.1 in the low noise condition, and 0.5 in the high noise condition.
[6]The decay rate d = .5, the base-level offset $\beta = 15$, the maximum association strength mas = 10

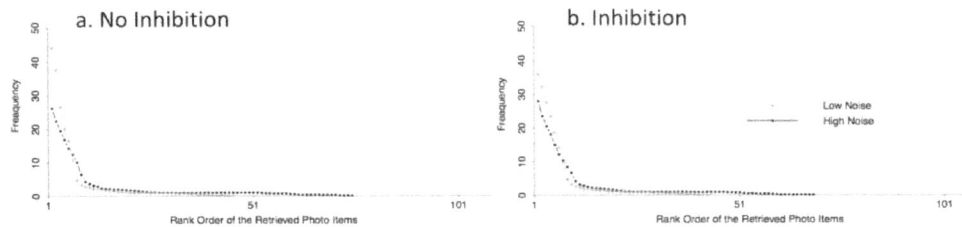

Figure 3. Freaquency distributions of retreived items

or the alpha wave of EEG (electroencephalogram). It may also be possible to reward a model by using bio-signals for pleasantness [19] to modulate the utility values for photo retrieval rules. We believe that realizing these interfaces would provide an effective means of guiding a user's mental time travel, naturally estimating parameters concerning cognitive and emotional healthiness.

ACKNOWLEDGMENTS

This research is suppoted by JSPS KAKENHI Grant Number 15H01615, and the Center of Innovation Program by Japan Science and Technology Agency, JST.

REFERENCES

1. J. R. Anderson. 2007. *How can the human mind occur in the physical universe?* Oxford University Press, New York.

2. J. S. Damoiseaux. 2012. Resting-state fMRI as a biomarker for Alzheimer's disease? *Alzheimer's Research & Therapy* (2012), 4–8.

3. C. L. Dancy, F. E. Ritter, K. A. Berry, and L. C. Klein. 2015. Using a cognitive architecture with a physiological substrate to represent effects of a psychological stressor on cognition. *Computational and Mathematical Organization Theory* 21, 1 (2015), 90–114.

4. J. Gemmell, G. Bell, R. Lueder, S. Drucker, and C. Wong. 2002. MyLifeBits: Fulfilling the Memex vision. In *Multimedia '02: Proceedings of the tenth ACM international conference on multimedia.* 235–238.

5. S. Hodges, L. Williams, E. Berry, S. Izadi, J. Srinivasan, A. Butler, G. Smyth, K. Narinder, and W. Ken. 2006. SenseCam: A retrospective memory aid. In *Ubicomp 2006: Ubiquitous computing, proceedings*, P Dourish and A Friday (Eds.). 177–193.

6. E. Isaacs, A. Konrad, A. Walendowski, T. Lennig, V. Hollis, and S. Whittaker. 2013. Echoes from the past: how technology mediated reflection improves well-being. In *Proceedings of the SIGCHI Conference on Human Factors in Computing Systems.* 1071–1080.

7. C. Lebiere and B. J. Best. 2009. Balancing long-term reinforcement and short-term inhibition. In *Proceedings of the 31st Annual Conference of the Cognitive Science Society.*

8. J. Morita, T. Hirayama, K. Mase, and K. Yamada. 2016. Modeling Autobiographical Memory from Photo Libraries. In *Proceedings of the 14th International Conference on Cognitive Modeling.* 243–245.

9. A. Newell. 1994. *Unified Theories of Cognition.* Harvard University Press.

10. T. C. Ormerod, J. Mariani, N. J. Morley, T. Rodden, A. Crabtree, J. Mathrick, G. Hitch, and K. Lewis. 2005. Mixing research methods in HCI: Ethnography meets experimentation in image browser design. In *EHCI-DSVIS 2004.* 112–128.

11. M. E. Raichle, A. M. MacLeod, A. Z. Snyder, W. J. Powers, D. A. Gusnard, and G. L. Shulman. 2001. A default mode of brain function. *Proceedings of the National Academy of Sciences* 98 (2001), 676–682.

12. S. Ramirez, X. Liu, C. J. MacDonald, A. Moffa, J. Zhou, L. Roger, R. L. Redondo, , and S. Tonegawa. 2015. Activating positive memory engrams suppresses depression-like behaviour. *Science* 552 (2015), 335–339.

13. F. E. Ritter. 2009. Two cognitive modeling frontiers: emotions and usability. *Transactons for the Japanese Society for Artificial Intelligence* 24, 2 (2009), 241–249.

14. C. Routledge, T. Wildschut, C. Sedikides, and J. Juhl. 2013. Nostalgia as a resource for psychological health and well-being. *Social and Personality Psychology Compass* 7, 11 (2013), 808–818.

15. D. L. Schacter. 2002. *The Seven Sins of Memory: How the Mind Forgets and Remembers.* Houghton Mifflin.

16. D. L. Schacter, D. R. Addis, and R. L. Buckner. 2007. Remembering the past to imagine the future: the prospective brain. *Nature Review Neuroscience* 8, 9 (2007), 657–661.

17. R. Simon and M. Engström. 2015. The default mode network as a biomarker for monitoring the therapeutic effects of meditation. *Frontiers in Psychology* (2015).

18. W. Wagenaar. 1986. My memory: A study of autobiographical memory over six years. *Cognitive Psychology* 18 (1986), 225–252.

19. S. R. Waldstein, W. J. Kop, L. A. Schmidt, A. J. Haufler, D. S. Krantz, and N. A. Fox. 2000. Frontal electrocortical and cardiovascular reactivity during happiness and anger. *Biological Psychology* 55 (2000), 3–23.

20. K. Yasuda, K. Kuwabara, K. Kuwahara, S. Abe, and N. Tetsutani. 2009. Effectiveness of personalised reminiscence photo videos for individuals with dementia. *Neuropsychological Rehabilitation: An International Journal* 19 (2009), 603–619.

Exploring Gaze in Interacting with Everyday Objects with an Interactive Cup

Siti Aisyah binti Anas, Shi Qiu, Matthias Rauterberg, Jun Hu
Eindhoven University of Technology,
Department of Industrial Design,
5600 MB, Eindhoven, The Netherlands
{s.a.b.anas, sqiu, g.w.m.rauterberg, j.hu}@tue.nl

ABSTRACT

Our eye gaze is important during social interactions. It can generate significant social cues in nonverbal communication. The feeling of being look back when we are gazing at someone influences our social behaviour. In this paper, we propose an interactive coffee cup that is responsive whenever a person is fixating on it. Taking the user's gazing behaviour as our system input modality, we want to create an environment where a person may establish social interaction with an everyday object whenever he/she is looking at it. To make an object *visible* to the user's eyes and for the user to feel connected with the object, it is expected that the object to possess distinctive characteristics that can acknowledge the user that it is aware of being look at. By combining the recent technology of eye trackers, mechanical design and embedded electronics, we want to explore the possibility of nonverbal social interaction between a person and inanimate object that will respond when a person is looking at it to allow social interaction and to create a sense of emotional bond between the two.

Author Keywords

Eye tracking; gaze sensitive object; emotional object; human-object interaction.

ACM Classification Keywords

H.5.m. Information interfaces and presentation (e.g., HCI): Miscellaneous;

INTRODUCTION

Communication is known as the bedrock of any successful relationship, either personal or professional. It is important to acknowledge that it is our nonverbal communication (our eye contact, gesture, facial expression, the tone of voice and posture) that speaks louder. The ability to interpret and adopt nonverbal communication is the most compelling tool that can help people to relate to one another and to build better relationships.

HAI '16, October 04-07, 2016, Biopolis, Singapore
ACM 978-1-4503-4508-8/16/10.
http://dx.doi.org/10.1145/2974804.2980494

Nonverbal communication contributes significantly to conversations and interactions. Since visual modality is dominant for most people and the fact that the eyes serve as the focal points of the body, eye contact is an essential type of nonverbal communication. Our eyes reflect our interest, honesty, trust and comfort when communicating with others. Having good eye contacts during conversation is key to creating positive connections with others. When a person tries to initiate interaction with another person, eye contact must come first. Eye contact is known as one of the most compelling social signals which can boost human's physiological arousal [10]. However, humans tend to feel that they are making eye contacts with other humans but not with objects. A website called What The Face: Objects That Look Back, invite people to upload pictures of everyday objects that appear to have human emotions [4]. All of these objects unintentionally show that they have the characteristics of a human face with eyes. Whenever they look at these objects, they felt that the object is staring back at them which influence their behaviour towards the objects. However, since most of the objects do not have eyes, it is hard to define if we can have eye contact with it or not. These objects remain invisible because they are not responsive towards our eye gaze. According to James Elkin, we should not confine our vision to things with eyes. In his opinion, vision should be universal, and every object has its own eyes, full of vision even if they are not [3]. Can a person experience the feeling of being look back from an object even if the object does not have any eyes? What if the object can react and display behaviours when a person is looking at it, will he/she experience the feeling of being look back from the object and influence their behaviour towards the object?

RELATED WORK

EmotoCouch [8] is an emotional couch that could display six emotional states (excited, happy, calm, depressed or sad, and angry). The emotion was identified based on the Circumplex emotion model. It used different colours of lights, irregular patterns of the cushion cover and the sense of touch (haptic feedback) to expressed range of emotions to people surrounding the couch. The couch could show an angry designed when the couch was under pressure hearing people arguing or showed excited designed when a family was sitting together to encourage family time. Sneaky Kettle [6] was a kettle which liked to play and party by rotating around its axis. Its behaviour depended on the type of rotations and the timing. The kettle knew that it was there to boiled water and not to have fun. However, it will sneakily start to move when there was no human presence. This kettle became more daring and braved enough to move, once it gets to know the user. The user may found this behaviour appealing for a moment but became bothered with it which make the kettle started to isolate itself and just moved when nobody was around. The user felt that this product had a soul. Emotional Objects [7] focused on three modified everyday objects with the purpose to effectively point out their dynamic connection with heat. A tea cup that vibrated when the tea was getting cold, a metal chair uncovered its desired to be warm and comfortable when people sitting in it and a pan with a handle became difficult to hold when it is excessively hot, making it impossible to touch using our bared hand. These unique characteristics allowed these object to promote meaningful interactions with their users by changing their normal state towards surrounding environment which could create an emotional bond between object and the user.

MOTIVATION

This research is motivated to create opportunities for social interaction between a person and an object by utilising the user's eye gaze in the physical world. Previous studies related to gaze interaction were mostly confined to the digital or virtual environment whether as an input modality to interact with an object while playing video games [9] or to point or select an object in human-computer interaction [5]. In this research, an eye tracker is used to detect user's gaze and to help the object to understand how it should react based on the gaze data it has retrieved from the eye tracker. By applying simple mechanical behaviours, we intend to design the object to have its personality traits. Will the user aware that their gaze is making the object react? If the user can realise the characteristic shown by the objects, will the objects affect the user's emotions? Does this experience create an emotional bond between object and the user?

INTERACTIVE COFFEE CUP

Coffee Cup with Dynamic Behaviour towards Human Gaze

We might not have notice that objects do express emotional response when we look at it based on the shape, colour or size [2] but these characteristics are fixed and unchangeable. That is why it is often the case that people are not entirely aware of it. Whether we realise it or not, these objects are communicating to us openly, actively or indirectly, but we were hoping to have a real interaction with them [1].

A coffee cup is the first everyday object chosen for this research because it is a common object we use in our daily life. Since people are already familiar with the cup, we do not have to introduce the function and how to use the cup. Normally, when we arrive at our workplace, the first thing that we do is to have a cup of coffee to start the day. Then, we place the cup within our eyesight. If we want to take another sip of coffee, we look at the cup, pick it up and take another sip. It is a one-sided behaviour between a person and the object. However, what if we implement the coffee cup

with dynamic behaviour that can show movements to express its emotional state, the experience of using the cup can be new and different. A cup that can move up to indicate "are you looking at me?" when the user looks at it, or it will go back to its initial state as shown in Figure 1 if the user turns his/her gaze around and focus on the other things around.

If the user maintains his/her gaze at the cup after it moves up, it will turn itself around and make sure the handle of the cup is pointing towards the user to offer "would you like to have

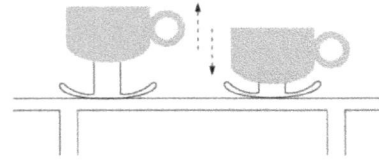

Figure 1. Coffee cup acknowledging the user with the presence of the gaze by moving up and back to its initial state.

a cup of coffee?" as shown in Figure 2.

The cup itself can express its shyness when the user staring at it for a longer time or it might try to distract the user by

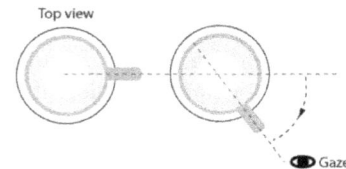

Figure 2. Coffee cup offering the user a cup of coffee to initiate social behaviour.

doing something naughty or ridiculous just to grab the attention so that they can develop visual contact between the two.

Prototype

Figure 3 shows the exploded view of the prototype for the interactive coffee cup. The coffee cup and the cup holder itself were modelled using Rhino3D and fabricated in the Ultimaker 3D printer. The cup holder has a slot to hold the handle. This slot is necessary for the user to know which suitable position to place the coffee cup back after they used it. We used acrylic plastic for the mechanical part and design it by using Adobe Illustrator software for laser cutting. To control the movement of the cup, we decided to use gears as part of the working mechanism. We implement rack and pinion gear systems in the prototype to enable the cup to move up and down. It combines a pair of gears which can convert rotary motion to linear motion. The pinion is a typical round gear, and the rack is a straight bar with jagged teeth in it. When the pinion rotates, it causes the rack to move corresponding to the pinion, thereby makes the cup move up if the pinion rotates clockwise, or move down if the pinion rotates counter clockwise. The cup holder is directly fixed to a flat round surface and attach to a servo horn to control the desired angle of the coffee cup. A servo motor controls this servo horn to enable the coffee cup to rotate to a precise angular position by transmitting a coded signal to the servo. If the coded signal change, the angular position of the cup will change accordingly.

Hardware and Software

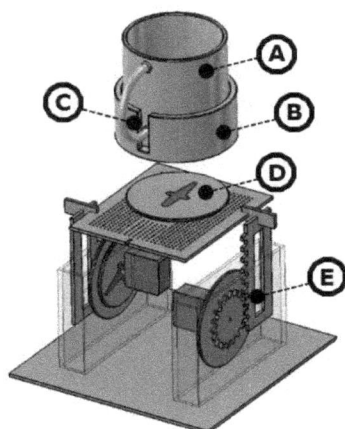

Figure 3. Exploded view of the interactive coffee cup. A: the coffee cup; B: the cup holder to hold the securely on top of the base; C: slot to grip the handle of the cup; D: the base of the coffee cup to control the angle of the cup; E: rack and pinion to control the movement of the cup (up and down).

To track user's gaze in real time, we are required to use an eye tracker to measure the eye positions and eye movements. The Eye Tribe Tracker is one of the affordable devices that can observe and evaluate human attention. It comes with software that can measure the eye gaze defined by a pair of (x,y) coordinate with an average efficiency of 0.5 to 1° of visual angle. This software is based upon an open Application Program Interface (API) design that allows the client applications to interact with the underlying tracker server to obtain gaze data in both raw and smoothed forms. However, this device is meant to be used for desktops, laptops and tablets where we need to fix it the displays. For this research, we use it to measure visual attention on real objects in real environments.

We used Java software to program the system to manipulate the 2D coordinate and make it suitable to be embed in the 3D environment to create an engaging experience by depending on user's eye gazes. We wrote a list of commands in the code, and if the eye gaze point of the user corresponds to the location of the coffee cup, taking into consideration the duration of each visual fixation, the system will transmit the appropriate command wirelessly using Bluetooth.

An Arduino microcontroller is used to control the behaviour of the coffee cup. Three servo motors and a Bluetooth module are connected to the Arduino. Once Arduino receives a certain command via Bluetooth from the system (Java program), it processes the command and controls the servo motor accordingly. The coffee cup will only interact with the user if the user manages to have a visual contact with the cup.

SYSTEM OVERVIEW

This system consists of an Eye Tribe tracker that calculates the location of user's gaze point by extracting information from the person's face and eyes. A computer that acts as a server to extract the data gathered by the Eye Tribe tracker. A Sparkfun Bluetooth mate gold module, an Arduino microcontroller development board, three servo motors and a coffee cup (Figure 4).

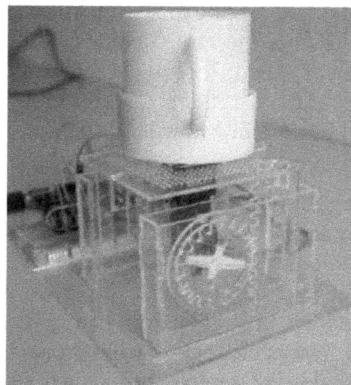

Figure 4. Working prototype of the interactive cup that reacts to human eye gaze.

Figure 5 shown the overview of the system. The location of the interactive coffee cup is pre-determined and must be within the eye tribe tracker's evaluation view. The position of the user is also important and must be in parallel to the tracker's tracking area. It is necessary to centre align the eye tracker and adjust it towards the user's face for the maximum trackability. When the user gazes at the coffee cup, the Eye Tribe will extract the coordinates of the gaze and compare them to the pre-determined position of the coffee cup. If the the point of gaze and the position of the coffee cup matches, the system will sent a command to the Arduino via Bluetooth. Arduino will control the dynamic behaviour of the coffee cup according to the user's gaze to enhance certain desirable characteristics of the interaction.

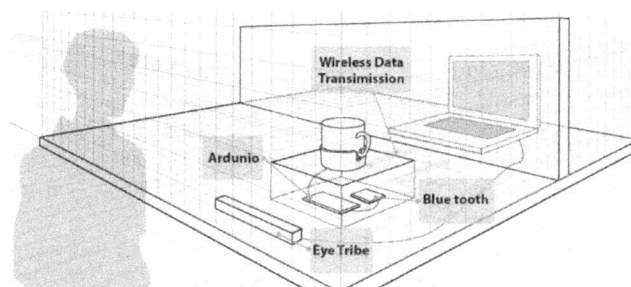

Figure 5. Overview of the system.

SCENARIO

Here we present a scenario that shows how the interactive coffee cup socialises with people in their daily life.

"Nick works for an advertising company, and he loves to drink coffee. Whether it is to wake him up or to keep him focused while being stuck at work, sitting down with a nice cup of coffee helps him get by. The cup he uses is not an ordinary cup. This cup has its feeling and will react whenever he looks at it. It can acknowledge him by moving up if he look at the cup and if he looks at it long enough, the cup will turn with the handle facing towards him with the purpose to offer him to have a sip of coffee. However, if he stares at the cup without any intention to drink the coffee, the cup will feel disappointed and start to turn away from him slowly. When the temperature of the hot coffee drop and Nick gaze at the cup, the cup will vibrate to let him know that he should drink the coffee before the coffee getting colder. Nick feels that the cup knew that he is looking at it because the cup can react to his gaze and have its personality traits which affect his emotion and behaviour towards the cup."

CONCLUSION

An interactive coffee cup with dynamic behaviour investigates how a simple everyday object can create human-object relationship by reacting to user's eye gaze. Even though the coffee cup does not have any eyes, we expect the behaviour embedded in it somehow can give the users the feeling of being look back as if they have a social interaction with another person. By implementing such experience, this responsive objects can give a different perspective in evoking meaningful social interactions between a person and an everyday object.

ACKNOWLEDGEMENT

We thank our colleagues at the Design Intelligence research group who offer suggestions and ideas for this project. This research received funding from the Ministry of Higher Education, Malaysia and Universiti Teknikal Malaysia Melaka (UTeM).

REFERENCES

[1]   Antonelli, P. 2011. *Talk to Me: Design and the Communication between People and Objects.* The Museum of Modern Art.

[2]   Biamino, G. and Cena, F. 2011. Social Awareness and User Modeling to Improve Objects Intelligence. *Proceedings of the 2011 IEEE/WIC/ACM International Conferences on Web Intelligence and Intelligent Agent Technology - Volume 03* (Washington, DC, USA, 2011), 118–121.

[3]   Elkins, J. 1997. *The Object Stares Back. On the Nature of Sensing.* Simon and Schuster, Inc.

[4]   Horse Head Production. What the Face. 2008. Retrieved August 16, 2015 from http://www.wtface.com.

[5]   Kangas, J., Špakov, O., Majaranta, P. and Raisamo, R. 2013. Defining gaze interaction events. *CHI 2013 Workshop on "Gaze Interaction in the Post-WIMP World* (Paris, France, Apr. 2013), 1–4.

[6]   Van Krieken, B., Desmet, P.M.A., Aliakseyeu, D. and Mason, J. 2012. A sneaky kettle: Emotionally durable design explored in practice. *Out of Control – Proceedings of the 8th International Conference on Design and Emotion* (Central Saint Martins College of Art & Design, London, UK, 2012), 1–5.

[7]   Marco van Hout. Sustaining the Human-Object Relationship. 2009. Retrieved April 17, 2015 from http://www.design-emotion.com/2009/07/24/sustaining-the-human-object-relationship/.

[8]   Mennicken, S., Brush, A.J.B., Roseway, A. and Scott, J. 2014. Exploring Interactive Furniture with EmotoCouch. *Proceedings of the 2014 ACM International Joint Conference on Pervasive and Ubiquitous Computing: Adjunct Publication* (Seattle, Washington, 2014), 307–310.

[9]   Sundstedt, V. 2012. *Gazing at Games:An Introduction to Eye Tracking Control.* Morgan & Claypool.

[10]   Suomen Akatemia (Academy of Findland). Personality Shapes the Way Our Brains React to Eye Contact. 2015. Retrieved August 31, 2015 from http://www.sciencedaily.com/releases/2015/06/1506 05081615.htm.

ChiCaRo: Tele-presence Robot for Interacting with Babies and Toddlers

Masahiro Shiomi
ATR-IRC
Kyoto, 619-0288, Japan
m-shiomi@atr.jp

Kasumi Abe
JSPS Research Fellow/University of Electro-Communications
Tokyo, 182-8585, Japan
k_abe@apple.ee.uec.ac.jp

Yachao Pei, Tingyi Zhang, Narumitsu Ikeda, Takayuki Nagai
University of Electro-Communications
Tokyo, 182-8585, Japan
{pei.yachao, louisa, ikeda_n}@apple.ee.uec.ac.jp, tnagai@ee.uec.ac.jp

ABSTRACT

This paper reports a tele-presence robot named ChiCaRo, which is designed for interaction with babies and toddlers. ChiCaRo can physically interact with babies and toddlers by moving around and using its small hand. We conducted a field trial at a playroom where babies and toddlers can freely play to investigate ChiCaRo's effectiveness. In the experiment adult participants interacted with their babies and toddlers by ChiCaRo and another robot. The adult participants evaluated ChiCaRo highly in the context of remote interaction with their babies and toddlers.

Author Keywords

Tele-presence robot; human-robot interaction; babies and toddlers

ACM Classification Keywords

H.5.2. User Interfaces – *Interaction styles*

INTRODUCTION

Child-robot interaction is one active research topics in robotics. For example, Tanaka et al. developed an educational application for Pepper (Softbank. Co. Ltd) to learn with children [1] and proposed a care-receiving robot concept, which enables children to learn by teaching the robot, instead of being taught by the robot [2]. They also conduct a field trail by using child-operated telepresence robot [3]. Kim et al. have investigated the effectiveness of videoconference technology by comparing between telepresence robot and a simple video system for children [4]. Shiomi et al. installed a social robot in an elementary school science classroom for a month to investigate whether a robot could increase children's interest in science [5]. Komatsubara et al. also investigated a social robot to determine whether it can clarify children's understanding of science in classrooms [6]. Social robots are also used as educational tools for children with autism spectrum disorders [7].

Interaction with babies/toddlers is another growing research topic in the human-robot interaction research field. For example, Fink et al. developed a robotic toy box that encourages young children to pick up their toys and investigated the robot's effectiveness through a WOZ technique [8]. Abe et al. investigated play strategies for children by gathering interaction data between children and a tele-operated robot controlled by a preschool teacher [9]. Hieida et al. investigated the effects of shaking hands in interaction between a tele-operated robot and kindergarteners [10].

However, these research works mainly focused on developing functions for autonomous communication robots to interact with them. Or, their interest is not babies/toddlers, mainly targeted of school-age children. Different from these research works, we developed a tele-presence robot for interacting with babies/toddlers by considering its appearances and functions. In this paper, we report the effectiveness of the developed proto-type tele-presence robot named ChiCaRo (Child-Care Robot).

HAI '16, October 04-07, 2016, Biopolis, Singapore
ACM 978-1-4503-4508-8/16/10.
http://dx.doi.org/10.1145/2974804.2980496

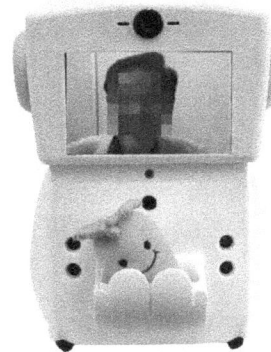

Fig. 1 ChiCaRo with a carrot-like toy

ChiCaRo

We developed a tele-presence robot named ChiCaRo (Fig. 1), which is 350 mm (height) x 270 mm (width) and weighs 4 kg. It has a 7-inch LCD monitor as a head (2 DOFs) and differential wheels for movement (2 DOFs). ChiCaRo has a small hand-like device (width: 103.5 mm, radius: 60 mm) on its front that can open and shut. This device is used to receive toys from children, to beckon them, and attract their attention. Six touch sensors and four infrared based distance sensors ensure safety, and one color sensor tracks the person with whom it is interacting. ChiCaRo is equipped with a stick PC (MS-NH1-AMZN, MouseComputer) for video chat, Arduino Mega and Nano for motor control and color as well as touch and distance sensor processing.

EXPERIMENT

Participants

In our experiments, 27 people (12 adults and 15 children whose ages ranged from one to six) participated. Some families participated together. Adult participants were paid 4,000 yen (about 34 dollars, including transportation expenses). 12 adult participants (eight women and four men, four of whom are grandparents and eight parents) answered questionnaires.

Environment

The experiment room was about 40 m^2, big enough to accommodate more than ten people (five adults and five children). We installed two web cameras for recording and showing the images to the operator. Toys, books, and chairs are available in the room for participants to play with and/or sit on.

Conditions

The study was with a within-participants design with the following two conditions:

ChiCaRo Condition: In this condition, adult participants used ChiCaRo to remotely interact with their children. Before starting this condition, they moved to an operation space. The experiment time was a maximum of ten minutes, but if the children were scared by the robot, the session was immediately ended.

Alternative Condition: In this condition, adult participants used Romo[1] to remotely interact with their children. The reason of why we used Romo as an alternative robot is because Romo can be used as a tele-operated robot for adult participants to interact with babies/toddlers due to its small size. We controlled it with iPod touch and official software that enables the adult participants to see the video image from Romo, navigate it, and select various behaviors of animated characters.

Procedures

In the experiment, we asked participants to act freely in the environment for two hours. In the first hour, the children became acclimated, and the adults learned about the tele-operation systems of ChiCaRo and Romo. After explaining this information, the adult participants filled out informed consent forms, which were approved by IRB. In the second hour, we asked the adult participants to control ChiCaRo or Romo and interact with their children. After tele-operation of either robot, the adult participants controlled the other robot and interacted again with their children after five minutes.

Adult participants answered questionnaires after controlling both robots. The order of the tele-operation robot was counterbalanced.

Measurements

We investigated *intention to use* in this study. This scale consists of three items that were adapted from Heerink et al. [11], including, "I'm planning to use this robot for the next few days."

RESULT

Figure 2 shows the questionnaire result for intention to use. We conducted a one-way repeated-measure ANOVA; a significant main effect was revealed between conditions ($F(1,11)=14.955$, $p=.003$, partial $\eta^2=.576$). This means that the adult participants evaluated ChiCaRo higher from the intention to use viewpoint than Romo. The Cronbach's alpha statistics of intention to use were 0.873 and 0.948 in the ChiCaRo and Romo conditions, which are within a good range.

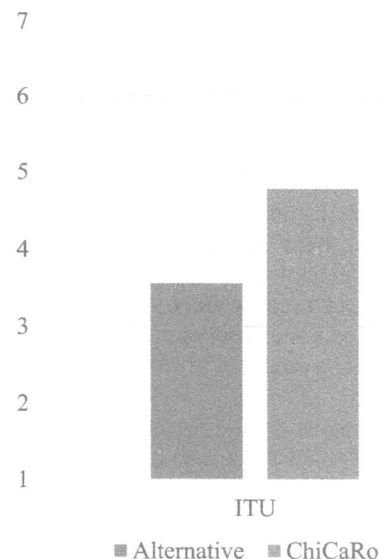

Fig. 2 Questionnaire results

[1] http://www.romotive.com

CONCLUSION

This paper presents a tele-presence robot, ChiCaRo, which is designed for remotely interacting with babies and toddlers. We implemented video chat, navigation, safety, and a hand-like device to realize rich remote interaction between operators and babies/toddlers and to support operations through autonomous functions. We conducted an experiment in a realistic context in a playroom with both adults and children participants. We investigated intention to use of ChiCaRo and compared it to an existing robotic toy that can also be controlled by operators. The result revealed that adult participants prefer ChiCaRo.

ACKNOWLEDGMENTS

This research work was supported by JSPS KAKENHI Grant Number 15H05322, 16K12505, and Grant-in-Aid for JSPS Fellows 15J11597.

REFERENCES

1. F. Tanaka, K. Isshiki, F. Takahashi, M. Uekusa, R. Sei, and K. Hayashi, "Pepper learns together with children: Development of an educational application," in Humanoid Robots (Humanoids), 2015 IEEE-RAS 15th International Conference on, pp. 270-275, 2015.
2. F. Tanaka, and S. Matsuzoe, "Children teach a care-receiving robot to promote their learning: Field experiments in a classroom for vocabulary learning," *Journal of Human-Robot Interaction*, vol. 1, no. 1, 2012.
3. F. Tanaka, T. Takahashi, S. Matsuzoe, N. Tazawa, and M. Morita, "Child-operated telepresence robot: a field trial connecting classrooms between Australia and Japan," in 2013 IEEE/RSJ International Conference on Intelligent Robots and Systems, pp. 5896-5901, 2013.
4. N. Kim, J. Han, and W. Ju, "Is a Robot better than Video for Initiating Remote Social Connections among Children?," *Journal of Institute of Control, Robotics and Systems*, vol. 20, no. 5, pp. 513-519, 2014.
5. M. Shiomi, T. Kanda, I. Howley, K. Hayashi, and N. Hagita, "Can a Social Robot Stimulate Science Curiosity in Classrooms?," *International Journal of Social Robotics*, vol. 7, no. 5, pp. 641-652, 2015.
6. T. Komatsubara, M. Shiomi, T. Kanda, H. Ishiguro, and N. Hagita, "Can a social robot help children's understanding of science in classrooms?," in Proceedings of the second international conference on Human-agent interaction, Tsukuba, Japan, pp. 83-90, 2014.
7. S. Boucenna, A. Narzisi, E. Tilmont, F. Muratori, G. Pioggia, D. Cohen, and M. Chetouani, "Interactive Technologies for Autistic Children: A Review," *Cognitive Computation*, vol. 6, no. 4, pp. 722-740, 2014.
8. J. Fink, S. Lemaignan, P. Dillenbourg, P. R, tornaz, F. Vaussard, A. Berthoud, F. Mondada, F. Wille, and K. Franinović, "Which robot behavior can motivate children to tidy up their toys?: design and evaluation of "ranger"," in Proceedings of the 2014 ACM/IEEE international conference on Human-robot interaction, Bielefeld, Germany, pp. 439-446, 2014.
9. K. Abe, C. Hieida, M. Attamimi, T. Nagai, T. Shimotomai, T. Omori, and N. Oka, "Toward playmate robots that can play with children considering personality," in Proceedings of the second international conference on Human-agent interaction, Tsukuba, Japan, pp. 165-168, 2014.
10. C. Hieida, K. Abe, M. Attamimi, T. Shimotomai, T. Nagai, and T. Omori, "Physical embodied communication between robots and children: An approach for relationship building by holding hands," in Intelligent Robots and Systems (IROS 2014), 2014 IEEE/RSJ International Conference on, pp. 3291-3298, 2014.
11. M. Heerink, K. Ben, V. Evers, and B. Wielinga, "The influence of social presence on acceptance of a companion robot by older people," *Journal of Physical Agents*, vol. 2, no. 2, pp. 33-40, 2008.

Mutual Adaptation between a Human and a Robot Based on Timing Control of "Sleep-time"

Masahiro Kitagawa
Hokkaido University
Hokkaido, Japan
ktgw-wgtk@complex.ist.hokudai.ac.jp

Benjamin Luke Evans
Hokkaido University
Hokkaido, Japan
benjamin@complex.ist.hokudai.ac.jp

Nagisa Munekata
Hokkaido University
Hokkaido, Japan
munekata@complex.ist.hokudai.ac.jp

Tetsuo Ono
Hokkaido University
Hokkaido, Japan
tono@complex.ist.hokudai.ac.jp

ABSTRACT

In our research, we made a system in which a robot acquires motions from a human's motions and repeats the motion when the human communicates with the robot. By controlling the timing of the robot's imitation, we verified an effect of Mutual Adaptation between human and robot.

As a result of the experiment in which we controlled the imitation timing, some experiment participants were influenced and changed their motion. We found in some cases the robot could affect human's motion by imitating that human's motion.

Author Keywords
Android; human-robot interaction; robot

ACM Classification Keywords
1.2.9 Robotics: Commercial robots and application

INTRODUCTION
In recent years, thanks to the development of robotics, we have seen many robots developed for commercial purposes, such as Softbank's personal robot Pepper[1], and Aldebaran's small humanoid robot NAO[2]. The development of these robots has enabled the introduction of robots into society and has made them more familiar in our daily lives. This can lead people to a world where people will communicate with robots more and more.

Not only verbal communication but also nonverbal communication has important roles in the communication between human and human. In our daily life, we tend to communicate with other people with some syntonic motions. For example, we can see human talks to someone nodding or with some gesture each other. To communicate smoothly in this way, people need to use rhythmical motions corresponding to the opponent's motion.[3]

Figure 1: Example of Experiment Performance

In our research, we redefined this nonverbal communication and we made a system in which a robot imitates a human using rhythmical and syntonic motions to communicate with the human. Using this system, we were able to see the effect of mutual adaptation between human and the robot.

RELATED WORK
Many studies about sympathetic motions by robots have been researched[4][5][6]. In particular, Komagome et al. observed in an experiment that motions of a robot propagate to research subjects[7]. In this experiment, they used the humanoid communication robot Robovie-ver2. They proposed a method to acquire and capture a human's motion information within real time using Microsoft's KINECT sensor[8].

In previous research, we defined physical synchronism also using a KINECT sensor. We used Robovie-R ver3 and Pepper as humanoid robots to move with humans.
Using this robot, we investigated the effects caused by robots when they change the timing of when they begin rhythmical and syntonic motions.

EXPERIMENT
In our work, we have defined "Sleep-time" and "Motion-time". "Sleep-time" is the time between the start of human movement and the start of the robot's movement. "Motion-time" is the time from when the robot starts to move until it finishes moving and acquires the some pose as that of the human.

Before this experiment, we conducted preliminary experiments where we changed these two parameters and verified the effect of these parameters using a humanoid robot. We recognized that "Sleep-time" influenced to the human's feeling stronger than "Motion-time". In this paper, we focused on "Sleep-time" and looked into its effect on humans.

Experiment Participants

The experiment consisted of 18 participants. Their ages were between 6-50 years old. 6 participants were male and 12 were female.

Experiment Environment

We used Pepper as the robot. This extended the variety of possible motion and improved the precision of imitation as compared to using Robovie-R ver3. Pepper also has a face-tracking function, which we used. Experiment participants and the robot stood side by side in order to give participants a strong impression that the robot was watching them and would follow their lead.

To acquire the motion of experiment participants, we used a KINECT-V2 sensor. We made a system in which the robot imitates the participants using the data of the participant's joints acquired from the KINECT-V2 sensor.

When the robot repeated the motion of participants, the system complemented the movement of the robot by calculating the Bezier curve. This allowed the robot to move safely. Using this function, the robot was able to move smoothly.

Experiment Procedures

In this experiment, the robot imitated the human's motions every 300ms. After the robot continued imitating for about 1 minute, the robot posed differently from the participant and pointed to right of the participant. We expected that this would influence the behavior of participants. At the end of this experiment, we interviewed the experiment participants and reviewed the video taken with a video camera.

Experimental Results

As a result of this experiment, 13 out of 18 experiment participants found the last motion of the robot strange. We were able to get participants to notice that the motion of the robot had changed, but we were not able to alter and lead the human's gaze by pointing to the right. Only 5 participants looked at their right when the robot pointed in that direction.

As a result of the interview from participants, regarding the last motion in which the robot pointed to the right, some participants said that they felt the robot had errored because the robot didn't imitate them. Other said that they felt the robot must be lonely to pose different from them. We believe this occurred because the system generated a relationship between the robot and some participants.

DISCUSSION and CONCLUSION

We altered the robot in a previous experiment from the humanoid robot Robovie-R ver3 to Pepper, so that the robot could move more smoothly and the precision of imitation could be improved. This emphasized the impression participants received from the robot's imitation.

We believe it is necessary to improve the precision of the robot's imitation more. We have three ideas to solve this problem. First, we need to shorten "Sleep-time" farther. Second, we need to make a more appropriate function in which the system can complement the movement of the robot better because the body of Pepper is different from the body of humans. Third, we need to expand the range where the robot can move

We found in some cases that the robots could affect human's motion by imitating that human's motions. It can be considered that the effect of a robot being able to lead a human's motion or gaze will be emphasized though mutual adaptation.

ACKNOWLEDGEMENT

This work was supported by JSPS Grant-in-Aid for Scientific Research on Innovative Areas Number JP26118006.

REFERENCES

1. Pepper: http://www.softbank.jp/robot/consumer/products/ [Accessed 14 July 2016]

2. NAO: http://www.revast.co.jp/service/humanoid/type03.html [Accessed 14 July 2016]

3. Y. Takaoka, M. Ozeki, and N. Oka; Toward ideal mutual adaptation in Human-Robot Interaction, HAI 2013, pp176-179, (2013).

4. Y. Takahashi and K. Sakakibara; Real-time joint angle estimation for a humanoid robot to imitate human motion using particle filter, JSAI Technical Report, SIG-Challenge-042-05, (2015)

5. C. Saito, H. Takahashi and H. Okada; How does human-robot imitation influence the subject's familiarity to the robot? -Investigation from gaze and questionnaire.-, HAI 2011, II-1A-6, (2011).

6. T. Ichijo , N. Munekata and T. Ono; Unification of Demonstrative Pronouns in a Small Group Guided by a Robot, HAI 2014, pp229-232, (2014).

7. D. Komagome, M. Suzuki, T.Ono and S.Yamada; RobotMeme -A Proposal of Human-Robot Mimetic Mutual Adaptation-, the 16th IEEE International Symposium, pp427-432, (2007)

8. Kinect sensor: http://www.xbox.com/ja-JP/kinect [Accessed 14 July 201

Simulation of a Tele-operated Task under Human-Robot Shared Control

Longjiang Zhou, Keng Peng Tee and Zhiyong Huang
A*Star Institute for Infocomm Research
Singapore
{zhoul, kptee, zyhuang}@i2r.a-star.edu.sg

ABSTRACT

This poster presents simulation of a tele-operated shared controlled robot task that is integrated with a generic simulator of RADOE (Robot Application Development and Operating Environment). A customized and extendable Rviz interface plugin is designed and applied to import models, do s imulation, enable real robot operation, and communicate with other projects by clicking related buttons. In the simulation process, the robot model in the simulator is controlled and visualized by human operator using an Omega 7 haptic device and automatic method, i.e., the shared control. After the simulation is conducted and satisfied, the system will send back a signal to the real robot system to execute the operation task; otherwise, simulation of the shared control process will be continued until satisfaction. We provide a simulation of a drawing task on the surface of a sphere.

Author Keywords

Robotics simulation; end-effectors; teleoperation motion planning.

ACM Classification Keywords

I.6.m. Simulation and Modeling: Miscellaneous.

INTRODUCTION

In application tasks with uncertainties in the pre-programmed settings (e.g. work piece location, size, orientation), it is difficult to achieve reliable robot operation under full autonomy, due to technical challenges in robotic perception, motion planning or control in the presence of uncertainties. On the other hand, humans are more adept in perception and cognition than robots, and can easily spot errors during operation. Human-robot shared control systems allow for more complex operations to be performed reliably due to complementary proficiencies between human and robot [1][2][3]. This approach is particularly useful for tele-operation tasks in which impoverished human depth

HAI '16 , October 04-07, 2016, Biopolis, Singapore
ACM 978-1-4503-4508-8/16/10.
http://dx.doi.org/10.1145/2974804.2983316

perception of the remote environment can be compensated by the robot's local sensing and automatic surface tracking behavior [4]. For example, in a task of drawing on a curved surface, the robot automatically controls the distance and orientation with respect to the surface, while the human performs the drawing motion easily as if it is on a flat plane.

To reduce the development time and cost, robotics simulators are used widely to simulate the behaviours of components and control programs so as to improve operation performance and robustness of the robots, especially for robots applied in special areas [5][6]. Of these software, commercial simulators [7][8] generally have high quality and reliability, but they increase the economic burdens to ordinary users. In comparison, open-source simulators [9] [10] decrease the development time and cost by providing an open and free communication platform for researchers. ROS (Robot Operating System) [11] is an open-source simulator which applied Rviz as its visualization tool and it also integrated Gazebo [12] for modelling and physical simulation of rigid bodies. However, the Gazebo was separated from ROS from Gazebo 1.9. So our team has developed the RADOE [13], a generic industrial robotics simulation platform with a user-friendly interface, to makeup this gap.

With respect to simulating tele-operated shared control tasks, the challenge is to incorporate another platform with both human and automatic control strategies, running on a different operating system. In our case, the tele-operated shared control drawing task is running on Microsoft Windows, and the RADOE simulation is running on Linux Ubuntu. We solved it by designing and implementing a wrapper, a software API based on TCP/IP protocol [15]. Through the wrapper, the trajectory of robot by tele-operated shared control is transmitted to RADOE simulation platform.

This poster introduces RADOE software and its integration with a tele-operated, human-robot shared controlled robotic drawing task [4] to show how the RADOE is applied in the development of industrial robotics simulation.

OVERALL STRUCTURE OF SIMULATION SYSTEM

The RADOE simulator has an overall structure as shown in Figure 1. The RADOE software is installed in a central PC, which may have multiple robots attached to it. The RADOE PC performs task definition and monitoring, which may require inputs from the environment sensors connected to it. It then performs the operation task by sending the required robot motion commands to the robots through the corresponding robot motion controller.

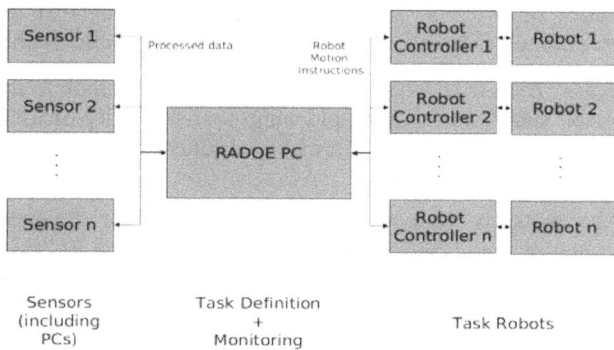

Figure 1. System structure of the RADOE simulator.

The framework of the shared controlled robot drawing system under study in this poster is shown in Figure 2. The human operator uses an Omega 7 haptic device to tele-operate the writing task of the Kuka robot on the surface of a flat plate. The writing procedure and results are displayed on the screen with Windows system to guide the robot motion control through the haptic device.

Figure 2. Structure of physical robot drawing system.

DISPLAY AND SIMULATION PROCEDURE OF RADOE

The framework of the RADOE simulator is shown in Figure 3. There are three regions of the simulator. The right hand side is the Gazebo display, the middle side is the Rviz display, and the left hand side is the "Displays" panel of the Rviz. For this panel, the upper part is the original settings provided by the Rviz software, and the lower part is a customized Rviz plugin interface developed by ourselves for the purpose of the specific project. If the "Import Robot" button is clicked, the user can freely select and import the robot into the simulation platform. The example in this figure is "rrbot", a simple 3-linked robot. The user can also click the "Import Environment" button to import some proper environment objects to the simulator. When the "Simulate" button is clicked, the user can simulate the motion trajectory control by running a bash script file which stores the predefined joint trajectories.

Note that the Rviz and Gazebo displays can be operated separately while at the same time they are integrated to make use of advantages of both softwares.

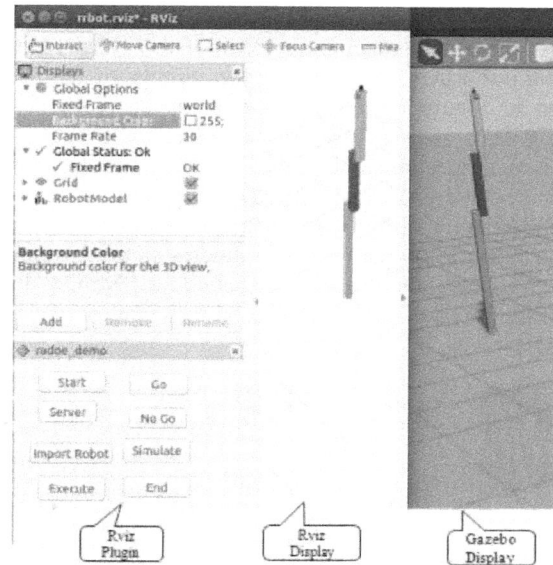

Figure 3: Displays of Rviz and Gazebo with Rviz Plugin interface.

SIMULATION OF THE SHARED CONTROLLED ROBOT TASK

The RADOE simulator has tried to incorporate lots of industrial robot models into the simulation platform [13]. In this poster, another application of the RADOE simulator is addressed. The KUKA LBRiiwa industrial robot with 7 axis is used to write some characters on the surface of a sphere under the control of a haptic device through tele-operation [4].

To realize this simulation task of robotic drawing system, we need to use the haptic device as the input of the simulator instead of the real robotic drawing system. Another issue we should solve is that the robot drawing system works in Windows system, while the RADOE simulator works in Linux Ubuntu system. Moreover, the control input of the real robot drawing system is the position of the end-effector, while the ROS Rviz cannot provide inverse kinematics solver for the joint trajectory control. So we will replace the Rviz with MoveIt [14], which provides motion planning resources for the operation task.

The overall structure of the kuka tele-operated drawing system is shown in Figure 4. The real robot drawing system with its Windows software (server) is linked to the RADOE simulator with Linux software (client) through the TCP/IP protocol, as shown in Figure 5. In the "radoe_demo" panel of Figure 3, the "Start" button is used to start the Client terminal that is linked to the RADOE simulator, and the "Server" button is used to start the server terminal that is linked to the real robot operation system. The server and client terminals communicate with each other automatically through the TCP/TP protocol [15]. When the server sends request of simulation to client, the operator on the client site will control the motion of robot end-effector by the Omega

7 haptic device as shown in Figure 4. When the pen tip on the end-effector touches the surface of the sphere, markers will be published to symbolize the writing of the pen, as shown in Figure 6. If the end-effector can complete the writing task successfully, the operator will click "Go" button to send command to the server site so that the real robot is allowed to execute the drawing task. Otherwise, if the end-effector fails to finish the writing task for certain reasons such as collision with obstacles or the unreachable spot of the task, the operator will click the "No Go" button to tell the server not to do operation task control of the real robot.

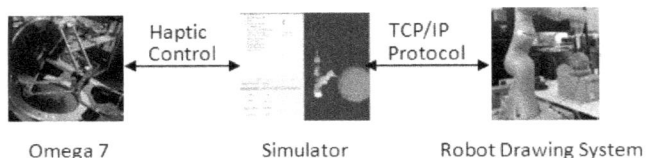

Figure 4: Overall structure of Kuka tele-operated drawing system with simulation.

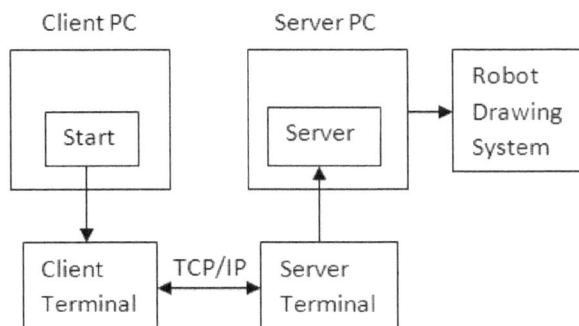

Figure 5: TCP/IP Protocol for the Robot Drawing System.

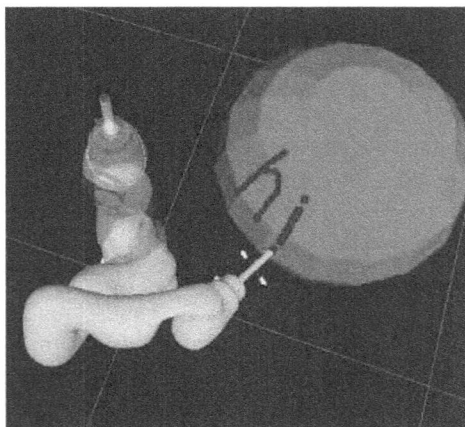

Figure 6: Simulation of Kuka drawing task on the surface of a sphere.

CONCLUSION

This poster put forward an approach to integrate the RADOE simulator with a tele-operated, human-robot shared controlled robot drawing system. A TCP/IP protocol has been established for communication between the RADOE simulator (as a client) and the real robot drawing system (as a server). The simulator can accept command from the server to implement the simulation task under the control of a haptic device and send back signals to the server to tell if the execution of robot task is feasible or not.

Future work will continue to implement and complete the overall simulation system and improve the quality of user-friendly interface through formal user study.

ACKNOWLEDGMENTS
This work is supported by the Agency for Science, Technology and Research (A*STAR) Industrial Robotics Programme Grant 12251 0 0001 and Grant 12251 00008. The authors would like to give thanks to Dr Wu Yan, Mr Chua Yuanwei, Mr Aditya Narayanamoorthy and Mr Ng Kam Pheng for their supportive work.

REFERENCES
1. Robert Riener, Alexander Duschau-Wicke, Alexander Konig, Marc Bolliger, Martin Wieser, and Heike Vallery. 2009. Automation in rehabilitation: How to include the human into the loop. In *Proceedings of the World Congress on Medical Physics and Biomedical Engineering*, 180–183.

2. Yanan Li, Keng Peng Tee, Shuzhi S. Ge, and Haizhou Li. 2013. Building companionship through human-robot collaboration. In *International Conference on Social Robotics*, 1-7.

3. Yanan Li, Keng Peng Tee, Wei Liang Chan, Rui Yan, Yuanwei Chua, and Dilip K. Limbu. 2015. Continuous Role Adaptation for Human–Robot Shared Control. *IEEE Transactions on Robotics* 31, 3:672-681.

4. Yan Wu, Wei Liang Chan, Yanan Li, Keng Peng Tee, Rui Yan and Dilip K. Limbu. 2015. Improving Human-Robot Interactivity for Tele-operated Industrial and Service Robot Applications. In *Proceedings of the IEEE 7th International Conference on Cybernetics and Intelligent Systems and IEEE Conference on Robotics, Automation and Mechatronics* (CIS/RAM' 15), 153 – 158.

5. Bing L. Luk, David S. Cooke, Stuart Galt, Arthur A. Collie, and Sheng Chen. 2005. Intelligent legged climbing service robot for remote maintenance applications in hazardous environments. *Robotics and Autonomous Systems* 53, 2: 142-152.

6. Louis Whitcomb, Dana Yoerger, Hanumant Singh, and Jonathan Howland. 1999. Advances in Underwater Robot Vehicles for Deep Ocean Exploration: Navigation, Control, and Survey Operations. In *Proceedings of the Ninth International Symposium on Robotics Research*, 346-353.

7. Peter I. Corke. 1995. A computer tool for simulation and analysis: the robotics toolbox for MATLAB. In *Proceedings of the 1995 National Conference of the Australian Robot Association*, 319–330.

8. Logic Design Inc. Programming with RoboLogix. Retrieved from: http://www.robologix.com/programming_robologix.php

9. Tim Laue, Kai Spiess, and Thomas Rofer. 2005. SimRobot - A General Physical Robot Simulator and its Application in RoboCup. In *Proceedings of the Robot Soccer World Cup Symposium,* 173-183.

10. Benjamin Balaguer, Stephen Balakirsky, Stefano Carpin, Mike Lewis, and Christopher Scrapper. 2008. USARSim: a validated simulator for research in robotics and automation. In *IEEE/RSJ Workshop on "Robot Simulators: Available Software, Scientific Applications, and Future Trends".*

11. Steve Cousins, Brian Gerkey, Ken Conley, and Willow Garage. 2010. Sharing Software with ROS [ROS Topics]. *IEEE Robotics & Automation Magazine* 17, 2: 12-14.

12. Nathan Koenig and Andrew Howard. 2004. Design and use paradigms for Gazebo, an open-source multi-robot simulator. In *Proceedings of the IEEE International Conference of Intelligent Robots and Systems* (IROS' 04), 2149-2154.

13. Longjiang Zhou, Renjun Li, Kam Pheng Ng, Aditya Narayanamoorthy, and Zhiyong Huang. 2016. A robotics simulator platform for RADOE. In *Proceedings of the IEEE International Conference on Control, Automation and Robotics (ICCAR'16),* 44–48.

14. Ioan A. Sucan and Sachin Chitta. 2013. Moveit!. Retrieved in 2013 from http://moveit.ros.org.

15. Silver Moon. 2012. Server and client examples with C sockets on Linux. Retrieved on July 30, 2012 from http://www.binarytides.com/server-client-example-c-sockets-linux/.

Evaluation of a Substitution Device for Emotional Labor by using Task-Processing Time and Cognitive Load

Takeomi Goto
Graduate School of System and
Information Engineering, University
of Tsukuba
1-1-1, Tenno-dai, Tsukuba, Japan
s1620779@u.tsukuba.ac.jp

Hirotaka Osawa
Faculty of Engineering, Information
and Systems, University of Tsukuba
1-1-1, Tenno-dai, Tsukuba, Japan
osawa@iit.tsukuba.ac.jp

ABSTRACT

Nowadays, physical and intellectual labor can be substituted by robotics and information technology. However, emotional labor, which causes mental stress to the workers, has not been substituted yet. Therefore, we propose a method called *emotional cyborg* that substitutes human-emotional representation with the use of attachable devices. In this study, we used AgencyGlass, a device that substitutes the function of human eyes. We conducted a preliminary study to measure the task-processing time and the subject's cognitive load during the use of AgencyGlass. The result suggests that the AgencyGlass can perform joint attention similar to humans; however, its attentional shift is weaker than in humans.

Author Keywords

emotional cyborg; human–agent interaction; human interface

ACM Classification Keywords

H.5.m. Information interfaces and presentation (e.g., HCI): Miscellaneous;

INTRODUCTION

The goal of our research is to complement human emotional labor. Nowadays, labor is categorized into physical, mental, and emotional labors. Although physical and mental labors have been substituted with information technology, emotional labor has not been substituted yet. For example, the labor of nurses, cabin attendants, and teachers is classified as emotional labor. In emotional labor, workers are required to adjust their facial expressions to adapt to customer's requests without considering their real emotions. For example, cabin attendants always have to be hospitable and smile if a customer complains about anything. In the field of nursing, it is more effective if a nurse's thoughts are similar to those of the patient [1]. The difference between a worker's inner emotions and facial expressions (required by customers) causes psychological load and finally results in a depressive symptom called "burn-out."

We propose a new approach, in which a human agent's facial emotional expression to humans is substituted by replacing human's face parts with an agent using HAI technologies. We consider this method to decrease workers' psychological load during emotional labor.

In this study, we used "AgencyGlass": a substitution device for emotional labor that looks like glasses. In addition, we assessed the difference between the functioning of an AgencyGlass and human's eyes [2]. To assess AgencyGlass, we conducted an experiment in which a subject interacts with the experimenter equipped with the AgencyGlass while performing a task. Further, we assessed the effect on the subject's task-processing time and psychological load.

EXPERIMENT

Device

We developed and explicated the AgencyGlass (Figure 1) in our previous study. We added a function that tracks the subject's eye direction detected by Omron OKAO-Vision module [3]. This module can detect the direction of eyes in the range of 1.3 m: 50° in the horizontal direction and 40° in the vertical direction, and outputs visual line angles.

Figure 1:AgencyGlass

Description

Subjects were provided with a calculation task, which involved the multiplication and addition of two integers.

HAI '16, October 04-07, 2016, Biopolis, Singapore
ACM 978-1-4503-4508-8/16/10.
http://dx.doi.org/10.1145/2974804.2980517

When the experimenter showed the subjects the calculation question, the movement conditions of the experimenter's eyes were as follows: (1) gazing: the experimenter gazes at the subject; (2) showing: the experimenter indicates the question through eye movement; and (3) tracking: the experimenter tracks subject's eyes direction. Further, the experimenter's facial conditions can be categorized in two: (H) original eyes and (G) those of AgencyGlass. Each subject performed tasks with six conditions. In this paper, we represent each condition by using H1–H3 and G1–G2.

Condition (2) was set according to "gaze-triggered attention." This refers to the function in which the human eye direction can divert other's attention [4]. Condition (3) was set according to "joint attention," which is function someone look at something other looking and human recognize each other [5].

Procedure
Subjects were provided calculation tasks on three boards labeled "A," "B," and "C" placed to the subjects' right, in front, and left, respectively. Numbers from six to nine were written on each board by using different colors and font sizes (Figure 2). The subjects were then provided with the calculation task by using board name and color, such as "Add A red and B blue." The experimenter's eye movement and gaze differed in each condition. Six calculation questions were given to a subject per condition.

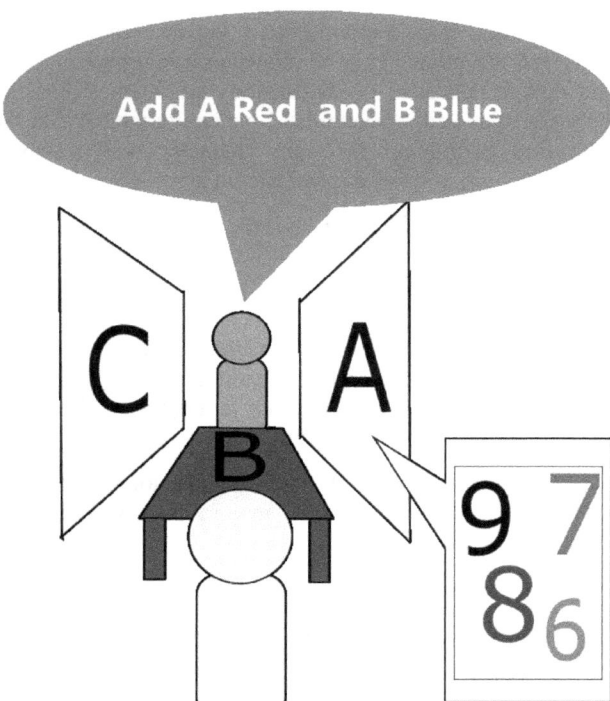

Figure 2: Experimental condition

After performing each conditional task, the subjects filled NASA-TLX and PANAS questionnaires, which were provided to assess load of the task and subject's psychological state (positive and negative feeling) per condition, respectively.

During condition G2, AgencyGlass were controlled by experiment comparison who hide himself from subject. During condition G3, we used the OKAO-Vision module to track a subject's eye direction.

Participants
There were 10 participants for the experiment. Their ages ranged from 21 to 25 years. Nine were male and one was female.

Hypothesis
The hypothesis of this experiment is that if there are significant differences between human eyes and AgencyGlass in any evaluation, AgencyGlass has functional problems.

RESULT
The task score was calculated according to the NASA-TLX questionnaire and the psychological evaluation was concuted based on the PANAS questionnaire (as positive or negative score). The task-processing time was measured using a stopwatch from experiment video. The calculation of the task-processing time started when the subjects were provided the question to when they answered.

The differences between human eyes and AgencyGlass were evaluated by a paired t-test between same eye movement conditions at $p = 0.05$ level (Figures 3–6). The results of the paired t-test show significant differences between the task scores of H2 and G2 (task score: average of difference = -11.189, $t = -2.984$, d$f = 9$, and p < .05. Positive score: average of difference = 1.800, $t = 1.094$, d$f = 9$, and p<.05. Negative score: average of difference = -5.400, $t = -3.499$, d$f = 9$, and p < .05). Similar differences were observed between H2 and G2 (i.e., H2–G2: average of difference = -0.408, $t = -2.020$, d$f = 9$, and $p < .1$). Furthermore, H3–G3 significantly affected the task-processing time (i.e., H3–G3: average of difference = -0.239, $t = -2.003$, d$f = 9$, and $p < .1$). The other pairs did not show significant difference for any evaluation.

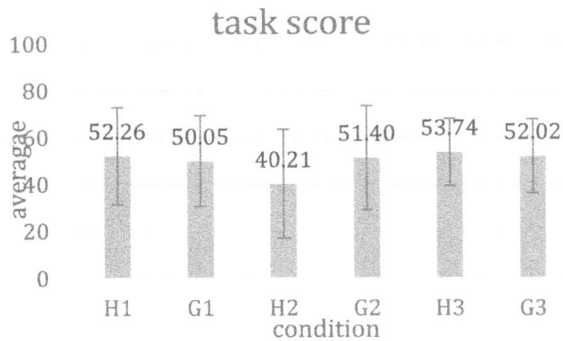

Figure 3: Average of task score

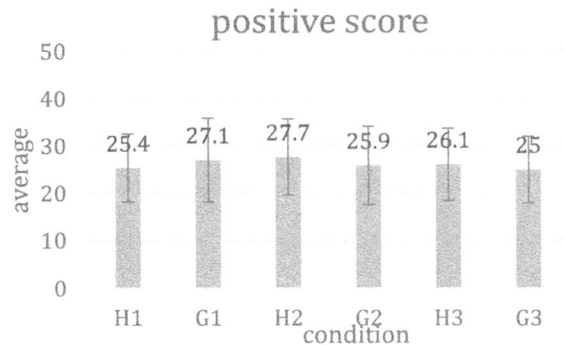

Figure 4: Average of positive score

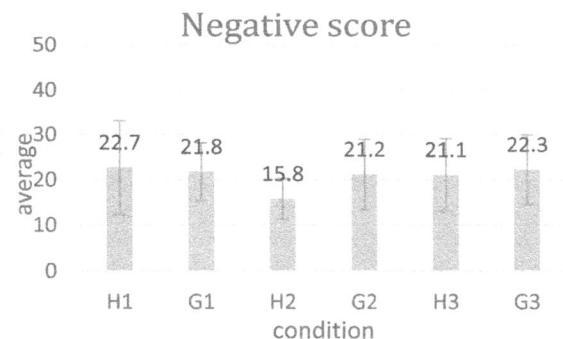

Figure 5: Average of negative score

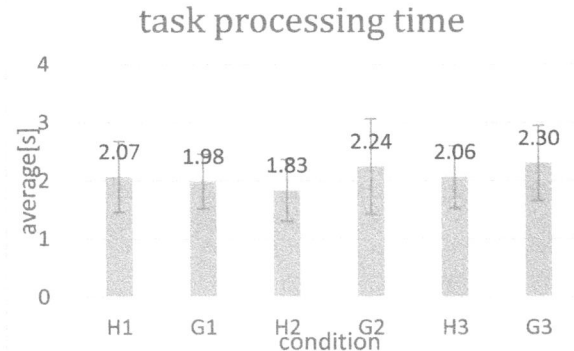

Figure 6: Average of task-processing time

DISCUSSION

For G2, the paired t-test confirmed that the task-processing time was slower than for H2. When the experimenter wore the AgencyGlass, the paired t-test did not show significant differences in any pairs. Therefore, we estimated that the gaze-triggered attention of AgencyGlass is weaker than in human eyes. This could also be because the calculation task was difficult and there was significant difference between the task, positive, and negative scores of H2 and G2.

Moreover, Friesen's study showed a simple character drawn by using circles and lines could cause gaze-triggered attention [4]. Thus, the mismatch between AgencyGlass and human face is because of the gaze-triggered attention being weak when experimenter wore the device. Because of disharmony of AgencyGlass or between eyes and AgencyGlass, we contemplated that the sensation of human face-like character was lost and subjects could not feel gaze-triggered attention.

The following points can be the reasons behind this phenomenon.

(1) Discomfort of images on AgencyGlass

Eyes image on AgencyGlass was of a different size and position than the experimenter's original eyes, and thus did not integrate eyebrows, which are important in expressing emotions.

The eye direction of AgencyGlass looked extreme and did not exactly look toward boards during the experiment.

(2) Discomfort of design

However, we designed AgencyGlass as a glass, wiring was bare and the frame was thick.

In G3, the paired t-test showed that the task-processing time was slower than in H3. As the other evaluation items did not show significant difference, we hypothesized that AgencyGlass has the possibility to perform joint attention like a human. The difference between the task-processing time could be because the eye-tracking system showed approximately 1 s delay. This delay might impede a subject's calculation.

IMPROVEMENT PLAN

To solve the aforementioned problems, we propose the following plan.

(1) Images

We will position and size the eye images on the AgencyGlass to match with original human eyes and add eyebrow images. Furthermore, we will subdivide eye direction of AgencyGlass more fully.

(2) Design

We will detach battery and microcomputer in the frame of the AgencyGlass and mount body inconspicuous position, hide wiring, and paint the AgencyGlass black, similar to a pair of glasses.

(3) Eyes tracking

We will build a faster eye-tracking system.

Thus, we will be able to develop an AgencyGlass more similar to human eyes.

CONCLUSION

In this study, we proposed an "emotional cyborg" method to reduce psychological loads during emotional labor, and developed the AgencyGlass. We performed experiments to assess the functional difference between AgencyGlass and human eyes. that is, the subjects were made to interact with an experimenter wearing the AgencyGlass by solving calculation questions. Thus, we realized that the gaze-triggered attention function of the AgencyGlass was weaker than in human eyes, and AgencyGlass has the possibility to perform joint attention like humans. In addition, we discovered functional and design problems in the AgencyGlass.

Our plan is to improve the function and design of AgencyGlass and develop a device more similar to human eyes.

ACKNOWLEDGEMENTS

This work was partially supported by JSPS KAKENHI 26118006A.

REFERENCES

[1]   A.R.Hochschild, "The Managed Heart:Commercialization of Human Feeling," *University of California Press*, 1983. .

[2]   H. Osawa, "Emotional cyborg: complementing emotional labor with human-agent interaction technology," in *Proceedings of the second international conference on Human-agent interaction - HAI '14*, 2014, pp. 51–57.

[3]   "Image Sensing Compponent (OMRON-HVC)." .

[4]   C. K. Friesen and A. Kingstone, "The eyes have it! Reflexive orienting is triggered by nonpredictive gaze," *Psychon. Bull. Rev.*, vol. 5, no. 3, pp. 490–495, Sep. 1998.

[5]   C. Moore and P. Dunham, *Joint Attention: Its Origins and Role in Development*. 2014.

A Web-based Platform for Collection of Human-Chatbot Interactions

Lue Lin
Ngee Ann Polytechnic
535 Clementi Road,
Singapore, 599489
llue97@hotmail.com

Luis Fernando D'Haro
Institute for Infocomm Research
1 Fusionopolis Way #21-01
Singapore, 138632
luisdhe@i2r.a-star.edu.sg

Rafael E. Banchs
Institute for Infocomm Research
1 Fusionopolis Way #21-01
Singapore, 138632
rembanchs@i2r.a-star.edu.sg

ABSTRACT

Over recent years, the world has seen multiple uses for conversational agents. Chatbots has been implemented into ecommerce systems, such as Amazon Echo's Alexa [1]. Businesses and organizations like Facebook are also implementing bots into their applications. While a number of amazing chatbot platform exists, there are still difficulties in creating data-driven-systems as they large amount of data is needed for development and training. This paper we describe an advanced platform for evaluating and annotating human-chatbot interactions, its main features and goals, as well as the future plans we have for it.

Author Keywords

Chatbots; conversational agents; evaluation; annotations; crowd source.

ACM Classification Keywords

D.3.2 Python, H.5.3 Web, Algorithms, Experimentation, and Human Factors.

INTRODUCTION

Since the proposal of the Turing test in 1950, Artificial Intelligence has been a topic of interest in the scientific community. Since then, multiple chat agents has been developed, tested, and deployed. While many may not realize it, such agents are already part of our everyday lives. They range from simple bots integrated in IRC to complex virtual assistants such as Siri [4] or Cortana.

One of the earliest chat agents, ELIZA [10], was implemented using regular expressions. This basic approach makes use pattern matching techniques to pick an answer from a set of predefined responses; ELIZA was then improved as well as modified and the technology was later used in software such as games and in creating new chatbots such as ALICE [9]. While such technology is efficient and easy to implement, it is not capable of processing utterances that are not defined in its heuristics, or rather the answers could not be contextually relevant.

More recent chatbots do not make use of hard coded question/response pair and instead the response is chosen or generated using machine learning algorithms [2], [6] or [8]. These agents are capable of considering not just the current turn but also the dialog context without the need for the developer to anticipate and provide an answer for all possible user inputs. However, this technology requires a huge training set that the system can use to learn suitable answers. But this requirement for data could be an issue since the data provided in the training set may be inappropriate. For instance, they could be too broad like a corpus extracted from movies scripts [3] or too specific like interactions on an IT helpline [7] therefore not suitable for normal conversations with people.

In addition, human to human interactions could be unsuited for training limited conversational agents since they are difficult to analyze or clean, people could over-expect a better performance from the chatbot if its answers are too natural. Another problem is when using unsupervised human-collected dialog is that some interactions could contain non appropriated comments. For instance, Tay, a bot released on Twitter designed to imitate the behaviors of a 19-year old girl was released by Microsoft on the 23rd of March, 2016. This bot was then promptly taken off-line and suspended in the short time frame of 16 hours after deployment due to inflammatory tweets coming from it. Tay's controversial tweets were the results of learning from un-moderated tweets by users with malicious intent.

Considering this kind of issues, the need for annotated and moderated data exists. However, the task of annotating data is tedious and time consuming. Also, annotated data could be of interest to a limited group of people, but it would be useful to motivate normal users to contribute with the annotations and in moderating the data. On the other hand, there are also confidentiality issues which could limit Chatbot providers to share their data with the research community. As such, we are proposing a solution to several of these problems in the form of a Web-based platform called WebChat. With the proposed platform, we aim to allow easier access to chat information, as well as facilitate the annotation and evaluation of the collected data.

HAI'16, October 4--7, 2016, Biopolis, Singapore.
ACM ISBN 978-1-4503-4508-8/16/10.
http://dx.doi.org/10.1145/2974804.2980500

In this paper, we will discuss the features and functions that WebChat can provide, as well as future plans for this platform. The paper provides first an overview of the main features included in our platform; then, we describe annotation scheme, the gamification and rewards ideas, and finally, we present our future plans and conclusions.

SYSTEM OVERVIEW AND CAPABILITIES

This section focuses on the architecture of WebChat, as well as its features and purpose.

System Architecture

Server:

The web server is written in Python, utilizing the Tornado framework. Tornado is chosen for its scalability as well as its lightweight nature.

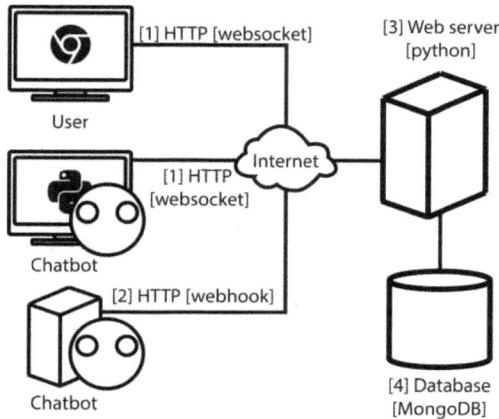

Figure 1. Overview of WebChat architecture

As seen from Figure 1, the main method of communication between the server and client will be made via JSON messages sent with HTTP Websockets or simple POST requests (via Webhooks). Storage of data on the server is implemented with a NoSQL database (MonngoDB).

Chatbot:

The main form of communication between the server and chatbots will be made using HTTP protocols in JSON format. Chatbot skeletons are publicly available in the platform to allow quick development of new chatbots or easy integration of existing ones. The 2 main types of messages sent to the server from the chatbot will be join and chat. Sending leave messages is optional.

Client:

Users can access WebChat through web browsers supporting websockets. Users can be classified in 2 types: regular and privileged. A regular user is just interested on chatting with any chatbot, while privileged users are those who provide chatbots or provide manual annotations of existing sessions. In order to provide rewards to both kinds of users, our platform implements some elements of

gamification and privileges as described later. Figure 2 shows the main interface where users can select the chatbot they want to chat with from the list of available chatbots.

Features

Chat

A chatbot can be in multiple rooms at once. Once a user selects the chatbot, both the chatbot and the client will be added to the chat room. The room will be closed and the conversation recorded in the database as soon as the user or the chatbot leaves the room.

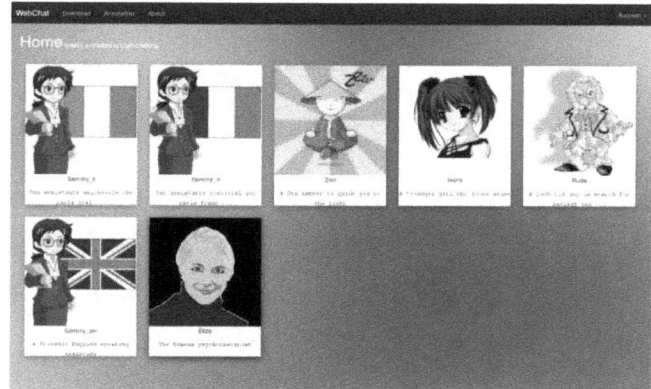

Figure 2. Main interface with available chatbots

Dialogue annotation

The objective of data annotation is to produce data that is suitable to be used as testing/training sets for intelligent systems. There are several ways utterances can be evaluated in chatbot-human interactions, including, but not limited to: fluency, spelling and dictation, as well as sentence structure [5]. WebChat annotates the obtained utterances based on these four attributes:

a. Subjectivity: The annotator must determine if the answer in the current turn is suitable or valid given the context/dialogue state.

b. Polarity: Polarity can be classified into 3 categories: positive, neutral, and negative. This attribute is collected to be used for further processing such as classification of utterances into implicit/explicit response or for emotion recognition.

c. Offensiveness: As the name implies, the utterance can be annotated for the presence of offensive words or comments.

d. Swear: The utterance may contain vulgarity.

Since the task of annotating data could be slow and tedious. WebChat aims to alleviate this by providing users a clean and efficient way to perform annotation. Figure 3 shows the user interface for annotating a turn. Users have the choice of either using the buttons to annotate each individual metrics, or use the number keys on the keyboard to select the options. Pressing the tab or enter key automatically focuses the next input field to allow quicker inputs from the user. Feedback can be provided for each attribute in the fields provided. Automatic annotation has been implemented based on the python module `Textblob`. Assuming that the optimal option has been selected, the user just need to do is to click on the submit button.

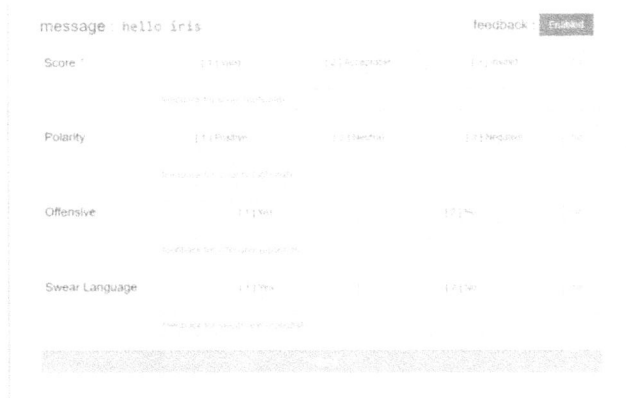

Figure 3. Annotation interface

Gamification/Incentivisation

Annotating data could be a boring and time-consuming task. To promote users to contribute with the annotations, a point system has been implemented. Tasks such as chatting, evaluating, as well as annotating will grant users a certain amount of points that they can use to download previously recorded chat sessions. Here, two types of points considered: basic points and annotator points. Basic points can only be used to download plain text sessions only, while annotator points allow users to download both plain text sessions as well as annotated data for that session. The number of points to be credited is calculated based on the number of messages exchanged with the robot and the number of annotated turns in the session.

Download

As mentioned before, users will be allowed to download previous chat sessions based on the amount of points that they have. A basic user can only download sessions without annotations. An annotator or a chatbot provider on the other hand can download the chat session as well as the annotations of the chat. Downloads can come in several formats, such as XML or JSON.

FUTURE PLANS AND CONCLUSIONS

This section talks about the future plans for WebChat, as well as the conclusion for this paper.

Future plans

Currently we are considering the following plans to improve specially the user experience as well as to facilitate the data annotation and evaluation.

a.   Garner support from the general public via additional rewards. Right now, the need for annotated data mainly applies for researchers and developers. However, we plan to provide coupons or vouchers to the regular public — in exchange for regular or annotated points.

b.   Branching out to multiple platforms: Right now, users can only access the platform is by using a browser; however, we are working on the integration with chat services such as Facebook Messenger or Telegram.

c.   Events. Events will be held on the website from time to time based on certain themes in order to promote given chatbots or to get additional points. For instance, chatbots that bears relation to Santa Claus will be featured during Christmas / The holiday season.

d.   Better pre-annotation: Instead of using the Textblob module, specialized classifiers can be used.

Conclusion

In this paper, we have introduced WebChat, up to the best of our knowledge, the first crowd-source initiative to collect and annotate human-chatbot interactions. The platform includes several resources with the goal of being easy to use for regular people, implementation of different baseline chatbots, communication protocols and messages to allow a quick incorporation of new or existing chatbots, mechanisms for annotating and evaluating chats, as well as the possibility of downloading all this data that can be used to improve chatbots or for different kind of social studies related with the interactions between humans and chatbots.

Finally, an important goal of this paper is to encourage researchers to provided chatbots and annotations for this platform, and more importantly, allowing both the general public and special interest groups to use the platform to enhance the process of data collection.

ACKNOWLEDGEMENTS

We thank all people who have interacted with the chatbots and those who perform annotations on existing dialogues.

REFERENCES

1.   Alexa. Amazon, 2016. https://developer.amazon.com/alexa.

2.   Rafael E. Banchs, Haizhou Li. IRIS: a Chat-oriented Dialogue System based on the Vector Space Model. 2012.

3.   Rafael E. Banchs. Movie-DiC: a movie dialogue corpus for research and development. In Proceedings of the 50th Annual Meeting of the Association for Computational Linguistics: Short Papers-Volume 2, pp. 203-207. Association for Computational Linguistics, 2012.

4.   Jerome R Bellegarda. Spoken language understanding for natural interaction: The SIRI experience. In Natural

Interaction with Robots, Knowbots and Smartphones, p. 3–14. Springer. 2014.

5. Dascalu, Mihai, Stefan Trausan-Matu, and Philippe Dessus. Utterances assessment in chat conversations. Research in Computing Science 46, 2010: pp. 323-334.

6. Alessandro Sordoni, Michel Galley, Michael Auli, Chris Brockett, Yangfeng Ji, Margaret Mitchell, Jian-Yun Nie, Jianfeng Gao, and Bill Dolan. A neural network approach to context-sensitive generation of conversational responses. arXiv:1506.06714. 2015.

7. David C. Uthus, and David W. Aha. The Ubuntu Chat Corpus for Multiparticipant Chat Analysis. AAAI Spring Symposium: Analyzing Microtext. 2013.

8. Oriol Vinyals, Quoc Le. A Neural Conversational Model. 2015.

9. Richard S. Wallace, Be Your Own Botmaster. ALICE A.I. Foundation, 2005.

10. Joseph Weizenbaum, ELIZA—a computer program for the study of natural language communication between man and machine. 1966.

The Optimum Rate of Mimicry in Human-Agent Interaction

Yumiko Shinohara,
Misa Yoshizaki,
Atsushi Hirota,

Katsuhiro Kubo,
Tomomi Takahashi,
Yukiko Nishizaki
Kyoto Institute of Technology
Matsugasaki, Sakyo-ku
Kyoto 606-8585, Japan
yumiko.shinohara.918@gmail.com

Momoyo Nozawa,
Hirofumi Hayakawa,
Natsuki Oka

ABSTRACT

The importance of building rapport between a human and an agent is increasing with the burgeoning development of robot technology. Several recent studies have focused on the chameleon effect, using psychological concepts to investigate human-agent interaction. However, the validity of the chameleon effect in human-agent interaction is controversial. Few studies have explored the influence of individual cognitive ability and the rate of mimicry on the human-agent interaction. We explored the optimal rate of mimicry and the relationship between mimicry rate and individual empathic ability. We controlled the amount of agent mimicry and examined the effect on participants classified as high- and low-perspective takers. We found that, overall, participants preferred agents that mimicked their behavior 83% of the time. Moreover, high-, but not low-, perspective takers tended to be influenced by the mimicry rate.

Author Keywords

The chameleon effect; mimicry; perspective taking; human-agent interaction; impression of robot

ACM Classification Keywords

I.2.0. General: Cognitive simulation

INTRODUCTION

As robot technology advances and the amount of human-agent interaction increases, methods for facilitating smooth interactions have received considerable attention. Previous studies have applied the chameleon effect to human-agent interaction [1, 2]. The chameleon effect refers to the mimicry of posture or behavior of one's interaction partners, which facilitates interactions and increases likeability between partners in human-human interaction [3]. In previous investigations of human-agent interactions, the agent mimicked (mirrored) the participant's nonconscious behavior. By comparing differences among three conditions (mirror, non-mirror, static) of the agent, the investigators found that mirroring appeared to have a positive influence on the anthropomorphic perception of a robot [1]. However, mirroring did not influence the likability rating of the agent.

The problem appeared to be that the amount of the participant's behavior could not be controlled effectively, and it is likely that differences in the amount of nonconscious behavior affected the amount of mimicry. Furthermore, the cognitive facet of empathy (i.e., perspective taking) was found to affect the results such that empathic individuals exhibited the chameleon effect to a greater extent than did other individuals [3]. Furthermore, it is not clear whether mimicking every aspect of the participant's behavior is effective for human-agent interactions.

We determined the optimal rate of behavioral mimicry by controlling the amount of agent mimicry, and examined the effect of individual differences in perspective-taking ability on the rate of mimicry. We hypothesized that the optimal rate of behavioral mimicry in human-agent interaction is between 50 and 100%, because of the previous study [3]. Furthermore, we hypothesized that individual differences in perspective-taking ability contributed to the chameleon effect in human-agent interaction.

METHODS

Participants

The participants included 80 university students (69 males and 11 females) between the ages of 18 and 24 ($M = 21.8$, $SD = 0.93$). All participants agreed to the treatment of protection of personal data.

Apparatus and materials

The experiment was conducted in a prefabricated dark room with a desk and chair for the participant in the center of the room. The humanoid Nao T14 (*Aldebaran-Robotics, France*) and a monitor (*GW2255, Ben Q Corporation, Japan*) were on the desk (Figure 1).

All sessions were videotaped in their entirety for the assessment of participant behavior. The participant and Nao robot were visible through the lens of the camera, and an experimenter positioned outside the experimental room

HAI '16, October 04-07, 2016, Biopolis, Singapore
ACM 978-1-4503-4508-8/16/10.
http://dx.doi.org/10.1145/2974804.2980506

controlled the Nao robot's choices according to those of the participant.

To test our hypothesis that perspective-taking affects the favorability rating of a mimicking agent, we used the perspective-taking subscale of Interpersonal Reactivity Index (IRI) [4, 5] to classify the participants as high or low perspective takers.

The participants were asked to complete a post-experiment questionnaire comprised of nine attributes (Human like, Friendly, Lifelike, Lively, Warm, Empathetic, Kind, Interactive, and Cheerful) [6, 7, 8] to evaluate their feeling toward the Nao robot. Each attribute was rated on a six-point scale from 1 (describes the Nao robot very well) to 6 (does not describe the Nao robot at all).

Figure 1. The experiment room

Procedure

Participants were asked to complete the IRI and rate the favorability of a robot or machine a few days before the experiment. During the experiment, each participant was required to complete the emotional-susceptibility subscale of the Multidimensional Empathy Scale (MES) [9] and the communication and social subscale of the Autism-Spectrum Quotient (AQ) [10, 11]. The experimenter provided a brief introduction while standing in front of the desk and told the participant to watch the Nao robot during the experiment.

Study phase

The participant and the Nao robot were given voice instructions to answer six "yes/no" questions with a nod or shake of the head (Table 1). Then they were instructed to answer six additional questions ("Which do you like?") by pointing a finger at the monitor. In this phase, the Nao robot answered each of the 12 questions after the participant and mimicked the participant's response 50 (6/12), 66 (8/12), 83 (10/12) or 100% of the time. The rate of mimicry was predetermined for each participant.

Observation phase

The participant and Nao robot were instructed to answer eight additional questions by pointing a finger at one of two similar objects on the monitor (Figure 2). In contrast to the study phase, the Nao robot answered these questions first,

and we noted whether the participant chose the same image as the Nao robot.

	Questions
Q1	Do you like *Natto*?
Q2	Do you have a fear of heights?
Q3	Do you like carbonated drinks?
Q4	Do you like alcohol?
Q5	Do you like animated cartoons?
Q6	Do you like sport?

Table 1. Yes/no questions.

Evaluation phase

After completion of the study and observation phases of the experiment, the experimenter returned to the experimental room with the post-experiment questionnaire and asked the participant to complete it and to call the experimenter when finished.

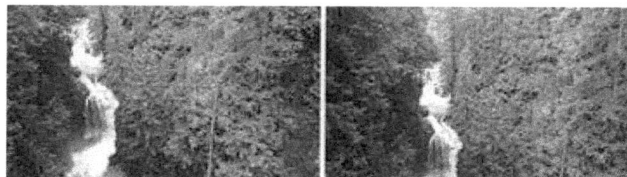

Figure 2. Example images used in the observation phase

RESULTS

Perspective-taking groups

We divided participants into two groups according to their score on the IRI perspective-taking subscale. The median score was 17.4; thus, those with a score higher than 17 were classified as high perspective takers (n = 40) and the remaining 40 participants were classified as low perspective takers.

Each perspective-taking group was then divided into four groups according to the rate of mimicry (50%, 66%, 83%, 100%) so that the distribution of perspective-taking abilities and the number of participants under each mimicry condition were equal (n = 10).

A participant who did not look at the Nao robot during the experiment was excluded from the high-perspective, 83% condition.

Likeability of the agent

The across-participant mean scores for the nine attributes according to mimicry rate are shown in Figure 3. An analysis of variance (*ANOVA*) was used to assess the effect of mimicry rate on the attribute scores. Mimicry rate had a significant effect on the friendly attribute score, such that the friendly rating was significantly higher in the 50% ($M = 3.7$, $SD = 1.34$) than in the 83% ($M = 2.63$, $SD = 0.76$), $F(3, 75) = 2.61$, $p = .03$) group. Lower mean values indicate greater feelings of friendliness toward the NAO robot. No

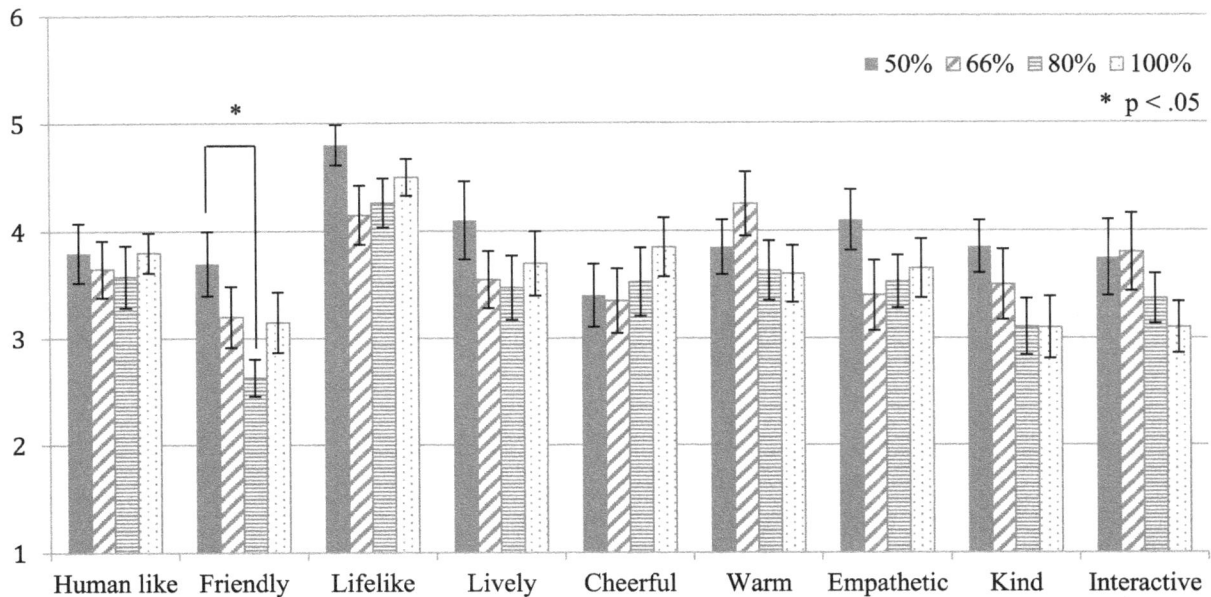

Figure 3: The evaluation of impression. Mean values of the nine items for the four rates of mimicry by the Nao robot (50%, 66%, 83%, 100%) on six-point scales running from 1 (describe e the Nao robot well) to 6 (does not describes the Nao robot very well)

significant differences were found for the other attributes. We conducted separate ANOVAs on the high- and low-perspective taking groups to assess the effect of perspective-taking ability on the friendly attribute score (Figure 4). The analysis revealed a marginally significant difference between the 50% ($M = 3.70$, $SD = 1.1$) and 83% ($M = 2.44$, $SD = 0.50$; $F(3, 35) = 2.72$, $p = .07$) conditions in high-perspective taking group, whereas no significant mimicry rate differences were found in the low-perspective taking group.

With the exception of the friendly attribute, the mimicry rate had no significant effect on the attribute scores in either perspective-taking group.

Changes in participant behavior

We used an ANOVA to assess differences among participant choices in the observation phase according to mimicry rate in the study phase. The analysis revealed no significant differences, suggesting that participants did not change their behavior in response a mimicking agent.

DISCUSSION

Participants under the 83% mimicry condition rated the robot as more friendly than did those under the 50% mimicry condition. We found no significant differences among the other subscales (i.e., MES), suggesting that the chameleon effect is valid in human-agent interactions, and that the optimal rate of mimicry is around 83%.

Furthermore, high-perspective takers under the 83% mimicry condition showed a marginally significant tendency to rate the Nao robot as friendly compared with those under the 50% condition. In contrast, mimicry rate had no effect on

the perception of friendliness in the low-perspective taker group. These findings support our hypothesis that perspective-taking contributes to the chameleon effect in human-agent interactions, suggesting that high-perspective takers are more likely to be influenced by the amount of agent mimicry than low-perspective takers.

Several possible factors may explain why agent mimicry did not change the behavior of the participants. First, the participants may not have considered the robot likable enough to warrant choosing the same answer. The links between favorability rating and conformity have not been well studied; therefore, the significance of this possibility is unclear. Second, during the observation phase of our study, the suitability of the questions and response options wasn't confirmed in advance. Thus, other factors may have influenced the results. Third, it is likely that some participants realized that the agent was intentionally mimicking their choice, thus invalidating the chameleon effect.

Furthermore, it is possible that emotional susceptibility influenced the results. We used the emotional-susceptibility subscale of the MES to assess the effect of emotional susceptibility on the participants' behavior. The correlation coefficient was calculated separately for all conditions to control for mimicry rate and perspective-taking ability. The analysis revealed no correlation between emotional susceptibility and the number of responses corresponding to those of the robot [12], indicating that our findings were not affected by emotional susceptibility.

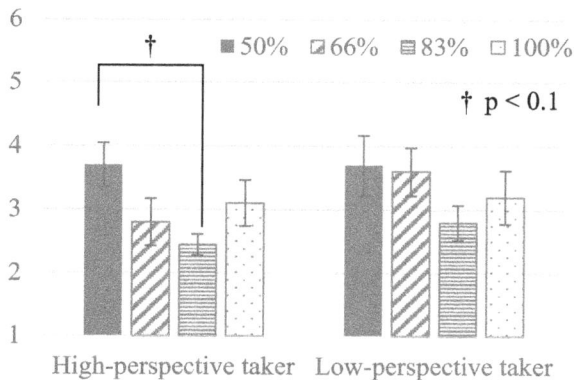

Figure 4. Mean values of the scale of Friendly for the four rate of mimicry and the perspective taking aspect.

CONCLUSION

We investigated the optimal rate of mimicry necessary for a favorable human-agent interaction according to cognitive empathic ability.

Our findings supported our hypotheses that an optimal rate of mimicry for human-agent interactions exists and that, as in human-human interactions, the effect is related to perspective-taking ability. We found that people tend to have friendly feelings toward a robot when it mimicked their choices 83% of the time. Furthermore, high-perspective takers were more strongly influenced by the rate of mimicry than were low-perspective takers.

Our findings can be used to enhance human-agent interactions. For instance, our finding of an optimal mimicry rate suggests that mimicry rates can be standardized to increase the rapport between humans and agents, to use robot technology more effectively.

REFERENCES

1. Luis A. Fuente, Hannah Ierardi, Michael Pilling, and Nigel T. Crook. October 2015. Influence of Upper Body Pose Mirroring in Human-Robot Interaction. Social Robotics Volume 9388 of series Lecture Notes in Computer Science pp 214-223.

2. Yugo Takeuchi and Yasuhiro Katagiri. May 2000. Inducing Social Agreement Responses toward Interface Agent. Transactions of Information Processing Society of Japan, 42: 1257-1266, (in Japanese).

3. Tanya L. Chartrand and John A. Bargh. 1999. The Chameleon Effect: The Perception-Behavior Link and Social Interaction. *Journal of Personality and Social Psychology*, 76, 6, 893-910

4. Mark H. Davis. 1980. A Multidimensional Approach to Individual Differences in Empathy. *JSAS Catalog of Selected Documents in Psychology*, 1980, 10, p.85.

5. Kohei Nomura, Seiki Akai and Kazunori Morikawa. 2015. Pilot Japanese Interpersonal Reactivity Index. In *The Japanese Psychological Association*, (In Japanese).

   http://www.myschedule.jp/jpa2015/img/figure/90691.pdf

6. Christoph Bartneck, Dana Kulic, Elizabeth Croft, and Susana Zoghbi. 2009. Measurement Instruments for the Anthropomorphism, Animacy, Likability, Perceived Intelligence, and Perceived Safety of Robots. *International Journal of Social Robotics*, 1(1) (2009), 71-81.

7. Misa Yoshizaki, Toshimasa Takai, Eri Takashima, Yusuke Suetsugu, Atsushi Hirota, Shogo Furuhashi... 2015. Effect of Embodied Cognition on an Impression of a Robot. Human Agent Interaction (HAI 2015).

8. Hiroko Kamide, Tomohito takubo, Kenichi Ohara, Yusushi Mae, and Tatuo Atai. 2013. Impressions of Humanoids: The Development of a Measure for Evaluating a Humanoid. *International Journal of Social Robotics* (2014) 6:33-44.

9. Suzuki Yuki, Kino Kazuyo. 2008. Development of the Multidimensional Empathy Scale (MES): Focusing on the Distinction between Self- and Other-Orientation. The Japanese Association of Educational Psychology, (in Japanese)

10. Akio Wakabayashi, Yoshikuni Tojo, Simon Baron-Cohen, and Sally Wheelwright. The Autism-Spectrum Quetient (AQ) Japanese version: Evidence from high-functioning clinical froup and normal adults. *The Japanese Journal of Psychology, 2004*, 75, 1, 78-84, (in Japanese).

11. Baron-Cohen, S., Wheelwright, S., Skinner, R., Martin, J., & Clubley, E. 2001. The Autism-Spectrum Quotient (AQ): Evidence from Asperger syndrome/ high-functioning autism, males and females, scientists and mathematicians. *Journal of Autism and Developmental Disorders,* 31, 5-17.

12. Guilford, J. P. 1956. Fundamental statistics in psychology and education. New York: McGraw Hill.

Smart Mobile Virtual Characters: Video Characters vs. Animated Characters

Sinhwa Kang†, Andrew W. Feng†, Mike Seymour‡, and Ari Shapiro†
†USC Institute for Creative Technologies, Playa Vista, USA
‡University of Sydney, New South Wales, Australia
†kang,feng,shapiro@ict.usc.edu; ‡mike.seymour@sydney.edu.au

ABSTRACT

This study investigates presentation techniques for a chatbased virtual human that communicates engagingly with users via a smartphone outside of the lab in natural settings. Our work compares the responses of users who interact with an animated 3D virtual character as opposed to a real human video character capable of displaying backchannel behaviors. The findings of our study demonstrate that people are socially attracted to a 3D animated character that does not display backchannel behaviors more than a real human video character that presents realistic backchannel behaviors. People engage in conversation more by talking for a longer amount of time when they interact with a 3D animated virtual human that exhibits backchannel behaviors, compared to communicating with a real human video character that does not display backchannel behaviors.

ACM Classification Keywords

I.2.12 Artificial Intelligence: Distributed Artificial Intelligence—Intelligent agents; J.4 Computer Applications: Social and Behavioral Sciences—Psychology.

Author Keywords

virtual humans; agents; smartphones; chat applications; nonverbal behavior; self-disclosure; rapport; reciprocity; facial expressions

INTRODUCTION

Interactive 3D characters and agents are an important part of many games, simulations and other interactive, digital experiences. A traditional method of generating such characters involves generating the 3D models and control algorithms using 3D production tools and real-time 3D simulation platforms such as game engines. Recently, mobile devices have become important platforms for communication and entertainment. Modern mobile platforms are typically powerful enough to run real-time 3D simulations like their desktop counterparts.

To clarify, we use the term *3D* to refer to the type of media and process that is used to generate the final content, although the final result is display in 2D on a screen. This is in contrast to a virtual reality environment or holographic display environment where the content is seen in 3D directly.

An alternative method to creating an interactive 3D character that can respond to a user is to use a series of 2D video clips captured from a 2D camera trained on an actor and to arrange the resulting video clips in a directed graph structure that determines which clip will be played depending on the state of the character and the conversation. For example, a single video clip can be played when the character asks a question, then another to respond to a user, then another for the character to wait for a response. By playing a video clip that is appropriate to the interaction using consistent camera framing, a set of video clips can be dynamically arranged to yield the perception of interactivity. We term this style of interaction *interactive video graphs*, as the state of the simulation in combination with the connectivity of the graph dynamically determines the next video to be played, yielding a dynamically changing presentation for the purpose of interactivity. Figure 1 shows the similarities and differences between a 3D-generated state-based architecture and the *interactive video graph* approach we are presenting.

Researchers in computer graphics and human modeling have been attempting to generate 3D animated characters that can match the behavioral and visual fidelity of a real person. Often the result can elicit the uncanny valley effect where the appearance and behavior of the virtual characters can not match those of a real person to a sufficient degree, causing a repulsion to such characters. Therefore, we wanted to discover a novel way to respond to the issue. We investigated how users felt when interacting with a real human video character via *interactive video graphs* that matched their appearance and behavior, compared to a human-looking but not photorealistic 3D animated character. We conjecture that people would expect a video character to respond better without any discrepancy between appearance and behavior, compared to a 3D animated character.

The ultimate goal of our study is to explore the best practice of implementing feasible characters in social interactions using a smartphone as the medium of communication.

HAI'16, October 4–7, 2016, Biopolis, Singapore.
ACM 978-1-4503-4508-8/16/10.
http://dx.doi.org/10.1145/2974804.2980511

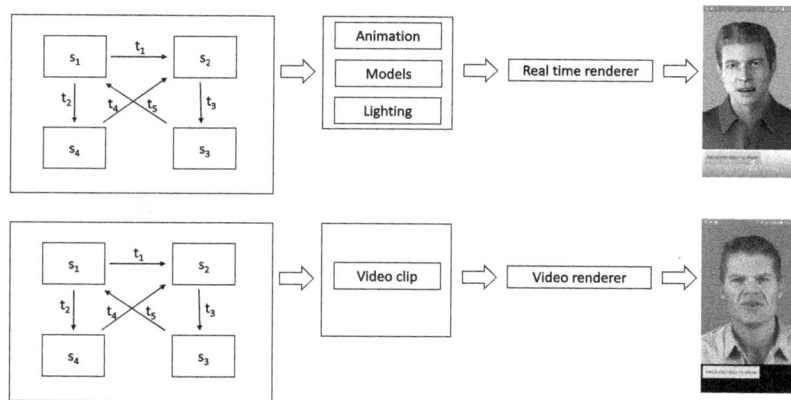

Figure 1: A state-transition graph for 3D characters (above) and for an interactive video graph for video-based characters (below). The s represent states, while the t represent transitions from those states. In the case of the interactive video graph, the video clip shown is directly related to the current state. In contrast, the 3D character's appearance is rendered by combining several inputs.

ARCHITECTURE

The character used two types of behaviors: 1) speaking behaviors and 2) listening behaviors with backchannel feedback. For a video-based character, we recorded numerous videos of a human asking questions and responding to speech. The video-based character's listening behaviors included a real human's generic listening behaviors such as facial expressions, head nodding, eyebrow raises, and slight smiles. For the 3D animated character, the speaking behaviors were generated by using the recorded voice of the real human, then nonverbal behaviors such as head movements, lip synch to speech and gestures were generated automatically from a automatic behavior generating system [5] during runtime executed on a real-time 3D virtual character system [1]. The listening behaviors, which included head nods, slight smiles and eyebrow raises, were generated while the user was speaking. The user interacted with the application in our study by pressing a button marked 'Click and hold to speak' during his/her speaking turn. We had the user explicitly indicate when he/she was speaking in order to reduce errors during regulation of speaking turns between the virtual human and the user. The speech was captured by the mobile device's microphone, then sent to a cloud file storage (Amazon Web Services) for offline transcription.

EXPERIMENTAL EVALUATION

Our study evaluates a more flexible and advanced stand-alone application that was available on Google Nexus (any versions greater than 5) or Samsung Galaxy (any versions greater than S5) and released via the Google Play Store. We conducted the study by recruiting paid participants via Qualtrics who had access to a smartphone, were willing to participate in a chat with a virtual human, and could fill out online questionnaires on their smartphone before and after each interaction.

This study examined users' perceptions and reactions to a virtual human based on various presentation types: (1) video with nonverbal backchannels, (2) video without nonverbal

backchannels, (3) animation with nonverbal backchannels, (4) animation without nonverbal backchannels, and (5) audio-only. To test a comparison between the presence and absence of characters of any type, an audio-only condition was added to the design. In our study, we manipulated realistic nonverbal backchannels to investigate the effect of behavioral realism on the interaction between users and virtual characters. The nonverbal backchannels included facial expressions, head gestures, gaze, and other upper body movements. Because users were asked to use the button 'Click and Hold to Speak' when they answered each question, we designed nonverbal backchannels as a way to intentionally increase users' self-disclosure and comfort, rather than other functions such as turn-taking. Users answered a total of twenty four questions with increasing intimacy asked by the virtual human (e.g. "What are your favorite sports?"). We borrowed the structure and context of the questions from the studies of Kang and colleagues [2]. Since smartphones were treated as an icon of emotionally engaged communication [3], the conversation scenario in our study imitated casual chats in the format of an interview in a counseling situation to maintain the emotionally engaged interaction. During the conversation, the virtual human responded to users' utterances with its own back stories in order to reciprocate intimate information sharing and advance the conversation (e.g. "I like to play very active sports like basketball and tennis.").

Participants and Procedure

A total of 95 participants (25% men, 75% women; average 38 years old) were randomly assigned to one of 5 conditions: video with nonverbal backchannels (N=20; 25% men, 75% women), video without nonverbal backchannels (N=19; 26% men, 74% women), animation with nonverbal backchannels (N=20; 30% men, 70% women), animation without nonverbal backchannels (N=18; 11% men, 89% women), and audio-only (N=18; 35% men, 65% women). The participants were given $10 compensation when they completed the study. Participation required a total of 35 minutes on an individual basis. The pre-questionnaire included questions pertaining to users' demographics. There were two types of the post-questionnaires. All users received the first post-questionnaire, which included metrics to rate their perception of virtual rapport with and social attraction toward a virtual human. The second post-questionnaire was also given to all users regardless of participating in another conversation with a virtual human for the 12 additional questions. It gauged the driving factors behind the users' choice to continue or not continue conversing with the virtual human. It was mandatory to complete the first session and two post-questionnaires to get compensation, but the second conversation was optional. This was done in order to effectively observe whether users enjoyed conversing with the virtual human.

Measurements

For subjective measures, in the first post-questionnaire, we utilized Social Attraction to measure users' feelings of attraction toward a virtual human. The measure consisted of 6 items whose examples included "I would like to have a friendly chat with a virtual human." We also measured Virtual Rapport to assess users' feelings of rapport with a virtual human. The measure consisted of 17 items whose examples included "I felt I had a connection with a virtual human." In the second post-questionnaire, we further asked an additional question related to likelihood to converse with the virtual human in the future (e.g. "I would look forward to another conversation with the virtual human."). These scales contained a Likert-type 5-point metric for items. All the scales described above showed good reliability (Social Attraction: Cronbach's alpha = .873, Virtual Rapport: Cronbach's alpha = .940). For objective measures, we analyzed users' feedback derived from their voice input. The data was categorized into three types: 1) the number of questions that a user answered (by asking the user to enter the last question that he/she answered), 2) negative reasons for quitting the conversation, and 3) the average number of words in answers (total number of words in each user's answers divided by the number of questions answered).

RESULTS

Results for the subjective measures

We performed a Between-Subjects ANOVA. The results [$F_{(4, 90)}=2.75$, $p=.033$] with a Tukey HSD Test demonstrate that users reported more social attraction to a 3D animated character without nonverbal backchannels (M=3.91, SD=.98) significantly more than a video character with nonverbal backchannels (M=2.93, SD=1.03), see Figure 2 (a). We found a trend that is similar to the results for social attraction in users' feeling of rapport, although the result is not statistically significant. Users reported their feeling of rapport more when they interacted with the 3D animated character without nonverbal backchannels, compared to interacting with the video character with nonverbal backchannels that is reported in Figure 2 (b). We did not find statistically significant difference for the additional question related to likelihood to converse with the virtual human in the future. These results indicate that people were socially attracted more to 3D animated characters when they did not present backchannel behaviors, compared to video characters that displayed backchannel behaviors.

Results for the objective measures

To measure the length of the conversation, we used the number of the additional questions that the user answered after the first 12 mandatory ones before stopping. We performed a Between-Subjects ANOVA with a Tukey HSD Test. Our results [$F_{(4, 90)}=2.19$, $p=.076$] demonstrate that users tended to answer more questions when they interacted with a 3D animated character that demonstrated nonverbal backchannels (M=23.35, SD=2.68), compared to interacting with a video character that did not exhibit nonverbal backchannels (M=18.58, SD=5.98). A Tukey HSD Test shows the difference is statistically significant. Results are reported in Figure 2, (c). We also examined users' reasoning for quitting the conversation using a binary measure (negative reasons and non-negative reasons). The items for a negative reason of quitting conversation included: "Feel a little uncomfortable talking to him" and "I am no longer interested." To analyze this data, we ran a Chi-square test to explore the associations between the two categorical variables. We did not find statistically significant differences among the conditions. However, we discovered notable trends that are presented in Figure 2, (d). The results show that users were more likely to cite negative reasons for not completing all 24 questions when interacting with the video character that did not present nonverbal backchannels while not citing any negative reasons at all when interacting with the 3D animated character that displayed nonverbal backchannels. There was no statistical significance for the average number of words in answers. The results indicate that people interacted with the 3D animated character that presented nonverbal backchannels for a longer amount of time, compared to interacting with the video character that did not display the backchannels.

DISCUSSION

We investigated whether the visual fidelity of a virtual human would encourage people to talk for a longer amount of time when the virtual human was displayed on the small screen of a smartphone. We additionally explored how the behavioral realism of a virtual human would affect the interaction by manipulating its nonverbal backchannels. In our study, the nonverbal backchannels were realistic, but less synchronized to the intended message of the speaker since speech recognition technology was not used in this interaction. It is notable that nonverbal backchannels are important to socialization and communication, but only when they are appropriate and synchronized to the intended message of the speaker [6]. However, our findings demonstrate that people are more inclined toward 3D animated characters in social interactions regardless of exhibiting backchannels than video characters presenting less synchronized backchannel behaviors. We contend that people grant more leniency with respect to behavioral anomalies in the 3D animated character as opposed to the video character. We further argue that people expect a real human video to exhibit synchronized backchannels as they might perceive the video character like a real human. MacDorman et al. [4] notes that slight imperfections in realistic characters could yield uncanny valley effects, and people might evaluate the realistic characters more negatively than cartoonish characters. In the same vein, we argue people would feel the uncanny valley

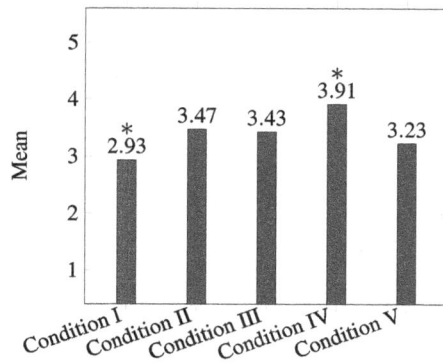

(a) Social Attraction, * p<.05)

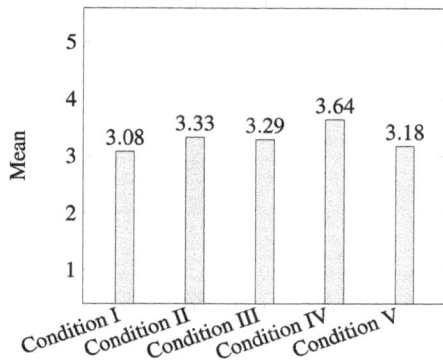

(b) Virtual Rapport

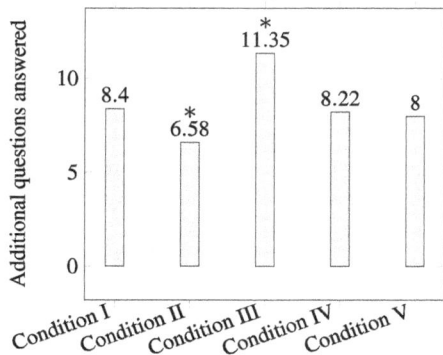

(c) Number of questions answered beyond the required amount before quitting, * p<.05)

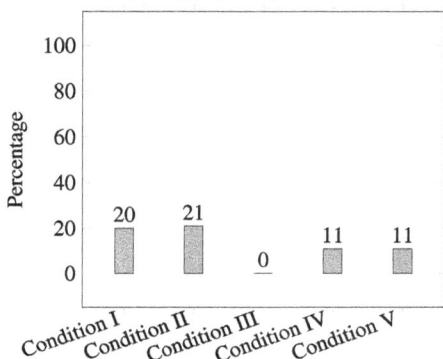

(d) Negative Quit Reasons

Figure 2: Results for subjective (a and b) and objective (c and d) measures in each of 4 conditions: (Condition I: video with backchannels, Condition 2: video without backchannels, Condition III: 3D with backchannels, Condition IV: 3D without backchannels, Condition V: audio-only.

more with a video character than a 3D character if the video character do not convey synchronized backchannels.

Based on the results of our current study, it is hard to confirm what form of a virtual character would elicit smartphone users' engagement in communication with a virtual character more. Our long term research goals include determining the effectiveness of using interactive video graph-based characters against using entirely 3D-based characters. While the final appearance of the two methods can be differentiated to the user as a matter of photorealism, the method of generating such content is vastly different. A finding that one method is more or less effective than another would be of interest to those developing such user interfaces and applications. Likewise, a finding that they are both equally or similarly effective would also be of interest, making them interchangeable as a means of interaction. In our study, we did not find definitive answers to those questions, and for future work we intend to perform larger study that can better differentiate the effectiveness of such practices.

ACKNOWLEDGMENTS

This work was supported by Institute for Information & communications Technology Promotion (IITP) grant (No. R0184-15-1030, MR Avatar World Service and Platform Development using Structured Light Sensor) funded by the Korea government (MSIP).

REFERENCES

1. Andrew W Feng, Anton Leuski, Stacy Marsella, Dan Casas, Sin-Hwa Kang, and Ari Shapiro. 2015. A Platform for Building Mobile Virtual Humans. In *Intelligent Virtual Agents*. Springer International Publishing, 310–319.

2. Sin-Hwa Kang, Andrew W Feng, Anton Leuski, Dan Casas, and Ari Shapiro. 2015. The Effect of An Animated Virtual Character on Mobile Chat Interactions. In *Proceedings of the 3rd International Conference on Human-Agent Interaction*. ACM, 105–112.

3. Sin-Hwa Kang, James H Watt, and Sasi Kanth Ala. 2008. Social copresence in anonymous social interactions using a mobile video telephone. In *Proceedings of the SIGCHI Conference on Human Factors in Computing Systems*. ACM, 1535–1544.

4. Karl F MacDorman, Robert D Green, Chin-Chang Ho, and Clinton T Koch. 2009. Too real for comfort? Uncanny responses to computer generated faces. *Computers in human behavior* 25, 3 (2009), 695–710.

5. Stacy Marsella, Yuyu Xu, Margaux Lhommet, Andrew Feng, Stefan Scherer, and Ari Shapiro. 2013. Virtual character performance from speech. In *Proceedings of the 12th ACM SIGGRAPH/Eurographics Symposium on Computer Animation*. ACM, 25–35.

6. Ning Wang and Jonathan Gratch. 2010. Don'T Just Stare at Me!. In *Proceedings of the SIGCHI Conference on Human Factors in Computing Systems*. ACM, 1241–1250.

Software Architecture of a Humanoid Robot for Coaching Physical Exercises in Kinaesthetic Rehabilitation

Sao Mai Nguyen
Institut Mines Telecom and
Lab-STICC CNRS
Brest, France
nguyensmai@gmail.com

Philippe Tanguy
Institut Mines Telecom and
Lab-STICC CNRS
Brest, France

ABSTRACT

Assistive technology and and assistive robotics in particular may help to improve physical rehabilitation. We develop a robot coach capable of demonstrating rehabilitation exercises to patients, watch a patient carry out the exercises and give him feedback so as to improve his performance and encourage him. We propose a general software architecture for our robot coach, which is based on imitation learning techniques using Gaussian Mixture Models and on personalised audio feedback to patients.

ACM Classification Keywords

I.2 Artificial Intelligence: Robotics; I.2.6 Learning: Knowledge acquisition; I.2.1 Applications and Expert Systems: Natural language Interfaces

Author Keywords

Physical rehabilitation; Intelligent tutoring system; Robot coach; Imitation Learning; Gaussian Mixture Models

Acknowledgment: The research work presented in this paper is partially supported by the EU FP7 grant ECHORD++ KER-AAL and by the the European Regional Fund (FEDER) via the VITAAL Contrat Plan Etat Region.

Motivation

50 to 80% of the world population suffers at a given moment from back pain which makes it in the lead in terms of health problems occurrence frequency [9, 12]. It is the third cause of disabling condition in the 45-65 years old population, whose proportion in European societies keeps rising. This incurs growing concern, as medical professionals will not be able to face this increasing demand for healthcare.

A Robot Coach

Active rehabilitation is considered more effective than usual care [6]. To enable rehabilitation to an increasing number of elderly patients, we propose a robot coach for physical rehabilitation exercises. The long-term goal of this project is

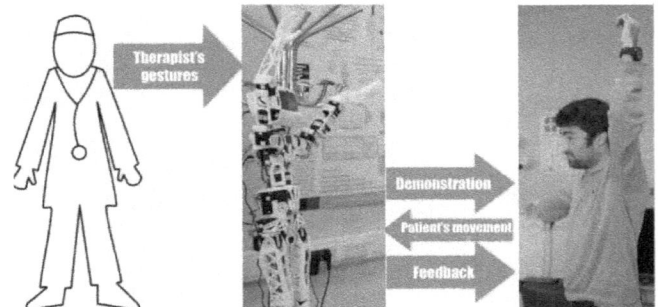

Figure 1. Timeline of the interactions between the therapist and the robot coach, and between the robot coach and the patient. After learning the specifications of the exercise from the therapist, the robot is capable of coaching by itself the patient, by making a demonstration of the specified exercise, assessing the patient's attempt and giving him his feedback.

to provide patients with a e-Health solution for personalised follow-up of long-term rehabilitation at home. We develop a robot coach capable of demonstrating physical exercises to patients, watch a patient carry out the exercises and give him feedback so as to improve his performance. It thereby provides physical and social connection which is not acquired via Virtual Reality systems. We propose a general software architecture for our robot coach, which is based on imitation learning techniques using Gaussian Mixture Models (GMM). Our system aims to be easily used by medical experts.

Approach

As a concrete example of the task scenario, as illustrated in Fig. 1, our e-Health robot will be able to:

- Let a physiologist select an exercise for the robot to coach

- Show a demonstration of the exercise to the patient

- Monitor the patient while he carries out his exercise

- Give a feedback to the patient to improve his performance and encourage him

Thus the patient and the robot will work together on a rehabilitation exercise assigned by the physiologist. Their interaction will rely on the advanced perception and action capabilities of the system, which enables the robot to show demonstrations of the exercise as well as monitor the movements of the patients and give him feedback on his mistakes.

State of the Art

Virtual reality has also contributed to the field of rehabilitation either through training programs for low back pain [10] or home based programs in elderly (VERA project San Diego). These programs have been demonstrated to improve the number of repetitions of movement compared to classic home based rehabilitation programs [1]. However, virtual reality agents evolve in their own world and lack social and physical connection with the user's world. On the contrary, robots have been considered as social mediators in different categories of clinical conditions like children with special needs or the elderly [8, 4]. Robot mediated physical exercises may improve the acceptance and adherence to active rehabilitation program and enhance the involvement in physical activities, owing to physical and social interaction between the robot and the patient.

Our approach for robotic systems coaching physical exercises is related to those presented in [3, 5] and [11].

Takenori *et al* [11] developed a system of imitation learning for daily physical exercises. The robot could learn new exercises from the therapists and be an exercise demonstrator. The communication was performed by voice and gesture in order to engage elderly people in the exercise activity. However, it could not provide feedback or active guidance to the patient. Fasola *et al.* in [3] and Goerer *et al.* [5] presented a socially assistive robot (SAR) to engage elderly users based on their intrinsic motivation or through HRI. They proposed an automatic evaluation of physical exercises by computing the distance between the user's current arm angles and the specified goal arm angles. This metric could be used in the simple setting where the patient can only move a few articulations, because their experimental setup required them to sit and only move the arms on the side. Moreover, it does not take into account the speed or the dynamics of the movement. It is ill-adapted to complex full-body exercises that can involve several parts of the body but not necessarily all parts. Recent studies have shown the importance of social aspects or personalization during physical exercises with robots.

We would like to focus on the intelligent tutoring system (ITS), and more specifically an algorithm capable of assessing which parts of the body are important to the exercise, and what are the acceptable ranges of freedom. We will develop a system for automatically assessing the movements of patients, to point out which parts of the movement need to be improved. More specifically we use probabilistic imitation learning algorithms to model each movement and detect errors.

PROPOSED SYSTEM

The Hardware

The system is composed with a Microsoft© Kinect v2 and an open source humanoid robot Poppy [7]. A demonstration video can be watched at http ://nguyens-mai.free.fr/roman2016.html.

The Computational Architecture

Figure 2 depicts the computational architecture with a humanoid robot during physical rehabilitation exercises. The

Figure 2. Overview of the computational architecture for the robot to learn a model of the exercise from the doctor's gestures, then to make demonstrations from the model, and to give feedback to the patient.

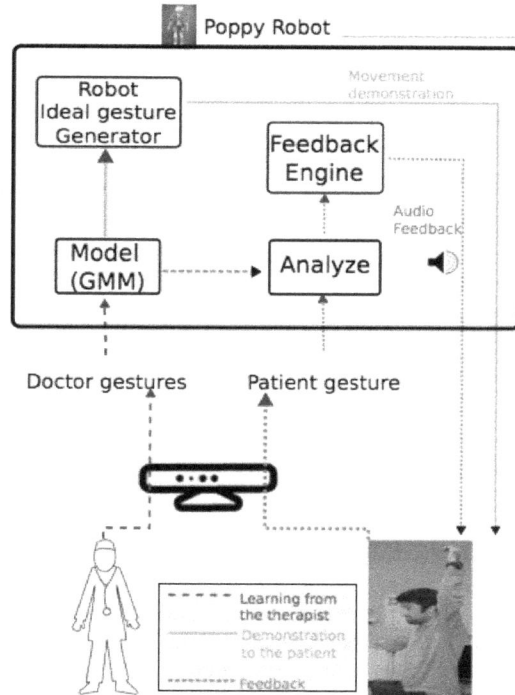

schema combines three different phases: learning, demonstration and feedback. In the first step, the therapist records in front of the camera several movements of the same exercise. These therapist's gestures enable the robot to learn a GMM with Expectation Maximization, as described in [2]. In the demonstration phase, the "ideal movement" can be generated in order to be reproduced by the robot, using Gaussian Mixture Regression (GMR).

Finally, during the exercise all movements done by the patient are recorded and analyzed for vocal feedback by the robot. At this stage the robot plays the role of a verbal coach to help the patient to perform the best movement for his rehabilitation. This part is realized with the *Feedback Engine* (section 1.4) and *Analyze* component.

The Intelligent Tutoring : Corrective Feedback

For the *Analyze* component, a metric of imitation allows the robot to assess the movement of a patient for each joint j automatically:

$$H_j = \delta_j^T W \delta_j \qquad (1)$$

where W represents parameters of the GMM and $\delta = x - \hat{x}$ is the difference between the observed attempt x and the generalised motion $\hat{x}$ (obtained by GMR). By applying Eq. 1 directly on the recorded motion, we obtain the overall quality of the observed attempt. The lower H_j, the better the imitation is. We arbitrarily set a threshold Δ to get the list of outstanding errors $E_j = \{(j, \delta_j), if H_j > \Delta\}$.

```
<?xml version="1.0" encoding="ISO-8859-1"?>
<resources>
<string name="arm-left-up">
Move your left arm higher
</string>
<string name="arm-left-down">
Move your left arm lower
</string>
<string name="arm-left-front">
Move your left arm more forward
</string>
...
```
Figure 3. XML file example: user feedback sentences

Furthermore, we compute the contribution to this error by each joint by computing $H_j = \delta_j^T W \delta_j$ with W representing parameters of the GMM and δ_j as the projection of δ on the subplane of the j-th dimension (δ_j is δ where all values are zeroed except for the jth component).

We arbitrarily set a threshold Δ to get the list of outstanding errors $E = \{(j, \delta_j), if H_j > \Delta\}$, to highlight only errors on data which have a high covariance. The robot thus helps the patient to improve on his most noticeable errors.

The Patient-Robot Interaction
This list of errors is sent to the Feedback Engine for audio feedback to translate this mathematical analysis into recommendation sentences for the Human-Patient Interaction. The system currently allows a one way interaction with the patient, using a text to speech server (MaryTTS) to provide vocal feedbacks. It takes as input the relevant changes produced during the comparison step between the ideal movement and the current patient movement and outputs a speech for vocal feedback. We developed a specific API on the server side in order to generate a specific and adapted movement correction with the following parameters:

- lang: country language, e.g. "en" for English.

- part: body member, e.g. arm.

- side: body side, e.g. left or right.

- position: gesture or movement advice to improve the exercise, e.g. "higher".

Those parameters allows to address specific sentences previously defined in a XML file. As shown Figure 3 each sentences are defined by a unique key name, e.g. "arm-left-up" corresponding to "Move your left arm higher".

The feedback engine takes as input the relevant changes produced during the comparison step between the ideal movement and the current patient movement. Then it transforms the relevant changes in order to use the text to speech API previously described.

We perform a verbal interaction denoted as *Feedback Engine*. The system allows to load different language dictionaries in form of XML files.

RESULTS
Dataset
We set up with the Kinect a database for 2 different physical exercises, including 6 different recordings for each exercise.

We obtained a model of exercise 1 using the 5 first recordings of exercise 1. We kept the 6th recording of exercise 1 for testing, as well as the recordings of exercise2. For the assessment of the patients' motions, we set $\Delta = 100$.

Modeling and Generating
The GMM model obtained is represented in fig. 4. This probabilistic representation is then used to generate an ideal movement, to be played by the robot coach to patients.

Assessing
The *Analyze* component outputs a general evaluation of the attempted imitation as a H value shown in Fig 5. The smaller H, the closer to the therapist's demonstrations the test attempt is. Here we arbitrarily consider that $H < \Delta$ is an acceptable attempt. As expected, the error is acceptable for d1 and d3, which are movements of exercise 1. On the contrary the error is very high for d2 where an error has been artificially introduced, and d4 which is a recording of a different exercise.

Moreover, our analysis finds out which joint positions are accountable for the errors. It shows that the robot was satisfied for d1 and d2, that is when the patient repeats correctly exercise 1. In the case of d2, where we added an offset on the x position of the joint named "rShoulder", we can verify that it reported correctly this error. In the case of d4, as the patient was executing another exercise, our system reported several errors.

Thus, our ITS reports correctly the errors seen in the attempted imitations. This output is then translated by the Feedback Engine into sentences for audio feedback.

DISCUSSIONS
In this paper, we have presented the concept of a general cognitive architecture for a robot coach for physical rehabilitation exercises, with both an intelligent tutoring system and a HRI. Using programming by demonstration as a probabilistic imitation learning algorithm, our robot coach is capable of learning new exercises from demonstrations by the therapists, then demonstrate exercises to the patient, and assess the performance of the patient and provide him with corrective feedback.

However, these are only preliminary results as this system does not yet run online. In particular, we plan on developing an interface to be able to switch seamlessly from the 'learning from the therapist' mode to the 'assessing the patient mode'. Second, in our tests the same person has acted as the therapist and the patient. We will need to address the correspondence problems when we face several users with different sizes and kinematic models.

REFERENCES
1. C Bryanton, J Bossé, M Brien, J McLean, A McCormick, and H. Sveistrup. 2006. Feasibility, motivation, and selective motor control: virtual reality compared to conventional home exercise in children with cerebral palsy. *Cyberpsychol Behav.* 9, 2 (Apr 2006), 123–8.

2. Sylvain Calinon, F. Guenter, and Aude Billard. 2007. On Learning, Representing and Generalizing a Task in a

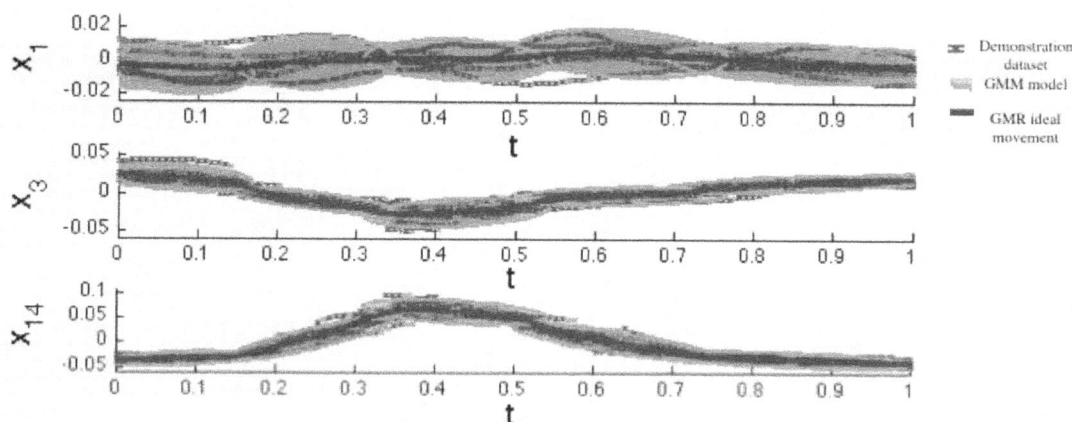

Figure 4. Modelling the demonstrations with GMM and generating an ideal movement with GMR. Are represented the results for 3 joint positions with respect to time (normalised values). The green ellipses plot a representation of the components of the GMM. The ideal trajectory (GMR) is represented with the thick blue line.

		d1	d2	d3	d4
H		11.0891	8.338e3	13.98	1.4933e3
E	rShoulder	[0,-0,-0]	[0.4,-0,-0]	[0,-0,-0]	[0,-0,-0]
	lElbow	[0,-0,-0]	[0,-0,-0]	[0,-0,-0]	[0,-4.5e-4,-2.0e-3]
	lShoulder	[0,0,-0]	[0,0,-0]	[0,0,-0]	[0,-0,-0.00029]
Audio feedback		Nothing	Move your right shoulder more to he right	Nothing	Move your left elbow lower, move your left elbow more forward, move your left shoulder more forward

Figure 5. Output of the analysis of test movements compared to the learned movement model. The analysis outputs both a global evaluation of the test movements, as well as a list of the outstanding errors for each joint position as a finer analysis. These figures are then interpreted by the robot to give an audio feedback

Humanoid Robot. *IEEE Transactions on Systems, Man and Cybernetics* 37, 2 (2007), 286–298.

3. Juan Fasola and Maja Mataric. 2013. A socially assistive robot exercise coach for the elderly. *Journal of Human-Robot Interaction* 2, 2 (2013), 3–32.

4. D Feil-Seifer and Maja Mataric. 2005. Defining Socially Assistive Robotics. In *Proceedings of the 2005 IEEE 9th International Conference on Rehabilitation Robotics.*

5. Binnur Görer, Albert Ali Salah, and H. Levent Akm. 2013. A Robotic Fitness Coach for the Elderly. In *4th International Joint Conference, AmI 2013.*

6. P Kent and P. Kjaer. 2012. The efficacy of targeted interventions for modifiable psychosocial risk factors of persistent nonspecific low back pain - a systematic review. *Man Ther.* 17, 5 (Oct 2012), 385–401.

7. Matthieu Lapeyre. 2014. *Poppy: open-source, 3D printed and fully-modular robotic platform for science, art and education.* Theses. Université de Bordeaux. https://hal.inria.fr/tel-01104641

8. P Marti, A Pollini, A Rullo, L Giusti, and E. Grönvall. 2009. Creative Interactive Play for Disabled Children. In *IDC.*

9. K. Mounce. 2002. Back pain. *Rheumatology* 41 (2002), 1–5.

10. M Roosink, BJ McFadyen, LJ Hébert, PL Jackson, LJ Bouyer, and C. Mercier. 2015. Assessing the perception of trunk movements in military personnel with chronic non-specific low back pain using a virtual mirror. *PLoS One* 10, 3 (Mar 2015), e0120251.

11. Obo Takenori, Loo Chu Kiong, and Kubota Naoyuki. 2015. Imitation Learning for Daily Exercise Support with Robot Partner. In *24th IEEE International Symposium on Robot and Human Interactive Communication.*

12. WHO. 2003. *The burden of musculoskeletal conditions at the start of the new millenium.* Technical Report. WHO, Geneva.

A Method to Alternate the Estimation of Global Purposes and Local Objectives to Induce and Maintain the Intentional Stance

Yoshimasa Ohmoto
Kyoto University
Kyoto, Japan
ohmoto@i.kyoto-u.ac.jp

Takashi Suyama
Kyoto University
Kyoto, Japan
suyama@ii.ist.i.kyoto-u.ac.jp

Toyoaki Nishida
Kyoto University
Kyoto, Japan
nishida@i.kyoto-u.ac.jp

ABSTRACT

The virtual world simulation has many advantages. However, the effects of the experience strongly influence the mental stance of the participants. To establish social relationships between a human and an artificial agent, the agent has to induce and maintain the intentional stance in its human partner. The purpose of this study was to investigate the method to induce the intentional stance in human participants of one-to-one human-agent interaction by using the alternating estimation of local objectives and global purposes by a network-connected two-layer model. We conducted an experiment to evaluate effect of the proposed method. The results suggested that this method was successful in inducing and maintaining the intentional stance over time.

ACM Classification Keywords

H.1.2. MODELS AND PRINCIPLES: User/Machine Systems; Human factors

Author Keywords

human-agent interaction; intentional stance; preference estimation.

INTRODUCTION

Interactive virtual agents have recently been developed in simulations of real-world events or processes designed for solving a problem, such as serious games and gamifications [2]. In virtual world simulation, we can conduct rehearsals or practice skills in specialized situations, extra-ordinary environments, and circumstances where no mistakes can be allowed. In addition, an individual's motivation to practice hard can be improved because, although serious, the game includes an entertainment aspect. The use of serious games is spreading widely in education, medical services, welfare, and fitness (e.g. [17]). In these applications, people acquire various techniques and abilities through game playing (e.g. [8]) and use games

HAI'16, October 4–7, 2016, Biopolis, Singapore.
Copyright © 2016 ACM ISBN 978-1-4503-4508-8/16/10 ...$15.00.
DOI: http://dx.doi.org/10.1145/2974804.2974828

for physical rehabilitation (e.g. [15]), and developers evaluate the user interface throughout the game [3].

The virtual world simulation has many advantages. However, the effects of the experience strongly influence the mental stance of the participants. For example, Lim and Byron reported that game players exhibited greater physiological arousal to otherwise identical interactions when other characters were introduced as an avatar (player-controlled characters) rather than an agent (characters controlled by the computer). We also focused on the mental stances that people infer when considering an agent, which can be defined as physical stance, design stance, and intentional stance [4]. When humans interact with each other, they usually assume the intentional stance, and they and their communication partner respect each other. When humans interact with a machine, they usually assume the design stance. In this case, they usually interact with the machine from a self-centred perspective because they do not consider the machine to have its own intentions. To establish social relationships between a human and an artificial agent, the agent has to induce and maintain the intentional stance in its human partner.

We considered the intentional stance and the design stance as follows. The intentional stance is a mental state in which people believe it is necessary for the interaction partner's behaviour estimation to take into account unobservable inner state parameters (e.g. a behaviour model, emotional aspects and decision-making strategies of the interaction partner). Therefore, people who assume the intentional stance pay attention to various interaction parameters in their interaction because they do not accurately identify what parameters are important to get acceptable results in the interaction. The design stance is a mental state in which people believe they can estimate the interaction partner's behaviour by the observable interaction parameters. Therefore, people who assume the design stance pay attention to only the observable parameters which are clearly related to the interaction. The big difference between the intentional stance and the design stance is people expect and accept that the results of the interaction are different when they provide same interaction behaviour to their interaction partner.

We examined previous studies to understand how to induce the intentional stance in human-agent interaction [12, 14] and found that the same could be achieved by presenting goal-oriented trial-and-error behaviour and by making the participants estimate the agent's behaviour model. In these studies, participants performed a multi-player game task in which two humans and an agent participated. In these cases, the participants generally assumed the intentional stance because the human participants mainly interacted with each other and the agent joined the interaction at crucial points. On the other hand, it is difficult to induce and maintain the intentional stance in one-to-one human-agent interaction, especially in virtual world, because humans may recognize the virtual world as an artificial environment, including the interactive agent that is completely controlled.

We believe that the following two reasons explain why the intentional stance could be induced and maintained in previous studies: the participants thought that the agents tried to achieve the goal of their activities by their heuristics, and the participants could understand the relationships between the agent's approaches for supporting the human's activities and the goals of the agent's activities. In other words, we hypothesize that providing their heuristics and the relationships between the heuristics and the interaction results can encourage the interaction partner to pay attention to the unobservable inner state of the agent. In one of our previous studies [13], we proposed a method to alternately propagate estimates of the objectives of the subordinate tasks (local objectives) and the purposes of the entire task (global purposes) during a collaboration task through interactions, using a network-connected two-layer model of emphasizing factors. We think that this method, which could provide consistency and coordination between local objectives and global purposes, is useful to enhance factors that induce and maintain the intentional stance. It is important for smooth interaction to understand the meta-rules to maintain the consistency and coordination, and the meta-rules are composed of some heuristics. Participants spontaneously speculate the meta-rules through the interaction and they pay attention to the unobservable inner state of the agent.

The present study aimed to investigate the method to induce and maintain the intentional stance in human participants of a one-to-one human-agent interaction. Therefore, we extended the alternating propagation of local objectives and global purposes by a network-connected two-layer model in a decision-making situation, to induce the intentional stance. We separately described the local objectives in local tasks and global purposes for the whole task. Then, through the human-agent interaction, the agent provided goal-oriented behaviour related to the global purposes, to support the local objectives in the local tasks. When agents can induce the intentional stance by the method, the human interaction partner can spontaneously consider the background of the interaction. For example, people accept advices from a healthcare agent because they naturally consider the reasons of the advices.

The present paper is organized as follows: In Section 2, we briefly introduce some related work. Section 3 contains an outline of the proposed method. Section 4 contains a description of our experiment that compared experimental and control groups, and presents our results. In Section 5, we discuss the achievements of this research and some future work. We give our conclusion in Section 6.

RELATED WORKS

Roubroeks [16] reported the occurrence of psychological reactance when artificial social agents are used to persuade people. In that study, participants read advice on how to conserve energy when using a washing machine. The advice was either provided as text-only, as text accompanied by a still picture of a robotic agent, or as text accompanied by a short film clip of the same robotic agent. The results of the experiment indicated that the text-only advice was accepted more than the advice with the still picture of the robotic agent or that with the short film clip of the robotic agent. The social agency theory proposes that more social cues lead to more social interaction, but, in this case, the result was the exact opposite. This is caused by differences in people's mental state with respect to humans or agents. These differences provide a critical barrier for an agent to cross before it can be accepted as a social partner. It is thus important that the mental state of people when they interact with agents is the same as that when they interact with humans.

Agents which collaboratively perform various tasks have been proposed in many studies, such as subordinate support agents when people perform tasks on their own initiative and automated attentive agents which automatically perform tasks in line with human's wishes [18]. We assumed that the intentional stance was partially induced in the participants in the collaborative task because, if not, the engagement for the collaboration would have been low and they might have failed in the collaboration.

Some mutually directable methods and concepts affect task performance [1, 10]. Mixed-initiative, for example, refers to a flexible interaction strategy where each agent can contribute to the task it does best. Furthermore, in general, the agents' roles are not determined in advance, but are opportunistically negotiated between them as the problem is being solved. In many cases, they merely provide a division of roles among interaction members; therefore, the consistency and coordination for performing the task are still managed by the main person.

Dindo et al. [5] proposed that humans use the intentional stance as a learning bias that sidesteps the (difficult) structure learning problem and bootstraps the acquisition of generative models for others' actions. They provided an example of how structure initialization can help in the learning of new parts of the model. In the example, they connected the action layer and intention layer by networks and identified the user's intentions from the sequence of the actions. This revealed that the network connected layered model is effective to estimate the intentions of human. They considered the intentional stance as a template of the structure generating the observed behavior. On the other hand, we consider the intentional stance itself is an important factor to determine interaction behaviours.

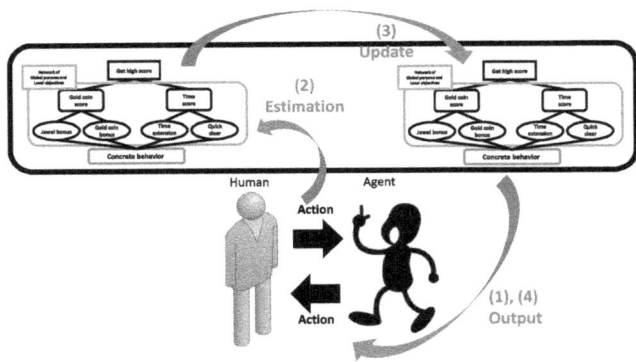

Figure 1. Outline of the method to alternate estimation by representing global and local goal-oriented behaviour.

A METHOD TO ALTERNATE ESTIMATION BY REPRESENTING GLOBAL AND LOCAL GOAL-ORIENTED BEHAVIOUR

Some methods induce the intentional stance, such as an agent resembling a human or an animal in appearance[7, 9, 6]. They mainly focused on inducing the intentional stance at the first impression. However, if the activities among the participants, including the agent, were not mutually influenced in collaborative long-term interaction, the participants would regard even in human-human interactions as 'mechanical' because it makes people think that they can estimate the interaction partner's behaviour by the observable interaction parameters.

In this study, we extended the alternating propagation of local objectives and global purposes in a decision-making situation to a situation in which the intentional stance is induced and maintained. We called this as AEGL (Alternate Estimation by representing Global and Local goal-oriented behaviour). AEGL separately describes the local objectives in local tasks and global purposes of the whole task. In addition, the method estimates the interaction partner's local objectives and global purposes based on the interaction responses. After the estimation, the method updates own local objectives depending on the estimated partner's global purposes. We expected that the interaction partner also estimates the agent's global purposes from its behaviour for the local tasks. We believed that this alternating process especially contributes to the maintenance of the intentional stance. Figure 1 shows the outline of this process.

In this study, the AEGL had lists of local objectives and global purposes, and the relational networks depending on the task. The parameters of the network nodes were updated in a correspondent interaction behaviour that included verbal and non-verbal responses. Subsequently, the parameters of the local objective nodes or global purpose nodes (referred to as 'intention nodes') were speculated based on the parameters of the network-connected nodes. We briefly explain the interaction process below.

First, an agent with AEGL determines its local objective based on weighted global purposes and provides appropriate behaviour to achieve the local objective. Subsequently, the agent estimates the interaction partner's local objectives based on the behaviour and responses. From the estimation, the agent updates the weights of estimated global purposes of the interaction partner. The parameters of the global purposes of the interaction partner and the agent are integrated and the agent modifies and determines its local objective based on the parameters.

The agent tries to support the interaction partner's local objectives, but the agent represents its global purposes through the local objective activities. The behaviour is modified through the interaction like a trial-and-error process. By repeatedly conducting the processes, the agent can create relationships between the agent's approaches for supporting the human's activities and the goals of the agent's activities.

EXPERIMENT

To investigate how the proposed method affects a user's impressions of the agent, we conducted an experiment using two agents: an 'AEGL agent' that provided interaction behaviour to the participants based on the AEGL and a 'goal-oriented agent' that performed goal-oriented actions. The AEGL agent dynamically estimated the participant's global purposes and modified the agent's local objectives. The goal-oriented agent prioritized its own global purposes. We assumed that if the alternating estimation could influence the mental stance of the participants more than providing goal-oriented behaviour, the AEGL agent could induce and maintain the intentional stance.

To evaluate this, we analyzed how the participants took care of the offer by the agent. The agent requested the participant to search its name cards. The participants could not find the name cards when they just completed their own purpose in the game. We assumed that, when the participants had an intentional stance toward the agent, they consciously searched the name cards. In addition, we asked the participants to complete a questionnaire after the experiment. We compared the experimental results of a group of participants who interacted with the 'AEGL agent' with those who interacted with the 'goal-oriented agent.'

Task

A participant and an agent participated in the collaborative game task. The task was a virtual a role playing game of escaping a dungeon. The purpose of the game was to get a high score. The game score was determined by the clear time, a number of scoring objects (gold coins) and bonus tasks (a number of jewels and time extension). The agent's name cards were not related to the score. The agent and the participant could communicate using predefined words. Some optimal solutions also existed.

The agent's primary global purpose was to gather bonus objects. Basically, the agent just searched and gathered jewels and quickly reached the goal. When the participant gathered gold coins, the agent also gathered the gold coins. When the participant reached the goal as quickly as possible, the agent gathered a minimal number of jewels. However, when the participant proposed to ignore the jewels, the agent refused the

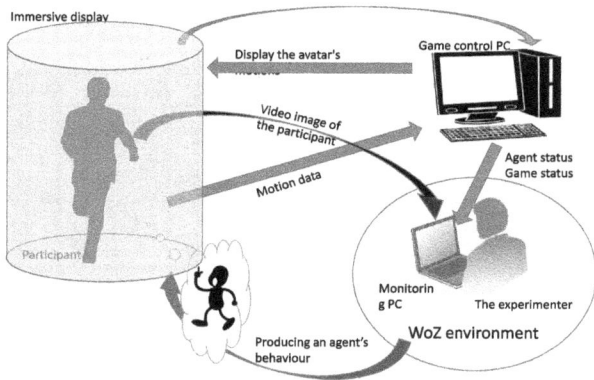

Figure 2. Experimental environment.

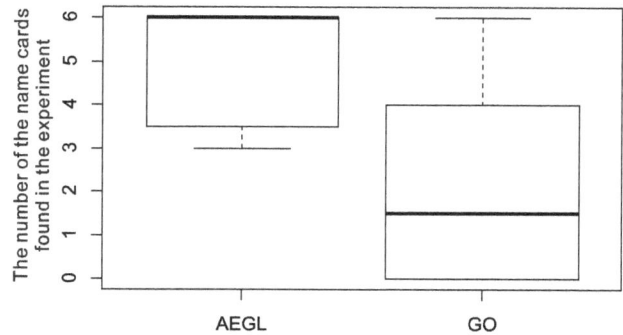

Figure 3. Result of the number of the name cards found in the experiment.

proposition. The goal-oriented agent did not change the strategy, but the AEGL agent dynamically changed the strategy based on the estimation of the participant's global purpose.

Experimental setting

The experimental setting has been shown in Figure . We used the Immersive Collaborative Interaction Environment (ICIE) [11] and Unity (http://unity3d.com/) to construct the virtual environment and the two agents. The ICIE uses a 360-degree immersive display composed of eight portrait orientation LCD monitors with a 65-inch octagonal screen. In this environment, participants could easily look around in the virtual space with a low cognitive load, similar to the real world.

The experimenter manually controlled the agent based on the predefined rules (Wizard of Oz). But, the behavior planning of the agent and the expressions of the multimodal behavior were automatically produced based on the method to alternate estimation by representing global and local goal-oriented behaviour.

Procedure

The interactive agent who joined the game was randomly selected. The frequency of intervention was the same for both agents. First, the participants were instructed regarding the experimental procedures. The experimenter provided the following instructions about the agent: 'The agent can recognize simple words. The agent has basic knowledge about the task. You can ask and propose how to perform the task. There are six task sessions in total'. The words which the agent could recognize were provided before the task started. After the instructions were provided, the experimenter started the game. The participant first performed a practice session and then performed five game sessions. Each game session lasted for eight minutes, with 1-minute rest intervals between sessions. The agent requested the participant to search the agent's name cards in fifth and sixth sessions. In both sessions, three name cards were provided but the name cards were different. The name cards were widely placed in the game field and they were hidden behind game objects. The experimenter has not provided any instructions regarding this request. On completion of the experiment, the participant completed a questionnaire.

Sixteen Japanese college students (11 men and 5 women) participated in the experiment. They were undergraduate students aged 19 to 33 years (an average of 21.9 years). All of them interacted with one of the agents for approximately 1 hour. Eight participants (6 men and 2 women) interacted with the AEGL agent (the 'AEGL group') and the rest interacted with the goal-oriented agent (the 'GO group').

Results

Analysis of the number of the agent's name cards found in the experiment

The experimenter had not provided prior instructions regarding the request for finding the name cards. Therefore, when the participants had an intentional stance toward the agent, they consciously searched the name cards in the game. To confirm the hypothesis, we asked the participants to state the agent's name after the experiment. The participants wrote down the characters of the name cards found in the game. We counted the number of name cards which were answered correctly. The number of name cards was six. We compared the results from the AEGL group with those from the GO group. These results have been shown in Figure 3. A Mann-Whitney U test showed that the number of name cards in the AEGL group was significantly more than that in the GO group ($p = 0.024$). This result suggests that the approach was successful in inducing the intentional stance.

Analysis of the questionnaires

The purpose of this analysis was to investigate how the method tested in the present study influenced the participants' subjective impressions. The participants rated the impressions of the agent on a seven-point scale, presented as ticks on a black line without numbers. We post-coded these scores from 1 to 7. We performed the Mann-Whitney U tests on the questionnaire data.

- **How carefully did you consider the agent's intentions?**
  This question was asked to confirm whether the participants considered the intentions of the agent. Participants presented their responses separately for the first half and second half of the experiment. The results have been shown in Figure 4 and Figure 5. In the first half of the experiment, the participants in the AEGL group took significantly less

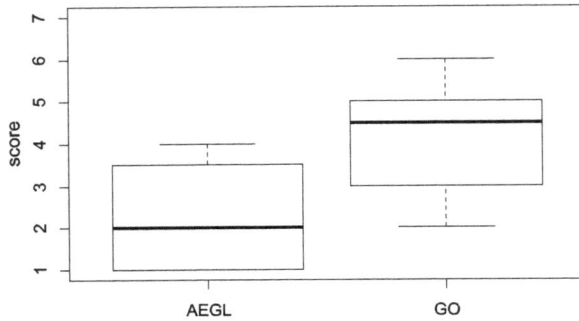

Figure 4. Result of the questionnaire "How carefully did you consider the agent's intentions?" for experimental sessions of the first half.

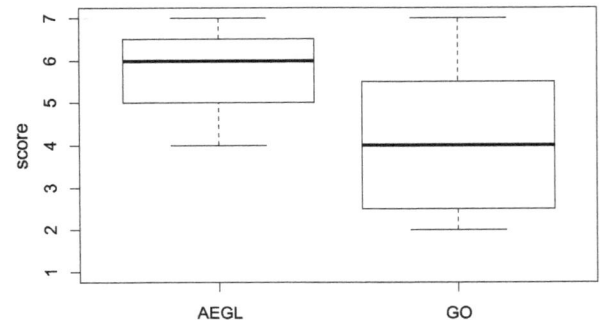

Figure 6. Result of the questionnaire "How strongly do you think that the agent has a definite goal?"

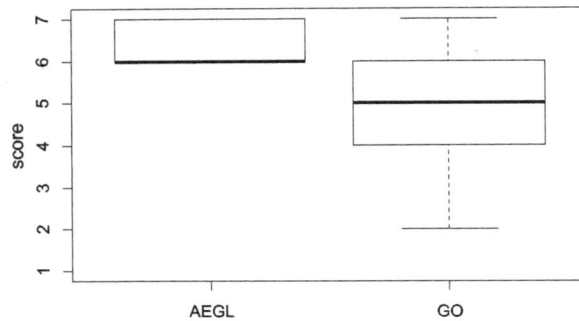

Figure 5. Result of the questionnaire "How carefully did you consider the agent's intentions?" for experimental sessions of the second half.

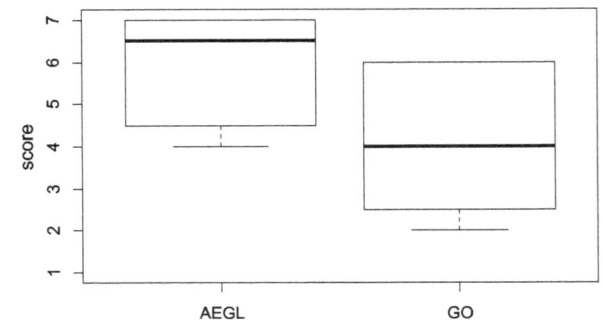

Figure 7. Result of the questionnaire "How strongly do you feel the agent tries to cooperate with you?"

care than did the participants in the GO group (p = 0.025). However, in second half of the experiment, the participants in the AEGL group took marginally more care than did the participants in the GO group (p = 0.052). In addition, we performed the Wilcoxon signed-rank test between the responses regarding the first and second half. In the AEGL group, the score for the second half was significantly higher than that for the first half (p = 0.0078), but there was no significant difference in the GO group (p = 0.22). This indicates that the AEGL agent could increase the degree of the intentional stance through the interaction and its influence was stronger than that of the GO agent.

- **How strongly do you think that the agent has a definite goal?**
  This question was asked to confirm whether the agent's behaviour was understood by the participants. The result has been shown in Figure 6. This shows that the intentionality of the AEGL agent was marginally higher than that of the GO agent (p = 0.080), but not significant. The result of AEGL group is very high, so we think this shows a ceiling effect. Anyway, the AEGL agent and the GO agent could represent their intentions through their interactions.

- **How strongly do you feel the agent tries to cooperate with you?**
  This question explored whether the participants were aware of the cooperative intention of the agent. The result has been shown in Figure 7. There was a significant difference

between the groups (p = 0.043), which suggests that the AEGL agent could provide its basic intention more effectively than the goal-oriented agent could. In our previous work [12], trial-and-error representation was effective in inducing the intentional stance. Indeed, in this regard, the changes of the global purpose of the AEGL agent provided the same effect as the trial-and-error representation.

Discussion

Analysis of the number of agent's name cards helped us confirm that the AEGL group greatly accommodated according to a request from the agent. They tried to search for all the name cards, but some of them gave up because of the time restriction. In contrast, four members of the GO group did not find a card, suggesting that they may have not tried to search for the cards. We think that the GO group members assumed the design stance and the AEGL group assumed the intentional stance. The AEGL could incite the participants to spend their time for the additional task which was not related to the game score. Dindo et al. [5] proposed that humans used as a leaning bias that sidestepped the structure learning problem. However, as we showed in this and previous studies, humans' interaction behaviour was changed depending on whether they assumed the intentional stance or not. Therefore, the induction of the intentional stance is one of the basic conditions to achieve natural human-agent interaction.

Analysis of the questionnaire data confirmed that the participants' mental stance in the AEGL group changed through the interaction but that of those in the GO group did not. In addition, the intentionality of the AEGL agent was marginally higher than that of the GO agent and the cooperativeness of the AEGL agent was significantly higher than that of the GO agent. These findings mean that goal-oriented behaviour was useful in inducing the intentional stance but the effect was static. When humans interact with the agent in a long-term task, the static effect will reduce along with time. We expect that the AEGL is one of the methods that do not reduce the effect of inducing and maintaining the intentional stance. It is important to continuously and mutually change the inner state, such as through AEGL, in natural long-term interactions. When an agent adopts an interaction framework which provides a division of roles among interaction members (e.g. Mixed-Initiative Interaction [1]), we expect that human interaction partners assume the design stance. In this case, the human-agent interaction will be optimized and task performance will become good. However, when the agent behaviour is updated for better performance, humans feel bad because they cannot estimate the new agent behaviour. This is similar to a problem that happened in a software interface update. If humans assume the intentional stance, they can accept the drastic changes more smoothly.

One of the limitation was that the two-layered relational networks were hand-corded depending on the task. In addition, the agent could not induce active interaction from the participants. In future, we need to consider the length of the interaction session. In this study, we conducted an experiment containing six short sessions. To apply the method to long-term interactions, we have to conduct an experiment containing long sessions and improve the interaction model to support development of the complex interaction.

CONCLUSION

The purpose of this study was to investigate the method to induce the intentional stance in human participants of one-to-one human-agent interaction by using the alternating estimation of local objectives and global purposes by a network-connected two-layer model. To evaluate the method, we implemented two types of agents: an AEGL agent (that mutually estimates and changes global purposes through the interaction), and a goal-oriented agent (that separately estimates the participant's intentions but does not change its global purpose). We conducted an experiment to evaluate effect of the proposed method. The results suggested that this method was successful in inducing the intentional stance and the AEGL is one of the methods that do not reduce this effect over time.

ACKNOWLEDGMENTS

This research is supported by Grant-in-Aid for Young Scientists (B) (KAKENHI No. 25870353) and Grant-in-Aid for Scientific Research on Innovative Areas (KAKENHI No. 26118002) from the Ministry of Education, Culture, Sports, Science and Technology of Japan.

REFERENCES

1. JE Allen, Curry I Guinn, and E Horvtz. 1999. Mixed-initiative interaction. *Intelligent Systems and their Applications, IEEE* 14, 5 (1999), 14–23.

2. J-P Briot, Marta de Azevedo Irving, Gustavo Mendes de Melo, José Eurico Filho Vasconcelos, Ines Alvarez, Sebastien Martin, and Wei Wei. 2011. A serious game and artificial agents to support intercultural participatory management of protected areas for biodiversity conservation and social inclusion. In *Culture and Computing (Culture Computing), 2011 Second International Conference on.* IEEE, 15–20.

3. Karen Collins, Kamen Kanev, and Bill Kapralos. 2010. Using games as a method of evaluation of usability and user experience in human-computer interaction design. In *Proceedings of the 13th International Conference on Humans and Computers.* University of Aizu Press, 5–10.

4. Daniel C Dennett. 1989. *The intentional stance.* MIT press.

5. Haris Dindo, Francesco Donnarumma, Fabian Chersi, and Giovanni Pezzulo. 2015. The intentional stance as structure learning: a computational perspective on mindreading. *Biological cybernetics* 109, 4-5 (2015), 453–467.

6. Winand H Dittrich and Stephen EG Lea. 1994. Visual perception of intentional motion. *PERCEPTION-LONDON-* 23 (1994), 253–253.

7. Batya Friedman, Peter H Kahn Jr, and Jennifer Hagman. 2003. Hardware companions?: What online AIBO discussion forums reveal about the human-robotic relationship. In *Proceedings of the SIGCHI conference on Human factors in computing systems.* ACM, 273–280.

8. M. Graafland, J. Schraagen, and M. Schijven. 2012. Systematic review of serious games for medical education and surgical skills training. 99, 10 (2012), 1322–1330.

9. Fritz Heider and Marianne Simmel. 1944. An experimental study of apparent behavior. *The American Journal of Psychology* (1944), 243–259.

10. Gary Klein, David D Woods, Jeffrey M Bradshaw, Robert R Hoffman, and Paul J Feltovich. 2004. Ten challenges for making automation a" team player" in joint human-agent activity. *IEEE Intelligent Systems* 19, 6 (2004), 91–95.

11. Toyoaki Nishida, Atsushi Nakazawa, Yoshimasa Ohmoto, and Yasser Mohammad. 2014. *Conversational Informatics: A Data-Intensive Approach with Emphasis on Nonverbal Communication.* Springer.

12. Yoshimasa Ohmoto, Jun Furutani, and Toyoaki Nishida. 2015a. Induction of intentional stance in human-agent interaction by presenting agent behavior of goal-oriented process using multi-modal information. In *COGNITIVE 2015: The Seventh International Conference on Advanced Cognitive Technologies and Applications.* IARIA, 90–95.

13. Yoshimasa Ohmoto, Asami Matsumoto, and Toyoaki Nishida. 2015b. The Effect of Alternating Propagation of Local Objective and Global Purpose by a Network-Connected Two-Layer Model of Emphasizing Factors. 246–251.

14. Yoshimasa Ohmoto, Suyama Takashi, and Toyoaki Nishida. 2016. Effect on the Mental Stance of an Agent's Encouraging Behavior in a Virtual Exercise Game. In *COGNITIVE 2016: The Eighth International Conference on Advanced Cognitive Technologies and Applications.* IARIA, 10–15.

15. P. Rego, P. M. Moreira, and L. P. Reis. 2010. Serious games for rehabilitation: A survey and a classification towards a taxonomy. In *Proceedings of the 5th Iberian Conference on Information Systems and Technologies (CISTI).* 1–6.

16. Maaike Roubroeks, Jaap Ham, and Cees Midden. 2011. When artificial social agents try to persuade people: The role of social agency on the occurrence of psychological reactance. *International Journal of Social Robotics* 3, 2 (2011), 155–165.

17. A. Väätänen S. Mokka, J. Heinilä, and P. Välkkynen. 2003. Fitness computer game with a bodily user interface. In *Proceedings of the second international conference on Entertainment computing.* 1–3.

18. Ben Shneiderman and Pattie Maes. 1997. Direct manipulation vs. interface agents. *interactions* 4, 6 (1997), 42–61.

Pedestrian Notification Methods in Autonomous Vehicles for Multi-Class Mobility-on-Demand Service

Evelyn Florentine [1], Mark Adam Ang[2], Scott Drew Pendleton[3], Hans Andersen[3], Marcelo H. Ang Jr.[3]

[1] Massachusetts Institute of Technology
Cambridge, MA, USA
evelynf@mit.edu

[2] nuTonomy
Singapore
mark@nutonomy.com

[3] National University of Singapore
Singapore
{scott.pendleton01, hans.andersen}@u.nus.edu, mpeangh@nus.edu.sg

ABSTRACT

In this paper, we describe methods of conveying perception information and motion intention from self driving vehicles to the surrounding environment. One method is by equipping autonomous vehicles with Light-Emitting Diode (LED) strips to convey perception information; typical pedestrian-driver acknowledgement is replaced by visual feedback via lights which change color to signal the presence of obstacles in the surrounding environment. Another method is by broadcasting audio cues of the vehicle's motion intention to the environment. The performance of the autonomous vehicles as social robots is improved by building trust and engagement with interacting pedestrians. The software and hardware systems are detailed, and a video demonstrates the working system in real application. Further extension of the work for multi-class mobility in human environments is discussed.

ACM Classification Keywords

H.1.2 User/Machine Systems: Human factors, Human information processing, Software psychology; H.5.m. Information Interfaces and Presentation (e.g. HCI): Miscellaneous; I.2.9 Robotics: Autonomous vehicles, Operator interfaces, Information Interfaces and Presentation

Author Keywords

Human-Robot Interface; Autonomous Vehicle; Pedestrian Interaction; Social Robotics; Light-Emitting Diode (LED); Robot Operating System (ROS); Arduino

INTRODUCTION

Mobility-on-Demand (MoD) services, such as car sharing or on demand taxi services have seen huge growth in the last few years with services such as Uber and Lyft [12]. Autonomous vehicles have long been awaited as the next generation of mobility especially in highly urbanized area such as Singapore. A truly "on-demand" mobility service can be realized by utilizing a fleet of autonomous vehicles throughout an urban environment.

Autonomous vehicles offer potential for additional safety, increased productivity, greater accessibility, better road efficiency, and positive impact to the environment. Research in autonomous vehicles has seen dramatic advances in recent years, due to the increases in available computing power and reduced cost in sensing and computing technologies. Competitions such as the 2007 DARPA Urban Challenge [15] have accelerated the field of autonomous vehicle design and the development.

In our previous work [11], we discussed the utility of having a multi-class autonomous vehicle fleet for a MoD system, through a simple usage case involving a road car (Mitsubishi iMIEV) and golf cars on the National University of Singapore campus. Both classes of vehicles are designed to utilize the same software architecture (with only low-level controls differing) and general sensor configuration, which are chosen for ease of fleet expansion. The functionality of the service was demonstrated in an uncontrolled environment open to real pedestrian and vehicular traffic. It is shown that while the car can operate at higher speeds on the road, the golf car has the flexibility of operating in pedestrian areas where cars are not allowed, thereby expanding the area coverage of the MoD service.

However, although autonomous vehicle (AV) technologies have been a popular topic of research for many years and several prototypes have already demonstrated impressive capabilities, pedestrian behavioural interactions with autonomous vehicles, especially with a multi-class fleet of AVs have not been thoroughly studied. This work serves as a preliminary investigation into autonomous vehicles as social robots, where audio and visual cues are provided to notify nearby human agents about the vehicle's intentions, and to acknowledgement them of the vehicle's perception.

Pedestrian-driver acknowledgement plays an integral role in road safety. Pedestrians and drivers communicate their intentions with each other through methods of eye contact, hand gestures and other nonverbal communication methods. This

HAI'16, October 4–7, 2016, Biopolis, Singapore.
Copyright © 2016 ACM ISBN 978-1-4503-4508-8/16/10 ...$15.00.
http://dx.doi.org/10.1145/2974804.2974833

has strong implications for the assurance of safety for pedestrians and other road users such as bicyclists as vulnerable road users. In 2009 the World Health Organization estimated that there are 1.2 million road traffic fatalities per year globally, 35 percent of which were pedestrians, 60 percent of which were vulnerable road users - pedestrians, bicyclists, and motorcyclists [10].

Figure 1. Hardware overview, highlighting primary retrofit additions to a Yamaha YDREX3 golf buggy made in order to enable autonomous capabilities. [Source: [12]

When pedestrians or other vulnerable road users must share the road with larger motor vehicles, they have good reason to seek assurance that drivers of larger vehicles are aware and will avoid them. This is also the case when smaller vehicles such as golfcarts are operating in pedestrian environments such as parks, airports, university campuses, etc. However, with the adoption of autonomous driving technologies, the relationship between pedestrian and driver has changed significantly. The pedestrian has no clear way of ensuring that the driver sees him moving around the vehicle as there is no driver. And the driver has no sure way of notifying the pedestrian of his intention to move on or slow down and let the pedestrian cross its path. As a result, the pedestrian may not feel safe with the idea of AVs, and the passenger inside the AV may not feel safe to ride in one.

In this work we describe methods of notifying the pedestrian as well as the autonomous vehicle's passengers of the vehicle's perception and motion intentions. A golf buggy is retrofitted with sensors and actuators in order to enable autonomous driving capabilities (Fig. 1). A speaker, an LED message board and a LED strip are used to communicate with the pedestrians. A touch screen is installed in the vehicle to access the booking system and visualizations.

This paper is organized as follows. In Section II, related work on autonomous vehicle acknowledgement of pedestrian will be reviewed. The hardware and software components of the system will be discussed in Section III. The future work and conclusion will be presented in Section IV.

RELATED WORKS

With the adoption of autonomous vehicles, the number of traffic accidents can be dramatically reduced. However, ethical questions have been risen by Bonnefon et. al [1] whenever an accident is inevitable, such as in situations where the vehicle

has to choose the lesser of two evils. The problem of ensuring pedestrian safety in the presence of road traffic is well acknowledged, with many research efforts focusing on autonomous vehicle perception such as pedestrian detection capabilities for AVs, as well as more advanced methods of reasoning about pedestrians' movements [13]. The perception capabilities provide the vehicle with situational awareness of its environment, however, pedestrians involved in the interaction may not be aware of the vehicle's perception capabilities/limitations.

As vehicles interact with pedestrians at road crossings, certain aspects of social robots apply. When operating smaller vehicles in pedestrian environments, the human-robot social interactions become even more frequent and varied. Two important metrics for human robot interaction in these social contexts are trust and engagement [14].

It has been observed that humans consistently read and interpret nonverbal cues similarly for robots as for people, and that cooperative human-humanoid tasks were performed more efficiently when gaze was incorporated in addition to more explicit forms of communication such as nodding and pointing [2]. Furthermore, eye contact has been shown to reduce miscommunication between a robot and human, where it was observed that humans benefited from knowing they were being watched [4]. Several humanoid robots have also been successful in achieving joint attention from the human and the robot through gaze [9].

Several other methods have been tested for representing the intention of a mobile robot, namely its intended direction and speed of motion via: lamps or blowouts [6], "eyeball" images or abstract signs on an omnidirectional display [7], and projected paths/symbols on the ground [8]. While these types of indications of intention could indeed be useful for a human to interact with a mobile robot, there is no direct insight into whether the robot is responding to the human's presence.

In this work, we display perception information, as well as mission state and intentions from a self-driving vehicle to nearby pedestrians. The autonomous vehicle is treated as a social robot and serves to enhance the social behaviours of driving, namely by fostering greater trust and engagement from humans who interact with it via audio and visual feedbacks.

METHODS AND RESULTS

In-Vehicle User Interface

We have designed a web-based booking system shown in Fig. 2 to accept mission requests. A mission ticket is created in the format of [*Pick-up Station, Drop-off Station*], where *Pick-up Station* and *Drop-off Station* correspond to the passenger's pick-up location and passenger's destination respectively. The mission ticket is then sent to the central server which manages the database of all tickets in the mission pool and assigns missions to each vehicle in the fleet by a simple first-come, first-served basis.

The assigned vehicle's mission planner finds a route between the given pick-up and drop-off point. Predetermined paths are stored in a directed graph. The route searching module

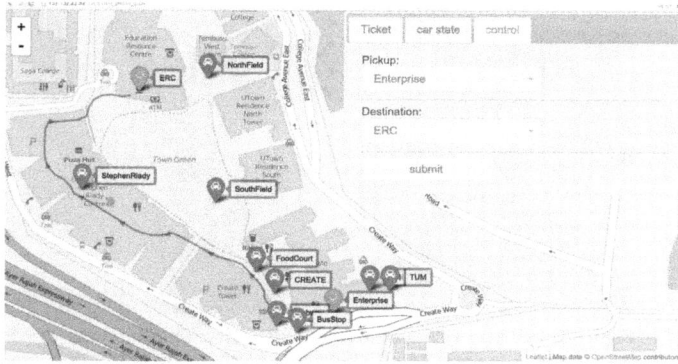

Figure 2. Online booking system for National University of Singapore's University Town, with 11 stations shown. The blue line represents the path the the passenger intends to travel which is from "Enterprise" station to "ERC" station.

performs a Dijkstra search over a directed graph of reference path segments reflecting the road network connectivity [5].

After assigning the reference paths for execution, the mission planner monitors the mission status. In our system, the mission statuses consist of *Mission Waiting, Approach Pick-Up, Arrive Pick-Up, Approach Destination, Arrive Destination, and Mission Infeasible.*

The passenger is then notified through both on-screen and on-board audio cues about the state of the current mission planner, and therefore can take appropriate action accordingly such as board/leave the vehicle safely, or understand whether or not the oncoming vehicle is reserved for him.

The dynamic virtual bumper (DVB), illustrated in Fig. 3 is utilized to generate an advisory speed for the vehicle's safe navigation in the presence of both the static and dynamic obstacles [12]. The DVB is a tube-shaped zone with its centerline as the vehicle's local path, with its width w_t and height h_t defined as a quadratic functions dependent on the vehicle's speed v_t.

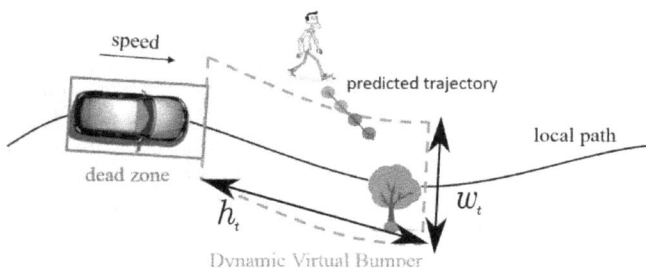

Figure 3. An illustration of the dynamic virtual bumper. [Source [12]]

$$w_t = w_0 + \alpha v_t^2$$
$$h_t = h_o + \beta v_t^2$$

where w_0 and h_0 are the static distance buffers and α and β are the coefficients that determine the growth rate of the dynamic virtual bumper as the velocity increases. LIDARs are used to detect obstacles in the vicinity. When an obstacle O_i is

detected within the DVB, the vehicle will generate an advisory speed of a new desired DVB, whose boundary is marked by the position of the nearest obstacle. Since the desired DVB is smaller than the current DVB upon encountering a nearby obstacle, the newly calculated target velocity will be smaller than the current velocity, thus the vehicle will be advised to slow down. The DVB accounts for the presence of both static and moving obstacles, where the considered obstacle set O is defined by the union of static obstacle and moving obstacles sets, $O = O_{static} \cup O_{moving}$. While O_{static} can be directly obtained from sensor measurement, O_{moving} has to be obtained from prediction of moving object trajectories around the vehicle, and therefore the DVB may frequently adjust in size when dynamic obstacles are present.

Figure 4. In-vehicle visualization of the moving obstacle detection and dynamic virtual bumper. The red box is the dynamic safety zone, and the red arrows are the velocity vectors of the detected moving obstacles.

The moving obstacle detection output, as well as the dynamic virtual bumper is also displayed on the screen inside the vehicle (Fig. 4), such that the passengers can understand the motion intention of the AV, as well as take preventive actions if there are failures in the vehicle's perception system.

Pedestrian Notification System

Figure 5. A retrofitted golfcart for autonomous functions, with pedestrian notification LED strip turned on. The blue color indicates no obstacle within close range, whereas red shows presence of a nearby obstacle. [Source [3]]

The motion intentions of the autonomous vehicles, such as the route destination and mission state, are conveyed to its surrounding through a LED message board. An audio cue in the form of music has also been broadcast through the speaker while the AV is driving autonomously to capture the attention of the surrounding pedestrians, who otherwise may not notice that the vehicle doesn't have a human driver.

A strip of LEDs has been installed along the outside of the vehicle to signal to pedestrians whether their presence has been perceived by the autonomous vehicle. Thus the pedestrians can receive acknowledgment from the AV via the change in LED color. A single planar LIDAR is used as the observation source of surrounding obstacles in the vehicle's vicinity. The LIDAR data could be associated to a particular LED using either polar or Cartesian mapping.

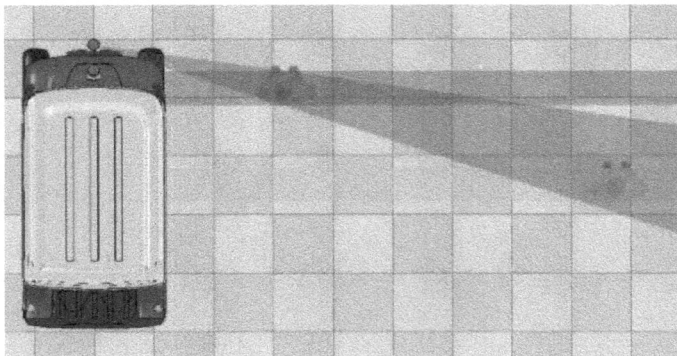

Figure 6. Visual comparison of Cartesian vs polar obstacle to LED position mapping. Note that both pedestrians shown in this scenario would fall within the same index range under polar mapping (blue area), but would fall within two different ranges for Cartesian mapping (near pedestrian in red front range, far pedestrian in green rear range). [Source [3]]

With polar mapping, the origin of the coordinate system would be the center of the associated LIDAR. Each LED corresponds to the LIDAR reading from certain angle ray traces, e.g. the blue triangular section in Fig. 6, and the display value is determined from the minimum radial distance measured by the LIDAR within the particular angle range.

With Cartesian mapping, the coordinate axes should be aligned to the primary axes of the vehicle. For example, the $+x$ direction can be defined as the forward direction of the vehicle, and $+y$ direction as perpendicular to the right of the vehicle with an origin point at the center of mass of the vehicle. Each of the two pedestrians shown in Fig. 6 would fall within two different ranges of x values, the near pedestrian in the red region and the far pedestrian in the green region, and then would be associated with two different sets of LEDs located along the right side of the vehicle, where the distance between the pedestrians and the right edge of the vehicle would be monitored and displayed on the LEDs.

In this scenario, depending on which mapping scheme is chosen, both pedestrian detection locations are either associated with the same set of LEDs (in the polar case) or different sets of LEDs (in the Cartesian case). The polar representation of the LIDAR data is used in this work since the associated ray

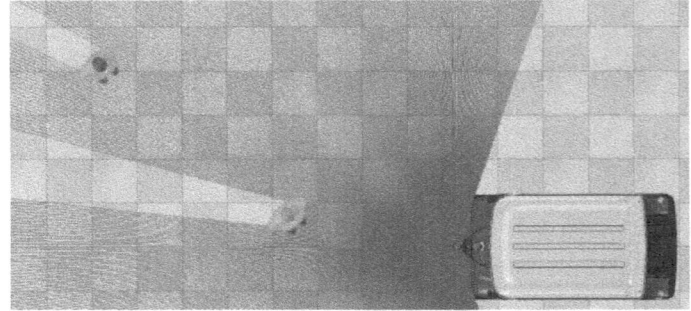

Figure 7. LIDAR ray traces shown in blue. Note that the closer proximity pedestrian is detected by 22 incident LIDAR rays in this case, while the further proximity pedestrian is detected by only 10 rays. Thus the corresponding number of LEDs associated with the detection would be approximately half for the far vs the near case. [Source [3]]

traces nearly overlap with the LED locations for close proximity pedestrians due to the placement of the LED strip on the vehicle, and this is the more straightforward approach to implement.

Let $R = \{r_1, r_2, \cdots, r_L\}$ be the ordered array of ray trace distance values, where L is the total number of ray traces in a singles scan, such that with LIDAR angular scan resolution ϕ, given a ray r_i scanning at an angle θ, the ray $r_{(i+1)}$ would correspond to the ray scanning at the angle $\theta + \phi$. Then a grouping can be assigned to each ray trace according to an array $K = \{k_1, k_2, \cdots, k_L\}$, where K is defined as

$$K = ceiling\left\{(1, 2, \cdots, L) * \frac{N}{L}\right\} \quad (1)$$

where N is the total number of LEDs used. This will result in N different groupings, such that $k_i = j$ would indicate that ray trace r_i will correlate to the j-th LED. Then the minimum value can be assigned for each grouping and stored in an array $D = \{d_1, d_2, , d_N\}$, where each value d_j is defined as

$$d_j = min\{r_i \forall i \in \{1, 2, \cdots, L\} | k_i = j\} \quad (2)$$

where $j \in \{1, 2, \cdots, N\}$

Once the minimum values are found, there is then some flexibility in deciding what color to display on the LED for each distance value. A continuous or discrete spectrum of colors could be used. For a continuous spectrum, far away obstacles could correspond to cool colors (blue, purple, etc.) and near could correspond to warm colors (red, yellow, etc.). For a discrete spectrum, one or several distance thresholds would be set such that within a specified range of distances, the LEDs would be set to a certain user defined fixed color. Otherwise the brightness of the LEDs could be varied such that the lights are dim or off for far away obstacle detections but bright for nearby obstacles. This varied brightness or on/off approach may reduce power consumption, though when no obstacles are present then there would not be an obvious indication that the system is operational.

A single discrete color changing threshold is chosen here, where the LEDs would be set to either blue color or red color according to a Boolean decision factor array $\gamma = \gamma_1, \gamma_2, \cdots, \gamma_N$

defined as

$$\gamma_j = (d_j < \delta) \qquad (3)$$

where δ is a user defined threshold distance, compared against the minimum distance value d_j. $\gamma_j = 0$ corresponds to a blue color setting for the j-th LED, and conversely $\gamma_j = 1$ indicates a red color setting for the j-th LED. Thus the blue lights are set to turn red to warn a pedestrian when they are closer to the golfcart (or more specifically the front LIDAR) than the red-light range. Note that the neighboring LED color assignments will continue to change as an obstacle approaches the golfcart even past the red-light range threshold. As an object moves closer to the golfcart, more LIDAR beams will detect that same object, hence more LEDs light up red Fig. 7.

The red-light range is set to 2.5 meters in the final chosen configuration. This value was set by manual tuning in a slow moving pedestrian environment. While it is difficult to specify an optimal value for the red-light range, this is correlated to pedestrian expectations for how close they need to be before the vehicle acknowledges them. If the threshold is set much higher, the system frequently detects other objects besides the pedestrian, which results in unintuitive large sections of red in the LED strip. Besides, the pedestrians may not typically be expecting to be detected at great distances away from the vehicle. When the threshold is set lower, the pedestrian had to stand too close to the car before the LEDs would turn red, hence they could be looking for acknowledgement from the vehicle earlier without receiving it.

A video showing the working system can be accessed at https://youtu.be/UmruwRx7dW4 [3]. It was observed that better pedestrian engagements were achieved with the combination of audio cues and perception acknowledgement system. The striking appearance of the LED and distracting music captured the pedestrian's attention to observe that the passing vehicle is operating autonomously, and therefore prompted the pedestrians to behave more consciously rather than paying attention to their electronic devices.

CONCLUSION AND FUTURE WORK
We have described methods of informing both the passengers and the pedestrians about the autonomous vehicle's perception status and intentions. In terms of pedestrian-robot social interaction, the audio cues and LED strips have proven to be useful as a warning/acknowledgement mechanism for the pedestrians that are very close to the car, garnering trust and engagement. However, this can be much further improved upon.

Using an LED strip to broadcast obstacle detections from a LIDAR was found to be an effective method to acknowledge pedestrian presence. The system is simple to create, uses little memory on the golfcart, and can be easily expanded. The LED strip can be extended to fit around the car and sync to more than one LIDAR so that a pedestrian can be "followed" by a section of red lights no matter what part of the car they are walking around. In order to do this, the obstacle detection mapping could use Cartesian coordinates, rather than polar. This project is both low-cost and unobtrusive, as it uses components that are already integral to the autonomous golfcart, such as the 2D LIDAR.

Further tests of the system under different conditions is also important as some notification methods may be more or less advantageous under certain unique circumstances that have not been encountered in our previous tests.

In the future, we would like to work on informing both the passengers and the pedestrian on the intended speed and exact direction that the vehicle is about to travel. This can be achieved by implementing more specific audio interactions, rather than just catchy noises to attract the pedestrians' attention, such that the visually impaired could infer more complete information on the intention of the vehicle. The transmission of concepts of safety zone and dynamic virtual bumper may also be useful to communicate to external agents.

Interactions between human drivers and autonomous vehicles as an aspect of social robotics should also be considered more carefully, with additional audio and visual cues options to be implemented and considered, such as external facing screens. The selection of the size of the visual cues has to be considered properly for them to not distract road users too much.

It would be advantageous to collect surveys and questionnaires from different categories of road users such as drivers, pedestrians, and motorcyclists in order to test whether these audio and visual cues would improve their trust of AVs on the road, and at which point do these methods become uncanny and distracting rather than helpful, as the end goal of autonomous vehicle development is for them to integrate seamlessly into the society such that human beings won't even notice that the vehicles drive themselves.

Further interactions in the framework of multi-class MoD can also be considered. Different classes of AVs interact at the boundaries between two differing environment types/deployment areas. Questions such as "how could one transfer between a car and a bus in a highly autonomous transportation system?" have not been widely discussed in the literature.

Acknowledgment
This research was supported by the Future Urban Mobility project of the Singapore-MIT Alliance for Research and Technology (SMART) Center, with funding from Singapore's National Research Foundation (NRF).

REFERENCES
1. Jean-François Bonnefon, Azim Shariff, and Iyad Rahwan. 2015. Autonomous Vehicles Need Experimental Ethics: Are We Ready for Utilitarian Cars? (2015). http://arxiv.org/abs/1510.03346

2. Cynthia Breazeal, Cory D Kidd, Andrea Lockerd Thomaz, Guy Hoffman, and Matt Berlin. 2005. Effects of Nonverbal Communication on Efficiency and Robustness of Human-Robot Teamwork. (2005).

3. Evelyn Florentine, Hans Andersen, Mark Adam Ang, Scott Drew Pendleton, Guo Ming, James Fu, and Marcelo H Ang Jr. 2015. Self-Driving Vehicle Acknowledgement of Pedestrian Presence Conveyed via Light-emitting Diodes. In *IEEE International Conference on Humanoid,*

Nanotechnology, Information Technology Communication and Control, Environment and Management (HNICEM).

4. Hiroshi Ishiguro, Tetsuo Ono, Michita Imai, and Takayuki Kanda. 2001. Development of an Interactive Humanoid Robot "Robovie" - An interdisciplinary research approach between cognitive science and robotics. *Proc. Int. Sympo. Robotics Research* (2001).

5. Wei Liu, Zhiyong Weng, Zhuangjie Chong, Xiaotong Shen, Scott Pendleton, Baoxing Qin, Guo Ming James Fu, and Marcelo H. Ang. 2015. Autonomous vehicle planning system design under perception limitation in pedestrian environment. In *2015 IEEE 7th International Conference on Cybernetics and Intelligent Systems (CIS) and IEEE Conference on Robotics, Automation and Mechatronics (RAM).* 159–166. DOI: http://dx.doi.org/10.1109/ICCIS.2015.7274566

6. Takafumi Matsumaru. 2006. Mobile robot with preliminary-announcement and display function of forthcoming motion using projection equipment. In *IEEE International Workshop on Robot and Human Interactive Communication.* 443–450. DOI: http://dx.doi.org/10.1109/ROMAN.2006.314368

7. T. Matsumaru, K. Akiyama, K. Iwase, T. Kusada, H. Gomi, and T. Ito. 2003a. Robot-to-human communication of mobile robot's following motion using eyeball expression on omnidirectional display. In *IEEE/ASME International Conference on Advanced Intelligent Mechatronics, AIM*, Vol. 2. 790–796. DOI: http://dx.doi.org/10.1109/AIM.2003.1225443

8. Takafumi Matsumaru, Hisashi Endo, and Tomotaka Ito. 2003b. Examination by Software Simulation on Preliminary-Announcement and Display of Mobile Robot's Following Action by Lamp or Blowouts. *IEEE International Conference on Robotics and Automation (ICRA)* 2 (2003), 771–777. DOI: http://dx.doi.org/10.1109/AIM.2003.1225440

9. Dai Miyauchi, Akio Nakamura, and Yoshinori Kuno. 2005. Bidirectional eye contact for human-robot communication. *IEICE Transactions on Information and Systems* E88-D, 11 (2005), 2509–2516. DOI: http://dx.doi.org/10.1093/ietisy/e88-d.11.2509

10. H Naci, D Chisholm, and T D Baker. 2009. Distribution of road traffic deaths by road user group: a global comparison. *Injury prevention : journal of the International Society for Child and Adolescent Injury Prevention* 15, 1 (2009), 55–59. DOI: http://dx.doi.org/10.1136/ip.2008.018721

11. Scott Pendleton, Zhuang Jie Chong, Baoxing Qin, Wei Liu, Tawit Uthaicharoenpong, Xiaotong Shen, Guo Ming James Fu, Marcello Scarnecchia, Seong-Woo Kim, Marcelo H. Ang, and Emilio Frazzoli. 2014. Multi-Class Driverless Vehicle Cooperation for Mobility-on-Demand. In *Intelligent Transportation Systems World Congress (ITSWC).* DOI: http://dx.doi.org/10.1017/CBO9781107415324.004

12. Scott Pendleton, Tawit Uthaicharoenpong, Zhuang Jie Chong, Guo Ming, James Fu, Baoxing Qin, Wei Liu, Xiaotong Shen, Zhiyong Weng, Cody Kamin, Mark Adam Ang, Lucas Tetsuya Kuwae, Katarzyna Anna Marczuk, Hans Andersen, Mengdan Feng, Gregory Butron, Zhuang Zhi Chong, Marcelo H Ang, Emilio Frazzoli, and Daniela Rus. 2015. Autonomous Golf Cars for Public Trial of Mobility-on-Demand Service. In *IEEE/RSJ International Conference on Intelligent Robots and Systems (IROS).* 1164–1171.

13. Baoxing Qin, Zhuang Jie Chong, Sooh Hong Soh, Tirthankar Bandyopadhyay, Marcelo H. Ang, Emilio Frazzoli, and Daniela Rus. 2014. A spatial-temporal approach for moving object recognition with 2D LIDAR. In *International Symposium on Experimental Robotics(ISER).*

14. Aaron Steinfeld, Terrence Fong, Michael Lewis, Jean Scholtz, Alan Schultz, David Kaber, and Michael Goodrich. 2006. Common Metrics for Human-Robot Interaction. *1st ACM SIGCHI/SIGART conference on Human-robot interaction (HRI '06)* (2006), 33–40. DOI: http://dx.doi.org/10.1145/1121241.1121249

15. C. Urmson, J. Anhalt, D. Bagnell, C. Baker, R. Bittner, M. N. Clark, J. Dolan, D. Duggins, T. Galatali, C. Geyer, M. Gittleman, S. Harbaugh, M. Hebert, T. M. Howard, S. Kolski, A. Kelly, M. Likhachev, M. McNaughton, N. Miller, and D Peterson. 2008. Autonomous driving in urban environments: Boss and the Urban Challenge. *J. Field Robotics* 25 (2008), 425–466. DOI: http://dx.doi.org/10.1002/rob

Estimating Person's Awareness of an Obstacle using HCRF for an Attendant Robot

Kenji Koide
Toyohashi University of Technology
1-1 Hibarigaoka, Tempaku,
Toyohashi, Aichi, Japan
koide@aisl.cs.tut.ac.jp

Jun Miura
Toyohashi University of Technology
1-1 Hibarigaoka, Tempaku,
Toyohashi, Aichi, Japan
jun.miura@tut.jp

ABSTRACT

This paper describes an estimation method of a person's awareness of an obstacle. We assume that the person's awareness influences the person's motion, and construct a model of the relationship between the awareness and the motion using HCRF. We extract a sequence of motion features from the person trajectory, and then classify whether the person is aware of the obstacle or not using the model. Awareness estimation experiments are conducted in order to validate the method and evaluate its performance. Since the method uses only the position and the velocity of the person, it can be applicable to mobile robots.

ACM Classification Keywords

H.1.2. MODELS AND PRINCIPLES: User/Machine Systems

Author Keywords

awareness estimation; sequence estimation; attendant robot

INTRODUCTION

Falls are the second leading cause of accidental deaths, worldwide and over 400 thousand persons die by falling every year [11]. In particular for the elderly, falling is one of the most common and often fatal accidents since their attentiveness tends to decrease and they are often unable to react to a falling situation. Our motivation is to develop a service robot which attends to an elderly person and protects them from such accidents.

If a person is not aware of an obstacle or a step, there is a high probability that he/she stumbles on it and falls. If we can estimate the person's awareness, we could assess the risk of falling, and an attendant robot could prevent such accidents by making the person have an awareness of an obstacle or a step. We consider that estimating a person's awareness is important for attendant robots.

HAI '16, October 04-07, 2016, Biopolis, Singapore
© 2016 ACM. ISBN 978-1-4503-4508-8/16/10. . . $15.00
DOI: http://dx.doi.org/10.1145/2974804.2974832

Our goal is to realize an attendant robot (see Fig.1). The robot estimates a person's awareness of surrounding environments while following her. If she is not aware of an obstacle, the robot takes an action, such as warning her or interposing itself between her and the obstacle, so that the obstacle attracts her attention. On the other hand, if the person is aware of it, the robot just continues to follow the person without hindering her motion.

Awareness estimation has been dealt with in several research domains. In driver assistance, in order to prevent accidents, the person's awareness of pedestrians is estimated from the driver's gaze and driving actions, such as accelerating, braking, and steering [1, 6]. In human-computer interaction, the person's awareness of other persons is estimated from the gaze and the head orientation of the person to realize a comfortable human assistance system [10, 2]. Those works show that gaze and head orientation reflect the person's awareness well. In the case of mobile robots, however, such information is not available or is difficult to obtain reliably. We can use only limited person information, such as the position and the velocity of a person.

Toward realizing an attendant robot, we propose a method of estimating the person's awareness of an obstacle. The purpose of this paper is to show that a person's awareness of an obstacle can be estimated by only observing his/her motion.

If a person is not aware of an obstacle, the person moves as if the obstacle were not there, and if the person is aware of it, the person changes his/her trajectory to avoid it. We, thus, consider that the person's motion is affected by the person's awareness of the obstacle and that the person's awareness can be estimated from their movement with respect to the obsta-

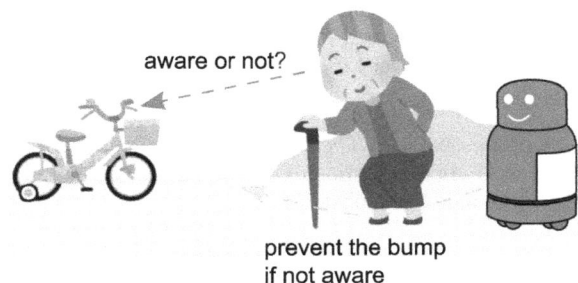

aware or not?

prevent the bump
if not aware

Figure 1. Attendant robot.

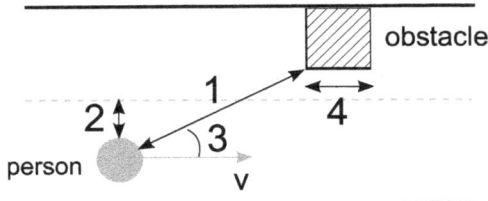

Figure 2. Person's motion features.

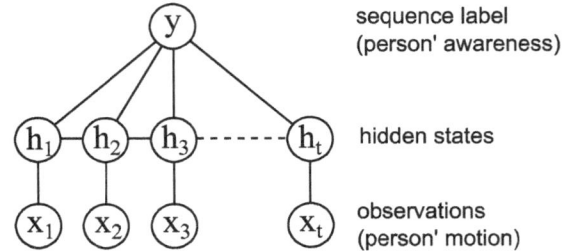

sequence label
(person' awareness)

hidden states

observations
(person' motion)

Figure 3. Person's awareness model.

cle. We first extract motion features from the person trajectory and model the relationship between the awareness and the motion using HCRF (Hidden Conditional Random Fields) [3]. We then estimate the person's awareness of the obstacle from the observed motion using the model. As a first step, we deal with a case where a person walks in a hallway and focus on estimating that person's awareness of an obstacle. We expect that the proposed framework can be extended to awareness of other things, such as a step, and more complicated environments.

The rest of the paper is organized as follows. The next section describes the estimation method for person's awareness of an obstacle. This is followed by an evaluation of the proposed method. Finally, conclusions are drawn, and future work is discussed.

ESTIMATING THE AWARENESS OF AN OBSTACLE

Using biometric information, such as gaze, is direct and the most common way to estimate a person's awareness [1, 2, 10]. Since such information is usually hard to obtain by mobile robots, we propose a method of estimating a person's awareness of an obstacle solely from a person's movement.

Person's Motion Features

In order to describe a person's motion with respect to an obstacle, we define the following four features (see Fig. 2).

1. Distance to the obstacle: When the person is close to the obstacle, the person's motion is affected strongly by the obstacle.

2. Distance to the skeleton of the hallway: This feature is designed to describe how the person's trajectory is affected by the obstacle. Since the person will move along the hallway if there is no obstacle, this feature will be changed by the existence of an obstacle.

3. Angle between the velocity vector and the vector from the person to the obstacle: This feature represents whether the person moves toward the obstacle or not. If the person is avoiding the obstacle, this feature will be large.

4. Size of the obstacle: The person's motion may be affected by several characteristics of the obstacle. We simply use its size to model the obstacle.

Person's awareness model using HCRF

We represent the motion of a person as $\mathbf{x} = \{x_1, x_2, \cdots, x_t\}$ which is a sequence of motion features with length t. Let y be

a binary label of a sequence denoting whether the person is aware of the obstacle or not. We assume that the person's motion is influenced by the condition of the person's awareness. This relationship can naturally be modeled using a sequence classifier, such as CRF (Conditional Random Fields) [9] and HCRF (Hidden Conditional Random Fields) [3]. In this work, we use HCRF to construct the model. We also use CRF as a baseline.

By introducing HCRF, we can model the relationship between the person's awareness and the person's motion as shown in Fig. 3. Following the work of [7], the relationship is modeled as:

$$P(y|\mathbf{x}, \theta) = \sum_{\mathbf{h}} P(y, \mathbf{h}|\mathbf{x}, \theta) = \frac{\sum_{\mathbf{h}} \exp^{\psi(y, \mathbf{h}, \mathbf{x}; \theta)}}{\sum_{y', \mathbf{h}} \exp^{\psi(y', \mathbf{h}, \mathbf{x}; \theta)}} \quad (1)$$

where θ is the parameter of the model, ψ is a potential function parameterized by θ. A sequence of hidden states $\mathbf{h} = \{h_1, h_2, \cdots, h_t\}$ is introduced as the possible hidden labels inside the model. In our model, the number of possible values of each hidden state is set to three.

The parameter θ is optimized using a stochastic descent method [3], and then, we estimate the label of the sequence as follows:

$$\arg \max_{y} P(y|\mathbf{x}, \theta) \quad (2)$$

We obtain observations every 0.5 [s] and use six consecutive observations as one sequence. The duration of a sequence is 3 [s]. We assume that the duration is long enough to describe the person's obstacle avoiding motion.

EXPERIMENTS

Person's motion measurement system

In order to measure a person's motion, we developed a measurement system using 3D LIDAR (Velodyne HDL-32e). The system first detects candidate objects of a human using a Euclidean clustering method, and then classify whether an object is an actual human or not using Kidono's shape descriptive features [4] and Adaboost classifier [8]. The detected people are tracked by a Kalman filter with a constant velocity model and global nearest neighbor data association [5]. Since the LIDAR provides very accurate range data, the system can reliably detect and track persons.

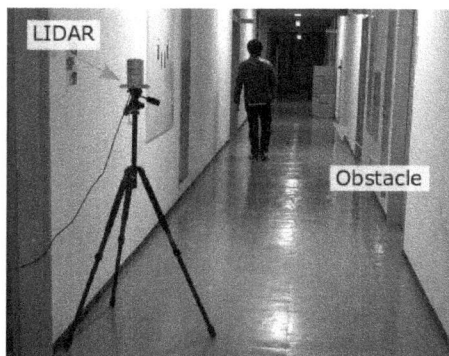

Figure 4. Experimental environment.

Table 1. Estimation Results.

Method	Precision	Recall	F1
CRF	0.743	0.745	0.744
HCRF	0.921	0.941	0.931

Awareness estimation experiments

Ideally, the HCRF model should be constructed from a person's motion data which contains both the situations where a person is aware and unaware of an obstacle. However, it is difficult to intentionally make situations where a person is unaware of an obstacle. Also, in the viewpoint of research ethics, it is illegal to conduct experiments in such situations since there is risk that the person will fall and sustain injury. We thus assume that there is no significant difference between the person's motions under situations where the person is unaware of an obstacle and where there is no obstacle. Therefore, we train the HCRF model from a person's motion data with and without obstacles.

We first collected a set of person trajectories with and without obstacles. Fig. 4 shows the experimental setting. The experiments were conducted in two kinds of settings; in the first one, an obstacle was placed in the hallway, and in the second, no obstacle was placed. Five persons walked in the hallway and avoided the obstacle if there was an obstacle. We measured the person's trajectory 30 times for each person with and without obstacles, respectively.

Fig. 5 shows the heatmap created from the measured trajectories. Red indicates where the persons passed on frequently, and blue indicates where the persons did not pass. The white circles indicate the size and the position of the obstacles. As we can see in Fig. 5, the person's motion is affected by the obstacles. If there is no obstacle, persons move straight along the hallway. On the other hand, if there is an obstacle, persons change their trajectories to avoid the obstacle.

In situations where a person is unaware of an obstacle, the person's motion is independent of the obstacle. To simulate the situation using the situations without obstacles, we randomly choose obstacle data from the situations with obstacles and extract the person's motion features as if there was a chosen obstacle. We train the HCRF model using the extracted features.

The set of the trajectories is divided into five parts, and one of them is used as a test set and the rest are used as a training set. The number of the motion sequences in the test set is 785, and the number of the sequences in the training set is 3146. Table 1 shows the estimation results. HCRF shows a better estimation performance than CRF, and in the case of HCRF, we achieve an estimation accuracy of 92.1%. Fig. 6 shows the relationship between the distance to the obstacle and the estimation accuracy. As a person get closer to an obstacle, the person's motion is influenced by the obstacle strongly, and the motion becomes distinguishable from when the case without the obstacle. As a result, the estimation accuracy increases. When the distance between the person and the obstacle is less than 4 [m], the method can estimate the person's awareness with an estimation accuracy of over 90%.

Online awareness estimation experiments

We measure three person's trajectories without obstacles and nine trajectories with obstacles for an online test. In order to validate the applicability of the proposed method to real attendant robots, we examine the point where the method judged that the person was aware of the obstacle.

Fig. 7 shows examples of the estimation results. Thick lines indicate the trajectory of a person and estimation results. Blue color indicates that the system is accumulating motion data and is not classifying the motion due to an insufficient amount of data. Green and red colors indicate that the person is unaware of the obstacle, and that the person is aware of the obstacle, respectively. In the case of Fig. 7(a), the system started to accumulate the person's motion data when the person entered into the environment. After a sufficient amount of motion data is accumulated, the system successfully classified the person's motion as being unaware of the obstacle. In the case of Fig. 7(b), after the accumulation of data was finished, the system classified the person's motion as being unaware of the obstacle. However, as the person got closer to the obstacle, within about 10 [m], the system judged that he was aware of the obstacle. When a person is close to an obstacle, the system reliably estimates the person's awareness since the identification accuracy increases as a person gets closer to an obstacle as shown in Fig. 6.

In all of the cases without obstacles, the classifier did not judge that the person was aware of the obstacle, and in all of the cases with obstacles, the classifier successfully judged that the person was aware of the obstacle before the person reached to the obstacle. Table 2 shows the statistics of the point where the classifier judged. The classifier can realize that a person is aware of an obstacle at a point about 8.5 [m] from the obstacle on average, and about 6.1 [m] at least. If the person is walking at 1.2 [m/s], the time to bump into the obstacle is about 5.1 [s]. If the robot takes preventative action within this time, it can avoid the collision. We consider that the robot can interact with the person within this duration if the robot approaches the person in advance. At least the robot can call the person to make the obstacle attract their attention within this duration.

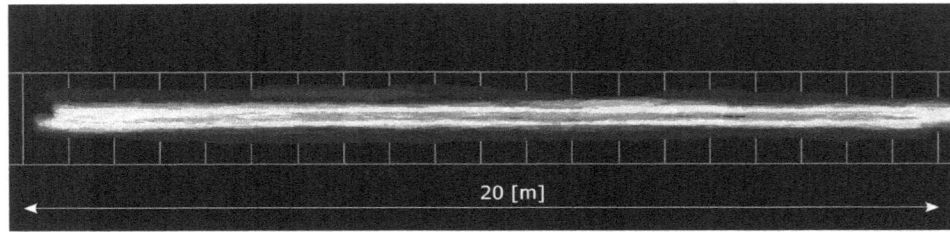

(a) Without obstacles.

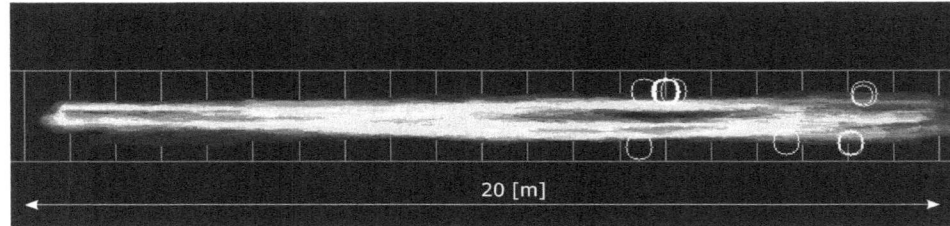

(b) With obstacles.

Figure 5. Heatmap of persons' trajectories. Red indicates where the persons passed on frequently, and blue indicates where the persons did not pass. The white circles indicate the size and the position of the obstacles.

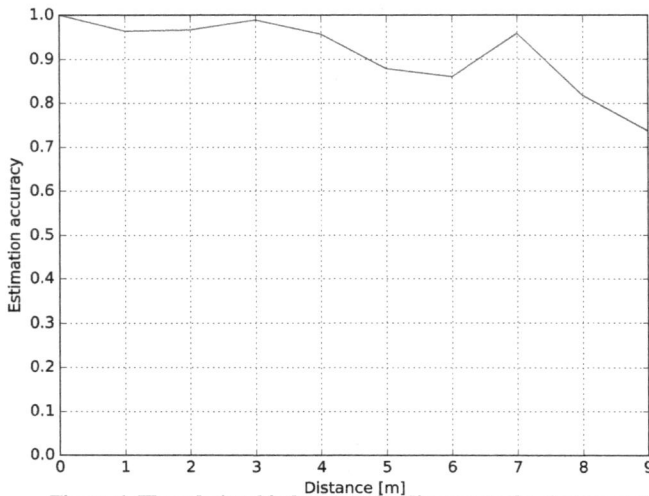

Figure 6. The relationship between the distance to the obstacle and estimation accuracy.

Table 2. Statistics of the point where the classifier judged that the person is aware of the obstacle.

	mean	std. dev.	min	max
distance [m]	8.53	1.88	6.09	11.41

CONCLUSION AND FUTURE WORK

This paper has described a method of estimating a person's awareness of an obstacle using only the person's motion. The method extracts motion features from their trajectory, and then classifies whether the person is aware of the obstacle or not using HCRF. We validated the method through real experiments and confirmed that the estimation is accurate enough.

Currently, we have developed only an estimation method of a person's awareness of an obstacle. Since the person may bump into not only just obstacles but also other persons, we

have to extend the method to be able to estimate person's awareness of other persons and work in more complicated environments. Also, motion planning with consideration of estimated awareness has also to be developed in order to realize socially acceptable attendant behavior.

ACKNOWLEDGEMENT

This work is in part supported by JSPS Kakenhi No. 25280093 and the Leading Graduate School Program R03 of MEXT.

REFERENCES

1. Tobias Bar, Denys Linke, Dennis Nienhuser, and J. Marius Zollner. 2013. Seen and missed traffic objects: A traffic object-specific awareness estimation. In *Proceedings of the 2013 IEEE Intelligent Vehicles Symposium (IV)*. IEEE.

2. Anup Doshi and Mohan M. Trivedi. 2010. Attention estimation by simultaneous observation of viewer and view. In *Proceedings of the 2010 IEEE Computer Society Conference on Computer Vision and Pattern Recognition - Workshops*. IEEE.

3. Asela Gunawardana, Milind Mahajan, Alex Acero, and John C. Platt. 2005. Hidden Conditional Random Fields for Phone Classification. In *Proceedings of the International Conference on Speech Communication and Technology*. International Speech Communication Association.

4. Kiyosumi Kidono, Takeo Miyasaka, Akihiro Watanabe, Takashi Naito, and Jun Miura. 2011. Pedestrian recognition using high-definition LIDAR. In *Proceedings of the 2011 IEEE Intelligent Vehicles Symposium (IV)*. IEEE.

5. Pavlina Konstantinova, Alexander Udvarev, and Tzvetan Semerdjiev. 2003. A study of a target tracking algorithm

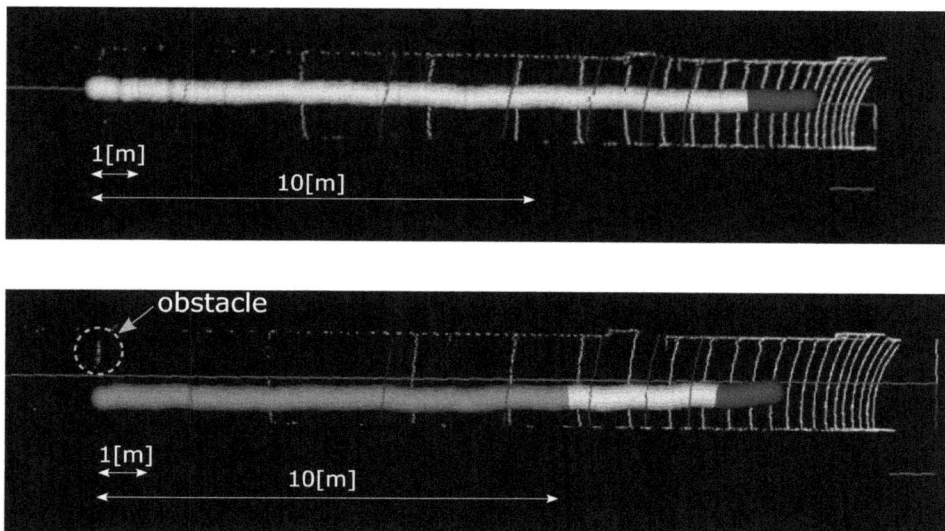

Figure 7. Examples of estimation results. Thick lines indicate the trajectory of a person and the estimation results. Blue color indicates that the system is accumulating motion data and is not classifying the motion due to an insufficient amount of data. Green and red colors indicate that the person is unaware of the obstacle, and that the person is aware of the obstacle, respectively.

using global nearest neighbor approach. In *Proceedings of the International Conference on Computer Systems and Technologies (CompSysTec ' 03)*. 290–295.

6. Minh Tien Phan, Vincent Fremont, Indira Thouvenin, Mohamed Sallak, and Veronique Cherfaoui. 2014. Recognizing Driver Awareness of Pedestrian. In *Proceedings of the 17th International IEEE Conference on Intelligent Transportation Systems (ITSC)*. IEEE.

7. Ariadna Quattoni, Michael Collins, and Trevor Darrell. 2004. Conditional random fields for object recognition. In *Advances in neural information processing systems*. 1097–1104.

8. Robert E. Schapire and Yoram Singer. 1998. Improved boosting algorithms using confidence-rated predictions. In *Proceedings of the Annual conference on Computational learning theory - COLT 98*, Vol. 37. ACM, 297–336.

9. Fei Sha and Fernando Pereira. 2003. Shallow parsing with conditional random fields. In *Proceedings of the 2003 Conference of the North American Chapter of the Association for Computational Linguistics on Human Language Technology - NAACL03*. ACL.

10. Rainer Stiefelhagen and Jie Zhu. 2002. Head orientation and gaze direction in meetings. In *Proceedings of the Extended Abstracts on Human Factors in Computing Systems - CHI02*. ACM.

11. WHO Media centre. 2012. Fact sheet 344: Falls. (oct 2012). http://www.who.int/mediacentre/factsheets/fs344/en/

Author Index